Understanding Social Problems

First Canadian Edition

Linda A. Mooney
East Carolina University

David Knox
East Carolina University

Caroline Schacht
East Carolina University

Adie Nelson
University of Waterloo

NELSON

THOMSON LEARNING™

AUSTRALIA   CANADA   MEXICO   SINGAPORE   SPAIN   UNITED KINGDOM   UNITED STATES

NELSON

™

THOMSON LEARNING

**Understanding Social Problems,
First Canadian Edition**

by Linda Mooney, David Knox,
Caroline Schacht, Adie Nelson

Editorial Director and Publisher:
Evelyn Veitch

Executive Editor:
Joanna Cotton

Marketing Manager:
Don Thompson

Project Editor:
Toni Chahley

Production Editor:
Tracy Bordian

Production Coordinator:
Hedy Sellers

Art Director:
Angela Cluer

Cover Design:
Katherine Strain

Cover Photos:
Photodisc

Copy Editor:
Dawn Hunter

Proofreader:
Madeline Koch

Compositor:
Alicja Jamorski

Printer:
Webcom

Canadian Cataloguing in Publication Data

Main entry under title:
Understanding social problems

1st Canadian ed.
Includes bibliographical references and index.
ISBN 0-17-616839-7

1. Social problems – Canada.
2. Canada – Social conditions – 1991– . 3. Social problems.
4. Social history. I. Nelson, Adie, 1958– .

HN103.5.U65 2000   361.1'0971
C00-931966-2

Brief Contents

Contents

CHAPTER 5   FAMILY PROBLEMS

SECTION 2   PROBLEMS OF HUMAN DIVERSITY

CHAPTER 6   THE YOUNG AND THE OLD

CHAPTER 7   GENDER INEQUALITY

SECTION 3   PROBLEMS OF INEQUALITY AND POWER

CHAPTER 10   THE HAVES AND THE HAVE-NOTS

CHAPTER 11   WORK AND UNEMPLOYMENT

CHAPTER 12   PROBLEMS IN EDUCATION

SECTION 4   PROBLEMS OF MODERNIZATION

CHAPTER 13   SCIENCE AND TECHNOLOGY

CHAPTER 14   POPULATION AND ENVIRONMENTAL PROBLEMS

Preface

Violence in the home, in the school, and in the street; impoverished living conditions for millions of people throughout the world; increasing levels of environmental pollution and depletion of the earth's natural resources; persistent conflict between and within nations; ongoing oppression of minorities; and the widening gap between the haves and the have-nots paint a disturbing picture of our modern world. In *A Guide for the Perplexed*, E. F. Schumacher asks whether a "turning around will be accomplished by enough people quickly enough to save the modern world" (quoted in Safransky 1990: 115). Schumacher notes that "this question is often asked, but whatever the answer given, it will mislead. The answer 'yes' would lead to complacency; the answer 'no' to despair. It is desirable to leave these perplexities behind us and get down to work."

In *Understanding Social Problems,* we "get down to work" by examining how the social structure and culture of society contribute to social problems and their consequences. Understanding the social forces that contribute to social problems is necessary for designing strategies for action—programs, policies, and other interventions intended to ameliorate the social problem.

ACADEMIC FEATURES

The three major sociological approaches, structural functionalism, symbolic interactionism, and conflict theory, are introduced in the first chapter and discussed and applied, where appropriate, to various social problems throughout the text. Other theories of social problems, as well as feminist approaches, are also presented where appropriate.

Emphasis on the Structure and Culture of Society

The text emphasizes how the social structure and culture of society contribute to and maintain social problems, as well as provide the basis for alternative solutions.

Review of Basic Sociological Terms

An overview of basic sociological terms and concepts is presented in the first chapter. This overview is essential for students who have not taken an introductory course and is helpful, as a review, for those who have.

Unique Organization

The order of the 15 chapters reflects a progression from a micro to a macro level of analysis, focusing first on problems of health care, drug use, and crime, and then broadening to the wider concerns of science and technology, population growth and environmental problems, and conflict around the world.

Two chapters merit special mention: "Sexual Orientation" (Chapter 9) and "Science and Technology" (Chapter 13). Whereas traditional texts discuss sexual orientation under the rubric of "deviance," this topic is examined in the section on problems of human diversity along with the related issues of age, gender, and racial and ethnic inequality. The chapter on science and technology includes such topics as biotechnology, the computer revolution, and the information highway. This chapter emphasizes the transformation of society through scientific and technological innovations, the societal costs of such innovations, and issues of social responsibility. This chapter is particularly relevant to students, many of whom have never known a world without computers.

Global Issues

We place emphasis on examining social problems from a global perspective. Each chapter contains a heading entitled "The Global Context," and we provide a number of "international data" boxes in each chapter.

Unique Chapter Format

Each chapter follows a similar format: the social problem is defined, the theoretical explanations are discussed, the consequences of the social problem are explored, and the alternative solutions and policies are examined. A concluding section assesses the current state of knowledge for each social problem.

Standard and Cutting-Edge Topics

In addition to problems that are typically addressed in social problems courses and texts, new and emerging topics are examined. Topics include violence against people with disabilities, the educational needs of exceptional children, the changing status of same-sex marriages, DNA testing in criminal investigations, telemedicine, cloning, bisexuality and biphobia, and environmental justice.

PEDAGOGICAL FEATURES

Student-Friendly Presentation

To enhance the book's appeal to students, the first Canadian edition includes material chosen for its relevance to students. In Chapter 1, for example, we present data on student activism; Chapter 2 highlights the "Health Concerns of Students." In Chapter 3, we have included a section on binge drinking and other alcohol-related problems on campus as well as the experience of homeless youths and substance abuse. Each chapter includes a social survey designed to help students assess their own attitudes, beliefs, knowledge, or behaviour regarding some aspect of a social problem. Students may also compare their responses with those from a larger sample. Examples include an Alcohol Attitudes Test, a Family Functioning Scale, an AIDS Knowledge Scale, and an Eco-Quiz.

National and International Data

National statistics and research data are presented throughout the text and offset as "National Data." Similar inserts called "International Data" present data from nations around the world.

Consideration Sections

Sections labelled "Consideration" provide unique examples, insights, implications, explanations, and applications of material presented in the text. These sections are designed to illuminate a previous point in a thought-provoking way.

The Human Side

To personalize the information being discussed, each chapter includes a feature entitled "The Human Side." These features encourage students to consider the reality of those whose lives have been affected by the social problem under discussion. We draw on the powerful words of Elijah Harper and Celia Haig-Brown, investigate the experience of street youths with drugs, and pay heed to the voices of gay and lesbian youths recounting their experiences with homophobia in schools.

Focus on Social Problems Research

Offset boxes called "Focus on Social Problems Research" present examples of significant research. These boxes demonstrate for students the sociological enterprise from theory and data collection, to results and conclusions. Examples of research topics covered include Canadians' beliefs about when divorce is justified (Chapter 5), students' openness to diversity (Chapter 8), and the socially constructed world of computer hackers (Chapter 13).

Focus on Technology

Also included are offset boxes called "Focus on Technology." These boxes present information on how technology may contribute to social problems and their solutions. For example, in Chapter 2, we focus on the burgeoning world of telemedicine. In Chapter 4, "Crime and Violence," the Focus on Technology feature highlights the use of DNA testing in criminal investigations. In Chapter 12, "Problems in Education," distance learning and the "new education" are examined.

Is It True?

Each chapter begins with five true or false items to stimulate student interest and thinking.

Critical Thinking

Each chapter ends with a brief section called "Critical Thinking" that raises several questions related to the chapter topic. These questions invite the student to use critical thinking skills in applying the information discussed in the chapters.

A CHAPTER-BY-CHAPTER LOOK

A partial list of the topics covered in this text follows.

Chapter 1: Thinking About Social Problems Collaborative research as an emerging methodology; student activism on campuses; and "sociological mindfulness."

Chapter 2: Illness and the Health Care Crises A new approach to measuring the health status of a population—disability-adjusted life year (DALY); health concerns of students; special populations; and telemedicine.

Chapter 3: Alcohol and Other Drugs Survey data on student drinking and "bingeing" behaviour; teenagers' use of inhalants; the medical use of marijuana debate; and tobacco suits and settlements.

Chapter 4: Crime and Violence The *International Crime Control Act*; pornography on the Internet; children who kill; and innovative criminal justice initiatives (e.g., community policing).

Chapter 5: Family Problems Violence and abuse in the family; elder abuse; premarital education proposals and policies; and divorce law reform.

Chapter 6: The Young and the Old Children and poverty; child prostitution; child pornography; physician-assisted suicide; and the feminization of poverty.

Chapter 7: Gender Inequality Cultural and structural sexism; attitudes toward feminism; men, women, and computer technologies; the wage gap; the men's movement.

Chapter 8: Race and Ethnic Relations The social construction of race; immigration; prejudice and discrimination; and hate crimes.

Chapter 9: Sexual Orientation Biphobia; gay and lesbian youth; socio-legal issues relating to sexual orientation including same-sex marriage; child custody; and reproductive rights.

Chapter 10: The Haves and the Have-Nots The Human Poverty Index (HPI); the extent and consequences of economic inequality; disability and poverty; the working poor; and the role of charity and nonprofit organizations in poverty alleviation.

Chapter 11: Work and Unemployment Child labour and child labour laws; labour unions; job burnout; corporate multinationalism; contingent workers; and cumulative trauma disorders and ergonomics in the workplace.

Chapter 12: Problems in Education Distance learning; special education; the soaring costs of higher education; the brain drain; alternative schools and home schooling.

Chapter 13: Science and Technology Postmodernism; the World Wide Web; the debate over partial birth abortions and cloning; deskilling versus upskilling; e-commerce; and science, ethics, and the law.

Chapter 14: Population and Environmental Problems Falling population levels in Europe; threatened biodiversity; environmental justice issues; environmentally induced illnesses; and "greenwashing."

Chapter 15: Conflict around the World Nuclear terrorism; Gulf War Syndrome; the Comprehensive Test Ban Treaty; and the increased threat of nuclear war.

ONLINE RESOURCES

Students: For a variety of resources that support this text, visit our Web site at **www.understandingsocialproblems.nelson.com**.

Instructors: Support material can be found at **www.understandingsocial problems.nelson.com/instructors**.

INSTRUCTOR'S TEST BANK

There are multiple-choice and true–false questions available for each chapter, all with page references. Also includes short-answer questions and essay questions for each chapter. Available upon adoption.

ACKNOWLEDGMENTS

This text reflects the work of many people. I would like to thank the following people for their contributions to the development of the first Canadian edition of this text: Peter Carrington, Toni Chahley, Joanna Cotton, Jim Curtis, Dawn Hunter, Ron Lambert, and Keith Warriner. For the assistance each offered, in various ways, I am most sincerely grateful. Additionally, I am indebted to those who read the manuscript in its various drafts and provided valuable insights and suggestions, many of which have been incorporated into the final manuscript:

Beverly Coulston, Fanshawe College
Trevor Harrison, University of Alberta
Richard Kerr, Durham College
Vicki Nygaard, University of Victoria
Subhas Ramcharan, University of Windsor

Finally, I am always interested in ways to improve the text and invite your feedback and suggestions for new ideas and material to be included in subsequent editions.

Adie Nelson
Department of Sociology
University of Waterloo
Waterloo ON N0L 0G0
E-mail address: <eds@watarts.uwaterloo.ca>

CHAPTER ONE

Thinking about Social Problems

Is It True?

1. For at least three decades, Canadians have identified the economy, unemployment, and crime as their foremost social concerns.

2. Before the nineteenth century, it was considered a husband's legal right and marital obligation to discipline and control his wife using physical force.

3. In seventeenth- and eighteenth-century England, tea drinking was considered a social problem.

4. Questions involving values, religion, and morality can be answered only through scientific research.

5. In a national survey of Canadians 18 and older, more than half agreed with the statement, "Anyone who works hard will rise to the top."

Answers: 1 = T, 2 = T, 3 = T, 4 = F, 5 = T

We enter the new millennium with our optimism for the future necessarily tempered by recognition of the persistence of such social problems as crime, unemployment, drug abuse, suicide, racism, sexism, and family violence. Consider, for example, that for the past three decades Canadians have consistently identified the economy, unemployment, and crime as primary areas of social concern. In 1995, the "top 10" social issues that Canadians viewed as "very serious" when asked to choose from a list were: the national debt (72 percent), unemployment (55 percent), the economy (54 percent), crime (46 percent), government incompetence (45 percent), child abuse (43 percent), AIDS (41 percent), juvenile delinquency (39 percent), family breakdown (36 percent), and violence (35 percent) (Bibby 1995: 94–5). In 1999, the *Maclean's* Year End Poll asked a random sample of 1200 adult Canadians to identify "the most important problem" facing our country. Almost one-third (31 percent) identified troubles besetting social services, assistance to the poor, health, and education. Dollar-and-cents difficulties in relation to unemployment and the economy were selected by 19 percent of respondents; 12 percent said taxation and the GST; and 10 percent, government debt and spending.

> It was the best of times, it was the worst of times; it was the age of wisdom, it was the age of foolishness; it was the epoch of belief, it was the epoch of incredulity; it was the season of light, it was the season of darkness; it was the spring of hope, it was the winter of despair.
>
> Charles Dickens, Novelist

International Data

A quarter of the world's population live in severe poverty.

SOURCE: Human Development Report 1997

A global perspective on social problems is even more troubling. In 1990, the United Nations Development Programme published its first annual *Human Development Report*, which measures the well-being of populations around the world according to a "human development index" (HDI). This index measures three basic dimensions of human development—longevity, knowledge (i.e., educational attainment), and standard of living. Recent data show that the human development index declined in 1996 in 30 countries, which was more than in any year since 1990 (*Human Development Report* 1997: 3).

Problems related to poverty and malnutrition, inadequate education, acquired immunodeficiency syndrome (AIDS) and other sexually transmitted diseases (STDs), inadequate health care, crime, conflict, oppression of minorities, environmental destruction, and other social issues are national and international concerns. Such problems present a threat and a challenge to our national and global society.

The primary goal of this text is to facilitate increased awareness and understanding of problematic social conditions in Canadian society and throughout the world. Although the topics covered in this text vary widely, all chapters share common objectives: to explain how social problems are created and maintained; to indicate how they affect individuals, social groups, and whole societies; and to examine programs and policies for change. We begin by looking at the nature of social problems.

WHAT IS A SOCIAL PROBLEM?

There is no universal, constant, or absolute definition of what constitutes a social problem. Rather, social problems are defined by a combination of objective and subjective criteria that vary across societies, among individuals and groups within a society, and across historical periods.

Objective and Subjective Elements of Social Problems

Although social problems take many forms, they all share two important elements: an objective social condition and a subjective interpretation of that social condition. The **objective element** of a social problem refers to the existence of a social condition. We become aware of social conditions through our own life experiences, through the media, and through education. We see homeless people in the streets and the faces of battered children in hospital emergency rooms. We read about employees losing their jobs as businesses downsize and factories close. We hear about corruption in high and low places. In television news reports, we see the anguished faces of parents whose children have been killed by drunk drivers.

The **subjective element** of a social problem refers to the belief that a particular social condition is harmful to society, or to a segment of society, and that it should and can be changed. We know that crime, drug addiction, poverty, racism, violence, and pollution exist. These social conditions become social problems only when a segment of society believes that these conditions diminish the quality of human life.

By combining these objective and subjective elements, we arrive at the following definition: A **social problem** is a social condition that a segment of society views as harmful to members of society and that is in need of remedy.

CONSIDERATION

Between 1933 and 1945, Hitler's Nazi regime killed more than 12 million Jews, homosexuals, people with mental and physical disabilities, and gypsies in death camps. Hitler's goal was to "clean" German society of "inferior" people so he could build a "master Aryan race." Why did the German population accept what Hitler was doing? Why did they not view the extermination of millions of people as a social problem? One reason is that, to some degree, Hitler kept the existence of the extermination camps hidden from the German population. Thus, to some extent, the objective condition was unknown. In addition, Hitler worked hard to influence how those Germans who were aware of the camps subjectively interpreted this social condition. Hitler's propaganda suggested that these were labour camps—not death camps. Germans who were aware of what was actually happening in the camps were encouraged to view the mass extermination as important and necessary for the future of Aryan society, rather than as a harmful social condition that should be stopped.

Variability in Definitions of Social Problems

Individuals and groups frequently disagree about what constitutes a social problem. For example, some Canadians view the availability of abortion as a social problem, while others view restrictions on abortion as a social problem. Similarly, some Canadians view homosexuality as a social problem, while others view prejudice and discrimination against homosexuals as a social problem. Such variations in what is considered a social problem are due to differences in values, beliefs, and life experiences.

Definitions of social problems vary not only within societies, but across societies and historical periods as well. For example, before the nineteenth century, it was a husband's legal right and marital obligation to discipline and control his wife using physical force. Today, the use of physical force is regarded as a social problem and a criminal offence rather than as a marital right.

Tea drinking is another example of how what is considered a social problem can change over time. In seventeenth- and eighteenth-century England, tea drinking was regarded as a "base Indian practice" that was "pernicious to health, obscuring industry, and impoverishing the nation" (Ukers 1935, cited in Troyer and Markle 1984). Today, the English are known for their tradition of drinking tea in the afternoon.

Because social problems can be highly complex, it is helpful to have a framework within which to view them. Sociology provides such a framework. Using a sociological perspective to examine social problems requires knowledge of the basic concepts and tools of sociology. In the remainder of this chapter, we discuss some of these concepts and tools: social structure, culture, the "sociological imagination," major theoretical perspectives, and types of research methods.

ELEMENTS OF SOCIAL STRUCTURE AND CULTURE

Although society surrounds us and permeates our lives, it is difficult to "see" society. By thinking of society in terms of a picture or image, however, we can visualize society and therefore better understand it. Imagine that society is a coin with two sides: on one side is the structure of society, and on the other is the culture of society. Although each "side" is distinct, both are inseparable from the whole. By looking at the various elements of social structure and culture, we can better understand the root causes of social problems.

Elements of Social Structure

The structure of a society refers to the way society is organized. Society is organized into different parts: institutions, social groups, statuses, and roles.

Institutions   An **institution** is an established and enduring pattern of social relationships. The five traditional institutions are family, religion, politics, economics, and education, but some sociologists argue that other social institutions, such as science and technology, mass media, medicine, sport, and the military, also play important roles in modern society.

Many social problems are generated by inadequacies in various institutions. For example, unemployment may be influenced by the educational institution's failure to prepare individuals for the job market and by alterations in the structure of the economic institution.

Social Groups   Institutions are made up of social groups. A **social group** is defined as two or more people who have a common identity, interact, and form a social relationship. For example, the family in which you were reared is a social group that is part of the family institution. The religious association to which you may belong is a social group that is part of the religious institution.

Social groups may be categorized as primary or secondary. **Primary groups**, which tend to involve small numbers of individuals, are characterized by intimate and informal interaction. Families and friends are examples of primary groups. **Secondary groups**, which may involve small or large numbers of individuals, are task-oriented and characterized by impersonal and formal interaction. Examples of secondary groups include employers and their employees, and store clerks and their customers.

Statuses   Just as institutions consist of social groups, social groups consist of statuses. A **status** is a position a person occupies within a social group. The statuses we occupy largely define our social identity. The statuses in a family may consist of mother, father, stepmother, stepfather, wife, husband, child, and so on. Statuses may be either ascribed or achieved. An **ascribed status** is one that society assigns to an individual based on factors over which the individual has no control. For example, we have no control over the sex, race, ethnic background, and socioeconomic status into which we are born. Similarly, we are assigned the status of "child," "teenager," "adult," or "senior citizen" based on our age—something we do not choose or control.

An **achieved status** is assigned based on some characteristic or behaviour over which the individual has some control. Whether you achieve the status of university graduate, spouse, parent, bank president, or prison inmate depends largely on your own efforts, behaviour, and choices. Your ascribed statuses may affect the likelihood of achieving other statuses, however. For example, if you are born into a poor socioeconomic status, you may find it more difficult to achieve the status of "university graduate" because of the high cost of a university education.

Every individual has numerous statuses simultaneously. You may be a student, parent, tutor, volunteer fundraiser, female, and have a physical disability. A person's **master status** is the status that is considered the most significant in a person's social identity. Typically, a person's occupational status is regarded as his or her master status. If you are a full-time student, your master status is likely to be "student."

Roles   Every status is associated with many **roles**, or the set of rights, obligations, and expectations associated with a status. Roles guide our behaviour and allow us to predict the behaviour of others. As a student, you are expected to attend class, listen, take notes, study for tests, and complete assignments. Because you know what the role of teacher involves, you can predict that your teacher will lecture, give exams, and assign grades based on your performance on tests.

A single status involves more than one role. For example, the status of prison inmate includes one role for interacting with prison guards and another role for interacting with other prison inmates. Similarly, the status of nurse involves different roles for interacting with physicians and with patients.

Elements of Culture

Whereas social structure refers to the organization of society, culture refers to the meanings and ways of life that characterize a society. The elements of culture include beliefs, values, norms, sanctions, and symbols.

Beliefs   **Beliefs** refer to definitions and explanations about what is assumed to be true. The beliefs of an individual or a group influence whether that individual or group views a particular social condition as a social problem. Does secondhand smoke harm nonsmokers? Are nuclear power plants safe? Does violence in movies and on television lead to increased aggression in children?

Our beliefs regarding these issues influence whether we view the issues as social problems. Beliefs not only influence how a social condition is interpreted, they also influence the existence of the condition itself. For example, men who believe that when a woman says "no," she really means "yes" or "maybe" are more likely to commit sexual assault than men who do not have these beliefs (Frank 1991). The Self and Society feature in this chapter allows you to assess your own beliefs about various social issues and compare your beliefs with national samples of Canadian adults 18 years of age and older, surveyed in 1975, 1985, and 1995.

Values   **Values** are social agreements about what is considered good and bad, right and wrong, desirable and undesirable. Frequently, social conditions are viewed as social problems when the conditions are incompatible with or contradict closely held values. For example, poverty and homelessness violate the value of human welfare; some types of crime contradict the values of honesty, private property, and nonviolence; racism, sexism, and heterosexism violate the values of equality and fairness.

Values play an important role not only in the interpretation of a condition as a social problem, but also in the development of the social condition itself. Sylvia Ann Hewlett (1992) explains how the values of freedom and individualism are at the root of many of our social problems:

> There are two sides to the coin of freedom. On the one hand, there is enormous potential for prosperity and personal fulfillment; on the other are all the hazards of untrammeled opportunity and unfettered choice. Free markets can produce grinding poverty as well as spectacular wealth; unregulated industry can create dangerous levels of pollution as well as rapid rates of growth; and an unfettered drive for personal fulfillment can have disastrous effects on families and children. Rampant individualism does not bring with it sweet freedom; rather, it explodes in our faces and limits life's potential. (pp. 350–1)

Absent or weak values may contribute to some social problems. For example, many industries do not value protection of the environment and thus contribute to environmental pollution.

Norms and Sanctions   **Norms** are socially defined rules of behaviour. Norms serve as guidelines for our behaviour and for our expectations of the behaviour of others.

There are three types of norms: folkways, laws, and mores. **Folkways** refer to the customs and manners of society. In many segments of our society, it is customary to shake hands when being introduced to a new acquaintance, to say "excuse me" after sneezing, and to give presents to family and friends on their birthdays. Although no laws require us to do these things, we are expected to do them because they are part of the cultural traditions, or folkways, of the society in which we live.

Laws are norms that are formalized and backed by political authority. A person who eats food out of a public garbage container is violating a folkway; no law prohibits this behaviour. However, throwing trash onto a public street is considered littering and is against the law.

Personal Beliefs about Various Social Problems

Indicate whether you agree or disagree with each of the following statements:

	AGREE	DISAGREE
1. There are some circumstances in which a doctor would be justified in ending a patient's life.	___	___
2. It should be possible for a pregnant woman to obtain a *legal* abortion if she wants it for any reason.	___	___
3. It should be possible for a pregnant woman to get a *legal* abortion if there is a strong chance of a serious defect in the baby.	___	___
4. The death penalty should be exercised in some instances.	___	___
5. Immigrants to Canada have an obligation to learn Canadian ways.	___	___
6. Marijuana should be legalized.	___	___
7. Homosexuality is "always wrong" or "almost always wrong."	___	___
8. Homosexuals are entitled to the same rights as other Canadians.	___	___
9. Birth control information should be available to teenagers who want it.	___	___
10. Natives have too much power in our nation's affairs.	___	___
11. There are racial and cultural groups that are discriminated against in my community.	___	___
12. Law enforcement is applied evenly to all those who break the law.	___	___
13. Anyone who works hard will rise to the top.	___	___
14. Corporations have far too much power in national life.	___	___
15. Bilingualism is a policy worth supporting.	___	___
16. In general, values in Canada have been changing for the worse.	___	___

PERCENTAGE* OF CANADIANS AGREEING WITH BELIEF STATEMENTS

	Percentage Agreeing in 1975, 1985, 1995		
Statement Number	*1975*	*1985*	*1995*
1. Doctor-assisted euthanasia	–	–	75
2. Abortion "on demand"	–	37	39
3. Abortion if "serious defect" in child	85	86	88
4. Use of death penalty	79	84	82
5. Assimilation expectations	85	–	88
6. Legalization of marijuana	27	–	31
7. Disapproval of homosexuality	72	71	52
8. Extending rights to homosexuals	–	76	67
9. Birth control information to teens	94	91	94
10. Natives have too much power	7	13	33
11. Racial and cultural discrimination	–	54	67
12. Law enforcement equitable	37	27	25
13. Self-efficacy	45	50	53
14. Corporations have too much power	83	73	69
15. Endorsement of bilingualism	49	53	55
16. Values changing for the worse	–	54	74

* Each Project Canada sample consists of a highly representative sample of approximately 1500 Canadian adults 18 and older.

SOURCE: *The Bibby Report: Social Trends Canadian Style* copyright © 1995 by Reginald W. Bibby. Reprinted by permission of Stoddart Publishing.

Some norms, called **mores**, have a moral basis. Violations of mores may produce shock, horror, and moral indignation. Both littering and child sexual abuse are violations of law, but child sexual abuse is also a violation of our mores because we view such behaviour as immoral.

All norms are associated with **sanctions**, or social consequences for conforming to or violating norms. When we conform to a social norm, we may be rewarded by a positive sanction. These may range from an approving smile to a public ceremony in our honour. When we violate a social norm, we may be punished by a negative sanction, which may range from a disapproving look to life in prison. Most sanctions are spontaneous expressions of approval or disapproval by groups or individuals—these are referred to as informal sanctions. Sanctions that are carried out according to some recognized or formal procedure are referred to as formal sanctions. Types of sanctions, then, include positive informal sanctions, positive formal sanctions, negative informal sanctions, and negative formal sanctions (see Table 1.1).

Table 1.1	Types and Examples of Sanctions

INFORMAL
Positive
Being praised by one's neighbours for organizing a neighbourhood-recycling program.
Negative
Being criticized by one's neighbours for refusing to participate in the neighbourhood-recycling program.

FORMAL
Positive
Being granted a citizen's award for organizing a neighbourhood-recycling program.
Negative
Being fined by the city for failing to dispose of trash properly.

Symbols A **symbol** is something that represents something else. Without symbols, we could not communicate with each other or live as social beings.

The symbols of a culture include language, gestures, and objects whose meanings are commonly understood by the members of a society. In our society, a red ribbon tied around a car antenna symbolizes Mothers Against Drunk Driving, a peace sign symbolizes the value of nonviolence, and a white hooded robe symbolizes the Ku Klux Klan. Sometimes people attach different meanings to the same symbol. The swastika is an ancient symbol or ornament that was supposed to bring good luck. However, its adoption as the official emblem of the Nazi Party and Nazi Germany has encouraged many to view it as a symbol of anti-Semitism, White supremacy, and bigotry.

The elements of the social structure and culture just discussed play a central role in the creation, maintenance, and social response to various social problems. One of the goals of taking a course in social problems is to develop an awareness of how the elements of social structure and culture contribute to social problems. Sociologists refer to this awareness as the "sociological imagination" or "sociological mindfulness."

THE SOCIOLOGICAL IMAGINATION

The **sociological imagination**, a term developed by C. Wright Mills (1959), refers to the ability to see the connections between our personal lives and the social world in which we live. When we use our sociological imagination, we are able to distinguish between "private troubles" and "public issues" and to see connections between the events and conditions of our lives and the social and historical context in which we live.

For example, that one man is unemployed constitutes a private trouble. That thousands of people are unemployed in Canada constitutes a public issue. Once we understand that other segments of society share personal troubles such as HIV infection, criminal victimization, and poverty, we can look for the elements of social structure and culture that contribute to these public issues and private troubles. If the various elements of social structure and culture contribute to private troubles and public issues, then society's social structure and culture must be changed if these concerns are to be resolved.

Rather than viewing the private trouble of being unemployed as resulting from an individual's faulty character or lack of job skills, we may understand unemployment as a public issue that results from the failure of the economic and political institutions of society to provide job opportunities to all citizens. Technological innovations emerging from the Industrial Revolution led to individual workers being replaced by machines. During the economic recession of the 1980s, employers fired employees so the firms could stay in business or could maximize profits, or both. Thus, in both these cases, social forces rather than individual skills largely determined whether a person was employed or not.

Another concept similar to "sociological imagination" is "**sociological mindfulness**." According to sociologist Michael Schwalbe (1998), sociological mindfulness is a way of paying attention to the social world. What do we see if we practise sociological mindfulness? Schwalbe answers:

> We see, for example, how the social world is created by people;...how people's behaviour is a response to the conditions under which they live; how social life consists of patterns...how power is exercised; how inequalities are created and maintained. (p. 4)

> Being sociologically mindful also means paying attention to the hardships and options other people face. If we understand how others' circumstances differ from ours, we are more likely to show compassion for them and to grant them the respect they deserve as human beings. We are also less likely to condemn them unfairly.... (p. 5)

> Part of being sociologically mindful of the constructedness of the social world is seeing the possibility of changing it. This means recognizing the possibility of acting differently, of choosing not to support arrangements that are harmful or unjust. (p. 23)...Being sociologically mindful, we thus see that human beings are both social products and social forces. (p. 25)

THEORETICAL PERSPECTIVES

Theories in sociology provide us with different perspectives with which to view our social world. A perspective is simply a way of looking at the world. A theory is a set of interrelated propositions or principles designed to answer a question or explain a particular phenomenon; it provides us with a perspective. Sociological theories help us to explain and predict the social world in which we live.

Sociology includes three major theoretical perspectives: the structural-functionalist perspective, the conflict perspective, and the symbolic interactionist perspective. Each perspective offers a variety of explanations about the causes of and possible solutions for social problems (Rubington and Weinberg 1995).

Structural-Functionalist Perspective

The structural-functionalist perspective is largely based on the works of Herbert Spencer, Emile Durkheim, Talcott Parsons, and Robert Merton. According to **structural-functionalism**, society is a system of interconnected parts that work together in harmony to maintain a state of balance and social equilibrium for the whole. For example, each of the social institutions contributes important functions for society: family provides a context for reproducing, nurturing, and socializing children; education offers a way to transmit a society's skills, knowledge, and culture to its youth; politics provides a means of governing members of society; economics provides for the production, distribution, and consumption of goods and services; and religion provides moral guidance and an outlet for worship of a higher power.

The structural-functionalist perspective emphasizes the interconnectedness of society by focusing on how each part influences and is influenced by other parts. For example, the increases in lone-parent and dual-earner families in part have contributed to the number of children who are failing in school because parents have become less available to supervise their children's homework. Because of changes in technology, colleges and universities are offering more technical programs, and many adults are returning to school to learn new skills that are required in the workplace. The increasing number of women in the workforce has contributed to the formulation of policies against sexual harassment and job discrimination.

CONSIDERATION

In viewing society as a set of interrelated parts, structural-functionalists also note that proposed solutions to a social problem may cause additional social problems. For example, the use of plea-bargaining was adopted as a means of dealing with overcrowded court dockets but resulted in "the revolving door of justice." Urban renewal projects often displaced residents and broke up community cohesion.

Structural-functionalists use the terms "functional" and "dysfunctional" to describe the effects of social elements on society. Elements of society are functional if they contribute to social stability and dysfunctional if they disrupt social stability. Some aspects of society may be both functional and dysfunctional for society. For example, crime is dysfunctional in that it is associated with physical violence, loss of property, and fear. However, according to

Durkheim and other functionalists, crime is also functional for society because it leads to heightened awareness of shared moral bonds and increased social cohesion.

Sociologists have identified two types of functions: manifest and latent (Merton 1968). **Manifest functions** are consequences that are intended and commonly recognized. **Latent functions** are consequences that are unintended and often hidden. For example, the manifest function of education is to transmit knowledge and skills to society's youth. However, public elementary schools also serve as babysitters for employed parents, and colleges and universities offer a place for young adults to meet potential mates. The babysitting and mate selection functions are not the intended or commonly recognized functions of education—hence, they are latent functions.

Structural-Functionalist Theories of Social Problems

Two dominant theories of social problems grew out of the structural-functionalist perspective: social pathology and social disorganization.

Social Pathology   According to the social pathology model, social problems result from some "sickness" in society. Just as the human body becomes ill when our systems, organs, and cells do not function normally, society becomes "ill" when its parts (i.e., elements of the structure and culture) no longer perform properly. For example, problems such as crime, violence, poverty, and youth crime are often attributed to the breakdown of the family institution, the decline of the religious institution, and inadequacies in our economic, educational, and political institutions.

Social "illness" also results when members of a society are not adequately socialized to adopt its norms and values. Persons who do not value honesty, for example, are prone to dishonesties of all sorts. Early theorists attributed the failure in socialization to "sick" people who could not be socialized. Later theorists recognized that failure in the socialization process stemmed from "sick" social conditions, not "sick" people. To prevent or solve social problems, members of society must receive proper socialization and moral education, which may be accomplished in schools, churches, workplaces, the family, and through the media.

Social Disorganization   According to the social disorganization view of social problems, rapid social change disrupts the norms in a society. When norms become weak or are in conflict with each other, society is in a state of **anomie** or normlessness. Hence, people may steal, physically abuse their partner or children, abuse drugs, commit sexual assault, or engage in other deviant behaviour because the norms regarding these behaviours are weak or conflicting. According to this view, the solution to social problems lies in slowing the pace of social change and strengthening social norms. For example, although the use of alcohol by teenagers is considered a violation of a social norm in our society, this norm is weak. The media portray young people drinking alcohol, teenagers teach each other to drink alcohol and they buy fake identification cards to purchase alcohol, and parents model drinking behaviour by having a few drinks after work or at a social event. Solutions to teenage drinking may involve strengthening norms against it through public education, restricting media depictions of youth and alcohol, imposing stronger sanctions against the use of fake IDs to purchase alcohol, and educating parents to model moderate and responsible drinking behaviour.

Conflict Perspective

Whereas the structural-functionalist perspective views society as comprising different parts working together, the **conflict perspective** views society as comprising different groups and interests competing for power and resources. The conflict perspective explains various aspects of our social world by looking at which groups have power and benefit from a particular social arrangement.

The origins of the conflict perspective can be traced to the classic works of Karl Marx. Marx suggested that all societies go through stages of economic development. As societies evolve from agricultural to industrial, concern over meeting survival needs is replaced by concern over making a profit, the hallmark of a capitalist system. Industrialization leads to the development of two classes of people: the bourgeoisie, or the owners of the means of production (e.g., factories, farms, businesses), and the proletariat, or the workers who earn wages.

The division of society into two broad classes of people—the "haves" and the "have-nots"—is beneficial to the owners of the means of production. The workers, who may earn only subsistence wages, are denied access to the many resources available to the wealthy owners. According to Marx, the bourgeoisie use their power to control the institutions of society to their advantage. For example, Marx suggested that religion serves as an "opiate of the masses" in that it soothes the distress and suffering associated with the working-class lifestyle and focuses the workers' attention on spirituality, God, and the afterlife rather than on such worldly concerns as living conditions. In essence, religion diverts the workers so that they concentrate on being rewarded in heaven for living a moral life rather than on questioning their exploitation.

Conflict Theories of Social Problems

There are two general types of conflict theories of social problems: Marxist and non-Marxist. Marxist theories focus on social conflict that results from economic inequalities; non-Marxist theories focus on social conflict that results from competing values and interests among social groups.

Marxist Conflict Theories   According to contemporary Marxist theorists, social problems result from the class inequality inherent in a capitalistic system. A system of "haves" and "have-nots" may be beneficial to the "haves" but often translates into poverty for the "have-nots." As we shall explore later in this text, many social problems, including physical and mental illness, low educational achievement, and crime, are linked to poverty.

In addition to creating an impoverished class of people, capitalism also encourages "corporate violence." Corporate violence may be defined as actual harm or risk of harm inflicted on consumers, workers, and the public because of decisions made by corporate executives or managers. Corporate violence may also result from corporate negligence, the quest for profits at any cost, and willful violations of health, safety, and environmental laws (Hills 1987). Our profit-motivated economy may provide encouragement for those who are otherwise good, kind, and law-abiding to participate knowingly in the manufacturing and marketing of defective brakes on jets, fuel tanks on automobiles, and unsafe contraceptive devices such as some intrauterine devices (IUDs). The profit motive has also caused individuals to sell defective medical devices, toxic pesticides, and contaminated foods to developing countries. Blumberg (1989) suggests that "in an economic system based exclusively on motives of self-interest and profit, such behaviour is inevitable" (p. 106).

Marxist conflict theories also focus on the problem of **alienation,** or powerlessness and meaninglessness in people's lives. In industrialized societies, workers often have little power or control over their jobs, which fosters a sense of powerlessness in their lives. The specialized nature of work requires workers to perform limited and repetitive tasks; as a result, the workers may come to feel that their lives are meaningless.

Alienation is bred not only in the workplace, but also in the classroom. Students have little power over their education and often find the curriculum is not meaningful to their lives. Like poverty, alienation is linked to other social problems, such as low educational achievement, violence, and suicide.

Marxist explanations of social problems imply that the solution lies in eliminating inequality among classes of people by creating a classless society. The nature of work must also change to avoid alienation. Finally, stronger controls must be applied to corporations to ensure that corporate decisions and practices are based on safety rather than on profit considerations.

Non-Marxist Conflict Theories Non-Marxist conflict theorists such as Ralf Dahrendorf are concerned with conflict that arises when groups have opposing values and interests. For example, antiabortion activists value the life of unborn embryos and fetuses; prochoice activists value the right of women to control their own bodies and reproductive decisions. These different value positions reflect different subjective interpretations of what constitutes a social problem. For antiabortionists, the availability of abortion is the social problem; for prochoice advocates, restrictions on abortion are the social problem. Sometimes the social problem is not the conflict itself, but rather the way that conflict is expressed. Even most prolife advocates agree that shooting doctors who perform abortions and blowing up abortion clinics constitute unnecessary violence and lack of respect for life. Value conflicts may occur between diverse categories of people, including non-Whites versus Whites, heterosexuals versus homosexuals, young versus old, liberals versus conservatives, and environmentalists versus industrialists.

Solutions to the problems that are generated by competing values may involve ensuring that conflicting groups understand each other's views, resolving differences through negotiation or mediation, or agreeing to disagree. Ideally, solutions should be win-win; both conflicting groups should be satisfied with the solution. However, outcomes of value conflicts are often influenced by power; the group with the most power may use its position to influence the outcome of value conflicts.

Symbolic Interactionist Perspective

Both the structural-functionalist and the conflict perspectives are concerned with how broad aspects of society, such as institutions and large social groups, influence the social world. This level of sociological analysis is called **macro sociology:** it looks at the "big picture" of society and suggests how social problems are affected at the institutional level.

Micro sociology, another level of sociological analysis, is concerned with the social psychological dynamics of individuals interacting in small groups. **Symbolic interactionism** reflects the micro-sociological perspective and was largely influenced by the work of early sociologists and philosophers such as Max Weber, George Simmel, Charles Horton Cooley, G. H. Mead, W. I. Thomas, Erving Goffman, and Howard Becker. Symbolic interactionism emphasizes that human behaviour is influenced by definitions and meanings that are created and maintained through symbolic interaction with others.

Sociologist W. I. Thomas ([1931] 1966) emphasized the importance of definitions and meanings in social behaviour and in its consequences. He suggested that humans respond to their definition of a situation rather than to the objective situation itself. Hence, Thomas noted that situations we define as real become real in their consequences.

Symbolic interactionism also suggests that our identity or sense of self is shaped by social interaction. We develop our self-concept by observing how others interact with us and label us. By observing how others view us, we see a reflection of ourselves that Charles Horton Cooley calls the "looking glass self."

Lastly, the symbolic interaction perspective has important implications for how social scientists conduct research. The German sociologist Max Weber (1864–1920) argued that to understand individual and group behaviour, social scientists must see the world from the eyes of that individual or group. Weber called this approach Verstehen, which in German means "empathy." Verstehen implies that in conducting research, social scientists must try to understand others' view of reality and the subjective aspects of their experiences, including their symbols, values, attitudes, and beliefs.

Symbolic Interactionist Theories of Social Problems

A basic premise of symbolic interactionist theories of social problems is that a condition must be defined or recognized as a social problem for it to be a social problem. Based on this premise, Herbert Blumer (1971) suggested that social problems develop in stages. First, social problems pass through the stage of "societal recognition"—the process by which a social problem, for example, drunk driving, is "born." Second, "social legitimation" takes place when the social problem achieves recognition by the larger community, including schools, churches, and the media. As the visibility of traffic fatalities associated with alcohol increased, so did the legitimation of drunk driving as a social problem. The next stage in the development of a social problem involves "mobilization for action," which occurs when individuals and groups, such as Mothers Against Drunk Driving, become concerned about how to respond to the social condition. This mobilization leads to the "development and implementation of an official plan" for dealing with the problem, involving, for example, highway checkpoints, lower legal blood-alcohol levels, and tougher penalties for drunk driving.

Blumer's stage development view of social problems is helpful in tracing the development of social problems. For example, although sexual harassment and date rape have occurred throughout the past century, these issues did not begin to receive recognition as social problems until the 1970s. Social legitimation of these problems was achieved when high schools, colleges and universities, churches, employers, and the media recognized their existence. Organized social groups mobilized to develop and implement plans to deal with these problems. For example, groups successfully lobbied for the enactment of laws against sexual harassment and the enforcement of sanctions against violators of these laws. Groups also mobilized to provide educational seminars on date rape for students and to offer support services to victims of date rape.

Some disagree with the symbolic interactionist view that social problems exist only if they are recognized. According to this view, individuals who were victims of date rape in the 1960s may be considered victims of a problem, even though date rape was not recognized at that time as a social problem.

Labelling theory, a major symbolic interactionist theory of social problems, suggests that a social condition or group is viewed as problematic if it is labelled as such. According to labelling theory, resolving social problems sometimes involves changing the meanings and definitions that are attributed to people and situations. For example, as long as teenagers define drinking alcohol as "cool" and "fun," they will continue to abuse alcohol. As long as our society defines the provision of sex education and contraceptives for teenagers as inappropriate or immoral, the teenage pregnancy rate in our country will continue to grow.

Table 1.2 summarizes and compares the major theoretical perspectives, their criticisms, and social policy recommendations as they relate to social problems. The study of social problems is based on research as well as theory, however. Indeed, research and theory are intricately related. As Wilson (1983) states,

> **Most of us think of theorizing as quite divorced from the business of gathering facts. It seems to require an abstractness of thought remote from the practical activity of empirical research. But theory building is not a separate activity within sociology. Without theory, the empirical researcher would find it impossible to decide what to observe, how to observe it, or what to make of the observations.... (p. 1)**

SOCIAL PROBLEMS RESEARCH

Most students taking a course in social problems will not become researchers or conduct research on social problems. Nevertheless, we are all consumers of research that is reported in the media. Politicians, social activist groups, and organizations attempt to justify their decisions, actions, and positions by citing research results. Because we are consumers of research, it is important to understand that our personal experiences and casual observations are less reliable than generalizations based on systematic research. One strength of scientific research is that it is subjected to critical examination by other researchers. The more you understand how research is done, the better able you will be to critically examine and question research, rather than to passively consume research findings. The remainder of this section discusses the stages of conducting a research study and the various methods of research used by sociologists.

Stages of Conducting a Research Study

Sociologists progress through various stages in conducting research on a social problem. This section describes the first four stages: formulating a research

Table 1.2   Comparison of Theoretical Perspectives

	Structural Functionalism	Conflict Theory	Symbolic Interactionism
Representative Theorists	Emile Durkheim Robert Merton Talcott Parsons	Karl Marx Ralf Dahrendorf	George H. Mead Charles Horton Cooley Erving Goffman
Society	Society is a set of interrelated parts; cultural consensus exists and leads to social order; natural state of society—balance and harmony.	Society is marked by power struggles over scarce resources; inequities result in conflict; social change is inevitable; natural state of society—imbalance.	Society is a network of interlocking roles; social order is constructed through interaction as individuals, through shared meaning, make sense out of their social world.
Individuals	Individuals are socialized by society's institutions; socialization is the process by which social control is exerted; people need society and its institutions.	People are inherently good but are corrupted by society and its economic structure; institutions are controlled by groups with power; "order" is part of the illusion.	Humans are interpretative and interactive; they are constantly changing as their "social beings" emerge and are moulded by changing circumstances.
Cause of Social Problem?	Rapid social change: social disorganization that disrupts the harmony and balance; inadequate socialization and/or weak institutions.	Inequality; the dominance of groups of people over other groups of people; oppression and exploitation; competition between groups.	Different interpretations of roles; labelling of individuals, groups, or behaviours as deviant; definition of an objective condition as a social problem.
Social Policy/ Solutions	Repair weak institutions; assure proper socialization; cultivate a strong collective sense of right and wrong.	Minimize competition; create an equitable system for the distribution of resources.	Reduce impact of labelling and associated stigmatization; alter definitions of what is defined as a social problem.
Criticisms	Called "sunshine sociology"; supports the maintenance of the status quo; needs to ask "functional for whom?" Does not deal with issues of power and conflict; incorrectly assumes a consensus.	Utopian model; Marxist states have failed; denies existence of cooperation and equitable exchange. Cannot explain cohesion and harmony.	Concentrates on micro issues only; fails to link micro issues to macro-level concerns; too psychological in its approach; assumes label amplifies problem.

question, reviewing the literature, defining variables, and formulating a hypothesis.

Formulating a Research Question   A research study usually begins with a research question. Where do research questions originate? How does a particular researcher come to ask a particular research question? In some cases, researchers have a personal interest in a specific topic because of their own life experience. For example, a researcher who has experienced spouse abuse may wish to do research on such questions as "What factors are associated with domestic violence?" and "How helpful are battered women's shelters in helping abused women break the cycle of abuse in their lives?" Other researchers may ask a particular research question because of their personal values—their concern for humanity and the desire to improve human life. Researchers who are concerned about the spread of human immunodeficiency virus (HIV) infection and AIDS may conduct research on such questions as "How does the use of alcohol influence condom use?" and "What educational

Collaborative Research as an Emerging Research Model

Collaborative research (also known as *participatory research*), refers to a research approach in which community activists and academicians work together in all phases of research, including identifying the research question, developing the research design, collecting and analyzing the data, presenting the results, and working with policy makers and practitioners in designing programs and policies.

Collaborative research is a win-win endeavour, benefiting professional researchers as well as community groups and organizations. Community groups often lack resources to conduct quality research. Through collaboration with university researchers, community activists and organizations gain access to financial and technical resources and discover the usefulness of using systematic research methods to analyze social problems and identify, implement, and evaluate solutions. Collaborative research provides "a means of putting research capabilities in the hands of the deprived and disenfranchised people so that they can transform their lives for themselves" (Park 1993: 1).

Through collaboration with community organizations and activists, academic researchers gain new insights into social problems and find new ways to use their skills and contribute to public well-being. Because collaborative research projects investigate the concerns of community organizations and practitioners, "the results are more likely to have relevance in solving pressing problems in today's society..." (Nyden et al. 1997: 4).

The collaborative research model not only helps achieve solutions to specific social problems, it also contributes to the redistribution of power in the creation of legitimate, scientific knowledge. The production of scientific knowledge has been largely controlled by researchers who are academic "experts" in their field, well versed in theories, and who have the technical knowledge and financial resources to conduct research. Research agendas and the production of legitimate, scientifically produced knowledge have been shaped and controlled by universities and by corporations and government agencies that have the economic resources to hire researchers and fund research projects. By involving practitioners, policymakers, and social activists in the research process, collaborative research offers a means to break

the university's monopoly on the production of knowledge and empowers community members to shape research based on the concerns of individuals and organizations facing the issues on a daily basis.

Given the movement toward downsizing and the fierce competition over scarce research funding dollars, there are certainly economic pressures encouraging community organizations and academic institutions to pool their resources. Publicly funded academic institutions are also under pressure to make direct contributions to social well-being and thus justify their public funding. Beyond the economic advantages of collaborative research, sociologist Phil Brown (1997) notes, "our task of integrating social science and social activism can help retain and rekindle the spirit of human betterment that has long been a part of sociology" (p. 101).

SOURCES: Brown, Phil. 1997. "Social Science and Environmental Activism: A Personal Account." In *Building Community: Social Science in Action*, edited by P. Nyden, A. Figert, M. Shibley, and D. Burrows, pp. 98–102. Thousand Oaks, Calif.: Pine Forge Press; Park, Peter. 1993. "What Is Participatory Research? A Theoretical and Methodological Perspective." In *Voices of Change: Participatory Research in the United States and Canada*, edited by P. Park, M. Brydon-Miller, B. Hall, and T. Jackson, pp. 1–19. Toronto, Ont.: Ontario Institute for Studies in Education Press.

strategies are effective for increasing safer sex behaviour?" Researchers may also want to test a particular sociological theory, or some aspect of it, to establish its validity or conduct studies to evaluate the effect of a social policy or program. Research questions may also be formulated by the concerns of community groups and social activist organizations in collaboration with academic researchers. Government and industry also hire researchers to answer questions such as "How many children are victimized by episodes of violence at school?" and "What types of computer technologies can protect children against being exposed to pornography on the Internet?"

CONSIDERATION

Many questions involving morals, values, and religion cannot be answered through scientific research. For example, scientific research cannot determine whether the death penalty or anything else is moral or immoral. Scientific research can, however, reveal information that may support or cause us to question our own moral judgments. Research can tell us how various segments of the population view capital punishment and what social and personal factors are associated with the different views. Research may also identify some of the social and economic consequences of allowing versus prohibiting capital punishment.

Reviewing the Literature   After formulating the research question, the researcher reviews the published material on the topic to find out what is already known about it. Reviewing the literature also provides researchers with ideas about how to conduct their research and helps them formulate new research questions. A literature review also serves as an evaluation tool, allowing a comparison of research findings and other sources of information, such as expert opinions, political claims, and journalistic reports.

Defining Variables   A **variable** is any measurable event, characteristic, or property that varies or is subject to change. Researchers must operationally define the variables they study. An **operational definition** specifies how a variable is to be measured. For example, an operational definition of the variable "religiosity" might be the number of times the respondent reports going to church or synagogue. Another operational definition of "religiosity" might be the respondent's answer to the question, "How important is religion in your life? (1 = not important, 2 = somewhat important, 3 = very important)."

Operational definitions are particularly important for defining variables that cannot be directly observed. For example, researchers cannot directly observe concepts such as "mental illness," "sexual harassment," "child neglect," "job satisfaction," and "drug abuse." Nor can researchers directly observe perceptions, values, and attitudes.

Formulating a Hypothesis   After defining the research variables, researchers may formulate a **hypothesis,** which is a prediction or educated guess about how one variable is related to another variable. The **dependent variable** is the variable that the researcher wants to explain; that is, it is the variable of interest. The **independent variable** is the variable that is expected to explain change in the dependent variable. In formulating a hypothesis, the researcher predicts how the independent variable affects the dependent variable. For example, Miles Corak (1998) predicted that the source of a parent's income (in this case, the father's) influenced the employment incomes of their grown-up children. His research found that the source of the father's income (e.g., paid work, self-employment, assets, government transfers) was strongly associated with the incomes of his adult children. In this example, the independent variable is source of father's income; the dependent variable is income of adult children.

CONSIDERATION

Some social problems act as independent variables in the production of other social problems. Social problems that produce many other social problems are called "primary social problems" (Manis 1974). For example, poverty is a social problem that leads to the secondary social problem of slum neighbourhoods, which in turn lead to the social problems of crime and addiction. In this example, "slum neighbourhoods" acts as both an independent and a dependent variable.

In studying social problems, researchers often assess the effects of several independent variables on one or more dependent variables. For example, Jekielek (1998) examined the impact of parental conflict and marital disruption (two independent variables) on the emotional well-being of children (the dependent variable). Her research found that both parental conflict and marital disruption (separation or divorce) negatively affect children's emotional well-being. However, children in high-conflict intact families exhibit lower levels of well-being than do children who have experienced high levels of parental conflict but whose parents divorce or separate.

Methods of Data Collection

After identifying a research topic, reviewing the literature, and developing hypotheses, researchers decide which method of data collection to use. Alternatives include experiments, surveys, field research, and secondary data.

Experiments   **Experiments** involve manipulating the independent variable to determine how it affects the dependent variable. Experiments require one or more experimental groups that are exposed to the experimental treatment(s) and a control group that is not exposed. After the researcher randomly assigns participants to either an experimental or a control group, she or he measures the dependent variable. After the experimental groups are exposed to the treatment, the researcher measures the dependent variable again. If participants have been randomly assigned to the different groups, the researcher may conclude that any difference in the dependent variable among the groups is due to the effect of the independent variable.

An example of a "social problems" experiment on poverty would be to provide welfare payments to one group of unemployed single mothers (experimental group) and no such payments to another group of unemployed single mothers (control group). The independent variable would be welfare payments; the dependent variable would be employment. The researcher's hypothesis would be that mothers in the experimental group would be less likely to have a job after 12 months than mothers in the control group would be.

The major strength of the experimental method is that it provides evidence for causal relationships; that is, how one variable affects another. A primary weakness is that experiments are often conducted on small samples, usually in artificial laboratory settings; thus, the findings may not be generalizable to other people in natural settings.

Surveys   **Survey research** involves eliciting information from respondents through questions. An important part of survey research is selecting a sample of those to be questioned. A **sample** is a portion of the population, selected to be representative so that the information from the sample can be generalized to a larger population. For example, instead of asking all abused spouses about their experience, you could ask a representative sample of them and assume that those you did not question would give similar responses. After selecting a representative sample, survey researchers either interview people, ask them to complete written questionnaires, or elicit responses to research questions through computers.

1. *Interviews*. In interview survey research, trained interviewers ask respondents a series of questions and make written notes about or tape-record the

respondents' answers. Interviews may be conducted over the telephone or face to face. For example, Statistics Canada's Violence Against Women Survey (VAWS) involved telephone interviews with more than 12 000 Canadian women 18 years of age and older. The women were asked about their experiences of sexual and physical violence since the age of 18. The findings indicated that 29 percent of ever-married women had experienced wife assault; that 16 percent had been kicked, hit, beaten, choked, had a gun or knife used against them, or been sexually assaulted; and that 11 percent had been pushed, grabbed, shoved, or slapped. Two percent of their respondents reported nonphysical assaults (e.g., being threatened or having something thrown at them) (Rodgers 1994).

One advantage of interview research is that researchers are able to clarify questions for the respondent and follow up on answers to particular questions. Researchers often conduct face-to-face interviews with groups of individuals who might otherwise be inaccessible. For example, some AIDS-related research attempts to assess the degree to which individuals engage in behaviour that places them at high risk for transmitting or contracting HIV. Street youth and intravenous drug users, both high-risk groups for HIV infection, may not have a telephone or address because of their transient lifestyle (Catania et al. 1990). These groups may be accessible, however, if the researcher locates their hang-outs and conducts face-to-face interviews. Research on homeless individuals may also require a face-to-face interview survey design.

The most serious disadvantages of interview research are cost and the lack of privacy and anonymity. Respondents may feel embarrassed or threatened when asked questions that relate to personal issues such as drug use, domestic violence, and sexual behaviour. As a result, some respondents may choose not to participate in interview research on sensitive topics. Those who do participate may conceal or alter information or give socially desirable answers to the interviewer's questions (e.g., "No, I do not use drugs").

2. *Questionnaires*. Instead of conducting personal or phone interviews, researchers may develop questionnaires that they either mail or give to a sample of respondents. Questionnaire research offers the advantages of being less expensive and time-consuming than face-to-face or telephone surveys. In addition, questionnaire research provides privacy and anonymity to the research participants. This reduces the likelihood that they will feel threatened or embarrassed when asked personal questions and increases the likelihood that they will provide answers that are not intentionally inaccurate or distorted.

The major disadvantage of mail questionnaires is that it is difficult to obtain an adequate response rate. Many people do not want to take the time or make the effort to complete and mail a questionnaire. Others may be unable to read and understand the questionnaire.

3. *"Talking" Computers*. A new method of conducting survey research is asking respondents to provide answers to a computer that "talks." Romer et al. (1997) found that respondents rated computer interviews about sexual issues more favourably than face-to-face interviews and that the former were more reliable. Such increased reliability may be particularly valuable when conducting research on drug use, deviant sexual behaviour, and sexual orientation as respondents reported the privacy of computers as a major advantage (Romer et al. 1997).

Field Research **Field research** involves observing and studying social behaviour in settings in which it occurs naturally. Two types of field research are participant observation and nonparticipant observation.

In participant observation research, the researcher participates in the phenomenon being studied to obtain an insider's perspective of the people or behaviour being observed, or both. Coleman (1990), a middle-class White male, changed clothes to live on the streets as a homeless person for 10 days. In nonparticipant observation research, the researcher observes the phenomenon being studied without actively participating in the group or the activity. For example, Dordick (1997) studied homelessness by observing and talking with homeless individuals in a variety of settings, but she did not live as a homeless person as part of her research.

Sometimes sociologists conduct in-depth detailed analyses or case studies of an individual, group, or event. For example, Skeen (1991) conducted case studies of a prostitute and her adjustment to leaving the profession, an incest survivor, and a person with AIDS.

The main advantage of field research on social problems is that it provides detailed information about the values, rituals, norms, behaviours, symbols, beliefs, and emotions of those being studied. A potential problem with field research is that the researcher's observations may be biased (e.g., the researcher becomes too involved in the group or individual to be objective). In addition, because field research is usually based on small samples, the findings may not be generalizable.

Secondary Data Research Sometimes researchers analyze secondary data, which are data that have already been collected by other researchers or government agencies or that exist in forms such as historical documents, police reports, hospital records, and official records of marriages, births, and deaths. For example, researchers may use information about job safety collected by workers' compensation boards (now called Workplace Safety and Insurance Boards in Ontario) to identify "dangerous occupations" in Canada. Although common sense might suggest that policing is an extraordinarily high-risk profession, it is actually quite safe. On average, there are 0.1575 deaths for every 1000 person-years of police work. Indeed, "working as a law enforcement officer is only marginally more dangerous than working as a biologist, an occupation in which there are 0.1570 deaths for every 1000 person-years worked" (Statistics Canada 1998: 231). In Canada, the three most dangerous occupations are, in order: the cutting and loading of rock, general mine labouring, and operating small rail engines. In addition, some occupations are also dangerous because they involve long-term exposure to harmful substances. Between 1988 and 1993, one in five work-related deaths in Canada occurred as the result of exposure to harmful substances such as poisons, chemicals, radiation, and asbestos (p. 232).

A major advantage of using secondary data in studying social problems is that the data are readily accessible, so researchers avoid the time and expense of collecting their own data. Secondary data are also often based on large representative samples. The disadvantage of secondary data is that the researcher is limited to the data already collected.

GOALS OF THE TEXT

This text approaches the study of social problems with several goals in mind.

1. *Provide an integrated theoretical background.* This text reflects an integrative theoretical approach to the study of social problems. More than one theoretical perspective can be used to explain a social problem because social problems usually have multiple causes. For example, youth crime is linked to (1) an increased number of youth living in inner-city neighbourhoods with little or no parental supervision (social disorganization), (2) young people having no legitimate means of acquiring material wealth (anomie theory), (3) youth being angry and frustrated at the inequality and racism in our society (conflict theory), and (4) teachers regarding youth as "no good" and treating them accordingly (labelling theory).

2. *Encourage the development of a sociological imagination.* Using data provided by the Canadian component of the International Social Survey Program (ISSP) in 1992–93, Curtis and Grabb (1999: 342) report that the majority of Canadians see success as based on individual attributes or abilities. That is, most Canadians, including those of less advantaged social statuses (e.g., women, the less-educated, and Canadians from poorer regions such as the Atlantic provinces) "endorse the idea that it is what an individual is or does, based on hard work, ambition and natural ability, along with the achievement of higher educational credentials, that helps a person get ahead." However, a major insight of the sociological perspective is that various structural and cultural elements of society have far-reaching effects on individual lives and social well-being. This insight, known as the sociological imagination or sociological mindfulness, enables us to understand how social forces underlie personal misfortunes and failures as well as contribute to personal successes and achievements. Each chapter in this text emphasizes how structural and cultural factors contribute to social problems. This emphasis encourages you to develop your sociological imagination by recognizing how structural and cultural factors influence private troubles and public issues.

3. *Provide global coverage of social problems.* The modern world is often referred to as a "global village." The Internet and fax machines connect individuals around the world, economies are interconnected, environmental destruction in one region of the world affects other regions of the world, and diseases cross national boundaries. Understanding social problems requires an awareness of how global trends and policies affect social problems. Many social problems call for collective action involving countries around the world; efforts to end poverty, protect the environment, control population growth, and reduce the spread of HIV are some of the social problems that have been addressed at the global level. Each chapter in this text includes coverage of global aspects of social problems. We hope that attention to the global aspects of social problems broadens your awareness of pressing world issues.

4. *Provide an opportunity to assess personal beliefs and attitudes.* Each chapter in this text contains a section called Self and Society, which offers you an opportunity to assess your attitudes and beliefs regarding some aspect of the social problem discussed. Earlier in this chapter, the Self and Society feature allowed you to assess your beliefs about a number of social problems and compare your beliefs with a national sample of Canadians.

5. *Emphasize the human side of social problems.* Each chapter in this text contains a feature called The Human Side, which presents personal stories of how social problems have affected individual lives. By conveying the private pain and personal triumphs associated with social problems, we hope to elicit a level of understanding and compassion that may not be attained through the academic study of social problems alone. This chapter's The Human Side presents stories about how students, disturbed by various social conditions, have participated in social activism.

6. *Encourage students to take prosocial action.* Individuals who understand the factors that contribute to social problems may be better able to formulate interventions to remedy those problems. Recognizing the personal pain and public costs associated with social problems encourages some to initiate social intervention.

Individuals can make a difference in society by the choices they make. Individuals may choose to vote for one candidate over another, demand the right to reproductive choice or protest government policies that permit it, drive drunk or stop a friend from driving drunk, repeat a racist or sexist joke or chastise the person who tells it, and practise safe sex or risk the transmission of sexually trans-

THE HUMAN SIDE

STUDENT ACTIVISM

Some people believe that to promote social change you must be in a position of political power or have large financial resources. However, the most important prerequisite for becoming actively involved in improving levels of social well-being may be genuine concern and dedication to a social "cause." The following vignettes provide a sampler of student activism—students making a difference in the world.

- In May 1999, hundreds of Chinese college students protested in Tiananmen Square in Beijing, China, because Chinese government officials would not meet with them to hear their pleas for a democratic government. These students boycotted classes and started a hunger strike. On June 4, 1989, thousands of students and other protesters were massacred or arrested in Tiananmen Square.
- In October 1969, less than four months after the "Stonewall Riots" in New York (an event that marked the symbolic beginning of the gay liberation movement), the first meeting of the first gay liberation organization in Canada, the University of Toronto Homophile Association (UTHA), was convened. In 1970, a group of eight gay students who perceived the need for an organization that would assist gays living in a heterosexual-dominated world formed Waterloo Universities Gay Liberation Movement (WUGLUM), a group encompassing both the University of Waterloo and Wilfrid Laurier University. In the autumn of 1971 in Saskatoon, the Gay Students Alliance became the first gay group in Saskatchewan. The following year, Gay McGill (originally GAY) became the first anglophone gay organization in Quebec. The costs of student activism at this

STUDENT ACTIVISM *(continued)*

time and on this issue were often steep. In 1975, Doug Wilson, a graduate student in education at the University of Saskatchewan, was prevented from teaching because of his public activity within the gay movement. Wilson attempted to pursue legal avenues of redress. However, although the Saskatchewan Human Rights Commission ruled in November 1975 that "sex" in the Human Rights Act included sexual orientation and launched formal proceedings against the University of Saskatchewan, proceedings were halted when the Saskatchewan Court of Queen's Bench ruled, in January of 1976, that the term "sex" in the Saskatchewan Human Rights Act did not include sexual orientation (Jackson and Persky 1982). Despite such past setbacks to the advancement of gay rights in Canada, organizations for lesbian, bisexual, gay, and transgendered peoples are now common on most campuses and provide such support services as "coming out" discussion groups and help lines, furnish educational materials, and organize a wide variety of social events.

- On December 6, 1989, the largest mass shooting in Canada occurred when 25-year-old Marc Lepine, armed with a Sturm Ruger Mini-14 semiautomatic rifle, knives, and bandoliers of ammunition, entered the École Polytechnique in Montreal and killed 14 female students and wounded 13 other students (9 women and 4 men). His rampage, which had deliberately targeted women, ended with his suicide. In the suicide note he left, Lepine wrote, "I have decided to send the feminists, who have always ruined my life, to their maker....I have decided to put an end to these viragos." This tragedy, which occurred in the University of Montreal's School of Engineering building, prompted the Canadian government to proclaim December 6 the National Day of Remembrance and Action on Violence Against Women. Since 1989, student activists across Canadian have held annual commemorative events to remember the women killed and to promote an end to violence in all its forms. For example, on the anniversary of the Montreal Massacre, the Engineering Undergraduate Society and the Association of Engineering at the University of British Columbia share a minute of silence and light candles in memory of the Montreal victims. In Nova Scotia, a Purple Ribbon campaign pays tribute to the murdered women, attempts to raise public awareness of violence against women, and collects donations to benefit transition houses for abused women and their children. The group Men for Change also formed in response to the tragedy, with the purpose of working toward an end to violence.

- In the early 1970s, U.S. citizen activist Ralph Nader launched PIRGs (Public Interest Research Groups) as a means of harnessing the energy and talent of students in solving social problems. Today, there are over 200 PIRG chapters in the United States and 19 in Canada (3 in B.C., 1 in Nova Scotia, 4 in Quebec, and 11 in

Ontario) funded through voluntary student fees. The goals of PIRGs are to motivate civic participation and responsibility by encouraging individuals to become informed, concerned, and active in their communities; to recognize and pursue integrative analyses of societal and environmental issues; to respect and encourage local and global ecosystem integrity; to encourage diversity and social equality for all people by opposing all forms of oppression; to work in a cooperative way, employing a consensual decision-making process and to work in solidarity with other like-minded environmental and social justice movements. PIRGs in Canada have produced a variety of issue-oriented publications and audio-visual materials on such topics as the food industry, acid rain, nuclear power, tenant rights, Ontario Hydro, freedom of information, and the management of toxic waste.

Students who are interested in becoming involved in student

activism, or who are already involved, might explore the Web site for the Center for Campus Organizing (1998)—an organization that supports social justice activism and investigative journalism on campuses. The organization recognizes that students and faculty, as part of an "affluent conscience constituency" (Carroll 1997: 11) have played critical roles in larger social movements for social justice in our society, including the Civil Rights movement, the anti–Vietnam War movement, the anti-Apartheid movement, the women's rights movement, and the environmental movement (Eyerman and Jamison 1991).

SOURCES: Carroll, William K. 1997. "Social Movements and Counterhegemony: Canadian Contexts and Social Theories." In *Organizing Dissent: Contemporary Social Movements in Theory and Practice*, edited by William K. Carroll, pp. 3–38. Toronto: Garamond Press; Center for Campus Organizing. December 12, 1998 <www.cco.org/about.html>; Eyerman, R., and A. Jamison. 1991. *Social Movements: A Cognitive Approach*. Cambridge: Polity Press; Jackson, Ed, and Stan Persky. 1982. *Flaunting It! A Decade of Gay Journalism from The Body Politic*. Vancouver: New Star Books.

National Data

The environmental movement's message to "Think globally, act locally" is being harkened to by many Canadians. In 1994, more than half of us could access recycling programs for paper, cans, glass bottles, and plastics and 8 out of 10 Canadians with such access recycled. In British Columbia and Ontario, about 9 out of 10 Canadians with access to recycling programs used them.
SOURCE: Statistics Canada 1998

mitted diseases. Individuals can also "make a difference" by addressing social concerns in their occupational role, as well as through volunteer work.

Although individual choices have an important impact, collective social action often has a more pervasive effect. For example, in 1971, engineer Jim Bohlen, lawyer Irving Stone, and law student Paul Cote formed the Greenpeace Foundation in Vancouver to protest U.S. unclear tests at Amchitka. In their first direct action, the 11 members of the Greenpeace Foundation set sail in a chartered trawler boat into the bomb testing range and, in so doing, managed to attract the interest of Canadians living downwind of the test site. The issue was subsequently brought before the U.S. Supreme Court; four additional tests that had been planned at Amchitka were cancelled. Since that time Greenpeace has continued in its pursuit of "a moratorium on all those things poisoning us" and become one of the largest environmental groups in the world with offices in Argentina, Australia, Austria, Belgium, Canada, Costa Rica, Denmark, Ireland, West Germany, Finland, France, Italy, Japan, Luxembourg, the Netherlands, New Zealand, Norway, Spain, Sweden, Switzerland, the United Kingdom and the United States. However, as Bohlen has himself remarked, "As individuals we are weak. Our strength is created by putting ourselves at risk" (in Nader et al. 1993: 100).

Schwalbe (1998) reminds us that we do not have to join a group or organize a protest to make changes in the world.

> We *can* change a small part of the social world single-handedly. If we treat others with more respect and compassion, if we refuse to participate in re-creating inequalities even in little ways, if we raise questions about official representation of reality, if we refuse to work in destructive industries, then we are making change. (p. 206)

UNDERSTANDING SOCIAL PROBLEMS

At the end of each chapter to follow, we offer a section entitled Understanding Social Problems in which we re-emphasize the social origin of the problem being discussed, the consequences, and the alternative social solutions. It is our hope that you will end each chapter with a "sociological imagination" view of the problem and how, as a society, we might approach a solution.

Sociologists have been studying social problems since the Industrial Revolution at the turn of the twentieth century. Industrialization brought about massive social changes: the influence of religion declined; families became smaller and moved from traditional, rural communities to urban settings. These and other changes have been associated with increases in crime, pollution, divorce, and juvenile delinquency. As these social problems became more widespread, the need to understand their origins and possible solutions became more urgent. The field of sociology developed in response to this urgency. Social problems provided the initial impetus for the development of the field of sociology and continue to be a major focus of sociology.

There is no single agreed-upon definition of what constitutes a social problem. Most sociologists agree, however, that all social problems share two important elements: an objective social condition and a subjective interpretation of that condition. Each of the three major theoretical perspectives in sociology—structural-functionalist, conflict, and symbolic interactionist—has its own notion of the causes, consequences, and solutions of social problems.

CRITICAL THINKING

1. People are increasingly using information technologies as a means of getting their daily news. Research indicates that news on the Internet is beginning to replace television news as the primary source of information among computer users (see Chapter 13). What role do the media play in our awareness of social problems, and will definitions of social problems change as sources of information change?

National Data

In the largest survey to ever investigate patterns of voluntarism and charitable giving, Statistics Canada found dramatic regional differences, with Quebec and Saskatchewan at either end of the scale. In 1997, Quebecers gave, on average, only $127 to charity; 22 percent of adults volunteered for charitable work, and 43 percent of Quebecers participated in community activities. In stark contrast, the average gift to charity in Saskatchewan was $308; 45 percent of adults volunteered, and 60 percent participated in community activities. Ontario occupied a middle position with 51 percent participating in community activities. The research also reported that strong family life translates into higher civic participation. Married people have the highest rates of civic participation in seven categories (work related; sports and recreation; religious; community and school groups; cultural and educational groups; fraternal and service organizations; and political parties) in all three provinces. Adults with adolescents aged 13 to 17 living at home have even higher rates of participation.

SOURCE: Picard 1999

2. Each of you occupies several social statuses, each one carrying an expectation of role performance, that is, what you should and should not do given your position. List five statuses you occupy, the expectations of their accompanying roles, and any role conflict that may result. What types of social problems are affected by role conflict?
3. Definitions of social problems change over time. Identify a social condition that is now widely accepted that might be viewed as a social problem in the future.

KEY TERMS

achieved status
alienation
anomie
ascribed status
beliefs
conflict perspective
dependent variable
experiment
field research
folkway
hypothesis
independent variable
institution
labelling theory

latent functions
law
macro sociology
manifest function
master status
micro sociology
mores
norms
objective element
operational definition
primary group
role
sample
sanctions

secondary group
social group
social problem
sociological imagination
sociological mindfulness
status
structural-functionalism
subjective element
survey research
symbol
symbolic interactionism
values
variable

Section 1

Problems of Well-Being

Section 1 deals with problems that are often regarded as private rather than public issues; that is, they are viewed as internally caused or as a function of individual free will. People often respond to these problems by assuming that the problem is the victims' fault—that in some way they have freely chosen their plight. In this set of problems, blame is most often attached to the individuals themselves. Thus, the physically and mentally ill (Chapter 2), the alcoholic and the drug addict (Chapter 3), the criminal and the delinquent (Chapter 4), and the divorced person and the child abuser (Chapter 5) are thought to be bad, weak, immoral, or somehow different from the average person. Consider the following scenarios.

A woman with a limited income decides not to fill an expensive prescription to be able to afford nutritious food for her children. When her condition worsens, she is blamed for failing to follow her doctor's orders to fill the pre-scription. As sociologists, we would say that the woman did not want to be sick, but rather chose what she perceived as the least of several unfortunate alternatives. In this case, factors that underlie her illness include poverty, the costs of medication not covered by government plans, and the value system that stresses parental responsibility and sacrifice.

A teenager from an urban lower-class neighbourhood decides to sell drugs rather than stay in school or get a regular job. Such a teenager is generally viewed as being "weak" or having "low" morals. Sociologists view such a person as a lower-class, poorly educated individual with few alternatives in a society that values success. Raised in an environment where the most successful role models are often criminals, legitimate opportunities are few, traditional norms and values are weak, and peer pressure to use and sell drugs is strong, what are his choices? He can pump gas or serve fast food for minimum wage, or he can sell drugs for as much as $5000 a week.

A mother comes home from work and finds her children playing and the house in disorder. She had told the children to clean the house while she was gone. She decides they need to be whipped with a belt because of their disobedience. The physical abuse she engages in is viewed as a reflection of her mental instability and her inability to control her temper. Research indicates, however, that fewer than 10 percent of identified child abusers are severely psychologically impaired. If being mentally unstable does not explain the majority of child abuse cases, what does explain them? A history of being abused as a child is the strongest independent predictor of who will be a child abuser as an adult. Additionally, the culture of society includes myriad beliefs that contribute to child abuse: acceptance of corporal punishment of children and the ambiguity surrounding what constitutes appropriate discipline, the belief that parental control is an inalienable right, and the historical and lingering belief that children are property.

A student drinks alcohol daily and often cuts classes. Although the public views such behaviour as a personal weakness, sociologists emphasize the role of the individual's socialization and society. For example, a disproportionate number of individuals with drinking problems were reared in homes where one or both parents drank heavily. In the general culture, media portrayals of drinking as desirable, fun, glamorous, and a source of status further promote drinking. Student culture itself often emphasizes bars and drinking parties as primary sources of recreation and affiliation.

These examples illustrate that many behaviours result more from social factors than from individual choice. To the degree that individuals do make choices, these choices are socially determined in that the structure and culture of society limit and influence individual choices. For example, customers in a restaurant cannot choose anything they want to eat; they are limited to what is on the menu. Sociologically, your social status—Black, White, male, female, young, old, rich, poor—determines your menu of life choices.

In each of the above examples, the alternatives were limited by the individual's position in the social structure of society and by the cultural and subcultural definitions of appropriate behaviour. While conflict theorists, structural-functionalists, and symbolic interactionists may disagree about the relative importance and mechanisms of the shared structure and culture of society in determining the problems identified, all would agree that society, not the individual, is the primary source of the solutions. In this and the following sections, we emphasize the importance of the social structure and culture of society as the sources of and the solutions to social problems.

CHAPTER TWO

Illness and Health Care

Is It True?

1. Individuals in Canada can expect to outlive citizens in almost every country except those in Switzerland, Sweden, and Japan.

2. Compared to other industrialized countries, Canada has the lowest infant death rate.

3. Accidents are the number one cause of death in Canada among individuals aged 15 to 25.

4. Suicide accounts for almost one-quarter of all teenage deaths in Canada.

5. First Nations and Inuit people have a rate of tuberculosis that is almost seven times the Canadian average.

Answers: 1 = T, 2 = F, 3 = T, 4 = T, 5 = T

In August 1997, Jeanne Calment, then the oldest woman in the world, died in France at the age of 122. When she was born in 1875, Thomas Edison had not yet discovered electricity; before she died, photographs from the planet Mars had been transmitted to Earth. During Jeanne Calment's lifetime, the world changed in unimaginable ways. One of the most profound changes over the last century has been the increase in the average length of life. Since the end of World War II, longevity of life in most developed and developing countries has increased by almost 25 years—the greatest increase seen in the history of humankind (LaPorte 1997).

Despite overall improvements in living conditions and medical care, health problems and health care delivery are major concerns of individuals, families, communities, and nations. Although technological advances in health care are increasing, disparities in health and access to health care between and within countries are also increasing (Creese et al. 1998).

In this chapter, we review health concerns in Canada and throughout the world. The World Health Organization (1946) defines **health** as "a state of complete physical, mental, and social well-being" (p. 3). Sociologists are concerned with how social forces affect and are affected by health and illness, why some social groups suffer more illness than others, and how health and health care can be improved.

> It is ironic that in some parts of the world hundreds of millions of people suffer daily from a lack of basic health care while in other parts millions of people spend money on things that are not healthy. Think what a billion dollars could do to help immunize people against deadly diseases in developing countries. A billion dollars is not much money—it is what Americans spend on beer every 12 days and what Europeans spend on cigarettes every five days.
>
> David Wright, "Telemedicine and Developing Countries"

THE GLOBAL CONTEXT: PATTERNS OF HEALTH AND DISEASE

The study of the distribution of disease within a population is called **epidemiology**. The field of epidemiology incorporates several disciplines, including public health, medicine, biology, and sociology. Sociologists who are **epidemiologists** are concerned with the social origins and distribution of health problems in a population and how patterns of illness and disease vary between and within societies. Next, we look at global patterns of morbidity, longevity, mortality, and disease burden.

Patterns of Morbidity

Morbidity refers to acute and chronic illnesses and diseases and the symptoms and impairments they produce. **Acute conditions** are short term; by definition, they can last no more than three months. **Chronic conditions** are long-term health problems. The rate of serious morbidity in a population provides one measure of the health of that population. Morbidity may be measured according to the incidence and prevalence of specific illnesses and diseases. **Incidence** refers to the number of *new cases* of a specific health problem within a given population during a specified period. **Prevalence** refers to the *total number of cases* of a specific health problem within a population that exist at a given time. For example, the incidence of HIV infection worldwide was 5.8 million in 1997, meaning that there were 5.8 million people newly infected with HIV in 1997. In the same year, the worldwide prevalence of HIV was 30.6 million, meaning that a total of 30.6 million people worldwide were living with HIV infection in 1997 (World Health Organization and the United Nations Joint Programme on HIV/AIDS 1998).

Morbidity statistics include data on the incidence and prevalence of mental disorders. The fourth edition of the *Diagnostic and Statistical Manual of Mental Disorders* defines a **mental disorder** as a "behavioural or psychological syndrome or pattern that occurs in an individual and that is associated with present distress (e.g., painful symptoms) or disability (i.e., impairment in one or more important areas of functioning) or with a significantly increased risk of suffering, death, pain, disability, or an important loss of freedom" (American Psychiatric Association 1944: xxi).

As we discuss later in this chapter, patterns of morbidity vary according to social factors such as poverty, education, sex, and race. Morbidity patterns also vary according to the level of development of a society and the age structure of the population. In the industrialized world, infectious and parasitic diseases have been largely controlled by advances in sanitation and immunizations. Noninfectious diseases such as cancer, circulatory diseases, mental disorders, respiratory diseases, and musculoskeletal diseases pose the greatest health threat to the industrialized world (World Health Organization 1997b). In developing nations, such as China and Mexico, infectious and parasitic diseases are more common than in industrialized countries, but chronic degenerative diseases are increasing. In the less developed countries, malnutrition, pneumonia, and infectious and parasitic diseases such as HIV disease, malaria (transmitted by mosquitoes), and measles are major health concerns.

In many countries, birthrates have declined over the last few decades (see Chapter 14). At the same time, improvements in sanitation and the development of medical technologies (such as vaccinations) have contributed to increased longevity. Declining birthrates and increased longevity have resulted in the aging of the world's population.

The aging of the world's population means that the most common health problems are becoming those of adults rather than those of children. Diseases that need time to develop, such as cancer, heart disease, Alzheimer's disease, arthritis, and osteoporosis, are becoming more common, and childhood illnesses, typically caused by infectious and parasitic diseases, are becoming less common. The shift from a society characterized by low life expectancy and parasitic and infectious diseases to one characterized by long life expectancy and chronic and degenerative diseases is called the **epidemiological transition**.

Patterns of Longevity

One indicator of the health of a population is the average number of years individuals born in a given year can expect to live, referred to as **life expectancy.** Worldwide, life expectancy has increased dramatically over the last half century (see Figure 2.1). However, wide disparities exist in life expectancy for different populations between and within societies. In 1998, Japan had the longest life expectancy: 80 years. In the same year, life expectancy was less than 40 in three countries (Malawi, Zambia, and Zimbabwe) (*Statistical Abstract of the United States: 1998*: Table 1345). In addition, more than 50 million people live in countries with a life expectancy of fewer than 45 years, and about 300 million people live in 16 countries where life expectancy actually decreased

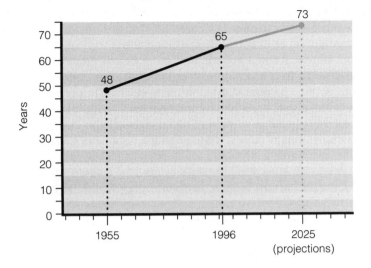

Figure 2.1

Global Life Expectancy, 1955–2025

SOURCE: *Fifty Facts from the World Health Report 1998*. World Health Organization. August 8, 1998 <www.who.int/whr/1998/factse.htm>. Reprinted by permission.

International Data

Canadians can expect to outlive citizens in almost every country except those in Switzerland, Sweden, and Japan. In Australia and Iceland, men have a slightly longer life expectancy than Canadian men do; in France, the life expectancy of women is slightly greater than among their Canadian counterparts.

SOURCE: Statistics Canada 1998

between 1975 and 1995 (World Health Organization 1998). In Canada, a girl born in 1995 can hope to celebrate her 81st birthday, a boy his 75th.

CONSIDERATION

A longer life does not necessarily mean a healthier life. Many older individuals spend their later years suffering from the pain and disability associated with chronic and debilitating diseases such as heart disease, cancer, diabetes, and mental disorders. The World Health Organization (1997b) suggests that **health expectancy**–defined as life expectancy in good health–is at least as important as life expectancy. Health expectancy refers to the average number of years an individual can expect to live in "good health."

Patterns of Mortality

Rates of **mortality** or death—especially those of infants, children, and women—provide sensitive indicators of the health of a population. Worldwide, the leading cause of death is infectious and parasitic diseases (World Health Organization 1998). In Canada, the leading causes of death for both women and men are cancer and cardiovascular diseases (Statistics Canada 1999).

Infant and Childhood Mortality Rates **Infant mortality rates**, the number of deaths of live-born infants under one year of age per 1000 live births (in any given year), provides an important measure of the health of a population. **Under-five mortality rates**, another useful measure of child health, refer to the number of deaths of children under age five. Between 1960 and 1996, there have been significant decreases in under-five mortality rates throughout the world (see Table 2.1). However, the childhood death rates of less developed countries are still extremely high compared to the childhood death rates in the developed world. In less developed countries, 7 out of 10 childhood deaths can be attributed to five main causes: pneumonia, diarrhea, measles, malaria, and malnutrition (World Health Organization 1997a).

International Data

Among the seven leading industrialized nations, Canada ranks fourth (behind the United States, Germany, and France) in health care spending as a proportion of gross domestic product (GDP) or the total value of all goods and services produced in a country.

SOURCE: Statistics Canada 1998

National Data

In 1995, 610 of every 100 000 Canadian newborns died before their first birthday. Of those who died, almost three-quarters suffered from birth defects or from complications at birth. When more specific causes of death are identified, sudden infant death syndrome emerges as the leading cause of death for children in Canada in their first year of life.

SOURCE: Statistics Canada 1998

Infant and child health is assessed not only by death rates, but by weight as well. Low-birth-weight babies (weighing 2500 grams or less) and underweight children are more likely to die early, and those who survive are more likely to suffer illness, stunted growth, and other health problems into adult life. Although about half of all newborns born in Canada in 1995 weighed 3400 grams or more, about 6 percent were of low birth-weight. The prevalence of low birth-weight babies also appears to have increased in Canada. In part, this may be the result of an increase in number of older women (who face a higher risk of having low birth-weight babies) having children (Statistics Canada 1998).

Table 2.1	Mortality Rates for Selected Countries, 1960 and 1996	
Canada	33	7
China	209	47
Ethiopia	280	177
France	34	6
India	236	111
Iran	233	37
Japan	40	6
Kenya	202	90
Mali	500	220
Mexico	148	32
Niger	320	320
Russian Federation	65	25
Sweden	20	4
United Kingdom	27	7
United States	30	8

SOURCE: UNICEF. 1998. *The State of the World's Children,* 1998. New York: UNICEF. Reprinted by permission.

International Data

In 1995, 27 percent of all children under five were underweight.

SOURCE: World Health Organization 1998

International Data

One-quarter to one-half of deaths among women in developing countries are attributed to pregnancy-related complications.

SOURCE: "Maternal Mortality: A Preventable Tragedy" 1998

Maternal Mortality Rates **Maternal mortality rates**, a measure of deaths that result from complications associated with pregnancy, childbirth, and unsafe abortion, also provide a sensitive indicator of the health status of a population. Maternal deaths are the leading cause of death for reproductive-age women in less developed countries.

The highest rates of maternal death are among African women. One of every 16 African women, compared with only 1 in 3700 North American women and 1 in 1400 European women, are at risk of dying from pregnancy, childbirth, or unsafe abortion ("Maternal Mortality: A Preventable Tragedy" 1998).

Several factors contribute to high maternal mortality rates in less developed countries. Good health care and adequate nutrition and sanitation are far less available in poorer countries. In addition, women in less developed countries experience higher rates of pregnancy and childbearing and begin childbearing at earlier ages. Thus, they face the risk of maternal death more often and before their bodies are fully developed (see also Chapter 14). Women in many countries also lack access to family planning services or do not have the support of their male partners to use contraceptive methods such as condoms. Consequently, many women resort to abortion to limit their childbearing, even in countries where abortion is illegal (see Chapter 13).

Illegal abortions in less developed countries have an estimated mortality risk of 100 to 1000 per 100 000 procedures (Miller and Rosenfield 1996). In contrast, the Canadian mortality risk for therapeutic abortions is very low. In 1995, 70 549 Canadian women had therapeutic abortions in hospitals, 35 650 had abortions performed in clinics in seven Canadian provinces and 459 Canadian women had abortions in the United States. The total abortion rate per 100 live births in Canada in 1995 was 28.2 (Health Canada 1999b).

Patterns of Burden of Disease

Researchers have developed a new approach to measuring the health status of a population. This new approach provides an indicator of the overall **burden of disease** on a population through a single unit of measurement that combines not only the number of deaths but also the impact of premature death and disability on a population (Murray and Lopez 1996). This comprehensive unit of measurement, called the **disability-adjusted life year (DALY)**, reflects years of life lost to premature death and years lived with a disability. More simply, one DALY is equal to one year of healthy life. A "premature" death is defined as one that occurs before the age to which the person could have expected to live if that person was a member of one of the world's longest-surviving populations (82.5 years for women; 80 years for men).

The Global Burden of Disease Study (Murray and Lopez 1996) calculated the burden of disease for various diseases and injuries. The study found that the burdens of mental illnesses, including depression, alcohol dependence, and schizophrenia, have been seriously underestimated by traditional approaches that focus on death and not on disability. The study also concluded that tobacco is a more serious threat to human health than any single disease, including HIV (see also Chapter 3).

SOCIOLOGICAL THEORIES OF ILLNESS AND HEALTH CARE

The sociological approach to the study of illness, health, and health care differs from medical, biological, and psychological approaches to these topics. Next, we discuss how three major sociological theories—structural-functionalism, conflict theory, and symbolic interactionism—contribute to our understanding of illness and health care.

Structural-Functionalist Perspective

The structural-functionalist perspective is concerned with how illness, health, and health care affect and are affected by changes in other aspects of social life. For example, the women's movement and changes in societal gender roles have led to more women smoking, drinking, and experiencing the negative health effects of these behaviours. Increased modernization and industrialization throughout the world have resulted in environmental pollution—a major health concern. The emergence of HIV and AIDS in the gay male population was a force that helped unite and mobilize gay rights activists in both Canada and the United States.

International Data

Out of an estimated 50 million pregnancies terminated worldwide every year, about 20 million are performed under unsafe and unsanitary conditions.

SOURCE: Abeysinghe 1998

International Data

Although mental illnesses are responsible for only about 1 percent of deaths, they account for almost 11 percent of disease burden worldwide.

SOURCE: Murray and Lopez 1996

According to the structural-functionalist perspective, health care is a social institution that functions to maintain the well-being of societal members and, consequently, of the social system as a whole. Illness is dysfunctional in that it interferes with people performing needed social roles. To cope with nonfunctioning societal members and to control the negative effects of illness, society assigns a temporary and unique role to those who are ill—the sick role (Parsons 1951). This role assures that societal members receive needed care and compassion, yet at the same time, the role carries with it an expectation that the person who is ill will seek competent medical advice, adhere to the prescribed regimen, and return as soon as possible to normal role obligations.

Structural-functionalists additionally explain the high salaries of physicians by arguing that society must entice people into the medical profession by offering high salaries. Without such an incentive, individuals would not be motivated to endure the rigours of medical training or the stress of being a physician.

Conflict Perspective

The conflict perspective focuses on how wealth, status, and power, or the lack thereof, influence illness and health care. Worldwide, the have-nots not only experience the adverse health effects of poverty, but they also have less access to quality medical care. In societies where women have little status and power, women's life expectancy is lower than in industrialized countries because of several social factors: eating last and eating less, complications from frequent childbearing and sexually transmitted diseases (because they have no power to demand abstinence or condom use), infections and hemorrhages following genital mutilation (which is practised in about 28 countries), and restricted access to modern health care (Lorber 1997). Consider, as well, that while public health measures, improved sanitation systems, proper housing, immunization, and antibiotics have virtually eliminated many of the infectious diseases (such as smallpox, tuberculosis, and cholera) that ravaged Canada's cities and towns in the nineteenth century, not all Canadians have equally benefited. Currently, one-fifth of all tuberculosis cases in Canada occur among First Nations people, largely due to crowded living conditions (with housing densities twice the national average), and poor nutrition. First Nations and Inuit people have a rate of tuberculosis that is almost seven times the Canada-wide average (Health Canada 1999b).

Medical research agendas are also shaped by wealth, status, and power. Although malaria kills twice as many people annually as does AIDS, malaria research receives less than one-tenth as much public funding as AIDS research (Morse 1998). Similarly, pneumonia and diarrheal diseases constitute 15.4 percent of the total global disease burden, but only 0.2 percent of the total global spending on research (Visschedijk and Simeant 1998). This disparity arises because northern developed countries, which provide most of the funding for world health-related research, do not feel threatened by malaria, pneumonia, and diarrheal diseases, which primarily affect less developed countries in Africa and Asia.

Worldwide, public health systems have been slower to address and more likely to neglect women's health issues than men's. For example, a year after the male impotence drug Viagra made its debut in 1998, the Constitutional Court in Colombia decreed that state-run health services must reimburse men needing the pill for impotence due to chronic or terminal diseases. In a country where the public health system is so overburdened that patients often have to provide their own syringes and people die of gangrene after amputation, it is disconcerting to note a high-court ruling that requires the government to pay for some men's use of a very expensive drug (*KW Record* 1999: A16). Women have also been excluded from participating in major health research studies that have looked at the relationship between aspirin use and heart disease or how cholesterol levels, blood pressure, and smoking affect heart disease (Johnson and Fee 1997).

The conflict perspective also focuses on how the profit motive influences health, illness, and health care. The profit motive underlies much of the illness, injury, and death that occur from hazardous working conditions and dangerous consumer products (see Chapter 11).

Symbolic Interactionist Perspective

Symbolic interactionists focus on (1) how meanings, definitions, and labels influence health, illness, and health care and (2) how such meanings are learned through interaction with others and through media messages and portrayals. According to the social construction of illness, "there are no illnesses or diseases in nature. There are only conditions that society, or groups within it, have come to define as illness or disease" (Goldstein 1999: 31). Psychiatrist Thomas Szasz (1970) argued that what we call "mental illness" is no more than a label conferred on those individuals who are "different," that is, who don't conform to society's definitions of appropriate behaviour.

Definitions of health and illness vary over time and between societies. In some countries, being fat is a sign of health and wellness; in others, it is an indication of mental illness or a lack of self-control. Before medical research documented the health hazards of tobacco, our society defined cigarette smoking as fashionable. Cigarette advertisements still attempt to associate positive images (such as youth, sex, and romance) with smoking to entice people to smoke. A study of top-grossing American films from 1985 to 1995 revealed that 98 percent had references that supported tobacco use and 96 percent had references that supported alcohol use (Everett et al. 1998).

A growing number of behaviours and conditions are being defined as medical problems—a trend known as **medicalization**. Hyperactivity, insomnia, anxiety, and learning disabilities are examples of phenomena that some view as medical conditions in need of medical intervention. Increasingly, "normal" aspects of life, such as birth, aging, sexual development, menopause, and death, have come to be seen as medical events (Goldstein 1999).

Symbolic interactionists also focus on the stigmatizing effects of being labelled "ill." Individuals with mental illnesses, drug addictions, physical deformities and disabilities, and HIV and AIDS are particularly prone to being labelled in negative ways. Having a stigmatized illness or condition often becomes a master status, obscuring other aspects of a person's social identity. One individual who uses a wheelchair commented: "When I am in my chair I am invisible to some people; they see only the chair" (Ostrof 1998: 36).

HEALTH CONCERNS OF STUDENTS

Next, we look at health problems that are primary health concerns among typical-age college and university students. These problems include automobile accidents,

HIV and other sexually transmitted infections, eating disorders, self-mutilation, and suicide. Use of alcohol, tobacco, and other drugs is also a major health concern and is discussed in Chapter 3; homicide is discussed in Chapter 4.

Motor Vehicle Accidents

In Canada, high rates for motor vehicle injury and crashes are strongly clustered in two age groups: 15 to 19 years of age and 20 to 24 years of age. Rates within these two groups are almost double the rates for the population as a whole (Health Canada 1999b). Men have a much higher risk of death or injury in motor vehicle accidents than do women. The most common accidents causing death are motor vehicle accidents and alcohol consumption is frequently involved in motor vehicle accidents (see Chapter 3).

HIV/AIDS and Other Sexually Transmitted Infections

Sexually transmitted infections (STIs), also known as sexually transmitted diseases (STDs), and their consequences are a major public health concern, especially for developing countries that lack resources for preventing and treating STIs. Many infected individuals—particularly women—experience no symptoms.

Chlamydia, a sexually transmissible bacterial infection that may affect the genitals, eyes, and lungs, is the most common STI in Canada, on college and university campuses, and in the world. Other STIs include gonorrhea, human papillomavirus (HPV), herpes, syphilis, and HIV/AIDS. Untreated STIs can have severe consequences, including uterine and fallopian tube infections, infertility, ectopic pregnancy (a potentially fatal pregnancy in which the fertilized egg begins to develop outside the uterus), chronic pain, cancer, and death.

Young adults are the age group at greatest risk of acquiring an STI because they are more likely to engage in intercourse without using condoms and to have multiple sex partners. According to the 1996–97 National Population Health Survey, among those Canadians aged 15 to 59 who were in a relationship of less than one year's duration, 16 percent reported that they had not used a condom the last time they had sex; 8 percent reported never using a condom. Among sexually active individuals aged 15 to 19, 51 percent of females and 24 percent of males reported having sex without a condom; among those 20 to 24 years of age, 53 percent of women and 44 percent of men reported having sex without a condom (Health Canada 1999b). A British Columbia survey also noted that although more than half of all 17-year-olds in that province were sexually active, fewer than 6 in 10 reported using a condom the last time they had sex (Statistics Canada 1998). Moreover, evidence suggests that beliefs about the effectiveness of a pregnancy prevention method may be generalized to beliefs about its efficacy for disease prevention. The Canadian *Youth and AIDS* study reported that only 27 percent of contraceptive pill users reported concurrent use of condoms. A secondary analysis of the college and university subset of the Canadian *Youth and AIDS* study (mean age 19.7 years) reported that those students with a greater number of sex partners were more likely to use oral contraceptive pills but less likely to use condoms. Of those who had 10 or more lifetime partners, regular condom use was reported by only 21 percent of males and 7.5 percent of females. Overall, regular condom use was reported by 24.8 percent of men and 15.6 percent of women (Boroditsky et al. 1996).

		Number of AIDS Cases in Thousands*	Rate of Growth 1996 to 1998
1	North America	890	18.7%
2	Latin America	1 400	7.7%
3	Caribbean	330	22.2%
4	Sub–Saharan Africa	22 500	60.7%
5	North Africa and Middle East	210	5.0%
6	Western Europe	500	−2.0%
7	Eastern Europe and Central Asia	270	440.0%
8	South and Southeast Asia	6 700	28.8%
9	East Asia and Pacific	560	460.0%
10	Australia and New Zealand	12	−7.7%

*As of Dec. 1998

Figure 2.2
The Spread of HIV

SOURCE: Ho, David. 1999. "And Will We Ever Cure AIDS?" *Time*, Canadian edition, November 8: 50. © Time Inc. Reprinted by permission.

One of the most urgent public health concerns around the globe is the spread of the human immunodeficiency virus (HIV), which causes acquired immunodeficiency syndrome (AIDS). Africa suffers the highest incidence of HIV/AIDS (see Figure 2.2). This chapter's Self and Society allows you to assess your knowledge of AIDS.

In Canada, men who have sex with other men are the group most at risk for developing HIV/AIDS, representing two-thirds of all AIDS cases reported among males in 1997. However, the proportion of cases attributed to this group peaked in 1987–88 and has been on the decline since that time. Worldwide, the predominant mode of HIV transmission is through heterosexual contact (Inciardi and Harrison 1997). In Canada, the number of HIV/AIDS cases attributed to heterosexual contact rose from 3 percent to 19 percent between 1987 and 1995. Although before 1993 there was 1 woman with AIDS for every 15 men, by mid-1997, the proportion of women had doubled. As well, the number of HIV/AIDS cases attributed to the sharing of needles by intravenous drug users climbed from 2 percent of cases diagnosed before 1992 to almost 20 percent in 1998. In British Columbia, intravenous drug users now constitute the group with the highest number of new HIV/AIDS infections. Among Aboriginals, injection drug use accounts for 54 percent of reported HIV/AIDS cases among women and 17.8 percent of reported cases among men (Statistics Canada 1998b).

Eating Disorders

Eating disorders are characterized by a persistent pattern of abnormal eating or dieting behaviour. These patterns are associated with significant emotional and physical disturbances. Two common eating disorders are anorexia nervosa and

International Data

As of June 30, 1998, 15 935 HIV/AIDS cases have been reported in Canada, all but 158 of them among adults. Since the disease was first diagnosed in Canada in 1982, 11 046 Canadians have died due to HIV/AIDS infection.

SOURCE: Statistics Canada 1998b

bulimia nervosa. **Anorexia nervosa** is characterized by weight loss, excessive exercise, food aversion, distorted body image, and an intense and irrational fear of body fat and weight gain. **Bulimia nervosa** is characterized by cycles of binge eating and purging (self-induced vomiting, and use of laxatives or use of diuretics or both). Eating disorders are much more common among women than they are among men. Unrealistic media portrayals of female attractiveness that emphasize thinness contribute to the prevalence of eating disorders among women.

Anorexia can cause a variety of physical problems, including anemia, kidney dysfunction, cardiovascular problems, and osteoporosis (inadequate bone calcium), and can lead to death. Bulimia can cause electrolyte and mineral imbalances, dental enamel erosion, disruption of normal bowel functions, tearing of the esophagus, rupturing of the stomach, and irregularities in heart rhythm that can be fatal. Treatment for eating disorders may involve psychotherapy, medications, nutritional counselling, medical treatment, and support groups.

If you think that a friend or a roommate may have an eating disorder, what should you do? The Academy for Eating Disorders (1997) recommends that you approach the person in private and express in a caring but straightforward way what behaviours or symptoms you have observed and what your concerns are. Say that you are worried and want to help, and give the person time to talk and express feelings. Listen without being judgmental. Provide information about resources for treatment and offer to go with the person and wait during the first appointment with a health care provider. If the person denies having a problem or refuses to get help, let the person know that you are still concerned and that you may bring the topic up again in the future.

Self-Mutilation

Self-mutilation, which has been variously referred to as self-injury, self-harm, or self-cutting has, until recently, been viewed as a rare or anomalous act outside prisons (Johnson and Britt 1967) or clinical settings (Ross and McKay 1979). However, Levenkron (1997, 1998) asserts that self-injuring has reached "epidemic" proportions in North America; Strong (1998) claims that self-mutilation should be seen as the "addiction of the 1990s." Indeed, Favazzo's (1998) estimate that the number of self-injurers is at least 750 per 100 000 North Americans translates into approximately a quarter of a million self-injurers in Canada and about two million self-injurers in the United States. Self-mutilation refers to "the direct, deliberate destruction or alteration of one's own body tissue without conscious suicidal intent" (Favazzo 1998). According to various writers (Alderman 1997; Levenkron 1997, 1998; Strong 1998), the average self-mutilator is a White female who begins to self-mutilate at age 14, continues self-injuring, often with increasing severity, into her late 20s, and is likely to also suffer from such other compulsive disorders as bulimia or alcoholism. For Miller (1995), self-cutting reflects a culturally sanctioned antagonism between women and their bodies: "Our bodies are always too fat, our breasts are too small, and the body becomes the object of our own violence." Others, however, dispute the suggestion that a gender divide exists in relation to self-mutilating behaviour and note that the support group Self-Mutilators Anonymous was started more than a decade ago by two men who were self-

AIDS Knowledge Scale

Indicate whether you think the following items are true or false.

	TRUE	FALSE
1. Hemophiliacs can get AIDS.	_____	_____
2. AIDS is an epidemic.	_____	_____
3. Only homosexuals get AIDS.	_____	_____
4. The virus that causes AIDS is called human immunodeficiency virus (HIV).	_____	_____
5. The AIDS virus can remain infectious outside the body for up to 10 days if it is at room temperature.	_____	_____
6. One can get AIDS by sharing a meal with a person who has AIDS.	_____	_____
7. People who have AIDS do not develop cancer.	_____	_____
8. Today, the blood supply in hospitals and blood donation centres is screened for the AIDS virus.	_____	_____
9. Impaired memory and concentration and motor deficits may occur in some AIDS patients.	_____	_____
10. One can get AIDS by sharing drug needles.	_____	_____
11. The AIDS virus may live in the human body for years before symptoms appear.	_____	_____
12. One can get AIDS from receiving blood or sperm from a donor who has AIDS.	_____	_____
13. By using a condom when having sex, one is always safe from contracting AIDS.	_____	_____
14. The HIV test is a blood test that can tell if a person has AIDS.	_____	_____
15. There is a cure for AIDS.	_____	_____
16. AIDS victims may show extreme tiredness, night sweats, fever, weight loss, diarrhea, etc.	_____	_____
17. One can get AIDS by having sexual intercourse with an infected person.	_____	_____
18. AIDS is spread by sneezing, coughing, or touching.	_____	_____
19. One can get AIDS by having sex with someone who uses intravenous drugs.	_____	_____
20. AIDS can be spread by having contact with towels or bed linens used by a person with AIDS.	_____	_____
21. An infected mother can give the AIDS virus to the baby during pregnancy and/or through breast-feeding.	_____	_____
22. More Canadian women than men have been infected by the AIDS virus.		

Scoring: The following items are true: 1, 2, 4, 8, 9, 10, 11, 12, 16, 17, 19, and 21. The following items are false: 3, 5, 6, 7, 13, 14, 15, 18, 20, and 22. The scale is scored by totalling the number of items answered correctly. Possible scores range from 0 to 22. The higher the score, the higher the degree of knowledge of HIV/AIDS.

SOURCE: Adapted from Goh, David S. 1993. "The Development and Reliability of the Attitudes towards AIDS Scale." *College Student Journal* 27: 208–14. The scale is on p. 214. Reprinted by permission of *College Student Journal*.

injurers. It has been suggested that self-injury may simply be less visible among men than among women (Walsh and Rosen 1999). That is, men may be better able than women to hide the evidence of self-mutilation or explain it away with reference to, for example, involvement in bar fights, hockey skirmishes, and so on.

Numerous attempts have been made to explain self-mutilating behaviour. It has been suggested that some individuals seek out the pain of self-mutilation to temporarily quell other deeper, more intolerable feelings of pain stemming from feelings of anger, sadness, or abandonment. Self-mutilation may also occur as an attempt to jolt oneself out of depressive states, to counter feelings of sadness, hopelessness, and emptiness, or to make the individual "feel alive." Additionally, it has been suggested that cutting oneself may release the body's own opiates (beta-endorphins) and that over time, self-injurers must hurt themselves more frequently and more violently to achieve the same degree of relief.

Suicide

Suicide is the second leading cause of death in Canada among young persons aged 15 to 19. In Canada, between 1986 and 1990, 13 out of every 100 000 young persons in the 13 to 19 age group killed themselves; suicide accounted for almost one-quarter of all teenage deaths. The suicide rate for 20- to 24-year-olds was 16 to 17 per 100 000 for the years 1993 to 1996 (see Figure 2.3). Although men are more likely than women are to complete suicide, women are at higher risk for suicide attempts. Most individuals who attempt or complete suicide give warning signs that they are thinking about killing themselves (see Table 2.2).

Figure 2.3
Suicide Rate among Youth, by Age, 15–24, Canada, 1970–96

SOURCE: Adapted from Statistics Canada, Health Statistics Division, *Health Indicators, 1999* (Statistics Canada Cat. No. 82-221-XCB).

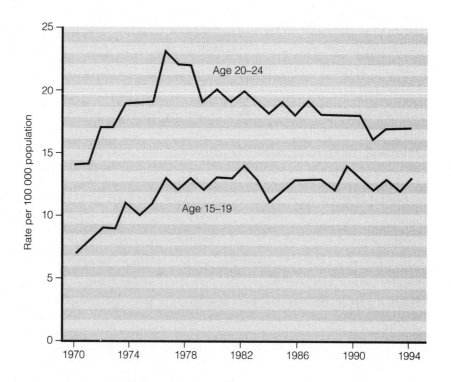

Table 2.2	Suicide Warning Signs

Verbal Signs
(Direct statements about suicide or indirect statements or subtle hints indicating a wish to die)

"I am going to commit suicide."
"I don't want to live anymore."
"You won't have to put up with me much longer."

"I don't think I can take it much longer."
"I wish I could go to sleep and never wake up."

Behavioural Signs

Sadness and crying
Changes in sleeping or eating patterns
Withdrawal from social interaction
Giving away personal possessions
Neglect of personal hygiene

Abusing alcohol or other drugs
Obtaining guns, ropes, or pills
Prior suicide attempts
Drop in grades
Taking risks, frequent accidents

Situational Signs

Loss of a relationship
Trouble with the law or at school
Presence of mental or serious physical illness
Recent suicide attempt by a friend or family member

Conflictual relationship with parents
Unwanted pregnancy
Disliked or stigmatized by peers

If you suspect that someone you know is contemplating suicide, there are three steps you can take ("Youth Suicide Prevention" 1998):

1. **Show you care.** Say something like "I'm concerned about you." "You mean a lot to me and I want to help." "Tell me about your pain." "I don't want you to kill yourself." "I'm on your side....We'll get through this."

2. **Ask questions.** In a direct, but caring way, ask questions such as, "Are you thinking about suicide?" "Are you thinking about harming yourself or ending your life?" "How long have you been thinking about suicide?" "Have you thought about how you would do it?" "Do you have the _____?" (insert the lethal means they have mentioned). "Do you really want to die? Or do you want the pain to go away?"

3. **Get help.** Call a local crisis hot line, psychiatrist, or psychologist, or other mental health professional. If the person has expressed an immediate plan or has access to a gun or other potentially deadly means, do not leave him or her alone; get help immediately by calling the police (or dial 911). Things you can say to the person at risk include the following: "You are not alone. Let me help you." "Together I know we can figure something out to make you feel better." "I will stay with you....I can go with you to where we can get some help." "Let's talk to someone who can help....Let's call the crisis line, now."

International Data

In 1991–93, the suicide rate for Canadian male youth was exceeded only in Australia and the Russian Federation among 10 industrialized countries; the female rate was higher than in all other countries except Sweden and the Russian Federation.

SOURCE: Health Canada 1999b

SOCIAL FACTORS ASSOCIATED WITH HEALTH AND ILLNESS

Public health education campaigns, articles in popular magazines, postsecondary-level health courses, and health professionals emphasize that to be healthy, we must adopt a healthy lifestyle. In response, many people have at

National Data

In 1996–97, the highest rate of unmet health care needs was reported by Canadians in the lowest income bracket. This relationship applied to both immigrant and Canadian-born individuals.

SOURCE: Health Canada 1999a

International Data

In developing countries, malnutrition is associated with 54 percent of all deaths of children under age five.

SOURCE: Visschedijk and Simeant 1998

least attempted to quit smoking, eat a healthier diet, and include exercise in their daily or weekly routine. However, health and illness are affected by more than personal lifestyle choices. In the following section, we examine how social factors such as poverty, education, race, and gender affect health and illness. Health problems related to environmental problems are discussed in Chapter 14.

Poverty

Poverty has been identified as the world's leading health problem by an international group of physicians ("Poverty Threatens Crisis" 1998). Poverty is associated with unsanitary living conditions, hazardous working conditions, lack of access to medical care, and inadequate nutrition (see also Chapter 10).

In Canada, socioeconomic status is related to numerous aspects of health and illness (Health Canada 1999b). People with lower family incomes tend to die at younger ages than those with higher incomes, and adults with low incomes are four to seven times as likely (depending on race, ethnicity, and sex) than those with higher incomes are to report fair or poor health. At each rung up the income ladder, Canadians have less sickness, longer life expectancies, and improved health. Poor persons are also more likely to report an unmet need for health care. In addition, research has found that low socioeconomic status is associated with increased risk of a broad range of psychiatric conditions (Williams and Collins 1999). Rates of depression and substance abuse, for example, are higher in the lower socioeconomic classes (Kessler et al. 1994). Why do poor people have higher rates of mental illness? One explanation suggests that lower-class individuals experience greater stress due to their deprived and difficult living conditions. Others argue that members of the lower class are simply more likely to have their behaviours identified and treated as mental illness.

CONSIDERATION

Poor health—either physical or mental—can cause, as well as result from, poverty. For example, individuals with poor mental or physical health have problems achieving high levels of education and difficulty obtaining and keeping employment.

Lower socioeconomic groups have higher rates of mortality, in part, because they have higher rates of health-risk behaviours such as smoking, alcohol drinking, being overweight, and being physically inactive. Other factors that explain the relationship between socioeconomic status and mortality in North America include exposure to environmental health hazards and inequalities in access to and use of preventive and therapeutic medical care (Lantz et al. 1998). Although in Canada access to universally insured care remains largely unrelated to income, many low- and moderate-income Canadians have limited or no access to health services such as eye care, dentistry, mental health counselling, and prescription drugs (Health Canada 1999a). In addition, the lower class tends to experience high levels of stress but has few resources to cope with it (Cockerham 1998). Stress has been linked to a variety of physical and mental health problems, including high blood pressure, cancer, chronic fatigue, and substance abuse.

Education

In general, low levels of education are associated with higher rates of health problems and mortality (National Center for Health Statistics 1998). For example, less educated women and men have higher rates of suicide. People with higher levels of education have better access to healthy physical environments, tend to smoke less, tend to be more physically active, and have access to healthier foods (Health Canada 1999a).

Low birth-weight and high infant mortality are also more common among the children of less educated mothers than among children of more educated mothers. This is partly because women with less education are less likely to seek prenatal care and are more likely to smoke during pregnancy.

One reason that lower education levels are associated with higher mortality rates is that individuals with low levels of education are more likely to engage in health-risk behaviours such as smoking and heavy drinking. The well educated, in contrast, are less likely to smoke and drink heavily and are more likely to exercise. However, research findings suggest that educational differences in mortality are best explained by the strong association between education and income (Lantz et al. 1998). While in 1994 nearly three-quarters of Canadians with a college or university education reported excellent or very good health, less than 50 percent of those without a high-school education did so. Consider as well that while about three-quarters of those in households of one or two who earned more than $60 000 reported that they were in good or excellent health, just over half of those in similar-size households living on $15 000 a year or less did so (Statistics Canada 1998).

Gender

As noted earlier, women in developing countries suffer high rates of mortality and morbidity due to the high rates of complications associated with pregnancy and childbirth. Women in all countries also suffer more severe and frequent complications of STIs, in part because women are biologically more susceptible than men are to becoming infected if exposed to an STI. In addition, STIs are less likely to produce symptoms in women and are therefore more difficult to diagnose until serious problems develop. The low status of women in many less developed countries results in their being nutritionally deprived and having less access to medical care than do men.

Before the twentieth century, the life expectancy of Canadian women was shorter than that of men because of the high rate of maternal mortality that resulted from complications of pregnancy and childbirth. Currently, however, Canadian women have a higher life expectancy than Canadian men have (see Figure 2.4).

Although women tend to live longer than men do, they have higher rates of illness and disability than do men (Verbrugge 1999). Prevalence rates for nonfatal chronic conditions (such as arthritis, thyroid disease, and migraine headache) are typically higher for women. However, men tend to have higher rates of fatal chronic conditions (such as high blood pressure, heart disease, and diabetes). Women also tend to experience a higher incidence of acute conditions, such as colds and influenza, infections, and digestive conditions. "In sum, women live longer than men but experience more illness, whereas men experience relatively little illness but die quickly when illness strikes" (Weitz

Figure 2.4
Life Expectancy at Birth, Canada, 1971–96

SOURCES: Statistics Canada, Health Statistics Division, special tabulations; Statistics Canada. 1998. "Deaths 1996." Statistics Canada Cat. No 11-001-XIE (*The Daily*, April 16, 1998).

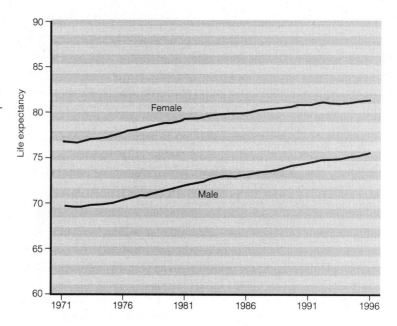

National Data

In 1994–95, more than one in four Canadians reported that they constantly felt themselves to be under high levels of stress. Working women, particularly those with young children, were especially vulnerable to stress as they attempted to juggle the simultaneous demands posed by parenting and work.

SOURCE: Statistics Canada 1998

1996: 56). Regarding mental health, men are more likely to abuse drugs and have higher rates of personality disorders, whereas women are more likely to suffer from mood disorders such as depression and anxiety (Cockerham 1998).

Women tend to have more non–life-threatening illnesses because of the stresses of routinized jobs, childcare, elder care, and housework. Men are more prone to chronic and life-threatening diseases, such as coronary disease, because they are more likely than women to smoke, use alcohol and illegal drugs, and work under hazardous conditions. Our culture socializes men to be aggressive and competitive and to engage in risky behaviours, which contribute to their higher risk of death from injuries and accidents. Although women are more likely to attempt suicide, men are more likely to succeed at it because they use deadlier methods.

CONSIDERATION

Although men are more likely to be victims of violence outside the home, in the home women are more likely to be victims (see also Chapter 5). Rose Weitz (1996) notes that "although neither health care workers nor the general public typically thinks of it as a health problem, women battering is a major cause of injury, disability, and death among…women worldwide." (p. 56)

We have previously noted that those who are less educated and have lower incomes face a greater risk of poor health. On occasion, these differences are striking. For example, "the differences between Canadian university graduates and those who have not finished high school are often on the order of twice the level of risk, and sometimes that extends to a three-fold differences (e.g., in the regular use of bicycle helmets), or even a four-fold difference (e.g., in smoking during pregnancy)" (Health Canada 1999b). A strong social status gradient also appears in relation to smoking, nicotine dependence, regular heavy drinking, regular physical activity, condom use with a new partner, sun protection, and intentions to alter lifestyle behaviours in the future to minimize health risk. Given the strong and consistent differences in lifestyle behaviours related to social status, it is not, perhaps, unexpected that rates of substance abuse are higher among First Nations peoples, homeless people (see Chapter 10), street youths (see Chapter 3), and those incarcerated in federal and provincial institutions than among the Canadian population as a whole (Canadian Centre on Substance Abuse 1999).

In Canada, the risks to health posed by inadequate income, welfare dependency, substandard living conditions, and stresses on mental health and well-being are manifestly apparent in the lives of First Nations peoples (Royal Commission on Aboriginal Peoples 1996). The life expectancy of Status Indians (i.e., those who names appear on the Indian Register maintained by the Department of Indian and Northern Affairs pursuant to the *Indian Act*) is seven to eight years shorter than for non-Aboriginal Canadians, and the infant mortality rate double that of the non-Aboriginal population. The rate of accidental death and injury among Aboriginal children is four times that of the non-Aboriginal population; death rates from causes such as birth defects, low birthweight, fetal alcohol syndrome, and respiratory illnesses are consistently and significantly higher among Aboriginal infants and children. Between 1986 and 1990, the suicide rate among Aboriginal children aged 10 to 11 was more than five times the rate found among non-Aboriginal children (National Forum on Health, n.d.). Indigenous Canadians also experience a heightened risk of violent death that increases from south to north and from east to west, and elevated rates of injuries, poisonings, and suicide. In British Columbia, the suicide rates on reserves are twice those found among off-reserve Indians (Canadian Centre for Substance Abuse 1999; Cooper et al. 1992). Among First Nation and Inuit males, the rates of violent death are especially high (Canadian Centre for Substance Abuse 1999).

Indigenous peoples also experience high rates of illicit drug use with First Nation and Métis youth more likely than non-Indigenous youth to use all types of drugs. Gfellner and Hundelby (1995) report that the use of solvents is also significantly higher among these youths than among non-Indigenous youths, and they estimate that the risk of developing an alcohol problem among Aboriginal youth is two to six times greater than that of other Canadians (Scott 1997). The prevalence of daily smoking among adult Indigenous Canadians occurs at about twice the rate found among the general Canadian population (Stephens 1994) and a national survey reported that 76 percent of Inuit women and 54 percent of Indian women smoked during pregnancy (Canadian Centre for Substance Abuse 1999).

Diabetes, which was virtually unknown among First Nations people before the 1940s, is now very prevalent, with age-standardized rates three times the national average. It is conservatively estimated that the rate of diabetes is two to three times higher among Aboriginal than among non-Aboriginal peoples (Health Canada n.d.[a]). In addition, while the annual number of new AIDS cases has levelled off among the general Canadian population, the number of AIDS cases identified among Aboriginal peoples has risen. A higher proportion of Aboriginal people diagnosed with AIDS are under 30 years of age than among the non-Aboriginal AIDS population (29.7 percent versus 18.0 percent) and the proportion of adult female Aboriginal AIDS cases is more than double that found within the non-Aboriginal population (15.1 percent versus 7.0 percent). In 1997 alone, 249 cases of AIDS (involving 210 males and 39 females) were reported among First Nations peoples (Health Canada n.d.[b]). This

National Data

A study conducted in 1997 on suicide in the Northwest Territories and Nunavut found that in a comparison of ethnic groups, the highest rate of suicide occurred among the Inuit at 79 per 100 000, compared with 29 per 100 000 for the Dene, and 15 per 100 000 for all other ethnic groups, comprising primarily non-Aboriginal persons.

SOURCE: Isaacs et al. 1998

chapter's *The Human Side* focuses attention on the health status of Canada's Indigenous peoples.

In 1994, the Interim Report of the Commission on Systemic Racism in the Ontario Criminal Justice System noted that health care and access to medical services, particularly during pregnancy, were of especial concern to Black female prisoners. These women reported that they were more harshly treated by correctional officers than were White women prisoners, were forced to do hard physical tasks in late stages of their pregnancies, and were not provided with the supplemental vitamins and extra servings of milk that are supposed to be given to all pregnant women in Canadian prisons.

SOURCE: Gittens et al. 1994

CONSIDERATION

Racial and ethnic prejudice and discrimination may induce psychological distress that adversely affects both physical and mental health status and increases the likelihood of violence and substance abuse. Moreover, **environmental racism** or the tendency for hazardous waste sites and polluting industries to be located in areas where the surrounding population is disproportionately Aboriginal or, in the United States, Black, may also contribute to lower levels of health. For example, in the 1980s, the mercury poisoning of the English-Wabigoon river system by local pulp and paper industries led to the virtual destruction of the Grassy Narrow Indians' lifestyle and means of livelihood (Shkilynk 1985).

PROBLEMS IN CANADIAN HEALTH CARE

Canada, like countries such as Great Britain, Sweden, Germany, and Italy, has a national health insurance system that is sometimes referred to as socialized medicine. Despite differences in how socialized medicine works in various countries, what is common to all systems of socialized medicine is that the government (1) directly controls the financing and organization of health services, (2) directly pays providers, (3) guarantees equal access to health care, and (4) allows some private care for individuals who are willing to pay for their medical expenses (Cockerham 1998). However, Canada does not truly have a system of "socialized medicine" in that Canadian physicians are not employed by the government. Rather, the majority of Canada's physicians are independent practitioners in independent or group practices. They are generally paid on a fee-for-service basis and submit their claims directly to the provincial health insurance plan for payment.

The origins of a universal health care system in Canada can be traced back to 1919 when William Lyon Mackenzie King first raised the idea of national, publicly funded health insurance as part of the Liberal Party platform. However, it took approximately half a century of intense debate and the persistent efforts of then-Saskatchewan premier Tommy Douglas, leader of the Co-Operative Commonwealth Federation (the precursor of the New Democratic Party), before the Canadian government would implement a universal health care system. In 1947 Douglas's government pioneered Canada's first universal hospital plan after testing prepaid medical insurance in the Swift Current health district and introducing a public insurance plan for hospital services. Public health care insurance also began in Saskatchewan with coverage provided for visits to and the services of physicians outside hospitals.

In 1956, the federal government of Canada offered to cost-share hospital and diagnostic services with the provinces and territories on a roughly 50-50 basis to encourage the development of hospital insurance programs. Although both private insurance companies and those within the medical profession opposed the attempt to establish a universal health care system and described Medicare as too expensive and as unfair to doctors, Douglas persevered in his efforts. On October 13, 1961, Douglas rose in the legislature and argued,

This is not a new principle. This has existed in nearly all of the countries of Western Europe. It has been in Great Britain since 1948; it has been in New Zealand since 1935; it has been in Australia. The little state of Israel that only came into existence in 1948 has today the most comprehensive health insurance in the world....To me it seems to be sheer nonsense to suggest that medical care is something which ought to be measured in dollars. When we're talking about medical care we're talking about our sense of values. Do we think human life is important?

In 1961, all of Canada's 10 provinces and two territories signed agreements establishing public insurance plans that provided universal coverage for at least in-hospital care that qualified for federal cost-sharing. However, it was not until 1972 that all Canadians received coverage for medical and hospital services under the *Hospital Insurance and Diagnostic Services Act* and the *Medical Care Act*. The *Canada Health Act* (1983) was later to supersede these acts.

Canada's health care system, known to Canadians as **Medicare**, provides access to universal comprehensive coverage for medically necessary in-patient and outpatient physician services. The role of the federal government in relation to health care is in the setting and administration of national principles for the health care system, assisting in the financing of provincial health services through fiscal transfers, and fulfilling certain functions for which it is constitutionally responsible. For example, the federal government is responsible for health service delivery to specific groups including veterans, Indigenous people living on reserves, members of the military, inmates of federal penitentiaries, and the Royal Canadian Mounted Police. However, the management and delivery of health services is the responsibility of each individual province or territory, which plans, finances, and evaluates the provision of hospital care, physician and allied health services, public health, and some aspects of prescription care. As such, our system of health care is perhaps best described as "12 interlocking provincial and territorial plans" (Statistics Canada 1998).

In 1964, the Hall Royal Commission on Services recommended that the provincial and federal governments introduce a medical program that would eradicate the disparities in Canada's health care system. The costs of the program were to be borne through taxation. The federal government agreed to share the costs equally with the provinces if each provincial plan satisfied five requirements:

1. Accessibility: reasonable access should be guaranteed to all Canadians.
2. Comprehensiveness: all necessary medical services should be guaranteed, without dollar limit, and should be available solely on the basis of medical need.
3. Universality: all Canadians should be eligible for coverage on uniform terms and conditions.
4. Portability: benefits should be transferable from province to province.
5. Administration by a public, nonprofit agency or commission. (Grant 1993: 401)

In 1972, these recommendations became law.

The formula for cost sharing between the provinces and the federal government was replaced in 1977 by per capita transfer to the provinces and territories, known as block funding. Under the *Established Programs Financing Act*, federal contributions were based on a uniform per capita entitlement and took the form of a tax transfer and cash payments. Because of this Act, the federal government reduced its contribution to Medicare from 50 percent to about 38 percent. Beginning in 1996–97, the federal government's contribution to provincial health and social programs was consolidated into a new single block transfer, the Canada Health and Social Transfer. To strengthen the health care system, it was announced in the 1999 Budget that the provinces and territories would receive an additional $11.5 billion over the period 1999–2000 to 2003–04 specifically for health care under the Canada Health and Social Transfer. The 1999 Budget additionally injected $1.4 billion over two years into such areas as research, technology, First Nations and Inuit health systems and programs, and enhancements to health promotion and health protection programs (Health Canada 1999b).

Among the Group of Seven (G7) industrialized countries, Canada ranks fourth in total health expenditures as a percentage of GDP (Health Canada 1999b). In 1996, Canada's total health expenditures were $75.3 billion, representing 9.2 percent of our gross domestic product (GDP), with hospitals accounting for the largest share ($25.9 billion or 34.3 percent), followed by expenditures for physicians ($10.7 billion or 14.3 percent) and drugs ($10.2 billion or 13.6 percent). Evidence suggests that our health care system is, in fact, accomplishing what it originally set out to do: eliminate inequality among Canadians in relation to health care services. For example, Gorey (1997, cited in Armstrong et al. 1998), reports that "compared to their Detroit counterparts, poor women in Toronto have a survival rate for breast cancer that is 30 percent higher, for ovarian cancer that is 38 percent higher and for cervical cancer that is 48 percent higher." He additionally notes that "Toronto women have survival rates more than 50 percent above that of women in Detroit's poorest districts for lung, stomach and pancreatic cancer," and that even after controlling for race and the standards used to measure poverty, the differences remain.

Although Canada's health care system ranks among the best systems in the world, some problems exist.

UNMET NEEDS

Although Canada's universal health insurance system is based on the premise that "all citizens will have access to the care they need within a reasonable time period" (Health Canada 1999b), there are no precise definitions of what constitutes "needed care" or a "reasonable time." Moreover, the findings of a survey conducted by the Canadian Medical Association (CMA 1999) suggest that Canadians perceived that access to a variety of health care services declined from 1996 to 1998 (Figure 2.5). Similarly, in the 12 months prior to their participation in the 1996–97 National Population Health Survey, approximately 5 percent of the Canadian population 12 years of age and older (1.2 million Canadians) required some health care or advice on at least one occasion and did not receive it. More than three-quarters of these needs were for physical health conditions (78 percent), with emotional health and injuries each reported by 9 percent of respondents. Those with the lowest income had approximately a 1 in 10 chance

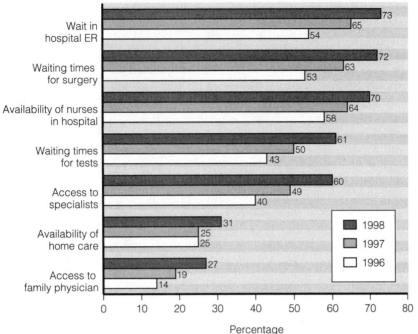

Figure 2.5

Canadians' Perceived Access to Health Care Services, 1998: Percentage Reporting Deteriorating Access in the Past Few Years

SOURCE: "Access to Health Care in Canada Report." Reprinted from and by the permission of the publisher, CMA, 1999; <www.cma.ca/advocacy/access/index.asp>. © 1999 Canadian Medical Association.

Chart data (Percentage), bars labelled 1998, 1997, 1996:

- Wait in hospital ER: 73, 65, 54
- Waiting times for surgery: 72, 63, 53
- Availability of nurses in hospital: 70, 64, 58
- Waiting times for tests: 61, 50, 43
- Access to specialists: 60, 49, 40
- Availability of home care: 31, 25, 25
- Access to family physician: 27, 19, 14

of having unmet needs compared with a 1 in 20 chance among those at the highest income level. Interprovincial variations in unmet health care needs ranged from a low of 3 percent among residents of Newfoundland and Quebec to a high of 8 percent in Alberta (Health Canada 1999b).

While hospital spending increased from $5.4 billion in 1975 to almost $26 billion in 1996, "the proportion of annual health-care spending devoted to hospital care actually declined over this period, from 44 percent to 34 percent" (Statistics Canada 1998a). Between 1986–87 and 1994–95, the number of public hospitals also declined by 14 percent and the number of available hospital beds dropped by nearly one-third. In response to rigorous budget cutbacks, hospitals have attempted to reduce their costs by closing hospital beds and increasing the number of day surgeries. For example, between 1986–87 and 1993–94, the number of people treated on an outpatient basis increased by 15 percent, while the number of days that inpatients stayed in public hospitals declined by 17 percent (Statistics Canada 1998). In addition, while emergency department use in Canada decreased 31 percent from 1991–92 to 1995–96, at least part of this decline is attributable "to the closing of hospital emergency departments, the opening of community walk-in clinics and urgent care centres, as well as the triaging of patients to appropriate services" (Health Canada 1999b).

Despite our universal health care system, it has also been noted that access to major medical procedures is much more limited than in the United States. Canada, with 10 percent of the population of the United States, has only 12 magnetic resonance imagers; in the United States, there are 1375. In all of Canada, only 11 facilities do open-heart surgery; in the United States, the number is 793 (Barnes 1990). There are queues for coronary bypass surgery and for ultrasound treatment of kidney stones (Blinick 1992). Provinces are also struggling to keep up with the demand for hospital beds for seniors who require long-term medical care. As of January 2000, approximately 10 000 Canadians

Income level and dental insurance are powerful determinants of accessibility to dental care: lower-income Canadians are the least likely to have dental insurance or to have visited a dentist during the past year. According to the National Population Health Survey, only 25 percent of Canadians in the low- to middle-income group had dental insurance and only 45 percent had visited a dentist during 1996–97. In contrast, 73 percent of high-income Canadians had dental insurance and 81 percent reported visiting a dentist during the previous year.

SOURCE: Health Canada 1999a

seniors (i.e., individuals 65 years of age and older) in Ontario, 7000 in British Columbia, 3000 in Quebec, and 1100 in Manitoba were on waiting lists for beds at publicly funded institutions (*Maclean's* 2000: 19).

Patients are not the only Canadians complaining of inadequate services. At the 1999 annual meeting of the CMA, physicians asserted that Canada was heading toward a critical shortage of doctors that will threaten patient safety and emphasized that there already exists a serious shortage of physicians in rural areas and within certain specialties such as anaesthesia, radiology, and obstetrics. It was noted that even in major Canadian cities such as Toronto, and even though, for example, Canadian cardiac surgeons work an average of 80 hours a week, patients are being forced to wait for needed surgery because of the shortage. They forecast that the situation will worsen as a large wave of aging baby boomers become increasingly reliant on the health care system and warn that by 2021, there will be only one doctor for every 718 patients (compared to the one doctor for every 548 patients in 1998). Canadian physicians blame the shortage of physicians on a 1992 decision by federal and provincial governments to:

- severely restrict the number of practising Canadian physicians;

- reduce Canadian medical school entry class sizes by 10 percent by the fall of 1993;

- cut national postgraduate medical training positions by 10 percent; and

- and recruit more medical graduates from foreign countries into Canada for postgraduate medical training. In 1983, there were 1887 first-year medical students at Canada's 16 medical schools; by 1997, the number had declined to 1577 (Kennedy 1999: A6).

Access to Dental Care

According to the 1996–97 National Population Health Survey, only slightly more than half of all Canadians (55 percent) have dental insurance. Having dental insurance is much more common among children, youths, and working-age adults than among Canadian seniors. Among those 75 years of age and older in Canada, only 25 percent of men and 17 percent of women report having dental insurance. Income differences in relation to dental care are particularly notable: those in the highest income group are about three times as likely to have dental insurance as those in the lowest category. There is also interprovincial variation in insurance coverage with slightly more than 60 percent of those in Ontario and Alberta having dental insurance versus lows of 40 and 43 percent in Quebec and Newfoundland, respectively. In Canada, dentists work independently of the health care system except where in-hospital dental surgery is required.

The High Cost of Medications

Except for medication received while in institutional care, prescription drugs, nonprescription drugs, and over-the-counter products (e.g., cough and cold remedies, oral hygiene products, and home diagnostic kits) are not covered by the *Canada Health Act*. Instead, payees include governments through pharmacare programs, private insurance (including insurance companies, employees, and unions) and patients paying out-of-pocket. According to the 1996–97 National Population Health Survey, the prescription drug costs of almost two-thirds (61 percent) of Canadians were covered to some extent by government plans or insurance, with the greatest percentage covered under private plans. At present, only four Canadian provinces provide universal drug plans; British Columbia is only province that uses a reference-based pricing scheme (which pays for only the lowest cost drug in each of three designated "therapeutic categories" to help reduce costs). In provinces without universal plans, Armstrong et al. (1998) note that "not only are many individuals left out, especially among the 'working poor,' but it is very difficult for any particular plan to control costs. At the same time, each of them faces unnecessarily high administrative costs." In consequence, the National Forum on Health has called our current drug plan situation "incompatible with Canada's vision for the health care system," and has recommended the establishment of a single-payer, publicly funded system for pharmaceuticals.

In 1993, the cost of prescription and nonprescription drugs in Canada was almost $10 billion dollars or 6.3 percent of the total economic burden of illness in Canada (Moore et al. 1997). Between 1975 and 1996, per capita spending on drugs increased by more than 100 percent in real terms and rose to $362 for every man, woman, and child (Armstrong et al. 1998). Armstrong et al. identify two additional reasons why Canada has experienced a dramatic increase in the amount spent on drugs. First, they note that "the Canadian government has in recent years provided special status to the brand-name pharmaceutical firms, protecting them from competition," a move that stands in stark contrast to earlier policies. In the 1960s, three investigations of the pharmaceutical industry in Canada (i.e., the Restrictive Trade Practices Commission 1963; the Hall Royal Commission on Health Services 1964; and the Harley Special Committee of the House of Commons on Drug Costs and Prices 1967) concluded that the cost of drugs in Canada was excessive and recommended government action to encourage price competition within the industry.

Nader et al. (1993) observe that these recommendations "were intended to deal with the seventeen-year patent periods for newly developed drugs granted to the mainly foreign-based multinational drug companies that dominated the Canadian drug industry. The extended period was seen as the root cause for the unduly high drug prices." In response, amendments were made to the *Patent Act* that "allowed companies that wished to import and sell generic equivalents of patented brand-name drugs to do so upon receipt of a 'compulsory licence' and upon payment of a 4 percent royalty to the company holding the patent for the particular drug" (p. 84–5). This amendment resulted in Canada possessing a unique compulsory licensing system. In May 1985, the system was credited by the federal government's Commission of Inquiry on the Pharmaceutical Industry with saving consumers at least $211 million in 1983 alone, without "a discernible negative impact on the profitability and rate growth of the pharmaceutical industry as a whole."

Nevertheless, the Canadian government, under the leadership of Prime Minister Brian Mulroney, decided to dismantle the compulsory licensing program, succumbing to pressure from the Reagan administration and large multinational drug companies (many of them from the United States). In its place, Bill C-22 was introduced, "which proposed a ten-year period of patent protection for new drugs, and the creation of a Drug Price Review Board, charged with controlling price increases" (Nader et al. 1993: 85). Opposition to this bill was extreme; 14 votes were held in the House of Commons, 46 different groups testified in 24 sessions of hearings before the standing committee responsible for the bill; opposition parties introduced 47 amendments to the bill when it was again debated in Parliament, and various groups including the Consumers Association of Canada, the Canadian Labour Congress, the National Action on the Status of Women, the Canadian Council on Social Development, the National Anti-Poverty Organization, the National Pensioners and Senior Citizens Federation, and the Canadian Federation of University Women opposed the bill—along with two-thirds of Canadians surveyed in polls. In August 1987, the Senate also rejected the bill by a vote of 40 to 0 and sent back an amended version to the House.

In October of that year, *The Globe and Mail* reported that, despite its repeated claims to the contrary, the Mulroney government "had agreed to pass Bill C-22 as part of the free-trade agreement with the U.S." and that the "Canadian government made the pledge in writing on October 3 in a signed but unreleased version of the deal" (Nader et al. 1993: 87). A further attempt by the Senate to submit a version of the bill (that would have seen a four-year patent protection period, continued compulsory licensing, and higher royalties to companies that do research in Canada) was thwarted within the House of Common. In the end, the Senate "'stepped back from the brink of constitutional crisis' and allowed the House version to become law" (p. 87). As Nader et al. observe, "Canada's unique compulsory licensing system for pharmaceuticals, a system that was among the best in the world in terms of controlling drug prices while compensating originators of new drugs, was dismantled in favor of the U.S. system of no price controls, and an extensive patent protection system" (p. 87).

A second reason for the massive increase in drug costs stems from the increasing reliance on drug-based therapies. Some of these drugs allow patients to either avoid institutional care altogether or allow them to leave hospital after shorter periods than was formerly the case. For example, **deinstitutionalization** programs, which release mentally ill persons from institutions into communities, are premised on the notion that the needs of these individuals can be met by a network of outpatient services combined with maintenance doses of drugs. However, evidence suggests that many such individuals are falling through the loosely assembled "net" of outpatient services and are simply being chemically "managed." More generally, Armstrong et al. (1998) report "[d]rugs are all too frequently over-used or inappropriately used."

Organ Replacement

In 1996, surgeons in Canada performed 1578 transplants of kidneys, hearts, lungs, and other organs. Nevertheless, between 1992 and 1996, more than 1000 individuals died while waiting for transplants. At the end of December 1997, there were 3072 Canadians waiting for an organ transplants. Between 1991 and 1997, the number of patients waiting for an organ transplant increased by 68 percent, with the largest number of those on waiting lists for transplants living in Ontario (48 percent), followed by Quebec (21 percent), and British Columbia (12 percent). Canada has one of the lowest organ donor rates of all developed countries. In 1996, Canada's donation rate was 14.1 donors per million population or almost half that of Spain (26.8 per million). Currently, men constitute the majority of transplant recipients (65 percent) in general and, in particular, among those who are recipients of heart transplants (84 percent) (Health Canada 1999b; Statistics Canada 1998).

STRATEGIES FOR ACTION: IMPROVING HEALTH AND HEALTH CARE

Because poverty underlies many of the world's health problems, improving the world's health requires strategies that reduce poverty—a topic covered in Chapter 10. Chapter 3 addresses problems associated with tobacco and illegal drugs, Chapter 11 addresses health hazards in the workplace, and Chapter 14 focuses on environmental health problems. Here, we discuss other strategies for improving health. These include global strategies to improve maternal and infant health, the use of computer technology in health care, and Canada's health care reform.

Improving Maternal and Infant Health

As discussed earlier, maternal deaths are a major cause of death among women of reproductive age in the developing world. In 1987, the Safe Motherhood Initiative was launched. This global initiative is a partnership of governments, nongovernmental organizations, agencies, donors, and women's health advocates working to protect women's health and lives, especially during pregnancy and childbirth. Improving women's health also improves the health of infants: 30 to 40 percent of infant deaths are the result of poor care during labour and delivery (Safe Motherhood Initiative 1998).

The Safe Motherhood Initiative advocates improving maternal and infant health by first identifying the powerlessness that women face as an injustice that countries must remedy through political, health, and legal systems. In many developing countries, men make the decisions about whether or when their wives (or partners) will have sexual relations, use contraception, or bear children. Improving the status and power of women involves ensuring that they have the right to make decisions about their health and reproductive lives.

Improving maternal and infant health requires educating women and communities about the importance of maternal health care and the health benefits of breast-feeding. A major priority is the provision of free or affordable maternal and infant health services with facilities located close to where women live. Such facilities should have an adequate number of trained staff and a continual supply of drugs and equipment.

Young adolescent girls are more likely to die during pregnancy and delivery, and children born to young adolescent girls are more likely to die during their first year of life. Thus, it is important to discourage pregnancy and childbearing at younger ages. One way to do this is to increase the minimum age for legal marriage. Delaying marriage often delays first births and can reduce the total number of pregnancies a woman has, which reduces her lifetime risk of maternal mortality and morbidity.

Promoting women's education, another health strategy, increases the status and power of women to control their reproductive lives, exposes women to information about health issues, and also delays marriage and childbearing. In 23 developing countries, women with a secondary education marry on

According to the National Population Health Survey, 4 percent of Canadians aged 12 and older (about one million people) reported a major depressive episode and were likely clinically depressed in 1996–97. Women were twice as likely as men were to be depressed and they experienced longer periods of depression. Young women between the ages of 15 and 19 were the most likely of any age-sex group to exhibit symptoms of depression.

SOURCE: Health Canada 1999b

Across Canada, health care authorities have shut down hospital beds despite the fact that a system to take care of discharged patients in the community is not in place. Between 1989 and 1999, the number of hospital beds available decreased by 28.4 percent. In Yukon, the number of hospital beds available decreased by 61.7 percent, in Saskatchewan, by 47.9 percent, in Nova Scotia, by 41.8 percent, in the Northwest Territories, by 40.6 percent, in PEI, by 36.1 percent, in Alberta, by 33 percent, in Ontario, by 31.1 percent, and Quebec by 28 percent.

SOURCE: Bergman 2000

THE HUMAN SIDE

AN EXCERPT FROM *NO ORDINARY PEOPLE*

Elijah Harper is a Canadian Ojibway-Cree leader, was chief of the Red Sucker Lake Band in Manitoba from 1978 to 1981, served in the Manitoba Legislature and as a provincial cabinet minister from 1981 to 1992, and was elected to the House of Commons in 1993. "To some Canadians, especially those of the First Nations, Elijah Harper is a hero…[and] known as the man who, almost singlehandedly, prevented the ratification of the Meech Lake Accord in 1990" (Morton and Weinfeld 1998: 32) in the belief that it did not adequately address the concerns of First Nations peoples. In this extract, taken from the introduction to his book *No Ordinary People*, Harper eloquently reminds us why health care is not simply the "private problem" of individuals. Individuals can only do so much; the larger responsibility is society's.

> As a Canadian and an aboriginal person, I could not support an amendment to the supreme law of the country that failed to recognize the place of all the founding cultures of the federation. The suffering of native people is too great.

> Aboriginal people in Canada die on average 10 years younger than other Canadians do. Three out of 10 aboriginal families have no furnaces or heat in their homes, yet Canada has one of the highest standards of living in the world. Thirty-four percent have no indoor plumbing; our homes are overcrowded and in poor condition. About 45 percent of aboriginal people are on social assistance. Few of our people are in secondary schools. Only 5 percent graduate from secondary school. In my province, Manitoba, aboriginal people comprise 7 percent of the population, yet they make up 45 percent of the jail population. Family income on reserves is about $10 000, less than half the national average. Alcoholism, drunkenness and solvent abuse are epidemic on some reserves, and we suffer the negative stereotyping that naturally follows from that. Unemployment is about 66 percent; on some reserves, it is as high as 90 percent. Even our languages are in danger. Many have already become extinct. Our religions were forbidden for long enough that much has been forgotten.

> But these are only statistics. I cannot bring to you the despair. I cannot bring to you the 15-year-old boy in Winnipeg who will never share a bright future because that child was so depressed by what he saw every day that he took his own belt and hanged himself.…We must attack our problems on two levels. We must attack them as individual problems and we must work to eradicate their origins. We must change personal circumstances and the system. We must build houses for the homeless, but we must also build better communities around them. We must cure the sick, but we must also eliminate the poor water, inadequate sanitation, poor nutrition and poverty that make our people sick. If we don't solve all our problems on those two levels, we will be eternally fighting against a current over which we have no control.

SOURCES: Excerpt from *Elijah: No Ordinary Hero*. Copyright © 1994 by Pauline Corneau. Published in Canada by Douglas and McIntyre. Reprinted by permission of the publisher.

average four years later than do those with no education ("Economic Growth Unnecessary for Reducing Fertility" 1998).

Finally, the Safe Motherhood Initiative recommends reforming laws and policies to support women's reproductive health and improve access to family planning services. This recommendation implies removing legal barriers to abortion—a highly controversial issue in many countries.

Health Promotion

For at least 25 years, federal policy has recognized the importance of individual behaviour as a determinant of health status. While in recent years the focus has shifted from individual behaviour to the socioeconomic determinants of behaviour, there is no doubt that health education remains an important health promotion strategy at the levels of the individual and of the broader population. Canadian health education stresses that good nutrition, exercise, and abstaining from smoking are important to good health, and it seems that many Canadians are heeding the message. For example, the National Population Health Survey reported that in the 12 months prior to the survey, just less than half (47 percent) of their respondents had changed some facet of their behaviour to improve their health, while slightly more than half (54 percent) recognized that some change was needed. Among the latter group, more than two-thirds (69 percent) indicated their intent to change their behaviour in the next year. Among those who recognized a need for change, the need most commonly identified was for greater amounts of exercise followed by reductions in smoking, improved nutrition, and weight loss. An absence of time and personal willpower were identified as the main barriers to making the desired lifestyle changes.

Within this survey, women were more likely than men to report having made changes in their personal behaviours in the year before the survey; women were also more likely to voice their intention to make such changes in the forthcoming year. However, differences based on gender were less notable than differences based on age. With increasing age, "[t]here was a general decline in behaviour change—whether actual, needed, or intended" (Health Canada 1999b). Individuals in Ontario were more likely to report behaviour changes in the previous year and the least likely to report any intended changes in future years. Residents of Quebec (79 percent), British Columbia (73 percent), and Alberta (61 percent) were the most likely to report intentions to change in the next year.

People with Disabilities

It would be a grave mistake to forget the necessity of ensuring the physical and social health of those who have physical or mental disabilities. Between 1995 and 1998, claims of discrimination on the grounds of disability formed about one-third of all complaints made to the Canadian Human Rights Commission. People with disabilities in Canada continue to face disadvantage in areas such as work, housing, support services, transportation, and income support. Moreover, depending on the specific nature of their disability, they may or may not have access to adequate health care and education services.

For example, when 17-year-old Calgarian Terry Urquhart was placed on a waiting list to receive a lung transplant, it marked the first time that anyone with Down's syndrome in Canada, and perhaps in the world, had been given serious consideration for a lung transplant. Although individuals with Down's syndrome commonly experience severe lung problems as part of their genetic disorder, Terry's parents were originally told that their son did not qualify for a transplant in that he failed to meet the program's written criterion of "satisfactory intelligence." It was not until his parents went to the media that Terry was placed on the waiting list. However, public reaction was not unequivocally in favour of Urquhart. Reportedly, "hundreds" of phone calls poured in to the University of Alberta Hospital in Edmonton to protest, with some threatening to destroy their donor cards if Terry received a lung transplant. Consider as well that only two decades ago, newborns with Down's syndrome often died in Canada because of physicians' recommendations that parents not correct a simple stomach blockage (Mitchell 1995: A10).

In November 1999, a group of Ontario families announced their intention to take the provincial government (specifically, the Health Minister, her ministry, and the Ministries of Education, Community and Social Services, and Children) to court in an attempt to gain health and educational services for their autistic children. Autism is a condition characterized by complete self-absorption and a reduced ability to respond or communicate with the outside world. In Ontario, autism is defined as a psychological condition even though some within the medical community would define it as a neurological disorder. If autism were classified as a brain disorder, the cost of treating it would be fully covered by Ontario's provincial health care program. However, because of the way autism is defined in that province, little government funding is available.

Graham (1999) has noted that "support programs and services available to persons with disabilities, which are so essential to viability within the wider community, vary enormously from one part of the country to another." He points out that in Lloydminster, which straddles the Saskatchewan–Alberta border, a person with a visual disability can obtain certain high-tech equipment on the Alberta side but not on the Saskatchewan side; "in other words, if you live in Saskatchewan you can get a white cane—but sorry, nothing high tech."

It has been suggested that a Canadian disability act is necessary to ensure that the rights and needs of people with disabilities in Canada are protected (Kerzner and Baker 1999). However, in the absence of such an act, organizations such as the Council of Canadians with Disabilities, the Canadian Association for Independent Living Centres, DAWN (the Disabled Actions Women's Network), the Coalition of Provincial Organizations of the Handicapped, and institutes such as the Roeher Institute, the Canadian Council on Rehabilitation and Work, the Canadian Centre on Disability Studies, and the National Aboriginal Clearing/Connecting House on Disability Issues attempt to ensure that both the health and social needs of peoples with disabilities are not ignored in Canada.

Computer Technology in Health Care

Computer technology offers numerous ways to reduce costs associated with health care delivery and to improve patient care. For example, public sexual health clinics of the future are expected to implement computer technology that will decrease the number of support staff, eliminate paperwork related to record keeping, supplement risk assessment of clients, and deliver interventions such as counselling and referrals (Conlon 1997). At one hospital, a computer information system used to store information and give treatment advice to physicians was successful in detecting 60 times as many adverse drug reac-

---

National Data

The majority of Canada's population of people with disabilities, who make up 15 percent of Canadians, live on incomes of less than $10 000 per year.

SOURCE: Graham 1999

The Emerging Field of Telemedicine

In December 1994, a Chinese college student named Zhu Ling became ill, experiencing such symptoms as dizziness, facial paralysis, and loss of hair. Doctors did not know what was wrong with her. After she lapsed into a coma, her friends at Beijing University posted a plea for help on the Internet, appealing to any medical professional anywhere for help in diagnosing Zhu Ling's mysterious illness. Shortly after the plea was posted (which included Zhu Ling's symptoms and photographs), an American doctor made the correct diagnosis of thallium poisoning. Doctors from all over the world consulted via the Internet on the best treatments for Zhu Ling, who eventually came out of her coma.

Zhu Ling's story illustrates just one of the numerous applications of **telemedicine,** which literally means "medicine at a distance." Telemedicine involves using information and communication technologies to deliver a wide range of health care services, including diagnosis, treatment, prevention, health support and information, and education of health care workers.

Types of Telemedicine Services
Telemedicine can involve the transmission of three main types of information: data, audio, and images. A patient's medical records or vital signs (such as heart rate and blood pressure) can be transmitted from one location to another. Many hospitals and clinics store their medical records electronically, allowing doctors to access information about their patients very quickly and to update patient data from a distance. Specialized medical databases, such as MEDLINE, can be accessed via the Internet and offer a valuable resource for health care practitioners and researchers. The public may also use the Internet to gain health information and support. The simplest telemedicine service is telephone consultation. Transmitting medical images—

either still or moving pictures—is another type of telemedicine. **Teleradiology,** or the transmission of radiological images (such as x-ray and ultrasound images) from one location to another for the purpose of interpretation or consultation, has become one of the most commonly used telemedicine services. **Telepathology** involves transmitting images of tissue samples to a pathologist in another location, who can look at the image on a monitor and offer an interpretation.

Benefits of Telemedicine
Telemedicine has the potential to improve public health by making health care available in rural and remote areas and by providing health information to health care workers and to the general population. In addition, "telemedicine allows the scarce resources of specialists and expensive equipment to be shared by a much greater number of patients. Doctors are no longer restricted by geographical boundaries; international specialists are able to spread their skills across continents, without leaving their own hospitals" (LaPorte 1997: 38).

Telemedicine can be used in training and educating health care professionals and providing health care workers with up-to-date health information. Telemedicine can also reduce health care costs by reducing the cost of travel to major health centres or to specialists and by reducing the length of hospitalization, since patients can be monitored at a distance.

Another benefit of telemedicine is the provision of health information and support services on the Internet, which helps empower individuals in managing their health concerns. Through e-mail, bulletin boards, and chat rooms, individuals with specific health problems can network with other similarly affected individuals. For example, a user keying in "breast cancer" on a popular search engine like AltaVista will find links to 134 215 related Web sites generated from nearly every country in the world. The Arthritis Society of Canada's

17 000-page site, with video and audio attachments showing the latest research findings and a store displaying more than 250 arthritis-related items for sale (including cutlery and bathroom aids), gets an average of 36 000 hits a day (McClelland 1999). This social support assists in patient recovery, reduces the number of visits to physicians and clinics, and "provides…individuals [with disabilities] with an opportunity to achieve levels of social integration that were simply not possible before" (LaPorte 1997: 33). At the same time, however, it is important to remember that not all Web sites are equally credible. To help steer Canadians through the jungle of Internet Web sites toward reliable, officially approved health information, Health Canada has set up the Canadian Health Network Web site <www.canadian-health-network.ca>, which gives access to more than 400 Canadian health organizations ranging from the Aboriginal Nurses Association to the Canadian Cancer Society and the Heart and Stroke Foundation of Canada. Although Toronto-based, the network has operating partners in Eastern and Western Canada to ensure that regional interests are represented. Other Canadian health sites on the Internet, some providing links to many other reliable sources include <222.hlth.gov.bc.ca/exsites/index.html>, the B.C. Ministry of Health; <www.achoo.com>, MNI Systems Corp., a health information technology company; <www.mtrl.toronto.on.ca/centres/chis/index.html>, Consumer Health Information Service, Toronto Reference Library; <www.arthritis.ca/new.html>, the Arthritis Society of Canada; and <www.alzheimer.ca>, the Alzheimer Society of Canada.

Telemedicine also offers indirect benefits to the larger society. Availability of health care in remote areas helps to (1) slow population migration and attract people back to previously abandoned areas, (2) attract skilled personnel to remote and rural areas with a positive impact on local and national economies, and (3) improve health indicators of a country, which improves the overall image of a country and attracts investment (LaPorte 1997).

The Future of Telemedicine

In the twentieth century, advances in public health have been largely due to improvements in sanitation and immunization. Advocates of telemedicine have forecasted that in the twenty-first century, improvements in public health will result from the increased uses of information technology (LaPorte 1997).

One of the unresolved issues in telemedicine concerns how to pay health care professionals for their telemedicine services. In 1996, Norway became the first country to introduce a telemedicine fee schedule, making it reimbursable by the National Health Service (Sethov 1997). Leaders of the telemedicine movement are working to establish payment guidelines, develop standard consent forms, and pass legislation and medical licensing policies that allow professionals to practise medicine across national and international boundaries.

Telemedicine holds the promise of improving the health of individuals, fami-

lies, communities, and nations. Whether or not telemedicine achieves its promise depends, in part, on whether resources are allocated to provide the technology and the training to use it.

SOURCES: LaPorte, Ronald E. 1997. Improving Public Health Via the Information Superhighway. University of Pennsylvania. June 8, 1998 <www.the-scientist.library.upenn.edu/yr1997/august/opin_97018.html>; Maclean's. 1999. "Web Advice." December 6: 65; McClelland, Susan. 1999. "Users Beware." Maclean's, June 21: 57–8; Sethov, Inger. 1997. "The Wonders of Telemedicine." April 8, 1998 <www.techserver.com/newsroom/ntn/info/111097/info10_14458_noframes.html>.

tions in patients as traditional methods ("Using Computers to Advance Health Care" 1996). This chapter's Focus on Technology describes additional uses of computers in health care.

UNDERSTANDING ILLNESS AND HEALTH CARE

As we have seen, patterns of health and disease vary widely between developed countries and less developed countries. The different types of health problems in developed versus less developed countries reflect their different socioeconomic statuses. Health problems are affected not only by economic resources, but also by other social factors such as aging of the population, gender, education, and race.

Our cultural values and beliefs emphasize the ability of individuals to control their lives through the choices they make. Thus, westerners view health and illness as resulting from individual behaviour and lifestyle choices, rather than resulting from social, economic, and political forces. We agree that an individual's health is affected by the choices that person makes—choices such as whether or not to smoke, exercise, engage in sexual activity, use condoms, wear a seatbelt, and so on. However, the choices individuals make are influenced by social, economic, and political forces that must be taken into account if the goal is to improve the health of not only individuals, but also of entire populations. Further, by focusing on individual behaviours that affect health and illness, we often overlook not only social causes of health problems, but social solutions as well. For example, at an individual level, the public has been advised to rinse and cook meat, poultry, and eggs thoroughly and to carefully wash hands, knives, cutting boards, and so on to avoid illness caused by *Escherichia coli* and salmonella bacteria. However, whether or not one becomes ill from contaminated meat, eggs, or poultry is affected by more than individual behaviours in the kitchen. Governmental actions can also offer solutions by providing for more food inspectors and stricter regulations on food industries.

While certain changes in medical practices and policies may help to improve world health, "the health sector should be seen as an important, but not the sole, force in the movement toward global health" (Lerer et al. 1998: 18). Improving the health of a society requires addressing diverse issues, including poverty and economic inequality, gender inequality, population growth, environmental issues, education, housing, energy, water and sanitation, agriculture, and workplace safety. Health promotion is important in not only the hospital, clinic, or doctor's office—it must also occur in the various settings where people live, work, play, and learn (Antezana et al. 1998).

CRITICAL THINKING

1. An analysis of 161 countries found that, in general, countries with high levels of literacy have low levels of HIV (World Health Organization and United Nations Joint Programme on HIV/AIDS 1998). However, in the region of the world affected the worst by HIV, sub-Saharan Africa, there is also a relationship between literacy rates and HIV, but the direction of the relationship is reversed. In this region, the countries with the highest levels of HIV infection are also those whose men and women are most literate. What are some possible explanations for this?

2. The Center for Disease Control and Prevention (CDC) recommend that people aged six and older engage regularly, preferably daily, in light to moderate physical activity for at least 30 minutes per day. Experts agree that if those "who lead sedentary lives would adopt a more active lifestyle, there would be enormous benefit to the public's health and to individual well-being" (Pate et al. 1995: 406). Yet, in a telephone survey of more than 87 000 adults, only about 22 percent reported being active at the recommended level; 24 percent reported that they led a completely sedentary lifestyle (that is, they reported no leisure-time physical activity in the past month). What social and cultural factors contribute to the sedentary lifestyle of many North Americans?

3. In many countries, drug injecting accounts for more HIV infections than sex does. Research evidence clearly suggests that needle exchange programs that provide sterile needles to intravenous drug users result in lower rates of HIV transmission (World Health Organization and United Nations Joint Programme on HIV/AIDS 1998). Should our government support such programs? Why or why not?

KEY TERMS

acute condition	epidemiologist	mental disorder
anorexia nervosa	epidemiology	morbidity
bulimia nervosa	health	mortality
burden of disease	health expectancy	prevalence
chronic condition	incidence	telemedicine
deinstitutionalization	infant mortality rate	telepathology
disability-adjusted life	life expectancy	teleradiology
year (DALY)	maternal mortality rate	under-five mortality rate
epidemiological	medicalization	
transition	Medicare	

CHAPTER THREE

Alcohol and Other Drugs

- The Global Context: Drug Use and Abuse
- Sociological Theories of Drug Use and Abuse
- Frequently Used Legal and Illegal Drugs
- Self and Society: Alcohol Attitude Test
- The Human Side: Mean Streets: Street Youths and Substance Abuse
- Societal Consequences of Drug Use and Abuse
- Focus on Technology: Drug Testing
- Treatment Alternatives
- Strategies for Action: Canada Responds
- Understanding Alcohol and Other Drugs

Is It True?

1. Between 1985 and 1999, there was a significant decline in the number of Canadians aged 15 and older who were smokers.

2. Impaired driving is one of the most common crimes committed by Canadians and a major cause of death in Canada.

3. Of all psychoactive drugs, alcohol is the only one whose consumption has been shown to increase aggression.

4. The most commonly used illicit drug in Canada is marijuana.

5. The Dutch have decriminalized small quantities of heroin and have one of the lowest addiction rates in Europe.

Answers: 1 = T, 2 = T, 3 = T, 4 = T, 5 = T

Substance abuse has an impact on many aspects of Canadian life—the home, the community, the health care system, the justice system and the economy.

Paul Garfinkel, CEO,
Centre for Addiction and
Mental Health,
and Jacques
LeCavalier,
CEO, Canadian
Centre on Substance
Abuse

In August 1995, 300 mourners gathered in a Montreal church for the funeral service of Daniel Desrochers. Daniel had been fatally injured when a bomb, planted in a drug dealer's vehicle by a rival gang, blew up, sending a steel fragment into his brain. He died four days later. Daniel had been playing in the street at the time of the explosion; he was 11 years old (*Maclean's* 1995: 23).

The abuse of alcohol and other drugs is a social problem when it interferes with the well-being of individuals or the societies in which they live—when it jeopardizes health, safety, work and academic success, family, and friends. Managing the drug problem is a difficult undertaking. In dealing with drugs, a society must balance individual rights and civil liberties against the personal and social harm that drugs contribute to crack-addicted babies, suicide, drunk driving, industrial accidents, mental illness, unemployment, and teenage addiction. When to regulate, what to regulate, and who should regulate are complex social issues. Our discussion begins by looking at how drugs are used and regulated in other societies.

THE GLOBAL CONTEXT: DRUG USE AND ABUSE

Pharmacologically, a **drug** is any substance other than food that alters the structure or functioning of a living organism when it enters the bloodstream. Using this definition, everything from vitamins to aspirin constitutes a drug. Sociologically, the term drug refers to any chemical substance that (1) has a direct effect on the user's physical, psychological, or intellectual functioning, (2) has the potential to be abused, and (3) has adverse consequences for the individual or for society. Societies vary in how they define and respond to drug use. Thus, drug use is influenced by the social context of the particular society in which it occurs.

Drug Use and Abuse around the World

Globally, drug use and abuse have increased over the past several decades. The production of opium has more than tripled since 1985; nine times the quantity of synthetic stimulants were confiscated in 1993 than in 1978; and in the past 10 years, seizures of most major drugs have increased dramatically. For example, 1996 cocaine seizures resulted in almost 228 metric tons of cocaine being confiscated worldwide (*World Drug Report* 1997). Further, individual indicators such as "emergency room visits, substance abuse related mortality cases, arrests of drug abusers, [and] number of countries reporting rising consumption levels—make clear that consumption has become a truly global phenomenon" (World Drug Report 1994, p. 29).

Italy decriminalized personal drug use and possession of small amounts of drugs in 1993 (*World Drug Report* 1997). The Netherlands, however, has had an official government policy of treating the use of such drugs as marijuana, hashish, and heroin as a health issue rather than a crime issue since the mid-1970s. Overall, this **"decriminalization"** policy has had positive results.

Although marijuana and heroin are readily available in Dutch cities, the use of both has declined over the years, as have the numbers of drug overdoses and HIV infections from intravenous drug use. The decline in the number of drug users may have occurred, in part, because addicts are free to seek help without fear of criminal reprisals.

Great Britain has also adopted a "medical model," particularly concerning heroin and cocaine. As early as the 1960s, English doctors prescribed opiates and cocaine for their patients who were unlikely to quit using drugs on their own and for the treatment of withdrawal symptoms. By the 1970s, however, British laws had become more restrictive, making it difficult for either physicians or users to obtain drugs legally. Today, British government policy provides for limited distribution of drugs to addicts who might otherwise resort to crime to support their habits.

In stark contrast to such health-based policies, other countries execute drug users, dealers, or both, or subject them to corporal punishment. The latter may include whipping, stoning, beating, and torture. Such policies are found primarily in less developed nations such as Malaysia, where religious and cultural prohibitions condemn any type of drug use, including alcohol and tobacco.

Drug Use and Abuse in Canada

According to officials and the media, there is a drug crisis in Canada—a crisis so serious that it demands that we engage in a "war on drugs." Canadians' concern with drugs, however, has varied over the years. Although in 1975 almost one in two Canadians (46 percent) identified drugs as a "very serious" problem in our country, by 1995, this figure had declined to about one in three (34 percent).

In Canada, the use of alcohol is much more widespread than the use of illicit drugs such as marijuana and cocaine, but our response to drug use is contradictory—condemning it on the one hand (e.g., heroin), yet encouraging and tolerating it on the other (e.g., alcohol). At various times in our history, many drugs that are illegal today were legal and readily available. In the nineteenth century and the early twentieth century, opium was routinely used in medicines as a pain reliever, and morphine was taken as a treatment for dysentery and fatigue. Amphetamine-based inhalers were legally available until 1949, and cocaine was an active ingredient in Coca-Cola until 1906, when it was replaced with another drug—caffeine (Witters et al. 1992). In the 1950s, anabolic steroids were viewed as "wonder drugs" that could enhance the well-being of sick and malnourished people, promote quick weight gain in cattle, and potentially provide a cure to cancer. It was arguably not until 1988, when Canadian athlete Ben Johnson lost his gold medal at the Seoul Olympics for taking a performance-enhancing drug, that many Canadians became aware that the use of anabolic steroids could be problematic. Even now, public opinion polls suggest Canadians are equivocal about whether steroid use should be viewed as socially problematic (Nuwer 1990: 23). Moreover, while the majority of Canadians (86 percent) indicate that they are aware of the health risks of environmental tobacco smoke (ETS), more than three million Canadians aged 12 and older (or 14 percent of the Canadian population) believe that there are no health risks for nonsmokers or have no opinion on the subject (Health Canada 1999: 155) (Figure 3.1). It would seem likely that among these Canadians, such measures as municipal bylaws that restrict public

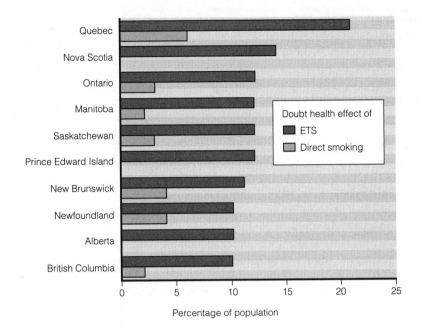

Figure 3.1
Skepticism about the Health Risks of Smoking, by Province, Age 12+, Canada, 1996–97

Note: Data suppressed for Nova Scotia, Prince Edward Island, and Alberta because of high sampling variability.

SOURCE: Health Canada. 1999. Statistical Report on the Health of Canadians: 155.

smoking or voluntary restrictions on smoking at home are viewed as ill conceived or unwarranted.

SOCIOLOGICAL THEORIES OF DRUG USE AND ABUSE

Most theories of drug use and abuse concentrate on what are called psychoactive drugs. These drugs alter the functioning of the brain, affecting the moods, emotions, and perceptions of the user. Such drugs include alcohol, cocaine, heroin, and marijuana. **Drug abuse** occurs when acceptable social standards of drug use are violated, resulting in adverse physiological, psychological, or social consequences. For example, when an individual's drug use leads to hospitalization, arrest, or divorce, such use is usually considered abusive. Drug abuse, however, does not always entail chemical dependency. **Chemical dependency** refers to a condition in which drug use is compulsive—users are unable to stop because of their dependency. The dependency may be psychological, in that the individual needs the drug to achieve a feeling of well-being, or physical, in that withdrawal symptoms occur when the individual stops taking the drug, or both.

Various theories provide explanations for why some people use and abuse drugs. Drug use is not simply a matter of individual choice. Theories of drug use explain how structural and cultural forces, as well as biological factors, influence drug use and society's responses to it.

Structural-Functionalist Perspective

Functionalists argue that drug abuse is a response to the weakening of norms in society. As society becomes more complex and rapid social change occurs, norms and values become unclear and ambiguous, resulting in **anomie**—a state of normlessness. Anomie may exist at the societal level, resulting in social strains and inconsistencies that lead to drug use. For example, research indicates that increased alcohol consumption in the 1830s and the 1960s was a response to rapid social change and the resulting stress (Rorabaugh 1979). Anomie produces inconsistencies in cultural norms regarding drug use. For example, while public health officials and health care professionals warn of the dangers of alcohol and tobacco use, advertisers glorify the use of alcohol and tobacco, and the government subsidizes alcohol and tobacco industries. Further, cultural traditions, such as giving away cigars to celebrate the birth of a child and toasting a bride and groom with champagne, persist.

Anomie may also exist at the individual level as when a person suffers feelings of estrangement, isolation, and turmoil over appropriate and inappropriate behaviour. An adolescent whose parents are divorcing, who is separated from friends and family as a consequence of moving, or who lacks parental supervision and discipline may be more vulnerable to drug use because of such conditions. Thus, from a structural-functionalist perspective, drug use is a response to the absence of a perceived bond between the individual and society, and to the weakening of a consensus regarding what is considered acceptable. Consistent with this perspective, Nylander et al. (1996) found that adolescents who reported that religion was important in their lives were less likely to use drugs than those for whom religion wasn't important.

Conflict Perspective

Conflict perspectives emphasize the importance of power differentials in influencing drug use behaviour and societal values concerning drug use. From a conflict perspective, drug use occurs as a response to the inequality perpetuated by a capitalist system. Societal members, alienated from work, friends, and family, as well as from society and its institutions, turn to drugs as a means of escaping the oppression and frustration caused by the inequality they experience. Further, conflict theorists emphasize that the most powerful members of society influence the definitions of which drugs are illegal and the penalties associated with illegal drug production, sales, and use.

For example, alcohol is legal because it is produced and often consumed by those who enjoy power, privilege, and influence. Consider that in 1996–97, the alcohol industry enjoyed sales of more than $11.38 billion, employed more than 14 000 people, and generated $3.34 billion in revenue for provincial governments as well as considerable federal revenue. During the same period, tobacco products generated more than $3.94 billion in revenue (CCSA 1999). Hackler (2000: 227) has suggested that the Canadian tobacco industry has also benefited from its ability to hire influential people such as Bill Neville, "chief of staff when Joe Clark was prime minister...a member of Brian Mulroney's election campaign committee for 1988,...[and] president of the Canadian Tobacco Manufacturer's Council since 1987." As Hackler observes, "Tobacco lobbies...are powerful and their goal is to increase drug use" (p. 224). Consider as well the irony: Of the $18.5 billion cost of substance abuse to the Canadian economy, the costs of legal drugs were the most significant, with tobacco accounting for $9.6 billion, alcohol $7.5 billion, and illicit drugs $1.4 billion (CCSA 1999).

Conversely, the consumption of "street drugs" such as cocaine and heroin is associated with the powerless and disenfranchised: the poor, minority group members, and, in particular, visible minorities. As Hackler (2000: 213) observes, "the societal demand to punish, stigmatize, and exclude users of certain substances is *not based on pharmacological evidence*" and that evidence of such damage "plays a secondary role in drug policy." The use of opium by Chinese immigrants in the 1800s provides an historical example. The Chinese, who had been brought to Canada to work on the railroads, regularly smoked opium as part of their cultural tradition. However, hostility to the use of opium emerged in part because of a labour surplus that followed the completion of railway construction and the diminished intensity of the Gold Rush. Green (1986) notes that before this time, in the midst of a labour shortage, "the Chinese were regarded as industrious, sober, economical and law abiding individuals" (p. 25). As jobs became scarce and the Chinese were viewed as competitors for the positions that existed, "the earlier friendly feelings toward the Chinese changed to hostility....There was a great demand that Chinese immigration be restricted or discontinued." (p. 24). Simultaneously, opium use, which had been previously viewed as, at worst, "an individual medical misfortune or personal vice, free of severe moral opprobrium" (p. 25), became defined as a significant social "evil." Morgan (1978) observes:

> The first opium laws ... were not the result of a moral crusade against the drug itself. Instead, it represented a coercive action directed against a vice that was merely an appendage of the real menace—the Chinese—and not the Chinese per se, but the laboring "Chinamen" who threatened the economic security of the white working class. (p. 59)

The criminalization of other drugs, including cocaine, heroin, and marijuana, follows similar patterns of social control of the powerless, political opponents, and/or minorities. In the 1940s, marijuana was used primarily by minority group members and carried with it severe criminal penalties. However, after White middle-class students began to use marijuana in the 1970s, various lobby groups sought to reduce the penalties associated with its use. Though the nature and pharmacological properties of the drug had not changed, the population of users was now connected to power and influence. Thus, conflict theorists regard the regulation of certain drugs and drug use itself as a reflection of differences in the political, economic, and social power of various interest groups.

Symbolic Interactionist Perspective

Symbolic interactionism, emphasizing the importance of definitions and labelling, concentrates on the social meanings associated with drug use. If the initial drug use experience is defined as pleasurable, it is likely to recur, and over time, the individual may earn the label of "drug user." If this definition is internalized so that the individual assumes an identity of a drug user, the behaviour will likely continue and may even escalate.

Drug use is also learned through symbolic interaction in small groups. First-time users learn not only the motivations for drug use and its techniques, but also what to experience. Becker (1966) explains how marijuana users learn to ingest the drug. A novice being coached by a regular user reports this experience:

I was smoking like I did an ordinary cigarette. He said, "No, don't do it like that." He said, "Suck it, you know, draw in and hold it in your lungs...for a period of time." I said, "Is there any limit of time to hold it?" He said, "No, just till you feel that you want to let it out, let it out." So I did that three or four times. (p. 47)

Marijuana users not only learn how to ingest the smoke, but also learn to label the experience positively. When certain drugs, behaviours, and experiences are defined by peers as not only acceptable but pleasurable, drug use is likely to continue.

Because they [first-time users] think they're going to keep going up, up, up till they lose their minds or begin doing weird things or something. You have to like reassure them, explain to them that they're not really flipping or anything, that they're gonna be all right. You have to just talk them out of being afraid. (Becker 1966: 55)

Interactionists also emphasize that symbols may be manipulated and used for political and economic agendas. "[A]meliorative programs which are imbued with...potent symbolic qualities...are virtually assured wide-spread public acceptance (regardless of actual effectiveness) which in turn advances the interests of political leaders who benefit from being associated with highly visible, popular symbolic programs" (Wysong et al. 1994: 461).

Biological Theories

Biological research has primarily concentrated on the role of genetics in predisposing an individual to alcohol abuse (Pickens and Svikis 1988). Research indicates that children of alcoholics have a 50 percent chance of becoming alcoholics themselves. At a recent International Conference on Genetics, one researcher stated that by looking at inherited traits, "we can predict [in] childhood with 80 percent accuracy who is going to develop alcoholism later in life" (AAP 1998). At the same time, many alcoholics do not have parents who abuse alcohol, and many alcoholic parents have offspring who do not abuse alcohol.

Biological theories of drug use hypothesize that some individuals are physiologically predisposed to experience more pleasure from drugs than others and, consequently, are more likely to be drug users. According to these theories, the central nervous system, which is composed primarily of the brain and spinal cord, processes drugs through neurotransmitters in a way that produces an unusually euphoric experience. Individuals not so physiologically inclined report less pleasant experiences and are less likely to continue use (Jarvik 1990).

Psychological Theories

Psychological explanations focus on the tendency of certain personality types to be more susceptible to drug use. Individuals who are particularly prone to anxiety may be more likely to use drugs as a way to relax, gain self-confidence, and ease tension. Those who have dependent personalities and have a compulsive need for love may be more inclined to use drugs to numb the frustration when other needs are not being met.

Psychological theories of drug abuse also emphasize that drug use is maintained by positive and negative reinforcement. Positive reinforcement occurs when drug use results in desirable experiences, such as excitement, pleasure, and peer approval. Negative reinforcement occurs when drug use results in the temporary alleviation of undesirable experiences, such as pain, anxiety, boredom, and loneliness.

FREQUENTLY USED LEGAL AND ILLEGAL DRUGS

Social definitions regarding which drugs are legal or illegal have varied over time, circumstance, and societal forces. In Canada, two of the most dangerous and widely abused drugs, alcohol and tobacco, are legal.

Alcohol

Canadians' attitudes toward alcohol have had a long and varied history (this chapter's Self and Society deals with attitudes toward alcohol). Although alcohol was a common beverage in early Canada, "the moral climate in Canada after the turn of the century was one in which middle class persons with strong religious convictions were willing to believe the worst of alcohol, tobacco and other drugs....The typical reaction to these perceived threats was to press for total prohibition" (Giffen et al. 1991: 150). Many have argued that the push for Prohibition was, in fact, a "moral crusade" (Gusfield 1963) against immigrant groups who were perceived as more likely to use alcohol. Today, Canada is experiencing a resurgence of concern about alcohol (Table 3.1). What has been called a "new temperance" has manifested itself in increased concern about fetal alcohol syndrome, teenage drinking, and calls for strict enforcement of drinking and driving regulations.

Alcohol is the most widely used and abused drug in Canada. Although most people who drink alcohol do so moderately and experience few negative effects, alcoholics are psychologically and physically addicted to alcohol and suffer various degrees of physical, economic, psychological, and personal harm. In 1994, 6504 Canadians (4681 men and 1823 women) died because of alcohol consumption: motor vehicle accidents, liver cirrhosis, and suicide accounted for the largest number of these deaths. In 1995–96, 80 946 Canadians (51 765 men and 29 181 women) were hospitalized because of alcohol-related problems: accidental falls, alcohol dependence syndrome, and motor vehicle accidents accounted for the largest number of alcohol-related hospitalizations (CCSA 1999).

In 1996–97, more than half (53 percent) of Canadians 12 years of age and older (12.7 million Canadians) reported drinking at least one alcoholic drink per month in the previous year. The largest proportion of regular drinkers (43 percent) reported consuming, on average, one to six drinks each week. Men were significantly more likely than women were to be regular drinkers (63 percent versus 43 percent), especially among those aged 15 to 44, where almost three-quarters of men (74 percent) and half of women (49 to 50 percent) were regular drinkers. Men who were regular drinkers were also more likely to drink more frequently and to report a higher average weekly consumption than women were. "Men were one and one half times more likely than women to drink 7–13 drinks each week (18% vs. 12%) and three times more likely to

If you strongly agree with the following statements, write in 1. If you agree, but not strongly, write in 2. If you neither agree nor disagree, write in 3. If you disagree, but not strongly, write in 4. If you strongly disagree, write in 5.

SET 1

_____   1. If a person concentrates hard enough, he or she can overcome any effect that drinking may have on driving.

_____   2. If you drive home from a party late at night when most roads are deserted, there is not much danger in driving after drinking.

_____   3. It's all right for a person who has been drinking to drive, as long as he or she shows no signs of being drunk.

_____   4. If you're going to have an accident, you'll have one anyhow, regardless of drinking.

_____   5. A drink or two helps people drive better because it relaxes them.

_____   *Total score for questions 1 through 5*

SET 2

_____   6. If I tried to stop someone from driving after drinking, the person would probably think I was butting in where I shouldn't.

_____   7. Even if I wanted to, I would probably not be able to stop someone from driving after drinking.

_____   8. If people want to kill themselves, that's their business.

_____   9. I wouldn't like someone to try to stop me from driving after drinking.

_____   10. Usually, if you try to help someone else out of a dangerous situation, you risk getting yourself into one.

_____   *Total score for questions 6 through 10*

SET 3

_____   11. My friends would not disapprove of me for driving after drinking.

_____   12. Getting into trouble with my parents would not keep me from driving after drinking.

_____   13. The thought that I might get into trouble with the police would not keep me from driving after drinking.

_____   14. I am not scared by the thought that I might seriously injure myself or someone else by driving after drinking.

_____   15. The fear of damaging the car would not keep me from driving after drinking.

_____   *Total score for questions 11 through 15*

SET 4

_____   16. The speed limit on the open roads spoils the pleasure of driving for most teenagers.

_____   17. Many teenagers use driving to let off steam.

_____   18. Being able to drive a car makes teenagers feel more confident in their relations with others their age.

_____   19. An evening with friends is not much fun unless one of them has a car.

_____   20. There is something about being behind the wheel of a car that makes one feel more adult.

_____   *Total score for questions 16 through 20*

Alcohol Attitude Test (*continued*)

SCORING

Set 1. —— 13–25 points: realistic in avoiding drinking-driving situations; 5–6 points: tends to make excuses to combine drinking and driving.

Set 2. —— 15–25 points: takes responsibility to keep others from driving when drunk; 5–9 points: wouldn't take steps to stop a drunk friend from driving.

Set 3. —— 12–25 points: hesitates to drive after drinking; 5–7 points: is not deterred by the consequences of drinking and driving.

Set 4. —— 19–25 points: perceives auto as means of transportation; 5–14 points: uses car to satisfy psychological needs, not just transportation.

SOURCE: Courtesy of National Highway Traffic Safety Administration. National Center for Statistics and Analysis, from *Drug Driving Facts*. Washington, DC: NHTSA, 1988.

Table 3.1 — **Public Opinion on the Importance of Alcohol Issues, Views on Alcohol Control Policies, and Attitudes toward Interventions, Canada 1994**

Importance of Alcohol Issues	Serious or very serious	A Problem but not serious	Not a problem	No opinion
Drinking and driving in the neighbourhood	25.8%	24.7%	41.7%	7.8%
Alcohol-related domestic violence	18.0	19.8	48.0	14.2
Alcohol-related public fights in the neighbourhood	16.7	23.1	53.4	6.9
Alcohol-related problems in the workplace	10.6	18.4	65.2	5.7

Opinion on alcohol control policies	Increased	Unchanged	Decreased	Not stated
Taxes on alcohol should be	25.4	44.8	25.4	4.5
The legal drinking age should be	38.3	54.7	4.1	2.9
Alcohol outlet hours should be	10.9	66.5	16.0	6.6
Government advertising against alcohol should be	48.8	34.4	12.9	3.8

	Yes	No	Not stated
Alcohol should be sold in convenience stores	30.0	66.8	3.3
There should be warning labels on alcoholic beverages	69.5	27.5	2.8

Attitudes toward intervention	Increased	Unchanged	Decreased	Not stated
Alcohol and drug prevention programs should be	74.4	18.0	2.6	4.9
Efforts to prevent drunk people from being served should be	75.5	15.3	5.2	4.0
Treatment programs should be	64.6	24.2	2.3	8.9

1.   Percentages are based on the number of respondents in the workforce. In 26.7 percent of the cases, the question was not applicable (for example, homemakers).

SOURCE: Adapted from Single, E. 1997. "Public Opinion on Alcohol and Other Drug Issues." In *Canada's Alcohol and Other Drug Survey 1994: A Discussion of the Findings,* edited by P. MacNeil and I. Webster (Vol. Cat: H39-336/1-1994E). Ottawa: Ministry of Public Works and Government Services Canada.

drink 14 or more drinks each week (13% vs 4%)" (Health Canada 1999: 171–2). Binge drinking, defined as the consumption of five or more alcoholic beverages on at least one occasion, is most common among youth. According to the 1996–97 NPHS, more than one-third (36 percent) of Canadians aged 20 to 24 who were current drinkers drank five or more drinks at least 12 times in the previous year and more than 1 in 10 (13 percent) did so 52 or more times in the previous year. Binge drinking is more prevalent among young Canadian men aged 15 to 19 (52 percent) than among young Canadian women (35 percent). However, the majority of both sexes in the 20- to 24-year-old age group (73 percent of men and 51 percent of women) reported at least one episode of binge drinking (Health Canada 1999: 171).

The National Population Health Survey reports a *positive* relationship between education and drinking. That is, as education increases, so too does the likelihood that Canadians are regular drinkers. "University graduates were most likely (61%) to drink at least once a month, while those with less than high school were least likely (44%) to do so." It additionally notes that the relationship between amount consumed and educational attainment "is similar, though less pronounced: with each successive level of education, the likelihood of having had one or more drinks weekly increased. However, university graduates were least likely to have had 14 or more drinks weekly" (Health Canada 1999: 172).

A recent study (Wechsler et al. 1998) of more than 17 000 college students at 140 four-year colleges and universities indicates that:

- In the two weeks before the survey, 44 percent of students had engaged in binge drinking.
- Seventy-three percent of men and 68 percent of women reported that getting drunk was an important reason for drinking.
- Students who were White, members of a fraternity or sorority, or athletes were the most likely to binge.
- Sixty-one percent of men and 39 percent of women drank alcohol on 10 or more occasions in the past 30 days.
- More than 80 percent of women and men reported having a hangover, more than 50 percent doing something they regretted later, more than 40 percent missing class due to drinking, and more than 30 percent getting behind in schoolwork because of drinking.

Not only were binge drinkers more likely to report using other controlled substances, but also the more frequently a student binged, the higher the probability of reporting other drug use. The most commonly reported other drugs used by frequent binge drinkers were, in order, cigarettes, marijuana, hallucinogens, and chewing tobacco (HHS 1998).

Tobacco

Although nicotine is an addictive psychoactive drug and the dangers of second-hand smoke form the basis for Canada's *Non-Smoker's Health Act*, tobacco continues to be one of the most widely used drugs in Canada. However, its use is decreasing. The results of 11 Statistic Canada surveys that asked questions about smoking from 1985 to 1999 indicate a significant decline of 10.3 percentage points in the smoking prevalence of Canadians aged 15 and older, with most of the decline occurring after 1994. However, there was a sig-

National Data

According to the National Population Health Survey, in 1996–97, the proportion of Canadian men and women who drank at least once per month rose steadily with increases in income. Men and women with higher incomes also tended to be heavier drinkers. Among men in the two lower-income levels who were drinkers, 24 percent reported at least one episode of heavy or "binge" drinking, compared with 43 percent of men in the highest income bracket. The rate of heavy drinking among women drinkers in the lowest income level was 13 percent. This rate dropped to 10 percent at the next income level, then slowly climbed to 19 percent at the highest income level.
SOURCE: Health Canada 1999

nificant and large increase of 6.5 percentage points in the current smoking rates for 15- to 19-year-olds between 1991 and January 1, 1994. Since 1994, there has been no significant change in the current smoking rate for youths (Statistics Canada 2000). According to the Canadian Centre on Substance Abuse (1999), 28.6 percent of Canadians aged 15 and older smoked cigarettes on either a daily or an occasional basis in 1996–97, with rates of use highest among those aged 20 to 24 (35.1 percent) and lowest among those aged 75 or older (11.2 percent).

Much of the concern about smoking surrounds the use of tobacco by young people (see Figure 3.2). While less than 1 percent (0.5) of Canadian youth aged 10 to 12 smoke, the prevalence of youth smoking rises rapidly to 22.2 percent among those aged 18 to 28 (CCSA 1999). Because more than 8 in 10 adult smokers acquire the smoking habit before the age of 20, smoking among teenagers can signify far more than youthful recklessness. In 1994, almost one-third of all Canadian 19-year-olds smoked and more than three-quarters of them smoked daily. Moreover, a long-term study of substance abuse among Canadian teenagers reported that between 1993 and 1995, the use of tobacco among this age group increased to 28 percent, its highest level since the early 1980s (Statistics Canada 1998: 110).

Leiss (1997) notes that although the prevalence of youth smoking fell by almost 25 percent between 1985 and 1990, by 1994 it had rebounded to its 1985 levels, "an outcome that most observers would attribute to the price reduction stemming from tax changes" (p. 7). In 1994, in an attempt to reduce cigarette smuggling, the federal government decreased tobacco taxes dramatically, an action that was followed by several provincial governments. However, smoking among Canadian teens since 1979 has been inversely related to the price of cigarettes. The Survey of Smoking in Canada conducted by Statistics Canada on behalf of Health Canada measured changes in smoking behaviour among respondents aged 15 and older following the tax reduction in early 1994 and four times between May 1994 and February 1995. The survey reported that 5 percent of 15- to 19-year-olds increased their level of smoking because of the price decreases, and 19 percent of those within this age group

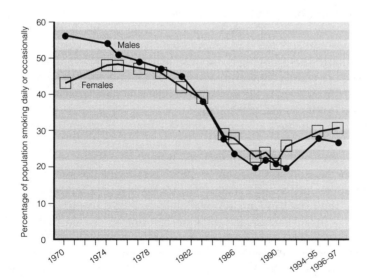

Figure 3.2
Prevalence of Smoking, by Sex, Age 15–19, Canada, 1970 to 1996–97
SOURCE: Health Canada 1999

The highest rate of smoking in Canada is reported by Aboriginal people and it is almost double the overall rate in the Canadian population as a whole. In 1997, adult smoking rates within the Aboriginal populations were highest among those aged 20 to 24 (72 percent) and 25 to 29 (71 percent). The use of smokeless tobacco by Aboriginal youth in the Northwest Territories and northern Saskatchewan also poses a significant health problem.
SOURCE: Health Canada 1999

In January 2000, Health Minister Allan Rock announced his intention to force tobacco manufacturers to dedicate half the front panel of every cigarette pack to any of 16 shocking images including stark close-ups of tumours and diseased lungs and mouths. In addition, a leaflet inside the package will list the toxic chemicals in tobacco smoke and advise smokers how to kick the habit. With more than two billion cigarette packs printed annually in Canada, these changes, considered to be among the toughest in the world, will amount to the biggest public-health campaign ever launched in Canada.
SOURCE: Fennell 2000

began smoking because of the reduced cost of doing so (Clark 1996: 5). Cigarette company polls also indicate that 97 000 more young Canadians were smoking at the end of 1996 than before the federal government cut cigarette taxes in 1994. It is estimated that underage smokers account for 3 percent of the industry's sales (*KW Record* 1997).

In 1997, Canada's *Tobacco Sales to Young Persons Act* (1993) was replaced by the *Tobacco Act*. In Canada, it is a summary conviction offence for any person to furnish (i.e., sell, give, or send) a tobacco product to a person under 18 in any public place (Solomon 1999: 11). The *Tobacco Act* also prohibits retailers from selling cigarettes in packages of fewer than 20, restricts the placement of tobacco machines, requires retailers to post signs indicating that giving or selling tobacco products to those under 18 is prohibited, and specifies that those who violate these provisions may be fined up to $3000 for a first offence and $50 000 for a subsequent offence. In addition, the Act governs the marketing activities of tobacco manufacturers and retailers, requires tobacco packaging to list certain information and to carry health warnings (the size, location, and colouring of which are governed by the regulation), and "severely limits all sponsorship, advertising and promotion of tobacco products" (p. 308). Although manufacturers who violate these provisions may face fines of up to $300 000 and a term of imprisonment of up to two years, these restrictions have been challenged by the tobacco industry as "unjustifiable infringements of their freedom of speech under section 2(b) of the *Canadian Charter of Rights and Freedoms*" (p. 308).

Tobacco was first cultivated by Indigenous people and used as part of their religious rituals. European settlers believed that tobacco had medicinal properties and its use spread throughout Europe, assuring the economic success of the colonies in the New World. Tobacco was initially used primarily through chewing and snuffing, but in time, smoking became more popular even though scientific evidence that linked tobacco smoking to lung cancer existed as early as 1859 (Feagin and Feagin 1994). Today, the health hazards of tobacco use are well documented and have resulted in the passage of federal laws that require warning labels on cigarette packages and prohibit cigarette advertising on radio and television (*Maclean's* 2000; Sheppard 1999). Smoking is associated with lung cancer, cardiovascular disease, strokes, emphysema, spontaneous abortion, premature birth, and neonatal death. In 1995, one is six deaths in Canada was caused by smoking; in that year, there were 34 728 deaths resulting from tobacco use and 500 345 years of potential life lost to tobacco use (CCSA 1999). It is estimated that smoking is responsible for at least one-quarter of all deaths in Canada of people between the ages of 35 and 84. As a cause of early death, smoking far outweighs the combined impact of suicide, vehicle crashes, and murder (Health Canada 1999: 308).

Despite increased awareness of the dangers of cigarettes, however, the tobacco industry continues to enjoy enormous revenues, in part because of its ability to influence public opinion and governmental policy.

At the same time, a smoking prohibition movement is gaining momentum. Organizations such as the Canadian Cancer Society, the Canadian Heart Association, and the Canadian Lung Association have sought to expose the fatal effects of tobacco and to encourage legislation banning its use. In Canada, the *Non-Smoker's Health Act* "severely restricts smoking on aircraft, trains and ships, and in Crown corporations, federal offices, banks, and other organizations under federal jurisdictions" (Solomon 1999: 208). This act requires that employers ensure that restrictions on smoking are followed and specifies fines of up to $1000 for a first offence and $10 000 for a subsequent offence for employees who violate it. Noting that restrictions on smoking bylaws can be almost as effective in discouraging cigarette use as raising tobacco taxes, many Canadian municipalities have enacted bylaws that restrict smoking in public settings. In 1995, an examination of 269 bylaws affecting most of the major Canadian municipalities indicated that 63 percent of Canadians or 17.9 million Canadians were covered by such restrictions. "Anti-smoking bylaws were most likely to specify municipal facilities, places of public assembly, service counters, and reception areas. Of the municipalities with bylaws, 68% made an explicit provision for enforcement and specified escalating fines for repeat offence" (Health Canada 1999: 63). Smoking is also completely restricted indoors and outdoors in more than 6 out of 10 Canadian schools (65 percent), 1 out of 2 day care centres, and almost 3 of 10 hospitals (29 percent). However, wide interprovincial variations do exist. In Ontario, total bans on school smoking are a provincial requirement, but such bans exist in only 15 percent of Quebec schools. In Newfoundland and Manitoba, 55 percent of licensed daycare centres have total indoor and outdoor smoking bans, but this is the case in only 24 percent of centres in the territories (Health Canada 1999: 63–4).

Although the tobacco companies have organized smoking rights organizations, the trend to restrict or ban tobacco use continues.

Marijuana

Although drug abuse ranks among the top concerns of many Canadians, surveys indicate that illegal drug use of all kinds is far less common than alcohol abuse. Marijuana remains the most commonly used and most heavily trafficked illicit drug in the world (*World Drug Report 1997*). According to the Canadian Centre on Substance Abuse (1999), cannabis is also the most commonly used illicit drug in Canada. In 1994, it was used by slightly more than 7 percent of Canadians aged 15 and older in the previous year; approximately one in four Canadians (23.1 percent) had used it at some point in their lives.

Marijuana's active ingredient is tetrahydrocannabinol (THC), which, in varying amounts, may act as a sedative or as a hallucinogen. An estimated 200 to 250 million people worldwide use marijuana, predominantly in Africa and Asia. Marijuana use dates back to 2737 B.C. in China and has a long tradition of use in India, the Middle East, and Europe. In North America, hemp, as it was then called, was used for making rope and as a treatment for various ailments. Nevertheless, in the 1920s, Judge Emily Murphy was the first to draw the attention of Canadians to "Marihuana—A New Menace" in her book, *The Black Candle*. "Although the drug was virtually unknown in Canada" at the time, Murphy's book suggested that marijuana had an insidious effect on its users and drove them "completely insane. The addict loses all sense of moral responsibility. Addicts to this drug, while under its influence, lose all sense of moral responsibility...are immune to pain...become raving maniacs and are liable to kill or indulge in any forms of violence to other persons, using the most savage methods of cruelty...without any sense of moral responsibility." To Murphy, all drugs, including marijuana, produced one predictable pattern: "moral degeneration, crime, physical and mental deterioration and disease, intellectual and spiritual wastage, and material loss through drug-induced negligence." However, as Green (1986: 31) has noted, racism appears to have been a "critical component" in Murphy's analysis of the drug problem. According to Murphy,

Canadian men are twice as likely as women to be current users of cannabis and one-and-a-half times as likely to be lifetime users of any illicit drug. The highest current use of cannabis is reported by men aged 15 to 24 (26 to 28 percent), while the highest lifetime use of any illicit drug is by males aged 20 to 34 (44 to 45 percent). After age 45, current use is negligible.

SOURCE: Health Canada 1999

narcotics were part of an international conspiracy "to injure the bright-browed races of the world" and a tactic used by "aliens of colour to bring about the degeneration of the white race." However, "[a]s a result of the considerable media attention devoted to *The Black Candle* and the paucity of challenge or contradictory statements, Murphy's conception of the scourge-like effects of drug use came to dominate Canadian narcotics ideology" (Green 1986: 33).

Marijuana use is most common among Canadian youth (CCSA 1999). Over the past 10 years, the number of young people who believe marijuana is dangerous has steadily declined and marijuana use among young people has steadily increased. A 1997 student survey in Manitoba reported that cannabis use had increased from 32 percent in 1993 to 44 percent in 1997. Research among students in New Brunswick also noted an increase from 17 percent in 1992 to 21 percent in 1996. In Nova Scotia, current use among students increased from 17 percent in 1991 to 32 percent in 1996. In Ontario, the Addiction Research Foundation reported a significant upward swing in cannabis use among students since 1993, with 29.2 percent reporting use in 1998 (compared with 12.7 percent in 1993). Among certain groups of young Canadians, cannabis use is even higher. For example, compared with others in the same age cohort, street youth in Canada report elevated rates of both illicit drug use and heavy drinking. In various studies, the percentage of street youth reporting cannabis use ranges from 66 percent to 88 percent, while between one-quarter and one-half report heavy drinking (Health Canada 1999).

Although the effects of alcohol and tobacco are, in large part, indisputable, there is less agreement about the effects of marijuana. Although the carcinogenic effects of marijuana are as lethal as nicotine's, other long-term physiological effects are unknown. An important concern is that marijuana may be a **gateway drug** that causes progression to other drugs such as cocaine and heroin. More likely, however, is that persons who experiment with one drug are more likely to experiment with another. Indeed, most drug users are polydrug users with the most common combination being alcohol, tobacco, and marijuana. For example, a Gallup Poll conducted for Health and Welfare Canada reports that marijuana smokers are twice as likely to smoke tobacco daily when compared to nonmarijuana smokers (66 percent versus 32 percent) and to drink alcohol on a monthly basis (98 percent versus 64 percent) (Eliany 1994). This chapter's The Human Side notes the role played by alcohol and other drugs in both the backgrounds and daily lives of Canada's street youths.

CONSIDERATION

On October 6, 1999, Health Minister Allan Rock issued an update to his department's June 9, 1999, report, *Health Canada's Research Plan on Marijuana for Medical Purposes* that indicated his department's commitment to both further research into the medical uses of marijuana and providing access to marijuana on compassionate grounds. He announced that 14 applications had been granted by Health Canada under Section 56 of the *Controlled Drugs and Substances Act*, that a review of another eight applications was near completion, and that a further 80 individuals had made inquiries to his department about obtaining such exemptions. Those people who obtain an exemption under Section 56 are allowed to cultivate or possess a controlled substance—activities that are otherwise illegal in Canada. Currently, exemptions are not available for caregivers or others (who may help in the cultivation of medical marijuana). Rock also announced that Health Canada would be actively engaging in ongoing consultations with, among others, potential applicants, physicians, and patient interest groups and that Health Canada had committed financial support to the Medical Research Council of Canada (MRC) to fund a five-year program of clinical research to evaluate the efficacy and safety of marijuana use.

Cocaine

Cocaine is classified as a stimulant and, as such, produces feelings of excitation, alertness, and euphoria. Although such prescription stimulants as metham-phetamine and dextroamphetamine are commonly abused, over the past 10 to 20 years societal concern over drug abuse has focused on cocaine. Such concerns have been fuelled by its increased use, addictive qualities, physiological effects, and worldwide distribution. More than any other single substance, cocaine has led to the present "war on drugs."

Cocaine, which is made from the coca plant, has been used for thousands of years, and anticocaine sentiment did not emerge until the early twentieth century in either the United States or Canada. In the United States, where cocaine was heavily used by urban Blacks, "stereotypes about the effects of cocaine—particularly in producing 'superhuman strength, cunning and effi-ciency'" coincided "with a wave of repressive measured defined to ensure the subordination of blacks" (Giffen et al. 1991: 14). In Canada, it has been suggested that efforts to suppress the nonmedical use of cocaine stemmed from a highly publicized cocaine scare in Montreal and, in particular, the pioneering efforts of a probation officer of the Montreal Children's Aid Society (pp. 37, 85). In 1911, the *Opium and Drug Act* confined the legal use of cocaine and morphine to medical prescriptions and made any other possession a criminal offence. Cocaine remains an illicit drug under the 1997 *Controlled Drug and Substances Act* (CDSA), even though its use and effects continue to be debated. For example, a 1982 *Scientific American* article suggested that cocaine was no more habit forming than potato chips (Van Dyck and Byck 1982). The percentage of Canadians reporting cocaine use was below 1 percent in both 1994 and 1993 (Figure 3.3). Its use is higher among Canadian men than among Canadian

International Data

Most of the world's coca leaf cultivation occurs in Peru, Columbia, and Bolivia, which combined account for 98 percent of the world's cocaine supply. World production of cocaine doubled between 1985 and 1995.

SOURCE: World Drug Report 1997

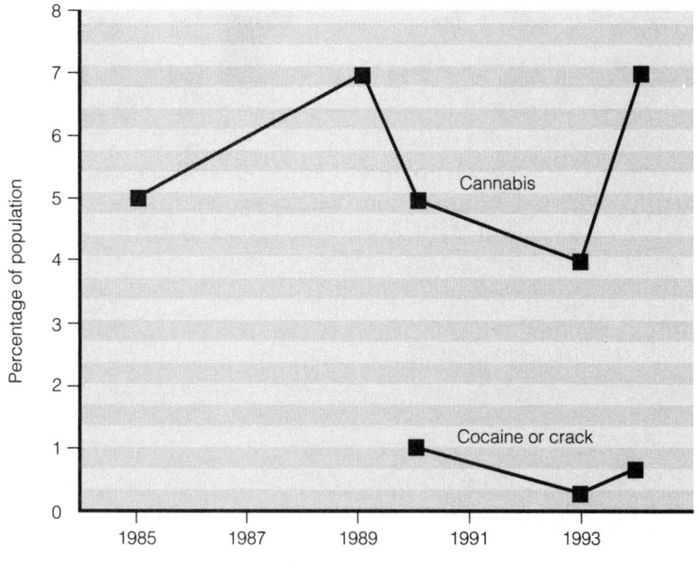

Figure 3.3

Trends in Cannabis and Cocaine/Crack Use, Age 15+, Canada, 1985–94

SOURCES: Adlaf, E. M. 1993. "Alcohol and Other Drug Use." In *Canada's Health Promotion Survey 1990: Technical Report*, edited by T. Stephens, T. Fowler, and D. Graham. Ottawa: Health and Welfare Canada, Minister of Supply and Services Canada (Cat. No. H39-363/2-1990E); Single, E., A. MacLennan, and P. Mac-Neil. 1994. *Horizons 1994: Alcohol and Other Drug Use in Canada*. Ottawa: Health Canada and the Canadian Centre on Substance Abuse (Cat. No. H39-307/2994E); MacNeil, P., and J. Webster. 1997. *Canada's Alcohol and Other Drugs Survey: A Discussion of the Findings*. Ottawa: Minister of Public Works and Government Services Canada.

women, highest among 25- to 34-year-olds (followed by 35- to 44-year-olds and 20- to 25-year-olds), and varies regionally, with British Columbia having the highest rates of use and Newfoundland the lowest (CCSA 1999).

Crack Cocaine Crack is a crystallized product made by boiling a mixture of baking soda, water, and cocaine. The result, also called rock, base, and gravel, is relatively inexpensive and was not popular until the mid-1980s. Crack is one of the most dangerous drugs to surface in recent years. Crack dealers often give drug users their first few "hits" free, knowing the drug's intense high and addictive qualities are likely to lead to returning customers. Recent data, however, suggest that the number of new users may be decreasing as young people begin to associate crack use with "burnouts" and "junkies" (ONDCP 1998b).

Other Drugs

Other drugs abused in Canada include hallucinogens (e.g., lysergic acid diethylamide [LSD], MDMA), narcotics (e.g., heroin), prescription drugs (e.g. tranquillizers, amphetamines), and inhalants (e.g., glue).

Hallucinogens

Hallucinogens may be classified as either natural, such as peyote, or synthetic, such as LSD. In either case, users report an altering of perceptions and thought patterns. Although the use of LSD has decreased in recent years, the use of so-called designer drugs such as MDMA and ketamine has increased. These drugs, marketed illegally under such names as "ecstasy," "China White," and "Special K," are not only dangerous but also expensive. Ketamine, an anesthetic for human and animal use, costs veterinarians $7 a vial, drug dealers $30 to $45 a vial, and drug users $100 to $200 a vial. Although the rate of hallucinogen use is low in Canada, a 1997 Ontario study survey reported that the use of such hallucinogens as mescaline and psilocybin (magic mushrooms) rose from 7 percent in 1995 to 13 percent in 1997. In like fashion, only 5.2 percent of Ontario students in 1991 reported using LSD at least once during the prior year, but by 1995, this figure had increased to 9.2 (Adlaf et al. 1995). These drugs, along with ecstasy, are closely associated with both the dance culture, "raves," and the "retro" revival of the late 1990s.

Heroin

In Canada, the most commonly injected drug is heroin. Although the precise number of illicit drug users who inject drugs is not known, it is estimated that in 1998 their numbers were between 50 000 and 100 000. Injected drug use is most common in Montreal, Toronto, and Vancouver, and is the primary risk factor in 18.3 percent of female AIDS cases in Canada and 3.7 percent of male AIDS cases (CCSA 1999). HIV prevalence has increased dramatically in many Canadian cities among inner-city intravenous drug users. According to members of the Killing Fields Campaign, Vancouver's skid-row neighbourhood in the downtown east side has the highest rate of HIV infection in the Western world, largely due to intravenous drug use. A study conducted in 1996 to track 1000 drug users in the area found that one in four were already infected with HIV, while another 20 percent were expected to become infected in 1997. First Nations persons are overrepresented in inner-city intravenous drug communities and AIDS cases within this population are more likely than non-Aboriginal cases to be attributed to intravenous drug use (19 percent versus 3 percent for

AN EXCERPT FROM *MEAN STREETS: YOUTH CRIME AND HOMELESSNESS*

In *Mean Streets: Youth Crime and Homelessness* (1997) Canadian sociologists John Hagan and Bill McCarthy describe the backgrounds and current experiences of homeless youths on the streets of two Canadian cities, Toronto and Vancouver. They report that substance abuse by parents and siblings is common in the backgrounds of these young people and that it is often coupled with poverty, neglect, and physical or sexual abuse.

Sebastian: "My parents threw me out....They're drug addicts. Hash, weed, coke, crack—everything....I didn't want to leave but they just threw me out. I had a huge fight with my dad. We'd fight 'cause I'd go, 'quit drugs,' and he would go 'no.'...I'd go, 'quit drinking.' He'd say 'no.' So we just argued about that most of the time. And one day he goes, 'I think its about time you leave, get on your own.' So I just left." (p. 25)

Robert: "Both my parents were alcoholics, and I had a younger sister and older brother, and, uh, it just got to a point...I mean, we used to get beat up at least four or five times a week. It got to a point where we'd hide and just wait for them to find us...and, um, finally I just couldn't take it anymore." (pp. 25–6)

Jeremy: "When I was 12, I was sent home from school, and my mom said, 'You're out of here' and I said, 'What do you mean?' and she goes, 'You're going to live with your father again.'

I said, 'Oh shit.' So I went down to my father's. My dad was an alcoholic, and he always abused me—physically. He'd punch me and stuff like that—throw me up against the walls. And like one night we were going at it, and I turned around, like he punched me a couple of times. I turned around and got a baseball bat out of the bedroom, and I hit him in the head, and then he got back up, and he started pounding on me big time. Well, the cops came and they took him, and they said 'You can go live with your mother, right?' My mother had already said, 'We don't want you,' so I said, 'Okay, I'm going to my mother's' and [instead] I went out in the streets." (p. 26)

Gord: "I started smoking dope when I was, like 8, 9 years old, like literally when I was 8 or 9 years old....Just, sittin' around the pool halls, you know, people giving you joints and stuff....My family was always poor. Like my mom was always poor. She was, you know, she was always on welfare. So, my older brother sold dope, did whatever he could to make money to help out and to take care of himself. I used to hang out in a pool hall....And all my brother's friends would get me to hold their dope and stuff, 'cause the cops would come in and I'd be playing video games, you know....After that it just, you know, I got to know when I was like 10, 10 years old I knew, you know, how to weigh out grams and knew there was sixteen ounces in a pound and twenty-eight grams in an ounce. So when I needed to make my own money, it just seemed totally natural because I knew so many people that would, just, give me dope and say, 'Okay, pay me when you can, right?' It was pretty easy actually. It seemed like the only logical thing to do." (p. 111)

Hagan and McCarthy's research additionally notes that drug use is a common part of the daily lives of homeless youths themselves; more than 80 percent of their respondents acknowledged smoking marijuana, 55 percent used crack or other chemicals, and 43 percent used cocaine. However, they note that drug use is simply one part of the "downward spiral of deviance, danger, and despair" that marks the lives of street youths.

Eva: "Oh, it was fun for a while—we met some really nice people, lots of partying—but down here [Vancouver's East Side] it was different. I found like, people were more violent, and everybody was into using hard drugs, and everything was just really different, and I ran into things, like I started prostituting and doing illegal stuff [using and selling heroin and armed robbery] and all kinds of crazy stuff down here." (pp. 113–4)

Jordy: "I was selling a bit of drugs here and there, stealing still, doing some shoplifting—videos and records from stores,

clothing, everything basically. Just being a hustler, man, just going out and hustling money wherever which way I could. If I could con some old man on the street for five bucks, I'd do it." (p. 115)

Alan: "Like when I walk down the street and I see people panhandling for money, like, I turn around and I look at them, and I go, 'Why are you sittin' here panhandling for money? Why don't you sell some drugs, or go rob someone or something', right? Why do you have to, like, sit there and ask everyone walkin' by for some money?'" (p. 53)

Kathy: "I beat this girl, really, really bad. I was on acid. I was just mad at the whole world. I just wanted anybody to beat up, and she was pouring, bleeding, and I was just hitting her with a steel bar and everything, and everybody's saying, 'What?' and I'm saying to everybody, 'Am I hurting her yet?' (p. 118)

Simon: "Fifty dollars that you make out there lasts about as long as five dollars does that you make from a paycheck....

With myself I am so ashamed or so mad, and I have really bad feelings about pulling tricks, you know, like I was being used enough sexually in my life, and then I subject myself to it again. So then I need to sedate how I'm feeling, so I usually go and get really drunk. So then 80 percent of

AN EXCERPT FROM *MEAN STREETS: YOUTH CRIME AND HOMELESSNESS*
(continued)

that money ends up being drinking money. And, like, you know, you have nothing to do all day and then having fifty bucks, you know, you're looking for a place to spend your money. You're looking for anything to entertain yourself." (p. 222)

Reprinted with the permission of Cambridge University Press.

Frequency of Alcohol use Among Street Youth
1988, 1991, and 1992

FREQUENCY	CANADA Radford et al. 1988 (N = 712)	TORONTO Smart et al. 1992 (N = 217)	HALIFAX Anderson 1991 (N = 201)
Never	12%	5%	11%
Less than once a month	19	22	11
Once a month	10	4	11
2 to 3 times a month	14	19	20
Once a week	14	9	8
2 to 3 times a week	22	22	25
4 to 6 times a week	n.a.	13	9
Every day	9	6	5

SOURCES: Adapted from *Canadian Profile 1999: Alcohol, Tobacco and Other Drugs*. 1999. Ottawa: Centre on Substance Abuse, Table 6.2, p. 184; Anderson, J. *A Study of "Out-of-the-Mainstream" Youth in Halifax, Nova Scotia*. 1993. Ottawa: Health and Welfare Canada, Health Promotion Directorate; Radford, J. L., A. J. C. King, and W. K. Warren. 1989. *Street Youth and AIDS*. Ottawa: Health and Welfare Canada; Smart, R. G., E. M. Adlaf, G. W. Walsh, and Y. M. Zdanowicz. 1992. *Drifting and Doing: Changes in Drug Use Among Toronto Street Youth, 1990–1992*. Toronto: Addiction Research Foundation.

Drug Problems Reported by Toronto Street Youth
during 1990, 1992

Drug Problem	1990 (N = 145)	1992 (N = 217)
Had blackouts or flashbacks	54%	48%
Concerned about drug use	45	40
Unable to stop when desired	43	25
Desire to use less	38	35
Drug-related arrest	26	34
Sought help	21	30
Medical problems	19	22
Received medical attention	13	21

SOURCES: Adapted from Canadian Centre for Substance Abuse. 1999. *Canadian Profile 1999*. Ottawa: Canadian Centre for Substance Abuse, Table 6.5, p. 187; Smart, R. G., E. M. Adlaf, K. M. Porterfield, and M. C. Canale. 1990. *Drugs, Youth and the Street*. Toronto: Addiction Research Foundation; Smart, R. G., E. M. Adlaf, G. W. Walsh, and Y. M. Zdanowicz. 1992. *Drifting and Doing: Changes in Drug Use Among Toronto Street Youth, 1990-1992*. Toronto: Addiction Research Foundation.

men, 50 percent versus 17 percent for women). In Canada, as in other countries, injection drug use is a major cause of the heterosexual transmission of HIV infection, hepatitis, and other infectious diseases (Health Canada 1999).

Prescription Drugs

Tranquillizers and antidepressants are often used in the treatment of psychiatric disorders. For example, Prozac, Valium, and Halcion are often prescribed for the treatment of insomnia, anxiety, and depression. In Canada, women are more likely than men are to use these types of drugs: 3.4 percent versus 2.0 for tranquillizers, 4.7 percent versus 2.5 percent for antidepressants, and 4.0 percent versus 2.9 percent for sleeping pills. Their use is also more common among the elderly than among the young. For example, Canadians over the age of 75 have the highest level of use of sleeping pills (10.6 percent) and antidepressants (5.3 percent), while those between the ages of 65 and 74 are most likely to use tranquillizers. The divorced, separated, or widowed in Canada are also more likely to use these drugs than those who are single or married, and the use of these drugs decreases as income increases (CCSA 1999). Despite the fact that these drugs are most often obtained through prescription, these drugs continue to be abused, and an illegal market for them persists.

Amphetamines are stimulants rather than "downers" and are legal when prescribed by a physician. Illegal use of amphetamines, made in clandestine laboratories, has increased in recent years. Worldwide, the production of amphetamines is increasing dramatically, with nine times the quantity seized by government officials in 1993 than in 1978 (*World Drug Report* 1997).

Inhalants

Common inhalants include lighter fluid, air fresheners, hair spray, glue, paint, and correction fluid, although there are more than 1000 other household products that are currently abused. Although the 1994 Canada's Alcohol and Other Drugs Survey reported that fewer than 0.1 percent of adult Canadians used solvents in the year before the survey, such estimates may fail to truly capture the numbers of Canadians who use solvents. Among those who used solvents, Canadians between the ages of 15 and 17 were the most frequent users. Regionally, solvents were used most by people in Quebec (0.2 percent), Ontario (0.1 percent), and Alberta (0.1 percent) (CCSA 1999). Solvent use is also considerably higher among Indian and Métis youth than among non-Indigenous populations (Gfellner and Hundelby 1995). Young people often use inhalants believing they are harmless, or that any harm caused requires prolonged use. Sudden sniff death syndrome, however, occurs instantly when the toxic fumes inhaled exceed certain levels of concentration (Join Together 1998).

SOCIETAL CONSEQUENCES OF DRUG USE AND ABUSE

Drugs are a social problem not only because of their adverse effects on individuals, but also because of the negative consequences their use has for society as a whole. Everyone is a victim of drug abuse. Drugs contribute to problems within the family and to crime rates, and the economic costs of drug abuse are enormous. Drug abuse also has serious consequences for health on both an individual and societal level.

Family Costs

The cost to families of drug use is incalculable. When one or both parents use or abuse drugs, needed family funds may be diverted to purchasing drugs rather than necessities. Children raised in such homes have a higher probability of neglect, behavioural disorders, and absenteeism from school, as well as lower self-concepts (Easley and Epstein 1991; Tubman 1993). Further, lower intelligence quotients (IQs) in toddlers have been linked to prenatal exposure to marijuana (Perkins 1997). Drug abuse is also associated with family disintegration. For example, alcoholics are seven times more likely to separate or divorce than nonalcoholics, and as much as 40 percent of family court problems are alcohol related (Sullivan and Thompson 1994: 347).

Abuse between intimates is also linked to drug use (Foster et al. 1994). In a study of 320 men who were married or living with someone, twice as many reported hitting their partner only after they had been drinking, compared with those who reported the same behaviour while sober (Leonard and Blane 1992). According to Statistics Canada's Violence Against Women Survey (VAWS), "women who are married or living with heavy drinkers are five times more likely to be assaulted by their partners than are women who live with non-drinkers" (Johnson 1996: 11). According to the findings of the VAWS, half of all wife batterers were drinking at the time they assaulted their wives; women who suffered very serious abuse were approximately twice as likely to report that their spouse had been drinking at the time. According to the findings of this survey, "the more a man drinks the greater the likelihood that drinking will be involved in incidents of assault against his wife" (p. 1).

> ## International Data
>
> In Great Britain, alcohol is a factor in 60 to 70 percent of all homicides, 75 percent of all stabbings, 70 percent of all beatings, and 50 percent of all fights and domestic assaults.
>
> SOURCE: Institute of Alcohol Studies 1997

Crime Costs

The drug behaviour of persons arrested, those incarcerated, and persons in drug treatment programs provides evidence of the link between drugs and crime. Drug users commit a disproportionate number of crimes. A study of chronic drug users found that 50 percent of both male and female addicts had engaged in illegal behaviour in the 30 days before the survey. However, as Roth (1994) has observed, "Of all psychoactive substances, alcohol is the only one whose consumption has been shown to commonly increase aggression." In 1998, a Canadian survey reporting on the use of drugs and alcohol within solved firearm homicides from 1991 to 1996 found that the accused was reported to have used alcohol in 20.6 percent of these homicides, to have used both alcohol and drugs in 12.3 percent, and to have used drugs alone in 4.5 percent (Department of Justice 1998).

CONSIDERATION

The relationship between crime and drug use is a complex one. Researchers disagree about whether drugs actually "cause" crime or whether, instead, criminal activity leads to drug involvement (Gentry 1995). Further, since both crime and drug use are associated with low socioeconomic status, poverty may actually be the more powerful explanatory variable. Studies on cocaine use among White, middle-class, and educated users indicate drugs and crime are not necessarily related (Waldorf et al. 1991). After extensive study of the assumed drug–crime link, Gentry (1995) concludes that "the assumption that drugs and crime are causally related weakens when more representative or affluent subjects are considered" (p. 491).

In addition to the hypothesized crime–drug use link, some criminal offences are drug defined: possession, cultivation, production, and sale of controlled substances; public intoxication; drunk and disorderly conduct; and driving while intoxicated. Since the 1990s, cannabis offences have risen while cocaine and heroin offences have declined. "In 1997, cannabis offences accounted for 72 percent of all drug crimes, compared with 58 percent in 1991. In contrast, cocaine accounted for 17 percent of all cases in 1997, down from 28 percent in 1991, and heroin accounted for about 2 percent of all cases, down marginally from 1991. Possession of cannabis alone accounted for almost half of all drug offences" (Statistics Canada 1999a). In addition, driving while intoxicated is one of the most common drug-related crimes in Canada and accounted for 15 percent of all cases heard in adult criminal court in the 1997–98 fiscal year. (See Figure 3.4 for statistics on who isn't driving while intoxicated in Canada.) However, there are some hopeful signs. Although police charged 70 587 persons with impaired driving offences in 1997, this was less than half the number charged in the early 1980s; since peaking in 1981, charges for impaired driving have decreased by 65 percent. In 1998, the rate of individuals charged with impaired driving decreased by 3.6 percent, marking the 15th consecutive annual decline. In all of the provinces and territories except for Manitoba and Nova Scotia (where small increases occurred), there was a decline in impaired driving offences in 1998. The highest rate of impaired drivers occurred in the Yukon with 1148 persons charged for every 100 000 population of those aged 16 and older; among the provinces, Saskatchewan had the highest rate (683) and Newfoundland the lowest (218). Among the nine largest census metropolitan areas (CMAs) in Canada, Edmonton had the highest rate (324) and Toronto the lowest (126). Since 1996, Winnipeg has been the only major CMA to report a significant increase in the

Figure 3.4

Motorists Who Always Arrange for a Designated Driver When Attending an Event Where Alcohol Will Be Consumed, by Province, Age 16+, Canada, 1996–97

SOURCE: Statistics Canada, *National Population Health Survey, 1996–97*, Cat. no. 82–567, special tabulations, Statistical Report on Health of Canadians.

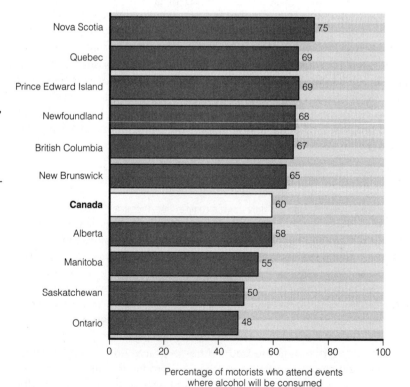

Percentage of motorists who attend events where alcohol will be consumed

number of impaired driving charges. The Winnipeg Police Service attributes this increase to public and private funding for enforcement programs that specifically target impaired driving.

Although some of the declines in the number of charges may be due to the increased use of roadside license suspensions by police, most indicators suggest a real decline in impaired driving in Canada. Thus, although 103 persons were charged in 1998 with impaired driving causing death, this figure actually represents the lowest level of such charges in a decade. Similarly, while 886 individuals were charged with impaired driving causing bodily harm, the number of such charges were down by 27.6 percent from 1989. The proportion of fatally injured drivers found to be legally impaired has also declined since the early 1990s (Statistics Canada 1999b).

Economic Costs

The economic costs of drug use are high. As reports by Health Canada (1999: 184) have noted, "The 'war on drugs' currently being waged by governments around the world consumes significant government resources in an attempt to deal with drug problems." In 1996, the Canadian Centre on Substance Abuse released a study that estimated that substance abuse cost more than $18.4 billion in Canada in 1992 or $649 per capita. The largest economic costs for alcohol, which accounted for $7.5 billion, were for lost productivity due to sickness and premature death ($4.14 billion), followed by law enforcement ($1.36 billion), and direct health care costs ($1.30 billion). The economics costs of tobacco amounted to more than $9.6 billion—including $6.8 billion for lost productivity and $2.68 billion for direct health care costs. The costs of illicit drug use were estimated to be $1.4 billion, including $823 million for lost productivity due to sickness and disease and $400 million spent on the costs of law enforcement. Concern that on-the-job drug use may impair performance or cause fatal accidents has led to drug testing. For many employees, such tests are routine, both as a condition for employment and as a requirement for keeping their job. This chapter's Focus on Technology reviews some of the issues related to drug testing and narcotics detection.

Other economic costs of drug abuse include the cost of homelessness, the cost of implementing and maintaining educational and rehabilitation programs, and the cost of health care. The cost of fighting the "war on drugs" is also enormous and likely to increase as organized crime develops new patterns of involvement in the illicit drug trade.

Health Costs

The physical health consequences of drug use for the individual are tremendous: shortened life expectancy; higher morbidity (e.g., cirrhosis of the liver, lung cancer); exposure to HIV infection, hepatitis, and other diseases through shared needles; a weakened immune system; birth defects such as fetal alcohol syndrome; drug addiction in children; and higher death rates. Death rates from drug-induced and alcohol-induced causes are significantly higher for males and First Nations peoples than for females and Whites (CCSA 1999; Health Canada 1999. However, the incidence of lung cancer in women has increased dramatically as their smoking rates have increased. In 1998, more Canadian women died from lung cancer (6500) than from breast cancer (5300); lung cancer

Drug Testing

The technology available to detect whether a person has taken drugs was used during the 1970s by crime laboratories, drug treatment centres, and the military. Today, employers in private industry have turned to chemical laboratories for help in making decisions on employment and retention, and parents and school officials use commercial testing devices to detect the presence of drugs. An individual's drug use can be assessed through the analysis of hair, blood, or urine. New technologies include portable breath (or saliva) alcohol testers, THC detection strips, passive alcohol sensors, interlock vehicle ignition systems, and fingerprint screening devices. Counter technologies have even been developed, for example, shampoos that rid hair of toxins and "Urine Luck," a urine additive that is advertised to speed the breakdown of unwanted chemicals.

Canadians are, perhaps, most familiar with drug testing in the context of international sporting events. For example, in August 1999, officials at the 1999 Pan American Games stripped the Canadian roller-hockey team of its gold medal when drug tests showed high levels of an anabolic steroid, Nadrolone, and two stimulants, ephedrine and pseudo-ephedrine, in the urine samples of the Canadian goaltender, Steve Vezina (Clark 1999: B14). However, some have suggested that testing for drugs should not be limited to athletes but extend to those in a variety of jobs, including, for example, air traffic controllers, police officers, technicians at nuclear power plants, doctors, nurses, and school bus drivers (McMillan 1991: 30).

While the majority of research focusing on the extent of on-the-job drug use has been conducted in the United States, where drug testing is more common than in other countries, Canadian research also suggests some cause for concern. For example, studies of power company employees reported rates of positive tests ranging from a low of 3 percent to 15 percent or higher (Canadian Centre for Substance Abuse 1999). A 1991 Canada Facts national survey found that more than one in five workers (22 percent) reported using alcohol on the job. A third study, conducted in Alberta (AADAC, 1992), found that more than one-third (36 percent) of workers reported having used an illegal drug at some time in their lives, 6.5 percent reported having used an illicit drug at least once in the past 12 months, 6.5 percent reported using cannabis, 1.1 reported the use of cocaine/crack, and 0.9 percent the current use of LSD, PCP, or other hallucinogens. Among those who used drugs at the workplace, the most typical employee was a young male worker in a relatively low-status position. The highest rates of current drug use were found among workers in the processing industry (12.9 percent) and the construction industry (12 percent) (CCSA 1999).

Some have suggested that if employees in any industry are using drugs, human lives may be in jeopardy because of impaired job performance. An alternative perspective is that drug testing may be harmful (O'Connor 1995; O'Keefe 1987; "This is a Test" 1998). First, the tests can be inaccurate because they may result in either "false positives" (the person who does not use drugs is identified as doing so) or "false negatives" (the person who uses drugs is identified as not doing so). The false-positives problem is serious: an innocent person could lose his or her job because of faulty technology. Second, urinalysis may also reveal that a person is pregnant, is being treated for heart disease, or has epilepsy. The person may want these aspects of his or her private life to remain private. Third, drug testing may violate basic human rights.

Drug testing could enable employers to detect drug use among employees and applicants. When combined with drug treatment programs, this might lead to the rehabilitation of drug abusers. However, Ackerman (1995) warns:

> To the individual drug user denied a job because of a positive urine test, and to the society on which he or she must remain (unemployed and) dependent, drug testing may compound the problems caused by drug addiction. (p. 487)

As a society, we are moving toward a policy of enforced drug testing for more and more segments of our society. Counterdrug technologies, such as high energy x-ray systems that are 50 to 70 times as powerful as a typical airport x-ray machine, are also being developed (NCJRS 1997), and there is little doubt that the production of drug-fighting technologies will continue. The question in a complex and increasingly diverse society is how to balance the rights of an individual with the needs of society as a whole.

SOURCES: Ackerman, Deborah L. 1995. "Drug Testing." In *Handbook on Drug Abuse and Prevention*, edited by Robert H. Coombs and Douglas Ziedonis, pp. 473–89. Boston: Allyn and Bacon; ADAC (Alberta Alcohol and Drug Abuse Commission). 1992. *Substance Use and the Alberta Workplace, the Prevalence and Impacts of Alcohol and Other Drugs, Final Report*. Edmonton: AADAC; *Canadian Profile 1999: Alcohol, Tobacco and Other Drugs*. 1999. Ottawa: Canadian Centre on Substance Abuse and Centre for Addiction and Mental Health; Clark, Campbell. 1999. "Vézina Says Sorry, but Not for Taking Banned Substances." *National Post*, August 3: B14; "Drug Testing in the Workplace." *Prevention Primer* <health.org>; McMillan, D. 1991. *Winning the Battle against Drugs*, New York: Franklin Watts; NCJRS (National Criminal Justice Resource Service). 1997. "Letter to The Honorable Benjamin A. Gilman." April 15 <www.ncjrs.org>; O'Keefe, Anne Marie. 1987. "The Case against Drug Testing." *Psychology Today* (June): 34–38; "This Is a Test: The Dilemmas of Drug Testing." 1998. *Issues in Ethics* 1: 1–3; *Vernonia School District v Wayne Acton et ux, Guardians ad Litem for James Acton*, 115 S. Ct. 2386, 132 L. ed. 2d 564 (1995).

accounts for almost one in three (32 percent) male cancer deaths and more than one in five female cancer deaths (22 percent) (Health Canada 1999).

Heavy alcohol and drug use are also associated with negative consequences for an individual's mental health. Longitudinal data on both male and female adults have shown that drug users are more likely to suffer from anxiety disorders (e.g., phobias), depression, and antisocial personalities (White and Labouvie 1994). Other data confirm that drug users, particularly in adolescence, have a higher incidence of suicide (Bureau of Justice Statistics 1992; Cooper et al. 1992). Marijuana, the drug most commonly used by adolescents, is also linked to short-term memory loss, learning disabilities, motivational deficits, and retarded emotional development.

The societal costs of drug-induced health concerns are also extraordinary. Health costs include the cost of disability insurance, the effects of secondhand smoke, the spread of AIDS, and the medical costs of accident and crime victims, as well as unhealthy infants and children. For example, infants are five times as likely to die from sudden infant death syndrome if adults smoke in their rooms (Klonoff-Cohen et al. 1995), and drug use by pregnant women increases the probability of complications for both mother and child (ONDCP 1998a).

TREATMENT ALTERNATIVES

Helping others to overcome chemical dependency is expensive. Persons who are interested in overcoming chemical dependency have several treatment alternatives from which to choose. Their options include hospitalization, family therapy, drug counselling, private and public treatment facilities, behaviour modification, community care programs, drug maintenance programs, and employee assistance programs. Two other commonly used rehabilitative techniques are 12-step programs and therapeutic communities.

Twelve-Step Programs

Both Alcoholics Anonymous (AA) and Narcotics Anonymous (NA) are voluntary associations whose only membership requirement is the desire to stop drinking or taking drugs. AA and NA are self-help groups in that they are operated by nonprofessionals, offer "sponsors" to each new member, and proceed along a continuum of 12 steps to recovery. These include an acknowledgment of one's helplessness over addiction and a recognition of a higher power as a source of help. In addition to the 12 steps, which require abstinence, humility, penance, and commitment, AA and NA members are immediately immersed in a fellowship of caring individuals with whom they meet daily or weekly to affirm their commitment. Some have argued that AA and NA members trade their addiction to drugs for feelings of interpersonal connectedness by bonding with other group members.

Symbolic interactionists emphasize that AA and NA provide social contexts in which people develop new meanings. Abusers are surrounded by others who convey positive labels, encouragement, and social support for sobriety. Sponsors tell the new members that they can be successful in controlling alcohol and drugs "one day at a time" and provide regular interpersonal reinforcement for doing so. Some AA members may also choose to take **Antabuse**, a prescribed medication, which when combined with alcohol produces severe nausea. Some alcoholics regard Antabuse as a "crutch," but others feel that anything that helps the alcoholic to remain sober should be used.

AA and NA have reputations as two of the most successful drug rehabilitation programs. However, because membership is voluntary and anonymous, accurate evaluation of these programs is difficult. Further, since the desire to change is a prerequisite for joining AA or NA, their success rates are artificially elevated, making other programs appear less successful.

Therapeutic Communities

In **therapeutic communities**, which house between 35 and 500 people for up to 15 months, participants abstain from drugs, develop marketable skills, and receive counselling. Synanon, which was established in 1958, was the first therapeutic community for alcoholics and was later expanded to include other drug users. The longer a person stays at such a facility, the greater the chance of overcoming the dependency. Symbolic interactionists argue that behavioural changes appear to be a consequence of revised self-definition and the positive expectations of others.

In the United States, Stay'N Out, a therapeutic community for the treatment of incarcerated drug offenders, has demonstrated its success in reducing recidivism. When participating in the program for at least nine months, only 23 percent of the inmates reoffended, compared with 50 percent of those not receiving treatment. The Cornerstone Program has also been successful with drug abusers in prison. Both programs include a holistic treatment approach that focuses on the social and psychological difficulties of returning to acceptable social roles (Lipton 1994: 336). However, in Canada, there are no therapeutic communities for the treatment of incarcerated drug users outside Quebec, which runs both the ECHO and STOP programs. Elsewhere, the two core substance abuse programs offered by Corrections Canada are the Offender Substance Pre-release Program (which involves approximately 32 three-hour counselling sessions offered over several months), and Choices (a cognitive-behavioural modification program that involves approximately 60 hours of counselling over three to four months).

STRATEGIES FOR ACTION: CANADA RESPONDS

Drug use is a complex social issue exacerbated by the structural and cultural forces of society that contribute to its existence. While the structure of society perpetuates a system of inequality creating in some the need to escape, the culture of society, through the media and normative contradictions, sends mixed messages about the acceptability of drug use. Thus, developing programs, laws, or initiatives that are likely to end drug use may be unrealistic. Nevertheless, numerous social policies have been implemented or proposed to help control drug use and its negative consequences.

Government Regulations

Drawing upon Solomon (1999), we will review some of the major federal and provincial alcohol and drug laws. In Canada, the importation and exportation of alcohol products, alcohol-related excise taxes, and broadcast advertising are regulated by the federal government. At present, the federal regulations prohibit broadcasting a range of messages, including those that encourage non-drinkers to consume alcohol; that direct their appeal to minors; that suggest that alcohol use is positively associated with social acceptance, personal accomplishment, or success in athletic or business endeavours; or that link the consumption of alcohol with high-risk activities. In addition, the provinces have some degree of control over the marketing and advertising of alcohol including such market practices as price discounting, drinking contests, the use of alcohol as prizes, or the dispensing of free drinks. The majority of provincial advertising regulations target lifestyle advertising that might otherwise encourage youths to drink, drink large amounts of alcohol, or drink and drive. Each province in Canada also regulates the control and sale of alcohol in its province. Currently, the legal drinking age in all Canadian provinces and territories is 19 with the exception of Quebec, Manitoba, and Alberta, where the minimum age is 18.

Under the Canadian *Criminal Code*, there are four specific types of drinking-and-driving offences. The first is "operating or having care or control of a motor vehicle while one's ability to drive is impaired by alcohol or a drug." The term "drug" is broadly defined here to include any substance, legal or illegal, which can cause impairment. The second type of offence is "[e]ngaging in impaired driving causing death or bodily harm." The 1985 introduction of this offence was intended to make the penalties for causing serious accidents while impaired harsher than those for "simply" driving while impaired. The maximum penalty for impaired driving causing bodily harm is 10 years' imprisonment and 10 years' driving prohibition; the maximum penalty for impaired driving causing death is 14 years' imprisonment and 10 years' driving prohibition. The third type is "[o]perating or having care or control of a motor vehicle with a blood alcohol concentration (BAC) over 0.08%." Even if you drive safely, driving with a BAC over this level is a criminal offence in Canada. The specific amount of alcohol that must be consumed to have a BAC over the specified level can vary depending on such factors as, for example, when the individual last ate, that person's weight and percentage of body fat, and how quickly the alcohol was consumed. Nevertheless, BAC can be determined through an analysis of a person's blood or urine. The final type of offence is "[f]ailing to provide breath or blood samples for analysis without a reasonable excuse." The term "reasonable excuse" refers to, for example, an inability to comprehend the demand or to physically comply with it. The minimum penalty for both the third and fourth types of offence is a $300 fine and a three-month driving prohibition for a first offence, 14 days' imprisonment and six months' driving prohibition for a second offence, and 90 days' imprisonment and a one-year driving prohibition for a subsequent offence. The maximum penalty when charged as a summary conviction offence is a $2000 fine, six months' imprisonment, and a three-year driving prohibition. As an indictable offence, the maximum penalty is five years' imprisonment, a three-year driving prohibition, and a fine of any amount that may be imposed by the court. Figure 3.5 shows the number of drinking-and-driving offences committed in Canada from 1987 to 1996.

In addition, provincial highway traffic legislation gives police the authority to stop vehicles in a random manner to determine whether the driver has been drinking; the provinces also have the authority to issue, suspend, revoke, and reinstate driving licences. The majority of Canadian provinces

Figure 3.5

Drinking-and-Driving Offences, Rates per 100 000 Population Aged 16 or Older, Canada, 1987 to 1996

SOURCES: Statistics Canada, Canadian Crime Statistics, 1987 to 1996 (Ottawa: Statistics Canada, Cat. No. 85-205, 1995, 1996, and 1997).

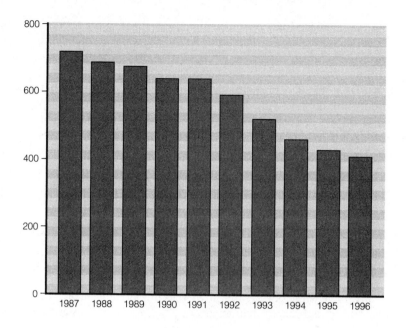

have created provisions for automatic provincial licence suspensions such that a person convicted of any federal drinking and driving offence is subject to an automatic mandatory provincial licence suspension. The length of the suspension for a first, second, or subsequent conviction varies in the different provinces and territories. For example, in Manitoba, a 12-month suspension is given for a first offence and a five-year suspension for a second; in Alberta and Saskatchewan, the respective time periods are one and two years, and, in the Yukon, three months and a year. Moreover, with the exception of Nova Scotia and Quebec, provincial legislation authorizes police to temporarily suspend a driver's licence at roadside if, for example, a driver refuses an officer's demand to provide a breath sample or registers a BAC of 0.95 or higher. In the majority of provinces, the duration of the suspension is 24 hours. Six provinces have enacted additional legislation that authorizes police to impose 90-day administrative licence suspensions (ALS) on those who register a BAC over 0.08 percent or refuse to provide a breath or blood sample. The provinces have also created several drinking-and-driving countermeasures, such as graduated licence programs for new drivers, which require that they abstain from drinking any alcohol prior to driving; vehicle impoundment programs to deter offenders from driving while prohibited or suspended; alcohol interlock programs, which involve the connection of a small breath-testing instrument to a vehicle that prevents it from being started or driven if the driver's BAC is over a preset limit; and mandatory remedial measures that require offenders to attend, for example, an alcohol awareness program for a first offence or, for a second or subsequent offence, undergo alcohol assessment or participate in a treatment program. The cost of participating in such programs is generally borne by the offender.

In Canada, the *Controlled Drugs and Substances Act* outlines the six federal criminal offences of possession, trafficking, possession for the purpose of trafficking, production, importing or exporting, and "prescription shopping."

While the penalties for possession vary depending on the type of drug, the maximum penalties under this act for the majority of offences are severe. For example, for "Schedule 1 Drugs" (i.e., cocaine, heroin, opium, phencyclidine, and those drugs that, prior to May 1997, were dealt with under the *Narcotics Control Act*), the maximum penalty for trafficking, possession for the purpose of trafficking, producing, and importing and exporting is life imprisonment. Life imprisonment is also the maximum penalty for importing or exporting any amount of any form of cannabis.

We earlier noted federal and provincial legislation that regulates tobacco in Canada. In addition to those previously noted, British Columbia has enacted legislation "to assist the provincial government and smokers in suing tobacco manufacturers to recover for tobacco-related costs, illness and disabilities. Moreover, the province has sued the manufacturers for the smoking-related costs that the government has incurred" (Solomon 1999: 309). Although similar legislation is being contemplated in other Canadian provinces, the tobacco companies have, not unexpectedly, challenged the constitutionality of this measure. Although there appears to be a movement toward treatment and prevention as indicated by funding specifics, there remains an emphasis on deterrence and "get tough" policies, particularly in dealing with large-scale traffickers and international offenders (Clinton 1998).

Despite all the attempts to regulate the use of alcohol and drugs, some would argue that the war on drugs has done more harm than good. Duke and Gross (1994) argue that the war on drugs, much like Prohibition, has only intensified other social problems: drug-related gang violence and turf wars, the creation of syndicate-controlled black markets, unemployment, the spread of AIDS, overcrowded prisons, corrupt law enforcement officials, and the diversion of police from other serious crimes. Consistent with conflict theory, still others argue that the "war on drugs" is a war on the poor, while the drug use of the affluent goes largely ignored (Duster 1995).

Further, our drug policies have implications that extend beyond domestic concerns and affect international relations and the economies of foreign countries. Distributing drugs worldwide requires a complex network of social actors. As the *World Drug Report* (1997) concludes:

> **The most prominent trafficking organizations appear to be characterized by highly centralized management control at the upper echelons, with compartmentalization of functions and task specialization at the lower levels. A seemingly endless stream of willing recruits for the most menial tasks provides the industry with a wide range of specialized personnel including chemists, chemical engineers, pilots, communication specialists, money launderers, accountants, lawyers, security guards and "hit men."**

Many of the countries in which drug trafficking occurs are characterized by government corruption and crime, military coups, and political instability. Some argue that trade sanctions should be imposed in addition to crop eradication programs and interdiction efforts. Others, however, noting the relative failure of such programs in reducing the supply of illegal drugs entering the country, argue that the "war on drugs" should be abandoned and that legalization is preferable to the side effects of regulation.

Legalization

Proponents for the **legalization** of drugs affirm the right of adults to make an informed choice. They also argue that the tremendous revenues realized from drug taxes could be used to benefit all citizens, that purity and safety controls could be implemented, and that legalization would expand the number of distributors, thereby increasing competition and reducing prices. Drugs would thus be safer, the number of drug-related crimes would be reduced, and production and distribution of previously controlled substances would be taken out of the hands of the underworld.

Those in favour of legalization also suggest that the greater availability of drugs would not increase demand. When a sample of 600 adults was asked, "If cocaine were legalized, would you personally consider purchasing it or not?" less than 1 percent reported that they would (Dennis 1993). Further, in countries where some drugs have been decriminalized, use has actually declined (Kort 1994). Finally, decriminalization of drugs would promote a medical rather than criminal approach to drug use that would encourage users to seek treatment and adopt preventive practices. For example, making it a criminal offence to sell or possess hypodermic needles without a prescription encourages the use of nonsterile needles that spread infections such as HIV and hepatitis.

Opponents of legalization argue that it would be construed as government approval of drug use and, consequently, drug experimentation and abuse would increase. Further, although the legalization of drugs would result in substantial revenues for the government, all drugs would not be decriminalized (e.g., crack), so drug trafficking and black markets would still flourish (Bennett 1993). Legalization would also require an extensive and costly bureaucracy to regulate the manufacture, sale, and distribution of drugs. Finally, the position that drug use is an individual's right cannot guarantee that others will not be harmed. It is illogical to assume that a greater availability of drugs will translate into a safer society.

Deregulation

The government has also approached the drug problem through **deregulation**. For example, in April 1999, the board of directors of the Association of Canadian Police Chiefs made a recommendation to the federal government that simple possession of marijuana and hashish be decriminalized. They suggested that this strategy would clear a backlog of drug cases in the courts and allow Canadian police services to focus their resources on more serious crimes like drug trafficking (Fife 1999). Currently, about 2000 Canadians go to jail every year for cannabis possession at a cost of approximately $150 per day per offender (CCSA 1999).

Canadian law currently allows distribution of methadone in treatment centres for heroin addicts. Methadone, a synthetic opiate, is taken orally and inhibits the euphoric effect of heroin, thus blocking the motivation for its use. The drug produces no "high," and the recovering addict can begin to lead a normal life. Persons in methadone maintenance programs also participate in family counselling and job training programs, both designed to help the addict make a successful return to society. A recent Drug Abuse Treatment Outcome Study conducted by the National Institute on Drug Abuse concludes that outpatient methadone treatment reduced heroin use by 70 percent, cocaine use by 48 percent, and crime by 57 percent, and increased full-time employment by 24 percent (DATOS 1998).

Collective Action

Social action groups such as Mothers Against Drunk Driving (MADD) have successfully lobbied legislators to raise the drinking age and to provide harsher penalties for driving while impaired.

MADD, with 3.5 million members and 60 chapters, has also put pressure on alcohol establishments to stop "two-for-one" offers and has pushed for laws that hold the bartenders personally liable if a served person is later involved in an alcohol-related accident. Even hosts in private homes can now be held liable if they allow a guest to drive who became impaired while drinking at their house. Most importantly perhaps, MADD seeks to change the meaning of alcohol use by, for example, redefining drunk driving "accidents" as violent crimes.

Sensitized to the danger of driving while impaired, some high-school principals and school boards have encouraged students to become members of Students Against Drunk Driving (SADD). Members often sign a formal pledge and put an emblem on their car to signify a commitment against alcohol. "Dry grads" also encourage students to refrain from drinking alcohol. To reduce the number of teenagers driving while drinking, local groups of parents have also organized parties at bowling alleys or school gyms as alternatives to high-school graduation parties.

Collective action is also being taken against tobacco companies by smokers, ex-smokers, and the families of smoking victims. They charge that tobacco executives knew more than 30 years ago that tobacco was addictive and concealed this fact from both the public and the government. Furthermore, they charge that tobacco companies manipulate nicotine levels in cigarettes with the intention of causing addiction. Recently, a Florida jury ordered a tobacco company to pay $1 million dollars—the largest settlement to date—to the family of a man who had died of lung cancer after smoking for 50 years (Mauro 1998).

UNDERSTANDING ALCOHOL AND OTHER DRUGS

In summarizing what we know about substance abuse, drugs and their use are socially defined. As the structure of society changes, the acceptability of one drug or another changes as well. As conflict theorists assert, the status of a drug as legal or illegal is intricately linked to those who have the power to define acceptable and unacceptable drug use. Rapid social change, anomie, alienation, and inequality undoubtedly further drug use and abuse. Symbolic interactionism also plays a significant role in the process—if people are labelled as "drug users" and expected to behave accordingly, drug use is likely to continue. If such behaviours or biological predispositions to use drugs are positively reinforced, the probability of drug involvement is even higher. Thus, the theories of drug use complement rather than contradict one another.

Drug use must also be conceptualized within the social context in which it occurs. In a study of high-risk youths who had become involved with drugs,

In Canada, almost two-thirds (64 percent) of those convicted of trafficking were sentenced to prison during the 1996–97 fiscal year; in contrast, only 13 percent of those convicted of drug possession were jailed. In 1996, almost 1 in 10 of the adult inmate population in Canada was in prison for a drug offence as their most serious offence.

SOURCE: Statistics Canada 1999a

Dembo et al. (1994) suggest that many youths in their study had been "failed by society":

> Many of them were born into economically strained circumstances, often raised by families who neglected or abused them, or in other ways did not provide for their nurturance and wholesome development....[F]ew youths in our sample received the mental health and substance abuse treatment services they needed. (p. 25)

However, many treatment alternatives, emanating from a clinical model of drug use, assume that the origin of the problem lies within the individual rather than in the structure and culture of society. Although admittedly the problem may lie within the individual at the time treatment occurs, policies that address the social causes of drug abuse provide a better means of dealing with the drug problem in Canada.

Prevention is preferable to intervention, and prevention must entail dealing with the social conditions that foster drug use. Some data suggest that poor adolescents are particularly vulnerable to drug involvement because of their lack of legitimate alternatives (Van Kammen and Loeber 1994):

> Illegal drug use may be a way to escape the strains of the severe urban conditions and dealing illegal drugs may be one of the few, if not the only, ways to provide for material needs. Intervention and treatment programs, therefore, should include efforts to find alternate ways to deal with the limiting circumstances of inner-city life, as well as create opportunities for youngsters to find more conventional ways of earning a living. (p. 22)

However, social policies dealing with drug use have been predominantly punitive rather than preventive.

In Canada and throughout the world, millions of people depend on legal drugs for the treatment of a variety of conditions, including pain, anxiety and nervousness, insomnia, depression, and fatigue. Although drugs used for these purposes are relatively harmless, the cultural message "better living through chemistry" contributes to alcohol and drug use and their consequences. These and other drugs are embedded in a political and economic context that determines who defines what drugs, in what amounts, are licit or illicit and what programs are developed in reference to them.

CRITICAL THINKING

1. Are alcoholism and other drug addictions a consequence of nature or nurture? If nurture, what environmental factors contribute to such problems? Which of the three sociological theories best explains drug addiction?
2. Measuring alcohol and drug use is often very difficult. This is particularly true given the tendency for respondents to acquiesce, that is, respond in a way they believe is socially desirable. Consider this and other problems in doing research on alcohol and other drugs, and how such problems would be remedied.

3. If, as symbolic interactionists argue, social problems are those conditions so defined, how might the manipulation of social definitions virtually eliminate many "drug" problems?

KEY TERMS

anomie
Antabuse
chemical dependency
decriminalization

deregulation
drug
drug abuse
gateway drug

legalization
MADD
therapeutic communities

CHAPTER FOUR

Crime and Violence

Is It True?

1. In 1997, only 12 percent of the 2.5 million *Criminal Code* incidents (excluding traffic offences) reported to Canadian police services involved violent crimes.

2. Although sociologists have different theories about the causes of crime, they agree that crime is always harmful to society.

3. The majority of Canadians believe that capital punishment should be exercised in some circumstances.

4. Less than 1 percent of Canadians regard prostitution as a "very serious" social issue.

5. The majority of Canadian homicide victims had some type of relationship with their murderers.

Answers: 1 = T, 2 = F, 3 = T, 4 = T, 5 = T

Unjust social arrangements are themselves a kind of extortion, even violence....

John Rawls,
"A Theory of Justice"

On November 22, 1999, the cover story of *Time* magazine directed attention to the Pokémon craze among children 12 years of age and under and pointedly drew attention to two incidents, one in Laval, Quebec, and the other in Long Island, New York, in which one preteen had stabbed another in a dispute over the collectible cards (Chua-Eoan and Larimer 1999). While the Pokémon craze is new, the suggestion that certain recreational activities lead to crime or are criminogenic is not. Olmsted (1988) has noted that, in the past, such diverse pastimes as billiards, parachuting, surfing, pinball, attending the theatre, amateur archaeology, horse racing, butterfly collecting, motorcycling, target shooting, and ballroom dancing have all been identified as morally disreputable and socially problematic activities. In the 1950s, a book entitled *Seduction of the Innocent* blamed the increase in crime in general, and juvenile delinquency in particular, on the reading of comic books (Gorelick 1992). Since that time, various social commentators have suggested that crime is best explained with reference to such activities as listening to rap music, watching certain television programs or cartoons, playing certain video games, or surfing the Internet. All attest to our continuing attempts to understand and prevent crime in our society.

The social problems of crime and violence rank among Canadians' foremost social concerns. Data derived from the 1993 General Social Survey, the 1996 International Criminal Victimization Survey (CVS), and national polls all suggest that Canadians believe that crime in general, and violent crime in particular, is on the increase and that they face an increasing likelihood of being a victim of crime within their own neighbourhoods (Fedorowycz 1999) (see Figure 4.1). Bibby (1995) reports that more than 85 percent of his respondents believed that there had been an increase in crime in Canada over the past five

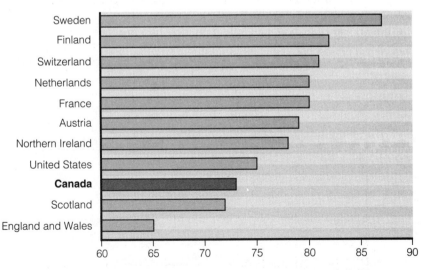

Percentage of population who report feeling "safe" or "fairly safe"
walking alone in the neighbourhood after dark

Figure 4.1
Feelings of Safety
SOURCE: Statistics Canada, "Juristat," Cat. No. 85-002-XPE.

years; in 1997, an August Reid–CTV News poll reported that almost 60 percent of Canadians believed that violent crime was on the increase. Yet, the national police-reported crime rate has actually fallen, decreasing in 1996 for the fifth consecutive year, while the violent crime rate declined for the fourth consecutive year.

This chapter examines crime rates as well as theories, types, and demographic patterns of criminal behaviour. The economic, social, and psychological costs of crime and violence are also examined. The chapter concludes with a discussion of social policies and prevention programs designed to reduce crime and violence in Canada.

THE GLOBAL CONTEXT: INTERNATIONAL CRIME AND VIOLENCE

Crime and violence rates vary dramatically by country. According to the United Nations Crime Survey, Canada's crime rate was the fourth highest among nine industrial countries (excluding the United States). However, while more than 2.6 million incidents (excluding traffic offences) were reported to Canadian police departments and services and confirmed as actual *Criminal Code* offences in 1996, our overall crime rate of approximately 8800 per 100 000 population was almost identical to what it was in the mid-1980s, and was about 15 percent lower than what it was in 1991. Although Canada's rate of violent crime has increased significantly over the past 15 years, it peaked in 1992 and has declined every year since that time (Figure 4.2). For example, the 1995 rate of 995 incidents per 100 000 population is 4 percent lower than the 1994 rate, which in itself was 3 percent lower than the rate in 1993. With the exception of Vancouver and Calgary, most major cities across Canada have witnessed a decline in the incidence of violent crime. Moreover, much of the earlier increase in Canada's violent-crime rates occurred because of the growth in the rate of the least serious form of assaults. In 1996, about 6 out of 10 of the 297 000 violent crimes reported to Canadian police were common assaults, an increase of approximately 40 percent since 1986 (Statistics Canada 1998a).

Although Canada's homicide rate is higher than in some European countries, it has consistently been about one-quarter of the U.S. rate. Canada's homicide rate has been gradually declining since the mid-1970s and, in 1998,

Figure 4.2

Violent, Property, and Other *Criminal Code* Incidents, Canada, 1987–97

SOURCE: *Uniform Crime Reporting Survey*, Canadian Centre for Justice Statistics, Statistics Canada; adapted from "Juristat," Cat. No. 85-002.

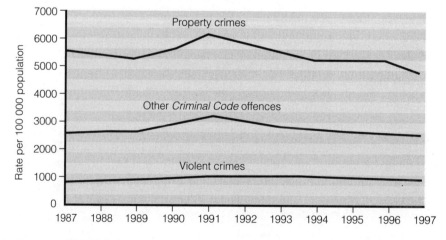

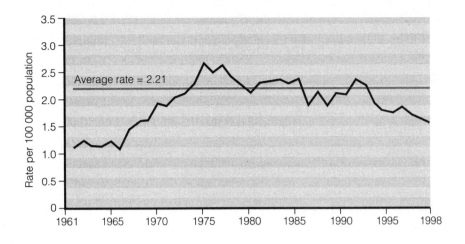

Figure 4.3
Homicide Rate, 1961–98
SOURCE: *Homicide Survey.* 1999. Canadian Centre for Justice Statistics; adapted from "Juristat," Cat. No. 85-002.

sank to its lowest rate in the past 30 years at 2.1 per 100 000 Canadians (Figure 4.3). To put this in perspective, while in 1996 there were 635 homicides in Canada, this figure is actually less than the number of homicides reported in some American cities. Moreover, "Canadians are 180 times more likely to die of either heart disease or cancer than homicide" (Statistics Canada 1998a).

The natures of crime and violence vary from country to country. Russian rubles, arms, and precious metals are smuggled out of that country daily; Chinese Triads operate in large cities worldwide, netting billions of dollars a year from prostitution, drugs, and other organized crime activities; Colombian cocaine cartels flourish and spread to sub-Saharan countries with needy economies; and Nigerian crime syndicates continue to defraud victims of billions of dollars through the promise of high returns on bogus investments (INTERPOL 1998; United Nations 1997). In an attempt to ensure that those involved in organized crime do not benefit from the profits of criminal activities, regardless of where such acts occurred, Canada has enacted laws that make it a criminal offence to possess the proceeds of crime. As Stamler (2000) points out, under section 462.3 of the Canadian *Criminal Code*, it is a criminal offence in Canada "to possess anything that was obtained or derived directly or indirectly from the commission of an indictable offence or from any act committed by an indictable offence." He notes that, when combined with the laws on conspiracy, this law "makes it possible to prosecute in Canada anyone who conspires to possess proceeds of crime within Canada, even if all the conspirators are outside of Canada." It is also a criminal offence for anyone (including bank employees and those employed in financial institutions) to launder the proceeds of crime.

SOURCES OF CRIME STATISTICS

It has been observed that "[t]here are no fewer than 600 federal statutes in force in Canada today" and that "[e]very year, federal Parliament, provincial legislatures, municipal councils and their agencies add thousands of new statutes, ordinances, rules and regulations to the plethora of laws which ensure justice for all Canadians" (Statistics Canada 1998a). From the *National Symbol of Canada Act*, which identifies the beaver as symbolic of Canadian sovereignty, to the *Income Tax Act*, whose rules and regulations are bound in an almost 2000-page volume amended yearly, our social life is bounded together by laws.

International Data

Despite its small size, in just nine months in 1998, drug control agents in Nepal arrested more than 1000 people, and seized 2495 kg of hashish, 1360 kg of cannabis, and 5.5 kg of heroin.
SOURCE: Shabad 1999

National Data

Average number of crimes reported each day in Canada in 1996:

Thefts under	
$5000:	2257
Breaking and	
entering:	1088
Assaults:	636
Motor vehicle	
thefts:	493
Impaired driving:	264
Drug offences:	180
Robberies:	87
Sexual assaults:	74
Homicides:	Less than 2

SOURCE: Statistics Canada, 1998a

Although there are 40 000 federal and provincial statutes and a broad range of municipal bylaws that define behaviour in violation of some penal law, "[u]nder the terms of the *Constitution Act*, only those offences defined by federal law can technically be called crimes" (Brantingham et al. 1995). Most of the behaviours that we would commonly recognize as crimes (e.g., assault, kidnapping, sexual assault, murder) are contained within the federal *Criminal Code*. Unlike the United States, which has many state *Criminal Code*s, Canada has a single criminal code.

A simple definition of **crime** would be "any act that violates the criminal law." For a violation to be a crime, however, the offender must have acted voluntarily and with intent and have no legally acceptable excuse (such as insanity) or justification (such as self-defence) for the behaviour. Three major types of statistics are used to measure crime: official statistics, victimization surveys, and self-report offender surveys.

Official Statistics

Since the establishment of the first modern police force, the London Metropolitan Police Force (Scotland Yard) in 1829, police agencies have collected information about crime. Systematic national police statistics have been collected since 1857 in England and Wales, since 1920 in Canada, and since 1930 in the United States (Brantingham et al. 1995). Since 1962, Canada has used a system called the Canadian Uniform Crime Reports (UCR) that was developed by Statistics Canada and the Canadian Association of Chiefs of Police "to provide a measure of reliability for crime statistics through providing police agencies with a standardized set of procedures for collecting and reporting crime information" (Evans and Himelfarb 2000).

Under the UCR system, information is collected monthly from more than 400 municipal police departments, services, and agencies across Canada on 91 detailed categories of crime and offences. This information is compiled and published each year with counts and calculated rates per 100 000 population presented for each province and territory and for Canada as a whole. Within UCRs, crimes known to the police are grouped into major categories of crime. For example, "Crimes of Violence" group together such acts as homicide, attempted homicide, assault, abduction, sexual assault, and robbery. "Property Offences" include such offences as breaking and entering, theft of motor vehicles, possession of stolen goods, fraud, and so on. Uniform Crime Reports additionally provide information on the numbers of persons charged with different types of offences, with separate counts for adults and youths, males and females. The crimes known to police are compiled and published annually in Canada by the Canadian Centre for Justice Statistics (CCJS), the operational arm of the National Justice Statistics Initiative (NJSI). Since its establishment in 1985, the mandate of the NJSI has been (a) "[t]o provide information to the justice community and the public on the nature and extent of crime and the administration of criminal justice in Canada," and (b) to direct energies toward "the production of useful information to support the legislative, policy, management and research agendae of the Partners, and to inform the public" (CCJS 1999).

These statistics have several shortcomings (DiIulio 1999). Not only do many incidents of crime go unreported, but also not all crimes reported to the police are recorded. Alternatively, some rates may be exaggerated. Motivation for such distortions may come from the public (e.g., demanding that something be done) or from political or organizational pressures (e.g., budget requests). For example, a police department may "crack down" on drug-related crimes in a given year. The result is an increase in the recorded number of these offences. Such an increase reflects a change in the behaviour of law enforcement personnel, not a change in the number of drug violations. Thus, official crime statistics may be a better indicator of what police are doing than what criminals are doing.

Victimization Surveys

Victimization surveys ask people if they have been victims of crime. As Fattah (1991) has noted, the first victimization surveys were carried out in the United States in the 1966 for the President's Commission on Law Enforcement and Administration of Justice. In the United States, the Department of Justice's National Crime Victimization Survey (NCVS), which is conducted annually, interviews nearly 83 000 people about their experiences as victims of crime. In contrast, victimization surveys in Canada have a much shorter history. As Fattah observes, "[n]o truly national victimization survey was done in Canada until the General Social Survey was carried out by Statistics Canada in 1988." In this survey, telephone interviews were carried out with respondents 15 years of age and older in all 10 provinces (territories were excluded) between January and February 1988. This method provided data on the criminal victimization experiences of 9870 individuals. In addition to national victimization surveys, the International Crime Victim Survey (ICVS) has attempted to collect standardized victimization data using the same questionnaire in many countries. The ICVS is the most comprehensive program of standardized sample surveys that examine householders' experience with crime, policing, crime prevention, and feelings of being unsafe in a large number of countries. Thus far, there have been three rounds of the ICVS, the first in 1989, the second in 1992, and the third in 1996–97. The first included 14 countries, plus the cities of Warsaw (Poland) and Surabaya (Indonesia). The second covered 11 industrialized countries, 13 developing countries, and 6 countries in transition (although in most cases, these were restricted to capital cities). The third covered 12 industrialized countries, all but 1 of the countries in Central and Eastern Europe, and 15 developing countries. In preparation for the next sweep in 2000, 92 surveys have been launched in 56 countries and, to date, 135 465 people have been interviewed. Although victimization surveys provide detailed information about crime victims, they provide less reliable data about offenders.

Self-Report Offender Surveys

Self-report surveys ask offenders about their criminal behaviour. The sample may consist of a population with known police records, such as a prison population, or it may include respondents from the general population, such as college students. Self-report data compensate for many of the problems associated with official statistics but are still subject to exaggerations and concealment. In this chapter's Self and Society, we provide one example of a self-report survey used by Canadian researchers to investigate criminality and delinquency among adolescent males.

CONSIDERATION

Self-report surveys reveal that virtually every adult has engaged in some type of criminal activity. Why then is only a fraction of the population labelled as criminal? Like a funnel, which is large at one end and small at the other, only a small proportion of the total population of law violators is ever convicted of a crime. For an individual to be officially labelled as a criminal, his or her behaviour must first be observed or known to have occurred. Next, the crime must be reported to the police. The police must then respond to the report, find sufficient evidence to substantiate that a crime has taken place, file an official report, and have enough evidence to make an arrest. The arrestee must then go through a preliminary hearing, an arraignment, and a trial and may or may not be convicted. At every stage of the process, an offender may be "funnelled" out. For example, for every 1000 burglaries that occur, only 495 are reported to the police, 72 lead to an arrest, 21 to a conviction, and 16 to an offender being incarcerated (Felson 1998: 7). If we review Figure 4.4, it becomes evident why research based on samples of incarcerated offenders may not have broad generalizability beyond inmate populations.

Figure 4.4
Caseload within the Canadian Criminal Justice System, 1996

[1] An offence is considered "actual" when, following an initial investigation, the police confirm that a criminal offence has occurred. An offence is "cleared" when police are satisfied that they have identified an offender. However, it may not be possible to lay a charge against an offender because he or she is dead, under age 12, has diplomatic immunity, is already in prison, and so on. If, in the view of the police, it is possible to lay a charge against an offender, the offence is cleared by charge.

[2] Includes secure custody only for young offenders and any custodial sentence for adults.

SOURCE: *Uniform Crime Reporting Survey, Adult Court Survey,* and *Youth Court Survey,* Canadian Centre for Justice Statistics, Statistics Canada. Adapted from "Juristat," Cat. no. 85–002.

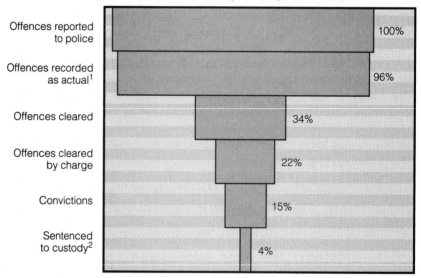

Total incidents reported to police = 2 832 800

- Offences reported to police — 100%
- Offences recorded as actual[1] — 96%
- Offences cleared — 34%
- Offences cleared by charge — 22%
- Convictions — 15%
- Sentenced to custody[2] — 4%

Percentage of police-reported offences

SOCIOLOGICAL THEORIES OF CRIME AND VIOLENCE

Some explanations of crime and violence focus on psychological aspects of the offender, such as psychopathic personalities, unhealthy relationships with parents, and mental illness. Other crime theories focus on the role of biological variables such as the central nervous system malfunctioning, vitamin or mineral deficiencies, chromosomal abnormalities, and a genetic predisposition toward aggression (see this chapter's Focus on Technology). Sociological theories of crime and violence emphasize the role of social factors in criminal behaviour and societal responses to it.

Montreal Self-Report Questions

During the past 12 months, did you:

	1 (Yes)	0 (No)
1. purposely damage or destroy musical instruments, sports supplies, or other school equipment?		
2. purposely damage or destroy public or private property that did not belong to you?		
3. take some school property worth $5.00 or more?		
4. purposely damage a school building (windows, walls, etc.)?		
5. take a motorcycle and go for a ride without the owner's permission?		
6. take a car and go for a ride without the owner's permission?		
7. purposely destroy a radio antenna, tires, or other parts of a car?		
8. "beat up" someone who hadn't done anything to you?		
9. take something from a store without paying?		
10. threaten to beat up someone to make that person do something he or she didn't want to do?		
11. get into a place (a movie, a game, or a performance) without paying the admission price?		
12. use a weapon (stick, knife, gun, rock, etc.) while fighting another person?		
13. use stimulants (speed, pep pills, etc.) or hallucinogens (LSD, STP, THC, etc.)?		
14. have a fistfight with another person?		
15. take something of large value (worth $50.00 or more) that did not belong to you?		
16. gamble for money with persons other than your family members?		
17. sell any kind of drugs?		
18. break into and enter somewhere to take something?		
19. carry a weapon (chain, knife, gun, etc.)?		
20. take something of some value (between $2.00 and $50.00) that did not belong to you?		
21. purposely set a fire in a building or in any other place?		
22. take and keep a bicycle that did not belong to you?		
23. take something of little value (worth less than $2.00) that did not belong to you?		
24. trespass anywhere you were not supposed to go (vacant house, railroad tracks, lumber yard, etc.)?		
25. use marijuana or hashish?		
26. make anonymous phone calls (not say who you were)?		
27. use opiates (heroin, morphine, opium)?		
28. send in a false alarm?		
29. buy, use, or sell something that you knew to be stolen?		

Criminal Activities Survey (*continued*)

30. drive a car without a driver's licence?
31. have sexual relations (other than kissing) with a person of the same sex?
32. skip school without a legitimate excuse?
33. have sexual relations (other than kissing) with a person of the opposite sex?
34. take part in a gang fight between adolescents?
35. run away from home for more than 24 hours?
36. tell your parents (or those who replace them) that you would not do what they ordered you to do?
37. take money from home without permission and with no intention of returning it?
38. get drunk on beer, wine, or other alcoholic beverages?
39. "fool around" at night when you were supposed to be at home?

SOURCE: LeBlanc, M., and M. Frechette. 1989. *Male Criminal Activity from Childhood through Youth: Multilevel and Developmental Perspectives*, pp. 195. New York: Springer-Verlag. © 1989 Springer-Verlag. Reprinted by permission.

Structural-Functionalist Perspective

According to Durkheim and other structural-functionalists, crime is functional for society. One of the functions of crime and other deviant behaviour is that it strengthens group cohesion:

> The deviant individual violates rules of conduct [that] the rest of the community holds in high respect; and when these people come together to express their outrage over the offense...they develop a tighter bond of solidarity than existed earlier. (Erikson 1966: 4)

Crime may also lead to social change. For example, an episode of local violence may "achieve broad improvements in city services...[and] be a catalyst for making public agencies more effective and responsive, for strengthening families and social institutions, and for creating public–private partnerships" (National Research Council 1994: 9–10).

While functionalism as a theoretical perspective deals directly with some aspects of crime and violence, it is not a theory of crime per se. Three major theories of crime and violence have developed from functionalism, however. The first, called **strain theory**, was developed by Robert Merton (1957) using Durkheim's concept of anomie, or normlessness. Merton argues that when legitimate means (for example, a job) of acquiring culturally defined goals (for example, money) are limited by the structure of society, the resulting strain may lead to crime.

Individuals, then, must adapt to the inconsistency between means and goals in a society that socializes everyone into wanting the same thing but only provides opportunities for some (see Table 4.1). Conformity occurs when individuals accept the culturally defined goals and the socially legitimate means of

Table 4.1	Merton's Five Types of Adaptation	
	Culturally Defined Goals	Structurally Defined Means
1. Conformity	+	+
2. Innovation	+	–
3. Ritualism	–	+
4. Retreatism	–	–
5. Rebellion	–/+	–/+

Key: (+) = acceptance of/access to; (–) = rejection of/lack of access to; (–/+) = rejection of culturally defined goals and structurally defined means and replacement with new goals and means.

SOURCE: Merton, Robert K. 1957. Reprinted with permission of The Free Press, a division of Simon and Schuster from *Social Theory and Social Structure* by Robert K. Merton. Copyright © 1957 by The Free Press: copyright renewed 1985 by Robert K. Merton.

achieving them. Merton suggests that most individuals, even those who do not have easy access to the means and the goals, remain conformists. Innovation occurs when an individual accepts the goals of society, but rejects or lacks the socially legitimate means of achieving them. Innovation, the mode of adaptation most associated with criminal behaviour, explains the high rate of crime committed by uneducated and poor individuals who do not have access to legitimate means of achieving the social goals of wealth and power.

Another adaptation is ritualism, in which the individual accepts a lifestyle of hard work, but rejects the cultural goal of monetary rewards. The ritualist goes through the motions of getting an education and working hard, yet is not committed to the goal of accumulating wealth or power. Retreatism involves rejecting both the cultural goal of success and the socially legitimate means of achieving it. The retreatist withdraws or retreats from society and may become an alcoholic, drug addict, or vagrant. Finally, rebellion occurs when an individual rejects both culturally defined goals and means and substitutes new goals and means. For example, rebels may use social or political activism to replace the goal of personal wealth with the goal of social justice and equality.

While strain theory explains criminal behaviour as a result of blocked opportunities, **subcultural theory** argues that certain groups or subcultures in society have values and attitudes that are conducive to crime and violence. Members of these groups and subcultures, as well as other individuals who interact with them, may adopt the crime-promoting attitudes and values of the group. For example, subcultural norms and values contribute to street crime. Sociologist Elijah Anderson (1994) explains that many inner-city youths live by a survival code on the streets that emphasizes gaining the respect of others through violence—the tougher you are and the more others fear you, the more respect you have in the community.

However, if blocked opportunities and subcultural values are responsible for crime, why don't all members of the affected groups become criminals? **Control theory** may answer that question. Hirschi (1969), consistent with Durkheim's emphasis on social solidarity, suggests that a strong social bond between individuals and the social order constrains some individuals from violating social norms. Hirschi identified four elements of the social bond: attachment to significant others, commitment to conventional goals, involvement in conventional activities, and belief in the moral standards of society. Several

National Data

Between 1977 and 1996, 12 666 people were victims of homicide in Canada, one-third of which involved family members (4193 victims). The largest category of family homicides during this period involved spouses (49 percent), followed by children killed by a parent (22 percent), and parents killed by a child (10 percent).

SOURCE: Statistics Canada 1998a

National Data

In 1997–98, Canada's youth courts processed 110 883 cases. Almost half of these cases involved property offences. Only one in five cases involved violent crimes and about half of those cases were common assaults.

SOURCE: Hendrick 1999

DNA Evidence

Increasingly, law enforcement officers in Canada, the United States, and Europe are using what is called DNA fingerprinting in the identification of criminal suspects. DNA stands for deoxyribonucleic acid, which is found in the nucleus of every cell and contains an individual's complete and unique genetic makeup. Developed in the mid-1980s, DNA fingerprinting is a general term used to describe the process of analyzing and comparing DNA from different sources to the DNA of a suspect. Evidence that can be used includes evidence found at a crime scene, such as blood, semen, hair, saliva, fibres, and skin tissue.

In the fall of 1998, the FBI initiated the Combined DNA Index System. This database contains the DNA fingerprints of 250 000 convicted felons and more than 4600 DNA samples from unsolved crime scenes. Despite the database being in operation less than two years, the "FBI claims that 200 outstanding cases have already been solved" (Kluger 1999: 1). In Canada, federal laboratories in Canada handled DNA evidence in the prosecution of 722 murders and 1289 assaults in 1995 alone (Statistics Canada 1998: 510). DNA analysis is helpful to not just to prosecutors 12 Canadian prisoners were released from custody on the strength of DNA evidence. DNA was used to vindicate Guy Paul Morin

and David Milgaard, long after they were wrongfully convicted of murders they did not commit (in 1992 and 1969 respectively).

Despite these success stories, there is tremendous concern about the use of DNA evidence and, specifically, questions about how donors would be selected and what methods of data collection would be used. Libertarians fear possible violations of civil rights, particularly after a recent court decision by a French judge who ruled that all men in a village would be DNA tested to locate the killer of a 13-year-old girl. In England, police officials legally take samples of blood or skin tissue from every criminal suspect (Gleick 1997: 3). In two recent murder cases, Canadian police officers conducted mass DNA screenings and asked hundreds of potential suspects to consent to testing. In the first, the 1998 stabbing of a female employee at an adult-video store in Sudbury, Ontario, Sudbury Regional Police officers took DNA from more than 400 possible suspects. In the second, the Port Alberni (British Columbia) RCMP examined DNA from 350 suspects in relation to the 1996 sexual assault and murder of an 11-year-old girl. While asking possible suspects to consent to testing is legal, some have expressed fear that it may go too far. For example, Toronto lawyer James Lockyer rhetorically asks what will happen to those who refuse to provide

samples and remarks, "That's where harassment might begin, if police don't take no for an answer." Toronto lawyer and forensic DNA authority Ricardo Federico additionally queries, "Is this what we want, having the science police knocking on everybody's door?" (*Maclean's* 1999: 13). Such concerns, in part, explain why, until recently, England had the only nationwide DNA databank in the world (Gleick 1997; Goldberg 1998).

Nevertheless, the future of DNA fingerprinting is likely to be bright. It's less expensive than ever before, predicted to be as low as $10 a test within a few years compared to earlier costs of $200 to $300. As technology has become increasingly sophisticated, the time it takes to conduct the analysis has decreased from weeks to days (Goldberg 1998). Further, even if DNA fingerprinting doesn't survive the legal scrutiny it's likely to come under (Tibbets 1999), it remains a valuable identification technique used in biology, archaeology, medical diagnosis, paleontology, and forensics.

SOURCES: Gleick, Elizabeth. 1997. "The Killer Left a Trace." *Time*, September 1: 150; Goldberg, Carey. 1998. "DNA Databanks Giving Police a Powerful Weapon, and Critics." *New York Times*, February 19: 1; Kluger, Jeffery. 1999. "DNA Detectives." *Time*, Canadian edition, January 11: 46–7; *Maclean's*. 1999. "Rounding up Suspects for Their DNA." December 13: 13; Statistics Canada. 1998. *Canada Yearbook 2000*. Ottawa: Ministry of Industry; Tibbets, Janice. 1999. "DNA Evidence Goes on Trial." *National Post*, December 15: A20.

empirical tests of Hirschi's theory support the notion that the higher the attachment, commitment, involvement, and belief, the higher the social bond and the lower the probability of criminal behaviour. For example, Laub et al. (1998) found that a good marriage contributes to the cessation of a criminal career. Further, Warner and Rountree (1997) report that local community ties, although varying by neighbourhood and offence, decrease the probability of crimes occurring.

Conflict Perspective

Conflict theories of crime suggest that deviance is inevitable whenever two groups have differing degrees of power; in addition, the more inequality in a society, the greater the crime rate in that society. Social inequality may lead individuals to commit crimes such as armed robbery and burglary as a means of economic survival. Other individuals, who are angry and frustrated by their low position in the socioeconomic hierarchy, may express their rage and frustration through crimes such as drug use, assault, and homicide.

According to the conflict perspective, those in power define what is criminal and what is not, and these definitions reflect the interests of the ruling class. Laws against vagrancy, for example, penalize individuals who do not contribute to the capitalist system of work and consumerism. Rather than viewing law as a mechanism that protects all members of society, conflict theorists focus on how laws are created by those in power to protect the ruling class. While wealthy corporations contribute money to campaigns to influence politicians to enact tax laws that serve corporate interests (Jacobs 1988), the "criminal justice system grows increasingly punitive as labour surplus increases," that is, as greater social control is felt to be needed (Hochstetler and Shover 1997).

Furthermore, conflict theorists argue that law enforcement is applied differentially, penalizing those without power and benefiting those with power. For example, female prostitutes are more likely to be arrested than are the men who seek their services. Unlike street criminals, corporate criminals are often punished by fines rather than by lengthy prison terms. Laws on "rape" originated to serve the interests of husbands and fathers who wanted to protect their property—wives and unmarried daughters.

Societal beliefs also reflect power differentials. For example, "rape myths" are perpetuated by the male-dominated culture to foster the belief that women are to blame for their own victimization, thereby, in the minds of many, exonerating the offender. Such myths include the notion that when a woman says "no" she means "yes," that "good girls" don't get raped, that appearance indicates willingness, and that women secretly want to be raped. Not surprisingly, in societies where women and men have greater equality, there are fewer rapes (Sanday 1981).

Symbolic Interactionist Perspective

Two important theories of crime and violence emanate from the symbolic interactionist perspective. The first, **labelling theory**, focuses on two questions: How do crime and deviance come to be defined as such, and what are the effects of being labelled as criminal or deviant? According to Howard Becker (1963):

> **Social groups create deviance by making rules whose infractions constitute deviance, and by applying those rules to particular people and labelling them as outsiders. From this point of view, deviance is not a quality of the act a person commits, but rather a consequence of the application by others of rules and sanctions to an "offender." The deviant is one to whom the label has successfully been applied; deviant behaviour is behaviour that people so label. (p. 238)**

Labelling theorists make a distinction between primary deviance, which is deviant behaviour committed before a person is caught and labelled as an offender, and secondary deviance, which is deviance that results from being caught and labelled. After a person violates the law and is apprehended, that person is stigmatized as a criminal. This deviant label often dominates the social identity of the person to whom it is applied and becomes the person's "master status," that is, the primary basis on which the person is defined by others.

Being labelled as deviant often leads to further deviant behaviour because (1) the person who is labelled as deviant is often denied opportunities for engaging in nondeviant behaviour, and (2) the labelled person internalizes the deviant label, adopts a deviant self-concept, and acts accordingly. For example, the teenager who is caught selling drugs at school may be expelled and thus denied opportunities to participate in nondeviant school activities (e.g., sports, clubs) and associate with nondeviant peer groups. The labelled and stigmatized teenager may also adopt the self-concept of a "druggie" or "pusher" and continue to pursue drug-related activities and membership in the drug culture.

The assignment of meaning and definitions learned from others are also central to the second symbolic interactionist theory of crime, **differential association**. Edwin Sutherland (1939) proposed that, through interaction with others, individuals learn the values and attitudes associated with crime as well as the techniques and motivations for criminal behaviour. Individuals who are exposed to more definitions favourable to law violation (e.g., "crime pays") than unfavourable (e.g., "do the crime, you'll do the time") are more likely to engage in criminal behaviour. Thus, children who see their parents benefit from crime, or who live in high-crime neighbourhoods where success is associated with illegal behaviour, are more likely to engage in criminal behaviour.

TYPES OF CRIME

Most Canadians would be understandably alarmed to hear that in 1997, 2.5 million *Criminal Code* incidents (excluding traffic incidents) were reported to Canadian police departments and agencies (Kong 1999). However, while it might be assumed that all these incidents were interchangeable with the dramatic cases reported on the nightly news, this is not the case. In 1997, more than half (58 percent) of these *Criminal Code* incidents involved property crimes, 12 percent involved violent crimes, and almost one in three (30 percent) involved other *Criminal Code* offences of which mischief, bail violations, and disturbing the peace were the most common.

Criminologists use the terms **conventional crime** or **street crime** to refer to "those traditional illegal behaviours that most people think of as crime" (Koenig 2000). Included here would be offences such as murder, sexual assault, assault, armed robbery, break and enter, and theft. In contrast, the term "non-conventional crimes" is employed with reference to such crimes as, for example, organized crime, white-collar crime, corporate crime, and computer crime.

Street Crime: Violent Offences

Violent crime includes homicide, attempted murder, assault, sexual assault, other sexual offences, abduction, and robbery. In 1997, violent crimes accounted for 12 percent of all *Criminal Code* offences. At the same time, however, the rate of violent crime in Canada decreased in 1997 for the fifth consecutive year. As Figure 4.5 indicates, common assaults (level 1), the least serious form of assault, account for 6 in 10 violent crimes. In 1997, the rate of youths charged with violent offences also decreased for the second consecutive year (Kong 1999). As Figure 4.6 indicates, youths in Canada are much more likely to commit property offences than crimes of violence.

Homicide refers to the willful or nonnegligent killing of one human being by another individual or group of individuals. Although homicide is the most serious of the violent crimes, it is also the least common, accounting for less than 1 percent of reported violent incidents in 1997 (Kong 1999) and 0.02 percent of the almost three million *Criminal Code* incidents reported to police in 1998 (Fedorowycz 1999). The majority of homicide victims had some type of relationship with their murderers and were killed over such issues as jealousy and money.

Historically, and continuing into the present, about two-thirds of homicide victims have been men as have almost 9 out of 10 (88 percent) of those accused of homicide. Fedorowycz (1999) notes that both the median and the average age of those accused of homicide in Canada has increased slightly over the past quarter century, and that in 1998, the most common single age (mode) for someone accused of homicide was 20 years. For both homicide and other

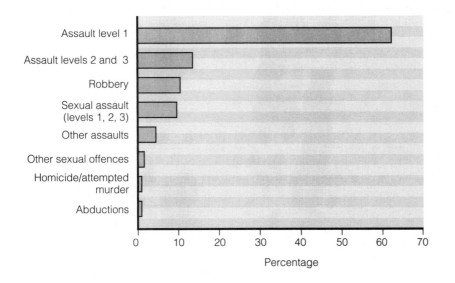

Figure 4.5
Violent Crime Categories, Canada, 1997

SOURCE: *Uniform Crime Reporting Survey*, Canadian Centre for Justice Statistics, Statistics Canada. Adapted from "Juristat," Cat. no. 85–002.

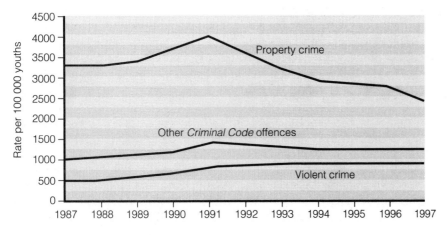

Figure 4.6
Rate of Youths Charged, 1987–97

SOURCE: *Uniform Crime Reporting Survey*, Canadian Centre for Justice Statistics, Statistics Canada.

violent crimes, the highest risk group for offending are those 16 to 34 years old. In 1998, this age group accounted for approximately two-thirds of those accused of homicide. Hackler (2000) notes that the majority of homicides committed among marginal groups in North America (e.g., First Nations people, African-Americans) are intraracial.

Other forms of violent crime are sexual and nonsexual assaults. Both types of assault are distinguished by several categories. In relation to nonsexual assault these categories are: common assault (level 1), assault with a weapon or causing bodily harm (level 2), and aggravated assault (level 3) in which the victim is wounded, maimed, or disfigured. In addition, the *Criminal Code* outlines other types of assaults including those committed on a peace officer, an officiating member of the clergy, the Queen, an internationally protected person, and so on.

Sexual assaults are also classified into one of three levels that are distinguished by the degree of physical harm to the victim: level 1 sexual assault, level 2 sexual assault (sexual assault with a weapon, threats to a third party, or causing bodily harm), and level 3 aggravated sexual assault (in which an offender, in committing a sexual assault, wounds, maims, disfigures, or endangers the life of the victim). In relation to both types of assaults, sexual and nonsexual, the least serious are the most common. For example, in 1997, common assaults, which consist of such behaviour as pushing, slapping, punching, in-person verbal threats, and threatening acts or gestures, accounted for almost 8 in 10 assaults. In that year, police also classified 97 percent of reported incidents of sexual assault as level 1 assaults.

In 1997, there were 27 063 incidents of sexual assault and 222 210 incidents of assault reported to Canadian police departments. Females accounted for more than 8 in 10 (84 percent) victims of sexual assault in that year. Although females and males were equally likely to be victims of assault, females were somewhat more likely than males to be victims of common assault (53 percent versus 47 percent respectively), while males were more likely than females to be victims of assault with a weapon and aggravated assault (66 percent versus 34 percent). Victims of sexual assault were likely to be younger than victims of nonsexual assault were. Almost 60 percent of sexual assault victims were less than 18 years old. The median age for female victims of sexual assault was 17 years and for male victims, 11 years. In contrast, the median age of nonsexual assault victims was 26 years for males and 29 years for females.

The most common assailants in cases of sexual assaults against females were casual acquaintances (33 percent); a family member, including a spouse or ex-spouse (27 percent); and a stranger (23 percent). Male victims were most likely to be sexually assaulted by a casual acquaintance (42 percent), a family member (29 percent), or a stranger (13 percent). In sexual assaults involving very young female victims (i.e., those under the age of 12), the perpetrator was most likely to be a family member (49 percent). Among male victims of this age, the perpetrator was equally likely to be a casual acquaintance (39 percent) or a family member (39 percent). In relation to assaults, females were most often assaulted by a spouse (43 percent) or an acquaintance (18 percent). Among male victims, the most common assailant was a stranger (39 percent) or an acquaintance (34 percent).

Over the past decade, increasing attention has been directed to **acquaintance rape**—sexual assaults committed by someone the victim knows. The term is somewhat misleading as it does not appear within the *Criminal Code* of

Canada and the act so described is actually subsumed within the three levels of sexual assault already noted. Nevertheless, it has been reported that although sexual assaults committed by acquaintances are the most likely to occur, they are the least likely to be reported and the most difficult to prosecute. Unless the sexual assault is what Williams (1984) calls a **classic rape**—that is, the offender was a stranger who used a weapon and the attack resulted in serious bodily harm—victims hesitate to report the crime out of fear of not being believed. In addition, the increased use of "rape drugs" such as Rohypnol or "Roofies," which renders its victims unconscious, may lower reporting levels even further. It is estimated that only 1 in 10 sexual assaults are reported each year.

Robbery, although involving theft, also involves force, the threat of force, or putting a victim in fear, and is thus considered a violent crime. In 1997, robberies accounted for 1 in 10 violent crimes. In that year, 29 590 robberies occurred. Since 1991, robberies involving firearms have declined, while robberies involving other weapons (e.g., knives) have increased. In 4 out of 10 robberies committed in 1997, no weapon was used. Robberies are committed by young people: in 1997, the median age of female offenders was 16 and of male offenders, 21. More than 6 in 10 victims of robbery in 1997 were male (Kong 1999). As with sexual assault, victims who resist a robbery are more likely to stop the crime but are also more likely to be physically harmed.

Street Crime: Property Offences

Property crimes involve acts committed with the intent to gain property that do not involve the use or threatened use of violence. Examples of property crime include theft, breaking and entering, motor vehicle theft, fraud, and possession of stolen property. Property crimes have declined in recent years, with the 1997 rate 18 percent lower than the rate five years ago. As indicated in Figure 4.7, theft under $5000 was the most common type of property crime in 1997.

After steadily increasing for more than a decade, the rate of motor vehicle theft decreased by 3 percent in 1997. However, the current rate is 14 percent higher than five years ago and almost 80 percent higher than it was a decade ago. Kong (1999) points out that "[i]n particular, there has been a large increase in the number of 'trucks' stolen in recent years," a category that includes minivans and sport utility vehicles. Given that most motor vehicles are stolen by youths for joy rides, it is not perhaps surprising that about three-quarters of all stolen vehicles are recovered within 48 hours. Of those charged with motor vehicle theft in 1997, more than 4 in 10 (43 percent) were youths aged 12 to 17.

Breaking and entering, which was the second most common category of property offences in 1997, entails entering a structure, usually a house (63 percent in 1997) with the intent to commit a crime while inside. Official statistics indicate that 373 355 incidents of breaking and entering were reported to the police in 1997 (Kong 1999). Four in 10 persons charged with this offence in 1997 were youths. In 1996, the average loss to homeowners and tenants was $5034 and for businesses, $5162. In that year, "property losses associated with B and Es cost the insurance industry about $398 million" in Canada.

Vice Crimes

Vice crimes are illegal activities that have no complaining party and are therefore often called **victimless crimes**. Vice crimes include using illegal drugs, communicating for the purposes of prostitution, illegal gambling, and the possession, distribution, or sale of child pornography.

"In Canada, all pornography which involves children is illegal, regardless of the medium, and this is applicable to Internet child pornography" (CCJS 1999). However, in January 1999, in a case involving a 66-year-old man, John Sharpe, who had been charged with possession of child pornography after police raided his home and seized CDs, photos, and writings about child pornography, B.C. Supreme Court judge Justice Duncan Shaw ruled that possessing child pornography should not be a crime because laws against it violate *Charter* provisions that guarantee freedom of thought, belief, opinion, and expression. In his 33-page decision, the judge wrote that a person's belongings are "an expression of that person's essential self" and that "only assumption," not evidence, supports the idea that materials advocating sex crimes with children actually prompt people to do such things. Moreover, the judge wrote that "[t]he intrusion into freedom of expression and the right of privacy is so profound that it is not outweighed by the limited beneficial effects of the prohibition" (cited in Bailey 1999: A4). In turn, the country's child pornography legislation was struck down in British Columbia; although Shaw's ruling became law in that province, it was not binding on other provincial courts.

In January 2000, the Supreme Court of Canada heard an appeal of this case. While government lawyers argued that the rights of children should supersede *Charter of Rights'* guarantees to privacy and freedom of expression, a lawyer for the B.C. Civil Liberties Association, John McAlpine, argued that the court "would drive a stake through the heart of liberty" if it sided with the position of the government lawyers. Although two judges, Charles Gonthier and Claire L'Heureux Dube responded by saying that freedom of expression is not an absolute right, a decision on this case had not been announced at the time this book went to press (*Maclean's* 2000: 40).

A lack of a consensus also characterizes both national and international reactions to prostitution and gambling. For example, Bibby (1995) has observed that "prostitution is not an issue Canadians have been seeing as particularly pressing." He points out that while one in five Canadians identified "prostitution" as an issue they regarded as "very serious" in 1985, a decade later, it was mentioned by less than 1 percent. While prostitution is not illegal in Canada, it is an offence to publicly communicate with another person for the purpose of buying or selling sexual services; since 1985, the law has clearly applied to both buyers and sellers. In contrast, in the Netherlands, the Prostitution Information Centre in Amsterdam offers a six-day course on "prostitution as a career option," and the Australia Council of Trade Unions recently recognized women in prostitution as a labour sector (CATW 1997). Similarly, in the United States, many states have legalized gambling, including casinos in Nevada, New Jersey, and Connecticut, as well as state lotteries, bingo parlours, horse and dog racing, and jai alai. However, in Canada, the *Criminal Code* prohibits individuals from keeping a common gaming house or common betting house, from being found "without lawful excuse" in such settings, renting or leasing premises to be used as such and, among other things, specifies that people may not import, make, buy, sell, rent, lease, hire or keep, exhibit, or employ any device or apparatus for the purpose of recording or registering bets or selling a pool, or any machine or device for gambling or betting. Although a series of exemptions to these laws are also contained within the *Criminal Code*, some have argued that there is little difference between "illegal" and "legal" gambling. Observing the success of legal gambling in Canada, conflict theorists might suggest that the difference is simply in who is profiting from the wager placed. In this chapter's The Human Side, we focus on some of the pros and cons of legalized gambling in Canada.

Organized crime refers to criminal activity conducted by members of a hierarchically arranged structure devoted primarily to making money through illegal means. Many of these activities include providing illegal goods and services such as drugs and gambling, as well as the coercion of legitimate businesses for profit. For example, organized crime groups may force legitimate businesses to pay "protection money" by threatening vandalism or violence.

The traditional notion of organized crime is the Mafia—a national band of interlocked Italian families—but members of many ethnic groups engage in organized crime. Other organized crime groups in Canada include Chinese Triads, the Colombian Mafia, outlaw motorcycle gangs, the Russian Mafia, and other ethnic-based drug trafficking groups. Their activities include drug trafficking, prostitution, terrorism, extortion, and such violent crimes as serious assaults and homicide (Stamler 2000).

Organized crime also occurs at the international level, such as smuggling illegal drugs and arms. Since the fall of the Soviet Union, it is estimated that as much as 25 percent of the Russian gross national income is from organized crime activities generated by 5600 separate crime groups. Today, organized crime is considered "...one the most important political problems in Russia..." whereby a "...Russian citizen's personal safety" can no longer be guaranteed (Shabalin et al. 1995).

White-Collar Crime

White-collar crime includes both occupational crime, where individuals commit crimes in the course of their employment, and corporate crime, where corporations violate the law in the interest of maximizing profit. Occupational crime is motivated by individual gain. Employee thefts of merchandise (pilferage) and money (embezzlement) are examples of occupational crime. Price-fixing, antitrust violations, and fraud are examples of corporate crime, that is, crime that benefits the organization. Table 4.2 summarizes some of the major categories of white-collar crime.

Corporate violence, a form of corporate crime, refers to the production of unsafe products and the failure of corporations to provide safe working environments for their employees. Corporate violence is the result of negligence, the pursuit of profit at any cost, and intentional violations of health, safety,

Table 4.2	Types of White-Collar Crime		
Crimes against Consumers	**Crimes against Employees**	**Crimes against the Public**	**Crimes against Employers**
Deceptive advertising	Health and safety violations	Toxic waste disposal	Embezzlement
Antitrust violations	Wage and hour violations	Pollution violations	Pilferage
Dangerous products	Discriminatory hiring practices	Tax fraud	Misappropriation of government funds
Manufacturer kickbacks	Illegal labour practices	Security violations	Counterfeit production of goods
Physician insurance fraud	Unlawful surveillance practices	Police brutality	Business credit fraud

"HEADS YOU WIN, TAILS YOU LOSE": LOTTERIES IN NEWFOUNDLAND

Heads

Since its inception in 1976, Atlantic Lottery Corporation (ALC) has paid out over $2.5 billion in prizes through games carried by the 6000 lottery retailers in Atlantic Canada. More importantly, it has turned over more than $2.4 billion in net profit to its shareholders—the four provinces of Atlantic Canada. Not only have lotteries fattened personal bank accounts...they have added millions of dollars in provincial government revenue. In the last five years, the government has made a net profit of $387.1 million from all Atlantic Lotto games. In the fiscal year of 1998–99, the lotteries brought home a staggering $89.9 million. These gambling profits are dumped into the general coffers for the province's operating budget. The money is then redistributed as funding for such areas as education, health and social programs.

Who is really making these dividends possible? None other than the hard-working Newfoundlanders dreaming of making a killing on the lottery. The 1998–99 *Annual Report of the Atlantic Lottery Corporation* reveals that total lottery sales in this province amounted to $239.7 million....Newfoundlers spent $27.2 million on Lotto 6/49 tickets last year, as well as $7.9 million on Lotto 6/49 TAG, $8.6 million on Super 7, and a whopping $61.3 million on breakopens (Nevadas). But the best seller surpasses the others in sales by a wide margin—Video Lottery machines (VLTs) accounted for $84.5 million of last year's sales.

VLTs were introduced to Newfoundland bars in 1990. Under the guidelines set by the government, the prize payout range for these machines is not less than 80% and no more than 96% of the credits wagered. The bars and the government originally split the profits 65/35 for shareholder and retailers. Later, the government changed these terms to get a larger share of the profits. Today, the profit sharing stands as 24.75% going to the retailers and 75.25% going to the province. However, if net revenue exceeds $400 000, the split becomes 19.8% for the retailers and 80.2% for the government....

Tails

Nearly everyone dreams of being a winner. It's amazing how convenience stores on Wednesday, Friday, and Saturday nights can become packed to the gills around cut-off time for purchasing Lotto 6/49 on Super 7 tickets....Most people will admit to dabbling in lotteries from time to time....[However the] need to wager has a variety of labels: problem gambling, pathological gambling, even maladaptive gambling behaviour....

The majority of problem gamblers are addicted to Video Lottery, described by ALC as "a product [that] provides interactive entertainment as well as the chance to instantly win small cash prizes." Granted, the maximum bet is $2.50 and the maximum payout is $500 per game. Unfortunately, there is no way to regulate how many times a person plays. No one can pinpoint exactly why VLTs are a bigger problem, but it can be said that across the country addiction hotlines get more calls about Video Lottery addiction than any other lottery.

"HEADS YOU WIN, TAILS YOU LOSE": LOTTERIES IN NEWFOUNDLAND
(continued)

In Alberta, 60% of calls to the provincial gambling hotline are from VLT addicts. The Addictions Foundation of Manitoba claims 85% of their hotline calls are VLT-related; government agencies in Quebec, Saskatchewan, and New Brunswick also field more calls concerning this form of problem gambling than any other. Excluding British Columbia, Prince Edward Island, Northwest Territories, and Yukon, the sum of provincial spending on gambling problems across the country was $4.8 million in 1995–96....

Tales of addicted gamblers are sad. There are those who spend their entire paycheque in one day. Players who fear losing their machine have been known to wear Depends (absorbent under-garments) or go on the spot rather than take bathroom breaks. Gambling parents have left their children locked inside their cars while they played the slots. When the money is long gone, desperate gamblers turn to crime as a means to support their addiction. Too many fall into a depression because they have lost their assets, their jobs, their family, and some commit or attempt suicide.

If these stories lend thought that only lower-income people gamble uncontrollably because they are wishing for the money they never had, think again. In 1997, a high-ranking civil servant in the criminal justice department lost his job because of an obsession with VLTs....

Individuals, organizations, and government have suggested several approaches to curbing VLT addictions. Portions of the public believe banning the machines altogether is the answer; others say the bar owners should "cut off" a gambler like they would a drunken patron. Social service organizations believe in the power of public awareness campaigns, and the government's solution is funding programs. In 1997, the provincial government [of Newfoundland] introduced a recovery program especially for gamblers to be run by Addictions Services, Department of Health and Community Services. This program operates on the yearly $150 000 government grant and $150 000 from Beverage Newfoundland and Labrador Association.

SOURCE: Abridged from Stuckless, Janice. 1999. "'Heads You Win, Tails You Lose': Lotteries in Newfoundland." *Downhomer* 12 (6), November: 16–9.

National Data

In 1996, the majority (82 percent) of Canadian households gambled some money, spending an average of $423 during the year. Among households that gambled, those with incomes of less than $20 000 spent an average of $296 or about 2.2 percent of their total household income. Those with $80 000 or more spent an average of $536, only 0.5 percent of their total income.

SOURCE: Statistics Canada 1998b

and environmental regulations. General Motors (GM) C-K model pickup trucks built between 1973 and 1987 were fitted with side-mounted fuel tanks. Unlike other vehicles, the fuel tanks were not protected by the frame, resulting in what consumer groups have called the "the most lethal auto defect in U.S. history" (Zagaroli 1997). While it is estimated that more than 800 people have burned to death in side-impact collisions because of the defect, more than four million trucks remain on the road. The National Highway Traffic Safety Administration agreed not to recall the trucks after GM (U.S.) agreed to fund a $51 million auto safety program (AP 1998).

More recently, GM was ordered to pay $4.9 billion (U.S.) to six people who were severely burned when their car exploded in flames after a rear-end collision. In court, lawyers for the plaintiffs produced a internal GM study that

National Data

Against All Odds

The chances of winning any prize in Ontario's Lotto 6/49 are slim, let alone an average $2 million jackpot. Even the odds of winning the minimum $10 fifth prize for just three correct numbers are the same as flipping six heads on a coin in a row.

Prize	Odds	Equivalent Number of Successive Heads
Jackpot	13 983 815 to 1	24 heads in a row
Second prize	2 330 635 to 1	21 heads in a row
Third prize	55 490 to 1	16 heads in a row
Fourth prize	1031 to 1	10 heads in a row
Fifth prize	56 to 1	6 heads in a row

SOURCE: Schofield 1996: 53. Reprinted by permission.

acknowledged that the gas tanks in the Chevrolet Malibu and El Camino, the Pontiac Grand Am, and Oldsmobile Cutlass were mounted in unsafe positions—27 centimetres from the rear bumper. However, the GM study had also pointed out that it would be cheaper to settle lawsuits that might arise from accidents in which victims were fatally burned (calculated to be $2.40 per car produced) than to change where the tanks were placed (calculated to be $8.59 per car produced). Here again, a profit-motivated decision was made and the placement of the gas tanks in these cars remained unaltered from 1979 to 1983. The foreman of the jury that ruled on this case later commented to the press, "If they had no regard for the lives of people in their cars, they should be held liable for it." Although the award was both the biggest product-liability award and the largest personal injury verdict in U.S. history, legal experts observed that the enormous punitive award was unlikely to stand on appeal. They noted that "[e]ven with awards in the tens of millions, it is rare for a plaintiff to actually get anything close to the jury's verdict" (White 1999).

In the United States, the National Commission on Product Safety estimates that there are 110 000 permanently disabling injuries, 30 000 deaths, and millions of serious injuries each year as a result of unsafe consumer products (Barkan 1997: 336). In many cases, corporate executives are aware that the products are unsafe. Another example is the Ford Pinto, which had a defective gas tank that exploded in rear-end collisions. Hundreds of burn deaths occurred before the problem was revealed to the public. Yet, the Ford Motor Company knew of the dangers of the car and made a profit-motivated decision to do nothing:

> **The $11 repairs for all Pintos would cost $137 million but 180 burn deaths and 180 serious burn injuries and 2100 burned vehicles would cost only $49.5 million (each death was figured at $200 000, and each injury at $67 000). Therefore, the company could anticipate a savings or profit [by doing nothing] of $87.5 million. (Hills 1987: 425)**

In Canada, some have argued that the term "**corporate murder**" (Swartz 1978) is an appropriate label for deaths resulting in such circumstances. Among the best-known cases are the failures of administrators within the Johns-Manville Corporation to alert workers to the serious health hazards posed by asbestos. Hagan (2000) notes that although these hazards have been recognized "since the turn of the century,…people working with it were not informed, and the government bureaucracy and the medical community ignored the hazard." Similarly, he notes the 1992 explosion at the Westray coal mine in Pictou County, Nova Scotia, which killed 26 miners instantly, "was not an accident, but…the result of conscious decisions by those responsible for the safety of the miners." An official inquiry into the disaster resulted in a report tellingly entitled *The Westray Story: A Predictable Path to Disaster*. In it, Justice Richard concludes that the managers at Westray had "displayed a certain disdain for safety and appeared to regard safety-conscious workers as the wimps in the organization" (in Hagan 2000).

Computer Crime

Computer crime refers to any violation of the law in which a computer is the target or the means of criminal activity. Seventy to 90 percent of all cases of computer crime are committed by employees (Albanese and Pursley 1993; Lewis 1998). Conklin (1998) has identified several examples of computer crime:

- In 1996, two individuals were charged with theft of 80 000 cellular phone numbers. Using a device purchased from a catalogue, the thieves picked up radio waves from passing cars, determined private cellular codes, reprogrammed computer chips with the stolen codes, and then, by inserting the new chips into their own cellular phones, charged calls to the original owners.
- A programmer made $300 a week by programming a computer to round off each employee's paycheque down to the nearest 10¢ and then to deposit the extra few pennies in the offender's account.
- An oil company illegally tapped into another oil company's computer to get information that allowed the offending company to underbid the other company for leasing rights.
- In 1995, Kevin Mitnick was arrested for breaking into an Internet service provider's computer system and stealing 20 000 credit card numbers.

CONSIDERATION

With the increased popularity and use of the Internet, there has also been an associated increase in the use of the Internet to support criminal activity. In 1996, a six-year-old California girl's accusations of sexual abuse led to an FBI investigation of the "Orchid Club," a chat room where people interested in child pornography shared pictures and other information. In July of 1996, 13 men were indicted, and arrest warrants were issued for several others in Finland, Canada, and Australia. Other crimes tied to the Internet include advertising of illegal products (e.g., prostitution, drugs, pornography), fraud, illegal distribution of copyrighted materials (e.g., books, tapes, compact discs [CDs], computer software), and illegal lotteries and gambling (CATW 1997; Hughes 1997).

National Data

In 1997–98, 16- and 17-year-olds accounted for 51 percent of cases processed in the youth courts of Canada. Cases involving 14- and 15-year-olds accounted for somewhat more than a third (37 percent), while those involving 12- and 13-year-olds represented 12 percent.

SOURCE: Hendrick 1999

Young Offenders

In Canada, the *Young Offenders Act* (1984) governs the conduct of youths between the ages of 12 and 18. While its predecessor, the *Juvenile Delinquency Act* (JDA) of 1908, directed that "as far as practicable every juvenile delinquent shall be treated, not as a criminal, but as a misguided and misdirected youth...needing aid, encouragement, help, and assistance," the principal aims of the *YOA* are to hold young persons who break the law accountable for their actions, to protect society from criminal behaviour, and to protect the legal rights of young offenders. In 1997, 111 736 youths aged 12 to 17 were charged with *Criminal Code* offences; more than half (53 percent) faced charges in relation to property crimes, 20 percent were charged with violent crimes, and the remainder were charged with other *Criminal Code* offences (e.g., mischief and offences against the administration of justice). In contrast, a decade ago, 69 percent of youths were charged with property offences and 9 percent with violent offences. Kong (1999) observes that much of the difference can be explained by increases in the number of youths charged with common (level 1) assault and decreases in the numbers charged with theft and break and enter. Although the past decade has witnessed a 179 percent increase in the rate of female youths charged with violent crimes (compared to an 85 percent increase among male youths), it is important to remember that this is largely due to the relatively small numbers of women charged with violent acts. That is, an increase from two to four persons charged is a 100 percent increase. The rate of female youths charged with violent crime in 1997 was 472 per 100 000 population; among male youths it was 1328 per 100 000 population (Kong 1999).

DEMOGRAPHIC PATTERNS OF CRIME

Although virtually everyone violates a law at some time, persons with certain demographic characteristics are disproportionately represented in the crime statistics. Victims, for example, are disproportionately young, lower-class, minority males from urban areas. Similarly, the probability of being an offender varies by gender, age, race, social class, and region.

National Data

In almost half (48 percent) of the cases processed in the youth courts of Canada in 1997–98, probation was the most serious sentence ordered. Custodial sentences were ordered in one-third of cases with convictions; in three-quarters of those cases, the custodial sentence given was three months or less.

SOURCE: Hendrick 1999

Gender and Crime

Both official statistics and self-report data indicate that males commit more crimes than females. Why are males more likely to commit crime than females? One explanation is that society views female lawbreaking as less acceptable and thus places more constraints on female behaviour: "women may need a higher level of provocation before turning to crime—especially serious crime. Females who choose criminality must traverse a greater moral and psychological distance than males making the same choice" (Steffensmeier and Allan 1995: 88).

Further, data suggest that males and females tend to commit different types of crimes. Men, partly because of more aggressive socialization experiences, are more likely than women are to commit violent crimes. Table 4.3 indicates the percentage of persons charged, by gender and age, in 1998. Females are less likely than males to commit serious offences, and the monetary value of female involvement in theft, property damage, and illegal drugs is typically less than that for similar offences committed by males. Nevertheless, a growing number of women have become involved in characteristically male criminal activities such as gang-related crime and drug use.

CONSIDERATION

Feminist criminology focuses on how the subordinate position of women in the social structure affects female criminality. For example, violent female offenders, although few in number, are more likely to be married and less likely to have a history of offending than their male counterparts. This suggests the possibility that violent female offenders may be recruited into crime by their husbands (Barlow 1993). Medna Chesney-Lind (1996) reports that arrest rates for runaway juvenile females are higher than for males not only because they are more likely to run away as a consequence of sexual abuse in the home, but also because police with paternalistic attitudes are more likely to arrest female runaways than male runaways. Feminist criminology thus adds insights into understanding crime and violence often neglected by traditional theories by concentrating on gender inequality in society.

Table 4.3 — **Percentage of Persons Charged, by Gender and Age, 1998**

	Age Group by Gender				Total by Age Group	
	Adults		Youth[1]			
	Male	Female	Male	Female	Adults	Youth
Homicides	87%	13%	96%	4%	88%	12%
Attempted murder	88	12	96	4	88	12
Assaults	85	15	70	30	85	15
Sexual assaults	98	2	97	3	85	15
Other sexual offences	97	3	97	3	86	14
Abduction	55	45	100	0	96	4
Robbery	91	9	85	15	64	36
Total violent crime	**86**	**14**	**74**	**26**	**84**	**16**
Break and enter	94	6	90	10	60	40
Motor vehicle theft	93	7	86	14	58	42
Fraud	70	30	67	33	93	7
Theft over $5000	79	21	83	17	81	19
Theft $5000 and under	70	30	67	33	73	27
Total property crime	**77**	**23**	**78**	**22**	**72**	**28**
Mischief	88	12	89	11	66	34
Arson	81	19	87	13	59	41
Prostitution	46	54	10	90	97	3
Offensive weapons	92	8	92	8	79	21
Total *Criminal Code*	**82**	**18**	**77**	**23**	**78**	**22**
Impaired driving[2]	90	10	88	12	99	1
Cocaine–possession	82	18	68	32	95	5
Cocaine–trafficking	84	16	72	23	95	5
Cannabis–possession	90	10	89	11	83	17
Cannabis–trafficking	84	16	89	11	85	15

(1) Canadians between the ages of 12 and 17. (2) Includes impaired operation of a vehicle causing death, causing bodily harm, alcohol rate of 80 mg failure, or refusal to provide a breath or blood sample.
SOURCE: *Uniform Crime Reporting Survey*, Canadian Centre of Justice Statistics, Statistics Canada. Cat. no. 11–008. Winter 1995, Number 39, page 19.

Age and Crime

In general, criminal activity is more prevalent among younger persons than among older persons. Figures 4.7 and 4.8 show the distribution of persons accused of property and violent offences, by age, in 1997. Although those aged 12 to 17 represent only 8.1 percent of the total Canadian population, they are overrepresented among those accused of criminal acts, particularly property offences. More than half (56 percent) of those accused of property crimes in 1997 and more than one-third (37 percent) of those accused of violent incidents in that year were under the age of 25 (Kong 1999).

Kong (1999) observes that the "prevalence of offending increases to a peak in teenage years and then decreases during one's twenties." She points out that the decline in the crime rate in recent years (e.g., from 1992 to 1997) has been accompanied by a decrease in the proportion of those aged 15 to 24 within the

Figure 4.7

Persons Accused of Violent Crime by Age, 1997

Nonrandom sample of 179 police agencies representing 18 percent of the national volume of crime. The data are not nationally representative.

SOURCE: Statistics Canada, "Persons Accused of Violent Crime by Age, 1997," adapted from *Juristat*, Cat. No. 85-002.

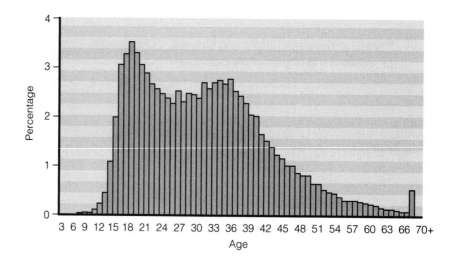

Figure 4.8

Persons Accused of Property Crime by Age, 1997

SOURCE: Statistics Canada. Adapted from *Juristat*, Cat. No. 85-002.

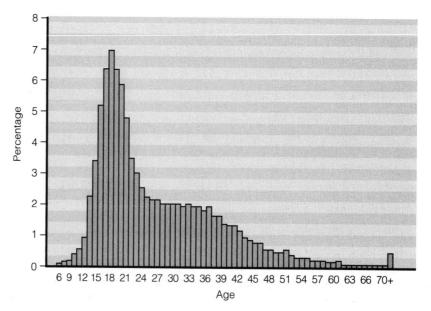

Canadian population. From 1986 to 1991, the number of individuals within this age category fell from 4.5 million to 4.1 million.

Why is criminal activity more prevalent among individuals in their teens and early 20s? One reason is that juveniles are insulated from many of the social and legal penalties for criminal behaviour. Younger individuals are also more likely to be unemployed or employed in low-wage jobs. Thus, as strain theorists argue, they have less access to legitimate means for acquiring material goods.

Some research suggests, however, that high-school students who have jobs become more, rather than less, involved in crime (Felson 1998: 120). In earlier generations, teenagers who worked did so to support themselves or their families. Today, teenagers who work typically spend their earnings on recreation and "extras," including car payments and gasoline. The increased mobility associated with having a vehicle also increases opportunities for criminal behaviour and reduces parental control.

Race, Social Class, and Crime

Race is a factor in who is arrested. The overrepresentation of Aboriginal peoples in the Canadian criminal justice system has been commented on by various commissions and task forces for more than three decades. Although Aboriginal peoples represent 2 percent of the adult population in Canada, they represented 15 percent of all sentenced admissions to provincial custody, 12 percent of all provincial probation intakes, and 17 percent of admissions to federal prisons in 1997–98 (Reed and Roberts 1999). Based on a one-day snapshot survey of all inmates in Canada's adult correctional facilities, Robinson et al. (1999) point out that Aboriginal persons accounted for 17 percent of adult inmates. In provincial and territorial facilities, 18 percent of inmates were Aboriginal peoples, and in federal facilities, 14 percent. The overrepresentation of Aboriginal peoples is particularly notable in the Prairie provinces of Canada (see Figure 4.9). Consider, for example, that while Aboriginals represent 9 percent of Manitoba's population, they account for 61 percent of the inmate population. In Alberta, where Aboriginals make up 4 percent of the provincial population, they account for more than one-third (34 percent) of inmates. As Table 4.4 indicates, there are only minor differences in the offence characteristics reported for Aboriginal and non-Aboriginal inmates.

La Prairie (1996) reports that, based on a review of the literature, Aboriginal inmates are more likely than non-Aboriginal inmates to be younger, to have had more extensive contact with both the criminal justice and correctional system, to come from more dysfunctional backgrounds and to serve prison sentences for defaulting on court-ordered fines. Aboriginal women, she notes, are particularly overrepresented in Canada's correctional institutions. Griffiths et al. (1994) earlier found that, based on their research on urban Aboriginal crime, Aboriginals are more likely than non-Aboriginals to be accused of either a property offence or violent crime.

Further, Hartnagel (2000) notes that other potential explanations for the overrepresentation of Aboriginal peoples within the Canadian criminal justice system include: "conflict between the values of Aboriginal culture and the dominant Canadian culture"; the social and economic aftermath of colonization and oppression; "the commission by Aboriginals of types of offences more likely to result in a justice system response; and a decline in interdependency

National Data

Although Aboriginal people constitute only 3 percent of the Canadian population, they accounted for 15 percent of all federal prison admissions and 16 percent of all provincial and territorial admissions in 1996–97.

SOURCE: Statistics Canada 1998a

Table 4.4 **Distribution of Offence Types by Aboriginal Status**

		Crimes Against the Person						
	# of inmates	Homicide/ Attempt Murder	Social Assault	Serious Assault	Minor Assault	Robbery	Other violent	Total
Provinces/Territories								
Aboriginal	3 941	3	8	12	7	8	2	40
Non-Aboriginal	17 406	4	6	5	5	9	3	32
CSC								
Aboriginal	1 964	23	20	10	–	21	4	79
Non-Aboriginal	11 865	24	12	3	–	25	8	72
Total Aboriginal	**5 905**	**10**	**12**	**11**	**5**	**12**	**3**	**53**

		Property Crimes				
	# of inmates	B and E	Theft	Fraud	Other property	Total
Provinces/Territories						
Aboriginal	3 941	18	8	2	7	35
Non-Aboriginal	17 406	18	8	5	6	37
CSC						
Aboriginal	1 964	13	1	–	2	16
Non-Aboriginal	11 865	12	1	–	2	15
Total Aboriginal	**5 905**	**16**	**6**	**2**	**5**	**28**
Total Non-Aboriginal	**29 271**	**16**	**5**	**3**	**4**	**28**

		Other *Criminal Code* (CC)/Federal Statutes					
	# of inmates	Weapons Offences	Admin & Justice	Impaired Offences	Drug Offences	Other CC/Fed	Total
Provinces/Territories							
Aboriginal	3 941	2	4	6	6	7	26
Non-Aboriginal	17 406	3	4	6	6	12	31
CSC							
Aboriginal	1 964	–	–	1	2	1	5
Non-Aboriginal	11 865	–	–	1	9	3	13
Total Aboriginal	**5 905**	**2**	**3**	**5**	**5**	**5**	**19**
Total Non-Aboriginal	**29 271**	**2**	**2**	**4**	**7**	**8**	**24**

– nil or zero

1 Only the most serious offence (MSO) is recorded.
2 Data were missing for 2332 provincial/territorial inmates (10 percent) and 33 CSC inmates (<1 percent)
SOURCE: Robinson et al. 1999

in Aboriginal communities, resulting in cultural dislocation and the decline of informal mechanisms of social control."

Nevertheless, it is inaccurate to conclude that race and crime are causally related. First, official statistics reflect the behaviours and policies of criminal justice actors. Thus, the high rate of arrests, conviction, and incarceration of Aboriginals may be a consequence of individual and institutional bias (e.g., police prejudice) not only against Aboriginals, but also against the lower class in general. Second, race and social class are closely related in that Aboriginals are overrepresented in the lower classes. Since lower-class members lack legitimate means to acquire material goods, they may turn to instrumental, or eco-

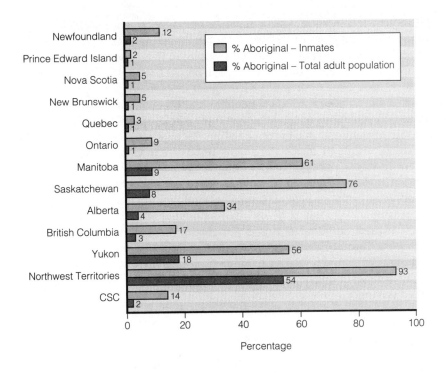

Figure 4.9

Aboriginal Persons—Proportion of Adult Population and Inmates by Jurisdiction

SOURCE: Robinson et al. 1999.

nomically motivated, crimes. Further, while the "haves" typically earn social respect through their socioeconomic status, educational achievement, and occupational role, the "have-nots" more often live in communities where respect is based on physical strength and violence, as subcultural theorists argue. Thus, the apparent relationship between race and crime may be, in part, a consequence of the relationship between these variables and social class.

Region and Crime

In Canada, the distribution of crime varies by region. Historically, an east–west distinction has been noted with crime rates in the Atlantic provinces and Quebec lower than those in Ontario and crime rates higher still in the Western provinces. Moreover, the rates of crime in Yukon and the Northwest Territories have traditionally been higher than those in the provinces.

Beginning in 1993, some variation in this pattern has been noted, with Alberta reporting rates of crime that are much lower than its neighbouring provinces. In 1997, provincial crime rates in Canada were lowest in Newfoundland (5571 per 100 000 population) and highest in British Columbia (12 870 per 100 000). In that year, and consistent with previous years, the highest rates of violent crime were reported in Manitoba, Saskatchewan, and British Columbia, and the lowest rates of crime reported in Quebec. Among census metropolitan areas, Thunder Bay had the highest rate of violent crime (1810 incidents per 100 000 population), followed by Regina (1638), Winnipeg (1456), Saskatoon (1397), and Victoria (1385); the lowest occurred in Sherbooke (410) and Trois-Rivières (488). In 1997, British Columbia had the highest reported rate of property crimes, followed by Saskatchewan and Manitoba; among CMAs, Regina reported the highest rate of property crime and Saint John the lowest (Kong 1999).

Although folk wisdom might suggest that there is more crime in larger cities than in small cities or towns, this is not, in fact, the case. While greater numbers of crime do, indeed, occur in larger than in smaller cities, this must be set against the greater number of people living in such areas. Leonard (1999) notes that, "[i]n 1996, 61% of Canadians lived in 24 major metropolitan areas (cities that have at least 100 000 people), and 61% of Canada's 2.6 million *Criminal Code* violations occurred within these metropolitan areas. Thus, a proportionate amount of crime occurred within the big cities as it did outside." In like fashion, although many Canadians believe that violent crime is more prevalent in Canada's major metropolitan areas than in its small towns, this perception is also inaccurate. As Leonard points out, "in 1995, 58% of violent crime occurred in the 24 biggest [Canadian] cities, which accounted for 61% of the population." While it may also be supposed that Canada's largest cities have the highest crime rates, this is not always the case. For example, from 1991 to 1995, Toronto, Canada's largest metropolitan area, had rates for the following offences that were generally lower than both the CMA average and the national average: homicide, arson, break and enter, motor vehicle fraud, and impaired driving.

COSTS OF CRIME AND VIOLENCE

Crime does not only or most primarily result in physical injury and loss of life or property; other, less tangible costs are incurred. Although the immediate victims of criminal acts bear the costs of crime most acutely, the economic, social, and psychological costs of crime may be experienced by a far broader constituency.

Economic Costs of Crime and Violence

Conklin (1998: 71–72) suggests that the financial costs of crime can be classified into at least six categories. First are direct losses from crime such as the destruction of buildings through arson, of private property through vandalism, and of the environment by polluters. Second are costs associated with the transferring of property. Bank robbers, car thieves, and embezzlers have all taken property from its rightful owner at tremendous expense to the victim and to society. For example, in 1993, computer thieves stole nearly $2 billion worth of copyrighted software programs over the Internet, and in 1995 an estimated $250 million worth of CDs and cassette tapes were illegally copied in China (Faison 1996; Meyer and Underwood 1994).

A third major cost of crime is that associated with criminal violence, such as the loss of productivity of injured workers and the medical expenses of victims. Fourth are the costs associated with the production and sale of illegal goods and services, that is, illegal expenditures. The expenditure of money on drugs, gambling, and prostitution diverts funds away from the legitimate economy and enterprises and lowers property values in high-crime neighbourhoods. Fifth is the cost of prevention and protection, that is, the millions of dollars spent on house alarms, security devices, weapons for protection, bars for windows, timers for lights, automobile security systems, and the like.

Finally, there is the cost of the criminal justice system. Figure 4.10 indicates the distribution of government spending on justice services in Canada in

1994–95. In that year, the government of Canada spent almost $10 billion on justice services: $5.8 billion on policing, $1.7 billion on courts, legal aid and prosecution, and $2.4 billion on youth and adult correctional services. It should be noted, however, that this figure underestimates the costs of crime; not included in these figures are the expenses incurred in building prisons or for other capital expenditures, nor those monies spent on justice policy research or victim compensation programs. The National Crime Prevention Council reports that, based on their formula, which factors in the costs of "unreported crime, the cost of property damage and insurance pay-outs, health care and hospitalization, voluntary caregiver long-term costs, the installations of private security systems and other cautionary measures taken to prevent victimization," the cost of crime in Canada in 1996 was approximately $46 billion (Statistics Canada 1998a).

Social and Psychological Costs of Crime and Violence

Crime and violence entail social and psychological, as well as economic, costs. According to the 1996 International Crime Victimization Survey, Canadians are less likely than those in Sweden, Finland, Switzerland, the Netherlands, France, Austria, Northern Ireland, or the United States to report that they feel safe walking alone in their neighbourhoods after dark. When asked what they felt the chances were of someone breaking into their home in the coming year, 30 percent of Canadians felt this was "likely" or "very likely"—a figure that was the third highest among the 11 Western industrialized countries surveyed. Approximately one-quarter of Canadians (24 percent) reported that, for safety reasons, they avoided certain places or people when out alone after dark and almost 8 out of 10 Canadians (78 percent) reported possessing at least one of seven home security measures: a burglar alarm, special door locks, special

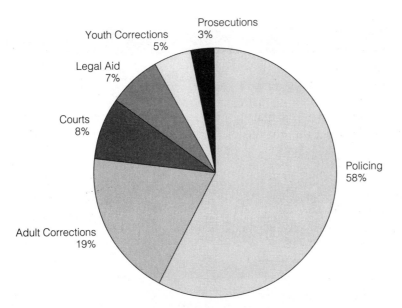

Total Expenditures: $10 billion
Total per Capita: $340

Figure 4.10
Government Spending on Justice Services, Canada, 1994–95
SOURCE: Canadian Centre for Justice Statistics, Statistics Canada.

National Data

In 1996–97, total expenditures on legal aid were $536.1 million or $17.90 per Canadian. In that year, there were 824 451 applications submitted for legal aid assistance; of this number, 510 914 were approved.

SOURCE: Johnstone and Thomas 1999

window or door grills, a watchdog, a high fence, a neighbourhood watch scheme, or a caretaker or security guard (see Table 4.5) (Besserer 1999).

In various ways, it is evident that fear of crime and violence affects community life:

If frightened citizens remain locked in their homes instead of enjoying public spaces, there is a loss of public and community life, as well as a loss of "social capital"—the family and neighbourhood channels that transmit positive social values from one generation to the next. (National Research Council 1994: 5–6)

White-collar crimes also take a social and psychological toll at both the individual and the societal levels. Moore and Mills (1990) state that the effects of white-collar crime include "(a) diminished faith in a free economy and in business leaders, (b) loss of confidence in political institutions, processes and leaders, and (c) erosion of public morality" (p. 414). Crime also causes personal pain and suffering, the destruction of families, lowered self-esteem, and shortened life expectancy and disease.

STRATEGIES FOR ACTION: RESPONDING TO CRIME AND VIOLENCE

In addition to economic policies designed to reduce unemployment and poverty, numerous social policies and programs have been initiated to alleviate the problem of crime and violence. These policies and programs are directed toward children at risk of being offenders, community crime prevention, media violence, and criminal justice policies.

Table 4.5 **Use of Household Security Measures**

(% households)	Special Door Locks	Watchdog	Watch Scheme	Special Grills	High Fence	Burglar Alarm	Caretaker/ Security Guard
Austria	38	14	2	12	6	6	1
Canada	**52**	**27**	**34**	**20**	**19**	**19**	**12**
England and Wales	68	25	47	27	41	27	4
Finland	..	..	..	..	..	..	..
France	35	22	42	14	13	14	13
Netherlands	68	16	9	11	13	14	13
Northern Ireland	33	24	2	12	14	11	–
Scotland	62	23	28	21	29	25	3
Sweden	39	12	6	7	2	6	1
Switzerland	28	13	4	11	1	5	6
United States	59	36	38	22	14	21	8
Average	48	21	21	16	15	14	6

– nil or zero
.. figures not available

SOURCE: *International Crime Victimization Survey 1996*

Youth Programs

Early intervention programs acknowledge that it is better to prevent crime than to "cure" it once it has occurred. Preschool enrichment programs, such as the Perry Preschool Project, have been successful in reducing rates of aggression in young children. After random assignment of children to either a control or experimental group, experimental group members received academically oriented interventions for one to two years, frequent home visits, and weekly parent–teacher conferences. When control and experimental groups were compared, the experimental group had better grades, higher rates of high-school graduation, lower rates of unemployment, and fewer arrests (Murray et al. 1997).

Recognizing the link between youthful offenders and adult criminality, many anticrime programs are directed toward at-risk youths. These prevention strategies, including youth programs such as Boys and Girls Clubs and the national Aboriginal Head Start program are designed to keep young people "off the streets," provide a safe and supportive environment, and offer activities that promote skill development and self-esteem. According to Gest and Friedman (1994), housing projects with such clubs report 13 percent fewer juvenile crimes and a 25 percent decrease in the use of crack.

Finally, many youth programs are designed to engage juveniles in non-criminal activities. While sports are probably the most common example, other recreation-based programs entail music, theatre arts, dance, and the visual arts. One such program was developed in Chicago in 1991. Aimed at the city's thousands of inner-city, unemployed, low-income youths between the ages of 14 and 21, "Gallery 37" now provides more than 2000 paid apprenticeship positions with local artists. The program is so successful that similar programs now exist in 16 U.S. cities as well as Adelaide, Australia, and London, England (OJP 1998).

Community Programs

Neighbourhood Watch programs, Block Parents, Crime Stoppers, and Operation Identification involve local residents in crime-prevention strategies. The objective of such programs is to reduce crime by heightening community involvement in crime-prevention strategies. Neighbourhood Watch programs, which are developed with the help of local police departments or services, offer advice on how residents may best protect their homes and belongings and encourage participants to watch out for and report suspicious activities in their neighbourhoods to the police. Some communities also offer alternative dispute resolution (ADR) centres. These centres encourage community members who are involved in a conflict to meet with mediators to discuss their conflicts and try to find a mutually agreeable resolution.

Community victim–offender dispute resolution programs are premised on the idea that by bringing victimizers and their victims together in face-to-face settings, both will benefit. For example, if committing a crime requires, to varying degrees, that an offender discounts the consequences of his or her act on the victim or blames the victim (e.g., "she's got insurance to cover the loss," "he was asking for it"), it is thought that face-to-face meetings will encourage a sense of personal culpability and compassion for the victim. Similarly, if the *hindsight effect* encourages victims to overestimate the extent to which they could have avoided victimization (Janoff-Bulman et al. 1985), confronting one's victimizer may result in a lessened amount of self-blame. Moreover, insofar as those who have experienced criminal victimization are likely to demonstrate a heightened fear of crime, it may prove personally empowering to see one's victimizer as simply another human being.

Media Violence

Violence is portrayed in music lyrics, music videos, video games, cartoons, television series, and movies. Consider, for example, such wildly popular "shooter" video games as the Duke Nukem series, Marathon, Descent, and Quake. In Duke Nukem 3D, the shooter moves through pornography stores where triple-X sex posters are used for target practice and Duke, his gun ever ready, directs prostitutes to "Shake it, baby." In this game, bonus points are awarded for the murder of these women; one level of the game features naked women tied to columns pleading, "Kill me; kill me." A 1996 report found that 85 percent of premium channel shows, 59 percent of basic cable shows, and 44 percent of broadcast channel shows included at least one act of violence (Farhi 1996). Such media images may desensitize individuals to violence and serve as models for violent behaviour. Exposure to television violence is associated with increased aggressive behaviour and decreased sensitivity to the pain and suffering of others (Comstock 1993; Murray 1993).

It has also been suggested that the way in which the media report crime may exacerbate public fearfulness. According to the Center for Media and Public Affairs, an analysis of the ABC, NBC, and CBS nightly newscasts from 1990 through 1996 revealed that while coverage of crime ranked sixth from 1990 to 1992, it skyrocketed to first place after that with 7448 stories devoted to crime in a four-year period. Approximately 1 out of every 20 American network news stories over that four-year period was about a murder, suggesting an unprecedented electronic crime wave (Kurtz 1997). It is evident that cable television need not only bring us *Frasier* and *Ally McBeal*. Moreover, according to the National Media Archive, a division of the Fraser Institute, which examined 98 Canadian supper-hour TV newscasts that were aired on three dates in 1997 (July 25, August 28, and September 24), "chaos news" (the term used to refer to news reports on crime, accidents, and natural disasters) accounted for 22 percent of local Canadian TV news items. In comparison to the United States, Canadian newscasts are more likely than American newscasts to feature news about government and governance (25.5 percent versus 13.1 percent) and "soft news" (e.g., general human interest stories, stories about entertainment, the arts, and culture) (27.3 percent versus 20.3 percent). American stations are also much more likely to lead or begin their newscasts with a report on crime, accidents or disasters; 72 percent of U.S. newscasts, versus 34.7 of Canadian newscasts, lead off with chaos news.

Criminal Justice Policy

The criminal justice system is based on the principle of **deterrence**, that is, the use of harm or the threat of harm to prevent unwanted behaviours. It assumes that people rationally choose to commit crime, weighing the rewards and consequences of their actions. Thus, the recent emphasis on "get tough" measures holds that maximizing punishment will increase deterrence and cause crime rates to decrease. Research indicates, however, that the effectiveness of deterrence is a function of not only the severity of the punishment, but the certainty and swiftness of the punishment as well. Further, "get tough" policies create other criminal justice problems, including overcrowded prisons, and, consequently, the need for plea-bargaining and early release programs.

Capital Punishment With capital punishment, the state (the federal government in Canada) takes the life of a person as punishment for a crime. Although capital punishment has not been used in Canada since 1962 and was formally abolished in this country in 1976, the state, of course, retains the right to bring it back. Since the 1970s, Gallup polls have consistently noted that the majority of Canadians believe that the courts are too lenient with offenders: in 1995, approximately 85 percent of a national random sample of Canadians maintained that the courts did not deal harshly enough with criminals, particularly young offenders, and about 82 percent believed that the death penalty should be exercised in some instances. While support for the reinstatement of capital punishment is somewhat lower in Quebec and marginally higher in the Prairie provinces, on a national level, support for the death penalty has been remarkably consistent over time. Consider, for example, that in the fall of 1943, Gallup reported that 80 percent of Canadians were in favour of capital punishment. At present, there are only small reported differences between women and men, and younger and older Canadians in their level of support for capital punishment (Bibby 1995).

Proponents of capital punishment argue that executions of convicted murderers are necessary to convey public disapproval and intolerance for such heinous crimes. Opponents of capital punishment believe that no one, including the state, has the right to take another person's life and that putting convicted murderers behind bars for life is a "social death" that conveys the necessary societal disapproval.

Proponents of capital punishment also argue that it deters individuals from committing murder. Critics of capital punishment hold, however, that since most homicides are situational and are not planned, offenders do not consider the consequences of their actions before they commit the offence. Critics also point out that the United States has a much higher murder rate than Canada or Western European nations that do not practise capital punishment and that death sentences are racially discriminatory.

Capital punishment advocates suggest that executing a convicted murderer relieves the taxpayer of the costs involved in housing, feeding, guarding, and providing medical care for inmates. Opponents of capital punishment argue that the principles that decide life and death issues should not be determined by financial considerations. In addition, taking care of convicted murderers for life may actually be less costly than sentencing them to death, due to the lengthy and costly appeal process for capital punishment cases (Garey 1985; "Myths" 1998).

Nevertheless, those in favour of capital punishment argue that it protects society by preventing convicted individuals from committing another crime, including the murder of another inmate or prison official. Opponents contend, however, that capital punishment may result in innocent people being sentenced to death. According to Radelet et al. (1992), at least 139 innocent people were sentenced to death in the United States between 1985 and 1990. Twenty-three of these people were eventually executed.

International Data

According to the 1996 International Crime Victimization Survey, among 11 Western industrialized countries, Canada had the highest percentage (80 percent) of the public who believed that the police in their area were doing a good job at controlling crime, followed by the United States (77 percent), Scotland (69), England and Wales (68), Northern Ireland (63), Sweden (62), France (56), Finland (55), Austria (55), and the Netherlands (45).

SOURCE: Besserer 1999

National Data

On an average day in 1996–97, there were 34 200 inmates in Canada's prisons and penitentiaries; in an average month, there were more than 117 000 individuals on conditional release from Canadian correctional facilities.

SOURCE: Statistics Canada 1998a

Rehabilitation versus Incapacitation

Another important debate focuses on the primary purpose of the criminal justice system: Is it to rehabilitate offenders or to incapacitate them through incarceration? Both **rehabilitation** and **incapacitation** are concerned with recidivism rates, or the extent to which criminals commit another crime. Advocates of rehabilitation believe recidivism can be reduced by changing the criminal, whereas proponents of incapacitation think it can best be reduced by placing the offender in prison so that he or she is unable to commit further crimes.

Societal fear of crime has led to a public emphasis on incapacitation, a demand for tougher mandatory sentences, a reduction in the use of probation and parole, support of a "three strikes and you're out" policy, and truth-in-sentencing laws (DiIulio 1999). While incapacitation is clearly enhanced by longer prison sentences, rehabilitation may not be. Rehabilitation assumes that criminal behaviour is caused by sociological, psychological, and/or biological forces rather than being solely a product of free will. If such forces can be identified, the necessary change can be instituted. Rehabilitation programs include education and job training, individual and group therapy, substance abuse counselling, and behaviour modification. While the evaluation of rehabilitation programs is difficult and results are mixed, incapacitation must of necessity be a temporary measure. Unless all criminals are sentenced to life, at some point about 98 percent will be returned to society.

Gun Control In 1995, the majority of victims of violent crime in Canada did not encounter a weapon (72 percent) and only 2 percent encountered a firearm. Of the approximately 1100 deaths caused by firearms in 1995, almost 8 in 10 (81 percent) of firearm deaths were the result of suicide; firearm homicides represented only 13 percent of all firearm deaths in Canada in that year.

While approximately one-third of homicides involve a firearm each year, the type of firearm used has changed in the past two decades. From 1975 to 1990, slightly less than 3 in 10 (29 percent) firearm homicides involved handguns and just more than 6 in 10 (61 percent) involved shotguns and rifles. Since 1991, however, handguns have accounted for about one-half of all firearm homicides. The use of handguns in homicides is most common in Canada's large urban areas, with handguns responsible for three-quarters of all firearm homicides in Toronto, Montreal, and Vancouver (Leesti 1999).

In 1977, Bill C-51, which introduced stricter gun control provisions, was passed in Canada. It introduced new firearm offences, increased penalties for gun-related offences, mandatory and discretionary prohibitions from possessing firearms, and additions to the categories of prohibited and restricted weapons. Two years later, additional changes in the bill came into effect with the introduction of the Firearm Acquisition Certificate (FAC), a requirement that allows for the screening of would-be gun purchasers, and the Firearm and Ammunition Business Permit systems. In the late 1980s, the government began drafting legislation designed to further strengthen gun control laws in Canada and, in 1991, Bill C-17 was passed. The intent of Bill C-17 was to enhance the FAC screening process; to strengthen both prohibition orders and regulations that required the safe storage, handling, display, and transportation of firearms; and to deter would-be offenders from using firearms in the commission of criminal acts.

The most recent legislation in this area, Bill C-68, resulted in the creation of a new *Firearms Act* in 1995 and in the amendment of the Canadian *Criminal Code*. These changes require all firearm owners and users to be licensed and to register all the firearms they possess. Additional changes include the creation of new offences for gun smuggling and trafficking, the prohibition of a number of different types of handguns, and the introduction of mandatory penalties for those employing firearms in the commission of a crime (Leesti 1999). Under the Canadian *Criminal Code*, prohibited weapons offences include carrying, pointing, or possessing such prohibited weapons as sawed-off or automatic firearms, silencers, or spring knives. Restricted weapon offences include carrying, pointing, or possessing restricted weapons without permits.

According to a 1991 Angus Reid survey on firearm ownership in Canada based on a representative, random survey of 10 000 Canadian households, at least one firearm was owned in almost one-quarter (23 percent) of Canadian households, with rifles and shotguns most common. Within private households that year, there were 3.1 million rifles and 2.3 million shotguns. The most common reason given for the ownership of such weapons was "hunting." In addition, data compiled from the Firearms Registration and Administration Section of the RCMP indicates that there are almost one million handguns registered in Canada; "target shooting" and "collecting" were the most commonly given reasons for ownership of handguns. It is evident, however, that these numbers may well underestimate the number of firearms currently in circulation in Canada.

Law Enforcement Agencies Police policies and practices can also affect crime rates. Seagrave (1997) noted that the mission statements of every Canadian police force in the 1990s contained evidence of formal commitment to the concept of community policing. Community-oriented policing involves collaborative efforts among the police, the citizens of a community, and local leaders. As part of community policing efforts, officers speak to citizens groups, consult with social agencies, and enlist the aid of corporate and political leaders in the fight against neighbourhood crime (COPS 1998; Lehrur 1999).

Officers using community-policing techniques often employ "practical approaches" to crime intervention. Such solutions may include what Felson (1998) calls "situational crime prevention." Felson argues that much of crime could be prevented simply by minimizing the opportunity for its occurrence. For example, cars could be outfitted with unbreakable glass, flush-sill lock buttons, an audible reminder to remove keys, and a high-security lock for steering columns (p. 168).

Finally, programs aimed at crime victims now exist in almost all police departments in Canada. Victim assistance programs are designed to provide crime victims with details on the progress of their case, facilitate the return of property to rightful owners, and act as a referral agency to other support groups in the local community. Often heavily dependent on volunteers, such services may signal the development of a partnership between the police and a local community agency or institution. In Ottawa, the Salvation Army works in collaboration with the Ottawa Police Department to supply victim services. In Montreal, the University of Montreal, in cooperation with the Montreal Urban Community Police, operates the Integrated Victim Assistance program (Seagrave 1997).

National Data

In Canada, the minimum requirements for most police departments are at least 18 years of age, a grade 12 education or its equivalency, a valid driver's licence in good standing, proficiency in either English or French, the absence of a criminal record, good vision and hearing, and physical and mental fitness.
SOURCE: Swol 1999

National Data

In 1996, women had greater representation in private security than in public police services. In that year, they accounted for about one in five private investigators and security guards but merely 13 percent of police officers.
SOURCE: Swol 1999

What can we conclude from the information presented in this chapter? Research on crime and violence supports the contentions of both functionalists and conflict theorists. The inequality in society, along with the emphasis on material well-being and corporate profit, produces societal strains and individual frustrations. Poverty, unemployment, urban decay, and substandard schools, the symptoms of social inequality, in turn lead to the development of criminal subcultures and definitions favourable to law violation. Further, the continued weakening of social bonds between members of society and society as a whole, the labelling of some acts and actors as "deviant," and the differential treatment of minority groups at the hands of the criminal justice system encourage criminal behaviour.

While crime and violence constitute major social problems in society, they are also symptoms of other social problems, such as poverty and economic inequality, racial discrimination, drug addiction, an overburdened educational system, and troubled families. The criminal justice system continues to struggle to find effective and just measures to deal with crime and criminal offenders. Many citizens and politicians have embraced the idea that society should "get tough on crime." Get-tough measures include building more prisons and imposing lengthier mandatory prison sentences on criminal offenders. Advocates of harsher prison sentences argue that "getting tough on crime" makes society safer by keeping criminals off the streets and deterring potential criminals from committing crime. However, skeptics are not convinced. As one argues:

> Prison...has a minimal impact on crime because it is a response after the fact, a mop-up operation. It doesn't work. The idea of punishing the few to deter the many is counterfeit because potential criminals either think they're not going to get caught or they're so emotionally desperate or psychologically distressed that they don't care about the consequences of their actions. (Rideau 1994: 80).

Prison sentences may not only be ineffective in preventing crime, they may also promote it by creating an environment in which prisoners learn criminal behaviour, values, and attitudes from each other.

Rather than getting tough on crime after the fact, some advocate getting serious about prevention:

> The only effective way to curb crime is for society to work to prevent the criminal act in the first place....Our youngsters must be taught to respect the humanity of others and to handle disputes without violence. It is essential to educate and equip them with the skills to pursue their life ambitions in a meaningful way. As a community, we must address the adverse life circumstances that spawn criminality. (Rideau 1994: 80)

Re-emphasizing the values of honesty, responsibility, and civic virtue is a basic line of prevention with which most agree.

National Data

In 1996, although visible minorities accounted for 10 percent of the employed labour force in Canada, they were underrepresented among those who were employed as police officers (3 percent). In that year, Aboriginals were well represented. Although Aboriginal persons represented only 1.7 percent of the employed labour force, they represented 3.0 percent of all police officers.

SOURCE: Swol 1999

National Data

During 1997–98, the most frequently occurring offence in adult criminal court was impaired driving, which accounted for 15 percent of all offences and almost 90 percent of all traffic cases.

SOURCE: Brookbank and Kingsley 1999

However, as William DeJong (1994) has observed:

If we are truly committed to preventing violence, we must do more than teach individual children how to survive in the dysfunctional environments in which they are growing up. We must also strive to change those environments by addressing the broader social, cultural, institutional, and physical forces that are at work. (p. 9)

CRITICAL THINKING

1. Crime statistics are sensitive to demographic changes. Suggest how the aging of the Canadian population may affect Canadian crime rates as we move into the twenty-first century.
2. Some countries have high rates of gun ownership and low crime rates. Others have low rates of gun ownership and low crime rates. What do you think accounts for the differences between these countries?
3. One of the criticisms of crime theories is that they do not explain all crime, all of the time. Identify the theories of crime that are most useful in explaining categories of crime, for example, white-collar crime, violent crime, sex crimes, and so on. Explain your choices.
4. The use of technology in crime-related matters is likely to increase dramatically over the next several decades. DNA testing, and the use of heat sensors, blood-detecting chemicals, and computer surveillance are just some of the ways science will help fight crime. As with all technological innovations, however, there is the question, "Who benefits?" Are there gender, race, and class implications of these new technologies?

KEY TERMS

acquaintance rape	crime	rehabilitation
classic rape	deterrence	strain theory
computer crime	differential association	street crime
control theory	incapacitation	subcultural theory
conventional crime	labelling theory	victimless crimes
corporate murder	organized crime	white-collar crime

CHAPTER FIVE

Family Problems

Is It True?

1. Since the 1970s, most Canadian women have been delaying their first childbirth until their late 20s and early 30s.

2. One in eight Canadians over the age of 15 provides some kind of care for others who are dealing with a long-term health care problem or a physical limitation.

3. If current rates are maintained, about 3700 out of every 10 000 marriages will end in divorce.

4. Only 1 in 10 Canadians believes that an unfaithful partner or lack of love and respect are sufficient reasons to divorce.

5. In Canada, a husband who forces his wife to have sex is committing a criminal offence.

Answers: 1 = T, 2 = T, 3 = T, 4 = F, 5 = T

An unhealthy culture cannot have healthy families.

Mary Pipher,
"The Shelter of Each
Other:
Rebuilding Our
Families"

Politicians often point to the "breakdown" of the family as one of the primary social problems in the world today—a problem of such magnitude that it leads to such secondary social problems as crime, poverty, and substance abuse. Although strengthening family relationships and values is frequently offered as the principal solution to such problems, sociologists argue that family problems and their solutions are rooted in the structure and culture of society. For example, the structure of the economic institution requires many parents to work long hours, often without benefits. Without a national childcare system, such as those in France and Sweden, employed parents of young children must often leave their offspring with inadequate or no supervision. Parents and spouses who are stressed by long work hours, poor working conditions, and little pay often bring their stress home, contributing to child abuse, spouse abuse, and divorce.

Families in Canada are also influenced by cultural factors. For example, the North American value of **individualism**, which stresses the importance of individual happiness, contributes to divorce as spouses leave marriages to pursue their individual goals. In other countries, such as India, the cultural value of **familism** encourages spouses to put their family's welfare above their individual and personal needs.

In this chapter, we look at some of the major social problems facing Canadian families—domestic violence, divorce, unmarried childbirth, and teenage parenthood. Prior and subsequent chapters in this text discuss other problems facing families, including poverty, lack of affordable housing, illness and inadequate health care, drug abuse, inequality in education, prejudice and discrimination, and problems in balancing work and family demands.

THE GLOBAL CONTEXT: FAMILIES OF THE WORLD

Family is a central aspect of every society throughout the world, but family forms are diverse. Although the only legal form of marriage in Canada is between one woman and one man, other societies practise polygamy, a form of marriage in which there are more than two spouses. Other societies legally recognize same-sex unions.

Family values, roles, and norms are also highly variable across societies. For example, in most Western countries, fathers are expected to be the child's primary adult male figure in terms of nurturance, socialization, and economic support. Yet, in some African societies, the mother's brother—the child's uncle—fulfils such a role. Unlike in Western societies, in some Asian countries, some marriages are arranged by the parents who select mates for their children. Another traditional Asian practice is for the eldest son and his wife to move in with the son's parents, where his wife takes care of her husband's parents. In some societies, it is normal for married couples to view each other as equal partners in the marriage, whereas in other societies social values dictate that wives be subservient to their husbands. The role of children also varies across societies. In some societies, children are expected to work full-time to help support the family (see discussion of child labour in Chapter 11).

It is clear from the previous discussion that families are shaped by the social and cultural context in which they exist. Next, we look at variations in Canadian families.

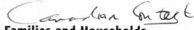

Variations in Canadian Families and Households

The term "family" stems from word **famulus**, the Latin word for "servant" (Gottlieb 1993). The word *familia* was used in classical times to refer to the live-in staff of a household, and from there, it came to mean the housestaff or the members of it. The term **"pater familias"** was so commonly used to refer to a "householder" that it took on the connotation of "an ordinary citizen." **Mater familias** was also commonly used to refer to the "woman of the house" in the sense of the person who directed its domestic affairs. These terms may sound foreign to modern ears, but they provide a hint that defining what is and is not a "family" has varied over time and space.

For the Canadian census, an **economic family** is a group of individuals sharing a common dwelling unit who are related by blood, marriage (including common-law relationships), or adoption. This definition also alerts us to some of the changes that have occurred recently in relation to the family. As Figure 5.1 indicates, between 1981 (the first time a Canadian census reported common-law marriages) and 1996, the number of such unions tripled. In 1996, almost two million Canadians lived common law. In Quebec, almost one couple in four is in a common-law relationship. Moreover, the growth in lone-parent families has also changed the face of Canadian families. In 1996, there were 1.1 million lone-parent families, 83 percent of which were headed by women.

In addition, questions on remarriage were asked for the first time by Statistics Canada in 1995 and the results indicate that there are about 430 000 stepfamilies in Canada, about 10 percent of all couple families with children. The composition of stepfamilies suggests the plurality of Canadian families. In 1995, slightly more than half of all Canadian stepfamilies consisted of a mother, her children, and a stepfather; 10 percent were composed of a father, his children, and a stepmother; and more than a third were reconstituted or blended families. A **blended family** consists of remarried spouses with at least one of the spouses having a child from a previous relationship.

Consider as well that in May 1999, the Supreme Court of Canada ruled that an Ontario law that excluded gays and lesbians from a definition of common-law couples was unconstitutional. Soon after the court's decision, the

Figure 5.1
Changing Family Structures
SOURCE: Statistics Canada 1998a

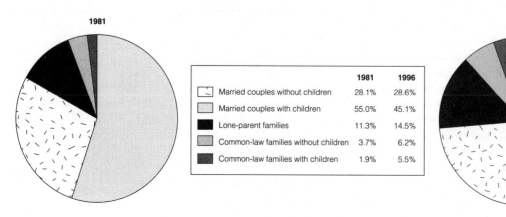

	1981	1996
Married couples without children	28.1%	28.6%
Married couples with children	55.0%	45.1%
Lone-parent families	11.3%	14.5%
Common-law families without children	3.7%	6.2%
Common-law families with children	1.9%	5.5%

Ontario government passed an omnibus bill that amended 67 of its laws to include same-sex couples. Other provinces reportedly plan to make similar changes (see Chapter 9). As variations in family forms have become more common, many family scholars are advocating new cultural and legal definitions of the family. Geile (1996) suggests that "recognition as 'family' should...not be confined to the traditional two-parent unit connected by blood, marriage, or adoption, but should be extended to include kin of a divorced spouse...same-sex partners, congregate households of retired persons, group living arrangements, and so on" (pp. 103–4).

Increasingly, social and legal policy and court decisions are expanding the concept of family to include unmarried living-together couples and same-sex couples who live together and view themselves as a family.

Although marriage and family forms have become diversified, marriage and family are still important to most Canadians. An examination of the sociological theories of the family will provide a framework for our discussion of various problems related to the family.

SOCIOLOGICAL THEORIES OF THE FAMILY

Three major sociological theories of the family—structural-functionalism, conflict theory, and symbolic interactionism—explain different aspects of the family.

Structural-Functionalist Perspective

The structural-functionalist perspective emphasizes that families perform functions that are important for the survival of society. Families replenish the population through reproduction and contribute to the socialization and education of youth. Well-functioning families also provide emotional and physical care for their members.

The structural-functionalist perspective is also concerned with how other institutions affect families. The educational, health care, religious, economic, and political institutions each affect families and their members.

Conflict Perspective

Conflict theory focuses on how wealth and power influence marriages and families. Within families, the unequal distribution of power among women, men, and children may contribute to spouse and child abuse. The unequal distribution of wealth between men and women, with men traditionally earning more money than women, contributes to inequities in power and fosters economic dependence of wives on husbands. The term **patriarchy** refers to male-dominated families. Families have traditionally been dominated by men, with the wife taking her husband's name, family residence defined by the husband's place of work, and the standard of living dictated by the male's income.

Conflict theorists emphasize that social programs and policies that affect families are largely shaped by powerful and wealthy segments of society. The interests of corporations and businesses are often in conflict with the needs of families. Hewlett and West (1998) note that corporate interests undermine family life "by exerting enormous downward pressure on wage levels for young, child-raising adults" (p. 32). Government, which is largely influenced by corporate interests through lobbying and political financial contributions, enacts policies and laws that serve the interests of for-profit corporations, rather than families.

Symbolic Interactionist Perspective

Symbolic interactionism emphasizes that human behaviour is largely dependent on the meanings and definitions that emerge out of small group interaction. Divorce, for example, was once highly stigmatized and informally sanctioned through the criticism and rejection of divorced friends and relatives. As societal definitions of divorce became less negative, however, the divorce rate increased. The social meanings surrounding single parenthood, cohabitation, and delayed childbearing and marriage have changed in similar ways. As the definitions of each of these family variations became less negative, the behaviours became more common.

Symbolic interactionists also point to the effects of labelling on one's self-concept and the way the self-fulfilling prophecy can affect family members' behaviour toward one another. The **self-fulfilling prophecy** implies that we behave according to the expectations of others. When family members label children as "bad" or "stupid," children may internalize these labels and view themselves as "bad" or "stupid." For some children, a negative self-concept and the self-fulfilling prophecy contribute to violence, crime and delinquency, school failure, and mental health problems such as depression and anxiety. As the following section explains, painful criticism of spouses, children, and elders may constitute a form of domestic abuse.

Figure 5.2
Importance of Family and Career, by Age and Gender
SOURCE: Bibby 1995

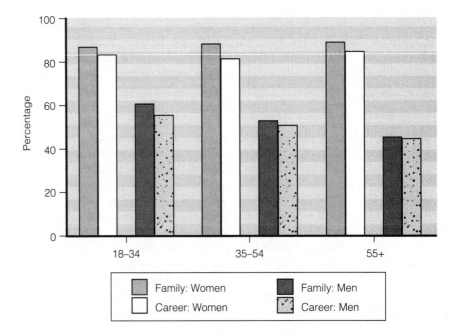

VIOLENCE AND ABUSE IN THE FAMILY

Although marriage and family relationships provide many individuals with a sense of intimacy and well-being, for others these relationships involve violence and abuse causing terror, pain, injury, and, for some, death. Domestic abuse can take various forms besides physical violence, including verbal and emotional abuse, and sexual abuse. **Neglect**, another form of abuse, includes failure to provide adequate attention and supervision, food and nutrition, hygiene, medical care, and a safe and clean living environment.

Violence and Abuse in Marriage and Cohabiting Relationships

Although both men and women may be victims of abuse by intimate partners, domestic violence primarily involves female victims. Police incident reports and victimization surveys consistently note that women are overwhelmingly more likely than men to be the victims of police-reported conjugal violence and domestic homicide. Based on data obtained from 15 Canadian police departments, Trevethan and Samagh (1992) report that there are clear gender differences among the victims of the most violent crimes, as well as noting that men and women tend to be the victims of different types of offences. Seventy-five percent of the reported adult violent-crime victims were victims of assault. Women were more likely to be victims of assault at the hands of their husbands or ex-husbands (52 percent), while men were more likely to be assaulted by strangers (44 percent). However, not all sociologists agree that it is necessarily women who are more likely than men to be abused in an intimate relationship.

For example, Brinkerhoff and Lupri's (1988) study of 562 married or cohabiting relationships in Calgary found wife-to-husband violence to be more prevalent than husband-to-wife violence, as measured by both an overall violence scale and a severe violence scale. The rate for the former was found to be more than double the rate of the latter. Strauss and Gelles (1990) claim that "assaults by women on their male partners occur at about the same rate as assaults by men on their female partners, and women initiate such violence about as often as men" (p. 110). Gelles (1993) argues that "more women [are] using violence towards men than what shelter data indicate" (p. 32). Nevertheless, any notion of gender equality vanishes when it comes to the effects of violence (Pagelow 1992). As Straus (1992) emphasizes, even though she may throw the coffeepot first, generally he lands the last and most damaging blows. Many more wives than husbands need medical attention because of intimate violence (Dobash and Dobash 1992, 1995).

Physical abuse and emotional abuse, no doubt, are factors in many divorces. In addition to affecting the happiness and stability of relationships, abuse affects the physical and psychological well-being of the victim. Empirical research on heterosexual married or cohabiting couples additionally finds that intimate violence follows certain "social channels," thus making some men and women more likely to be abusers—or victims—than others. The highest rates of marital violence are found among families with low incomes and low educational levels; blue-collar workers and individuals under age 30; families in which the husband is unemployed; families with above-average numbers of children; families living in large urban areas; individuals who have no religious affiliation; and individuals who believe in and uphold traditional gender roles

Family Functioning Scale

INSTRUCTIONS

Every family has strengths and capabilities, although different families have different ways of using their abilities. This questionnaire asks you to indicate whether your family is characterized by 26 different qualities. Please read each statement, and then circle the response that is most true for your family (people living in your home). Please give your honest opinions and feelings. Remember that your family will not be like all the statements.

How is your family like the following statements:

	NOT AT ALL	A LITTLE	SOMETIMES	USUALLY	ALMOST ALWAYS
1. We make personal sacrifices if they help our family.	1	2	3	4	5
2. We usually agree about how family members should behave.	1	2	3	4	5
3. We believe that something good always comes out of even the worst situations.	1	2	3	4	5
4. We take pride in even the smallest accomplishments of family members.	1	2	3	4	5
5. We share our concerns and feelings in useful ways.	1	2	3	4	5
6. Our family sticks together no matter how difficult things get.	1	2	3	4	5
7. We usually ask for help from persons outside our family if we cannot do things ourselves.	1	2	3	4	5
8. We usually agree about the things that are important to our family.	1	2	3	4	5
9. We are always willing to pitch in and help each other.	1	2	3	4	5
10. We find things to do that keep our minds off our worries when something upsetting is beyond our control.	1	2	3	4	5
11. We try to look at the bright side of things no matter what happens in our family.	1	2	3	4	5
12. We find time to be together even with our busy schedules.	1	2	3	4	5
13. Everyone in our family understands the rules about acceptable ways to act.	1	2	3	4	5
14. Friends and relatives are always willing to help whenever we have a problem or crisis.	1	2	3	4	5
15. Our family is able to make decisions about what to do when we have problems or concerns.	1	2	3	4	5
16. We enjoy time together even if it is doing household chores.	1	2	3	4	5

	NOT AT ALL	A LITTLE	SOMETIMES	USUALLY	ALMOST ALWAYS
17. We try to forget our problems or concerns for a while when they seem overwhelming.	1	2	3	4	5
18. Family members listen to both sides of the story during a disagreement.	1	2	3	4	5
19. We make time to get things done that we all agree are important.	1	2	3	4	5
20. We can depend on the support of each other whenever something goes wrong.	1	2	3	4	5
21. We usually talk about the different ways we deal with problems and concerns.	1	2	3	4	5
22. Our family's relationships will outlast our material possessions.	1	2	3	4	5
23. We make decisions like moving or changing jobs for the good of all family members.	1	2	3	4	5
24. We can depend on each other to help out when something unexpected happens.	1	2	3	4	5
25. We try not to take each other for granted.	1	2	3	4	5
26. We try to solve our problems first before asking others to help.	1	2	3	4	5

(May be duplicated without permission with proper acknowledgment and citation.)

SCORING

Circling a 5 represents the optimum family functioning response in terms of family strengths. Circling a 1 represents the least optimum family functioning response. The scale was administered to 206 mothers and 35 fathers of preschool children. The majority of items had average ratings between 3.00 and 4.00.

SOURCE: Trivette, Carol M., Carl J. Dunst, Angela G. Deal, Deborah W. Hamby, and David Sexton. 1994. "Family Functioning Style Scale" in *Supporting and Strengthening Families: Volume 1—Methods, Strategies and Practices*, Chapter 10 "Assessing Family Strengths and Capabilities," edited by Carl J. Dunst, Carol M. Trivette, and Angela G. Deal, p. 139. Cambridge, Mass.: Brookline Books. Permission to reproduce granted in text.

(Gelles 1980). As well, cohabitators tend to have higher rates of intimate violence than do married and dating couples (Stets 1991; Stets and Straus 1989). One longitudinal study (O'Leary et al. 1989) finds that the likelihood of abuse occurring in a marriage is three times greater if abuse also occurred during the courtship phase of a relationship than if abuse did not occur during courtship. In addition, according to statistics provided by the DisAbled Women's Network (DAWN) in Toronto, women with disabilities face an increased risk of both sexual and physical abuse and find their emotional and physical safety jeopardized by the inaccessibility of support services (Health Canada 1999).

Intimate violence may also occur within gay and lesbian relationships. Waterman et al. (1989), in their study of a nonrandom sample of 34 gay and 36 lesbian college students found that 18 percent of the gay men and 40 percent of the lesbians reported having experienced violence within their current or most recent relationships. A third of the lesbians reported they had been subject to forced sex by their current partner. Two-thirds of Chesley et al.'s (1991) nonrandom sample of 189 women in Toronto, the majority of whom were White, middle-class lesbians possessing some college or university education (76 percent), reported knowing lesbians who had experienced abuse within an intimate relationship. One in five respondents perceived themselves as "survivors of some form of psychological, physical and/or sexual violence in their lesbian relationships" (Ristock 1991: 76) and three out of four felt abuse is a problem within the lesbian community.

Recognition that the most dangerous time for a victim of intimate violence was after leaving a violent relationship helped fuel the 1993 enactment of a law against "criminal harassment." This law is directed against "stalking" behaviours that may stem from a variety of motives including the adamant refusal of one relational partner "to believe that the relationship has ended" (Kong 1997). Stalking or criminal harassment includes repeatedly following, communication (via cards, letters, e-mails, and so on), or uttering direct or indirect threats or promises of violence or forcible intimacy.

According to research conducted by the Canadian Centre for Justice Statistics that analyzed the relationship of the victim and the stalker in 5023 incidents (more than 90 percent of which came from Ontario and Quebec), 8 out of 10 of the victims of criminal harassment were women, and more than half (58 percent) were stalked by an ex-husband, boyfriend, or current husband (Kong 1997). Another one-quarter of the women victims were stalked by casual acquaintances, and the rest by other family members, stranger, or coworkers. In contrast, almost half of the 977 male stalking victims were stalked by a casual acquaintance, usually another male, while 11 percent were stalked by coworkers. Few of the male victims of criminal harassment were stalked by an ex-wife or girlfriend.

Violence between intimate partners or ex-partners may also include unintentional death and intentional murder. Silverman and Kennedy (1993) observe that approximately 40 percent of all homicides that have occurred in Canada over the past 30 years have involved family members. Annual rates of spousal homicide in Canada remained relatively constant between 1974 and 1992, with the ratio of wives killed by their husbands to husbands killed by their wives being 3.2 to 1. A married woman was nine times more likely to be killed by her spouse than by a stranger. While women in Canada are more likely to be killed by husbands or ex-husbands (48 percent), men are more likely to be killed by acquaintances (53 percent) rather than by a wife or ex-wife, another family member, a friend, a business relation, or a stranger (Trevethan and Samagh 1993). Between 1974 and 1992, men also committed 94 percent of all familicides in Canada. **Familicide** refers to a form of spousal homicide in which the offender not only kills a spouse, but also kills one or more of a couple's children at the same time (Wilson and Daly 1994). Crawford et al. (1997) report that, between 1991 and 1994, an average of 40 women died each year in Ontario, 71 percent of them at the hands of a current or former husband, a cohabiting partner, or a boyfriend. Silverman and Kennedy (1993)

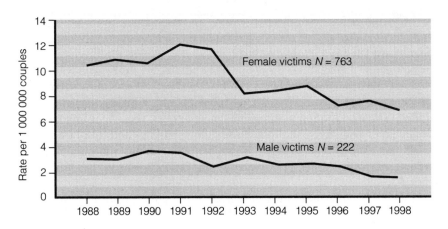

Figure 5.3
**Spousal Homicide Rate,
1988–98**
SOURCE: *Homicide Survey.* 1999. Canadian
Centre for Justice Statistics.

emphasize that most spousal homicides are the culmination of an escalating sequence of spousal violence and not a sudden isolated event.

The pattern described for the early 1990s has remained relatively constant, although the number of spousal homicides have steadily declined from 12 wives per million couples (which includes common-law, separated, or divorced couples) in 1991 to 7 per million in 1998. See Figure 5.3 for spousal homicide rates for 1988 to 1998. For husbands, the rate has decreased from four per million couples in 1990 to two per million in 1998.

Fedorowycz (1999) suggests this decline "may primarily be the result of reduced exposure to abusive or violent relationships as a consequence of the changing living arrangements of men and women, improvements in the economic status of women, and increases in the availability of domestic violence services (e.g., safe houses or shelters, counselling, financial aid)." However, women remained the most likely victims of lethal violence in spousal relationships, accounting for four out of five victims. In 1998, 46 women were killed by a current legal or common-law spouse and 11 were killed by a former (separated or divorced) spouse; women were almost five times more likely to be killed by a spouse (former or current) than a stranger. In that year, 13 men were killed by a spouse; in 12 cases, the perpetrator was a current spouse and in one case, a former spouse. In 6 out of 10 spousal homicides in that year, the couple were known to police as having a history of domestic violence; this was true for 7 out of 10 incidents involving a female victim and half of those incidents involving a male victim. In addition to those who were killed by a spouse, an additional 10 women were killed by either a boyfriend or an ex-boyfriend (versus two males killed by intimates other than spouses). Overall, more than half (55 percent) of female victims and 6 percent of male victims in 1998 were killed by someone whom, at some time, had been an intimate partner.

Domestic violence is also a primary cause of homelessness. One study found that half of homeless women and children were fleeing from abuse ("Domestic Violence and Homelessness" 1998). According to Novac et al. (1996), homelessness and violence are inextricably linked for women. They observe that "homeless women with histories of family disruption and abuse distinguish being housed from being safe, so that homelessness is a problem for women, but is also a strategy for escaping violence. The relationship between violence and homelessness among women is complex, since there is also a great risk of violence when women are homeless."

About 40 percent of battered women are abused during their pregnancy, resulting in a high rate of miscarriage and birth defects (North Carolina Coalition Against Domestic Violence 1991). Witnessing marital violence is related to emotional and behavioural problems in children and subsequent violence in their own relationships (Busby 1991). Children may also commit violent acts against a parent's abusing partner. According to the Violence Against Women Survey (VAWS), children witness violence against their mothers in about 40 percent of violent marriages, including more than 50 percent of the cases in which the women fear for their lives. The VAWS additionally reported that "women who were exposed to wife battering while growing up had rates of violence directed at them by their own husbands that were almost twice as high as women who grew up in non-violent environments" (Johnson 1996: 176).

Child Abuse

Child abuse refers to the "physical or mental injury, sexual abuse, negligent treatment, or maltreatment of a child under the age of 18 by a person who is responsible for the child's welfare…" (Willis et al. 1992: 2). The most common type of reported child abuse is neglect. Table 5.1 describes family assaults against children in Canada in 1996.

Reviews of research on the effects of child abuse suggest that abused children tend to exhibit aggression, low self-esteem, depression, and low academic achievement (Gelles and Conte 1991; Lloyd and Emery 1993). Adults who were physically abused as children may exhibit low self-esteem, depression, unhappiness, anxiety, an increased risk of alcohol abuse, and suicidal tendencies. Physical injuries sustained by child abuse cause pain, disfigurement, scarring, physical disability, and death.

Among adolescent females, sexual abuse is associated with lower self-esteem, higher levels of depression, antisocial behaviour (e.g., running away from home, illegal drug use), and suicide attempts (Morrow and Sorrell 1989). Sexually abused girls are also more likely to experience teenage pregnancy,

Table 5.1

Family Assaults against Children and Youth, by Type of Assault, by Sex[a] of Victim, and by Accused–Victim Relationship, Canada 1996

	Sexual assault			Physical assault		
	Total	Against Females	Against Males	Total	Against Females	Against Males
	0	440	0	3 328	1 855	1 473
Percent	100	100	100	100	100	100
Parent	43	42	48	64	59	70
Other immediate family[b]	28	29	24	21	21	21
Extended family[c]	27	27	28	7	6	8
Spouse of victim	1	2	1	8	14	1

a Cases where the sex of the victim was unknown were excluded.
b "Immediate family" includes natural, step, half, foster, and adopted siblings.
c "Extended family" includes others related by blood or marriage (e.g., grandparents, aunts, uncles, cousins).
SOURCES: *Assaults against Children and Youth in the Family.* 1997. Statistics Canada, Canadian Centre for Justice Statistics. Ottawa: Statistics Canada (Cat. No. 85-00-XPE, Vol. 17, No. 11) (data from *Revised Uniform Crime Reporting Survey*); Health Canada 1999.

have higher numbers of sexual partners in adulthood, acquire sexually transmitted infections, and experience forced sex (Browning and Laumann 1997; Stock et al. 1997).

Adult males who were sexually abused as children tend to exhibit depression, substance abuse, and difficulty establishing intimate relationships (Krug 1989). Sexually abused males also have a higher risk of anxiety disorders, sleep and eating disorders, and sexual dysfunction (Elliott and Briere 1992).

Elder Abuse

Elder abuse includes physical abuse, psychological abuse, financial abuse (such as improper use of the elder's financial resources), and neglect. Elder neglect includes failure to provide basic health and hygiene needs such as clean clothes, doctor visits, medication, and adequate nutrition. Neglect also involves unreasonable confinement, isolation of elderly family members, lack of supervision, and abandonment. In 1996, those 65 years of age and older were victims in only two percent of violent crimes reported to police; however, family members were involved in one in five of all violent crimes against older adults, with children and spouses accounting for the majority of perpetrators (44 percent and 34 percent, respectively). According to police statistics, the percentage of violent crimes committed by family members against seniors has remained constant since 1993, and spouses and children continued to account for the majority of accused in such cases (Health Canada 1999; Statistics Canada 1998a).

Factors Contributing to Domestic Violence and Abuse

Research suggests that cultural, community, and individual and family factors contribute to domestic violence and abuse (Willis et al. 1992).

Cultural Factors In many ways, our culture tolerates and even promotes violence. Violence in the family stems from our society's acceptance of violence as a legitimate means of enforcing compliance and solving conflicts at personal, national, and international levels (Viano 1992). Violence and abuse in the family may be linked to cultural factors such as violence in the media (see Chapter 4), acceptance of corporal punishment, gender inequality, and the view of women and children as property.

1. *Acceptance of corporal punishment.* Many mental health professionals and child development specialists argue that corporal punishment is ineffective and damaging to children. Yet, many parents accept the cultural tradition of spanking as an appropriate form of child discipline. Moreover, section 43 of the Canadian *Criminal Code* specifies that "[e]very schoolteacher, parent, or person standing in the place of a parent is justified in using force by way of correction toward a pupil or child, as the case may be, who is under his care, if the force does not exceed what is reasonable under the circumstances." In effect, this section allows children to be assaulted by their parents and teachers, provided that the force used in the assault is "reasonable" and for the child's "correction." One of the leading decisions used by our courts to interpret section 43 (made by the Quebec Court of Appeal in 1971) specifies that "the mere fact that the children dis-

ciplined suffered contusions and bruises is not in itself proof of exercise of undue force."

Unlike such countries as Austria, Cyprus, Denmark, Finland, Italy, Norway, and Sweden where the use of corporal punishment in the home or school is against the law, Canadian law specifically allows for the corporal punishment of children. Indeed, recent court rulings have deemed punishment that results in temporary marks on the skin of a child or discolouration lasting for several days to be "reasonable." For example, in ruling on a Manitoba case in which a stepfather had kicked his stepson downstairs and pulled a clump of hair out of the child's head, the judge commented that such punishment was "mild, indeed, compared to the *discipline* I received in my home" (emphasis added); in New Brunswick, the actions of a teacher who directed karate blows, including ones to the faces of four teenage boys, were deemed acceptable by a second Canadian judge who remarked that the behaviour "would instill respect in the students"; in British Columbia, a teacher was acquitted of assault "even though he had hit a 13-year-old male student in the head with a hammer" (Reform Watch 1997). Robertson (1994) observes that the following punishments are allowed by Section 43 of the *Code*.

- strapping on hands, shoulders, buttocks, legs
- hitting with straps, belts, sticks, extension cords, rulers
- causing bruises, welts, abrasions, swelling, nose bleeds, chipped teeth
- slapping on face, pushing, pulling, grabbing, shaking, kicking with stocking feet

Even when the use of corporal punishment is judged to be other than reasonable, Canadians would still seem uncertain about what should be done about it. In a Gallup poll, 14 percent of those surveyed reported "*personal* awareness of a *serious* incidence of physical abuse of children by a parent." However, more than one-third (37 percent) took no action whatsoever to intervene (Conway 1990: 83).

At various times, groups have called for the repeal of section 43. Most recently, a 1999 report by the Canadian Coalition for the Rights of the Child called *How Does Canada Measure Up?* charged that by failing to repeal this section of the Code, Canada was systematically violating articles of the United Nations Convention on the Rights of the Child (to which Canada is a signatory). The Convention on the Rights of the Child, adopted by the United Nations in 1989, and ratified by every country except the United States and Somalia, is often described as the most comprehensive human rights document in history. The convention has been included in the constitutions of 20 countries. A further 32 countries worldwide have modified their laws to comply with its terms. Section 19 of the U.N. Convention enjoins signatories to take legislative measures to protect children from all forms of physical or mental violence, injury, or abuse.

2. *Gender inequality.* Traditional male gender roles have taught men to be aggressive. Traditionally, men have also been taught that they are superior to women and that they may use their aggression toward women because "women need to be put in their place." Traditional female gender roles have also taught women to be submissive to their male partner's control.

Anderson (1997) found that men who earn less money than their partners are more likely to be violent toward them. "Disenfranchised men then must rely on other social practices to construct a masculine image. Because it is so clearly associated with masculinity in…[our] culture, violence is a social practice that enables men to express a masculine identity" (p. 667).

3. *View of women and children as property.* Before the late nineteenth century, a married woman was considered the property of her husband. A husband had a legal right and marital obligation to discipline and control his wife using physical force. The expression "rule of thumb" can be traced to an old English law that permitted a husband to beat his wife with a rod no thicker than his thumb. This "rule of thumb" was originally intended as a humane measure to limit how harshly men could beat their wives. This traditional view of women as property may contribute to men doing with their "property" as they wish.

   The view of women and children as property also explains marital rape and father–daughter incest. Historically, the penalties for rape were based on property right laws designed to protect a man's property—his wife or daughter—from rape by other men; a husband or father "taking" his own property was not considered rape (Russell 1990). In the past, a married woman who was raped by her husband could not have her husband arrested because marital rape was not considered a crime.

CONSIDERATION

In some countries, husbands are permitted by law to use physical force against their wives. In some societies, **"honour murder"** of wives is practised when a man suspects his wife of being unfaithful. **Dowry deaths** in other countries may occur when the wife brings an insufficient dowry into the marriage.

Community Factors Community factors that contribute to violence and abuse in the family include social isolation and inaccessible or unaffordable health care, day care, elder care, and respite care facilities.

1. *Social isolation.* Living in social isolation from extended family and community members increases a family's risk for abuse. Isolated families are removed from material benefits, care-giving assistance, and emotional support from extended family and community members.

2. *Inaccessible or unaffordable community services.* Failure to provide medical care to children and elderly family members (a form of neglect) is sometimes due to the lack of accessible or affordable health care services in the community. Failure to provide supervision for children and adults may result from inaccessible day care and elder care services. Without elder care and respite care facilities, socially isolated families may not have any help with the stresses of caring for elderly family members and children with special needs.

Individual and Family Factors Individual and family factors that are associated with domestic violence and abuse include a family history of violence, drug and alcohol abuse, poverty, and fatherless homes.

1. *Family history of abuse.* Most parents who abuse or neglect their children were themselves abused or neglected as children (Gelles and Conte 1991).

However, many adults who were abused as children do not continue the cycle with their own children.

2. *Drug and alcohol abuse.* Sacco and Kennedy (1994) point out that alcohol, drugs, and other intoxicants play a role in the commission of many violent crimes, including homicide. O'Keefe (1997) found that higher use of alcohol and other drugs was also associated with violence in high-school dating relationships. Alcohol increases aggression in some individuals and enables the offender to avoid responsibility by blaming the violent behaviour on alcohol.

3. *Poverty.* Abuse in adult relationships occurs among all socioeconomic groups. However, Kaufman and Zigler (1992) point to a relationship between poverty and child abuse:

    Although most poor people do not maltreat their children, and poverty, per se, does not cause abuse and neglect, the correlates of poverty, including stress, drug abuse, and inadequate resources for food and medical care, increase the likelihood of maltreatment. (p. 284)

4. *Stepfather families.* Numerous studies show that children are more likely to be sexually abused by a stepfather or mother's boyfriend than by their biological father (Blankenhorn 1995). This is largely because stepfathers and mothers' boyfriends are not constrained by the cultural incest taboo that prohibits fathers from having sex with their children.

STRATEGIES FOR ACTION: PREVENTING AND RESPONDING TO FAMILY VIOLENCE AND ABUSE

Strategies to prevent family violence and abuse can be applied at three different levels (Gelles 1993; Harrington and Dubowitz 1993). **Primary prevention** strategies target the general population, whereas **secondary prevention** strategies target groups thought to be at high risk for family violence and abuse. **Tertiary prevention** strategies target families who have experienced abuse; these strategies are designed to reduce the adverse effects of abuse and stop the abuse from happening again.

Primary Prevention Strategies Public education and media campaigns that target the general population may help reduce domestic violence by conveying the criminal nature of domestic assault and offering ways to prevent abuse ("When you are angry at your child, count to 10 and call a friend..."). Ultimately, though, to prevent or reduce family violence, elements of our culture that contribute to such violence must change. Parents and educators must be taught and encouraged to use methods of child discipline that do not involve physical punishment. Violence in the media must be curbed or eliminated, and traditional gender roles and views of women and children as property must be replaced with egalitarian gender roles and respect for women and children.

This chapter's The Human Side also suggests that we may have to broaden our understanding of what a family is and challenge misleading stereotypes about people with disabilities—their intelligence, their credibility, and their sexuality—if we are to be effective in both preventing violence within families and responding to it when it occurs.

Other strategies include reducing violence-provoking stress by reducing poverty and unemployment and providing adequate housing, nutrition, medical care, and educational opportunities.

Secondary Prevention Strategies Families that are at risk of experiencing violence and abuse include low-income families, parents with a history of depression or psychiatric care, single parents, teenage mothers, parents with few social and family contacts, individuals who experienced abuse in their own childhood, and parents or spouses who abuse drugs or alcohol. Secondary prevention strategies, designed to prevent abuse from occurring in high-risk families, include parent education programs, parent support groups, individual counselling, substance abuse treatment, and home visiting programs.

In response to studies that noted that family violence is more prevalent in Aboriginal communities, the federal government allotted $7 million to the funding of short-term community-based projects related to family violence in Indian and Inuit communities as part of the Family Violence and Child Sexual Abuse Initiatives. More than 180 projects, focusing on public awareness, training, community workshops, and research and program development, were funded in Native communities across Canada in the 1990s and care was taken to respect the strategies of intervention preferred within Aboriginal communities. Often, Aboriginal peoples do not view the problem of family violence as one of an offender–victim relationship so much as one of community dysfunction, of which family violence is but a symptom. In consequence, solutions to the problem are viewed in terms of a holistic, community-wide healing process planned, developed, and implemented by Aboriginal peoples. Programs and manuals to combat various forms of family violence, such as *Let the Healing Begin: Breaking the Cycle of Child Sexual Abuse in Our Communities* (McEvoy 1990), are often written for people of average reading ability, illustrated with numerous pictures, drawings, and cartoons that depict only Indigenous peoples, and blend psychological ideas with traditional practices. For example, it is not uncommon to have workshops dealing with issues of abuse begin with a prayer and a sharing circle or a smudge ceremony using the local root. Communities may also use naming ceremonies and feasts to celebrate different points of healing or encourage survivors to take part in sweat lodges to ask for help for themselves and others. The Medicine Wheel, which explains that a healthy person must use all four parts of himself or herself—physical, mental, emotional, and spiritual—is also favoured as a healing tool with many versions of the Wheel used in counselling programs.

CONSIDERATION

It has been suggested that the perceived need for healing within Aboriginal communities makes the position of both victim and perpetrator of abuse interchangeable and lessens the likelihood that a term of imprisonment will be seen as an appropriate response on the part of the court in sentencing an offender. Some maintain that "shaming" an offender may be a more powerful tool in reducing acts of family violence than the formal processes of arrest, conviction, and incarceration (Braithwaite 1989; Mugford and Mugford 1991). However, others would argue that acts of sexual or physical assault and incest must be recognized as, first and foremost, criminal acts and be treated as such by the courts (Razack 1994).

National Data

A nonrandom sample survey of Canadian women with disabilities conducted by the DisAbled Women's Network found that 40 percent had been raped, abused, or assaulted and that more than half (53 percent) who had been disabled from birth or early childhood had been abused. Only 10 percent of women who reported abuse sought help from transition houses; only half of those women were accommodated.

SOURCE: Riddington 1989

National Data

A study conducted by the Addiction Research Foundation found that women who are assaulted by their male partners are 74 percent more likely to rely on sedatives and 40 percent more likely to take sleeping pills than women who are not assaulted are.

SOURCE: Groenveld and Shain 1989

FAMILY VIOLENCE AGAINST WOMEN WITH DISABILITIES

Probably the single biggest factor affecting the incidence of family violence against women with disabilities is the extent of these women's "families." Women with disabilities must often depend on a variety of people to provide them with assistance in carrying out their everyday lives. For this reason, their "family" is understood to include not only parents, husbands, boyfriends, and other relatives, but also friends, neighbours, and caregivers. Caregivers can include attendants, interpreters, homemakers, drivers, doctors, nurses, teachers, social workers, psychiatrists, therapists, counsellors, and workers in hospitals and other institutions. This large number of people and the intimate physical and emotional contact involved in the care they provide, greatly increase the risk of abuse to persons with disabilities.

Women who live in institutional settings, and women who are multiply or profoundly disabled, are most vulnerable to abuse because they are more dependent upon even larger numbers of people, and less able to get away. It is estimated that women with disabilities are 1.5 to 10 times as likely to be abused as women without disabilities are, depending on whether they live in the community or in institutions.

While a disability can make it more difficult for a woman to escape or report abuse, social attitudes toward persons with disabilities are probably a bigger factor in her increased vulnerability to violence. The way in which society views persons with disabilities handicaps these women in many ways:

- They tend to be viewed and treated as children, as lacking intelligence.
- They may be trained to be compliant and are sometimes punished for assertiveness or for challenging authority figures. This is in direct contrast to the street-proofing taught to many children in schools.
- Women with disabilities are considered to be non-sexual and are often not given sex education, which can result in an inability to distinguish between abusive behaviour and normal or necessary forms of touching.
- They may be considered incompetent witnesses by police and the courts, particularly if they have difficulty or require assistance in communicating.
- When they do report abuse, they may not be believed....

Prevalence of Abuse

- Research has only just begun in this area, but indications are that women and children with disabilities are one of the most highly victimized groups in our society.
- A survey conducted in 1985 by DAWN Canada (DisAbled Women's Network) found that violence and fear of violence were the most critical issues facing women with disabilities.
- The degree of risk of sexual abuse of persons with disabilities appears to be at least 150% of that for individuals of the same sex and similar age without disabilities.

FAMILY VIOLENCE AGAINST WOMEN WITH DISABILITIES
(continued)

- It is estimated that only 20% of the cases of sexual abuse involving disabled people are ever reported to the police, community service agencies, or authorities....

Barriers to Obtaining Help

It is extremely difficult for any abused woman to leave a situation of abuse....Battering undermines self-esteem and can make a woman feel she is somehow responsible for her own abuse. For a woman with a disability, this situation is even more difficult. She may be dependent on her abuser for affection, communication, and financial, physical, and medical support. If she reports the abuse, she may risk poverty and loss of housing. She may fear she will not be heard or believed if she speaks out. She may face further violence, institutionalization, or loss of her children if she seeks help. She may not have access to information about existing support services for victims of violence. Even if she has this information, many sources of support may not be accessible. She may not be able to contact the police or women's shelters because they do not have communication devices such as Telecommunication Devices for the Deaf (TDDs). She may not be able to physically leave her situation because of a lack of accessible transportation. Her lack of options may leave her feeling so powerless and despairing that suicide seems the only viable choice. And if she seeks help in dealing with suicidal thoughts or attempts, she is unlikely to find counselling that takes account of her own reality....

SOURCE: Abridged from "Family Violence against Women with Disabilities." 1993. National Clearinghouse on Family Violence. Ottawa: Minister of Supply and Services Canada.

Tertiary Prevention Strategies What social interventions are available to families that are experiencing abuse or neglect? Abused women and children may seek relief at a shelter or "safe house" for abused women. Shelters provide abused women and their children with housing, food, and counselling services. Safe houses are private homes of individuals who volunteer to provide temporary housing to abused women who decide to leave their violent homes. Battered men are not allowed to stay at women's shelters, but many shelters help abused men by providing money for a motel room, counselling, and support services. Some communities have abuse shelters for victims of elder abuse.

Abused or neglected children may be removed from the home. Provincial child welfare laws permit abused or neglected children to be placed in out-of-home care, such as foster care. However, a preferred approach is to prevent family breakup when desirable and possible without jeopardizing the welfare of children in the home. Family preservation programs are in-home interventions for families who are at risk of having a child removed from the home due to abuse or neglect.

Alternatively, a court may order an abusing spouse or parent to leave the home. Abused spouses or cohabiting partners may obtain a restraining order prohibiting the perpetrator from going near the abused partner. However, legal

National Data

In relation to all divorces granted in Canada in 1995, the court (either through decisions in contested cases or simple ratification of informal, uncontested arrangements), awarded legal custody of children to the mother in 67.6 percent of cases, to the father in 10.9 percent, to the mother and father jointly in 21.4 percent, and to neither in 0.2 percent of the cases.

SOURCE: Statistics Canada 1997b

action does not always protect victims of family violence. Research conducted in the United States reports that nearly 4 in 100 violent offenders sentenced to local jail for intimate violence were on probation or under a restraining order at the time they committed the offence (U.S. Department of Justice 1998). Canadian courts have been notably reluctant to curtail the access of abusive spouses to their children; the courts have held that a husband's commission of assault upon his wife does not invalidate his application for child custody or the claim that he is a "good father." In situations in which a restraining order prohibits the abusive partner from establishing contact with a current or former spouse, the order itself may be unknowingly breached when the abused spouse voluntarily allows the abusive partner into the home to pick up or deliver their children.

DIVORCE

As Figure 5.4 indicates, the number of divorces per 100 000 population in Canada, known as the **crude divorce rate,** rose from 137.6 in 1971 to 278.0 in 1981, reached a peak of 307.8 in 1989, and declined to 262.2 in 1995 (Statistics Canada 1997a). Individual and relationship factors that contribute to divorce include incompatibility in values or goals, poor communication, lack of conflict resolution skills, sexual incompatibility, extramarital relationships, substance abuse, emotional or physical abuse or neglect, boredom, jealousy, and difficulty coping with change or stress related to parenting, employment, finances, in-laws, and illness. Other demographic and life course factors that are predictive of divorce include marriage order (second and subsequent marriages are more prone to divorce than first marriages), cohabitation (couples who live together before marriage are more prone to divorce), teenage marriage, premarital pregnancy, and low socioeconomic status.

Figure 5.4

Divorces, Canada, 1971–96

SOURCES: Statistics Canada, Divorce in the 1990s, *Health Reports 1997,* 9(2): 53–8 (Statistics Canada Cat. No. 82-003-XPB); Statistics Canada, Health Statistics Division, special tabulations.

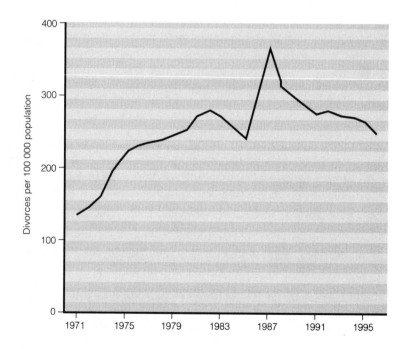

Various social factors also contribute to the increased rate of divorce over the past three decades. These include the following structural and cultural forces.

1. *Changing family functions.* Before the Industrial Revolution, the family constituted a unit of economic production and consumption, provided care and protection to its members, and was responsible for socializing and educating children. During industrialization, other institutions took over these functions. For example, the educational institution has virtually taken over the systematic teaching and socialization of children. Today, the primary function of marriage and the family is the provision of emotional support, intimacy, affection, and love. When marital partners no longer derive these emotional benefits from their marriage, they may consider divorce with the hope of finding a new marriage partner to fulfil these needs.

2. *Increased economic autonomy of women.* Before 1940, most wives were not employed outside the home and depended on their husband's income. During World War II, Canada needed women in the labour force. Today, the employment rate among married women is higher than in previous decades.

   Wives who are unhappy in their marriage are more likely to leave the marriage if they have the economic means to support themselves. Unhappy husbands may also be more likely to leave a marriage if their wives are self-sufficient and can contribute to the support of the children.

3. *Increased work demands.* Another factor influencing divorce is increased work demands and the stresses of balancing work and family roles. Workers are putting in longer hours, often working overtime or taking second jobs. Many employed parents—particularly mothers—come home to work a "second shift"—the work involved in caring for children and household chores. Balancing work and family roles can lead to marital tension and resentment, as reflected in the following excerpt:

> My husband's a great help watching our baby. But as far as doing housework or even taking the baby when I'm at home, no. He figures he works five days a week; he's not going to come home and clean. But he doesn't stop to think that I work seven days a week. Why should I have to come home and do the housework without help from anybody else? My husband and I have been through this over and over again. Even if he would just pick up things from the kitchen table and stack the dishes for me, that would make a big difference. He does nothing. On his weekends off, I have to provide a sitter for the baby so he can go fishing. When I have a day off, I have the baby all day long without a break. He'll help out if I'm not here, but the minute I am, all the work at home is mine. (quoted in Hochschild 1997, pp. 37–8)

4. *Liberalized divorce laws.* Before 1968, adultery was the only grounds for divorce in Canada, except in Nova Scotia, where cruelty was sufficient grounds even before Confederation (Morrison 1987). The 1968 *Divorce Act* expanded the "fault grounds" under which a divorce could be granted. In addition to adultery, proof that one's partner had engaged in prohibited activities such as mental or physical cruelty, gross addiction to alcohol or

other drugs, sodomy, bestiality, and homosexual acts, entitled the petitioner to an immediate divorce. The 1968 *Divorce Act* introduced what are often termed **no-fault** grounds that allowed couples to divorce without requiring them to stipulate their specific reason for doing so. In these cases of "marital breakdown," couples were required to live apart for a three-year period before applying for a divorce and jointly consent to being divorced. In the event that one party did not wish to be divorced, the court required that five years pass from the time of separation before applying for divorce. In addition, Morton (1990: 213) notes that "[a]s an added protection for the economically dependent spouse in cases of unilateral separation, courts were given the discretion to refuse a divorce if a 'granting of the decree would be unduly harsh or unjust or would affect the making of reasonable arrangements for the maintenance [financial support] of the spouse.'"

The 1968 *Divorce Act* represented a compromise that sought to satisfy those who felt that marriage should not be regarded as a terminal condition and those who felt that divorce was unacceptable on moral or religious grounds. However, in seeking to satisfy everyone, the Act satisfied virtually no one. The Act placed a strong emphasis on the virtues of reconciliation, with the lawyers for each spouse legally obliged to discuss reconciliation with their clients. Divorce trial judges were also required to determine whether the couple's reconciliation was possible. However, for those who felt that the law should support marriage, the availability of no-fault provisions for divorce was seen as unduly liberal. In contrast, others charged that the fault grounds were too narrow. It was also noted that the disparate degrees of access to divorce provided by fault cases and no-fault cases promoted a degree of fraud and duplicity among those who did not wish to wait for three years before they were legally divorced. For example, Morton (p. 213) observed that "most fault divorces were adultery cases and...these cases were really consent divorces disguised to allow the spouses to avoid the three-year waiting period" (p. 213).

In 1985, a new divorce act became law. It was drafted in response to many of the criticisms outlined above, but again has not proven immune to controversy. Under the new *Divorce Act,* there is only one ground available for divorce—marital breakdown—but this is defined in three ways: (1) the spouses have lived apart for one year; (2) one of the spouses has committed an act of adultery; (3) one spouse has treated the other with mental or physical cruelty. While proof of fault entitles couples to an immediate divorce, those opting for a one-year separation "may apply for a divorce any time after separation to ensure that their case is heard soon after the year is up" (Morton 1990: 214).

5. *Cultural values.* Our values also contribute to divorce. In the pursuit of individual happiness, spouses and children may be left behind. This chapter's Focus on Social Problems Research examines a number of socio-demographic characteristics that affect Canadians' beliefs about the conditions that justify getting a divorce.

The perceived value of marriage has also changed. The increased social acceptance of nonmarital sexuality, nonmarital childbearing, cohabitation, and singlehood reflect the view that marriage is an option, rather than an inevitability. The view of marriage as an option, rather than as an imperative, is mirrored by the view that divorce is also an acceptable option. Divorce today has less social stigma than in previous generations.

When Is Divorce Justified?

Recognizing that "little in known about why some marriages succeed and others fail," Judith A. Frederick and Jason Hamel (1998) sought to explore sociodemographic characteristics that affect Canadians' beliefs about the conditions that justify divorce. To do so, they used data collected by the 1995 General Social Survey on family and social support. This survey sampled approximately 11 000 Canadians aged 15 and older and living in the 10 provinces, excluding full-time residents of institutions. Frederick and Hamel focused on a question in which respondents were asked whether "…you think the following reasons are sufficient for splitting up a marriage or common-law relationship" (see table). The 10 reasons that followed this question fell into three broad categories: (1) abusive or disrespectful behaviour toward a partner; (2) "experiential issues" such as conflict over money,

household chores and raising the children; and (3) issues related to fertility (e.g., an inability to have children or disagreement about the specific number of children desired). Respondents were also asked if they would stay in a union "for the sake of their children."

The researchers adopted the three broad age groupings earlier used by Michael Adams (1997). The term "Elders" was used to refer to those respondents born before 1946, "Boomers," those born between 1946 and 1965, and "Gen-Xers," people born after 1965. In his earlier work, Adams had suggested that gender, age, and income largely determine the values of Elders and that their society tended to be supportive of such well-established institutions as marriage. In contrast to Elders, Boomers were more affluent, educated, well travelled, and informed. They were also more apt to challenge then venerate the institution of marriage and the values that it represents. Finally, Gen-Xers

were seen as less affluent than their parents were and more likely than other groups to view marriage as irrelevant.

Based on their research, Frederick and Hamel report that most Canadians (more than 95 percent), regardless of their age, agree that abusive behaviour, infidelity, and disrespect toward a partner justify divorce. Indeed, Elders, Boomers, and Gen-Xers displayed near unanimity on this issue. In relation to a partner who drank too much, the level of agreement declined. Nevertheless, nearly three out of four felt this situation to be sufficient grounds for divorce. In addition, the majority of Canadians (approximately 60 percent) reported that they would not stay in a bad marriage for the sake of their children, with Boomers the least likely to say they would do so. Within this study, men were more inclined than women were to want to remain married for the sake of their children (almost 60 percent of men versus less than a third of women).

What Justifies Divorce?

	Gen-Xers 15–20	Boomers 30–49	Elders 50 and over	Total % of population aged 15 and over
Fundamental Issues				
Abusive behaviour from the partner	95	95	94	95
Unfaithful behaviour from the partner	89	85	89	88
Lack of love and respect from the partner	86	86	87	88
Partner drinks too much	68	73	80	74
Experiential Issues				
Constant disagreement about how the family finances should be handled	28	40	49	40
Unsatisfactory sexual relationship with the partner	21	37	45	35
Unsatisfactory division of household tasks with the partner	12	16	21	17
Conflict about how the children are raised	14	17	21	17
Fertility Issues				
Inability to have children with the partner	8	12	17	13
Disagreement about the number of children to have	3	6	11	7
Would stay for the children	44	39	52	43

SOURCE: Statistics Canada 1995; General Social Survey 1995

The three groups were found to differ most in relation to experiential issues—"that is, dealing with finances, sexual relationships, household chores and raising children." The researchers found that with increased age (and experience of such problems), the less tolerant Canadians are. While slightly more than 6 out of 10 Elders (61 percent) viewed such issues as valid reasons for divorce, only about 1 in 2 (55 percent) Boomers and Gen-Xers (49 percent) agreed. The authors also report that "[f]ewer people think that divorce is justified by infertility or the number of children to have than by conflict over the way the children are being raised." While 13 percent viewed the inability to have children as a valid reason for ending a marriage, an even smaller percentage (7 percent) felt that disagreement over the number of children to have was a valid reason to divorce. Elders were more than twice as likely as Gen-Xers to agree that these issues justified terminating a marriage.

In addition, Frederick and Hamel found that marital history influences Canadians' views about divorce with people who have remained in their first marriage taking a less liberal view than those who had not. Those who had only been married once and remained married and those who were widowed were the least likely to view any of the issues presented to them as sufficient to justify divorce. Perhaps predictably enough, those who were separated, divorced, in a common-law union, or remarried were more likely to view divorce as a viable option.

SOURCE: Frederick, Judith A., and Jason Hamel. 1998. "Canadian Attitudes to Divorce." *Canadian Social Trends* (Spring) 48: 6–10.

Consequences of Divorce

When parents have bitter and unresolvable conflict, or if one parent is abusing the child or the other parent, divorce may offer a solution to family problems. However, divorce often has negative effects for ex-spouses and their children and contributes to problems that affect society as a whole.

Health Consequences Divorce tends to have deleterious physical and psychological health consequences on ex-spouses. Divorce is associated with anxiety and psychological distress, unhappiness, loneliness, depression, illness, and suicide (Heim and Snyder 1991; Kitson and Morgan 1991; Song 1991; Waite 1995).

Economic Consequences While both women and men experience a drop in income following divorce, women may suffer more. Forty percent of divorcing women lose half of their family income, whereas fewer than 17 percent of men experience this degree of loss (Arendell 1995).

Effects on Children Although divorce following high conflict may actually improve the emotional well-being of children relative to staying in a conflicted home environment (Jekielek 1998), for many children parental divorce has detrimental effects. With only one parent in the home, children of divorce, as well as children of never-married mothers, tend to have less adult supervision compared with children in two-parent homes. Lack of adult supervision is related to higher rates of juvenile delinquency, school failure, and teenage pregnancy (Popenoe 1993). A survey of 90 000 teenagers found that the mere physical presence of a parent in the home after school, at dinner, and at bedtime significantly reduces the risk of teenage suicide, violence, and drug use (Resnick et al. 1997). Based on a review of 37 studies involving more than 81 000 adults who had experienced the divorce of their parents, researchers found that adult children of divorced parents experienced lower levels of psychological well-being (depression, low life satisfaction), family well-being (low marital quality, divorce), socioeconomic well-being (low educational attainment, income, and occupational prestige), and poorer physical health (Amato and Keith 1991).

CONSIDERATION

Concern about the effects of fatherlessness on children has overshadowed the issue of how child absence affects fathers. Many divorced fathers are overwhelmed with feelings of failure, guilt, anger, and sadness over the separation from their children (Knox 1998). If separation from their children causes anguish to fathers, why do some divorced fathers sever all ties with their children? Hewlett and West (1998) explain that "visiting their children only serves to remind these men of their painful loss, and they respond to this feeling by withdrawing completely" (p. 169).

STRATEGIES FOR ACTION: RESPONDING TO THE PROBLEMS OF DIVORCE

Two general strategies for responding to the problems of divorce are (1) strategies to prevent divorce and strengthen marriages and (2) strategies to strengthen postdivorce families.

Divorce Prevention Strategies

One strategy for preventing divorce is to require or encourage couples to participate in premarital education before getting married. Some have proposed legislation requiring or encouraging premarital education (Clark 1996; Peterson 1997). Proposed policies include mandating premarital education, lowering marriage licence fees for those who participate, and imposing delays on issuing marriage licences for those who refuse premarital education.

Researchers have found that couples who participated in a widely used couples' education program called PREP (the Prevention and Relationship Enhancement Program) had a lower divorce and separation rate five years after completing the program compared with couples who did not participate (Stanley et al. 1995). PREP couples also showed significant improvement in conflict management, maintained higher levels of marital satisfaction, and reported significantly lower levels of aggression than did the controls.

Some family scholars and policymakers advocate strengthening marriage by reforming divorce laws to make divorce harder to obtain. In most cases, these measures are designed to make breaking up harder to do by requiring proof of fault (e.g., adultery, abuse) or extending the waiting period required before divorce is granted (Brienza 1996).

Opponents argue that **divorce law reform** measures would increase acrimony between divorcing spouses (which harms the children as well as the adults involved), increase the legal costs of getting a divorce (which leaves less money to support any children), and delay court decisions on child support and custody and distribution of assets.

In the United States, a novel idea arose when, in June 1997, the Louisiana legislature became the first in that nation to pass a law creating a new kind of marriage contract. Under the new law, couples can voluntarily choose between the standard marriage contract that allows a no-fault divorce (after a six-month separation) and a "covenant marriage" that permits divorce only under condition of fault or after a marital separation of more than two years. Couples who choose a **covenant marriage** must also get premarital counselling. Representative Tony Perkins, who sponsored the bill, believes the new law will prevent potentially weak marriages. Perkins explains:

> When a man says he wants a no-fault marriage and a woman says she wants a covenant marriage, that's going to raise some red flags. She's going to say "What? You're not willing to have a lifelong commitment to me?" (Louisiana Divorce 1997: 1)

However, it is too early to assess the effect of Louisiana's new covenant marriage law.

Strengthening Postdivorce Families

Negative consequences of divorce for children may be minimized if both parents continue to spend time with their children on a regular and consistent basis and communicate to their children that they love them and are interested in their lives. Parental conflict, in either intact families or divorced families, negatively influences the psychological well-being of children (Demo 1992, 1993). By maintaining a civil coparenting relationship during a separation and after divorce, parents can minimize the negative effects of divorce on their children. However, about 20 percent of separated and divorced spouses have an angry, hostile relationship (Masheter 1991).

What can society do to promote cooperative parenting by ex-spouses? One answer is to encourage, or even mandate, divorcing couples to participate in **divorce mediation**. In divorce mediation, divorcing couples meet with a neutral third party, a mediator, who helps them resolve issues of property division, child custody, child support, and spousal support in a way that minimizes conflict and encourages cooperation. Children of mediated divorces adjust better to the divorce than children of litigated divorces do (Marlow and Sauber 1990). In the United States, for example, an increasing number of jurisdictions and states have mandatory child-custody mediation programs, whereby parents in a custody or visitation dispute must attempt to resolve their dispute through mediation before a court will hear their case.

Another trend aimed at strengthening postdivorce families is the establishment of parenting programs for divorcing parents (Shapiro and Schrof 1995). Such programs emphasize that it is important for both parents to remain involved in their children's lives. Such programs also teach parents skills to help their children adjust to the divorce and advise parents to avoid expressing hostility or criticism toward the ex-spouse in front of the children. In Canada, the B.C. Ministry of the Attorney General is piloting a "Parenting after Separation" program for separated and divorced couples with children.

LONE PARENTHOOD

In 1996, 14.5 percent of all Canadian families were headed by a lone parent (Statistics Canada 1997c: 2). Whereas lone-parent families in the first half of the twentieth century were primarily the product of the death of a parent

National Data

Among First Nations people, the rate of out-of-wedlock births is 60 percent higher than the national average.
SOURCE: Fleras and Elliott 1996

(Oderkirk and Lochhead 1992) occasioned by wars, mortalities associated with childbirth, and generally more hazardous living conditions, widowed people raising children alone accounted for only 20 percent of lone-parent families in 1996 (Statistics Canada 1996).

Over the course of this century, increasing numbers of women have chosen to give birth and raise children on their own, without undertaking marriage. Because of this trend, 24 percent of solo mothers in 1996 had never been married. While the issue of teen pregnancies (Figures 5.5 and 5.6) continues to generate considerable concern, at present in Canada, solo parenting is most likely the product of marital dissolution (either separation or divorce), after which child custody is typically granted, either formally or informally, to one parent only (mothers overwhelmingly). Approximately 83 percent of all lone-parent families are headed by women, as of 1996, an increase from 74 percent in 1941 (Ram 1990: 52). Compared to lone-parent fathers, lone-parent mothers are more likely to be younger, less well educated, have lower earnings and less income, and responsible for younger-aged children (Oderkirk and Lochhead 1992). Twenty-six percent of lone-parent family income in 1997 came from government transfers in 1997; in that year, the average income for lone-parent families headed by women was $25 445. For the sake of comparison, it can be noted that the average income in two-parent families was $64 814 in that year and in male-led, lone-parent families $40,974 (Health Canada, 1999).

In Chapter 10, we deal more fully with the "feminization of poverty." Here we shall focus on only aspect of solo parenthood: that which affects those who are teenagers and unmarried.

Social Factors that Encourage Unmarried Parenthood

Since 1969, birth control measures have been legal in Canada. Before 1969, these measures "were illegal if practiced for birth control rather than for an acceptable 'medical' reason—to prevent venereal disease or to deal with problems of menstrual irregularity" (Conway 1990: 213). However, even within contemporary society, cultural inhibitors remain that would seem to discourage young women from acknowledging their participation in sexual activities. Often, teenaged girls fail to use contraceptives simply because to obtain them, they have to acknowledge that they are sexual to either their parents, doctors, or strangers such as pharmacists. In consequence, Hacker (1992) has reported that "most teenage pregnancies occur in the first six months of sexual activity, and...seeking contraception typically is delayed from nine to 12 months after intercourse has been initiated" (p. 16).

Despite the availability of the pill and the increasing use of the more radical technique of sterilization, statistics show that the rate of illegitimate births is rising. Between 1931 and 1960, out-of-wedlock births accounted for approximately 4 percent of births in Canada; in 1983, they accounted for 16 percent and in 1990, they accounted for 22 percent (Gairdner 1991). While the pregnancy rate among every other age group of fertile women is decreasing, the teenage pregnancy rate is increasing. From 1985 to 1993, pregnancy rates for Canadian teenagers 15 to 19 increased from 41 to 48 per 1000. In 1994, there were 48.8 pregnancies for every 1000 women aged 15 to 19, a rate that has not been seen in Canada since the 1970s. In contrast to the situation among teen mothers in the 1970s, however, teen mothers in the 1990s are more likely to be single (25 percent in 1974 versus 81 percent in 1994). By 1997, the teen

<aside>
National Data

In Canada, the pill has been replaced by sterilization as the most popular form of birth control among Canadian women aged 18 to 49.

SOURCE: Balakrishnan et al. 1995
</aside>

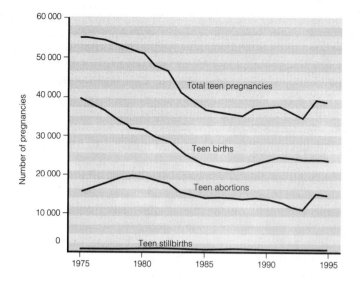

Figure 5.5

Teenage Pregnancies, Births, and Abortions, Canada, 1975–95

SOURCES: Statistics Canada, Health Statistics Division, *Health Indications, 1999* (Cat. No. 82-221-XCB); Statistics Canada, Health Statistics Division, *Births and Deaths, 1995;* Health Canada 1999

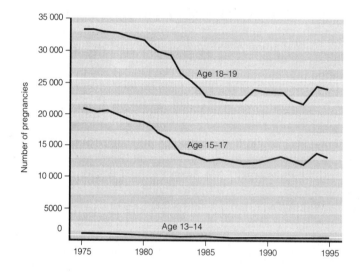

Figure 5.6

Teenage Pregnancies, Age 13 to 19, Canada, 1975–95

SOURCES: Statistics Canada, Health Statistics Division, *Health Indications, 1999* (Cat. No. 82-221-XCB); Statistics Canada, Health Statistics Division, *Births and Deaths, 1995;* Health Canada 1999.

pregnancy rate had increased to 59.2 (Crawford 1997). However, the number of live births to teenagers is down because the proportion of pregnancies ending in abortion is up. This proportion almost doubled between 1974 and 1994 from 26 to 45 percent.

Various reasons have been suggested to explain why teens opt for parenthood. Some have suggested that a perceived lack of future occupational opportunities contributes to teenage parenthood (Luker 1996). Teenage females who do poorly in school may have little hope of success and achievement in pursuing educational and occupational goals. They may think that their only remaining option for a meaningful role in life is to become a parent. In addition, some teenagers feel lonely and unloved and have a baby to create a sense of feeling needed and wanted.

The most rapid rise in single parenthood is among older, educated, professional women, although they still represent only a small fraction of all single mothers (Ingrassia 1993). Most would prefer to be married before having a child, but feel that their biological clock will not wait (Sapiro 1990).

Increased social acceptance of cohabitation also contributes to unmarried parenthood. Births to cohabiting couples are technically considered unwed births, even though the parents are living together.

Social Problems Related to Teenage and Unmarried Parenthood

Teenage and unmarried childbirth are considered social problems because of the consequences typically associated with them. These include the following:

1. *Poverty for single mothers and children.* Many unmarried mothers, especially teenagers, have no means of economic support or have limited earning capacity. Single mothers and their children often live in substandard housing and have inadequate nutrition and medical care. The public bears some of the economic burden of supporting unmarried mothers and their children, but even with public assistance, many unwed and teenage parents often struggle to survive economically.

2. *Poor health outcomes.* Teenage and unmarried women are less likely to seek prenatal care and more likely than older and married women to smoke, drink alcohol, and take drugs. These factors have adverse effects on the health of the baby. Indeed, babies born to unmarried or teenage mothers are more likely to have low-birthweights and to be born prematurely. Children of teenage and unmarried mothers are also more likely to be developmentally delayed. These outcomes are largely a result of the association between teenage and unmarried childbearing and poverty.

3. *Low academic achievement.* Low academic achievement is both a contributing factor and a potential outcome of teenage parenthood. Teenage mothers are at risk for dropping out of school and, consequently, have a much higher probability of remaining poor throughout their lives. Since poverty is linked to unmarried parenthood, a cycle of successive generations of teenage pregnancy may develop.

4. *Children without fathers.* Shapiro and Schrof (1995) report that children who grow up without fathers are more likely to drop out of school, be unemployed, abuse drugs, experience mental illness, and be a target of child sexual abuse. They also note that "a missing father is a better predictor of criminal activity than race or poverty" (p. 39). Popenoe (1996) believes that fatherlessness is a major cause of the degenerating conditions of our young.

STRATEGIES FOR ACTION: INTERVENTIONS IN TEENAGE PREGNANCY

Some interventions regarding teenage childbearing aim at prevention, while others attempt to minimize its negative effects. One preventive intervention is to provide sex education and family planning programs before unwanted or unintended pregnancy occurs. Schools, churches, family planning clinics, and public health departments may offer sex education programs. Research on the effectiveness of such programs in preventing pregnancy is disheartening,

International Data

The social acceptance of unmarried couples having children varies widely throughout the world. Acceptance of this lifestyle ranges from 90 percent or more in parts of Western Europe to less than 15 percent in Singapore and India.

SOURCE: Global Study of Family Values 1998

National Data

Within Canada, the total fertility rate—the average number of live births per women—declined slightly from 1995, from 1.71 children per woman to 1.64.

SOURCE: Statistics Canada 1998a

however. Stout and Rivara (1989) reviewed five studies and concluded that school-based sex education programs have little or no effect on reducing teenage pregnancy. However, programs that include sex education curricula with easily accessible health clinics (Jacobs and Wolf 1995) have resulted in decreases in adolescent pregnancy rates.

One obstacle to sex education in the schools is the fear that teaching youth about sex and contraception actually encourages sexual activity. However, the World Health Organization reviewed 35 controlled studies of sex education programs and found that students who participated in the programs did not initiate intercourse at an earlier age than students in the control group that were exposed to no programs (Berne and Huberman 1996).

Other programs aim at both preventing teenage and unmarried childbearing and minimizing its negative effects by increasing the life options of teenagers and unmarried mothers. Such programs include educational programs, job training, and skill-building programs. Other programs designed to help teenage and unwed mothers and their children include public welfare prenatal programs to help ensure the health of the mother and baby, and parenting classes for both teenage fathers and unmarried mothers.

In this chapter, we have focused on only a few topics related to family concerns—violence and abuse, divorce, and teenage and unmarried parenthood. However, families are affected by numerous other problems, discussed elsewhere in this text—problems such as crime; disease, illness, and inadequate health care; alcohol and drugs; gender inequality; prejudices against racial, ethnic, and sexual-orientation minorities; poverty; war; and problems at the workplace.

UNDERSTANDING FAMILY PROBLEMS

Societal definitions of the family have changed with increased acceptance of many previously stigmatized behaviours, such as cohabitation, divorce, and nonmarital parenthood. As these behaviours have become more socially acceptable, they have also become more common.

The impact of family problems, including divorce, abuse, and nonmarital childbearing, is felt not only by family members, but also by the larger society. Family members experience such life difficulties as poverty, school failure, low self-esteem, and mental and physical health problems. Each of these difficulties contributes to a cycle of family problems in the next generation. The impact on society includes large public expenditures to assist single-parent families and victims of domestic violence and neglect, youth crime, and low academic achievement of children who are struggling to cope with family problems.

Family problems can best be understood within the context of the society and culture in which they occur. Although domestic violence, divorce, and teenage pregnancy and unmarried parenthood may appear to result from individual decisions, these decisions are influenced by myriad social and cultural forces.

Given the social context of family problems, it is important that we look to social intervention for solutions. Perhaps with more economic and social supports and more "family-friendly" workplaces, families would be less likely to experience violence and abuse and divorce. Politicians have enormous power in shaping policies that affect families.

CRITICAL THINKING

1. Some scholars and politicians argue that "stable families are the bedrock of stable communities." Others argue that "stable communities and economies are the bedrock of stable families." Which of these two positions would you take and why?

2. Is individualism necessarily incompatible with familism? Why or why not?

3. Research has suggested that secondhand smoke from cigarettes represents a health hazard for those who are exposed to it. Consequently, smoking is now banned in many public places and workplaces. Indeed, with the start of the year 2000, a provincewide smoking ban took effect in British Columbia. Under the new rules—the toughest in Canada—smoking is prohibited in all institutions that employ people, including bars and restaurants, unless owners can provide separately ventilated rooms designed for smokers. Do you think that parents should be banned from smoking in enclosed areas (home or car) to protect their children from secondhand smoke? Do you think that smoking in enclosed areas with one's children present should be considered a form of child abuse? Why or why not?

4. Some judges are imposing "shame sentences" on convicted spousal abusers. For example, an abusive husband may be ordered to publicly apologize to his wife on the steps of City Hall or to go to a local mall carrying a sign that reads, "I went to jail for assaulting my wife. This could be you" ("In the News" 1998). What do you think about these types of "shame sentences" for batterers?

5. When divorcing parents participate in mediation, the mediator does not speak of "child custody" and "visitation." Rather, the mediator uses phrases such as "parenting plan" and "plan for spending time with your children." Why do you think mediators use terms such as "parenting plan" and "plan for spending time with your children" rather than the terms "child custody" and "visitation?"

KEY TERMS

blended family
child abuse
covenant marriage
crude divorce rate
divorce law reform
divorce mediation
dowry death
economic family

familicide
familism
famulus
honour murder
individualism
mater familias
neglect
no-fault divorce

pater familias
patriarchy
primary prevention
secondary prevention
self-fulfilling prophecy
tertiary prevention

Section 2

Problems of Human Diversity

People are diverse. They vary on many dimensions, including age, gender, sexual orientation, and race and ethnicity. In most societies, including Canada, these characteristics are imbued with social significances and are used to make judgments about an individual's worth, intelligence, skills, and personality. Such labelling creates categories of people who are perceived as "different" by others as well as by themselves and, as a result, are often treated differently.

A **minority** is a category of people who have unequal access to positions of power, prestige, and wealth in a society. In effect, minorities have unequal opportunities and are disadvantaged in their attempt to gain societal resources. Even though they may be a majority in terms of numbers, they may still be a minority sociologically. Before Nelson Mandela was elected president of South Africa, South African Blacks suffered the disadvantages of a minority even though they were a numerical majority of the population.

Terms that may apply to minorities include stereotyping, prejudice, and discrimination. A **stereotype** is a set of assumptions or generalizations about the characteristics of a group of persons. **Prejudice** is an attitude, often negative, that causes someone to prejudge an individual. **Discrimination** is differential treatment by members of the majority group against members of the minority that has a harmful effect on members of the subordinate group. The groups we will discuss in this section are all victims of stereotyping, prejudice, and discrimination.

Minority groups usually have certain characteristics in common. For example, members of a minority group generally know that they are members of a minority, stay within their own group, have relatively low levels of self-esteem, are disproportionately represented in the lower socioeconomic strata, and are viewed as having negative traits. Other characteristics of specific minority groups are identified in the accompanying table.

In the following chapters, we discuss categories of minorities based on age (Chapter 6), gender (Chapter 7), race and ethnicity (Chapter 8), and sexual orientation (Chapter 9). Although other categories of minorities exist (e.g., people with disabilities, religious minorities), we have chosen to concentrate on these four groups because each is surrounded by issues and policies that have far-reaching social, political, and economic implications.

Nine Characteristics of Four Minorities

	Old/Young	Women	Racial and Ethnic Minorities	Homosexuals
1. Status ascribed based on	Age	Sex	Race/ethnicity	Sexual orientation
2. Visibility	High	High	High	Low
3. Attribution of minority status (correctly or incorrectly) based on	Hair Skin elasticity Size Posture	Anatomy Shape	Skin colour Facial features Hair	Mannerisms Style of dress
4. Summary image	Dependent	Weak	Inferior	Sick or immoral
5. Derogatory and offensive terms	Old codger Brat	Bitch Whore	Nigger Paki	Faggot Dyke
6. Control through feigning various characteristics*	Frailty Helplessness	Weakness	Ignorance	Heterosexuality
7. Discrimination	Yes	Yes	Yes	Yes
8. Victims of violence	Yes	Yes	Yes	Yes
9. Segregation	Yes	Yes	Yes	Yes

* Being aware of their lack of power, minority group members may try to exert control by feigning certain characteristics. For example, slaves could not tell their owners, "I'm not going to plough the fields—do it yourself!" However, by acting incompetent, slaves may have avoided the work. Gays may attempt to pass as straight by bragging about heterosexual conquests. The elderly in nursing homes whose family members might otherwise not visit may feign illness in the hope of eliciting a visit. The problem with these acts is that they contribute to and stabilize the summary images.

CHAPTER SIX

The Young and the Old

Is It True?

1. The elderly are more likely to be victims of crime than the young are.
2. The older a person, the less likely that person is to define a particular age as old.
3. It is estimated that three million children in Canada arrive at school hungry.
4. In Canada, there has been a steady increase in the percentage of seniors with low income.
5. By 2041, almost one-quarter of the Canadian population will be aged 65 or older, nearly double the proportion in 1995.

Answers: 1 = F, 2 = T, 3 = T, 4 = F, 5 = T

O ne paradox in life is that the young want to be older and the old want to be younger. Toddlers want to be "old enough to go to school" with their brothers and sisters, children want to be "old enough to go to the mall" by them-

selves, teenagers speak of "being old enough to drive," and the elderly reminisce about the "good old days" and complain of "being too old." Sociologically, at what age are people "old"? What does being "old enough" mean? How much time is there between being "not old enough" and being "too old"?

Although age diversity is often celebrated (e.g., birthdays, high-school graduation, retirement), there are countless examples of how social life oppresses children and devalues the elderly. The young and the old represent major population segments of Canadian society. In this chapter, we examine the problems and potential solutions associated with youth and aging. We begin by looking at age in a cross-cultural context.

THE GLOBAL CONTEXT: THE YOUNG AND THE OLD AROUND THE WORLD

The young and the old receive different treatment in different societies. Differences in the treatment of the dependent young and old have traditionally been associated with whether the country is developed or less developed. Although there are proportionately more elderly in developed countries than in less developed ones, these societies have fewer statuses for the elderly to occupy. Their positions as caretakers, homeowners, employees, and producers are often usurped by those aged 18 to 65. Paradoxically, the more primitive the society the more likely that society is to practise **senilicide**—the killing of the elderly. In some societies, the elderly are considered a burden and left to die or, in some cases, actually killed.

Not all societies treat the elderly as a burden. Scandinavian countries provide government support for in-home care workers for elderly who can no longer perform such tasks as cooking and cleaning. Eastern cultures such as Japan revere their elderly, in part, because of their presumed proximity to honoured ancestors. This attitude is in stark contrast to that of North American youth who view the elderly as "culturally irrelevant" (Kolland 1994). Japanese elders sit at the head of the table, enter a room first, bathe first, and are considered the head of the family. While Canada celebrates Mother's Day and Father's Day, Japan has Respect for Elders Day.

Societies also differ in the way they treat children. In less developed societies, children work as adults, marry at a young age, and pass from childhood directly to adulthood with no recognized period of adolescence. In contrast, in industrialized nations, children are often expected to attend school for 12 to 16 years and, during this time, to remain financially and emotionally dependent on their families.

Because of this extended period of dependence, Canada treats "minors" differently from adults. Juveniles have a separate justice system and minimum ages for driving, drinking alcohol, joining the military, entering into a contract,

International Data

One-fifth of the world's elderly population is Chinese. By 2020, there will be more than 230 million elderly Chinese, about 15.6 percent of their total population.

SOURCE: DHHS 1998

marrying, dropping out of school, and voting. These limitations would not be tolerated if placed on individuals because of sex or race. Hence, **ageism**, the belief that age is associated with certain psychological, behavioural, or intellectual traits, at least in reference to children, is significantly more tolerated than sexism or racism in Canada.

Despite this differential treatment, people in our country are fascinated with youth and being young. This was not always the case. The elderly were once highly valued—particularly older men who headed families and businesses. Younger men even powdered their hair, wore wigs, and dressed in a way that made them look older. Remember, however, that in 1901, only 5.05 percent of the population was 65 or older; almost 45 percent of the population was 19 or under. In that year, the median age of the Canadian population (excluding Newfoundland) was 22.7 years (Novak 1997). Being old was rare and respected; to some it was a sign that God looked favourably on that individual.

One theory argues that the shift from valuing the old to valuing the young took place during the transition from an agriculturally based society to an industrial one. Land, which was often owned by elders, became less important, as did their knowledge and skills about land-based economies. With industrialization, technological skills, training, and education became more important than land ownership. Called **modernization theory**, this position argues that as a society becomes more technologically advanced, the position of the elderly declines (Cowgill and Holmes 1972).

CONSIDERATION

Using participant observation techniques, Cahill (1993) recorded the treatment of children in public places for nearly 300 hours over a two-year period. He observed that children are, for example, restricted in the places they can go, are often discouraged from eating in some restaurants, and are excluded from some apartment complexes. Further, public accommodations do not adequately meet the needs of children—pay telephones, sinks, and water fountains are out of children's reach. Cahill concludes that such limitations, as well as the segregation of children in schools, limits communication between children and adults, creating differences in their respective social worlds. The result is "…a distinct [youth] subculture of which adults are only vaguely aware…" (p. 400).

YOUTH AND AGING

Age is largely socially defined. Cultural definitions of "old" and "young" vary from society to society, from time to time, and from person to person. For example, the older a person, the less likely that person is to define a particular age as old. In a national study of more than 2503 men and women aged 18 to 75, 30 percent of those under 25 responded that "old" is between 40 and 64 years of age. Only 8 percent of those over the age of 65 reported that 65 was old (Clements 1993). In ancient Greece or Rome, where the average life expectancy was 20 years, a person was old at 18; similarly, a person was old at 30 in medieval Europe.

Age is also a variable that has a dramatic impact on a person's life (Matras 1990 identified 1 to 4):

1. Age determines life experiences, since the date of birth determines the historical period in which a person lives. As Harrigan (1992) notes, 50 years ago we couldn't have imagined any need for metal detectors to be installed at school entrances.
2. Different ages are associated with different developmental stages (physiological, psychological, and social) and abilities. Ben Franklin observed, "at 20 years of age the will reigns; at 30 the wit; at 40 judgment."
3. Age defines roles and expectations of behaviour. The expression "act your age" implies that some behaviours are not considered appropriate for people of certain ages.
4. Age influences the social groups to which one belongs. Whether one is part of a sixth grade class, a labour union, or a seniors' bridge club depends on age.
5. Age defines legal status. It defines when you can get a driver's licence, vote, get married without your parents' permission, and become eligible for social security benefits.

Childhood, Adulthood, and Elderhood

Every society assigns different social roles to different age groups. **Age grading** is the assignment of social roles to given chronological ages (Matras 1990). Although the number of age grades varies by society, most societies make at least three distinctions: childhood, adulthood, and elderhood.

Childhood The period of childhood in our society is from birth through age 17 and is often subdivided into infancy, childhood, and adolescence. Infancy has always been recognized as a stage of life, but the social category of childhood only developed after industrialization, urbanization, and modernization took place. Before industrialization, infant mortality was high because of the lack of adequate health care and proper nutrition. Once infants could be expected to survive infancy, the concept of childhood emerged, and society began to develop norms in reference to children. In Canada, child labour laws prohibit children from being used as inexpensive labour, educational mandates require that children begin school by the age of six or seven, and the criminal law impose severe penalties for the sexual exploitation of children.

Adulthood The period from age 18 through 64 is generally subdivided into young adulthood, adulthood, and middle age. Each status involves dramatic role changes related to entering the workforce, getting married, and having children. The concept of "middle age" is a relatively recent one that has developed as life expectancy has been extended. Some people in this phase are known as members of the **"sandwich generation"** since they are often emotionally and economically responsible for both their young children and their aging parents.

Elderhood At age 65, a person is likely to be considered elderly, a category that is often subdivided into the young-old, old, and old-old. Membership in one of these categories does not necessarily depend on chronological age. The growing number of healthy, active, independent elderly is often considered the young-old, whereas the old-old are less healthy, less active, and more dependent.

By 2041, an estimated 23 percent of the population will be aged 65 and older, nearly double the proportion in 1995.

SOURCE: Statistics Canada 1998a

SOCIOLOGICAL THEORIES OF AGE INEQUALITY

Three sociological theories help explain age inequality and the continued existence of ageism in Canada. These theories—structural-functionalism, conflict theory, and symbolic interactionism—are discussed in the following sections.

Structural-Functionalist Perspective

Structural-functionalism emphasizes the interdependence of society—how one part of a social system interacts with other parts to benefit the whole. From a functionalist perspective, the elderly must gradually relinquish their roles to younger members of society. This transition is viewed as natural and necessary to maintain the integrity of the social system. The elderly gradually withdraw as they prepare for death, and society withdraws from the elderly by segregating them in housing such as retirement villages and nursing homes. In the interim, the young have learned through the educational institution how to function in the roles surrendered by the elderly. In essence, a balance in society is achieved whereby the various age groups perform their respective functions: the young go to school, adults fill occupational roles, and the elderly, with obsolete skills and knowledge, disengage. As this process continues, each new group moves up and replaces another, benefiting society and all of its members.

This theory is known as **disengagement theory** (Cummings and Henry 1961). Some researchers no longer accept this position as valid, however, given the increasing number of elderly who remain active throughout life (Riley 1987). In contrast to disengagement theory, **activity theory** emphasizes that the elderly disengage in part because they are structurally segregated and isolated, not because they have a natural tendency to do so. For those elderly who remain active, role loss may be minimal. In studying 1720 respondents who reported using a senior centre in the previous year, Miner et al. (1993) found that those who used the centre were less disengaged and more socially active than those who did not use it.

Conflict Perspective

The conflict perspective focuses on age grading as another form of inequality as both the young and the old occupy subordinate statuses. Some conflict theorists emphasize that individuals at both ends of the age continuum are superfluous to a capitalist economy. Children are untrained, inexperienced, and neither actively producing nor consuming in an economy that requires both. Similarly, the elderly, although once working, are no longer productive and often lack required skills and levels of education. Both young and old are considered part of what is called the dependent population; that is, they are an economic drain on society. Hence, children are required to go to school in preparation for entry into a capitalist economy, and the elderly are forced to retire.

Other conflict theorists focus on how different age strata represent different interest groups that compete with one another for scarce resources. Debates about funding for public schools, child health programs, social security, and Medicare largely represent the conflicting interests of the young versus the old.

Symbolic Interactionist Perspective

The symbolic interactionist perspective emphasizes the importance of examining the social meaning and definitions associated with age. The elderly are often defined in stereotypical ways, contributing to a host of myths surrounding the inevitability of physical and mental decline. Table 6.1 identifies some of these myths.

Table 6.1	Myths and Facts about the Elderly

Health

Myth: The elderly are always sick; most are in nursing homes.

Fact: In 1994, almost three out of four seniors aged 65 and older and living at home rated their health as good to excellent. Among seniors aged 85 and older, more than three in four rated their health as good or very good. Although the likelihood that an individual will live in some type of special-care home for the aged (e.g., nursing homes, hospitals, etc.) increases with age, only 1.4 percent of men and 1.7 percent of women between the ages of 65 and 74 lived in such institutions. Among those 85 and older, about one-quarter of men and slightly more than a third of women (36.3 percent) lived in special-care homes (Novak 1997; Statistics Canada 1998a).

Automobile Accidents

Myth: The elderly are dangerous drivers and the most likely age group to die in car accidents.

Fact: Although older drivers are more likely to be seriously injured or to die in car crashes than are most of their younger counterparts, the worst record is actually held by the youngest drivers. According to Statistics Canada, the mortality rate for drivers aged 65 or older is 27.2 per 100 000. Although that rate falls to 14 deaths per 100 000 for drivers aged 25 to 64, the rate climbs to 40.6 per 100 000 for those aged 15 to 19 (Canadian Press 1999: B11). Up to age 75, older drivers tend to drive fewer miles than younger drivers and compensate for their reduced reaction time by driving more carefully. Nevertheless, the normal processes of aging, diminishing vision and hearing and decreasing attention spans, may interfere with the ability to drive a car (Carney 1989). Using 1996–97 data, Statistics Canada reports that 34 percent of seniors with vision problems and 37 percent of those with manual dexterity problems were licensed to drive. As well, 26 percent of seniors with a serious cognitive problem hold a driver's licence (Canadian Press 1999: B11).

Mental Status

Myth: The elderly are senile.

Fact: Although some of the elderly learn more slowly and forget more quickly, most remain oriented and mentally intact. Only 20 to 25 percent develop Alzheimer's disease or some other incurable form of brain disease. Senility is not inevitable as people age.

Crime

Myth: The elderly are more likely to be victims of crime than the young are.

Fact: Although older people express more fear of crime than younger people do, "studies in Britain, the United States, and Canada show that older people run less risk of victimization than any other group" (Novak 1997). While evidencing low rates of victimization in general, Plouffe (1991) suggests that the elderly may run a higher risk of being victimized by consumer fraud. According to the National Advisory Council on Aging, factors that may create a higher risk of fraud among the elderly include: "a lack of information, social isolation, and [a] lack of wariness in business relations" (Novak 1997).

continued

| Table 6.1 | Myths and Facts about the Elderly (continued) |

Sexuality
Myth: Sexual satisfaction disappears with age.
Fact: Many elderly persons report sexual satisfaction. For example, in a study of 61 elderly men (average age of 71, both with and without sexual partners), sexual satisfaction was rated at an average of 6.3 on a scale where 1 = no satisfaction and 10 = extremely high satisfaction (Mulligan and Pagluta 1991).

Adaptability
Myth: The elderly cannot adapt to new working conditions.
Fact: A high proportion of the elderly are flexible in accepting change in their occupations and earnings. Adaptability depends on the individual: many young are set in their ways, and many older people adapt to change readily.

SOURCES: Binstock, Robert H. 1986. "Public Policy and the Elderly." *Journal of Geriatric Psychiatry* 19: 115–43; Canadian Press. 1999. "Older Drivers More at Risk." *KW Record*, November 17: B11; Carney, James. 1989. "Can a Driver Be Too Old?" *Time*, January 16: 28; Mulligan, T., and R. F. Pagluta Jr. 1991. "Sexual Interest, Activity and Satisfaction among Male Nursing Home Residents." *Archives of Sexual Behaviour* 20: 199–204; Novak, Mark. 1997. *Aging and Society: A Canadian Perspective*, 3d ed. Scarborough, Ont.: Nelson.

Media portrayals contribute to the negative image of the elderly. The young are typically portrayed in active, vital roles and are often overrepresented in commercials. In contrast, the elderly are portrayed as difficult, complaining, and burdensome and are often underrepresented in commercials. A recent study of the elderly in popular films from the 1940s through the 1980s concluded that "older individuals of both genders were portrayed as less friendly, having less romantic activity, and enjoying fewer positive outcomes than younger characters at a movie's conclusion" (Brazzini et al. 1997: 541).

The elderly are also portrayed as childlike in terms of clothes, facial expressions, temperament, and activities—a phenomenon known as **infantilizing elders** (Arluke and Levin 1990). For example, young and old are often paired together. When Grandpa Simpson baby-sits Bart and his siblings, he invariably falls asleep before Bart's baby sister, Maggie. Jack Lemmon and Walter Matthau in *Grumpy Old Men* get "cranky" when they get tired and, in the *Odd Couple II*, lose their luggage, direction, money, and car during a cross-country trip. Finally, the elderly are often depicted in role reversal, cared for by their adult children as in the situation comedies *Golden Girls* and *Frazier*.

Negative stereotypes and media images of the elderly engender **gerontophobia**—a shared fear or dread of the elderly, which may create a self-fulfilling prophecy. For example, an elderly person forgets something and attributes that behaviour to age. A younger person, however, engaging in the same behaviour, is unlikely to attribute forgetfulness to age given cultural definitions surrounding the onset of senility. Thus, the elderly, having learned the social meanings associated with being old, may themselves perpetuate the negative stereotypes.

PROBLEMS OF YOUTH IN CANADA

By the year 2001, there will be an estimated 1.9 million children under the age of five, 2.1 million between the ages of five and nine, 2.1 million between the ages of 10 and 14, and 2.1 million between the ages of 15 and 19, for a total of 8.2 million "youth" in Canada (Statistics Canada 1998a). In spite of the presumed benefits of being young, numerous problems are associated with childhood. Further, some of our most pressing social problems can be traced to early childhood experiences and adolescent behavioural problems (Weissberg and Kuster 1997).

Not surprising, what happens to children is increasingly defined as a social problem. This chapter's Focus on Social Problems Research highlights a recent Canadian study that examines the importance of parenting style to child development.

Children and the Law

Historically, children have had little control over their lives. They have been "double dependent" on both their parents and the state. Indeed, our ancestors regarded children as property. Beginning in the 1960s, however, the view that children should have more autonomy became popular and was codified in several legal decisions.

The dominant view of children today, as expressed by the courts as well as by the public, involves taking "a protective stance toward children rather than empowering children to care for themselves" ("Children's Legal Rights" 1993: 342; Regoli and Hewitt 1997). Examples of protective legislation include requiring child abuse prevention and treatment programs, and ensuring education for children with disabilities. Every province and territory in Canada has a stated commitment to integrated, inclusive education for children with disabilities. In addition, the ***Young Offenders Act (YOA),*** which governs the conduct of Canadian youths under the age of 18, notes in its Declaration of Principles that "young people should not in all accounts be held accountable in the same manner or suffer the same consequences for their behaviours as adults." Toward that end, the *Young Offenders Act* dilutes strict criminal responsibility with the principle of "mitigated accountability." Thus, the Declaration of Principles also states that young offenders "require supervision, discipline and control but...also have special needs and require guidance and assistance" and that "where it is not inconsistent with the protection of society, taking no measures or taking measures other than judicial proceedings under this Act should be considered for dealing with young persons who have committed offences" (see Figure 6.1).

The *Young Offenders Act* also outlines that the rights and freedoms of young persons include a right to the "least possible interference" that is consistent with the protection of society, having regard for the needs of young people and the interests of their families. The Act allows for "alternative measures" in lieu of trial and punishment, prohibits the publication of the names of young offenders (except in exceptional circumstances such as, for example, if a youth is at large and considered by a judge to be "dangerous to others"), and restricts access to juvenile records. It also includes a variety of legal safeguards, for example, guarantees of legal representation, special provisions to ensure there is no improper questioning of a youth by police or other persons in positions of authority, and provisions for the notification of parents or other appropriate adults when a youth is arrested. All of these safeguards augment the rights extended to all Canadians under the *Charter of Rights and Freedoms.*

IS CHILD DEVELOP-MENT MORE AFFECTED BY PARENTING THAN BY SOCIAL CLASS?

Good parenting has a more profound effect on children than [do] poverty or affluence, a Canadian researcher has found in a landmark study that compared the childrearing practices of the rich and the poor. "The effects of parenting far outweigh the effects of social-class background," said Prof. Douglas Willms, director of the University of New Brunswick's Atlantic Centre for Policy Research.

No group has a monopoly on strong child-rearing skills—or questionable ones. Weak practices are found in near-equal measure among the rich, the middle class, and the poor, according to the study, written by Prof. Willms and Ruth Chao of the University of California, Riverside. It is to be published soon in Prof. Willms' book, *Vulnerable Children*. "For too long we've characterized poor families and single-parent families as the source of children with behaviour problems and low academic achievement," said Prof. Willms said in an interview. "It's really not the case. What really matters is parenting practices: how they parent, how much they've engaged with their children, how responsive they are, how much they monitor behaviours, and so on." The authors say their study, based on a representative sample of 2- to 11-year-olds, challenges the notion of a "culture of poverty," the widespread belief that the poor are doing such a bad job of raising their children that they are dooming them to live on society's margins. However, if the study means less stigma for poor parents, it also suggests an explosive political result: an end to targeted programs for the poor, and a move to share resources with the middle class and affluent. "If you have targeted programs that try to address the problems of low-income families, single-parent families, and so on, you're only going to reach a small proportion of vulnerable children. That's one of the fundamental messages of this research," said Prof. Willms....

Parents were asked 25 questions to determine how they ranked on four scales, each measuring positive childrearing practices. The first scale, Rational (also known as Consistent), included questions such as, "How often do you get annoyed with [your child] for saying or doing something he/she is not supposed to do?" and "How often do you think that the kind of punishment you give him/her depends on your mood?" The questions on the second scale, Responsive, included, "How often do you praise [your child] by saying something like 'Good for you!' or 'What a nice thing you did!'...The third scale, Firm approach, included, "When you give him/her a command or order to do something, what proportion of the time do you make sure that he/she does it?" The fourth scale, Reasons with child, was based on a single question, "When [your child] breaks the rules or does things that he/she is not supposed to do, how often do you: (a) Calmly discuss the problem? and (b) Describe alternative ways of behaving that are acceptable?" Parents were ranked out of five on each scale...and placed into one of four categories, which co-author Douglas Willms describes as tendencies, rather than rigid groupings....

The study had several surprising findings about how Canadians are raising their children.

- Just one-third of Canadian parents can be characterized as "authoritative"–the most skilled, according to the authors, at raising their children in a fair, firm way. Children of authoritative parents are the most likely to do well in school and the least likely to develop behavioural problems. These parents had slightly higher than average income, education levels, and job prestige. However, parents from all backgrounds could be found within this group.
- One in seven parents of preschool children are struggling. Prof. Willms labels them "permissive-irrational," meaning that they often ignore bad behaviour and are not consistent in disciplining

their children. The same proportion of parents of school-age children is in a slightly different category, even less skilled, which the authors call "irresponsible," because they scored uniformly low on four key parenting scales. These parents had slightly lower than average levels of income, education, and job prestige—but again, families from all backgrounds fell into this category.
- Parents become steadily less responsive toward their children once they reach the age of four. At the same time, responsiveness is growing more, not less important to children's development....

The study is part of a massive Canadian effort to understand what makes some children thrive in school or turn to drugs and crime. The National Longitudinal Survey of Children and Youth, sponsored by the federal government, is tracking thousands of children from birth to age 11....The longitudinal survey has already found that poor children tend to fall behind the children of the middle and upper classes in school and develop more emotional problems. (Children of single parents, too, have more emotional and behavioural problems, no matter what financial status.) On the other hand, there are more middle-class children than [there are] poor children with problems, because the middle class is the larger group. Prof. Willms and Prof. Chao set out to find whether the childrearing styles of Canadians differ according to their social class. They then looked at whether the most skilled parents were producing children who were most likely to thrive. Beyond that, they wanted to know whether the most skilled parents among the poor are raising children who do better in school and suffer fewer social problems than the average poor child.

SOURCE: Abridged from Fine, Sean. 1999a. "Child Development More Affected by Parenting than Social Class." *The Globe and Mail*, October 4: A4.

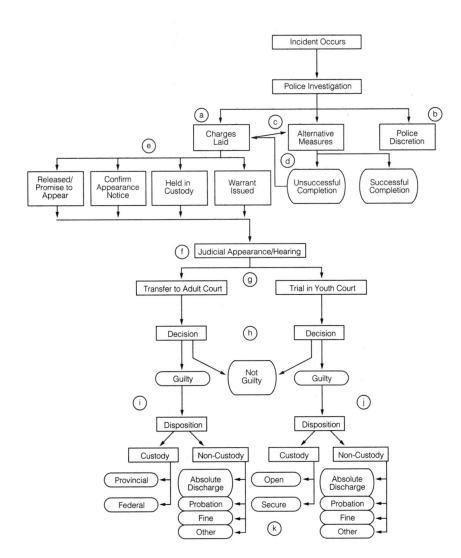

Figure 6.1
Justice Process for Youths
SOURCE: Statistics Canada. 1998. *Canada Yearbook*. Ottawa: Ministry of Industry.

Canada has adopted the *Hague Convention on the Civil Aspects of International Child Abduction* and the program "Our Missing Children" to protect abducted children from crossing international borders. Canada is also a signatory to the United Nations Convention on Children's Rights, a treaty that has been described as "the most comprehensive human rights document ever adopted by the international community," and ratified by all but two countries in the world. which ones!

As required under Article 44 of the Convention, in 1999 the Canadian Coalition for the Rights of Children issued its first five-year nongovernmental progress report to the United Nations. Entitled *The UN Convention on the Rights of the Child: How Does Canada Measure Up?*, the report concluded that Canada meets most of its obligations under the UN Convention on the Rights of the Child. It notes, for example, that children's right to education is assured in Canadian legislation, which provides for primary and secondary schooling and requires all children to attend school. It acknowledges that the *Canada Health Act* provides free universal health care for all Canadians; that refugee children are eligible for health care, education, and settlement services in Canada; and that our provincial and territorial governments have a duty to intervene to protect a child at risk from abuse or neglect. At the same time, however, the report concludes that Canada had some way to go before full compliance with the Convention is achieved. Among their findings:

- Canada has not honoured its commitment to spend 0.7 percent of its GNP on international aid;
- Statistics and information on federal programs and policies for children are unclear and unreliable. For example, there are no national statistics on child abuse and neglect in Canada and there is insufficient information about how to prevent child maltreatment. This lack of information constrains the development of effective services.
- Canadian legislation rarely recognizes children specifically and there are few redress mechanisms available to them. As such, children's fundamental freedoms are very dependent on the goodwill of adults. Rights education is not part of our schools' core curricula and children's convention rights have not been widely promoted in Canada. In child welfare cases, the child's best interests are weighed against parental rights. In other areas, children's "best interests" are ignored or interpreted without considering the views of children at all. The general principle of maximum survival and development is not assured for our most vulnerable children, such as children with disabilities, Aboriginal children, and children in the care of the state.
- Where a child lives often determines the degree to which his or her rights are met. There can be significant differences in the programs and services children receive in different parts of the country. Home care services for families of children with disabilities vary widely and there is no effort to create standards or even to define basic services. Child welfare services are often fragmented and uncoordinated within jurisdictions, with resources unevenly allocated across regions. For Aboriginal children living on reserves, the delivery of services is further complicated by jurisdictional disputes.
- Resources for children's programs and services are often stretched or unstable. Cutbacks to education funding and the closing of schools have undermined access to and the quality of education, especially in special education, citizenship, social studies, and arts education. Child welfare services have taken a back seat to budget cuts in some provinces, despite growing caseloads, chronic waiting lists, and worker burnout. Even with the high number of Aboriginal children affected by disabilities, the delivery of services in Aboriginal communities is generally poor or nonexistent. Canada has had little success in reducing child poverty, and 19.8 percent of children under the age of 18 live in low-income families (Figure 6.2).
- Aboriginal children have a disability rate that is more than twice the national average. Aboriginal children are at greater risk of school failure than other Canadian children. A disproportionate number of Aboriginal children are victims of abuse and neglect compared to non-Aboriginal children. The suicide rate among Aboriginal youth is about five times the national average.
- An estimated 535 000 children and youth under age 20 have some form of disability. Children with disabilities have varying opportunities to live "full

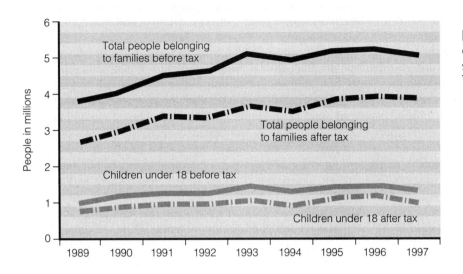

Figure 6.2
Canadians in Poverty
SOURCE: Fine 1999b: A1.

and decent lives" and the supports and services they need are not considered an entitlement but a privilege. Many families of children with disabilities do not receive adequate assistance. Early identification and intervention services are not universally available and the right to appropriate education in the most enabling environment is not guaranteed.

- Abused and neglected children continue to fall through the cracks in our child welfare systems. Inquests and inquiries into the deaths of children who were killed by their parents speak of inadequate risk assessments, insufficient training for social workers, a lack of service coordination and information sharing, a shortage of placement facilities, failed foster placements, a crisis orientation, and a lack of long-term planning for children who are in the care of the state.

- The refugee determination system is slow and the long wait unduly prolongs uncertainty in the lives of children and their families. Family reunification is rarely dealt with in a positive and expeditious manner. The interests of children are not taken into account in decisions to deport their parents. Children, even if born in Canada, do not have to be considered in the deportation hearings of their parents.

- Discrimination against people because of disability is prohibited by federal and provincial legislation but people with disabilities, and children in particular, still experience prejudice. Young people with disabilities experience more abuse and violence than those without disabilities. In addition, many disability issues are examined from the adult perspective and the special needs of children are overlooked. For example, provincial building codes include accessibility standards but they were not designed with children in mind.

- The few complaint mechanisms that are available to children and youth tend to be difficult to access.

Economic Discrimination

Children are discriminated against in terms of employment, age restrictions, wages, and training programs. Traditionally, children worked on farms and in factories but were displaced by the Industrial Revolution. In the 1880s, the

National Data

In 1999, the Ontario government tabled its controversial *Safe Streets Act*, aimed at banning squeegee kids and aggressive panhandlers. Offenders are subject to fines of up to $500; repeat offenders face penalties of as much as $1000 or six months in jail.

SOURCE: *Maclean's* 1999a: 41

National Data

Of the 4.5 million people in the greater Toronto area, about 50 000 children receive food from food banks, up from 33 000 in 1989.

SOURCE: Fine 1999b

National Data

Teens living in families with incomes below $30 000 a year are twice as likely to smoke as teens living in high-income families. Poor teens are also twice as likely to drop out of school as teens from families with high incomes.

SOURCE: Ross et al. 1996

Factory Acts "curbed the employment of both women and children on the grounds of protecting their health" (Krahn and Lowe 1993), and by 1929, children under age 14 were legally excluded from factory and mine employment in most provinces. Although the law was designed to protect children, it was also discriminatory in that it prohibited minors from having free access to jobs and economic independence. No such law exists for any other age group.

Young people in Canada often find it difficult to obtain any employment. In 1996, more than one out of every five Canadians between the ages of 15 and 24 had never held a job and the unemployment rate for this group was approximately 16 percent. A high rate of youth unemployment is not unique to Canada but part of an international trend, with young people in European countries finding it as difficult or more difficult to find work. This difficulty is also encountered in relation to summer employment. Between 1989 and 1997, the unemployment rate for students seeking summer jobs rose from 11.2 percent to 16.7 percent. Compared to previous years, young people are now more likely to only get part-time rather than full-time summer jobs. In 1997, just less than a third of 15- to 16-year-olds (32 percent) worked during the summer; in 1989, almost twice as many had summer jobs (Statistics Canada 1998a).

Worldwide, there is also evidence that when global economic decisions are made, children suffer. Bradshaw et al. (1992) observed that the global debt crisis has led the world's business community to pressure developing countries into financial strategies that directly affect the well-being of children. For example, funding for immunization programs for children is often cut out of economic necessity. "This potential relationship between international debt and children's quality of life is one of the most important sociological issues in poor countries today" (p. 630).

Because of economic discrimination at both the individual and the institutional level, many children live in poverty. Some children in Canada face a heightened risk of poverty. For example, in 1995, three out of five Aboriginal children under the age of six were in low-income families, compared with a national rate of slightly more than one in four. Among Aboriginal children aged 6 to 14, the incidence of low income was 48 percent, more than double the national average. In that year, 45 percent of children under the age of six in the visible minority population were in low-income families (compared with 26 percent for all Canadians) (Statistics Canada 1998c).

According to the National Longitudinal Survey of Children and Youth, one-quarter of children aged four and five from low-income households (less than $30 000 a year) scored poorly on verbal tests that indicate readiness to learn. In contrast, only 15.6 percent of those children from middle-income households and 9.2 percent of higher-income children scored poorly on these tests. In addition, this survey reported that 14.6 percent of low-income children were in households that were ranked as "dysfunctional." Only 7.5 percent of children in middle-income homes and 5 percent of children in high-income homes were similarly identified. The survey also found that approximately 15 percent of those in the lowest of four income groups had problems with aggression, depression, anxiety, or hyperactivity. Of those who were not in the poorest group, only 9 percent suffered behavioural problems. Finally, about 7 percent of those who were in the poorest groups had failed a grade. Among those who were not in the poorest group, only 2 percent had failed a grade (Fine 1999b).

CONSIDERATION

The rate of child poverty increased by 45 percent between 1989 and 1995; in 1996, 1.5 million children were living in "straitened circumstances"—an increase of 60 percent since 1989. Childhood poverty is related to school failure (Fields and Smith 1998), negative involvement with parents (Harris and Marmer 1996), stunted growth, reduced cognitive abilities, limited emotional development (Brooks-Gunn and Duncan 1997), and a higher likelihood of dropping out of school (Duncan et al. 1998).

Kids in Crisis

Childhood is a stage of life that is socially constructed by structural and cultural forces of the past and present. The old roles for children as labourers and farm helpers are disappearing, yet no new roles have emerged. While being bombarded by the media, children must face the challenges of an uncertain economic future, peer culture, music videos, divorce, incidents of abuse, poverty, and crime. Parents and public alike fear children are becoming increasingly involved with sex, drugs, alcohol, and violence. Some even argue that childhood as a stage of life is disappearing (Adler 1994).

Although some argue that children are pessimistic about their future and are living in fear (Ingrassia 1993), this chapter's The Human Side describes the growth of one organization for children, launched by a Canadian youth, that is run by children and devoted to improving the lives of children worldwide.

DEMOGRAPHICS: THE "GREYING OF CANADA"

The population of Canada, as in many other countries around the world is "greying," that is, getting older. Here, the definition of "older" is age 65 or beyond. Figure 6.3 suggests how Canada's population will age in the years to come.

The number of elderly is increasing for three reasons. First, the 10 million baby boomers born between 1947 and 1967 are getting older. Second, life expectancy has increased as a result of better medical care; sanitation, nutrition, and housing improvements; and a general trend toward modernization. Finally, lowered birthrates contribute to a higher percentage of the elderly. Since the proportion of the elderly is influenced by such variables as the number of baby boomers, life expectancy, and birthrates, different countries have different proportions of the elderly. Western Europe and the Scandinavian countries have a higher percentage of the elderly; Canada, the United States, Japan, Israel, and the former Soviet Union have lower percentages.

Age Pyramids

Age pyramids are a way of showing in graph form the percentage of a population in various age groups. In 1901 the Canadian age pyramid looked very much like a true pyramid: the base of the pyramid was large, indicating that most people were in their younger years, and the top of the pyramid was much smaller, showing that only a small percentage of the population was elderly. By

FREE THE CHILDREN: CHILDREN HELPING CHILDREN

Free the Children, an international children's organization with members in more than 20 countries, was founded in 1995 by Craig Kielburger, a 16-year-old Canadian. Kielburger first became an advocate for children's rights when he was 12 years old and read about the murder of a child from Pakistan who had been sold into bondage as a carpet weaver. Free the Children is a registered nonprofit charitable organization whose mission statement identifies as its two main goals (1) to free children from poverty, exploitation, and abuse, and (2) to give children a voice, leadership training, and opportunities to take action on issues that affect them on a local or an international level. Only youth under the age of 18 within the organization vote on decisions regarding policy and projects and act as spokespersons for children or for the organization. Free the Children is also very particular about the adults who work for them. They demand that the adults who work with them respect the fact that FTC is a children's organization run by children for children and *not* an organization run by adults for children.

Kielburger has received many awards for his work, including the State of the World Forum Award and the Roosevelt Freedom Medal. He was named a Global Leader of Tomorrow at the World Economic Forum in Davos, Switzerland, and Ambassador of the First Children's Embassy in Sarajevo. His organization has also flourished and more than 100 000 children have participated in FTC's campaigns and activities. These include:

- A "Friendship School Campaign." To date, students have raised funds to construct 20 schools in Latin America. They have put together and shipped more than 5000 school kits to South Africa, the Philippines, Latin America, and India. Their Millennium Challenge is to build 100 schools and to ship 100 000 school kits to children by the year 2001.

- Young people from FTC have raised money to set up a piping and reservoir system to bring clean water from the mountains into two villages in Waslala, Nicaragua, and to build one medical clinic. They have shipped more than $200 000 in medical supplies to the area.

- FTC raised more than $100 000 for the construction of a live-in rehabilitation and education centre for freed bonded child labourers in Alwar, India. The centre, which accommodates up to 100 children at any given time, provides counselling, education, medical aid, and vocational training, and seeks to facilitate the reintegration of these children into society. The rehabilitation centre was completed in the fall of 1998 and is operated by the South Asian Coalition of Child Servitude (SACCS).

- During the Kosovo crisis, students in more than 100 schools put together 10 000 kits of health care and hygiene items, 8000 stuffed animals, 2000 baby kits, and gathered 50 000 items of clothing for Balkan refugees. The health kits were distributed to children in camps in Kosovo, Belgrade, and North America.

FREE THE CHILDREN: CHILDREN HELPING CHILDREN *(continued)*

- Free the Children has also bought arable land and farming equipment for 15 fatherless families in Nicaragua to set up a coffee cooperative. It is believed that the children in these families will benefit if their mothers are allowed to improve their socioeconomic status and to grow their own food.

  Free the Children has helped to convince members of the business community to adopt codes of conduct regarding child labour. They have also lobbied governments to change laws to better protect children from sexual exploitation. Approximately 90 percent of the money raised by FTC goes directly to projects.

SOURCE: Adapted and abridged from the Free the Children Web site at <www.freethechildren.org/>.

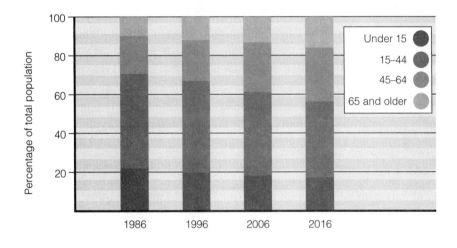

Figure 6.3
Percent of Total Population
SOURCE: "A Changing People" 1999

the year 2041, Canada's "pyramid" will look quite unlike a pyramid and reflect the aging of the Canadian population (see Figure 6.4a and 6.4b).

The number of people at various ages in a society is important because the demand for housing, education, health care, and jobs varies as different age groups, particularly baby boomers, move through the pyramid. For example, as Canada "greys," colleges and universities will recruit older students, advertisements will be directed toward older consumers, and elderly housing and medical care needs will increase.

Age and Region

In Canada, certain areas of the country have older populations than others, and five regions in particular can be identified: a large area that involves parts of Manitoba and Saskatchewan (where more than 17 percent of the population is over the age of 65); the Okanagan Valley and the Victoria–Vancouver region in British Columbia; a ring of Ontario townships surrounding Toronto; and a block of counties in southwest Nova Scotia. At present, Saskatchewan has proportionally more seniors than any other province; the territories have the lowest proportion of seniors. Among urban centres, the Victoria and the St. Catharines-Niagara census metropolitan areas have the highest proportion of seniors.

Figure 6.4a

Canadian Population Pyramids, Age and Sex, 1901

SOURCE: Wayne W. McVey Jr., and Warren E. Kalbach. 1995. *Canadian Population*. Scarborough: Nelson Canada

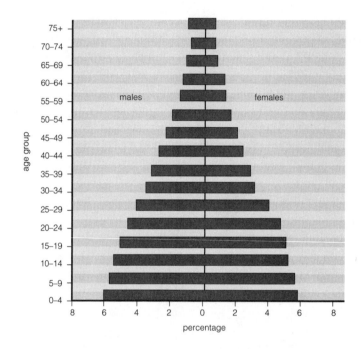

Figure 6.4b

Canadian Population Pyramids, Age and Sex, 2041[a]

[a] low = population growth projection based on 1991 census data

SOURCE: George, M. V., M. J. Norris, F. Nault, S. Loh, and S. Y. Dai. 1994. *Population Projections for Canada, Provinces, and Territories 1993–2016*. Ottawa: Minister of Industry, Science and Technology

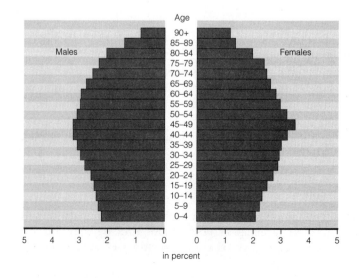

In some cases, areas of the country have "aged" due to out-migration by the young. The large proportion of the elderly in Saskatchewan is due to this factor. In contrast, other areas of the country exert considerable appeal for the elderly because of, for example, a temperate climate and the notable presence of other elderly people. Such factors draw many elderly people to such areas as Victoria, Vancouver, and the Okanagan Valley. Consider as well that, while Winnipeg lacks the temperate climate found in Victoria, its ability to furnish suitable housing and necessary services provides an incentive for the in-migration of elderly people from its hinterlands. Figure 6.5 provides a map of what the projected median age will be in various parts of the country in 2005. It is notable that those areas populated with a high proportion of Indigenous people will be younger, on average, than other parts of the country. Because of birth rates that are higher than the Canadian average and lower life expectancies, Indigenous people as a group are younger than non-Indigenous peoples in Canada are.

Age and Gender

In Canada, elderly women outnumber elderly men. The 1991 sex ratio for Canadians aged 65 to 74 was 82 men for every 100 women. Because differences increase with advanced age, at ages 75 to 84 there are 66 men for every 100 women, and at ages 85 and over, there are 44 males for every 100 females (Gee 1995). Men die at an earlier age than women do for both biological and sociological reasons—heart disease, stress, and occupational risk (see Chapter 2). The fact that women live longer results in a sizable number of elderly women who are poor. Not only do women generally make less money than men do, but with increasing age and the higher mortality of men, women are more likely to find themselves living alone on a reduced income.

According to the National Council of Welfare (1995), encroaching poverty often necessitates that women sell their family home and move to rental or institutional settings. In addition, the risk of poverty for elderly women remains significant in that relatively few have access to additional private-sector pensions (i.e., nongovernment) such as those provided by employers to employees. Findings derived from Statistics Canada's Labour Market Activity Survey and prepared specifically for the Canadian Advisory Council on the Status of Women (Townson 1995) indicate that only slightly more than one-third (35.3 percent) of women, versus 41.0 percent of men, in the Canadian labour force were covered by company pension plans. Certain groups, such as First Nations women and women with disabilities, are particularly unlikely to be covered by a private pension plan. The likelihood of poverty is particularly pronounced among elderly women with disabilities (Ross et al. 1994).

Age and Social Class

How long a person lives is influenced by social class. In general, the higher the social class, the longer the person lives, the fewer the debilitating illnesses suffered, the greater the number of social contacts and friends, the less likely to define oneself as "old," and the greater the likelihood of success in adapting to retirement. Higher social class is also related to fewer residential moves, higher life satisfaction, more leisure time, and more positively self-rated health. Functional limitations such as problems with walking, dressing, and bathing are

Figure 6.5
Median Age, 2005
SOURCE: "A Changing People" 1999.

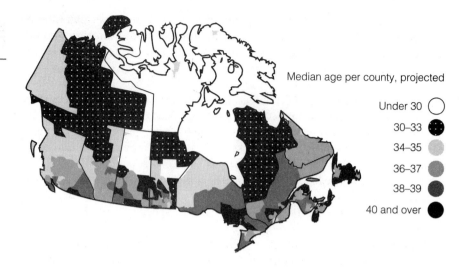

Median age per county, projected

Under 30	○
30–33	●
34–35	◐
36–37	◑
38–39	◕
40 and over	●

also lower among higher income groups (Seeman and Adler 1998). In short, the higher one's socioeconomic status, the longer, happier, and healthier one's life.

PROBLEMS OF THE ELDERLY

Many of the problems of the elderly can be traced to the ideology of ageism. In response to this ideology, Betty Friedan (1993) advocates abandoning the cultural emphasis on youth and moving toward "the fountain of age." She suggests looking

> into this new period of life with openness, with change, with vitality....It's time to look at age on its own terms, and put names on its values and strengths, breaking through the definition of age solely as deterioration or decline from youth. The problem is how to break through the cocoon of our illusory youth and risk a new stage in life, where there are no prescribed roles, no models, nor rigid rules or visible rewards—how to step out into the true existential unknown of these years of life now open to us and find our own terms for living them. (p. 69)

Friedan's book *The Fountain of Age* (1993) suggests that most North Americans view the aging process with fear and anxiety over what is believed to be inevitable physical and mental decline. She argues that the problem is not age per se, but the inability to look beyond youth to the possibilities of creative aging. Friedan warns, however, that the elderly cannot reach their full potential if society's barriers, both structural and cultural, remain.

Lack of Employment

What one does (occupation), for how long (work history), and for how much (wages) are important determinants of retirement income. Indeed, employment is important because it provides the foundation for economic resources later in life. Yet, for the elderly who want to work, entering and remaining in the labour force may be difficult because of negative stereotypes, lower levels of education, reduced geographical mobility, fewer employable skills, and discrimination. Novak (1997: 197) notes that at least three economic forces lead Canadian workers to retire at age 65:

> **First, some workers with good pension plans may earn more money in retirement than if they keep on working. Taxes, the cost of commuting, clothes, lunches, and other work-related expenses may make work an expensive option.**
>
> **Second, most private pension plans begin to pay full benefits at age 65...[and] many occupational pension plans penalize a person for staying on past retirement age....**
>
> **Third, OAS/GIS payments start at age 65, as do the Canada and Quebec Pension Plan payments. A person who works past age 65 will still get these benefits, but will lose a large portion of them through higher taxes.**

Those who wish to enter the workforce at an older age or who, because of financial necessity, find it necessary to re-enter the labour force after retirement may be stymied in their attempts. The most common reason that workers over age 45 give for ending their job search is the perception that no work is available. Corroborating this perception to some degree is the fact that, from 1976 to 1994, the average time that unemployed 45- to 64-year-olds were out of work doubled from 17 weeks to 33 weeks. At present, older workers who look for work are likely to be unemployed for almost twice as long as those aged 15 to 24 (Statistics Canada 1998a). Although employers cannot advertise a position by age, they can state that the position is an "entry level" one or that "two to three years' experience" is required (Knoke and Kalleberg 1994).

Retirement

Retirement is a relatively recent phenomenon. Before social security, individuals continued to work into old age. Today, the proportion of retirees under age 60 is double the rate it was in the late 1970s and one-quarter of all new retirees are between the ages of 55 and 59. Between 1975 and 1991, the number of working Canadians in their late 50s dropped 14 percent; in Australia the equivalent drop was 20 percent and in the United States, 5 percent. In 1984, the Quebec Pension Plan reduced its minimum age requirements for retirement benefits to age 60 and, in 1987, the Canadian Pension Plan followed suit. However, the desire to remain financially independent and a lack of confidence in the social security system may encourage many workers to remain in the labour force longer than the minimum age requirements allow (Simon-Rusinowitz et al. 1996).

Retirement can be difficult in that "work" is often equated with "worth." A job structures one's life and provides an identity; the end of a job culturally signifies the end of one's productivity. Retirement may also involve a dramatic decrease in personal income.

In spite of the potential problems with retirement, most people retire willingly. In a study of Finnish adults 35 and older, 55 percent of the workers said they would stop work immediately on reaching retirement age (Huuhtanen and Piispa 1996). Most retirees report enjoying retirement and having a greater sense of well-being than younger people who are still working (Russell 1989). Some workers benefit from **phased retirement**, which permits them to withdraw gradually. As the number of elderly and, thus, the number of retirees increase, it will become easier to retire: there will be more retirement communities, senior citizen discounts, and products for the elderly. Negative stereotypes of the retired elderly may also change.

Retirement Income

In 1996, the elderly and children were the groups most likely to be classified as low income. However, this was not true for elderly people living in families. Indeed, in that year, the elderly in families were the *least* likely to be low income (8 percent), while children under the age of 18 were the most likely. In the last four decades, seniors in Canada have benefited from rising incomes. While in 1951, the average senior earned slightly more than half the income of Canadians of working age, in 1995, the average senior earned $20 300 or almost $84 for every $100 earned by working-aged Canadians (Statistics Canada 1998a).

At present, Canada's retirement income system is composed of three tiers: (1) governmental benefits such as Old Age Security (OAS) and the Guaranteed Income Supplement (GIS) designed to forestall the likelihood of poverty by furnishing all seniors with a taxable, flat-rate benefit (adjusted every three months as the Consumer Price Index increases) paid monthly regardless of their work histories or life circumstances; (2) the government-sponsored Canada Pension Plan (CPP) and the Quebec Pension Plan (QPP), which are designed to provide workers with a retirement income based on their pre-retirement earnings from ages 18 to 65; and (3) private savings, which include employer-sponsored private pensions plans, private investments, and Registered Retirement Savings Plans (RRSPs) (Townson 1995: 27). During the 1996–97 fiscal year, CPP, OAS, and GIS benefits cost the federal government $38 billion; in 1996, the Quebec government paid out $3.4 billion in QPP benefits.

In April 1999, the maximum monthly OAS pension was $411.23. While, in general, both men and women become eligible to receive OAS benefits at age 65, some exemptions do exist. For example, since 1989, those Canadian seniors whose net incomes exceed $50 000 yearly are required to repay some or all of their OAS benefits. As well, immigrants who have lived in Canada for fewer than 10 years are eligible for only partial benefits.

The GIS was introduced in 1966 to assist those seniors with little or no income other than their OAS pension. The amount given depends on the pensioner's income, marital status, and spouse's income. In general, the maximum GIS is reduced by $1 for every $2 of income a person has above the OAS pension. For example, in April 1999, a single pensioner without personal income would receive OAS benefits of $411.23 per month and a monthly GIS of $488.72. If the individual had a private pension providing $400 a month, the GIS would be reduced by $200 a month. Spouse's Allowance (SPA) is available to those between the ages of 60 and 64 whose spouses have died or those with low income whose spouses receive an OAS pension. The amount given depends on a pensioner's income and marital status. In April 1999, the maximum SPA benefit for widows and widowers was $747.45 and $729.56 for spouses of OAS pensioners.

Although GIS and OAS benefits are unrelated to an individual's prior income history, CPP/QPP benefits are directly based on a person's income earned between the ages of 18 and the time they claim retirement (between the ages of 60 and 70), and proportionately reflect their prior income patterns. In 1997, the CPP and the QPP covered 3.2 million Canadians. In that year, they additionally offered benefits to 350 000 persons with disabilities and 1.3 million survivors of people who had contributed to the plans.

Although full benefits do not begin until age 65, partial CPP/QPP payments can be received by retired persons between ages of 60 and 64, and a person can wait until age 70 to begin receiving enhanced payments. Those who start collecting at 60 receive 70 percent of the amount they would be entitled to receive at age 65. For those who delay retirement, an additional half a percentage point is added for each month past age 60 that retirement is delayed. Accordingly, those who postpone retirement to age 70 would receive 130 percent of their full (age 65) income. Increasingly, however, concern has been expressed over whether our social security system will be adequate to provide benefits for the rising numbers of elderly in the decades to come.

CONSIDERATION

The term **"new ageism"** refers to viewing the elderly as a burden on the economy and, specifically, on the youth of Canada. Younger workers are concerned that the size and number of benefits given to the elderly, particularly as the baby boomers move through the ranks, will drain the social security system. If that is the case, the government will have to increase taxes, decrease benefits, or find new sources of revenue. Concern in other countries over "equity between the generations" has already affected public policy. For example, in Japan government benefits can be taken back if redistribution is necessary; in Australia employee pension plans are mandatory;, and in South Korea workers must save 35 percent of their income for retirement in anticipation of government shortfalls (Peterson 1997).

Health Issues

The biology of aging is called **senescence**. It follows a universal pattern but does not have universal consequences. "Massive research evidence demonstrates that the aging process is neither fixed nor immutable. Biologists are now showing that many symptoms that were formerly attributed to aging—for example, certain disturbances in cardiac function or in glucose metabolism in the brain—are instead produced by disease" (Riley and Riley 1992: 221). Biological functioning is also intricately related to social variables. Altering lifestyles, activities, and social contacts affects mortality and morbidity. For example, a longitudinal study of men and women between 70 and 79 found that regular physical activity, higher numbers of ongoing positive social relationships, and a sense of self-efficacy enhanced physical and cognitive functioning (Seeman and Adler 1998).

Biological changes are consequences of either **primary aging** due to physiological variables such as cellular and molecular variation (e.g., grey hair) or **secondary aging**. Secondary aging entails changes attributable to poor diet, lack of exercise, increased stress, and the like. Secondary aging exacerbates and accelerates primary aging.

Many of the elderly are healthy, but as age increases, health tends to decline. Between 1990–91 and 1995–96, the total number of hospital separations among all age groups in Canada decreased except among those aged 65 and older (Health Canada 1999). The average length of hospital stay also increased significantly with age. While the average length of stay was 11 days, most age groups fell well below this. However, the 55 to 64 age group reached this level and elderly Canadians surpassed it (23 days for those 75 and over). Indeed, the Canadian average is actually skewed toward the older age groups (Health Canada 1999).

Some evidence suggests that health care may be rationed on the basis of age in Canada. For example, in what is believed to be the first large-scale Canadian study to examine treatment for heart attacks among the elderly, the researchers concluded that "[t]he older you are, the less likely you are to be treated." The research, conducted by Paula Rochon, of the Baycrest Centre for Geriatric Care in Toronto and the Institute for Clinical Evaluative Science, and published in the November 1999 issue of the *Canadian Medical Association Journal*, tracked more than 15 500 heart-attack patients aged 66 and older in Ontario between April 1993 and March 1995. The findings of this research indicated that almost half (48 percent) of Canadian seniors were not getting life-saving drugs that greatly improve the chances of survival after a heart attack. Among the 5453 heart-attack patients deemed to be the best candidates for beta-blocker therapy, 30 percent were not provided with these drugs. Women were significantly less likely than men to receive drugs, and seniors who lived in long-term care facilities were twice as likely not be treated with them. The study also reported that older, frailer patients were three times as likely not to be treated with beta-blocker therapy when compared to those seniors aged 66 to 74. Moreover, older seniors who received the beta-blockers were often prescribed doses that were lower than what is considered medically acceptable (Arnold 1999).

An estimated 7 percent of Canada's 3 795 121 seniors currently require institutional care, and 10.3 percent require some form of home care. Generally, publicly funded home care is free, while the per-day cost to patients to live in publicly funded institutions is between $25 and $90, based on income.

The statistics in Table 6.2, supplied by the provinces and Statistics Canada, record the number of people aged 65 and over in each province; the number of beds at publicly funded institutions; the number of people on waiting lists for those beds; the number of people receiving some form of home care; the maximum number of hours or dollars of publicly funded home care for non–acute-care clients; and the number of people on home-care waiting lists. Figures for private nursing homes and private home care are not available.

Quality of Life

While some elderly do suffer from declining mental and physical functioning, many others do not. Being old does not mean being depressed, poor, and sick. Interestingly, research indicates that the elderly may be less depressed than the young are, with several studies concluding that the elderly may have the lowest depression rates of all age groups. Other research suggests that depression is "curvilinear" with age, that is, highest at the extremes of the age continuum (DeAngelis 1997).

| Table 6.2 | Demand for Senior Care by Province, 2000 |

BRITISH COLUMBIA

Number of seniors	155 610
Long-term care beds	24 707
Waiting list	about 7000
Total receiving home care	about 105 000 per year
Maximum hours	unlimited
Waiting list	none

ALBERTA

Number of seniors	294 610
Long-term care beds	13 767
Waiting list	not available
Total receiving home care	65 199 per year
Maximum hours	will fund up to $3000 per month
Waiting list	not available

SASKATCHEWAN

Number of seniors	148 757
Long-term care beds	8981
Waiting list	not available
Total receiving home care	22 816 per year
Maximum hours	not available
Waiting list	not available

MANITOBA

Number of seniors	155 610
Long-term care beds	9206
Waiting list	1100
Total receiving home care	about 32 000 per year
Maximum hours	unlimited
Waiting list	none

ONTARIO

Number of seniors	1 444 009
Long-term care beds	56 990
Waiting list	about 10 000
Total receiving home care	about 400 000 per year
Maximum hours	60 to 120 per month
Waiting list	11 000

QUEBEC

Number of seniors	927 132
Long-term care beds	about 49 000
Waiting list	less than 3000
Total receiving home care	339 000 per year
Maximum hours	42 per week
Waiting list	none

NOVA SCOTIA

Number of seniors	123 830
Long-term care beds	5877
Waiting list	not available
Total receiving home care	12 000 per year
Maximum hours	not available
Waiting list	none

Table 6.2	Demand for Senior Care by Province, 2000 (continued)
NEW BRUNSWICK	
Number of seniors	97 574
Long-term care beds	4143
Waiting list	about 83
Total receiving home care	12 974 per month
Maximum hours	will fund up to $2040 per month
Waiting list	none
PRINCE EDWARD ISLAND	
Number of seniors	18 285
Long-term care beds	933
Waiting list	55
Total receiving home care	2200 per year
Maximum hours	28 per week
Waiting list	not available
NEWFOUNDLAND/LABRADOR	
Number of seniors	62 082
Long-term care beds	2958
Waiting list	480
Total receiving home care	850 per month
Maximum hours	will fund up to $2268 per month
Waiting list	292

SOURCE: *Maclean's* 2000

Among the elderly who are depressed, two social factors tend to be in operation. One is society's negative attitude toward the elderly. Words and phrases such as "old," "useless," and "a has-been" reflect cultural connotations of the aged that influence feelings of self-worth. The roles of the elderly also lose their clarity. How is a retiree supposed to feel or act? What does a retiree do? As a result, the elderly become dependent on external validation that may be weak or absent.

The second factor contributing to depression among the elderly is the process of growing old. This process carries with it a barrage of stressful life events all converging in a relatively short period. These events include health concerns, retirement, economic instability, loss of significant other(s), physical isolation, job displacement, and increased salience of the inevitability of death due to physiological decline. All of these events converge on the elderly and increase the incidence of depression and anxiety.

Living Arrangements

The elderly live in a variety of contexts, depending on their health and financial status (see Figure 6.6). Most elderly do not want to be institutionalized but prefer to remain in their own homes or in other private households with friends and relatives.

Although many of the elderly poor live in government housing or apartments with subsidized monthly payments, the wealthier aged often live in retirement communities. Often, these planned communities are very expensive, but they offer various amenities and activities, have special security, and are restricted by age. One criticism of these communities is that they segregate the elderly from the young and discriminate against younger people by prohibiting them from living in certain areas.

Those who cannot afford retirement communities or who may not be eligible for subsidized housing often live with relatives in their own home or in the homes of others. Other living arrangements include shared housing, modified independent living arrangements, and nursing homes. With shared housing, people of different ages live together in the same house or apartment; they have separate bedrooms but share a common kitchen and dining area. They share chores and financial responsibilities. The advantage of this pattern is that it integrates age groups and utilizes skills, talents, and strengths of both the young and of the old.

In modified independent living arrangements, the elderly live in their own house, apartment, or condominium within a planned community where special services such as meals, transportation, and home repairs are provided. Skilled or semiskilled health care professionals are available on the premises, and call buttons are installed so help can be summoned in case of an emergency. The advantage of this arrangement is that it provides both autonomy and support for people who are too ill or have too many disabilities to live alone. The individual can still maintain some independence even when ill.

Nursing homes are residential facilities that provide full-time nursing care for residents. Nursing homes may be private or public. Private facilities are very expensive and are operated for profit by an individual or a corporation. Public facilities are nonprofit and are operated by a governmental agency, religious organization, or the like. Nursing home residents are not typical of the elderly: they are likely to be widowed, or quite ill, or over 80, or without family to take care of them (Kinsella and Taeuber 1993). The elderly with chronic health problems are also more likely to be admitted to nursing homes. Nursing homes vary dramatically in cost, services provided, and quality of care.

National Data

Canadians most likely to provide some unpaid senior care in 1996 were aged 45 to 54 (23 percent). However, Canadians aged 55 to 64 are especially more likely to provide 10 or more unpaid hours of senior care.

SOURCE: Health Canada 1999

National Data

Women are more likely than men are to provide some senior care (19 versus 14 percent), with the largest disparity found among those providers aged 45 to 54 (27 percent of women and 19 percent of men).

SOURCE: Health Canada 1999

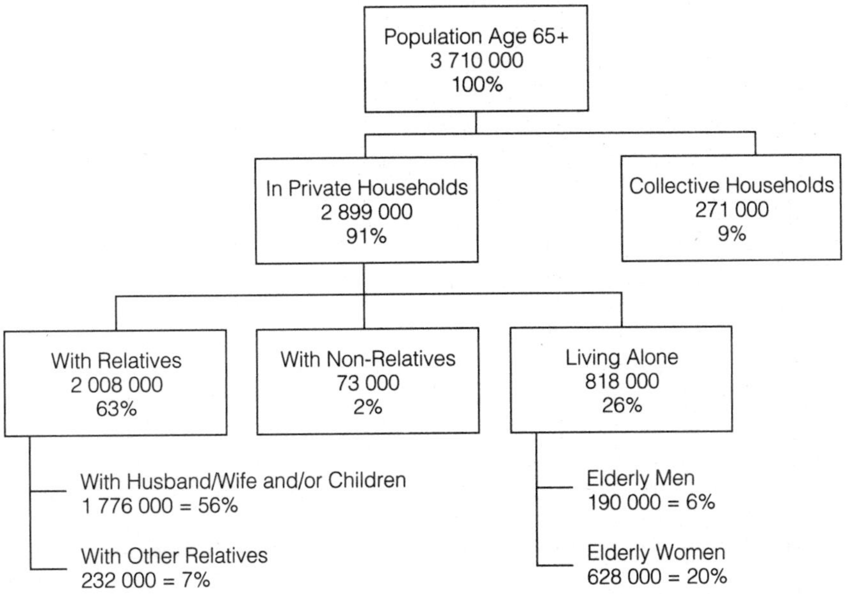

Population Age 65+
3 710 000
100%
In Private Households
2 899 000
91%
Collective Households
271 000
9%
With Relatives
2 008 000
63%
With Non-Relatives
73 000
2%
Living Alone
818 000
26%
With Husband/Wife and/or Children
1 776 000 = 56%
With Other Relatives
232 000 = 7%
Elderly Men
190 000 = 6%
Elderly Women
628 000 = 20%

Figure 6.6
Living Arrangements for Seniors, 1991

Notes: "In private households" refers to a person who occupies a private dwelling.

"Collective households" refers to a person who occupies a collective dwelling such as a home for the aged, nursing home, or hospital.

SOURCE: Vanier Institute of the Family. 1994. *Profiling Canada's Families*, p. 117

PHYSICIAN-ASSISTED SUICIDE AND SOCIAL POLICY

Everyone's parents may experience a significant drop in quality of life and a total loss of independence due to illness, accident, or, more typically, aging. Adult children or spouses are often asked their recommendations about withdrawing life support (food, water, or mechanical ventilation), starting medications to end life (intravenous vasopressors), or withholding certain procedures to prolong life (cardiopulmonary resuscitation). The recommendation of family members is sometimes given considerable weight in the ultimate decision of the caregiver or attending physician. Seventy-six percent of the caregivers in one study said that "family preference" was the most important factor influencing the restriction of technological interventions (Randolph et al. 1997). However, most family recommendations are based on the physician's recommendations to limit care or request such limitations (Luce 1997). When the physician and family member are in conflict about what to do, the physician usually defers to the preference of the family member (Prendergast and Luce 1997).

It is a fundamental principle of Canadian law that every adult who is capable of decision-making has the right to consent to or refuse medical treatment, even if the result of the decision is life threatening. However, this general right to self-determination is not absolute and in cases of a medical emergency, medical treatment may proceed on the basis of a legal principle called "implied consent" or necessity. However, even in a medical emergency, physicians may be obliged to follow a person's prior instructions with respect to the refusal of medical treatment. For example, in the case of *Mallette v. Shulman*, the Ontario court of appeal upheld the refusal of a life-saving blood transfusion by a woman who was uncon-

scious but who had previously signed a "no blood products card" because of her religious objections to blood transfusions. This case is often pointed to as offering recognition of 'living wills.' In a **living will**, people declare whether they want all possible medical intervention or limits placed on treatment should they become incapacitated. The purpose of a living will is to enable individuals to make their own decisions and ensure that others are aware of these decisions. In Canada, Nova Scotia was the first province to pass a law providing for advance care directives. This 1988 act, entitled the *Medical Consent Act*, allows a capable adult to authorize another adult to provide substitute consent for or give other directives in relation to medical treatment. Quebec has also passed this type of "proxy model" of advance care directive. Manitoba, Ontario, British Columbia, and Alberta have additionally evidenced some level of support for such measures.

A second case, that of *Nancy B.* in Quebec, is also significant in this discussion. In this case, Nancy B., a young woman in her early 20s, was stricken with Guillain-Barre syndrome, which, in her case, proved unusually debilitating. After Nancy B. was maintained on a respirator for months, unable to breathe, she asked her doctors to take her off the respirator. A judge was called to her bedside to hear her submission and, ultimately, granted her request. The respirator was turned off and she died under mild sedation. In this case, the action of her doctor was considered palliative in nature and, as such, it was concluded that no contravention of the criminal code had occurred.

Although 6 percent of a sample of U.S. physicians reported that they had complied with the request of a patient for assisted suicide (Meier et al. 1998), the official positions of both the Canadian and the American Medical Associations are that physicians must respect the patient's decision to forego life-sustaining treatment but

that they should not participate in patient-assisted suicide. Physician-assisted suicide (PAS) is often distinguished from **euthanasia**, the deliberate taking of an individual's life at that individual's request (Zalcberg and Buchanan 1997). However, at times, the distinction between the two can be somewhat vague. For example, a special Senate committee on euthanasia, headed by Liberal senator Joan Neiman, was struck in the aftermath of the case of Sue Rodriquez, a Vancouver woman suffering with a degenerate nerve disease whose request for physician-assisted suicide was denied by the Supreme Court of Canada. (Despite their ruling, Rodriquez committed suicide, aided by an unknown doctor, in February 1994.) Although in June 1995 the Senate committee narrowly recommended against legalizing physician-assisted suicide and voluntary euthanasia, it remains a criminal offence to counsel, aid, or abet suicide.

Arguments against PAS focus on who has the right to decide that a person may die. The practice is subject to abuse: for example, one spouse may encourage a physician to kill the other to be relieved of a burden and inherit a lot of life insurance money. When euthanasia is defined as the deliberate ending of a life by a second person based on that second person's judgment about the quality of that life, ethical issues are raised. An objection to formalizing and legalizing the current practice of medical euthanasia is that this recognition may lead to toleration of deliberately ending the lives of members of minorities, certain ethnic groups, or individuals with mental illnesses, or the elderly—the "slippery slope" argument (Allen 1998).

Euthanasia remains controversial. A team of researchers identified the attitudes of elderly individuals (patients) and their family members toward PAS (Koenig et al. 1996). Forty percent of the elderly individuals had positive attitudes toward PAS, and 59 percent of the relatives expressed favourable attitudes. Patients who opposed

PAS were more likely to be women, Black individuals, and those with less education.

Physician-assisted suicide has been legal in Holland for 10 years, but there have been some abuses. Though physicians are required by law to report their involvement in PAS, 60 percent of physicians in one study did not do so. In addition, more than half had suggested euthanasia to patients who were not necessarily terminally ill. One-fourth of the physicians did not have the consent of the patient even though many of the patients were competent to make such a decision (Hendin et al. 1997).

SOURCES: Allen, F. C. L. 1998. Euthanasia: Why Torture Dying People When We Have Sick Animals Put Down? *Australian Psychologist* 33: 12–5; Hendin, Herbert, C. Rutenfrans, and Z. Zylicz. 1997. "Physician-Assisted Suicide and Euthanasia in the Netherlands: Lessons from the Dutch." *Journal of the American Medical Association* 277: 1720–3; Koenig, H. G., D. Wildman-Hanlon, and K. Schmader. 1996. "Attitudes of Elderly Patients and Their Families toward Physician-Assisted Suicide." *Archives of Internal Medicine* 156: 2240–8; Luce, J. M. 1997. "Withholding and Withdrawal of Life Support: Ethical, Legal, and Clinical Aspects." *New Horizons* 5: 30–7; Meier, D. E., C. A. Emmons, S. Wallenstein, T. Quill, S. Morrison, and C. Cassel. "A National Survey of Physician-Assisted Suicide and Euthanasia in the United States." *New England Journal of Medicine* 338: 1193–1201; Prendergast, T. J., and J. M. Luce. 1997. "Increasing Incidence of Withholding and Withdrawal of Life Support from the Critically Ill." *American Journal of Respiratory and Critical Care Medicine* 155: 15–20; Randolph, A. G., M. B. Zollo, R. S. Wigton, and T. S. Yeh. 1997. "Factors Explaining Variability among Caregivers in the Intent to Restrict Life-Support Interventions in a Pediatric Intensive Care Unit." *Critical Care Medicine* 25: 435–9; Zalcberg, J. R., and J. D. Buchanan. 1997. "Clinical Issues in Euthanasia." *Medical Journal of Australia* 166: 150–2.

Victimization and Abuse

Although abuse may take place in private homes by family members, the elderly, like children, are particularly vulnerable to abuse when they are institutionalized. For example, Brithe Jorgensen in *Crimes Against the Elderly in Institutional Care* (1986) reported that even when administrators were aware of cases that warranted criminal charges for assault, theft, or breach of the home's legal obligations to provide proper care, no reports were made to the police. Similarly, Pillemer and Hudson (1993) conducted interviews with a random sample of nursing home staff and found that 40 percent admitted that during the previous year, they had abused patients psychologically and 10 percent admitted to abusing them physically.

At present, British Columbia, Saskatchewan, Manitoba, Nova Scotia, and New Brunswick have enforced provincial standards at retirement homes as a condition of licensing. However, Ontario, which is one of the few provinces that do not regulate retirement homes, has experienced disarming reports of abuse within such facilities.

Whether the abuse occurs within the home or in an institution, the victim is most likely to be female, widowed, White, frail, and over 75. The abuser tends to be an adult child or spouse of the victim who misuses alcohol (Anetzberger et al. 1994). Some research suggests that the perpetrator of the abuse is more often an adult child who is financially dependent on the elderly victim (Boudreau 1993). Whether the abuser is an adult child or a spouse may simply depend on whom the elder victim lives with.

Many of the problems of the elderly are compounded by their lack of interaction with others, loneliness, and inactivity. This is particularly true for the old-old. The elderly are also segregated in nursing homes and retirement communities, separated from family and friends, and isolated from the flow of work and school. A cycle is perpetuated—being poor and old results in being isolated and engaging in fewer activities. Such withdrawal affects health, which makes the individual less able to establish relationships or participate in activities.

This chapter's Self and Society allows you to assess your attitudes and beliefs about elder abuse.

International Data

By the year 2020, there will be more than 230 million elderly Chinese with fewer young people to support them because of the one-child policy begun in the 1970s. The Chinese constitution mandates that "adult children have a responsibility to support their elderly parents."

SOURCE: DHHS 1998

National Data

In 1995, about 250 000 Canadians lived in long-term health care institutions. The majority were aged 65 or older and had entered the facility within the previous two years.

SOURCE: Statistics Canada 1998a

Attitudes and Beliefs about Elder Abuse

Researcher Michael J. Stones has created a research tool, the Elder Abuse Aptitude Test (EAAT), to study attitudes and beliefs about elder abuse. Fill out the EAAT below and total your score to assess your attitudes and beliefs. The EAAT will also sensitize you to the many types of abuse that older people can face.

The following statements refer to how people sometimes act toward seniors. They only refer to behaviour by someone a senior has reason to trust. That person could be a relative or someone who takes care of the senior. That person could also be someone paid to help the senior or look after the senior's affairs, such as a doctor, a nurse, or homemaker, or lawyer. The questions do not refer to how strangers treat seniors.

Please indicate whether the actions below are (1) not abusive, (2) possibly abusive, (3) abusive, (4) severely abusive, or (5) very abusive toward a senior if done by someone a senior has reason to trust. Remember that the questions don't apply to acts by a stranger. Circle a number next to each statement, such that:

1 = not abusive
2 = possibly abusive
3 = abusive
4 = severely abusive
5 = very severely abusive

A person a senior has reason to trust who

1. Steals something a senior values	[1]	[2]	[3]	[4]	[5]
2. Makes a senior pay too much for things like house repairs or medical aids	[1]	[2]	[3]	[4]	[5]
3. Pushes or shoves a senior	[1]	[2]	[3]	[4]	[5]
4. Lies to a senior in a harmful way	[1]	[2]	[3]	[4]	[5]
5. Opens a senior's mail without permission	[1]	[2]	[3]	[4]	[5]
6. Pressures a senior to do paid work when that senior doesn't want to	[1]	[2]	[3]	[4]	[5]
7. Doesn't take a senior places that a senior has to go (like a doctor's appointment)	[1]	[2]	[3]	[4]	[5]
8. Withholds information that may be important to a senior	[1]	[2]	[3]	[4]	[5]
9. Unreasonably orders a senior around	[1]	[2]	[3]	[4]	[5]
10. Doesn't provide a senior with proper clothing when needed	[1]	[2]	[3]	[4]	[5]
11. Tells a senior that he or she is "too much trouble"	[1]	[2]	[3]	[4]	[5]
12. Fails to provide proper nutrition for a senior	[1]	[2]	[3]	[4]	[5]
13. Disbelieves a senior who claims to be abused without checking that claim	[1]	[2]	[3]	[4]	[5]

How did you score? How did your classmates score? Stones reports average scores of 4.07 for 22- to 40-year-olds; 3.85 for 41- to 64-year-olds; and 3.50 for 65- to 83-year-olds. How do you think people from other backgrounds or with little knowledge of elder abuse would score?

SOURCES: Stones, M. J. 1994. *Rules and Tools: The Meaning and Measurement of Elder Abuse: A Manual for Milestones.* Newfoundland. Reprinted with permission, Stones, M. J., and D. Pittman. 1995. "Individual Differences in Attitudes about Elder Abuse: The Elder Abuse Attitude Test (EAAT)," *Canadian Journal on Aging* 14 (Supp. 2): 61–71. Novak, Mark. 1997. *Aging and Society: A Canadian Perspective,* 3rd ed. Scarborough, ON: Nelson.

STRATEGIES FOR ACTION: THE YOUNG AND THE OLD RESPOND

Activism by or on behalf of children or the elderly has been increasing in recent years and, as the number of children and elderly grow, such activism is likely to escalate and to be increasingly successful. For example, global attention to the elderly led to 1999 being declared the "International Year of Older Persons" (DHHS 1998), while "the first nearly universally ratified human rights treaty in history" deals with children's rights (UNICEF 1998). Such activism takes several forms, including collective action through established organizations and the exercise of political and economic power.

Collective Action

Countless organizations work on behalf of children, some of which we have already noted. Others include Access to Justice Network, Amnesty International, Adoption Council of Canadians, Canadian Child Care Foundation, Child and Family Canada, Children's Defense Fund, Childwatch, Defence for Children International, Save the Children-Canada, and UNICEF. Many successes take place at the local level where parents, teachers, corporate officials, politicians, and citizens join together in the interests of children.

Similarly, more than a thousand organizations work toward realizing political power, economic security, and better living conditions for the elderly. These organizations include the Seniors Computer Information Project (Manitoba), Saskatchewan Seniors Mechanism, Alberta Senior Citizens Sport and Recreation Association, Council on Aging of Ottawa-Carleton, Alberta Council on Aging, Assemblée des aînés francophones du Canada, The Canadian Senior Citizens' Information and Services Centre, National Advisory Council on Aging, Golden Age Association (Montreal), Society for the Retired and Semi-Retired (Edmonton), Elder Adult Resource Services (EAR) (Edmonton), and the Canadian Association of Retired Persons (CARP).

One of the earliest and most radical groups in North America was the Gray Panthers, founded in 1970 by Margaret Kuhn. The Gray Panthers in the United States were responsible for revealing the unscrupulous practices of the hearing aid industry, persuading the National Association of Broadcasters to add "age" to "sex" and "race" in the Television Code of Ethics statement on media images, and eliminating the mandatory retirement age. In view of these successes, it is interesting to note that the Gray Panthers, with only 50 000 to 70 000 members, is a relatively small organization when compared with the Canadian Association of Retired Persons (CARP).

CARP is Canada's largest 50-plus lobby group with more than 370 000 members. A nonprofit association that does not accept funding from any government body, CARP speaks out on a wide range of issues important to those over 50. Its mandate is "to protect what we have and improve our lifestyle" <www.fifty-plus.net/join/index-cfm>. Services of the CARP include discounted mail-order drugs, investment opportunities, travel information, volunteer opportunities, a *Spamhunter's Resource Guide* offering practical advice for dealing with unwanted advertising offers and news updates on issues of concern to those 50 and older. The goal of GLARP, the Gay and Lesbian Association of Retiring Persons, is to raise money to develop gay and lesbian retirement communities and retirement resorts (GLARP 2000).

National Data

Adults over 65 were victims in 2 percent of violent crimes in 1996, and one-fifth of these involved family members. Overall, adult children (44 percent) and spouses (34 percent) were responsible for the majority of family violence cases involving seniors.

SOURCE: Statistics Canada 1998b

Political and Economic Power

Children are unable to hold office or to vote. Nevertheless, child advocates, acting on behalf of children, have wielded considerable political influence in such areas as childcare, education, health care reform, and crime prevention. At the same time, aging baby boomers may be particularly well situated, because of their numbers, to advance their concerns. Indeed, demographer David Foote has argued that by 2005 the concerns of aging baby boomers "will dominate Canada...as much as their thirty-something angst mirrored the economic woes of the 1980s and their forty-something prudence reflected the government cost cutting of the 1990s" (Nikiforuk 1999).

One economist, noting that the elderly's economic power is considerable, has referred to the elderly as a "revolutionary class." (Thurow 1996). Advertisers actively seek the discretionary income of the elderly. Minkler (1989) observed that one favourable outcome of such a marketing focus is a more positive image of the elderly. Better products and services for older Canadians are also benefits. To the extent that future political issues are age based and the elderly are able to band together, their political power may increase as their numbers grow over time (Matras 1990; Thurow 1996).

In 1997, representatives of Canada, the United States, France, Germany, Italy, Canada, England, Japan, and Russia met for the first time to discuss the sociopolitical implications of the world's aging population. The summit stressed the importance of nations' learning from one another "to promote active aging through information exchanges and cross-national research" (DHHS 1998).

UNDERSTANDING THE YOUNG AND THE OLD

What can we conclude about youth and aging in Canadian society? Age is an ascribed status and, as such, is culturally defined by role expectations and implied personality traits. Society regards both the young and the old as dependent and in need of the care and protection of others. Society also defines the young and old as physically, emotionally, and intellectually inferior. Because of these and other attributions, both age groups are sociologically a minority with limited opportunity to obtain some or all of society's resources.

Although both the young and the old are treated as minority groups, different meanings are assigned to each group. In general, however, the young are more highly valued than the old are. Functionalists argue that this priority on youth reflects the fact that the young are preparing to take over important statuses while the elderly are relinquishing them. Conflict theorists emphasize that in a capitalist society, both the young and the old are less valued than more productive members of society are. Conflict theorists also point out the importance of propagation, that is, the reproduction of workers, which may account for the greater value placed on the young than the old. Finally, symbolic interactionists describe the way images of the young and the old intersect and are socially constructed.

The collective concern for the elderly and the significance of defining ageism as a social problem have resulted in improved economic conditions for the elderly. Currently, they are one of society's more powerful minorities. Research indicates, however, that despite their increased economic status, the elderly are still subject to discrimination in such areas as housing, employment, and medical care and are victimized by systematic patterns of stereotyping, abuse, and prejudice.

In contrast, the position of children has steadily declined as evidenced by a general increase in poverty, homelessness, and unemployment (see Chapters 10 and 11). Wherever there are poor families, there are poor children. Further, age-based restrictions limit their entry into certain roles (e.g., employee) and demand others (e.g., student). While most of society's members would agree that children require special protections, concerns about quality-of-life issues and rights of self-determination are only recently being debated.

Age-based decisions are potentially harmful. If budget allocations were based on indigence rather than age, more resources would be available for those truly in need. Further, age-based decisions may encourage intergenerational conflict. Government assistance should not be thought of as a zero-sum relationship—the more resources one group gets, the fewer resources another group receives.

Social policies that allocate resources based on need rather than on age would shift the attention of policymakers to remedying social problems rather than serving the needs of special interest groups. Age should not be used to negatively affect an individual's life any more than race, ethnicity, gender, or sexual orientation. While eliminating all age barriers or requirements is unrealistic, a movement toward assessing the needs of individuals and their abilities would be more consistent with the ideal of equal opportunity for all.

CRITICAL THINKING

1. In many ways, society discriminates against children. Children are segregated in schools, in a separate justice system, and in the workplace. Identify everyday examples of the ways in which children are treated like "second-class" citizens in Canada.
2. Age pyramids pictorially display the distribution of people by age. How do different age pyramids influence the treatment of the elderly?
3. Regarding children and the elderly, what public policies or programs from other countries might be beneficial to incorporate in Canada? Do you think policies from other countries would necessarily be successful here?
4. How might the "fountain of age" described by Friedan be accomplished in society? In what ways does gender effect definitions of the "fountain of age"?

KEY TERMS

activity theory	infantilizing elders	primary aging
age grading	living will	sandwich generation
age pyramids	minority	secondary aging
ageism	modernization theory	senescence
disengagement theory	new ageism	senilicide
euthanasia	phased retirement	Young Offenders Act
gerontophobia	prejudice	(YOA)

CHAPTER SEVEN

Gender Inequality

Is It True?

1. Researchers have observed that elementary- and secondary-school teachers pay more attention to girls than they do to boys.

2. Worldwide, women are less likely to be able to read and write than men.

3. Since 1961, the greatest single change to the face of the Canadian labour force has been the substantial growth in the number of employed women in general and, in particular, employed women with children.

4. In Canada, 9 out of 10 persons diagnosed as suffering from eating disorders are women.

5. Women in Canada occupy a greater percentage of legislative positions than do women in any other country in the world.

Answers: 1 = F, 2 = T, 3 = T, 4 = T, 5 = F

The term "gender inequality" begs the question, "Unequal in what way?" Depending on the issue, both women and men can be victims of inequality.

When income, career advancement, and sexual harassment are the focus, women are most often disadvantaged; but when life expectancy, mental and physical illness, and access to one's children following divorce are considered, it is often men who are disadvantaged. In this chapter, we seek to understand inequalities in both genders.

In the previous chapter, we discussed the social consequences of youth and aging. This chapter looks at **sexism**—the belief that there are innate psychological, behavioural, and intellectual differences between women and men and that these differences connote the superiority of one group and the inferiority of the other. As with age, such attitudes often result in prejudice and discrimination at both the individual and the institutional level. Individual discrimination is reflected by the physician who will not hire a male nurse because the physician believes that women are more nurturing and empathetic and are, therefore, better nurses. Institutional discrimination, that is, discrimination built into the fabric of society, is exemplified by the difficulty some women experience in finding employment; they may have no work history and few job skills because of living in traditionally defined marriage roles.

Discerning the basis for discrimination is often difficult because gender, age, sexual orientation, and race intersect. For example, First Nations people, members of visible minorities, and men and women with disabilities earn yearly incomes well below the Canadian average (Moreau 1991: 28). Consider as well that in 1995, women of colour earned just over half (51 percent) of what White men earned and only 60 percent of what men of colour earned (Das Gupta 1996: 7). Such **double** or **triple jeopardy** occurs when a person is a member of two or more minority groups. In this chapter, however, we emphasize the impact of gender inequality. **Gender** refers to the social definitions and expectations associated with being female or male and should be distinguished from **sex**, which refers to one's biological identity.

THE GLOBAL CONTEXT: THE STATUS OF WOMEN AND MEN

Although societies vary in the degree to which they regard men and women as equals, the 1997 United Nations Human Development Report concludes that "no society treats its women as well as its men" (p. 39). To assess the views on gender equality of a hundred university students from 14 countries (Canada, England, Finland, Germany, India, Italy, Japan, Malaysia, the Netherlands, Nigeria, Pakistan, Singapore, Venezuela, and the United States), Williams and Best (1990a) developed a series of 30 statements reflecting traditional and modern gender role positions. Agreement with such statements as "the man's job is too important for him to get bogged down with household chores" reflected a traditional orientation. Agreement with such statements as "marriage should not interfere with a woman's career any more than it does with a

National Data

According to national Canadian surveys, there has been a shift in attitudes toward women since the mid-1970s. While 34 percent of Canadians in 1975 agreed with the statement that "Married women should not be employed if their husbands are capable of supporting them," in 1995, only 10 percent of Canadians agreed with the statement. In 1975, 22 percent of Canadians agreed with the statement "Women should take care of running their homes and leave running the country up to the men"; in 1995, only 10 percent expressed this sentiment.
SOURCE: Bibby 1995

man's" reflected a modern orientation. Results indicate that the more highly developed the country, the more modern its gender role ideology.

Thus, in many underdeveloped countries, women do much of the physical labour, are forbidden to own land, can be divorced through the mere act of repudiation, and earn as little as half of what a man earns. Even in countries where women have achieved some measure of success, gender inequality is evident. Although more than 69 percent of all physicians in the countries of the former Soviet Union are female, they constitute 90 percent of all pediatricians but only 6 percent of all surgeons (O'Kelly and Carney 1992). The subordinate status of women in many underdeveloped countries is further evidenced by the practice of female genital mutilation.

Clitoridectomy and infibulation are two forms of female genital mutilation. In a clitoridectomy, the entire glans and shaft of the clitoris and the labia minora are removed or excised. With infibulation the two sides of the vulva are stitched together shortly after birth, leaving only a small opening for the passage of urine and menstrual blood. After marriage, the sealed opening is reopened to permit intercourse and delivery. After childbirth, the woman is often reinfibulated. Worldwide, about 85 to 115 million women and girls have undergone genital mutilation (McCammon et al. 1998).

The societies that practise clitoridectomy and infibulation do so for a variety of economic, social, and religious reasons. A virgin bride can inherit from her father, thus making her an economic asset to her husband. A clitoridectomy increases a woman's worth because a woman whose clitoris is removed is thought to experience less sexual desire and therefore to be less likely to be tempted to have sex before marriage. Older women in the community also generate income by performing the surgery so its perpetuation has an economic function (Kopelman 1994: 62). Various cultural beliefs also justify female genital mutilation. In Muslim cultures, for example, female circumcision is justified on both social and religious grounds. Muslim women are regarded as inferior to men: they cannot divorce their husbands, but their husbands can divorce them; they are restricted from buying and inheriting property; and they are not allowed to have custody of their children in the event of divorce. Female circumcision is one expression of the inequality and low social status women have in Muslim society.

Inequality in Canada

Although attitudes toward gender equality are becoming increasingly liberal, Canada has a long history of gender inequality. Women have had to fight for equality: the right to vote, equal pay for comparable work, quality education, entrance into male-dominated occupations, and legal equality. Even today, most Canadians would agree that our society does not treat women and men equally. As discussed later, many national statistics support the belief that men and women are not treated equally: women have lower incomes; hold fewer prestigious jobs; remain concentrated in traditionally female-dominated fields of study at universities, community colleges, and trade apprenticeship programs; and are more likely than men are to live in poverty.

Our perceptions of the characteristics of men and women also reflect the inequality between the sexes. A Gallup poll asked whether various characteristics were "generally more true of men or more true of women" (DeStefano and Colasanto 1990). Respondents most frequently described men, in rank order, as aggressive, strong, proud, disorganized, courageous, confident, independent, ambitious, selfish, and logical. In contrast, women were most often described as emotional, talkative, sensitive, affectionate, patient, romantic, moody, cautious, creative, and thrifty. Notice that none of the top 10 characteristics was the same. About half of the respondents thought that biological factors were responsible for the differences, and half thought the differences were due to sociocultural factors.

SOCIOLOGICAL THEORIES OF GENDER INEQUALITY

Both structural-functionalism and conflict theory concentrate on how the structure of society and, specifically, its institutions contribute to gender inequality. However, these two theoretical perspectives offer opposing views of the development and maintenance of gender inequality. Symbolic interactionism focuses instead on the culture of society and how gender roles are learned through the socialization process.

Structural-Functionalist Perspective

Structural-functionalists argue that preindustrial society required a division of labour based on gender. Women, out of biological necessity, remained in the home performing such functions as bearing, nursing, and caring for children. Men, who were physically stronger and could be away from home for long periods, were responsible for providing food, clothing, and shelter for their families. This division of labour was functional for society and, over time, became defined as both normal and natural.

Industrialization rendered the traditional division of labour less functional, although remnants of the supporting belief system persist. Today, because of daycare facilities, lower fertility rates, and the less physically demanding and dangerous nature of jobs, the traditional division of labour is no longer as functional. Thus, modern conceptions of the family, to some extent, have replaced traditional ones—families have evolved from extended to nuclear, authority is more egalitarian, more women work outside the home, and there is greater role variation in the division of labour. Functionalists argue, therefore, that as the needs of society change, the associated institutional arrangements also change.

Conflict Perspective

Many conflict theorists hold that male dominance and female subordination are shaped by the relationship men and women have to the production process. During the hunting and gathering stage of development, males and females were economic equals, each controlling their own labour and producing needed subsistence. As society evolved to agricultural and industrial modes of production, private property developed and men gained control of the modes of production while women remained in the home to bear and care for children. Male domination was furthered by inheritance laws that ensured that ownership would remain in their hands. Laws that regarded women as property ensured that women would remain confined to the home.

As industrialization continued and the production of goods and services moved away from the home, the male–female gap continued to grow—women had less education, lower incomes, and fewer occupational skills and were rarely owners. World War II necessitated the entry of large numbers of women into the labour force, but in contrast to previous periods, many did not return home at the end of the war. They had established their own place in the workforce and, facilitated by the changing nature of work and technological advances, now competed directly with men for jobs and wages.

Conflict theorists also argue that the continued domination of males requires a belief system that supports gender inequality. Two such beliefs are that (1) women are inferior outside the home (e.g., they are less intelligent, less reliable, and less rational) and (2) women are more valuable in the home (e.g., they have maternal instincts and are naturally nurturing). Thus, unlike functionalists, conflict theorists hold that the subordinate position of women in society is a consequence of social inducement rather than the biological differences that led to the traditional division of labour.

Symbolic Interactionist Perspective

Some scientists argue that gender differences are innate, but symbolic interactionists emphasize that through the socialization process, both females and males are taught the meanings associated with being feminine and masculine. Gender assignment begins at birth, when a child is classified as either female or male. However, the learning of gender roles is a lifelong process whereby individuals acquire society's definitions of appropriate and inappropriate gender behaviour.

Gender roles are taught in the family, the school, and peer groups, and by media presentations of girls and boys and women and men. Most important, however, gender roles are learned through symbolic interaction as the messages others send us reaffirm or challenge our gender performances. As Lorber (1998: 213) notes:

> Gender is so pervasive that in our society we assume it is bred into our genes. Most people find it hard to believe that gender is constantly created and recreated out of human interaction, out of social life, and is the texture and order of social life. Yet gender, like culture, is a human production that depends on everyone constantly "doing gender...."

Conceptions of gender are, thus, socially constructed as societal expectations dictate what it means to be female or what it means to be male. Although race and class variations exist, in general, women are socialized into expressive or nurturing and emotionally supportive roles and males are more often socialized into instrumental or task-oriented roles. These roles are then acted out in countless daily interactions as the boss and the secretary, the doctor and the nurse, and the football player and the cheerleader "do gender."

GENDER STRATIFICATION: STRUCTURAL SEXISM

As structural-functionalists and conflict theorists argue, the social structure underlies and perpetuates much of the sexism in society. **Structural sexism**, also known as "institutional sexism," refers to the ways in which the organization of society, and specifically its institutions, subordinate individuals and groups based on their sex classification. Structural sexism has resulted in gender differences in educational attainment, income levels, and occupational and political involvement.

Education and Structural Sexism

Literacy rates worldwide indicate that women are less likely to be able to read and write than males. In developing countries, the literacy rate for females is 61 percent compared to 79 percent for males (United Nations 1997). In Canada, however, the proportionate number of women enrolled full-time at universities has increased noticeably over the past decades. In 1964–65 less than one-third (31 percent) of full-time undergraduates were women; in 1994–95 women accounted for 54 percent of full-time university undergraduates and 53 percent of full-time college students (Normand 1995; Statistics Canada 1998a). While some traditionally male-dominated fields are no longer male dominated (e.g., in 1994–95, 70 percent of the students in veterinary medicine were women and equal numbers of men and women were studying medicine), women's participation levels in mathematics, engineering, and the physical and applied sciences remain relatively low. For example, in 1994–95, male computer science students outnumbered women by more than four to one at Canadian universities, and only one in five full-time undergraduate engineering students was a woman (Statistics Canada 1999a: 157–8). In addition, while women's proportional participation remains constant at the master's degree level, the proportions drop noticeably in most fields of study at the doctoral level with the exception of the social sciences. Only in the traditionally female-dominated field of education do women account for the majority of doctoral students (see Table 7.1).

National Data

Of all full-time enrolments at community colleges, women constitute the primary student component in programs such as secretarial services (96 percent), educational and counselling services (90 percent), and nursing (89 percent). Women are only highly visible for their relative rarity in programs related to the natural sciences (32 percent), mathematics and computing sciences (30 percent), and engineering and related technologies (12 percent).

SOURCE: Normand 1995

Table 7.1	Women as a Percentage of Full-Time Enrolment, by Field and Level of Study, Canada, 1992–93		
	Undergraduate	Master's	Doctoral
Health professions	68	62	43
Education	67	66	60
Fine and applied arts	62	59	46
Humanities	61	56	46
Agriculture/biological sciences	59	50	33
Social sciences	54	47	45
Mathematics/physical sciences	30	27	19
Engineering/applied sciences	19	18	11

SOURCE: Adapted from Normand 1995: 19

One explanation for why women earn fewer doctoral degrees than men is that women are socialized to choose marriage and motherhood over long-term career preparation (Olson et al. 1990). From an early age, women are exposed to images and models of femininity that stress the importance of domestic family life. When 821 undergraduate women were asked to identify their lifestyle preference, less than 1 percent selected being unmarried and working full-time. In contrast, 53 percent selected "graduation, full-time work, marriage, children, stop working at least until youngest child is in school, then pursue a full-time job" as their preferred lifestyle sequence (Schroeder et al. 1993: 243). Only 6 percent of 535 undergraduate men selected this same pattern.

Structural limitations also discourage women from advancing in the educational profession itself. In 1996, women outnumbered men in elementary and kindergarten teaching positions by approximately four to one and were approximately equal in number to male teachers at the postsecondary level, but they were outnumbered by men as university professors by about two to one (Statistics Canada 1998b). Women seeking academic careers may also find that promotion in higher education is more difficult than it is for men. Long et al. (1993) examined the promotions of 556 men and 450 women with Ph.D.s in biochemistry. They found that women were less likely to be promoted to associate or full professor, were held to a higher standard than men, and were particularly disadvantaged in more prestigious departments. Throughout Canada, women are less likely than men are to be full professors (the highest rank) and when employed as full professors, earn less on average than men who are full professors. On average, female academics earn 82 percent of the salary of male academics of comparable rank (Henslin and Nelson 1997).

Income and Structural Sexism

When data were first collected in 1967 in Canada on female-to-male earnings, the ratio stood at 58.4 percent. Since that time, it has increased notably. For example, during 1989 to 1993, the ratio increased from 66 percent to 72 percent because of both an increase in average female earnings and a stalling in average male earnings. In 1994, men's earnings improved significantly as the result of a surge in employment in the higher-wage goods-producing industries and the earnings ratio fell to 69.8 percent. "In short, recent variations in the ratio have been due more to improving or faltering earnings for men than to changes in the earnings for women" (Statistics Canada 1997a). In 1996, women working in full-year, full-time jobs earned an average $30 717, while comparably employed men earned, on average, $41 848; the earnings ratio was 73.4 (Statistics Canada 1997b). In 1997, women earned, on average, 80 cents for every dollar earned by men: female workers earned an average of $15.10 an hour while male workers received $18.80 an hour (Statistics Canada 1999g). The hourly wage gap between men and women is widespread among individuals of all ages, educational levels, occupations, and industries. However, it varies for different groups. For example, in 1997, single women who had never been married earned 96 cents for every $1 earned by their male counterparts. Women with a university education earned 85 cents for every dollar earned by their male counterparts, and women without a high-school diploma earned only 69 cents for every $1 earned by their male counterparts (Statistics Canada 1999e).

Generally, the higher one's education is, the higher one's income is. As in Canada, there is a general trend worldwide for income differences between men and women to decrease as educational differences between the two decrease (Wootton 1997; Educational Indicators 1998). For example, Statistics Canada (1994) reports that, based on their analysis of survey data that focused on three graduating classes of university and community college students in 1982, 1986, and 1990, the gender gap among postsecondary graduates has narrowed in recent years. Among 1990 university graduates, they report, women are doing slightly better than their male counterparts after controlling for experience, job tenure, education, and hours of work. Among community college graduates, a small gender gap of about 3.5 percent on an hourly wage basis was reported. However, for all graduates, the wage gap tended to increase with age, even after controlling for previous work experience.

According to a Canadian study based on data obtained from the Survey of Labour and Income Dynamics, women's lower amount of actual work experience appears to have a significant bearing on the persistent wage gap between men and women. While many possible reasons for the wage gap exist, including differences in work experience, education, major field of study, occupation, and industry of employment, this study reported that about 18 percent or almost one-fifth of the wage gap reflected the fact that women generally have less experience than their male counterparts, supervise other employees less often, and are involved in administrative decisions less frequently. Several other factors were also associated with the wage gap, including differences in job tenure and the fact that men are more likely to graduate from programs leading to higher-paying jobs and earnings. Table 7.2 illustrates the persistence of the gender wage gap in the average earnings of full-year, full-time workers in the 25 highest paying and the 25 lowest paying occupations in Canada in 1995.

Tomaskovic-Devey (1993) examined the income differences between males and females and found that the percentage of females in an occupation was the best predictor of an income gender gap—the higher the percentage of females, the lower the pay. Supporting this observation, a team of researchers (Kilbourne et al. 1994) analyzed data from the National Longitudinal Survey that included more than 5000 women and more than 5000 men. They concluded that occupational pay is gendered and that "occupations lose pay if they have a higher percentage of female workers or require nurturant skills" (p. 708).

Two hypotheses are frequently cited in the literature to explain why the income gender gap continues to exist. One is called the **devaluation hypothesis**. It argues that women are paid less because the work they perform is socially defined as less valuable than the work performed by men. The other hypothesis, the **human capital hypothesis**, argues that female–male pay differences are a function of differences in women's and men's levels of education, skills, training, and work experience.

Tam (1997), in testing these hypotheses, concludes that human capital differences are more important in explaining the income gender gap than the devaluation hypothesis is. Marini and Fan (1997) also found support for the human capital hypothesis, although their research supports a third category of variables as well. They found that organizational variables (characteristics of the business, corporation, or industry) explain, in part, the gender income gap. For example, on career entry, women and men are channelled by employers into sex-specific jobs that carry different wage rates.

Table 7.2

Average Earnings of Full-Year, Full-Time Workers in the 25 Highest-Paying and 25 Lowest-Paying Occupations, by Sex, Canada, 1995

	Average Earnings ($)		
	Both Sexes	Men	Women
All Occupations	37 556	42 488	30 130
Total: 25 highest paying occupations[1]	**80 206**	**86 139**	**58 943**
Judges	126 246	128 791	117 707
Specialist physicians	123 976	137 019	86 086
General practitioners and family physicians	107 620	116 750	81 512
Dentists	102 433	109 187	71 587
Senior managers: Goods production, utilities, transportation, and construction	99 360	102 971	58 463
Senior managers: Financial, communications carriers, and other business services	99 177	104 715	71 270
Lawyers and Quebec notaries	81 617	89 353	60 930
Senior managers trade, broadcasting, and other services	79 200	84 137	48 651
Primary production managers (except agriculture)	76 701	78 421	48 479
Securities agents, investment dealers, and traders	75 911	90 391	47 323
Petroleum engineers	72 543	73 657	56 506
Chiropractors	68 808	71 032	56 764
Engineering, science, and architecture managers	68 235	69 792	53 138
University professors	68 195	72 532	55 909
Senior managers: Health, education, social, and community services, and membership organizations	68 187	78 012	56 190
Air pilots, flight engineers, and flying instructors	67 581	68 219	43 991
Geologists, geochemists, and geophysicists	66 210	68 116	51 151
Utilities managers	64 816	66 239	52 564
School principals and administrators of elementary and secondary education	64 513	66 837	60 394
Optometrists	64 419	73 920	48 337
Insurance, real estate, and financial brokerage managers	64 197	73 419	46 070
Commissioned police officers	63 518	64 865	50 011
Senior government managers and officials	63 195	69 477	49 667
Supervisors: mining, and quarrying	62 537	62 768	0
Information systems and data processing managers	62 387	64 999	53 140
Total: 25 lowest paying occupations[1]	**17 729**	**20 238**	**16 564**
Inspectors and testers, fabric, fur, leather products manufacturing	20 001	25 396	18 507
Light duty cleaners	19 991	23 829	18 125
Early childhood educators and assistants	19 772	25 074	19 586
Pet groomers and animal care workers	19 716	24 467	17 398
Taxi and limousine drivers and chauffeurs	19 664	19 845	16 756
Visiting homemakers, housekeepers, and related occupations	19 607	24 751	19 063
Hotel front desk clerks	19 220	20 364	18 575
Cooks	19 054	20 224	17 607
Maitre d'hotel and hosts/hostesses	18 873	24 649	17 336
Kitchen and food service helpers	18 799	17 320	19 697
Hairstylists and barbers	18 292	22 867	16 755

Table 7.2	Average Earnings of Full-Year, Full-Time Workers in the 25 Highest-Paying and 25 Lowest-Paying Occupations, by Sex, Canada, 1995 (continued)		
Painters, sculptors, and other visual artists	18 188	20 421	14 982
Tailors, dressmakers, furriers, and milliners	17 850	24 686	16 026
General farm workers	17 756	19 990	13 825
Estheticians, electrologists, and related occupations	17 658	22 889	17 462
Sewing machine operators	17 613	20 664	17 340
Cashiers	17 553	20 557	16 977
Ironing, pressing, and finishing occupations	17 322	19 297	16 499
Artisans and craftspersons	16 943	20 555	13 565
Bartenders	16 740	18 899	14 940
Harvesting labourers	16 426	18 683	14 465
Service station attendants	16 203	16 520	14 947
Food service counter attendants and food preparers	15 487	17 912	14 681
Food and beverage servers	14 891	18 192	13 861
Babysitters, nannies, and parents' helpers	12 713	15 106	12 662

1 Although athletes were in the 25 highest paying occupations and trappers and hunters were in the 25 lowest paying occupations, their very small numbers rendered their income statistics unreliable. Hence, the individuals in these occupations were excluded from this table.

SOURCE: Adapted from Statistics Canada 1998d

Work and Structural Sexism

Work is highly gendered. As a group, women tend to work in jobs where there is little prestige and low or no pay, where no product is produced, and where women are the facilitators for others. Women are also more likely to hold positions of little or no authority within the work environment. Investigating the gender gap in organizational authority in seven countries (Australia, Canada, Japan, Norway, Sweden, United Kingdom, and United States), Wright et al. (1995: 419) conclude that in every country, "women are less likely than men to be in the formal authority hierarchy, to have sanctioning power over subordinates, or to participate in organizational policy decisions." Women of colour, First Nations women, and women with disabilities may be even less likely to hold positions of power. For example, in contrast to visible minority men, who are found concentrated in either professional occupations or service jobs (in both cases at higher proportions than Canadians overall), visible minority women are more likely than Canadian women as a whole to be concentrated in manual labour work (Moreau 1991: 28). Consider as well that women with disabilities aged 15 to 64 are less likely than men with disabilities (41 percent versus 56 percent) to be employed (Shain 1995: 10).

No matter what the job, if a woman does it, it is likely to be valued less than if a man does it. For example, in the early nineteenth century, 90 percent of all clerks were men, and being a clerk was a very prestigious profession. As the job became routine, in part because of the advent of the typewriter, the pay and prestige of the job declined and the number of female clerks increased. Today, female clerks predominate, and the position is one of relatively low pay and low prestige.

International Data

Between 1950 and 1995, the percentage of women in the labour force increased dramatically worldwide: 22 percent in North America, 15 percent in Latin America, 10 percent in Europe, and 5 percent in Asia. The percentage of women in the labour force between 1950 and 1995 in Africa remained unchanged.

SOURCE: United Nations 1997

The concentration of women in certain occupations and men in other occupations is referred to as **occupational sex segregation**. Table 7.3 presents the distribution of full-time male and female workers by their major occupational categories. However, a more precise identification of where men and women work is also possible. In 1996, the top 10 most frequent occupations of Canadian women in the labour force were: retail salesperson (5.2 percent of the female labour force), secretaries (4.8 percent), cashiers (3.6 percent), registered nurses (3.4 percent), accounting clerks (3.4), elementary-school teachers (2.9 percent), food servers (2.7 percent), general office clerks (2.6 percent), babysitters or nannies (2.1 percent), and receptionists (1.8 percent). The top 10 most frequent occupations for Canadian men in the labour force were: truck drivers (2.9 percent of the male labour force), retail salespersons (2.8 percent), janitors (2.4 percent), retail trade managers (2.3 percent), farmers (2.3 percent), sales representatives or wholesale trade (1.7 percent), motor vehicle mechanics (1.6 percent), material handlers (1.5 percent), carpenters (1.5 percent), and construction trade helpers (1.3 percent) (Statistics Canada 1998b: 6).

It is notable that for women, the majority of the top 10 jobs are concentrated in the clerical, sales, service, nursing, and elementary-school teaching categories. Indeed, with the exception of New Brunswick and Quebec, retail

Table 7.3	Employment by Occupation and Sex, 1997, Population 15 Years of Age and Older			
	Number in Thousands and % of Total Employed			
	Males		**Females**	
Occupational Category	Number	%	Number	%
Managerial, administrative	1066.1	13.94	863.6	13.73
Natural sciences, engineering, and mathematics	489.2	6.40	129.8	2.06
Social sciences	110.6	1.45	198.6	3.16
Religion	30.4	0.40	9.5	0.15
Teaching	136.5	3.09	423.9	6.74
Medicine and health	156.7	2.05	595.7	9.47
Artistic, literary, and recreational	179.7	2.35	150.8	2.40
Clerical occupations	398.6	5.21	1528.3	24.29
Sales occupations	756.2	9.89	660.8	10.50
Service occupations	797.0	10.42	1082.0	17.20
Farming, horticultural, and animal husbandry	329.4	4.31	124.8	1.98
Fishing and trapping	29.5	0.39	2.6	0.04
Forestry and logging	51.4	0.67	3.1	0.05
Mining and quarrying	65.0	0.85	2.2	0.03
Processing	271.8	3.55	85.3	1.36
Machining	230.3	3.01	14.8	0.24
Fabricating, assembling, and repairing	905.1	1.83	240.3	3.82
Construction trades	683.4	8.93	21.6	0.34
Transport equipment operating	484.0	6.33	51.4	0.82
Material handling	253.6	3.32	69.8	1.11
Other crafts	124.3	1.63	32.8	0.52

SOURCE: Adapted from Statistics Canada 1998a

sales was the most frequently occurring occupation in 1996 for women in all of the Canadian provinces; in New Brunswick and Quebec, the most common occupation for women was secretarial positions (Statistics Canada 1998b: 6). It is also noteworthy that although the top 10 occupations for women, taken together, accounted for almost a third (32.5 percent) of the total female labour force, the top 10 occupations for men account for only 20.3 percent of the total male labour force. Women tend to be more highly concentrated within fewer occupations while men are more evenly distributed across a larger range of occupations.

In some occupations, sex segregation has decreased in recent years. For example, the proportion of female doctors and dentists rose from 18 percent in 1982 to 26 percent in 1993 (Best 1995: 33). Indeed, the number of female dentists almost doubled from 800 in 1990 to 1500 in 1995. Moreover, while women accounted for only 17 percent of all earners in the 25 highest paying occupations in Canada in 1990, by 1995 this figure had increased to 22 percent (Statistics Canada 1998d).

Despite these and other changes, women are still heavily represented in low-prestige, low-wage, **"pink-collar" jobs** that offer few benefits. Consider, for example, that in 1995, women accounted for about three out of every five individuals who worked full year, full time in the 25 lowest paying occupations in Canada. The average earnings of women in these occupations was $16 564 (Statistics Canada 1998d). Moreover, women in higher-paying jobs are often victimized by a **glass ceiling**—an invisible barrier that prevents women and other minorities from moving into top corporate positions. A recent study of Fortune 500 companies found that less than 11 percent of all seats on the Fortune 500 company boards are held by women (Klein 1998). Interestingly, Cianni and Romberger's investigation (1997) of visible minority women and men in Fortune 500 companies indicates that gender has more of a role in "organizational treatment" than race.

Sex segregation in occupations continues for several reasons (Martin 1992; Williams 1995). First, cultural beliefs about what is an "appropriate" job for a man or a woman still exist. For example, in an examination of gender-role orientations and attitudes toward women as managers among a sample of 194 Canadian business students (71 female and 123 male undergraduate and graduate students), Burke (1994) reports that the men exhibited significantly more negative attitudes toward women as managers than did the women. He suggests that this "augurs badly" for women in at least three ways: (1) as colleagues, these men would be unlikely to endorse initiatives to develop women's careers or, perhaps, actively endorse "backlash" strategies, (2) these men are unlikely to provide women with mentorship or sponsorship and may act as poor role models for other men, and (3) these individuals are unlikely to support the career aspirations of their spouse or female partner.

In addition, because of gender socialization, men and women learn different skills and acquire different aspirations. Opportunity structures for men and women and the expectations placed on them also vary. For example, women may be excluded by male employers and employees who fear the prestige of their profession will be lessened with the entrance of women, or who simply believe that "the ideal worker is normatively masculine" (Martin 1992: 220).

Finally, since family responsibilities primarily remain with women, working mothers may feel pressure to choose professions that permit flexible hours and career paths, sometimes known as "mommy tracks." Thus, for

International Data

In the Ukraine, the second largest country in Europe, women comprise 69 percent of the white-collar labour force but hold only 5 percent of the managerial, director, or department head positions.

SOURCE: Tserkonivnitska 1997

A recent Canadian survey indicates that 59 percent of men and 67 percent of women agreed or strongly agreed that an employed mother could establish just as warm and secure a relationship with her child as a mother who did not engage in paid employment. However, 59 percent of the men and 51 percent also agreed or strongly agreed that a preschool child was likely to suffer if both parents were employed.

SOURCE: Ghalam 1997

According to the Survey of Income and Labour Dynamics, women who return to paid work within two years of giving birth have higher incomes, higher job statuses, and longer tenure than those women who do not return to work do. Those who return to work are also more likely to be in a unionized job and to be living with a partner.

SOURCE: Statistics Canada 1999f

example, women dominate the field of elementary education, which permits them to be home when their children are not in school. Nursing, also dominated by women, often offers flexible hours.

CONSIDERATION

Although women entering professions dominated by men are at a disadvantage, the reverse is not true. Williams (1995) interviewed 76 men and 23 women in four traditionally female professions—elementary-school teacher, librarian, nurse, and social worker. She found that men who work in traditional female occupations often receive preferential treatment in hiring and promotion decisions. Williams concludes that men take their "superior" status with them, even into female-dominated professions.

Politics and Structural Sexism

In 1868, when the first federal general election was held, only men who owned a specified amount of property were allowed to vote; in 1885, the *Electoral Franchise Act* defined a "person" who was eligible to vote as a male who was of other than Mongolian or Chinese origin. While the 1917 *Wartime Election Act* granted wives, sisters, and mothers of servicemen the right to vote, it was not until 1918 that Canadian women won the right to vote in federal elections (Frank 1994). Women over the age of 21 were granted the right to vote in provincial elections in 1916 in Manitoba, Saskatchewan, and Alberta; in 1917, in British Columbia and Ontario; in 1918 in Nova Scotia; in 1919 in New Brunswick; in 1922 in Prince Edward Island; in 1925 in Newfoundland (where initially this right was limited to women over the age of 25); and in 1940 in Quebec (Whitla 1995: 320–2). These rights were first granted to White women; women from certain other ethnic groups did not receive the franchise until later years. For example, Mossman (1998: 181) observes that "prior to 1960, aboriginal women (and men) in Canada were entitled to vote only if they gave up their Indian status, a status defined by the federal *Indian Act*." While an Aboriginal women became automatically "enfranchised" if she married a White man, "it was only in the 1970s that aboriginal women's claims to equality under the *Indian Act* were tested in the Supreme Court of Canada."

Table 7.4 provides information on women's representation in parliamentary legislatures and in cabinet positions within those parliaments in 26 countries. The relative absence of women in politics worldwide is a consequence of structural limitations. "No gender-specific training is required to be a parliamentarian. Neither public speaking, nor the ability to represent the opinions of the electorate, nor the art of winning public confidence requires exclusively masculine traits. But politics remains an obstacle course for women" (United Nations Development Programme 1995: 83).

There are some signs that Canada is on the road to achieving gender equality in politics. For example, in June 1993, Kim Campbell was elected Conservative Party leader and, by ascension shortly after, became Canada's first female Prime Minister (for an admittedly limited term of less than six months). Some years earlier, in December 1989, the election of Audrey MacLaughlin as leader of the NDP signalled the first time a Canadian women had been elected as the leader of a national political party. Nevertheless, in general, the more important the political office, the lower the probability a woman will hold it.

Table 7.4		Women in National Legislatures in Selected Countries, in Percentage			
Legislature %	Cabinet %	Country	Legislature %	Cabinet %	Country %
41.0	52.0	Sweden	17.0	14.0	Switzerland
39.0	39.0	Norway	15.0	13.0	Belgium
34.0	39.0	Finland	14.0	13.0	Guatemala
33.0	35.0	Denmark	13.0	14.0	Philippines
30.0	31.0	Netherlands	11.0	29.0	United States
29.0	4.0	New Zealand	10.0	8.0	United Kingdom
26.0	12.0	Germany	9.0	4.0	India
23.0	30.0	Austria	8.0	0.0	Japan
23.0	12.0	Cuba	7.0	3.0	Russia
21.0	8.0	China	5.0	13.0	France
19.0	23.0	Canada	2.0	7.0	Pakistan
18.0	13.0	Australia	0.0	4.0	Mauritania
18.0	17.0	Spain	0.0	0.0	Kuwait

Note: Dates of data not specified in source.

SOURCE: Adapted from Neft and Levine 1997: 21–3

International Data

Worldwide, women hold about 10 percent of all seats in legislative bodies—12 percent in industrialized countries, 10 percent in developing countries, and 8 percent in transitional countries.

SOURCE: United Nations 1997

Running for office requires large sums of money, the political backing of powerful individuals and interest groups, and a willingness of the voting public to elect women. Hunter and Denton (1984) note that Canadian political parties have shown a marked tendency to nominate women only after they have suffered losses at the polls or to nominate women in "lost cause" ridings where another party enjoys the overwhelming support of voters. It is, then, political party-elites who hamper women "in securing nominations in the first place, and beyond this, in gaining nominations which carry a reasonable prospect of victory" (Stark 1992: 454). Moreover, minority women have even greater structural barriers to election and, not surprisingly, represent an even smaller percentage of elected officials.

Consider, for example, that while Mary Ellen Smith became, in 1918, the first woman to be elected to the Legislative Assembly in British Columbia and the first woman in the British Empire to serve as a cabinet minister, it was not until 1972 that a Black woman, Rosemary Brown, won a seat in that province. Brown was the first Black woman elected to any Canadian legislature. In 1991, Zanana Akande was the first Black woman to be elected to the Ontario legislature and also the first Black woman to become a cabinet minister in that province (Mandell 1995: 347).

Human Rights and Structural Sexism

In 1999, and for the sixth consecutive year, the United Nations Development Programme ranked Canada as the best country, among 174 nations surveyed, for such "quality of life" variables as health, education levels, life expectancy, and standard of living. However, when the UNDP employed the *Gender Empowerment Measure*, which focuses directly on women's advancement within a nation in terms of its political, economic, and professional life, our national rating declined from first to fourth place.

The status of women in Canada was addressed early by the 1970 Report of the Royal Commission on the Status of Women. The Report directed many of its recommendations to legislative reforms in the areas of the criminal law, tax and childcare allowances, social assistance, immigration, and family law. These recommendations were guided by the principle that women and men "having the same rights and freedoms, share the same responsibilities...[and] should have an equal opportunity to fulfil their obligation....[T]here should be equality of opportunity to share the responsibility to society as well as its privileges and prerogatives." However, while advocating, in general, that men and women should be treated identically (i.e., the "sameness standard" of equality), the Report acknowledged that, on occasion, equality might demand or necessitate "special" or "different treatment" of women. For example, because women can become pregnant, the "special needs" created by pregnancy might demand acknowledgment of difference (e.g., maternity leave) or a shift from "equality of treatment" (formal equality) to "equality of outcome" (substantive equality).

In various ways, Canadian laws have not always benefited men and women in equal fashion. Consider, for example, that until 1983, most women were denied the right to claim pregnancy benefits under the old *Unemployment Insurance Act* (Atcheson et al. 1984: 20–1); that until 1983, husbands who raped their wives were exempt from prosecution and conviction; and that before 1989, women could be fired from their jobs simply because they became pregnant. Consider as well, that while the courts have permitted "businessmen to deduct club fees because men like to conduct business with each other over golf," have held the purchase of a Rolls Royce "to be an incident of a professional expense" (because it enhances professional image), and have sustained claims that "making charitable contributions to enhance one's reputation in a community inheres in the business of manufacturing boxes" (Macklin 1992), Canada's *Income Tax Act* refuses to regard the cost of childcare as a legitimate "business deduction." Childcare costs are viewed officially as part of the process of parenting and, in particular, mothering.

Moreover, attempts to "de-gender" the law have not always proven to be fully effective. For example, in the case of *Murdoch v. Murdoch*, Irene Murdoch claimed that, based on her contribution of money and labour during 25 years of marriage, she was entitled to one-half of the property owned by her husband when they divorced. It was noted that her tasks while married had included "haying, raking, swathing, moving, driving trucks and tractors and teams, quietening horses, taking cattle back and forth to the reserve, dehorning, vaccinating, branding, anything that was to be done...just as a man would" (Dranoff in Mossman 1998: 187). The denial of Mrs. Murdoch's claim in the Supreme Court of Canada generated activism by groups concerned with women's rights and, by 1980, every Canadian province, with the exception of Quebec, had enacted legislation amending the arrangements for the distribution of property between spouses at the time of separation or divorce. Men and women were to be treated "equally."

Although the notion of "equal treatment" sounds fair, does treating those who are unalike the same result in equality? As Mossman (1998: 187) observes, "With the benefit of hindsight, many feminists now recognize that the reform legislation in common law provinces was fundamentally flawed, since it assumed that men and women had equal access to economic self-sufficiency." In the vast majority of cases, it is women who become the custodial parents of dependent children following marital breakdown. The constraints on full-time employment posed by the parental role, coupled with the wage gap, may continue to create substantive hardship for women upon divorce.

Gender discrimination can take other forms as well. For example, Hindu and Muslim law in India, Bangladesh, and some African and Arab countries limits the inheritance rights of widows and daughters (United Nations 1997). In Canada, having lower incomes, shorter work histories, and less collateral, some women have difficulty obtaining home mortgages or rental property. Sexism also occurs is science where women are excluded from the "inner circle" that stimulates research and financing (Zuckerman et al. 1991) and in the legal profession, where women are only half as likely as men to receive a partnership in their law firms—even women who graduated from quality law schools and received academic honours (Spurr 1990). The average female corporate lawyer makes $40 000 a year less than her male counterpart (Hagan 1990). Sexism can also take place in relation to the practice of science. For example, although it is bad science to test drugs on only one sex and assume the results apply to the other, antidepressants used to be tested only on male subjects, even though 70 percent of the drugs were prescribed for women.

Sexism can also have deadly effects. Consider that breast cancer, which kills one North American woman every 12 minutes, has often been discounted as simply a "woman's problem" and, until relatively recently, has been ignored by the media, politicians, medical researchers, and lobbyists. From 1991 to 1993, Canada's national newspaper, *The Globe and Mail*, made AIDS the topic of 600 stories, letters, editorials, and announcements; in contrast, breast cancer was written about only 39 times during this time. Hoy (1995) notes that although AIDS caused the death of fewer than 1000 Canadians in 1991 (while breast cancer caused the death of almost 5000 in that year), the Canadian government committed $38 million for AIDS education and prevention during the 1990–91 fiscal year; less than half a million was earmarked for breast cancer research. In 1993, Canada's health minister observed, "There are about one million women who face the problem and we spent $25 million. There are about 30 000 people with HIV in Canada and we are spending between $35 and $37 million a year. We need to keep perspective" (p. 29). Although breast cancer has been identified as "the disease that women fear the most" (p. 29), it is only recently that breast cancer has become "politicized" as a "woman's issue." The term "woman's issue" is itself intriguing, for it suggests that it is only women who should be concerned with the ravages of this disease.

CONSIDERATION

The Convention to Eliminate All Forms of Discrimination against Women (CEDAW), also known as the International Women's Bill of Rights, was adopted by the United Nations in 1979. CEDAW establishes rights for women not previously recognized internationally in a variety of areas, including education, politics, work, law, and family life. More than 161 countries have ratified the treaty, including every country in the Western Hemisphere and every industrialized nation in the world except Switzerland and the United States (CEDAW 1998; WOC Alert 1998).

THE SOCIAL CONSTRUCTION OF GENDER ROLES: CULTURAL SEXISM

As symbolic interactionists note, structural sexism is supported by a system of cultural sexism that perpetuates beliefs about the differences between women and men. **Cultural sexism** refers to the ways in which the culture of society—its norms, values, beliefs, and symbols—perpetuates the subordination of an individual or group because of the sex classification of that individual or group. Cultural sexism takes place in a variety of settings, including the family, the school, and the media, as well as in everyday interactions.

Family Relations and Cultural Sexism

From birth, males and females are treated differently. For example, the toys male and female children receive convey different messages about appropriate gender roles. Research by Rheingold and Cook (1975) revealed how traditional gender role stereotypes are reflected in children's rooms in middle-class homes. Girls' rooms contained dolls, floral prints, and miniature home appliances such as stoves and refrigerators. Boys' rooms were more often decorated with a military or athletic motif and contained such items as building blocks, cars, trucks, planes, and boats. Overall, boys had more toys, more educational toys, and a greater variety in types of toys than girls. This study was replicated more than 10 years later with the same results (Stoneman et al. 1986). The significance of these findings lies in the relationship between the toys and the activities they foster: active versus passive play. This chapter's Focus on Technology documents the negative consequences of seemingly harmless play differences.

National Data

Canadian women and men aged 25 to 44 who were employed full-time and had children under 19 each spent, on average, about 10 hours per day on total paid and unpaid work activities. However, women devoted 1.6 hours more per day to unpaid work than their male counterparts did.

SOURCE: Health Canada, 1999

Household Division of Labour   Girls and boys work within the home in approximately equal amounts until the age of 18, "when the 2-to-1 female to male ratio familiar to adults begins to emerge" (Robinson and Bianchi 1997: 4). Throughout adulthood, housework remains primarily a woman's responsibility (Merida and Vobejda 1998). The fact that women, even when working full time, contribute significantly more hours to home care than men is known as the "second shift" (Hochschild 1989). For example, in the Ukraine, women work an average of 73 hours per week—34 hours at the workplace and 39 hours at home. Men, on the other hand, work 60 hours a week—41 hours in the workplace and 19 hours at home (Tserkonivnitska 1997). Moreover, in Canada, Beatty et al. (1993), reporting on a sample of men and women who were 1991 business school graduates, note that while both women and men *hoped* they would have egalitarian relationships with their partners, both *expected* that the male partner's career would be of higher priority than the woman's and that the woman would undertake more of the "second shift" work of childcare, housework, and family maintenance.

Calasanti and Bailey (1991) offer three explanations for the continued traditional division of labour in families. The first explanation is the "time-availability approach." Consistent with the structural-functionalist perspective, this position emphasizes that role performance is a function of who has the time to accomplish certain tasks. Because women are more likely to be at home, they are more likely to perform domestic chores.

Women, Men, and Computers

Technology has changed the world in which we live. The technological revolution has brought the possibility of greater gender equality because, unlike tasks dominating industrialization, sex differences in size, weight, and strength are less relevant. Although feminists have long decried the gendering of technology, surely computers and other information technologies are gender neutral—or are they?

Before adolescence, boys and girls use computers equally. However, around the age of 13, cultural definitions of "computers are for boys" set in.

Because girls are less likely to play video games (to wit, "Game Boy"), software that appeals to girls is less likely to be manufactured—92 percent of video games have no female characters (O'Neal 1998)—leading to a self-fulfilling prophecy with very serious consequences.

In adolescence and beyond, girls are not as interested in computers as boys are. When they are interested, unlike boys who define it as a toy to explore, something that is fun, girls define computers as a tool to accomplish a task, a kind of homework helper (Breidenbach 19997: 69). If women do not pursue computer-based information technologies, they will have an "intellectual and workplace handicap that can only get worse as technology grows more prevalent" (Currid 1996: 114).

There are some signs of optimism, however. Recognizing the absence of competition and the potential profitability of products that target girls 8 to 17, various manufacturers are now scrambling to produce computer games for this market. Some

of these products, to be sure, are highly traditional in the messages they convey. For example, Mattel's computer version of "Clueless" allows players to select outfits for their game character from capacious clothes closets, do their makeup, or change their hair. Mattel's "Barbie" CD-ROMs (which include Barbie Magic HairStyler, Barbie Fashion Designer, Adventures with Barbie Ocean Discovery, and Barbie Storymaker) allow their user to "play dolls" and change Barbie's outfits and hairstyles on a computer screen. Mattel's "Talk With Me Barbie" doll comes with her own CD-ROM and allows Barbie to sit at her own pink computer (which, in turn, is plugged into a home computer). Other products targeted at young female users capitalize on successful television programs. For example, the advertising copy on the jacket of the Sabrina The Teenage Witch CD-ROM entices potential users to "explore Sabrina's world, including her bedroom, school, and even the Other Realm itself, filled with cool games and puzzles from Drell's wacky Wheel of Misfortune," "use Sabrina's hilarious Magic Tools," and obtain "your own official Witch licence." Such products do attempt, nevertheless, to challenge computers as the turf of the male hobbyist.

While women still lag behind in terms of overall Internet use (reportedly 57 percent male and 43 percent female), a 1997 ACNielsen Internet survey that targeted 13 000 people in 8000 households aged 12 and over reported that they were more female first-time Net users than male first-time users (53 percent versus 47 percent, respectively) and that the gender gap on the Internet was closing (Dhooma 1997: 49). Moreover, an increasing number of Web sites, run by or exclusively for women have appeared

including, the "all-female Starfleet Ladies Auxiliary and Embroidery/Baking Society" (Kantrowitz 1994); the United Nations of the Women's Movement <feminist.com>; the Canadian Woman site, <www.media-city.com/ canadianwoman>; Toronto Webgrrls, <www.webgrrls.com/ Toronto>, a networking organization for women interested in learning about the opportunities on the Internet and multimedia; On The Homefront, <home.istar.ca. mprovost/ homefrnt.htm>, a quarterly forum for stay-at-home women by stay-at-home women); Advancing Women, <www.advancingwomen.com>; Power Surge <members .aol.com/dearest/intro.htm>; and Women's Wire <www.women.com/ guide/#top>, which features daily headlines about women making the news, and information on relationships, fashion, business, and healthy living.

Some companies, such as Sun Microsystems and Hewlett-Packard, have begun aggressive recruitment and hiring programs for women and people of colour (Wilde 1997). However, for significant changes to take place regarding women, men, and computers, we must recognize that computers specifically, and technology in general, are not gender neutral and, in fact, have emerged and flourished within the context of a male-dominated industry.

SOURCES: Breidenbach, Susan. 1997. "Where Are All the Women?" *Network World* 14 (41): 68–9; Currid, Cheryl. 1996. "Bridging the Gender Gap: Women Will Lose out Unless They Catch up with Men in Technology Use." *Informationweek*, April 1: 114; DeBare, Ilana. 1996. "Women and Computing." Parts I, III–VI. *Sacramento Bee*. <www.sacbee.com/news/projects/ women>. Rashida, Dhooma. 1997. "A Growing Wave of Surfer Girls." *Toronto Sun*, April 7: 49. Grossman, Lev. 1999. "The War over Women on the Web." *Time Daily.* January 29, <www.time.com>; Kantrowitz, B. 1998. "Men, Women, and Computers." *Newsweek*, May 16: 48–55; O'Neal, Glenn. 1998. "Girls Often Dropped from Computer Equation." *USA Today*, March 10: D4; Wilde, Candee. 1997. "Women Cut through IT's Glass Ceiling." *Informationweek*, January 20: 83–6.

A second explanation is the "relative resources approach." This explanation, consistent with a conflict perspective, suggests that the spouse with the least power is relegated the most unrewarding tasks. Since men often have more education, higher incomes, and more prestigious occupations, they are less responsible for domestic labour. The husband who shouts at his wife, "I pay the bills, the least you can do is keep the house clean!" is expressing the relative resources ideology.

"Gender role ideology," the final explanation, is consistent with a symbolic interactionist perspective. It argues that the division of labour is a consequence of traditional socialization and the accompanying attitudes and beliefs. Females and males have been socialized to perform various roles and to expect their partners to perform other complementary roles. Women typically take care of the house, men the yard. This division of labour is learned in the socialization process through the media, schools, books, and toys. A husband's comment that washing the dishes is "women's work" reflects this perspective.

The School Experience and Cultural Sexism

Sexism is also evident in the schools. It can be found in the books students read, the curricula and tests they are exposed to, and the different ways teachers interact with students.

Textbooks A study by the University of the Philippines concludes that textbooks and other instructional material perpetuate gender stereotypes (UP 1997). In the materials examined, men were portrayed in more interesting and active roles, women's roles were defined by their relationship to men (e.g., wife, daughter), and males were more often pictured in illustrations. Similarly, Purcell and Stewart (1990) analyzed 1883 storybooks used in schools and found that they tended to depict males as clever, brave, adventurous, and income producing and females as passive and as victims. Females were more likely to be in need of rescue, and were also depicted in fewer occupational roles than males. In a study of 27 introductory psychology and 12 human development textbooks, Peterson and Kroner (1992) determined that the representation of the work, theory, and behaviour of males significantly exceeded that of females, and that "the picture presented in textbooks is that the majority of persons working in the various domains of psychology are men" (p. 31). Even textbooks that were designed to promote equality are characterized by "subtle language bias, neglect of scholarship on women, omission of women as developers of history and initiators of events, and an absence of women from accounts of technological developments" (American Association of University Women 1992: 63).

Teacher–Student Interactions Sexism is also reflected in the way teachers treat their students. After interviewing 800 adolescents, parents, and teachers in three school districts in Kenya, Mensch and Lloyd (1997) report that teachers were more likely to describe girls as lazy and unintelligent. "And when the girls do badly," the researchers remark, "it undoubtedly reinforces teachers' prejudices, becoming a vicious cycle." Similarly, in the United States Sadker and Sadker (1990) observed that elementary-school and secondary-school teachers pay more attention to boys than to girls. Teachers talk to boys more, ask them more questions, listen to them more, counsel them more, give them more extended directions, and criticize and reward them more frequently. Sadker and Sadker observed that this pattern continues at the postsecondary level.

Streaming and Destreaming Initiatives

Research has repeatedly noted that both the self-esteem of girls and their academic performance in certain subjects, such as mathematics and the physical sciences, begins to decline during late childhood and early adolescence (Gilligan et al. 1990). In a study of self-esteem among more than 1160 students in grades 6 through 10, girls were significantly more likely to have "steadily declining self-esteem," while boys were more likely to fall into the "moderate and rising" self-esteem group (Zimmerman et al. 1997). The reasons for these declines have been linked to the structure of the school system in general and, in particular, both the dynamics of teacher–student and peer interactions inside and outside the classroom. For example, Larkin (1994) reports that young Canadian women commonly complain of crotch grabbing, breast pinching, and being publicly "rated" at they walk down school corridors. According to Larkin, girls as young as 10 have reported that imitation "gang bangs" have occurred on school playgrounds (see also Gaskell and Willinsky 1995).

Recognizing that as children advance through the educational system, they generally become aware that certain subjects (English, art, music, history) are defined as "girls' subjects" while others (math, physics, chemistry, computers) are viewed as "boys' subjects," several Canadian school districts are experimenting with the introduction of "all-girl" math and science classes, which encourage young women to enter, and excel at, nontraditional areas of study. For example, O'Neill Collegiate and Vocational Institute in Oshawa, Ontario, introduced the STEM (science, technology, English, mathematics) program, which is designed to encourage more girls to pursue studies in these areas. Early reports on this program suggest that girls feel more comfortable about asking questions and voicing their opinions in same-sex classrooms because they do not have to fear teasing or insults from boys.

It has also been suggested that the same-sex classroom environment is "less distracting" than co-ed classes and allows students to concentrate more fully on their work (White 1996). As well, beginning in the 1980s and as the result of initiatives sponsored by the federal and provincial governments and various interest groups, a series of postsecondary programs were introduced at community colleges and similar institutions to encourage women to enter programs that traditionally did not have a large proportion of women. The available evidence suggests that such initiatives have been at least partially successful. While the proportion of women in trade and vocational programs in community colleges who were taking courses in the engineering and applied sciences rose only moderately between the mid-1980s and mid-1990s (from 6.2 percent in 1983–84 to 8.4 percent in 1995–96), the gains within other trade and vocational programs have been more significant. Thus, the proportion of women enrolled in electrical/electronic technology programs almost quadrupled from 2.7 percent in the 1983–84 academic year to 10.5 percent in 1995–96. In woodworking and carpentry, the proportion of women doubled over the same time period.

Nevertheless, in certain areas women remained highly underrepresented among student enrolments. For example, while the proportion of women in marine mechanics programs did increase during this period, it rose from 0.4

percent in 1983–84 to a mere 3.0 percent in 1995–96. In stark contrast, women in 1995–96 continued to account for 85 percent of student enrolments in the health sciences, a field which has, traditionally, been defined as "female" (Statistics Canada 1999b).

Media Images and Cultural Sexism

One concern voiced by social scientists in reference to cultural sexism is the extent to which the media portrays females and males in a limited and stereotypical fashion, and the impact of such portrayals. A recent study by Signorielli (1998) analyzed gender images presented in six media: television, movies, magazines, music videos, TV commercials, and print media advertisements. The specific programs, movies, videos, and so on selected were those most often consumed by 12- to 17-year-old girls, for example, the 25 most watched television shows. The results indicate:

- Other than magazines directed at teenage girls, the medium with the highest representation of women is television (45 percent), followed by TV commercials (42 percent), movies (37 percent), and music videos (22 percent).
- In general, media content stresses the importance of appearance and relationships for girls and women and of careers and work for boys and men.
- Across the six media, 26 to 46 percent of women are portrayed as "thin or very thin" in contrast to 4 to 16 percent of men; 70 percent of girls wanted to look like, fix their hair like, or dress like a character on television, compared with 40 percent of boys.
- In a survey of boys and girls, both agreed that "worrying about weight, crying or whining, weakness, and flirting" are characteristics associated more with girls than with boys, and that "playing sports, being a leader, and wanting to kiss or have sex..." are more often characteristic of male characters.

Language and Cultural Sexism

In subtle ways, both the words we use and the way we use them can reflect gender inequality. The term *nurse* carries the meaning of "a woman who..." and the term *engineer* suggests "a man who...." The embedded meanings of words, as symbolic interactionists note, carry expectations of behaviour.

Despite research that suggests females are most often the victims of negative stereotypes, at least one study concludes otherwise. Fiebert and Meyer (1997) had a sample of college students complete either the sentence "A woman is..." or "A man is...." Responses were then coded as either positive, negative, or neutral. Males were significantly more likely to be stereotyped negatively.

CONSIDERATION

The terms "broad," "chick," "old maid," and "spinster" convey information about age as well as attaching a stigma to the recipient. There are no comparable terms for men. Further, women have traditionally been designated as either Mrs. or Miss, while Mr. conveys no social meaning about marital status. Language is so gender stereotyped that the placement of female or male before titles is sometimes thought necessary as in the case of "female police officer" or "male prostitute." There is a movement away from sexist language. Both the *Canadian Journal of Sociology* and the *Canadian Review of Sociology and Anthropology* endorse the general guidelines contained in the publication. *On the Treatment of the Sexes in Research* by Margrit Eichler and Jeanne Lapointe, published by the Social Sciences and Humanities Research Council of Canada, and refer potential contributors to their journals to this document.

Virginia Sapiro (1994) has shown how male–female differences in communication style reflect the structure of power and authority relations between men and women. For example, women are more likely to use disclaimers ("I could be wrong but...") and self-qualifying tags ("That was a good movie, wasn't it?"), reflecting less certainty about their opinions. Communication differences between women and men also reflect different socialization experiences. Women are more often passive and polite in conversation; men are less polite, interrupt more often, and talk more (Tannen 1990).

International Data

In a survey of Russian youth, both male and female college students identified beauty and kindness as the ideal traits of a woman; strength and ability to provide for one's family were identified as the ideal traits of a man.

SOURCE: Attwood 1996

SOCIAL PROBLEMS AND TRADITIONAL GENDER ROLE SOCIALIZATION

Cultural sexism, transmitted through the family, school, media, and language, perpetuates traditional gender role socialization. Although gender roles are changing, traditional gender roles are still dominant and have consequences for both women and men:

> There is no denying that the gender system controls men too. Unquestionably, men are limited and restricted through narrow definitions of "masculinity."... They, too, face negative sanctions when they violate gender prescriptions. There is little value in debating which sex suffers or loses more through this kind of control; it is apparent that both do. (Schur 1984: 12)

These traditional socialization experiences lead to several social problems, including the feminization of poverty, social-psychological costs, health costs, and relationship problems.

Poverty

The main causes of what is often called the "feminization of poverty" are divorce (see Chapter 10), births to unwed mothers of limited financial means, and the lower wages paid to women in the labour force, particularly women with lower levels of education. Another major cause is the increasingly large numbers of elderly widows living on low income.

Using Canadian tax records, Laroche (1998) examined the experiences of individuals whose pre-tax total family income fell below the Low Income Measure (LIM) at least once between 1982 and 1993. She reports that "being a woman and living in a lone-parent family significantly increased the probability of falling below the threshold and remaining in a low income situation for a considerable amount of time" (p. 24). Table 7.5 indicates that low-income women with children could expect to spend 5.1 to 6.9 years out of 10 living below the LIM while male lone parents could expect to spend an average of 3.5 to 4.5 years in a low-income situation. Statistics Canada's Survey of Labour and

Income Dynamics, which focused on the experiences of Canadians in low-income situations between 1993 and 1996, also found that women, in general, and female lone parents in particular, were more susceptible to remaining in financially straitened circumstances. Of all the men who had a low weekly pay in 1993, about one-third (compared with 17 percent of women) had obtained a better paying job by 1995. Among female lone parents who had low earnings in 1993 and were still employed in 1995, only 12 percent had moved up from low-paying jobs. Among Canadians 65 years of age and older, about 7 percent of women (compared with 1 percent of men) lived in low-income situations on a continuous basis between 1993 and 1996 (Statistics Canada 1999c, 1998e) (see also Chapter 6).

As noted earlier, both individual and institutional discrimination contribute to the economic plight of women. Traditional gender socialization also contributes to poverty among women. Women are often socialized to put family ahead of their education and careers. Women are expected to take primary responsibility for childcare, which contributes to the alarming rate of female-headed lone-parent families in Canada. In 1997, when compared to children in two-parent families, children in female-headed lone-parent families were almost five times more likely to be in a low-income situation. In that year, more than half (56.0 percent) of non-elderly females lived below the "poverty line" (i.e., spent more than 54.7 percent of their income on food, shelter, and clothing) (Statistics Canada 1999d). A study of the relationship between martial status, gender, and poverty in the United States, Australia, Canada, and France indicates that never-married women compared to ever-married women in all four countries are more likely to live in poverty (Nichols-Casebolt and Krysik 1997).

Table 7.5	Time Spent below the LIM by Gender, Marital Status, and Number of Children		
	Average Number of Years below the LIM over Next 10 Years		
	One child	Two children	Three or more children
Women **Married**			
two incomes	2.8	1.9	2.2
one income	3.4	3.6	4.2
Divorced	5.2	5.5	6.2
Separated	5.9	6.2	6.9
Single	5.1	5.4	6.1
Men **Married**			
two incomes	1.8	2.0	2.4
one income	3.5	3.8	4.6
Divorced	3.6	4.0	4.7
Separated	3.4	3.8	4.5
Single	3.6	4.0	4.7

SOURCE: Laroche 1998

Social-Psychological Costs

Many of the costs of traditional gender socialization are social-psychological in nature. Reid and Comas-Diaz (1990) noted that the cultural subordination of women results in women having low self-esteem and being dissatisfied with their roles as spouses, homemakers or workers, mothers, and friends. However, not all researchers have found that women have a more negative self-concept than men do. Summarizing their cross-cultural research on the self-concepts of women and men, Williams and Best (1990b) found no consistency in the self-concepts of women and men in 14 countries: "[I]n some of the countries the men's perceived self was noticeably more favourable than the women's, whereas in others the reverse was found" (p. 152). More recent research also documents that women are becoming more assertive and desirous of controlling their own lives rather than merely responding to the wishes of others or the limitations of the social structure (Burger and Solano 1994).

Men also suffer from traditional gender socialization. Men experience enormous cultural pressure to be successful in their work and earn a high income. In a study of 601 adult men, those who reported feeling "more masculine" earned an average of $35 800; those who reported feeling less masculine earned an average of $28 300 (Rubenstein 1990). Further, as a consequence of traditional male socialization, males are more likely than females to value materialism and competition over compassion and self-actualization (Beutel and Marini 1995; McCammon et al. 1998). Traditional male socialization also discourages males from expressing emotion. In a study of emotional expression among American women and men, Mirowsky and Ross (1995) conclude that "men keep emotions to themselves more than women, and that women express emotions more freely than men" (p. 449).

Health Costs

On the average, men in Canada die about six years earlier than women, although sex differences in life expectancy have been shrinking (Statistics Canada 1998c). Traditional male gender socialization is linked to males' higher rates of heart disease, cirrhosis of the liver, most cancers, AIDS, homicide, drug-induced deaths, suicide, and motor vehicle accidents (Wilkins 1996).

Are gender differences in morbidity and mortality a consequence of socialization differentials or physiological differences? Although both nature and nurture are likely to be involved, social rather than biological factors may be dominant. As part of the "masculine mystique," men tend to engage in self-destructive behaviours—heavy drinking and smoking, poor diets, a lack of exercise, stress-related activities, higher drug use, and a refusal to ask for help. Men are also more likely to work in hazardous occupations than women are. For example, men are more likely to be miners than are women—an occupation with one of the highest mortality rates in Canada.

Relationship Costs

Gender inequality also has an impact on relationships. For example, negotiating work and home life can be a source of relationship problems. While men in traditional versus dual-income relationships are more likely to report being satisfied with household task arrangements, women in dual-income families are the most likely to be dissatisfied with household task arrangements (Baker et al. 1996). Further, the belief that your partner is not performing an equitable portion of the housework is associated with a reduction in the perception of spousal social support (Van Willigen and Drentea 1997).

There are also, of course, the practical difficulties of raising a family, having a career, and maintaining a happy and healthy relationship with a significant other. Successfully balancing work, marriage, and children may require a number of strategies, including (1) a mutually satisfying distribution of house-hold labour, (2) rejection of such stereotypical roles as "supermom" and "breadwinner dad," (3) seeking outside help from others (e.g., childcare givers, domestic workers), and (4) a strong commitment to the family unit.

Finally, violence in intimate relationships is gendered (see Chapters 4 and 5). Although men are more likely to be victims of violent crime, women are more likely to be victims of sexual assault and domestic violence. Violence against women reflects male socialization that emphasizes aggression and dom-inance over women.

STRATEGIES FOR ACTION: TOWARD GENDER EQUALITY

In September 1995, women and men from across the globe came together in Beijing at the United Nations' Fourth World Conference on Women to address issues concerning gender inequality and the status of women. Efforts to achieve gender equality have been largely fuelled by the feminist movement. Despite a conservative backlash, feminists, and to a lesser extent men's activist groups, have made some gains in reducing structural and cultural sexism in the work-place and in the political arena.

Grassroots Movements

Feminism and the Women's Movement In its early incarnation, the suffrage movement in Canada, or the "first wave" of feminism. "was less a 'woman's movement' than an attempt on the part of particular men and women, pre-dominantly urban professionals and entrepreneurs, to supervise [the moral development of] society" (Bacchi 1983: 13). First at the local level, and later at the national and provincial levels, thousands of upper- and middle-class women sought to ameliorate a host of social ills and became active in the tem-perance movement, in campaigns for religious instruction, better workplace conditions, improvements in public health and child welfare, and in the devel-. opment of living facilities for single women. Women's early activism in these areas was often linked to "women's auxiliaries, institutes and missionary soci-eties to spread the word of God" (Errington 1993: 73) established by Christian churches and forwarded as the philanthropic extension of women's "natural" expertise as wives, mothers, and "guardians" of moral virtue.

In 1876, Dr. Emily Howard Stowe founded the Toronto Women's Literary Club, an organization that "in 1883...took a name more revealing of its poli-tics: the Toronto Women's Suffrage Association" (Adamson et al. 1988: 33). Stowe's organization launched a campaign to demand the franchise for women at every political level and for women's rights to obtain entrance to and edu-cation within the prestigious occupations. However, when compared to their counterparts in the United States and England, early Canadian feminists were more likely to engage in a war of words than in firebrand tactics.

In the decades between the first and second waves of the feminist movement, the position of women did improve in Canadian society. Moreover, as Wine and Ristock (1991: 1) have suggested, "[p]erhaps the most impressive impact of the [women's] movement is the massive shift in the consciousness of the Canadian public in terms of affirmation of women's right to equality, including reproductive freedom, equal treatment in the workplace, and freedom from violence." However, it has been acknowledged that the second wave of the women's movement did not always nor consistently recognize, include, or champion the needs of all Canadian women equally. For example, women with disabilities often found their needs excluded or marginalized (Driedger 1993). Similarly, Wine and Ristock (p. 13) have observed that "though women's organizations provided some support,...[t]he activist work of Native women to change section 12(b) of the *Indian Act*, and its denial of treaty rights to Native women who married non-Native men...[was a] battle fought almost entirely by Native women." As Cassidy et al. (1998: 26) acknowledge in their discussion of "silenced and forgotten women"—First Nations women, Black women, immigrant women, women with disabilities, and poor women— it is only recently that the second wave of the women's movement "has finally begun to address criticisms that White, middle-class feminists have denied, dismissed, and denigrated the experiences of differently raced, abled, and classed women." To measure your attitudes toward feminism look at this chapter's Self and Society.

The Men's Movement As a consequence of the women's rights movement, men began to re-evaluate their own gender status. In *Unlocking the Iron Cage*, Michael Schwalbe (1996) examines the men's movement as both participant and researcher. For three years, he attended meetings and interviewed active members. His research indicates that participants, in general, are White middle-class men who feel they have little emotional support, who question relationships with their fathers and sons, and who are overburdened by responsibilities, unsatisfactory careers, and what is perceived as an overly competitive society.

As with any grassroots movement, several factions co-exist in the men's movement. Some men's organizations advocate gender equality; others developed to oppose "feminism" and what was perceived as male bashing. For example, the Promise Keepers are part of a Christian men's movement that has often been criticized as racially intolerant, patriarchal, and antifeminist. However, one female researcher and author who attended meetings incognito, that is, as a man, reports: "I'm struck with how close it all sounds like feminism" (Leo 1997).

Today, issues of custody and fathers' rights headline the men's rights movement and have led to increased visibility (Goldberg 1997). Many members of such groups argue that society portrays men as "disposable," and that as fathers and husbands, workers and soldiers, they feel that they can simply be replaced by other men willing to do the "job." They also hold that there is nothing male-affirming in society and that the social reforms of the last 30 years have "been the deliberate degradation and disempowerment of men economically, legally and socially" (NCFM 1998: 7).

International Data

The GDI Index (Gender-related Development Index) developed by the United Nations measures the success of a country in moving toward gender equality. In 1997, the top-ranked countries were Canada, Norway, Sweden, Iceland, and the United States. The lowest ranking countries were Sierra Leone, Nigeria, and Burkina Faso.

SOURCE: Human Development Report 1997

Attitudes Toward Feminism Scale

Following are statements on a variety of issues. Left of each statement is a place for indicating how much you agree or disagree. Please respond as you personally feel and use the following letter code for your answers:

A: Strongly Agree   **B: Agree**   **C: Disagree**   **D: Strongly Disagree**

_____ 1. It is naturally proper for parents to keep a daughter under closer control than a son.

_____ 2. A man has the right to insist that his wife accept his view as to what can or cannot be afforded.

_____ 3. There should be no distinction made between woman's work and man's work.

_____ 4. Women should not be expected to subordinate their careers to home duties to any greater extent than men.

_____ 5. There are no natural differences between men and women in sensitivity and emotionality.

_____ 6. A wife should make every effort to minimize irritation and inconvenience to her husband.

_____ 7. A woman should gracefully accept chivalrous attentions from men.

_____ 8. A woman generally needs male protection and guidance.

_____ 9. Married women should resist enslavement by domestic obligations.

_____ 10. The unmarried mother is more immoral and irresponsible than the unmarried father.

_____ 11. Married women should not work if their husbands are able to support them.

_____ 12. A husband has the right to expect that his wife will want to bear children.

_____ 13. Women should freely compete with men in every sphere of economic activity.

_____ 14. There should be a single standard in matters relating to sexual behaviour for both men and women.

_____ 15. The father and mother should have equal authority and responsibility for discipline and guidance of the children.

_____ 16. Regardless of sex, there should be equal pay for equal work.

_____ 17. Only the very exceptional woman is qualified to enter politics.

_____ 18. Women should be given equal opportunities with men for all vocational and professional training.

_____ 19. The husband should be regarded as the legal representative of the family group in all matters of law.

_____ 20. Husbands and wives should share in all household tasks if both are employed an equal number of hours outside the home.

_____ 21. There is no particular reason why a girl standing in a crowded bus should expect a man to offer her his seat.

_____ 22. Wifely submission is an outmoded virtue.

_____ 23. The leadership of a community should be largely in the hands of men.

_____ 24. Women who seek a career are ignoring a more enriching life of devotion to husband and children.

_____ 25. It is ridiculous for a woman to run a locomotive and for a man to darn socks.

_____ 26. Greater leniency should be adopted toward women convicted of crime than toward male offenders.

_____ 27. Women should take a less active role in courtship than men.

_____ 28. Contemporary social problems are crying out for increased participation in their solution by women.

_____ 29. There is no good reason why women should take the name of their husbands upon marriage.

_____ 30. Men are naturally more aggressive and achievement oriented than women.

_____ 31. The modern wife has no more obligation to keep her figure than her husband to keep down his waistline.

_____ 32. It is humiliating for a woman to have to ask her husband for money.

_____ 33. There are many words and phrases that are unfit for a woman's lips.

_____ 34. Legal restrictions in industry should be the same for both sexes.

_____ 35. Women are more likely than men to be devious in obtaining their needs.

_____ 36. A woman should not expect to go to the same places or to have quite the same freedom of action as a man.

_____ 37. Women are generally too nervous and high-strung to make good surgeons.

_____ 38. It is insulting to women to have the "obey" clause in the marriage vows.

_____ 39. It is foolish to regard scrubbing floors as more proper for women than mowing the lawn.

_____ 40. Women should not submit to sexual slavery in marriage.

_____ 41. A woman earning as much as her male date should share equally in the cost of their common recreation.

_____ 42. Women should recognize their intellectual limitations as compared with men.

List above reprinted by permission of Bernice Lott, Department of Psychology, University of Rhode Island.

SCORING

Score your answers as follows: A = +2, B = +1, C = –1, D = –2. Because half the items were phrased in a pro-feminist and half in an antifeminist direction, you will need to reverse the scores (+2 becomes –2, etc.), for the following items: 1, 2, 6, 7, 8, 10, 11, 12, 17, 19, 21, 23, 25, 26, 27, 30, 33, 35, 36, 37, and 42. Now sum your scores for all the items. Scores may range from –84 to +84.

INTERPRETING YOUR SCORE

The higher your score, the higher your agreement with feminist (Lott uses the term "women's liberation") statements. You may be interested in comparing your score, or those of your classmates, with those obtained by Lott (1973) from undergraduate students at the University of Rhode Island. The sample comprised 109 men and 133 women in an introductory psychology class, and 47 additional older women who were participating in a special continuing education for women (CEW) program. Based on information presented by Lott (1973), the following mean scores were calculated: men = 13.07, women = 24.30, and continuing education women = 30.67.

More recently, Biaggio et al. (1985) administered Lott's questionnaire to 76 students from a University of Idaho introductory psychology class and 63 community members randomly selected from the local phone directory. Although they did not present the scores of their respondents, they reported they did not find differences between men and women. Unlike Lott's students, in Biaggio et al.'s sample, women were not more pro-liberation than men were. Biaggio, Mohan, and Baldwin (p. 61) stated, "It seems that some of the tenets of feminism have taken hold and earned broader acceptance. These data also point to an intersex convergence of attitudes, with men's and women's attitudes toward liberation and child rearing being less disparate now than during the period of Lott's study." It would be interesting to determine whether there are differences in scores between members of each sex in your class.

SOURCES: Biaggio, M. K., P. J. Mohan, and C. Baldwin. 1985. "Relationships among Attitudes toward Children, Women's Liberation, and Personality Characteristics." *Sex Roles* 12: 47–62; Lott, B. E. 1973. "Who Wants the Children? Some Relationships among Attitudes toward Children, Parents, and the Liberation of Women." *American Psychologist* 28: 573–82.

Changes in the Workplace

Changes in the workplace are reflected in changes in the structure of the Canadian family. Since 1961, the greatest single change to the face of the Canadian labour force has been the substantial growth in the numbers of employed women in general and, in particular, employed women with children (Best 1995). Corporations have begun to accommodate changing gender roles and the increased emphasis on both work and family by offering a variety of new programs and benefits such as on-site childcare, part-time employment, job sharing, flextime, telecommuting, and assistance with elderly parents.

More women have also begun to enter traditionally male occupations. Williams (1995) suggests that this is an important and essential step on the road to gender equality, because it gives women more economic opportunities and helps to break down limiting stereotypes about women's capabilities. However, Williams warns that

> **Well-meaning efforts directed at getting women to be more "like men" run the risk of reifying the male standard, making men the ultimate measure of success. If the aim is gender equality, then men should be encouraged to become more "like women" by developing, or feeling free to express, interests and skills in traditionally female jobs. (p. 179)**

Public Policy

The introduction of policy changes and programs designed to eliminate gender inequality have not been without controversy. Here we direct attention to sexual harassment and employment equity and note some of the debates these issues have inspired on Canadian campuses in recent years.

Canadian case law has recognized that sexual harassment is a multifaceted phenomenon that may include sexual assault; unwanted touching or patting; leering, sexually suggestive gestures; demands for sexual favours; derogatory or degrading remarks; repeated and unwelcome sexual flirtations, advances, or propositions; the use of sexually degrading words to describe a person; sexist jokes that cause embarrassment; and displaying sexually offensive material. The Law Society of Canada notes that "[w]hether a particular type of conduct constitutes sexual harassment is sometimes difficult to determine" and that although "the severity of the conduct may be the most conclusive factor...what is determinative is a combination of frequency, severity and persistence" (in Mossman 1997: 244). This chapter's The Human Side suggests some of the difficulties that Canadian tribunals have faced in determining who is, and who is not, a victim of sexual harassment.

Sexual Harassment

There are two types of **sexual harassment**: (1) *quid pro quo*, in which an employer requires sexual favours in exchange for a promotion, salary increase, or any other employee benefit, and (2) the existence of a hostile environment that unreasonably interferes with job performance, as in the case of sexually explicit comments or insults being made to an employee. The Supreme Court

A CAMPUS DIVIDED

For months, the community of 20 000 scholars perched atop Burnaby Mountain has been getting its own crash course in the complexities of sexual harassment. At the centre of the storm have been the allegations of student Rachel Marsden that her former swim coach, Liam Donnelly—whom she says she saw romantically for 16 months beginning in May 1994—raped her while the two were on a date in September 1995. Donnelly has vigorously protested his innocence, publicly insisting that Marsden had aggressively pursued him with lewd e-mail messages in which she invited him for sex in her car, and with provocative photos slipped under his door.

When a formal university harassment panel heard the case [in the fall of 1996], Donnelly refused to take part, acting on legal advice that he says he now regrets taking. After a five-day hearing, he was found guilty of sexual harassment. Soon after, Donnelly asked president John Stubbs to grant him a private hearing. But Stubbs refused, and on May 23, the president fired the swim coach. Days later, Marsden was awarded $12 000 in compensation and full credit for a course she had failed to complete.

Now, it is that decision by Stubbs…that has become the flash point for campus debate. In a July 14 news release that took the Simon Fraser community by surprise, acting president David Gagan raised troubling questions about the case. Among other things, Gagan revealed that Marsden had developed a personal relationship with SFU harassment policy co-ordinator Patricia O'Hagan (who has since left the university)—and alleged that Stubbs knew of the relationship when he approved the panel's ruling. As well, Gagan stated that a draft of the panel's report had been shown to Marsden—by whom, it was not made clear—before a final version was released. Hours after Gagan dropped his bombshell, David Bond, chairman of SFU's board of governors…announced his intention to convene an emergency board meeting to discuss a plan of action.…

As if campus wags did not have enough to talk about, only days after Gagan's announcement Marsden broke her long silence. In a news release entitled *Rachel Sets the Record Straight*, and at a news conference on the front lawn of her home,… Marsden painted a colourful portrait of several of the steamier details of her alleged affair with the former swim coach. Describing herself as a "naive virgin" when she met Donnelly, she acknowledged sending provocative photos to the former swim coach. But, she said, they were not slipped under his door but "personally selected [by Donnelly] from my modelling portfolio." Marsden also admitted sending a torrid e-mail that invited the coach "to go inside me.…I could sit on your lap or we could do it lying down." Her explanation: it was "a very desperate attempt to entice him into meeting with me so that I could obtain accountability and an apology for the abuse, harassment, and rape I had suffered at his hands." And her announcement was not without contrition. "I realize that sending

A CAMPUS DIVIDED *(continued)*

this e-mail demonstrated poor judgement on my part," she wrote, "but unfortunately I had no faith in the criminal justice at the time, and I had no knowledge of the university harassment policy and procedures."

In a one-two punch, Marsden followed her defence with a spirited offence—offering to draw a detailed diagram of Donnelly's bedroom, name the brand of lubricant cream he prefers, and identify many of his sexual mannerisms. And she addressed head-on the issue of her personal relationship with the former harassment officer O'Hagan. The two had gone on a weekend river-rafting trip with members of O'Hagan's family, wrote Marsden, but only after her hearing had concluded. And she candidly acknowledged that O'Hagan "offered emotional support to me throughout a process which was extremely painful"—a role Marsden's supporters were quick to defend. After all, noted Joey Hansen, president of the Simon Fraser student society, "Hagan was not a member of the harassment panel itself, and had no part in writing the decision...."

Still, it was Stubbs, more than Marsden, who has been placed in the spotlight....Even before last week's turn of events, many on campus were demanding a formal review of his decision to fire Donnelly, including a group of professors who have been petitioning the board of governors to intercede. The reason for their anger: Stubb's steadfast refusal to listen to Donnelly's version of events—a decision that Stubbs

defended shortly after firing the swim coach. "Mr. Donnelly chose not to participate in the process," said the president in an interview. "My job is not to second-guess the panel, but to receive their report and consider it very carefully."

Many are now saying that is simply not good enough. "This has all been outrageous," insists criminology professor Neil Boyd, who served as chairman of the harassment panel between 1990 and 1993. "Donnelly had provocative photos and e-mails of Marsden offering him sex—things germane to the issue of whether she sexually harassed him....When you get that kind of evidence, the answer isn't to hide behind procedure, but to convene a new hearing." Others beg to differ. "When it comes to power at this place, students are on the lowest rung," says student president Hansen. "The president can't buckle just because a faculty member demands a re-hearing...."

Amid speculation over how events will unfold, at least some at Simon Fraser were voicing another concern: that on the scenic mountaintop campus, the trees had begun to obscure the forest. "Whoever wins or loses all these battles," student leader Hansen says, "it is pretty clear that women on this campus are going to be more reluctant than ever to come forward with claims of sexual harassment. It's pretty ironic, isn't it, that after all the time and energy expended, our campus may be a less safe place to learn than ever?"

SOURCE: Abridged from Dwyer, Victor. 1997. "A Campus Divided." *Maclean's* 10 (3): 42–4.

of Canada in *Janzen v. Platy Enterprises et al.* (1989) established as a point of law that sexual harassment can constitute discrimination on the basis of sex. Sexual harassment occurs at all occupational levels, and some research suggests that the number of incidents of sexual harassment is inversely proportional to the number of women in an occupational category (Fitzgerald and Shullman 1993). For example, female doctors (Schneider and Phillips 1997) and lawyers (Rosenberg et al. 1997) report high rates of sexual harassment, in the first case by male patients and in the second by male colleagues. In addition, it has become increasingly evident that sexual harassment is not restricted to the workplace but can also infect those settings where individuals prepare for entering the workplace. McDaniel and Roosmalen (1992) report that sexual harassment is a common experience among Canadian female university students and one structured by power differentials. They report that 40 percent of their female university-student sample had experienced sexual insults, 29 percent had received a sexual invitation, 10.8 percent had been sexually assaulted, and 7 percent had experienced sexual intimidation.

However, sexual harassment is not exclusively a "women's problem." Research suggests that approximately 15 percent of men are subject to sexual harassment (Henslin and Nelson 1997).

Employment Equity

The passage of the *Canadian Human Rights Act* in 1977 provided the legal foundation for **employment equity.** Section 16(1) of the *Canadian Human Rights Act* asserts that it is not a discriminatory practice to adopt or carry out a special program, plan, or arrangement designed to prevent, eliminate, or reduce disadvantages suffered by persons or groups because of race, national or ethnic origin, skin colour, religion, age, sex, family status, marital status, or disability by improving their opportunities in respect to goods, services, facilities, accommodations, or employment. Thus, the Act implicitly suggests that "employment equity" does not constitute "reverse discrimination." Rather, under the terms of reference of the Canadian Human Rights Commission, charged with administering the Act, an employment equity program may be required as part of the settlement of a complaint of discrimination, as a strategic attempt to forestall the future recurrence of discriminatory practices.

The 1986 proclamation of the *Employment Equity Act* in Canada, akin to the guidelines established in 1983 for the federal public service, requires all sizable employers (varyingly defined as having either 50 or 100 or more employees) within the federal sector to ensure that their procedures for hiring, firing, promotion, and training are equitable to all groups. The overall employment data are to be compiled and submitted to the Canada Employment and Immigration Commission and, through this procedure, to the Canadian Human Rights Commission. This body of data is made public to allow accountability of employers' attempts to ensure equality for the underrepresented groups within the workforce: women, visible minorities, people with disabilities, and First Nations people.

Nevertheless, opponents of employment equity have argued that, despite the intention of this initiative, this strategy will not quell discrimination, may well lead us back to the degrading colour/racial/gender consciousness of the past, and may latently function to create resentment of and hostility toward those groups that it seeks to help. Consider, for example, that in August 1999, academics from across Canada wrote letters to officials at Wilfrid Laurier University to protest a job posting for a psychology professor that specified that only women would be considered. "Obviously, at Laurier the commitment to...fairness and the pursuit of academic excellence takes a back seat to social goals like achieving a gender balance in departments. This bodes...ill for your institution, which has gone down in my estimation, as I'm sure it has in that of many academics," read one letter received by the institution. The gender-specific job posting was described by the chairperson of the psychology department at Laurier as an attempt to "address a gender imbalance" in the psychology department at that university; at the time of the posting, the department had 18 male professors and only four women professors.

Nevertheless, academics protesting the job posting also submitted numerous queries to the Ontario Human Rights Commission, questioning the university's use of Section 14 of the Ontario Human Rights Code, which stipulates that a special program may be implemented as long as it does not infringe on other rights—such as freedom from discrimination—and "is designed to relieve hardship or economic disadvantage." Although conceding that women have suffered job discrimination at universities in the past, critics of the gender-specific posting argued that women academics were "hardly a disadvantaged group" (*National Post* 1999: A4).

UNDERSTANDING GENDER INEQUALITY

Gender roles and the social inequality they create are ingrained in our social and cultural ideologies and institutions and are, therefore, difficult to alter. Nevertheless, as we have seen in this chapter, growing attention to gender issues in social life has spurred some change. For example, women who have traditionally been expected to give domestic life first priority are now finding it acceptable to be more ambitious in seeking a career outside the home. Men who have traditionally been expected to be aggressive and task oriented are now expected to be more caring and nurturing. Women seem to value gender equality more than men do, however, perhaps because women have more to gain. For instance, 84 percent of 600 adult women said that the ideal man is caring and nurturing; only 52 percent of 601 adult men said that the ideal woman is ambitious (Rubenstein 1990: 160).

However, men also have much to gain by gender equality. Eliminating gender stereotypes and redefining gender in terms of equality do not mean simply liberating women, but liberating men and our society as well. "What we have been talking about is allowing people to be more fully human and creating a society that will reflect that humanity. Surely that is a goal worth striving for" (Basow 1992: 359). Regardless of whether traditional gender roles emerged out of biological necessity as the functionalists argue or economic oppression as the conflict theorists hold, or both, it is clear today that gender inequality carries a high price: poverty, loss of human capital, feelings of worthlessness, violence, physical and mental illness, and death. Surely, the costs are too high to continue to pay.

CRITICAL THINKING

1. Some research suggests that "[men] and women with more androgynous gender orientations—that is to say, those having a balance of masculine and feminine personality characteristics—show signs of greater mental health and more positive self-images." (Anderson 1997: 34). Do you agree or disagree? Why or why not?
2. The chapter indicates that there is a "gender gap" in the number of men and women obtaining doctoral degrees. Why might this be?
3. What have been the interpersonal costs, if any, of sensitizing Canadian society to the "political correctness" of female–male interactions?
4. Why are women more likely to work in traditionally male occupations than men are to work in traditionally female occupations? Are the barriers that prevent men from doing "women's work" cultural, structural, or both? Explain.

KEY TERMS

cultural sexism
devaluation hypothesis
double or triple
   (multiple) jeopardy
employment equity
gender

glass ceiling
human capital
   hypothesis
occupational sex
   segregation
pink-collar jobs

sex
sexism
sexual harassment
structural sexism

CHAPTER EIGHT

Race and Ethnic Relations

Is It True?

1. Many anthropologists and other scientists have concluded that "races" do not really exist.

2. Canada holds the dubious distinction of being one of the world's largest mailing centres for hate literature.

3. In 1996, more than half of Canada's immigrants were from Asia and the Middle East.

4. When asked whether Canada's cultural diversity tends to enhance or erode the Canadian identity, a majority of Canadians responded that it "erodes Canadian identity."

5. In Sweden, it is against the law to give the Nazi salute.

Answers: 1 = T, 2 = T, 3 = T, 4 = F, 5 = T

In November 1999, five British Columbian skinheads entered guilty pleas to charges of manslaughter in a B.C. courtroom. The five had beaten an elderly caretaker to death at a Sikh temple in January 1998 in Surrey, B.C. The judge presiding at the sentencing hearing, Judge William Stewart of the provincial court, referred to the five as "social misfits," and noted that the victim, Nirmal Singh Gill, had been singled out for attack and "died simply because he was Indo-Canadian." Although the Crown had demanded that life terms be imposed upon the five men, Judge Stewart sentenced the convicted killers to 12 to 15 year terms of imprisonment (*Maclean's* 1999b: 33).

Although many Canadians may be startled to realize that there are individuals in Canada who would willfully kill another human being simply because of skin colour or ethnicity, many others would not be surprised. Consider as well, in this context, that in 1996, a poll based on 3000 telephone interviews in the United States and 3000 in Canada reported that 14 percent of Canadians and 22 percent of Americans reported that they "would rather have neighbours my own race"; 55 percent of Canadians and 67 percent of Americans agreed that "the number of immigrants should be reduced" (*Maclean's* 1996: 38).

In this chapter, we discuss the nature and origins of prejudice and look "under the rug" to uncover the extent of discrimination and its consequences for both racial and ethnic minorities. We also discuss strategies designed to reduce prejudice and discrimination. We begin by examining racial and ethnic diversity worldwide and in Canada, emphasizing first that the concept of race is based on social rather than biological definitions.

> We make a great mistake by associating the inheritance of physical characteristics with far more complex traits of human personality and behaviour.
>
> David Suzuki,
> Scientist,
> Science Educator,
> and Broadcaster

National Data

In 1999, the results of *Maclean's* year-end poll, based on the responses of 1200 adult Canadians randomly selected from all 10 provinces, indicated that almost one in two Canadians (49 percent) "strongly agreed" or "somewhat agreed" with the statement "We are allowing too many immigrants into our country."

SOURCE: *Maclean's* 1999c

THE GLOBAL CONTEXT: DIVERSITY WORLDWIDE

A first-grade teacher asks the class, "What colour are apples?" Most of the children answer red. A few say green. One boy raises his hand and says "White." The teacher tries to explain that apples can be red, green, or sometimes golden, but never white. The boy insists his answer is right and finally says, "Look inside" (Goldstein 1999). Like apples, human beings may be similar on the "inside," but are often classified into categories according to external appearance. After examining the social construction of racial categories, we review patterns of interaction among racial and ethnic groups and overview racial and ethnic diversity in Canada.

The Social Construction of Race

The concept of **race** refers to a category of people who are believed to share distinct physical characteristics that are deemed socially significant. Racial groups are sometimes distinguished based on such physical characteristics as skin colour, hair texture, facial features, and body shape and size. Some physical variations among people are the result of living for thousands of years in different geographical regions (Molnar 1983). For example, humans living in regions with hotter climates developed darker skin from a natural skin pigment, melanin, which protects the skin from the sun's rays. In regions with moderate or colder climates, people had no need for protection from the sun and thus developed lighter skin.

Cultural definitions of race have taught us to view race as a scientific categorization of people based on biological differences between groups of individuals. Yet, racial categories are based more on social definitions than on biological differences. Anthropologist Mark Cohen (1998) explains that distinctions among human populations are graded, not abrupt. Skin colour is not black or white, but rather ranges from dark to light with many gradations of shades. Noses are not either broad or narrow, but come in a range of shapes. Physical traits such as these, as well as hair colour and other both visible and invisible characteristics, come in an infinite number of combinations. For example, a person with dark skin can have any blood type and can have a broad nose (a common combination in West Africa), a narrow nose (a common trait in East Africa), or even blond hair (a combination found in Australia and New Guinea).

The science of genetics also challenges the notion of race. Geneticists have discovered that "the genes of black and white...[North Americans] probably are 99.9 percent alike" (Cohen 1998: B4). Furthermore, genetic studies indicate that genetic variation is greater within racially classified populations than between racial groups (Keita and Kittles 1997). Classifying people into different races fails to recognize that over the course of human history, migration and intermarriage have resulted in the blending of genetically transmitted traits. Thus, there are no "pure" races; people in virtually all societies have genetically mixed backgrounds.

The American Anthropological Association has passed a resolution stating that "differentiating species into biologically defined 'race' has proven meaningless and unscientific" (Etzioni 1997, 39). Scientists who reject the race concept now speak of **populations** when referring to groups that most people would call races (Zack 1998).

CONSIDERATION

The concept of race is so embedded in our culture that even those who advocate abandoning racial classification continue to use racial terminology. For example, in his book *The New Coloured People*, Spencer (1997) argues for abandoning racial classification, yet he uses racial terminology throughout the book (even in the last chapter entitled "Thou Shalt Not Racially Classify"). Keita and Kittles (1997) suggest that the concepts of biological race and racial categories continue to exist and to be used "in part, due simply to old habits. Categorical thinking is entrenched..." (p. 591).

Patterns of Racial and Ethnic Group Interaction

When two or more racial or ethnic groups come into contact, one of several patterns of interaction may occur, including genocide, expulsion or population transfer, slavery, colonialism, segregation, acculturation, assimilation, pluralism, and amalgamation. These patterns of interaction may occur when two or more groups exist in the same society or when different groups from different societies come into contact.

- **Genocide** refers to the deliberate, systematic annihilation of an entire nation or people. The European invasion of the Americas, beginning in the sixteenth century, resulted in the decimation of most of the original inhabitants of North and South America. For example, labelling Aboriginals as "savages" allowed early Canadian settlers and visiting fishermen to commit "atrocities of a most barbaric kind" upon the Beothuks of Newfoundland (Rowe 1977: 146). Indeed, some scholars have claimed that the eventual extinction of the Beothuk resulted from the "sport of Indian hunting": murder committed "for fun" (Horwood 1969) and for the payment of a bounty for each Beothuk killed (Such 1978: 62). Although some Native groups were intentionally killed, others fell victim to diseases brought by the Europeans. In the twentieth century, Hitler led the Nazi extermination of more than 12 million people, including more than six million Jews, in what has become known as the Holocaust. Recently, ethnic Serbs have attempted to eliminate Muslims from parts of Bosnia—a process they call "ethnic cleansing."

- **Expulsion or population transfer** occurs when a dominant group forces a subordinate group to leave the country or to live only in designated areas of the country. In the United States, the 1830 *Indian Removal Act* called for the relocation of eastern tribes to land west of the Mississippi River. The movement, lasting more than a decade, has been called the Trail of Tears because tribes were forced to leave their ancestral lands and endure harsh conditions, inadequate supplies, and epidemics that caused illness and death. During World War II, approximately 22 000 Japanese-born naturalized Canadians and foreigners were stripped of their rights, had their homes, property, and businesses confiscated, and were evacuated from British Columbia and resettled in internment camps. In addition, the "Deemed Suspect," refugees from Germany and Austria, were deported from England to Canada and interned here as "enemy aliens." Between 1940 and 1943, 2300 individuals "deemed suspect" were interned in Canada within eight camps (Columbo 1986). In 1979, Vietnam expelled nearly one million Chinese from the country because of long-standing hostilities between China and Vietnam.

- **Slavery** exists when one group treats another group as property to exploit for financial gain. The dominant group forces the enslaved group to live a life of servitude, without the basic rights and privileges enjoyed by the dominant group. In early American history, slavery was tolerated and legal for three centuries. In what is now Canada, slavery was practised by several Indian tribes on the Northwest Coast and by Europeans, beginning in 1500 in Newfoundland. By 1608, Black slaves were introduced by the French with the first slave transported directly from Africa sold in 1629. In New France, there were 3604 recorded slaves by 1759, 1132 of whom were Black, the remainder of whom were "panis" (Indians). The "right" of Canadians to own and sell Native people as slaves was declared on May 29, 1733. Canada prohibited the importation of slaves in 1793; that same year, an act of the Upper Canada legislature ruled that all children in its jurisdiction born to slaves after that year were to be free upon reaching the age of 25 and proposed the gradual emancipation of slaves. Although the last slave auction in Canada was held in 1797 in Montreal, slavery remained technically legal in most of

Canada until 1834 when it was abolished for the entire British Empire (Winks 1999).

- **Colonialism** occurs when a racial or ethnic group from one society takes over and dominates the racial or ethnic group(s) of another society. The European invasion of North America, the British occupation of India, and the Dutch presence in South Africa before the end of apartheid are examples of outsiders taking over a country and controlling the native population. As a territory of the United States, Puerto Rico is essentially a colony whose residents are U.S. citizens but who cannot vote in presidential elections unless they move to the mainland.

- **Segregation** refers to the physical separation of two groups in residence, workplace, and social functions. Segregation may be **de jure** (Latin meaning "by law") or **de facto** ("in fact"). For example, Blacks across Canada were treated as inferior from the time they began to settle here, prohibited from entering restaurants, hotels, and recreational facilities, and barred from most professions. In provinces such as Nova Scotia and Ontario, where Blacks were most concentrated, Blacks were often forced into segregated schools. The last segregated school in south western Ontario closed in 1956; however, it was 1975 before Windsor, Ontario, became the last municipality to desegregate its public facilities (Henry and Tator 1995: 321–2). In like fashion, because of a range of discriminatory legislation in B.C. "where anti-Asian sentiment was endemic from the 1850s to the 1950s" (Dreidger 1999: 1889), "Chinese, Japanese and South Asians could not vote, practice law or pharmacy, be elected to public office, serve on juries or work in public works, education or the civil service." Consider as well that the first Jew to be elected to a Canadian legislature, Ezekiel Hart, chosen in Trois-Rivières, Quebec, in 1807, was declared ineligible to sit in Parliament for the third session of the fourth Parliament of Lower Canada because he was Jewish. A year later, Hart was re-elected and again barred from sitting in Parliament because he was Jewish. Jews were declared ineligible to enter Canada for the totality of the French regime in Canada, and it was not until January 28, 1837, during the first session of the 14th Parliament of Lower Canada, that an act was passed that, in theory, conferred full civil rights on Jews. Anti-Semitism, however, was not extinguished, and in the 1920s and 1930s, Jews were automatically excluded from employment in major institutions such as banks and the police, barred from elite social clubs, beaches, and holiday resorts in Montreal, Toronto, and Winnipeg, and universities set limits on Jewish enrolment (Henry et al. 1995). Segregation is not unique to Canada. In Germany, for example, Turkish immigrants are concentrated in ghettos, and in Sweden, Greek, Chilean, and Turkish immigrants are largely isolated from the rest of the population.

- **Acculturation** refers to learning the culture of a group different from the one in which a person was originally raised. Acculturation may involve learning the dominant language, adopting new values and behaviours, and changing the spelling of the family name. In some instances, acculturation may be forced. For example, the 1977 passage of the French Language Charter (Bill 101) established French as the official language of Quebec and made French the legal language of work and the public sector. It also resulted in a situation in which educational instruction takes place almost exclusively in French, with English granted "secondary language status." Similarly, the Canadian government's policy of "aggressive civilization," which was designed to destroy all aspects of Aboriginal culture and which found expression in the creation of native residential schools is discussed in detail in Chapter 12.

- **Assimilation** is the process by which formerly distinct and separate groups merge and become integrated as one. There are two types of assimilation: secondary and primary. **Secondary assimilation** occurs when different groups become integrated in public areas and in social institutions, such as neighbourhoods, schools, the workplace, and in government. **Primary assimilation** occurs when members of different groups are integrated in personal, intimate associations such as friends, family, and spouses. The degree of acculturation and assimilation that occurs between majority and minority groups depends in part on (1) whether minority group members have voluntary or involuntary contact with the majority group and (2) whether majority group members accept or reject newcomers or minority group members. Groups that *voluntarily immigrate* and who are *accepted* by "host" society members will experience an easier time acculturating and assimilating than those who are forced (through slavery, frontier expansion, or military conquest) into contact with and are rejected by the majority group.

- **Pluralism** refers to a state in which racial and ethnic groups maintain their distinctness, but respect each other and have equal access to social resources. In Switzerland, for example, four ethnic groups—French, Italians, Germans, and Swiss Germans—maintain their distinct cultural heritages and group identities in an atmosphere of mutual respect and social equality. Similarly, a policy of cultural pluralism, or **multiculturalism,** is evidenced in the description of Canada as a "mosaic" of peoples, which dates back to 1922. Unlike the United States, which, since 1908, has been described by some as a unicultural "**melting pot,**" Canada encourages the expression of ethnic and other differences. Indeed, one of the most important recommendations of the Royal Commission on Bilingualism and Biculturalism, appointed in 1963, was that Canada's multicultural heritage be preserved. In a speech given in the House of Commons on October 8, 1971, then-Prime Minister Pierre Trudeau committed his government to "a policy of multiculturalism within a bilingual framework...as the most suitable means of assuring the cultural freedom of Canadians" (in Columbo 1986: 353). When launching its multicultural policy in 1971, the Canadian government confirmed its commitment to an ideal that acknowledged that Canada, while officially bilingual, had no "official" culture—that is, that none of the distinguishable cultures took precedence over the others.

    Multiculturalism attempts to foster a society in which diversity is viewed as valuable. In July 1988, the Conservative government passed a bill to introduce the *Canadian Multiculturalism Act.* This act sets forth the government's multiculturalism policy: to wit, "to recognize all Canadians as full and equal participants in Canadian society." Since 1972, there has been a minister responsible for multiculturalism and, since 1973, a Canadian Multiculturalism Council and a Multiculturalism Directorate within the Department of the Secretary of State. In 1991, a Department of Multiculturalism and Citizenship was established to emphasize that multiculturalism empowers minorities to pursue the dual goals of ethnicity and equality.

A 1999 survey of 2049 Canadians aged 18 and older, conducted by the Environics Research Group, asked respondents, "Do you think that Canada's cultural diversity tends to enhance or erode the Canadian identity." Almost 6 out of 10 (59 percent) felt it enhanced Canadian identity, with female respondents slightly more likely than males to express this attitude (60 percent versus 57 percent).

SOURCE: "A Changing People" 1999: 34

Currently, Canada's Multicultural Program, which is based on the goals of the Multicultural Policy and the Canadian *Multicultural Act*, has three fundamental goals: (1) identity: fostering a society that recognizes, respects, and reflects a diversity of cultures such that people of all backgrounds feel a sense of belonging and attachment to Canada; (2) civic participation: developing active citizens with both the opportunity and the capacity to participate in shaping the future of Canada and its communities; (3) social justice: building a society that ensures fair and equitable treatment and that respects the dignity of and accommodates peoples of all origins.

- **Amalgamation,** also known as **marital assimilation**, occurs when different ethnic or racial groups become married or pair-bonded and produce children. Although in most societies, the norm of **endogamy** influences individuals to marry within their social group, there is no doubt that miscegenation or interracial marriages have become more acceptable in Canada in the past few decades. Disapproval of Black–White marriage in Canada declined from 52 percent in 1968 to 34 percent in 1973 and 16 percent in 1988 (Reitz and Breton 1994: 80). Although both Canadians and Americans are becoming increasingly accepting of interracial marriage, Canadians, in general, are more approving than are Americans (Khokh 1995).

Visible Minorities in Canada

Before 1996, the Canadian census derived indirect information on the numbers and characteristics of persons who were visible minorities from responses to questions on ethnic or cultural origin. However, in 1996, the Canadian census introduced a new question that asked respondents directly if they were a member of one of the population groups defined by the *Employment Equity Act* as "visible minorities." That is, "persons, other than Aboriginal peoples, who are non-Caucasian in race or non-White in colour." Included under this definition are: Chinese, South Asians, Blacks, Arabs and West Asians, Filipinos, Southeast Asians, Latin Americans, Japanese, Koreans, and Pacific Islanders. Census respondents were asked to indicate their population group by checking one or more of 10 mark-in categories. Table 8.1 presents the results obtained.

Based on estimates prepared by Statistics Canada, by 2005, visible minorities will constitute 54 percent of the population of Toronto. It is also expected that the proportion of visible minorities in Canada will rise to 16 percent in 2005.

SOURCE: *Time* 1999

According to Statistics Canada (1998b), in 1996, 3.2 million persons or 11.2 percent of Canada's total population identified themselves as members of a visible minority. The largest visible minority populations in Canada were the Chinese (3 percent of Canada's total population), followed by South Asians (2.4 percent), and Blacks (2 percent). These three groups accounted for two-thirds of Canada's visible minority population in that year.

Approximately 3 out of every 10 individuals (29 percent) who identified themselves as members of a visible minority were born in Canada, and the rest were immigrants (68 percent) (see Figure 8.1). Approximately one-quarter (24 percent) of Canada's visible minority population was recent immigrants who arrived in Canada between 1991 and 1996. Reflective of historical immigration patterns, wide differences exist in the proportion of Canadian-born among visible minority groups. For example, in both Nova Scotia and New Brunswick, the majority of visible minorities are Canadian-born (69 percent and 56 percent, respectively) and reflect the settlement of Blacks in these two provinces in earlier generations. In 1996, approximately 65 percent of Japanese, 42 percent of Blacks, and 29 percent of South Asians living in Canada had been born in Canada.

Table 8. 1

Visible Minority Population by Group, 1996[1]

	Total Number	% of Total Population
Total visible minority population	3 197 480	11.2
Chinese	860 150	3.0
South Asian	670 585	2.4
Black	573 860	2.0
Arab/West Asian	244 665	0.9
Filipino	234 200	0.8
Latin American	176 975	0.6
Southeast Asian	172 765	0.6
Japanese	68 135	0.2
Korean	64 835	0.2
Visible minority not included elsewhere	69 745	0.2
Multiple visible minority	61 570	0.2

[1] Total population in 1996 was 28 528 125.

SOURCE: Census of Canada, Statistics Canada.

National Data

A 1998 Canadian Heritage survey of 40 Torontonians, aged 18 to 27, with one Black and one White parent, found their definition of race changed dramatically as they got older. While only 22.9 percent said they were biracial in elementary school, 59 percent identified themselves as such in high school, and 82.1 identified themselves as biracial at the time of the study.

SOURCE: Infantry 2000

Among other visible minority groups, approximately one-fourth were born in Canada. Because of high immigration levels in the 1990s, the proportion of recent immigrants among Canada's visible minority population is especially high in the provinces of British Columbia (27 percent) and Ontario (25 percent).

Considerable variation exists in the proportion of visible minorities within Canada's provinces and territories. Ontario and British Columbia, which contain half our country's total population, account for almost three-quarters of the visible minority population. Visible minorities account for 17.9 of the population in British Columbia, 15.8 percent in Ontario, and 10.1 percent in Alberta, but 0.7 percent in Newfoundland, and 1.1 percent in both Prince Edward Island, and New Brunswick. The majority of visible minorities (94 percent) live in one of Canada's 25 census metropolitan areas (CMAs). The term "census metropolitan area" refers to a very large urban area whose principal or

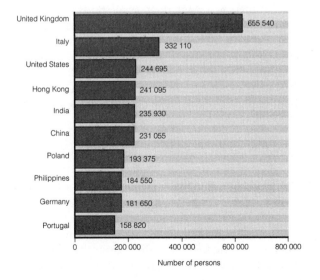

Figure 8. 1

Birthplace of All Immigrants as of 1996

SOURCE: Statistics Canada. 1997. 1996 Census: Immigration and Citizenship, *The Daily*, November 4 (Statistics Canada Cat. No. 11-001-XIE).

central city has a population of at least 100 000. In 1996, 7 of every 10 visible minority persons in Canada lived in three CMAs: Toronto, Vancouver, and Montreal.

In 1996, Toronto had the largest proportion of the total visible minority population in Canada (42 percent), followed by Vancouver (18 percent), and Montreal (13 percent). Visible minorities compose almost one-third of the total population of Toronto (32 percent) and Vancouver (31 percent). With the exception of Arab/West Asians and Japanese, Toronto is the home of the largest number of each of the visible minority groups in Canada. Approximately half of Canada's South Asians and Blacks and two-fifths of Canada's Chinese, Koreans, and Filipinos live in Toronto. Relatively high numbers of visible minorities also live in five other urban areas: Calgary (16 percent), Edmonton (14 percent), Ottawa-Hull (12 percent), Montreal (12 percent), and Winnipeg (11 percent).

Aboriginality

The *Constitution Act, 1981* defines "aboriginal peoples of Canada" as belonging to four major groups:

1. *Status Indians*: Persons whose names appear on the Indian Register maintained by the Department of Indian and Northern Affairs Canada under the *Indian Act* and who are registered as Indians for the purpose of special entitlements. In 1998, there were 627 435 status Indians who belonged to 608 bands. In that year, the largest Native band was the Six Nations of the Grand River, a band with a population of 19 894 and consisting of 13 registry groups: the Bay of Quinte Mohawks, Bearfoot Onondaga, Delaware, Konadaha Seneca, Lower Cayuga, Lower Mohawk, Niharondasa Seneca, Onondaga Clear Sky, Tuscarora, Upper Cayuga, Upper Mohawk, and Walker Mohawk.

2. *Nonstatus Indians*: Those whose Indian status has been extinguished for a variety of reasons and whose names do not appear on the Indian Register. In former times, Indians gave up their official status when they wanted to vote, to drink alcohol off the reserve, or (if they were women) to marry a non-Indian. In 1985, the federal government introduced Bill C-31, which enabled Indian women to regain their legal status if they had lost it by marrying men who did not possess Indian status. The bill also allowed all first-generation children of such marriages and any Indian who had enfranchised to regain their legal status as Indian. In consequence, the number of nonstatus Indians has dwindled.

3. *Métis*: The descendants of Indian and non-Indian unions (principally between Indians and Europeans and, prior to Confederation, between Indians and the French). Previously regarded as "halfbreeds," the Métis have sought to establish their status within Canadian society, past and present. For example, they have suggested that Louis Riel be regarded as the Métis' "Father of Confederation," and argued that Riel "intuitively sensed the future for Canada and wanted to guarantee a place for Métis people in that future" (Kilgour 1988: 48).

4. *The Inuit*: This term, meaning "the people," replaced "Eskimos," a Algonquian word meaning "eaters of raw flesh" that is now considered derogatory. The Inuit became the first Aboriginal group in Canada to achieve at least partial self-determination with the creation of Nunavut (Inuktitut for

"our land"). First proposed in 1976 as an Inuit homeland by the Inuit Tapirisat (an association of Inuit leaders), and established by the *Nunavut Act* of June 1993, Nunavut became a constitutional entity on April 1, 1999. About 80 percent of Nunavut's total population (approximately 27 000) are Inuit (Crauford-Lewis 1999: 1686).

In census years before 1996, the numbers of Aboriginal persons in Canada were ascertained from a question that asked respondents about their ancestry. For example, in the 1991 Canadian census, the question posed was, "To which ethnic or cultural group(s) did this person's ancestor's belong?" and respondents asked to report as many of their ethnic or cultural origins (e.g., English, French, German, and North American Indian) as applicable. In 1996, however, the census included both an ancestry and an identity question. The identity question was: "Is this person an Aboriginal person, that is North American Indian, Métis, or Inuit (Eskimo)?"

In 1996, 1 101 953 individuals in Canada reported Aboriginal ancestry as either a single response (477 630) or as part of a multiple response (624 423). North American Indian ancestry was reported by 867 225 and Métis or Inuit ancestry by 49 845 people. Based on responses to the identity question, there were 799 010 people who reported that they were either North American Indian (554 290), Métis (210 190), or Inuit (41 080). Because a small number of persons reported that they considered themselves members of more than one Aboriginal group, the total of these numbers slightly exceeds the total Aboriginal population. Note that because of problems with enumeration on 77 Indian reserves and settlements (with an estimated population of 44 000 persons), the numbers obtained in the 1996 census may underestimate Canada's Aboriginal population.

The status of Canada's Native peoples reflects the strains of almost 400 years of cultural domination, exploitation, and exclusion. The consequences are not surprising. Native people suffer the lowest levels of education, income, health, and employment in Canada. Social conditions on many Native reserves, the lands set aside for the exclusive use of status Indians, reflects the historical and political neglect that Canada has shown toward its Indigenous peoples. On many reserves, housing fails to meet the most basic structural standards. Less than half of on-reserve homes have sewer or water hook-ups and half can best be described as overcrowded (Frideres 1993). Although the federal budget of February 1999 committed $190 million over three years to new home-care programs and more extensive health monitoring in Aboriginal communities, the infant mortality rate among natives remains 1.7 times the national average. Native men on reserves die, on average, seven years sooner than other Canadians, and the life expectancy for Native women remains six years lower than the national norm (Health Canada 1999). It has been estimated that the suicide rate among the Aboriginal population averages two to seven times that of the Canadian population as a whole (Health Canada 1999).

Native people do not consider themselves simply part of the Canadian multicultural mosaic; rather, they seek recognition of their sovereign status as the ancestral occupants of Canada. In support of this position, the main conclusion of the 1996 Royal Commission on Aboriginal Peoples "was the need for a complete restructuring of the relationship between aboriginal and non-aboriginal peoples in Canada." Doerr (1999: 3) notes that their recommendations included:

governmental commitment to a new set of ethical principles...which acknowledged and respected aboriginal cultures and values, the historical origins of aboriginal nationhood and the inherent right to aboriginal self-determination.

that the further development of aboriginal governments should focus on aboriginal nations rather than single communities...[and] the establishment of an aboriginal parliament which would comprise aboriginal representatives and advise Parliament on matters affecting aboriginal peoples.

the need to significantly increase land holdings for First Nations in southern Canada...[and] a recommendation for an independent lands and treaties tribunal to oversee negotiations among federal, provincial and aboriginal governments on land issues.

adoption of aboriginal health and healing strategies, an aboriginal peoples international university, educational programs to support aboriginal self-government and public education initiatives to promote cultural sensitivity and understanding among non-aboriginals.

However, in its 1998 response to the Report, the federal government limited itself to pursuing four objectives: "renewing partnerships; strengthening aboriginal governance; developing a new fiscal relationship; and supporting strong communities, people and economies" (Doerr 1999: 4). The federal government also issued a Statement of Reconciliation, which expressed regret for past errors and a determination to learn from these errors, and committed $350 million to support community-based healing.

CONSIDERATION

Historically, various countries around the world have collected census data on the racial groups within their populations. For example, the first American census in 1790 divided the U.S. population into four groups: free White males, free White females, slaves, and other persons (including free Blacks and Indians). To increase the size of the slave population, the **"one drop of blood rule"** appeared, which specified that even one drop of Negroid blood defined a person as Black and, therefore, eligible for slavery. It is evident, however, that the one drop rule represents, at best, a very crude and inaccurate way of defining a person's "race."

Identifying a person as belonging to a specific "race"—or ethnicity—is not a simple task. For example, if you went back in your family history as far as the Norman Conquest of 1066, you would find yourself claiming 41 000 000 ancestors (Fitzhugh 1991: 290). With the passage of time, fewer if any individuals can claim that their racial or ethnic ancestry is "pure."

Ethnic Diversity in Canada

Ethnicity refers to a shared cultural heritage or nationality. Ethnic groups may be distinguished based on language, forms of family structures and roles of family members, religious beliefs and practices, dietary customs, forms of artistic expression such as music and dance, and national origin.

Two individuals with the same racial identity may have different ethnicities. For example, a Black Canadian and a Black Jamaican have different cultural, or ethnic, backgrounds. Conversely, two individuals with the same ethnic background may identify with different races. Consider for example, that while Jews in China may look Asian, some Jews in Sweden may be blue-eyed blondes or, in Ethiopia, be Black.

Canadians come from a variety of ethnic backgrounds. "Ethnic origin," as defined in the 1996 Canadian census, refers to ethnic or cultural ancestry and should not be confused with place of birth, citizenship, or nationality. Before 1996, the census question "To which ethnic or cultural group(s) did this person's ancestors belong" was accompanied by a list of the 15 most frequent ethnic origins. Respondents, in turn, were asked to mark as many from this list as applicable and were provided with two blank spaces in which they could indicate other ethnic origins that were not included on the list. However, for the 1996 census, the format of the ethnic origin question was modified. Rather than providing respondents with a list of answer categories, respondents were given four blank spaces in which to indicate single or multiple ethnic origins. In recognition of the fact that "Canadian" was the fifth most frequently reported ethnic origin in the 1991 census, "Canadian" was included, for the first time, among the examples given of how this question might be answered.

As might be expected, the inclusion of this example "resulted in a major change in the way ethnic origin origins were reported" (Statistics Canada 1998b). In 1996, 5.3 million individuals (19 percent of Canada's total population) reported their ethnic origin as simply "Canadian." In 1991, when "Canadian" was not listed as an option, only 3 percent identified their ethnic origin solely as Canadian, with an additional 1 percent listing it in combination with one or more other ethnic origins. Almost all of the people who reported "Canadian" in 1996 were Canadian-born and had French or English as their first language. Evidence also suggests that those who identified themselves as Canadian in 1996 were those who had, on earlier censuses, identified their ethnic origins as English or French. The highest proportion of people reporting their ethnic origin as Canadian occurred in places where comparatively little recent immigration has occurred and in regions of Canada that had been settled the earliest. For example, 21 percent of those in the Atlantic provinces and 38 percent of those living in Quebec gave "Canadian" as a single response.

In the 1996 census, 4.9 million people (17 percent of Canada's total population) reported British Isles–only ancestry while 2.7 million (9 percent) reported French-only ancestry. Approximately 2.9 million (10 percent) reported some combination of British Isles, French, or Canadian origin in that year. About 4.6 million people (16 percent of the population) reported an ethnic ancestry of either British Isles, French, or Canadian, in combination with some other ethnic origin. Among those who reported origins other than the British Isles, French, or Canadian (8.1 million or 28 percent of Canada's total population), 3.7 million reported European single origins, 1.3 reported single East and Southeast Asian origins, and 590 000 reported single South Asian origins.

Because of intermarriage, there has been an increase in the number of persons reporting more than one ethnic origin. In 1996, more than one in three (36 percent) reported more than one ethnic origin, with the highest proportion of multiple responses occurring in Prince Edward Island (52 percent) and the lowest proportion occurring in Quebec (17 percent). In general, groups that set-

Approximately 45 percent of high-school students in Richmond, B.C., speak a language other than English at home. In Brampton, Ontario, 33 languages are spoken in Brampton's 97 schools. In Toronto, the city clerk's office offers phone translations in no fewer than 148 languages.

SOURCE: *Time* 1999

tled more recently in Canada (i.e., persons with, for example, Caribbean, African, Arab, Latin American origins) were less likely to report multiple origins than those of Aboriginal, British Isles, French, or other European origins. Table 8.2 provides the 15 most commonly identified ethnic origins, either as the sole ethnic origin or as part of a mixed heritage.

Table 8.2	Visible Minority Population by Group, 1996		
	Total Responses	**Single Ethnic Origin**	**Multiple Ethnic Origin**
Total population	28 528 125	18 303 625	10 224 495
Canadian	8 806 275	5 326 995	3 479 285
English	6 832 095	2 048 275	4 783 820
French	5 597 845	2 665 250	2 932 595
Scottish	4 260 840	642 970	3 617 870
Irish	3 767 610	504 030	3 263 580
German	2 757 140	726 150	2 030 990
Italian	1 207 475	729 455	478 025
Aboriginal	1 101 955	477 630	624 330
Ukrainian	1 026 475	331 780	694 790
Chinese	921 585	800 470	121 115
Dutch	916 215	313 880	602 335
Polish	786 735	265 930	520 805
South Asian	723 345	590 145	133 200
Jewish	351 705	195 810	155 900
Norwegian	346 310	47 805	298 500

SOURCE: Census of Canada, Statistics Canada, 1996

CONSIDERATION

Statistics Canada's decision to include the ethnic category of "Canadian" has not been without controversy and researchers, government departments, and ethnic groups continue to debate the usefulness of the designation. Some have argued that the category should be dropped from the next census because it makes it difficult to obtain reliable information on the ethnic backgrounds of Canadians. According to Jack Jedwab, the head of the Association for Canadian Studies, injecting nationalism into the census only frustrates the work of researchers. "The sheer number of people who identify themselves as Canadians makes it difficult to determine how many people are not indicating their ethnic background" (*National Post* 1999a: A1). More recently, there has been considerable debate over whether the ethnicity question itself ought to be deleted from the Canadian census.

The Québécois

In Canada, we have traditionally spoken of the English and the French as "**charter groups**," a term that reflects the historical importance of these groups in Canada's history. Although the *British North America Act* of 1867 acknowledged and enshrined the rights and privileges of the French and the British as the founding or charter groups of Canadian society, "the history of English–French relations in Canada is one of competition between two collectivities engaged in constructing and maintaining a society" (Breton 1988: 557). Indeed, Lord Durham's 1839 description of this relationship as "two nations warring in the bosom of a single state" may still strike some as apt. As Behiels (1999: 909) has commented, "Observers of the continuing debate over Quebec's role within Confederation, and particularly the contemporary Quebecois secessionist movement, might be tempted to believe that Durham's assessment can be applied as a general principle to the entirety of the Canadian experience." However, he emphasizes that this would be a gross simplification of the situation and stresses that the character of francophone–anglophone relations has, in fact, "ebbed and flowed in response to changing socio-economic, political and ideological factors as well as to the commitment of Canada's majority and minority francophone communities to survival and equality."

During the period between Confederation and World War II, institution-building in Canada largely favoured the English. The development of the Canadian collective identity, Breton (1988) has argued, was not modelled on something uniquely "Canadian," but rather was decidedly "British" and "Protestant." Although in the English collectivity, immigration was pursued as the central means for ensuring the growth of the English-speaking population, in Quebec, the concern that French Catholics would be drowned in a British Protestant sea found expression in a natality policy that encouraged child-bearing. Nevertheless, with the influx of English-speaking merchants and settlers into Quebec, the English, although a statistical minority, gradually assumed power. Over time, this former minority transformed itself into an elite that dominated the economic cartels that emerged in the areas of finance, transportation, and staples. English-speaking groups came to dominate the Quebec economy and the politico-bureaucratic groups that strongly influenced the federal government.

Urban migration, a postwar industrial expansion, and reforms made during Quebec's Quiet Revolution in 1960 and 1966 encouraged a strong rise in Quebec nationalism. Under the leadership of Jean Lesage, the provincial government of Quebec initiated a broad range of structural and ideological reforms that increased the role of the state and reduced the authority and role of the Catholic Church. A steeply declining birthrate and an increase in the number of non-francophone immigrants (many of whom chose to use English at work and for the schooling of their children) reinforced the belief among francophones in Quebec that to survive as a French-speaking society, the French language would have to be aggressively promoted. Francophones became increasingly likely to equate their collective identity with the empowerment of Quebec itself. Those who had formerly referred to themselves as "canadien" or "canadien-français" increasing began to use the name "Québécois" and to assert their belief that Quebec was capable of directing and controlling its own future.

The victory of the Parti Québécois, a party dedicated to Quebec's achievement of independent nationhood, in the 1976 Quebec provincial election notified Canadians of both the strength of French nationalism within that province and of the depth of French-Canadian dissatisfaction. Neither the 1969 passage of Canada's *Official Languages Act*, nor the passage in 1977 of the French Language Charter (Bill 101) in Quebec, which established French as the only official language of education, work, and the public sector in that province, extinguished the perceived threat of assimilation.

Since then, "French Canada's attempt to redefine its role within Canada has produced vigorous public debate and considerable political turmoil" (Behiels 1999: 911). The desire to create a French homeland that is predominantly French in character is not, strictly speaking, a "new" idea but one that has circulated since at least the time of Confederation. However, it gained a sense of immediacy in the early 1990s when Lucien Bouchard's secessionist Bloc Québécois won 54 of the province's 75 seats. In 1994, the leader of the Parti Québécois, Jacques Parizeau, announced that a referendum on the concept of sovereignty-partnership would be held the following year. It was maintained that should Canada refuse "to negotiate an economic association with an independent Quebec following a majority vote...[that] Quebec would unilaterally declare its independence from Canada" (p. 912).

With polls suggesting a victory for secessionist forces, Prime Minister Jean Chrétien promised the Québécois a veto over all major constitutional changes and recognition of Quebec as a distinct society. When the referendum vote was held, just more than 50 percent voted "No" to secession and just less than 50 percent voted "Yes"—a wafer-thin rejection of sovereignty that Parizeau blamed on "money and the ethnic vote." A poll conducted in 1995 reported that one in three Canadians and one in two Quebecers believed that "the country...[would] cease to exist by the end of the decade" (*Maclean's* 1999c: 28).

In the aftermath of the referendum, the federal government passed a bill granting all five regions of Canada, including Quebec, a veto over future constitutional changes and a resolution supporting the concept of Quebec as a distinct society. The federal government also agreed to refer the question of whether or not Quebec had the absolute right to secede unilaterally from Canada to the Supreme Court of Canada. The Supreme Court of Canada later issued the unanimous ruling that Quebec did not have this right under Canadian constitutional law nor under international law. However, it was also the opinion of the Supreme Court that

> if Quebec voters demonstrated a clear, and not just a simple, majority on a straightforward question on outright secession, then Ottawa and the other provinces would have an obligation to enter into negotiations with the government of Quebec. They also pointed out that there was no guarantee that such negotiations would succeed or that the territory of the province of Quebec would remain intact if the negotiations succeeded since the rights of the majority had to respect those of the various minorities (Behiels 1999: 912).

The problem, however, was that the Supreme Court did not define what it meant by "clear" or "substantial." In November 1999, Prime Minister Jean Chrétien announced that his cabinet had agreed that the federal government would have to act to ensure these terms were clearly defined and tabled a draft bill, the *Clarity Act*, that set out the conditions under which Ottawa would negotiate the break-up of the country following a referendum win by Yes forces. Although the draft bill declared that a simple majority of 50 percent plus one would not be enough to trigger separation, it did not spell out exactly what percentage would be considered sufficient.

In response to this move by the federal government, Joseph Facal, Quebec's intergovernmental affairs minister announced that only Quebec's National Assembly could decide the wording of the referendum and the terms for leaving Canada. According to Facal, "Ottawa, inspired by a Soviet-style law, is trying to impose a real straightjacket on Quebec's political future. It's an assault without precedent on the democratic rights of the people of Quebec to chose the political future it wants to chose" (*National Post* 1999b: A11). For their part, the Bloc Québécois labelled the move "a crime against history"; Quebec premier Lucien Bouchard called Ottawa's move "a strain on Canada's democratic reputation in the eyes of the international community (*Maclean's* 1999c: 83).

An Angus Reid Survey of Quebec residents, released on December 14, 1999, found that 80 percent of those polled agreed that a clear referendum question was needed and 59 percent said that a clear majority—more than 50 percent plus one—was needed before Quebec could negotiate separation. A second poll, conducted by Ekos Research Associates in December 1999, found that only 30 percent of Quebecers would vote for outright independence in a referendum while 64 percent favoured the status quo. Only 17 percent of Quebecers, the lowest level ever reported in a survey, stated that they expected that Quebec would be a country in five years time (*National Post* 1999c: A7).

Canadian Immigration

Immigration is, arguably, the area of public policy that has had the greatest impact on Canada's history, economy, multicultural identity, and regional diversity. The growing racial and ethnic diversity of Canada is largely attributable to immigration. However, the history of Canada's immigration policies is far from exemplary. In the 1870s and 1880s, the active attempt to recruit immigrants to Canada for labour-intensive industries was accompanied by the emergence of regulations that sought to preserve Canada's "English stock" by restricting or denying entry to certain groups. These regulations reflected the sentiment that, while useful as labourers, certain groups were "undesirable" as permanent residents of Canada. For example, hostility toward Asians and a fear of the "yellow peril" is clear in the statement by Sir John A. Macdonald, Canada's first prime minister, that "a Mongolian or Chinese population in our country...would not be a wholesome element in this country" (in Sher 1983: 33). Later, Canada's 1910 *Immigration Act* gave the government the formal power to "prohibit for a stated period, or permanently, the landing in Canada...of immigrants belonging to any race unsuited to the climate or requirements of Canada." In addition, Troper (1999: 1140) notes that when rumours spread that a group of Black people were preparing to immigrate to Alberta from the United States,

> Federal authorities initiated an ingeniously simple scheme. Nothing in the *Immigration Act* specifically barred black Americans, but any immigrant could effectively be denied access to Canada for health reasons under the Act's medical provisions. The government merely instructed immigration inspectors and their medical aides along the American border to reject all blacks as unfit for admission on medical grounds. There was no appeal. Blacks were warned they should not waste their time and money by considering immigration to Canada.

Canada's *Chinese Immigration Act* of 1923 completely barred the Chinese from entering Canada and Chinese persons already in Canada were not allowed to sponsor family or relatives. In the same year, the federal government listed Poland, Yugoslavia, Hungary, and Romania as "non-preferred" countries for the purposes of immigration. Abella and Troper (1998: 108) emphasize that Canada's refusal to accept Jewish refugees from Hitler's Europe reflected the pervasive anti-Semitism of pre-war Canada. They note that when a senior Canadian official was asked by journalists how many Jewish refugees would be admitted after the war, his response was: "None is too many." "It is perhaps no surprise therefore that Canada had by far the worst record of any Western country for providing sanctuary to the Jews of Europe in the 1930s and 1940s" (Abella 1999: 90).

In 1947, Prime Minister William Lyon Mackenzie King pledged to remove "objectionable discrimination" from the *Immigration Act*. Certain blatantly discriminatory features of the Act were removed, but Canada's immigration policy still included "selective restriction." Preferred candidates were those who were British, Irish, French, or American. The Ministry of Citizenship and Immigration was to determine the suitability of other would-be immigrants in light of "the climate, educational, social, industrial, labour and other requirements in Canada." A person applying to immigrate to Canada could be declared "undesirable" because of "his peculiar customs, habits, modes of life, methods of holding property or his general inability to assimilate."

In the 1950s, the Canadian government, under pressure from other countries of the Commonwealth, began to relax its immigration policies. Some of the changes were simply cosmetic; for example, southern and eastern European countries were renamed "traditional sources" rather than "non-preferred." However, other changes were more substantive. The White Paper of 1966 and the Regulations of 1967 called for the abolishment of discrimination based on race, colour, religion, national origin, or gender. Immigration was to respond to Canada's need for workers, and cultural enrichment was added as part of Canada's immigration objectives. In addition, the White Paper noted Canada's commitment to the plight of international refugees.

Currently, the *Immigration Act* specifies three major objectives of immigration: (1) family reunification, (2) the fulfilment of Canada's international legal obligations and the compassionate and humanitarian treatment of refugees, and (3) the promotion of a strong and viable economy in all of Canada's regions. The three principal components of immigration in Canada are family class, independent (economic) immigration, and refugees (see Figure 8.2).

Family-class applicants are those who are sponsored by a family member already in Canada who agrees to assume responsibility for providing the sponsored immigrant with the necessities of life for as many as 10 years. Sponsors of anyone other than a spouse or dependent children must meet minimum income requirements.

Independent or *skilled workers* are assessed by a point system that looks at such factors as age, education, knowledge of one or both of Canada's official languages, specific vocational preparation, job training, occupation, arranged employment (in which cases the employers must show that there are no Canadians qualified to do the job and demonstrate that the working conditions and proposed wages are adequate), and designated occupations (a listing of occupations for which workers are in short supply in either specific provinces or regions). Canada also admits "business immigrants"—investors and entrepre-

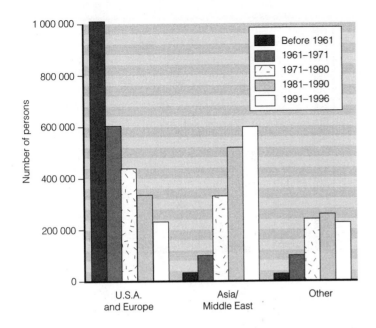

Figure 8.2
New Landed Immigrants,
by Class, 1981–96

SOURCE: Dumas, J., and A. Belanger. 1997.
Report on the Demographic Situation in Canada
1997: Current Demographic Analysis. Ottawa:
Statistics Canada, Demography Division (Statistics Canada Cat. No. 91-209) (original data
source: Citizenship and Immigration Canada)

neurs—based on either an approved investment or the applicant's ability and resolve to start a business that will create jobs for Canadians. Those seeking entry to Canada as self-employed people must contribute significant economic or other benefits to Canada.

The selection criteria used in assessing potential immigrants to Canada are subject to the Canadian Charter of Rights and Freedoms. Immigrants are to be selected without discrimination. Under the Canada-Quebec Accord on Immigration, Quebec holds sole selection powers for both refugees who are to be resettled from abroad and independent immigrants who desire to immigrate to Quebec.

In 1996, approximately five million persons (17 percent of the Canadian population) were immigrants and the largest proportion of immigrants were born in the United Kingdom (13 percent) or Italy (7 percent). Recently, Asia and the Middle East are increasingly furnishing greater numbers of Canada's immigrants. Between 1991 and 1996, 57 percent of those who immigrated to Canada were from either Asia or the Middle East, with high immigration from Hong Kong, the People's Republic of China, and India. In contrast, the numbers of individuals who immigrate from the United States and Europe have declined significantly (see Figure 8.3). The majority of Canada's immigrants in 1996 were independent class immigrants (56 percent), followed by family immigrants (30 percent). Approximately one in six immigrants in 1996 were classified as refugees.

Some notable differences are apparent between the immigrant population and the Canadian-born population. For example, 47 percent of immigrants who arrived in 1996 were between the ages of 24 and 44, and 22 percent were under the age of 14. Among the Canadian-born population, the respective figures are 33 percent and 21 percent. Twenty-seven percent of immigrants were over the age of 65, versus 11 percent of the total Canadian population. Compared to those who are Canadian-born, recent immigrants, regardless of their country of birth, tend to be in better health—a tendency that reflects the

Figure 8.3
Birthplace of All Immigrants, by Period of Immigration, 1996 Census

SOURCE: Statistics Canada. 1997. 1996 Census: Immigration and citizenship, *The Daily*, November 4 (Statistics Canada Cat. No. 11-001-XIE).

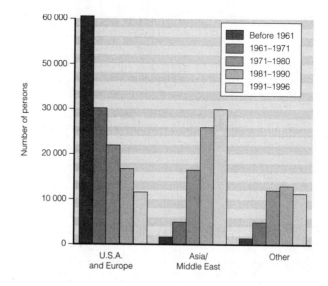

demands of our immigration requirements. In the 1994–95 National Population Health Survey, 50 percent of all immigrants aged 18 and older, versus 57 percent of those who were Canadian-born, reported a chronic health problem (e.g., allergies, joint problems), and 18 percent of immigrants, versus 22 percent of those who were Canadian-born, reported a long-term disability.

Canada is a signatory to the 1951 United Nations Convention Relating to the Status of Refugees. The *Immigration Act, 1976* and the 1992 amendments introduced by Bill C-86 additionally provide for the admission of "designated classes" on humanitarian grounds. A UN Convention **refugee** is defined as a person who "owing to a well-founded fear of being prosecuted for reasons of race, religion, nationality, membership in a particular social group or political opinion, is outside the country of his nationality and is unable, or owing to such fear, is unwilling to avail himself of the protection of that country." The term "designated classes" is used to refer to "a variety of refugee-like situations including mass outflows...disproportionate punishment for violation of strict exit controls (self-exiles) and, for specific countries, the internally displaced (political prisoners and oppressed people)" (Boyd 2000: 84).

As the number of refugee applicants has grown (see Table 8.3), some people have voiced the suspicion that many of these individuals are not legitimate refugees but simply individuals who are attempting to circumvent Canada's immigration regulations. Since the 1980s, Canada's refugee regulations and procedures have undergone a continual series of changes designed to prevent individuals who are simply "looking for a way around tough Canadian immigration regulations" from claiming refugee status (Troper 1999: 1141). Nevertheless, Canada's refugee policy became the subject of renewed controversy when, in the summer of 1999, four ships carrying approximately 600 Chinese arrived on British Columbia's coast after several months at sea. Unlike the United States, which may deport new arrivals within weeks if it rejects their claims for asylum, Canada reviews requests for refugee status in a typically long, drawn-out fashion. At the time this book went to press, two people had filled unsuccessful refugee claims, 74 had been rejected, four had withdrawn their claims, and about 450 were still being processed. Sixty-seven had disappeared—reputedly, to the United States (*Maclean's* 2000: 42).

CONSIDERATION

Managing Canada's increasing diversity has become a challenge for the federal government and municipal governments, for school boards, and for businesses. According to research conducted by the Privy Council Office, federal efforts will be required to fill an expanding gap in providing English training for the young and to match the skills of new immigrants to job openings. At the municipal level, there will be a challenge to deliver services to a multilingual population. The problem of figuring out who needs what is also essential. For example, immigrants from Vietnam have difficulty with the school system and, while 47 percent of new immigrants fall into a low-income bracket, those from Mexico and Central American suffer from unusually high rates of unemployment.

SOCIOLOGICAL THEORIES OF RACE AND ETHNIC RELATIONS

Some theories of race and ethnic relations suggest that individuals with certain personality types are more likely to be prejudiced against or to direct hostility toward minority group members. Sociologists, however, concentrate on the impact of the structure and culture of society on race and ethnic relations. Three major sociological theories lend insight into the continued subordination of minorities.

Structural-Functionalist Perspective

Functionalists emphasize that each component of society contributes to the stability of the whole. In the past, inequality between majority and minority groups was functional for some groups in society. For example, in the United States, the belief in the superiority of one group over another provided moral justification for slavery, supplying the South with the means to develop an agricultural economy based on cotton. Further, members of the majority perpetuated the belief that minority members would not benefit from changing structural conditions (Nash 1962). Thus, southern Whites felt that emancipation would be detrimental for Blacks, who were highly dependent upon their "White masters" for survival.

Table 8.3	Refugees to Canada, 1960–98							
1960	2 329	1970	1 361	1980	40 638	1990	36 093
1961	1 813	1971	614	1981	15 058	1991	35 891
1962	1 733	1972	5 204	1982	17 000	1992	36 943
1963	2 024	1973	2 381	1983	14 062	1993	24 835
1964	2 279	1974	1 656	1984	15 553	1994	19 739
1965	2 131	1975	6 109	1985	17 000	1995	26 789
1966	2 058	1976	5 576	1986	19 485	1996	28 552
1967	1 499	1977	3 670	1987	21 950	1997	25 324
1968	9 971	1978	3 038	1988	27 230	1998	22 831
1969	3 604	1979	27 894	1989	37 361		

SOURCE: Refugee's Branch, Citizenship and Immigration Canada

National Data

More than half of all immigrants in 1996 settled in Ontario, 21 percent in British Columbia, and 15 percent in Quebec.

SOURCE: Statistics Canada 1998a

Functionalists recognize, however, that racial and ethnic inequality is also dysfunctional for society (Schaefer 1998; Williams and Morris 1993). A society that practises discrimination fails to develop and utilize the resources of minority members. Prejudice and discrimination aggravate social problems such as crime and violence, war, poverty, health problems, unemployment, and drug use—problems that cause human suffering and financial burdens for individuals and society.

SELF & SOCIETY   Becoming a Canadian Citizen: Could You Pass the Test?

Canadian citizenship is a relatively new concept. It was not until after World War II that an independent Canadian citizenship was introduced. Before then, Canadians were considered British subjects residing in Canada, rather than Canadian "citizens." The introduction of Canada's *Citizenship Act* stemmed largely from the vision and efforts of Canadian cabinet minister Paul Martin Sr. On visiting a military cemetery in France in the closing months of WWII, Martin became deeply moved by the rows and rows of crosses that marked the graves of Canadian soldiers and by the fact that, despite their differences in religion or ethnicity, all had given their lives for a common cause. As a tribute to those who had fallen in battle, Martin began a campaign that culminated on January 1, 1947, in Canada's first *Citizenship Act.*

Generally, those who are born in Canada automatically become Canadian citizens. In addition, those who were born in another country after February 15, 1977, and who have at least one parent who was a Canadian citizen at the time of their birth, are Canadian citizens. However, others may apply to become Canadian citizens.

To apply for Canadian citizenship, you must be 18 years of age or older, a permanent resident, and be in Canada legally as a "permanent resident." You must have lived in Canada for at least three out of the four years right before the day you apply (this three-year residency requirement is waived in the case of children who are under the age of 18). Any time spent in Canada before becoming a resident is counted as half time if it falls within this four-year period; all the time spent in Canada since becoming a permanent resident counts as full time. An individual cannot become a Canadian citizen if that individual is or was in prison, on parole, or on probation in the past four years; convicted of an indictable offence in the past three years; charged with an indictable offence; under a deportation order and not currently allowed to be in Canada; currently facing charges under the *Citizenship Act;* or under investigation for a war crime or a crime against humanity, or if that individual has had their Canadian citizenship revoked in the past five years.

To become a Canadian citizen you must be proficient enough in either of Canada's official languages, English or French, to understand others and have them understand you. This translates into the ability to speak and understand spoken English or French or to be able to read and write in simple English or French. You must pass a written test that asks general questions about Canada's system of governance, its geography, history, and people, and the rights and responsibilities of citizenship. This citizenship test includes specific questions about the economy, geography, and history of the region in which the applicant resides. For those who are visually impaired, oral examinations are available. To pass the citizenship test, applicants must answer at least 12 out of 20 questions correctly.

Those who apply for and meet all the requirements for Canadian citizenship are sent a Notice to Appear to Take the Oath of Citizenship, which tells them when and where their citizenship ceremony will take place. At the ceremony, individuals take the Oath of Citizenship; those who wish to swear the oath of citizenship on their holy book are invited to bring it to the ceremony. At the citizenship ceremony, new Canadians receive a certificate of citizenship and a commemorative document that shows the date on which they became a Canadian citizen.

Becoming a Canadian Citizen: Could You Pass the Test?
(continued)

The following questions, taken from a larger list of sample questions that appear on the Web site of Citizenship and Immigration Canada, <www.cic.gc.ca>, are typical of those appearing on the written examination. Could you pass the test?

SAMPLE QUESTIONS

___ 1. Who are the Aboriginal peoples of Canada?

___ 2. What are the three main groups of Aboriginal peoples?

___ 3. From whom are the Métis descended?

___ 4. Who were the United Empire Loyalists?

___ 5. When did the *British North America Act* came into effect?

___ 6. Which four provinces first formed Confederation?

___ 7. List each province and territory and when each joined Confederation.

___ 8. When is Canada Day and what does it celebrate?

___ 9. What part of the Constitution legally protects the basic rights and freedoms of all Canadians?

___ 10. Name two fundamental freedoms protected by the Canadian Charter of Rights and Freedoms.

___ 11. List four rights Canadian citizens have.

___ 12. Which legal document recognizes the cultural diversity of Canadians?

___ 13. What are the two official languages of Canada?

___ 14. Which legal document protects the official language rights of Canadians?

Conflict Perspective

Conflict theorists emphasize the role of economic competition in creating and maintaining racial and ethnic group tensions. Majority group subordination of racial and ethnic minorities reflects perceived or actual economic threats by the minority. For example, although 15 000 Chinese were allowed to enter Canada as a pool of inexpensive labour for the building of the transcontinental railway, on its completion, they were treated as unwelcome guests. In 1885, the infamous "head tax" was imposed on every Chinese immigrant to Canada. Initially set at $50, the head tax was increased to $100 in 1900, and three years later to $500—an astronomical amount at that time—in an obvious attempt to restrict the entrance of Chinese and other Asians to Canada.

Further, conflict theorists suggest that capitalists profit by maintaining a surplus labour force, that is, having more workers than are needed. A surplus labour force ensures that wages remain low, because someone is always available to take a disgruntled worker's place. Minorities who are disproportionately unemployed serve the interests of the business owners by providing surplus labour, keeping wages low, and, consequently, enabling the owners to maximize profits.

Conflict theorists also argue that the wealthy and powerful elites foster negative attitudes toward minorities to maintain racial and ethnic tensions among workers. As long as workers are divided along racial and ethnic lines,

> **National Data**
>
> In Canada, the Oath of Citizenship is:
> "I swear (or affirm) that I will be faithful and bear true allegiance to Her Majesty, Queen Elizabeth the Second, Queen of Canada, Her Heirs and Successors, and that I will faithfully observe the laws of Canada and fulfil my duties as a Canadian citizen."

they are less likely to join forces to advance their own interests at the expense of the capitalists. In addition, the "haves" perpetuate racial and ethnic tensions among the "have-nots" to deflect attention away from their own greed and exploitation of workers.

Symbolic Interactionist Perspective

The symbolic interactionist perspective focuses on how meanings and definitions contribute to the subordinate position of certain racial and ethnic groups. The different connotations of the colours white and black are a case in point. The white knight is good, and the black knight is evil; angel food cake is white, devil's food cake is black. Other negative terms associated with black include black sheep, black plague, black magic, black mass, blackballed, and blacklisted. The continued use of such derogatory terms as Jap, Gook, Spic, Frog, Kraut, Coon, Chink, Wop, and Mick also confirms the power of language in perpetuating negative attitudes toward minority group members.

Research by Donakowski and Esses (1996) concludes that the labels used to refer to minority groups play a role in the attitudes that are expressed toward them. In their research, 108 Canadian university students responded to a questionnaire that assessed attitudes toward Native peoples, as well as three components of attitudes: stereotypes (characteristics attributed to the group), symbolic beliefs (beliefs that the group promotes or threatens cherished values, customs, and traditions), and emotions. Five different labels were used for the group: Aboriginal peoples, First Nations people, Native Canadians, Native Indians, and Native peoples. Among non-Native students, the term Aboriginal peoples was associated with the most positive attitude, followed by Native peoples, Native Indians, First Nations people, and Native Canadians.

Noting that attitudes toward Native peoples were less favourable when the labels Native Canadians and First Nations were used, the researchers conclude that this stemmed, in part, from the symbolic beliefs that came to mind in response to these labels. When labelled Native Canadians or First Nations people, Native peoples were viewed as more likely to threaten national unity than when the three other labels were used. The researchers conclude that, "it is possible that when the label First Nations People is used, individuals may be more likely to base their attitudes toward the group on beliefs about the political role of Natives in Canada (a Native activist organization in Canada goes by a similar name: 'Assembly of First Nations'...[and] remind people that Natives are now working within Canadian society toward more autonomy and political power" (p. 90).

Research conducted at a second Canadian university and based on a sample of 86 university students (36 Native, 50 non-Native) also found that the labels of ethnic identity commonly used for Native peoples in Canada by the media, government, and many nongovermental organizations were not commonly used by their Native respondents. Bowd and Brady (1998) report that their Native respondents were more likely to describe their own ethnic heritage using tribal terms rather than the identity labels employed by non-Natives. Their study also notes that regardless of ethnic identity label, Native respondents uniformly rated Natives more positively than did non-Natives.

The labelling perspective directs us to consider the role that negative stereotypes play in race and ethnicity. **Stereotypes** are exaggerations or generalizations about the characteristics and behaviour of a particular group. Negative stereotyping of minorities leads to a self-fulfilling prophecy. As Schaefer (1998: 17) explains,

> Self-fulfilling prophecies can be devastating for minority groups. Such groups often find that they are allowed to hold only low-paying jobs with little prestige or opportunity for advancement. The rationale of the dominant society is that these minority individuals lack the ability to perform in more important and lucrative positions. Training to become scientists, executives, or physicians is denied to many subordinate group individuals, who are then locked into society's inferior jobs. As a result, the false definition becomes real. The subordinate group has become inferior because it was defined at the start as inferior and was therefore prevented from achieving the levels attained by the majority.

PREJUDICE AND RACISM

Prejudice refers to an attitude or judgment, usually negative, about an entire category of people. Prejudice may be directed toward individuals of a particular religion, sexual orientation, political affiliation, age, social class, sex, race, or ethnicity.

At the extreme, racial prejudice takes the form of **racism**: the belief that certain groups or races are innately superior to other groups. The perception that certain groups have inferior traits serves to justify subordination and mistreatment of those groups.

Measuring Prejudice and Racism

The study and assessment of prejudice and racism usually involves two aspects: (1) the content of stereotypes and (2) people's reported willingness to interact with various racial and ethnic groups in specified social situations. For example, Emory Bogardus (1968) developed a social distance scale (frequently referred to as the Bogardus scale) that presents situations representing different degrees of social contact or social distance. The items, with their corresponding distance scores, follow. People are asked if they would be willing to admit various racial and ethnic groups

- to close kinship by marriage (1.00)
- to their club as personal neighbours (2.00)
- to their street as neighbours (3.00)
- to employment in their occupation (4.00)
- to citizenship in their country (5.00)
- as visitors only to their country (6.00)

A score of 1.00 for any group would indicate no prejudice toward that group. Comparing social distance scores across time suggests that prejudice has decreased over the last several decades (Schaefer 1998). However, Dovidio and Gaertner (1991) suggest that "what may have changed across time...is what people regard as socially desirable rather than racial attitudes per se" (p. 125).

In other words, survey data on racial attitudes may reflect what respondents view as "politically correct" rather than what people really believe or feel.

Modern Racism

A number of scholars believe that prejudice has not declined, but rather, has taken on a more subtle and complex form known as **modern racism**. Shipler (1998) explains:

> Today, when explicit discrimination is prohibited and blatant racism is no longer fashionable in most circles, much prejudice has gone underground. It may have diminished in some quarters, but it is far from extinct. Like a virus searching for a congenial host, it mutates until it finds expression in a belief, a statement, or a form of behaviour that seems acceptable. (p. 1)

People who have modern racist views have negative feelings toward minority groups but do not necessarily endorse the idea of genetic or biological inferiority or adhere to traditional stereotypes. The modern racist believes that serious discrimination in Canada no longer exists, that any continuing racial inequality is the fault of minority group members, and that employment equity policies are unfair and unjustified. "Modern racism tends to 'blame the victim' and place the responsibility for change and improvements on the minority groups, not on the larger society" (Healey 1997: 55).

Sources of Prejudice

Sources of prejudice include cultural transmission, stereotypes, and the media.

Cultural Transmission Prejudice is taught and learned through the socialization process. One of the first sources of prejudice is the family. Research indicates, for example, that parents who are prejudiced are more likely to have children who are also prejudiced. Other institutions also foster prejudice. Some religious doctrines teach intolerance of racial and ethnic groups. Further, school curricula have traditionally been Eurocentric—that is, biased toward White Europeans—often perpetuating the belief that minority group members are inferior.

Stereotypes Prejudicial attitudes toward racial and ethnic groups are often the result of stereotypes—exaggerations or generalizations about a category of individuals (Kawakami et al. 1998). These generalizations, which become deeply embedded in the culture, are either untrue or are gross distortions of reality.

CONSIDERATION

Shipler (1998) suggests that negative stereotyping of minorities enhances the self-esteem of majority group members. "If blacks are less intelligent, in whites' belief, then it follows that whites are more intelligent. If blacks are lazier, whites are harder working. If blacks would prefer to live on welfare, then whites would prefer to be self-supporting" (p. 3).

Media The media contribute to prejudice toward racial and ethnic minorities by portraying minorities in negative and stereotypical ways, or by not portraying them at all (Barlow 1998; Mann and Richey 1993; Mendelberg 1997; Oliver 1994). For example, Mosher (1998) notes that while the racialization of crime has a long history in Canada, it reached unprecedented levels in the 1980s, with the Canadian news media displaying an increasing tendency to attribute the social problem of crime to Blacks and Asians. To like effect, research by Claxton-Oldfield and Keefe (1999) on stereotypes about the Innu of Davis Inlet, Labrador, suggests the potency of the media in shaping public opinion about different racial and ethnic groups. In the first part of their research, a sample of 22 male and 56 female Newfoundland college students (aged 18 to 23) were asked to list the characteristics that came to mind about the Innu and to indicate where these impressions came from. At least 20 percent of the students described the Innu as being uneducated, alcoholic, poor, and isolated, and as gas-sniffers. The two most important sources for the students' impressions of the Innu were television and newspapers. In the second phase of their investigation, the researchers examined the image of the Innu in a daily Newfoundland newspaper for one year (January to December 1996). Headline analysis revealed that conflict and deviance words (e.g., gas-sniffing, sexual abuse, protest) appeared in 44 percent of the headlines of newspaper items about the Innu. The researchers conclude that stereotypes of the Innu mirror the images that are portrayed of them in the media.

An analysis of more than 2000 children's storybooks published between 1937 and 1993 revealed that only 15 percent had at least one Black character in the story (Pescosolido et al. 1997). The researchers found that the depiction of intimate, egalitarian, interracial interaction and the portrayal of Black adults as main characters were rare.

Some music also fuels racial hatred, especially among the industry's primary consumer group—youth. Consider the following music lyrics:

> ...Niggers just hit this side of town, watch my property values go
> down. Bang, gang, watch them die, watch those niggers drop like
> flies....—*Berserkr*

The Internet has provided another avenue for the proliferation of ideologies based on racial hatred. Web sites that represent racial hate groups are designed to recruit new members and give racists an empowering sense of community.

DISCRIMINATION AGAINST MINORITIES

While prejudice refers to attitudes, **discrimination** refers to behaviour that involves treating categories of individuals unequally. A person may be prejudiced and not discriminate; conversely, a person may discriminate but not prejudiced.

Individual versus Institutional Discrimination

Individual discrimination occurs when individuals treat persons unfairly or unequally because of their group membership. There are two types of indi-

National Data

According to national Canadian surveys conducted by Reginald Bibby, "over the past two decades a core of about 15 percent of Canadians have maintained that East Indians/ Pakistanis, other Asians, and Jews have "too much power in Canadian life." Since the mid-1980s, these surveys also report a growing perception that Natives and South Asians have "excessive power," despite their relative lack of power. Although the "too much power numbers are fairly small...they are disturbing because they indicate that pockets of bigotry continue to exist" (55–6).

SOURCE: Bibby 1995

National Data

Research into the adaptation experiences of 368 Chinese immigrant students from Hong Kong and 63 Black immigrant students from the Caribbean attending public high schools in Toronto during 1993–94, found that while immigrant students from Hong Kong adapted better academically than their Caribbean counterparts did, Caribbean students adapted better socially, culturally, and linguistically. Racial discrimination was reported by 25 percent of the students from Hong Kong and 17 percent of the Caribbean students.

SOURCE: Chow 1997

vidual discrimination—overt and adaptive. In **overt discrimination** individuals discriminate because of their own prejudicial attitudes. For example, a White landlord may refuse to rent to a First Nations family because of her own prejudice against Aboriginal peoples. Alternatively, a French-Canadian student who shares a dorm room with an English-Canadian student may request a roommate reassignment from the student housing office because he is prejudiced against anglophones.

Suppose a Vietnamese-Canadian family wants to rent an apartment in a predominantly White neighbourhood. If the landlord is prejudiced against the Vietnamese and does not allow the family to rent the apartment, that landlord has engaged in overt discrimination. However, what if the landlord is not prejudiced against the Vietnamese but still refuses to rent to a Vietnamese family? Perhaps that landlord is engaging in **adaptive discrimination**, or discrimination that is based on the prejudice of others. In this example, the landlord may fear that if he rents to a Vietnamese-Canadian family, other renters who are prejudiced against the Vietnamese may move out of the building or neighbourhood and leave the landlord with unrented apartments. Overt and adaptive individual discrimination may coexist. For example, a landlord may not rent an apartment to a Vietnamese family because of her own prejudices *and* the fear that other tenants may move out.

Institutional discrimination occurs when normal operations and procedures of social institutions result in unequal treatment of minorities. Institutional discrimination is covert and insidious and maintains the subordinate position of minorities in society. As conflict theorists emphasize, majority group members make rules that favour their own group.

Racial and ethnic minorities experience discrimination and its effects in almost every sphere of social life (Noh and Belser 1999; Stodolska and Jackson 1998). This chapter's The Human Side focuses on the longest individual case in the history of the Canadian Human Rights Commission, the complaint of Mary Pitawanakwat against her employer, the Canadian Secretary of State. It is surely ironic to note that it is this department that, in Canada, is responsible for promoting multiculturalism and supporting programs for minorities and women.

Next, we look at the extent and brutality of hate crimes against minorities.

Hate Crime Victimization

Perhaps the most brutal form of discrimination takes the form of **hate crimes**, acts of violence motivated by prejudice against racial, ethnic, religious, and sexual-orientation groups. The brutal murder of Nirmal Singh Gill described in the opening of this chapter exemplifies the horrific nature of some hate crimes. Hate crimes are often less severe than brutal murder, yet are nonetheless harmful, inhumane, and against the law. In Canada, section 718.2 of the *Criminal Code* provides that "evidence that [an offence] was motivated by bias, prejudice or hate based on race, national or ethnic origin, colour, religion, sex, age, mental or physical disability, sexual orientation or any other similar factor" is to be considered an aggravating circumstance in sentencing convicted offenders. For example, in the case of *R. v. Ingram and Grimsdale* (1977) 35 C.C.C. (2d) 376 (Ont. C.A.) at 379, it was held that "An assault which is racially motivated renders the offence more heinous. Such assaults, unfortunately,

WHEN WILL JUSTICE BE DONE?

On March 21, 1986, the same day Prime Minister Brian Mulroney signed the International Declaration to Combat Racism and Racial Discrimination, Mary Pitawanakwat was fired from her job as a social development officer with the Department of Secretary of State in Regina. Although the official reason given for Mary's firing was "incompetence," a Human Rights tribunal hearing...[eventually] concluded that a racist climate existed in the Regina Secretary of State office where Mary worked....

The only visible Aboriginal staff member in an office of 25, Mary's basic job description was to assist organizations in applying for funding from a variety of programs, assess applications, and make recommendations on funding and policy issues....When Mary went to work at Secretary of State in 1979, she was the first Aboriginal woman hired under the office's new affirmative action program for Aboriginal peoples. But as early as 1982, Mary was frustrated about racist comments in the office. For example, Mary says her direct supervisor, Regional Director Catherine Lane, had referred to Indians as "savages" and "god-damned Indians." When Mary finally complained to Lane about these remarks, Lane told her, "You're not going to use that against me." ...Andre Noque, the...Regional Director at Secretary of State in Regina [would later defend]...the use of the word "savage" [before the Human Rights Tribunal], saying "to me, 'savage' does not have that much of a negative connotation. To me 'savage' equals 'Indian.'"

Mary...[was later to tell] the tribunal that once she had spoken out about racism within the department, her work was purposely held up by her supervisors, causing delays in her casework; she said she was badgered about day-to-day tasks;...she said managers rolled their eyes when she spoke at staff meetings....She reported that her travel budget was curtailed, and her educational conferences and overtime were denied while other staff continued to enjoy these rights. Although Mary had one of the biggest client caseloads in the region, she reported that she was denied additional support when she asked for it....[Two coworkers later] testified at the tribunal that Mary's managers were out to get her....

From 1979 to 1982, Mary's performance appraisals had been "fully satisfactory" and "satisfactory," but by 1983, she was graded with "unsatisfactory." In 1984 and 1985, Mary filed two grievances for unfair performance appraisals and two for personal harassment, all four of which were denied. Another grievance was filed because Mary refused orders by her supervisor to monitor drug use and trafficking among her clients, claiming if the Secretary of State wanted a narcotics investigator, they should call the RCMP. But the only way a grievance could get to adjudicators was if there had been a violation of the collective agreement, or if the case involved a disciplinary action resulting in financial penalty. At the time, there was no provision in Mary's collective agreement for addressing sexual or racial harassment.

By 1983–84, Mary felt increasingly isolated within her office because of the attitudes, comments, and treatment she experienced in

National Data

Although analysis of the 1991 Canadian census suggests significant educational and occupational mobility among Canadian ethnic groups over the past decades, the extent of ethnic mobility in earnings has been quite different from that in education and occupation. While earning differences were not profound either among European groups or among visible minorities, substantial disparities existed between these two broad categories to the disadvantage of visible minorities. While traditionally the "Vertical Mosaic thesis" has emphasized ethnicity as a fundamental basis of social stratification in Canada and the "New Mosaic thesis" stresses ethnic mobility in socioeconomic status, it has been suggested that race has replaced ethnicity in Canada as a fundamental bases of stratification in earnings.

SOURCE: Lian 1996

Over the past decade, the Canadian Independent Living Movement has shown increasing recognition that not all people with disabilities, including those from diverse racial and cultural backgrounds, are being fully served by the practices and policies currently in place. The national umbrella organization is being challenged to provide independent living programs and services to people with disabilities who come from diverse ethnocultural backgrounds and cultures.

SOURCE: Pardo 1996

THE HUMAN SIDE

WHEN WILL JUSTICE BE DONE? *(continued)*

her workplace. When she approached the Canadian Human Rights Commission to complain, she was told she must first exhaust all "internal avenues of redress" before the Human Rights Commission would discuss her concerns. So, Mary sought support from colleagues and union staff and she spoke out at staff meetings.

…It seemed like a clear-cut case, but it was complicated by other factors. Some of those Mary accused of perpetuating racism were women active in the feminist, lesbian, and labour communities….Her supervisor was the person responsible for some of the funding to local feminist organizations and was considered by some in the women's community to be a feminist-insider in the department….It was a case that seemed to blur the lines of allegiance and the hierarchies of oppression for many people….

One week after she signed her complaint with the Canadian Human Rights Commission in November 1985, the Secretary of State recommended that Mary be "released" from her position for "incompetence." Her complaint with the Canadian Human Rights Commission was immediately put on hold. Mary appealed her firing and three months later, a one-man Public Service Commission Appeal Board ruled that the Secretary of State was justified in firing her.

In the summer of 1986, the Canadian Human Rights Commission decided it wouldn't hear Mary's complaint…saying her case had already been heard by the Appeal Board. In December 1986, Mary appealed to the Federal Court of Appeal to overturn the Human Rights Commission's refusal to hear her

discrimination case. After deliberating for almost a year, the Court ordered the Human Rights Commission to hear Mary's complaint. Eight months later…an investigation finally began….A year later, an investigator's report was submitted to the Human Rights Commission and in December 1989, the Human Rights recommended that the Human Rights Tribunal Panel appoint a tribunal to hear Mary's case. In January 1990, three tribunal members were appointed. Within a week, the Justice Department appealed to the Federal Court to cancel the tribunal, arguing again that Mary's case had already been heard. The Court overruled the department and the tribunal proceeded. On December 2, 1992, the Human Rights Tribunal signed its decision that the case of racial discrimination be brought forward….

At Mary's Human Rights tribunal…neither Mary's supervisor nor union shop steward recalled that any overt racism existed in the office. But coworker after coworker testified they often heard words like "Indian time," "scalping," "lazy Indian," "dirty Indian," "savages,"…"God-damn Indians, always wanting more," "God-damn Friendship Centre, they're at it again."…[A] senior clerk…who testified in support of Mary's claims at her 1985 Appeal Board Hearing and in 1991…says her boss warned her there would be consequences if she defended Mary at the hearings. She testified that management hounded Mary, hid files, criticized her unfairly, and made fun of her….[A second coworker] testified she was monitored and harshly punished for her continued support of Mary. She eventually took over nine months sick leave.

WHEN WILL JUSTICE BE DONE? *(continued)*

The tribunal recognized a degree of racism existed within the office and found...one of Mary's supervisors and the department guilty of "gross negligence." While acknowledging that her firing was unjust, Mary was awarded only two out of six years' lost salary....

In 1988, Mary...[was] diagnosed with breast cancer. She was treated with surgery,...cobalt, and chemotherapy treatments. Then Mary says, due to the illness and the stress of the situation, she reached a crisis point and was admitted to hospital for psychiatric treatment. Dr. John Chong, a university professor specializing in occupational stress,...was so incensed at what was happening to Mary that he drove to Regina from Hamilton to see that Mary was released from hospital. "What was happening to Mary was insane," recalls Chong. "What drug or therapy can cure racial harassment, sexual harassment, and economic harassment?"...[Nevertheless b]ecause part of Mary's time was spent undergoing psychiatric treatment in hospital, the tribunal reduced Mary's compensation to what she would have received on sick pay....

The tribunal also placed a stipulation that Mary would have to repay the financial assistance she [had] received under the Department of Indian Affairs when she [had gone] back to university after being fired. She was denied compensation for emotional distress or "hurt feelings" because, in the tribunal's opinion, Mary was partly to blame for her situation. In spite of the racism acknowledged by the tribunal, there was no acknowledgement that Mary personally suffered racial discrimina-

tion. In fact, the tribunal reprimanded Mary for taking so long in bringing her case before the Commission. The tribunal said Mary would have to relocate to another province if she wanted her job back because after all that had happened, it would be too difficult to reintegrate Mary into the Secretary of State office....

Mary maintains that the Tribunal didn't force the government or Secretary of State to stop the racism within the Regina office. Furthermore, she says, managers to whom insulting and demeaning comments and harassment have been attributed, have been promoted. No punitive actions were taken against those responsible for the harassment. [As of 1993] anti-racism education ordered by the tribunal for Secretary of State staff...[had] not taken place....Women coworkers who stood up for Mary and faced harassment years after for doing so were never written letters of apology....Mary plans to bring her case before the United Nations to force the Canadian government to eliminate systemic racism, much the same way the UN forced Canada to amend the *Indian Act* in 1985 to remove discriminatory measures against Indian women....She says..."I fight now for my children....I didn't bring my children into the world to have anyone be superior to them or so they would bear the brunt of other people's hatred. If it weren't for them....I might have accepted something less and stopped fighting long ago."

At a press conference following the tribunal's ruling, Sharon McIvor, an executive member of the Native Women's Association of Canada

WHEN WILL JUSTICE BE DONE? *(continued)*

(NWAC) called the tribunal's ruling harsh, unfair, offensive, and victim blaming. NWAC, which represents 13 provincial and territorial organizations and approximately 120 000 Aboriginal women across Canada, predicted that the ruling would discourage other employees from speaking out against racism within the workplace. According to McIvor, more Aboriginal employees have left the office since 1986 than have been recruited, a statistic she says supports Mary's charge of racial

harassment. The National Action Committee on the Status of Women (NAC) also strongly condemned the tribunal's ruling.…"If the decision of the tribunal stands, it shows the sham and bankruptcy of the whole Canadian human rights systems."

Editor's note: Her battle still ongoing. Mary Pitawanakwat passed away on July 10, 1995.

SOURCE: Adapted and abridged from Cowan, Mary Rose. 1993. "Will Justice Ever Be Done? Mary Pitawanakwat Case of Racial Discrimination against the Canadian Secretary of State." *Herizons*, Summer 7 (2): 16–20, 21–3.

invite imitation and repetition by others and incite retaliation. The danger is even greater in a multicultural, pluralistic urban society." In addition, Section 319 of the *Criminal Code* defines the willful promotion of hatred against any identifiable group (i.e., "any section of the public distinguished by colour, race, sexual orientation, religion, or ethnic group") and advocating genocide as criminal offences, punishable by up to two years imprisonment. Perhaps the best-known prosecution under the latter section of the Code is that of James Keegstra, a former Alberta high-school teacher who was accused of formenting hatred against the Jews in his classroom lectures. Keegstra was subsequently charged under the subsection of Canada's *Criminal Code* that prohibits hate propaganda other than in private conversations. The case was later appealed to the Supreme Court of Canada. In 1996, the Supreme Court ruled that although hate propaganda "formed part of protected freedom of expression pursuant to subsection 2(b) of the Canadian Charter of Rights and Freedoms" its prohibition was reasonable and "supported by international documents to which Canada is a party and sections 15 (equality) and 27 (multi-culturalism) of the Charter" (Beaudoin 1999: 1237).

In other cases, however, the attempt to curtail the spread of hate propaganda has been less successful. For example, after publishing a brochure entitled "Did Six Million Really Die?" that claimed that the Holocaust was a myth propagated from a worldwide Jewish conspiracy, Ernst Zundel was charged under section 181 of the *Criminal Code*, which makes the willful dissemination of false news a criminal offence. However, the Supreme Court of Canada ruled that this section of the code denied Zundel the right to freedom of expression, as guaranteed under the Canadian Charter of Rights and Freedoms, and that section 181 was not justified in a free and democratic society.

Roberts (1995) notes that "there has been little systematic research in Canada upon the nature and incidence of hate crimes" and considerable variability exists in the definitions of "hate crimes" employed by various Canadian police departments. He points out that although hate crime statistics have been systematically collected in the United States since 1990 when the U.S. Congress passed the *Hate Crimes Statistics Act* (which requires states to collect such data and submit them to the federal government), Canada "lags far behind other nations in this regard" and that any attempt to determine the number of hate crimes committed "must remain rather speculative." However, he reports that the majority of hate crimes recorded by Canadian police services were directed toward racial minorities (61 percent) followed by religious minorities (23 percent), gays or lesbians (11 percent), and ethnic minorities (5 percent).

Levin and McDevitt (1995) found that the motivations for hate crimes were of three distinct types: thrill, defensive, and mission. Thrill hate crimes are committed by offenders who are looking for excitement and attack victims for the "fun of it." Defensive hate crimes involve offenders who view their attacks as necessary to protect their community, workplace, or campus from "outsiders." Perpetrators of defensive hate crimes are trying to send a message that their victims do not belong in a particular community, workplace, or campus and that anyone in the victim's group who dares "intrude" could be the next victim. Mission hate crimes are perpetrated by offenders who have dedicated their lives to bigotry. In Levin and McDevitt's study of hate crimes in Boston, the most common type of hate crime was thrill hate crime (58 percent) followed by defensive hate crime (41 percent). The least common, but most violent, type of hate crime is mission hate crime. Levin and McDevitt describe the 1995 Oklahoma City bombing as "probably the quintessential mission hate crime, perpetrated by individuals whose lives had become consumed with hatred not only for the federal government but possibly for blacks and Jews as well" (p. 9).

Mission hate crimes are often committed by members of White supremacist organizations that endorse racist beliefs and violence against minority group members. The Ku Klux Klan, the first major racist, White supremacist group in the United States, began in Tennessee shortly after the Civil War. Klansmen have threatened, beat, mutilated, and lynched Blacks as well as Whites who dared to oppose them. White Aryan Resistance (WAR), another White supremacist group, fosters hatred that breeds violence. The following message is typical of one received by calling a White Aryan Resistance phone number (Kleg 1993: 205):

> This is WAR hotline. How long, White men, are you going to sit around while these non-White mud races breed you out of existence? They have your jobs, your homes, and your country. Have you stepped outside lately and looked around while these niggers...hep and jive to this Africanized rap music? While these Gooks and Flips are buying up the businesses around you?...This racial melting pot is more like a garbage pail. Just look at your liquor stores. Most of them are owned by Sand niggers from Iraq, Egypt, or Iran. Most of the apartments are owned by the scum from India, or some other kind of raghead....[Jews] are like maggots eating off a dead carcass. When you see what these Jews and their White lackeys have done, the gas chambers don't sound like such a bad idea after all. For more information write us at....

National Data

In an attempt to estimate the number of hate crimes committed annually in Canada, an extrapolation was made using data from Ottawa in 1994 as a starting point. In that year, 211 hate crimes were recorded by the Ottawa police department. On the assumption that only one in three such incidents is ever reported to police, this would suggest that there were actually 633 incidents committed. Since Ottawa accounts for only 7 percent of the total *Criminal Code* offences for the major urban centres in Canada, further extrapolation would suggest that the total number of hate crimes committed in nine urban centres (Halifax, Montreal, Ottawa, Toronto, Winnipeg, Regina, Calgary, Edmonton, Vancouver) would total 60 000.

SOURCE: Roberts 1995

Other racist groups known to engage in hate crimes are the Aryan Nations, Heritage Front, Canadian Liberty Net, Church of the Creator, the Identity Church Movement, neo-Nazis, and the skinheads. While Klan members have traditionally concealed their identities under white hoods and robes, racist skinheads are usually identifiable through their shaved heads, steel-toed boots, jeans, and suspenders. They often have tattoos of Nazi or satanic emblems.

CONSIDERATION

Not all skinheads are racists. Many youth have adopted the skinhead "look" and lifestyle but do not endorse racism or violence. One nonracist skinhead said: "Being a skinhead does not mean being a Nazi. I happen to have no hair, a black leather jacket, and army boots, and I get stopped all the time by people trying to preach nonviolence to me. I am a pacifist." (Quoted in Landau 1993: 43)

STRATEGIES FOR ACTION: RESPONDING TO PREJUDICE, RACISM, AND DISCRIMINATION

Next, we look at various strategies that address problems of prejudice, racism, and discrimination. These include multicultural education, political strategies, employment equity programs, and diversity training in the workplace.

Multicultural Education

Much educational material is biased toward White Europeans. For example, Zinn (1993) observes, "[T]o emphasize the heroism of Columbus and his successors as navigators and discoverers, and to de-emphasize their genocide, is not a technical necessity but an ideological choice. It serves, unwittingly, to justify what was done" (p. 355). **Multicultural education** focuses on the need to represent all racial and ethnic groups in the school curriculum (see also Chapter 12). With multicultural education, the school curriculum reflects the diversity of Canadian society and fosters an awareness and appreciation of the contributions of different racial and ethnic groups to Canadian culture. Multicultural education also works to dispel myths, stereotypes, and ignorance about minorities. One minority student commented: "What bothers me a lot is ignorance—people not realizing the difference between someone who's Japanese, someone who's Chinese, someone who's Korean, and just tending to classify them as one big word—Asian" ("In Our Own Words" 1996: 54). However, despite commonly expressed support for multicultural education, there has been a notable reluctance among teachers to integrate antiracist educational approaches in classroom practices. For example, as part of a large study of teachers, school administrators, and antiracist educator policy advisors in five urban schools across Canada, Solomon and Levine-Rasky (1996) analyzed 1002 survey questionnaires and an additional 227 information sheets completed by teachers in 57 elementary and secondary schools. They report that teachers' negative responses to antiracist education are based on their commitment to traditional pedagogic concerns, conservative political views, and conservative views on race and antiracism.

Many colleges and universities have made efforts to promote awareness and appreciation of diversity by offering courses and degree programs in racial and ethnic studies, and multicultural events and student organizations. Research suggests that college attendance tends to result in increased tolerance and support for diversity (Pascarella et al. 1996). This chapter's Focus on Social Problems Research feature presents a study that identifies various factors that influence first-year students' openness to diversity.

Political Strategies

Various political strategies have been implemented or suggested to reduce prejudice and discrimination. Although some individuals argue that laws cannot change attitudes, there is evidence that changing behaviours can change attitudes. When the military, schools, and housing were integrated, the attitudes of Whites toward non-Whites became more positive. Hence, there is a need for laws that prohibit discrimination, for those laws to be strictly enforced, and for sanctions to be imposed when the laws are violated. Another strategy to decrease discrimination involves increasing minority representation in government. This requires increasing political involvement, action, and participation.

Employment Equity

The proactive management of diversity in the workplace has been required by law in Canada since 1986, when the federal government passed the *Employment Equity Act*. This Act, with its uniquely Canadian approach to affirmative action, was passed in response to the recommendations of the Royal Commission on Equality in Employment (1984).

The legitimacy of **employment equity** stems from Canada's Human Rights Act and Charter of Rights and Freedoms. Both acknowledge the legality of special programs designed to "overcome disadvantages" or to ameliorate the past impact of discriminatory practices. The *Employment Equity Act* applies to all federal-regulated employers with 100 or more employees, public sector companies, federal contractors with at least 100 employees, and Crown corporations. These entities are now obligated to publish annual reports on the composition of their workforces, with particular reference to the work performed by women, visible minorities, people with disabilities, and Aboriginal peoples.

According to Harish Jain (1988), the three key components of employment equity are:

- A restructuring of Canada's labour force to reflect local demographic realities. Attempts are made to ensure that proportional numbers of designated minorities are represented throughout all income and occupational levels at ratios consistent with the proportion of these groups within the local or regional workforce.
- A comprehensive review process by the employer to identify and remove any discriminatory and systemic barriers to employment and promotion that might exist.
- A positive program for the recruitment, hiring, training, and promotion of all designated minority groups in recognition of their disadvantaged opportunities in the past.

What Influences Students' Openness to Diversity?

A study by Pascarella et al. (1996) sought to determine how students' openness to diversity is influenced by four different sets of factors: student background characteristics, environmental emphases of the institution attended, measures of the students' academic experience, and measures of students' social involvement.

Sample and Methods

The researchers collected data from 2290 first-year students at 18 colleges and universities. The dependent variable was a scale designed to measure openness to diversity (see scale). This scale not only assesses an individual's openness to cultural, racial, and value diversity, it also measures the extent to which an individual enjoys being challenged by different ideas, values, and perspectives.

Openness to Diversity/Challenge Scale

(Scored on a Likert-type scale: 5 = strongly agree to 1 = strongly disagree)

1. I enjoy having discussions with people whose ideas and values are different from my own.
2. The real value of a college/university education lies in being introduced to different values.
3. I enjoy talking with people who have values different from mine because it helps me understand myself and my values better.
4. Learning about people from different cultures is a very important part of my university/college education.
5. I enjoy taking courses that challenge my beliefs and values.
6. The courses I enjoy the most are those that make me think about things from a different perspective.
7. Contact with individuals whose background (e.g., race, national origin, sexual orientation) is different from my own is an essential part of my college/university education.
8. I enjoy courses that are intellectually challenging.

Four sets of independent variables were developed, each of which consisted of numerous measures. These included (1) precollege/preuniversity variables (including a measure of precollege/preuniversity openness to diversity and precollege/preuniversity academic ability), (2) environmental emphasis of the college/university (including a measure of the degree of racial discrimination at the institution), (3) student academic experiences (including number of social science courses taken and self-reported number of hours spent studying per week), and (4) student social/nonacademic experiences (including involvement in clubs and organizations and assessment of students' peer interactions and topics of conversation).

Findings

The precollege/preuniversity measure of openness to diversity/challenge had the strongest effect on openness to diversity/challenge after the first year of attendance. Women and non-White students had higher levels of openness to diversity/challenge than men and White students.

The extent to which students perceived their institution as having a nondiscriminatory racial environment had a positive impact on openness to diversity. Hours spent studying had a small positive effect, while the number of mathematics courses taken during the first year of college had a small negative impact.

Living on campus, participating in a racial or cultural awareness workshop, and hours worked per week had positive effects on openness to diversity/challenge, while joining a fraternity or sorority had a negative effect. In addition, "the more students interact with diverse peers and the greater the extent to which such interactions focus on controversial or value-laden issues that may engender a change in perspective or opinion, the greater one's development of openness to diversity and challenge" (p. 188).

The findings of this study suggest that colleges and universities that offer racial or cultural awareness workshops can foster students' appreciation and acceptance of cultural, racial, and value diversity. Encouraging openness to diversity may also be achieved by the institution establishing policies and programs that sensitize students and personnel to racial discrimination and demonstrate that such discrimination is not acceptable. Colleges and universities may also consider interventions to counteract the negative influence of membership in fraternities or sororities on openness to diversity.

Finally, the fact that precollege/preuniversity openness to diversity had the largest effect on openness to diversity among first-year students points to the need to foster openness to diversity in the elementary-school and secondary-school grades. This may be achieved through multicultural programs, educational approaches, and school policies that discourage and sanction prejudice and discrimination.

SOURCE: Based on Pascarella, Ernest T., Marcia Edison, Amaury Nora, Linda Serra Hagedorn, and Patrick T. Terenzini. 1996. "Influences on Students' Openness to Diversity and Challenge in the First Year of College." *Journal of Higher Education* 67(2): 174–93. Copyright 1996 by Ohio State University Press. All rights reserved. Used by permission.

With the passage of the *Multiculturalism Act* in 1988, Canada became the world's first officially multicultural society. The Act stipulated that all federal institutions and workplaces had to reflect and reinforce the diversity at the core of Canadian society. Federal agencies and bureaucracies were obligated to implement programs to improve minority representation so that they reflected the local demographics. Initiatives would also be established to improve minority access and make workplace treatment more equitable. As well, each institution was required to provide culturally appropriate services to the public.

Opponents argue that these programs constitute **reverse discrimination**. Some opponents are those who feel they have been treated unfairly because of efforts to provide minorities with educational and employment opportunities. Bobo and Kluegel (1993) argue that much of the White opposition to race-targeted policies such as employment equity is due to self-interest and prejudice. Some members of the targeted groups are also critical of employment equity, arguing that it perpetuates feelings of inferiority among minorities and fails to help the most impoverished of minorities (Shipler 1998; Wilson 1987).

CONSIDERATION

Shipler (1998) notes that "while most whites think that under affirmative action less qualified blacks are hired and promoted over more qualified whites, most blacks think that without affirmative action, less qualified whites are hired and promoted over more qualified blacks" (p. 3).

Some advocates of employment equity point to the moral and compensatory justification for such programs. In response to the charge that employment equity programs are as discriminatory to Whites as past conditions were to non-Whites, Herman Schwartz (1992) argues:

> No one can honestly equate a remedial preference for a disadvantaged (and qualified) minority member with the brutality inflicted on blacks and other minorities....The preference may take away some benefits from some white men, but none of them is being beaten, lynched, denied the right to use a bathroom, a place to sleep or eat, being forced to take the dirtiest jobs or denied any work at all, forced to attend...mind-killing schools, subjected to brutally unequal justice, or stigmatized as an inferior being. (pp. 193–4)

Other advocates suggest that employment equity provides minority role models. "Nonwhites in educational and professional positions where they were previously not present function as models for other, especially younger, members of their racial group who can identify with them and form realistic goals to occupy the same roles themselves" (Zack 1998: 51).

Diversity Training

Increasingly, corporations have begun to implement efforts to reduce prejudice and discrimination in the workplace through diversity training. Broadly defined, **diversity training** involves "raising personal awareness about individual 'differences' in the workplace and how those differences inhibit or enhance the way people work together and get work done" (Wheeler 1994: 10).

Currently, the programs and services offered by Correctional Services Canada to the 2710 male and 70 female federal Aboriginal offenders include elders' visits to institutions, the existence of Native liaison workers, spiritual ceremonies, and the increasing use of restorative justice initiatives including community involvement through healing circles and Aboriginal healing lodges that are designed to prepare offenders for their release into the community.

SOURCE: Coates 1999

Diversity training may address such issues as stereotyping and cross-cultural insensitivity, as well as provide workers with specific information on cultural norms of different groups and how these norms affect work behaviour and social interactions.

In a survey of 45 organizations that provide diversity training, Wheeler (1994) found that for 85 percent of the respondents, the primary motive for offering diversity training was to enhance productivity and profits. In the words of one survey respondent, "The company's philosophy is that a diverse work force that recognizes and respects differing opinions and ideas adds to the creativity, productivity, and profitability of the company" (p. 12). Only 4 percent of respondents said they offered diversity training out of a sense of social responsibility.

UNDERSTANDING RACE AND ETHNIC RELATIONS

After considering the material presented in this chapter, what understanding about racial and ethnic relations are we left with? First, we have seen that racial categories are socially constructed with no scientific validity. Racial and ethnic categories are largely arbitrary, imprecise, and misleading. While some scholars suggest we abandon racial and ethnic labels, others advocate adding new categories—multiracial and multiethnic—to reflect the identities of a growing segment of the Canadian population.

Conflict theorists and functionalists agree that prejudice, discrimination, and racism have benefited certain groups in society. It is also true, however, that racial and ethnic disharmony have created tensions that disrupt social equilibrium. Further, as symbolic interactionists emphasize, lowered expectations of minority group members, negative labelling, and the use of pejorative terms to describe racial and ethnic minority members contribute to their subordinate position.

Prejudice, racism, and discrimination are debilitating forces in the lives of minorities. In spite of these negative forces, many minority group members succeed in living productive, meaningful, and prosperous lives; many others cannot overcome the social disadvantages associated with their minority status and become victims of a cycle of poverty (see Chapter 10). Thus, alterations in the structure of society that increase opportunities for minorities—in education, employment and income, and political participation—are crucial to achieving racial and ethnic equality. Although government policies or regulations may provide structural opportunities for minorities, policies and regulations often do not change attitudes and beliefs about minority groups embedded in the culture. Changing cultural attitudes begins with the socialization process in the home and in the school. The same socialization process through which children learn prejudice and discrimination may be used to teach children acceptance, compassion, and appreciation for people with varied ethnic and racial backgrounds.

Harmonious racial and ethnic relations may also be achieved through increased contact with different racial and ethnic group members, and through multicultural education and diversity training. Civil rights activist Lani Guinier (1998) suggests that "the real challenge is to...use race as a window on issues of class, issues of gender, and issues of fundamental fairness, not just to talk about race as if it's a question of individual bigotry or individual prejudice. The issue is more than about making friends—it's about making change." However, as Shipler (1998) argues, making change requires that members of society recognize that change is necessary, that there is a problem that needs rectifying.

> One has to perceive the problem to embrace the solutions. If you think that racism isn't harmful unless it wears sheets or burns crosses or bars blacks from motels and restaurants, you will support only the crudest anti-discrimination laws and not the more refined methods....(p. 2)

CRITICAL THINKING

1. Burnet (1999) has noted that government policies of multiculturalism have been attacked "as a means of buttressing Anglo-Saxon dominance, by diverting the efforts of the non-French and the non-English from political and economic affairs into cultural activities." Do you agree with this criticism? Why or why not?

2. Lieberman (1997) asked university faculty members in five disciplines (biology, biological anthropology, cultural anthropology, psychological anthropology, and developmental psychology) to indicate agreement or disagreement with the statement "There are biological races in the species Homo sapiens." In each of the disciplines, women were more likely than men to reject race as a biological reality. Why do you think women in Lieberman's study were more likely than men to reject the concept of race?

3. Should race be a factor in adoption placements? Should people be discouraged from adopting a child who is of a different race than the adoptive parents are? Why or why not?

4. Under Swedish law, giving Nazi salutes is a crime (Lofthus 1998). Do you think that the social benefits of outlawing racist expressions outweigh the impingement of free speech? Do you think such a law should be proposed in Canada? Why or why not?

5. Do you think that there will ever be a time when a racial classification system will no longer be used? Why or why not? What arguments can be made for discontinuing racial classification? What arguments can be made for continuing it?

KEY TERMS

acculturation

adaptive discrimination

amalgamation

assimilation (primary
    and secondary)

charter groups

colonialism

de facto segregation

de jure segregation

discrimination

diversity training

employment equity

endogamy

ethnicity

expulsion

genocide

hate crime

individual discrimination

institutional
    discrimination

marital assimilation

melting pot

modern racism

multicultural education

multiculturalism

one drop of blood rule

overt discrimination

pluralism

population transfer

populations

prejudice

race

racism

refugees

reverse discrimination

segregation

slavery

stereotype

CHAPTER NINE

Sexual Orientation

Is It True?

1. The majority of Canadians say that gays should have equal rights in the workplace.
2. People who believe that gay individuals are born that way tend to be more tolerant of gays than are people who believe that gay individuals choose their sexual orientation.
3. Most countries throughout the world have laws that protect gay individuals from discrimination because of sexual orientation.
4. The American Psychiatric Association currently classifies homosexuality as a mental disorder.
5. Worldwide, most laws prohibiting homosexual behaviour apply to female rather than male homosexuality.

Answers: 1 = T, 2 = T, 3 = F, 4 = F, 5 = F

On October 6, 1998, Matthew Shepard, a 21-year-old student at the University of Wyoming, was abducted and brutally beaten. He was found tied to a wooden fence by two motor-cyclists who initially thought that he was a scarecrow. Matthew's skull had been smashed, and his head and face had been slashed. The only apparent reason for the attack: Matthew Shepard was gay. On October 12, Matthew died of his injuries. Media coverage of his brutal attack and subsequent death focused international attention on sexual-orientation minorities—gay men, lesbians, and bisexuals—and their treatment in society.

> I have friends. Some of them are straight....Year after year I continue to realize that the facts of my life are irrelevant to them and that I am only half listened to, that I am an appendage to the doings of a greater world, a world of power and privilege...a world of exclusion. "That's not true," argue my straight friends. There is only one certainty in the politics of power; those left out beg for inclusion, while the insiders claim that they already are. Men do it to women, whites do it to blacks, and everyone does it to queers.
>
> Gay Pride
> Parade Flier

It is beyond the scope of this chapter to explore how sexual diversity and its cultural meanings vary throughout the world. Rather, this chapter focuses on Western conceptions of diversity in sexual orientation. The term "**sexual orientation**" refers to the classification of individuals as heterosexual, bisexual, or homosexual based on their emotional and sexual attractions, relationships, self-identity, and lifestyle. **Heterosexuality** refers to the predominance of emotional and sexual attraction to persons of the other sex. **Homosexuality** refers to the predominance of emotional and sexual attraction to persons of the same sex. **Bisexuality** involves emotional and sexual attraction to members of both sexes.

In this chapter, we examine prejudice and discrimination toward homo-sexual (or gay) women (also known as lesbians), homosexual (or gay) men, and bisexual individuals. We begin by summarizing the legal status of lesbians and gay men around the world. Then, we discuss the prevalence of homosexuality, heterosexuality, and bisexuality, review biological and environmental explana-tions for sexual orientation diversity, and apply sociological theories to better understand societal reactions to sexual diversity. The chapter ends with a dis-cussion of strategies to reduce antigay prejudice and discrimination.

THE GLOBAL CONTEXT: A WORLD VIEW OF LAWS PERTAINING TO HOMOSEXUALITY

The International Lesbian and Gay Association (ILGA) sponsored a survey of 210 countries throughout the world (excluding the United States) to investi-gate laws and social attitudes regarding homosexuality (*ILGA Annual Report 1996–1997*). Data were not available for 19 countries. This survey found that female homosexuality was legal in 49 countries and illegal in 44 countries. Male homosexuality was legal in 58 countries and illegal in 84 countries. Thus, most laws prohibiting homosexual behaviour apply to male rather than to female homosexuality. Female homosexuality was not mentioned in the laws of 98 countries, whereas male homosexuality was not mentioned in the laws of 49 countries. In countries where homosexual behaviour is legal, ages of con-sent vary. In addition, in many countries where homosexuality is legal, there are no laws protecting lesbians and gay men from discrimination.

In general, oppression of gays is worse in Africa than in other regions of the world. However, in 1996, South Africa became the first country in the world to include in its constitution a clause banning discrimination based on sexual orientation. Canada, Fiji, and Ecuador also have constitutions that ban discrimination based on sexual orientation ("Constitutional Protection" 1999).

Social acceptance of homosexuality is generally higher in Europe than it is in the rest of the world. At least 12 European countries, as well as Canada, Brazil, and Australia, have national laws banning discrimination based on sexual orientation. In 1996, Buenos Aires, Argentina, also drafted a statute that included a clause recognizing "the right to be different" and condemning all forms of discrimination, including those based on sexual orientation (Sarda 1998).

In Hungary, same-sex couples may have a common-law marriage. In other European countries (Denmark, Iceland, Norway, Sweden, and the Netherlands), "registered partnership" laws convey legal status to same-sex couples ("Comparative Survey" 1998). The Netherlands is moving toward becoming the first nation in the world to let same-sex couples marry under regular marriage laws (*ILGA Annual Report* 1996–1997).

A global perspective on laws and social attitudes regarding homosexuality reveals that countries vary tremendously in their treatment of homosexuals— from intolerance and criminalization to acceptance and legal protection. Later in this chapter, we examine social attitudes and laws regarding homosexuality in Canada.

Prevalence of Homosexuality, Heterosexuality, and Bisexuality

The prevalence of homosexuality, heterosexuality, and bisexuality is difficult to determine. Because of embarrassment, a desire for privacy, or fear of social disapproval, many individuals are not willing to answer questions about their sexuality honestly. In addition, estimates of the prevalence of sexual orientations vary because of differences in the way researchers define and measure them. Classifying individuals as heterosexual, homosexual, or bisexual is not as clearcut as some people believe. People's self-identities may not correspond with their behaviour. For example, substantial numbers of individuals who view themselves as heterosexual have had same-sex attractions and relations. Definitional problems also arise from the fact that sexual attractions, behaviour, and self-identity may change over time.

Nevertheless, research data have yielded rough estimates of prevalence rates of homosexuality and bisexuality. In a national study of U.S. adults aged 18 to 59, researchers focused on three aspects of homosexuality: sexual attraction to persons of the same sex, sexual behaviour with people of the same sex, and homosexual self-identification (Michael et al. 1994). The researchers found that not all people who are sexually attracted to or have had sexual relations with individuals of the same sex view themselves as homosexual or bisexual.

Other data reflect the prevalence of same-sex sexual behaviour among a large sample of high-school students in Massachusetts (Faulkner and Cranston 1998). More than 3000 students in grades 9 through 12 completed a self-administered anonymous questionnaire that included the question: "The person(s) with whom you have had sexual contact is (are) (1) female(s), (2) males(s), (3) females(s) and male(s), (4) I have not had sexual contact with anyone." Of the sexually experienced students (which did not necessarily imply having had intercourse), 6.4 percent reported same-sex contact, either exclusively or bisexually. This survey found equal numbers of male and female individuals with same sex experience, and equal numbers of students reporting exclusively same-sex activity and bisexual experience.

Origins of Sexual Orientation Diversity: Nature or Nurture?

One of the prevailing questions raised regarding homosexuality and bisexuality centres on its origin or "cause." Despite the growing research on this topic, a concrete cause of sexual orientation diversity has yet to be discovered. Many researchers believe that an interaction of biological and environmental forces is involved in the development of one's sexual orientation (De Cecco and Parker 1995). After presenting research findings on the biological bases of sexual orientation, we look briefly at environmental explanations.

Biological Origins of Sexual Orientation Gays and gay rights advocates tend to support the position that homosexuality is an innate trait. In a national study of homosexual men, 90 percent believe that they were born with their homosexual orientation; only 4 percent believe that environmental factors are the sole cause (Lever 1994). Gallup poll findings reveal an increasing trend in the belief that homosexuality is inborn, from 13 percent in 1977 to 31 percent in 1996 (Saad 1996).

Biological explanations of sexual-orientation diversity usually focus on genetic or hormonal differences between heterosexuals and homosexuals. In an overview of genetics research on homosexual and heterosexual orientations, Pillard and Bailey (1998) conclude that genes account for at least half of the variance in sexual orientation. Their review of family, twin, and adoptee studies indicate that homosexuality (and thus heterosexuality) runs in families. However, the actual empirical research attempting to isolate a biological-cause basis for sexuality is less than convincing in its findings.

For example, science has yet to identify a "homosexuality" gene despite the assertion of some researchers, such as Hamer et al. (1993), who claim to have discovered *statistical* evidence for its existence. In their examination of 40 pairs of gay brothers, Hamer et al. note a significantly higher number (33 out of 40) than expected (20 out of 40) of the pairs shared matching DNA in a region called Xq28 at the tip of the X chromosome, a chromosome males genetically inherit from their biological mothers. The researchers focused on this chromosome after noting in previous research that more gay male relatives appear to be found on the mother's side of the family. Hamer and his research team did not actually isolate a specific gene, or even a specific set of genes, that exist within that chromosomal region; they only provided the statistics-based suggestion that such genes must be there. Nor do they specifically account for the homosexuality of those brothers who do not possess the matching DNA. Nor have Hamer et al. examined heterosexual brothers for the existence or nonexistence of matching DNA in the Xq28 region to determine whether heterosexual brothers are similar to or different from homosexual brothers (Peele and DeGrandpre 1995). Consider as well that the results of a recent Canadian study (Rice et al., 1999), based on 62 gay male sibling pairs and which analyzed the microsatellite markers at position Xq28, did not support Hamer's suggestion of a X-linked gene underlying homosexuality. Even though the evidence for any link among humans between genes, hormones (e.g., such as testosterone), and sexual behaviour is very unclear, researchers continue in the quest to isolate a biological cause for human sexuality. This chapter's Focus on Social Problems Research reviews one such recent effort. In judging such theories, it is important to consider the tremendous variation in actual, acceptable, and unacceptable sexual behaviour across the cultures of the world, both currently and historically, and how the sexual behaviour of individuals may change over their own lifetimes.

Environmental Explanations of Sexual Orientation According to Doell (1995), "…we all probably develop, from infancy, the capacity to have heterosexual, homosexual, or bisexual relationships" (p. 352). Environmental theories propose that such

FOCUS ON SOCIAL PROBLEMS RESEARCH

WHAT NEXT? SEXUAL ORIENTATION AND PENIS SIZE

A Canadian professor studying an apparent relationship between penis size and sexual orientation says gay men have longer members than heterosexual men. "If size matters, it may give us clues to sexual development," said Anthony Bogaert, a sexologist in the health studies department at Brock University in St. Catharines, Ontario….A study co-written by Prof. Bogaert and published in the June edition of the international journal Archives of Sexual Behaviour concluded that the average erect penis size of homosexuals is 16.64 cm (6.46 inches) but only 15.6 cm (6.14 inches) for heterosexuals.

The difference in length may suggest that biological factors, such as fluctuations in the levels of testosterone or other pre-natal hormones in the mother's womb, could influence the size of the penis and sexual orientation, the article says. "It may suggest some sort of biological factors involved in sexual orientation development, but the data are open to interpretation at this point," said Prof. Bogaert, who co-authored *The Relation between Sexual Orientation and Penile Size* with California State University psychology professor Scott Hershberger. "It's rather an interesting, titillating finding."

But Dr. Miriam Kaufman, a paediatrician at the Hospital for Sick Children in Toronto and an associate professor at the University of Toronto, questions why society needs studies that try to determine the reasons for homosexuality. "Any gay man will tell you that he has a longer penis than a straight man," laughed Dr. Kaufman, an expert in sexuality. "To start getting into things like measuring penis size is ridiculous. It's another group of people who will say, 'See, penis size is important.' "

The study relied on data collected between 1938 and 1963 by the Indiana-based Kinsey Institute for Research in Sex, Gender and Reproduction, which asked 4187 heterosexuals and 935 homosexuals to measure themselves with a ruler at home and mail in the lengths. The Kinsey data have been used for many research projects, but this appears to be the first attempt to determine sexual orientation based on penis size.

Dr. Kaufman called the data suspect, questioning the reliability of the participants' sexual orientations and their self-measurements. "Penis size is not exactly a value-neutral matter in our culture." Prof. Bogaert allowed there may be problems with people misrepresenting their size but he argued the Kinsey material has stood up to other medical studies and believes any exaggeration would come equally from gay and straight men—so the results can be relied upon.

The study also reported that factors such as education, height, and weight did not play a significant role in penis size, noting the circumference of the erect organ was also found to be larger for homosexuals (12.6 cm) than heterosexuals (12.2 cm). A more conclusive study would require clinical measurements, but Prof. Bogaert added it would take years to collect data from such a large sample size.

Prof. Bogaert argued that studies tracking the biological reasoning behind sexual orientation also give credence to those who insist that being gay is not a choice. [However,] Alison Kemper, executive director of the 519 Church Street Community Centre, a Toronto organization for gays and lesbians, called the study far-fetched and silly. "As if the variety of sexual orientations can be reduced to measurements…certainly not to a bunch of guys in the U.S. being sent off with rulers in the mid-twentieth century," said Ms. Kemper. She doubted the penis-length results would give gay men something to cheer about….

Prof. Bogaert said some gay publications have contacted him about the study. "I think they're likely interested because in this small, little realm, gay men win," said Prof. Bogaert, whose research has also included probing sexual orientation according to birth order. "But I don't think there has been a lot of rallying around the flag."

SOURCE: Abridged from Culbert, Lori. 1999. "Gays' Manhood Surpasses That of Straight Men: Study." *National Post*, September 28: A1, A10

factors as availability of sexual partners, early sexual experiences, and sexual rein-forcement influence subsequent sexual orientation. The degree to which early sexual experiences have been negative or positive has been hypothesized as influencing sexual orientation. Having pleasurable same-sex experiences would be likely to increase the probability of a homosexual orientation. For the same reason, early traumatic sexual experiences have been suggested as causing fear of heterosexual activity. However, a study that compared sexual histories of lesbian and heterosexual women found no differences in the incidence of traumatic experiences with men (Brannock and Chapman 1990).

CONSIDERATION

Beliefs about the causes of homosexuality are related to people's attitudes toward homosex-uals. A national poll of Americans found that "those who believe homosexuals choose their sexual orientation are far less tolerant of gays and lesbians and more likely to conclude homo-sexuality should be illegal than those who think sexual orientation is not a matter of personal choice" (Rosin and Morin 1999: 8).

SOCIOLOGICAL THEORIES OF SEXUAL ORIENTATION

Although sociological theories do not explain the origin or "cause" of sexual orientation diversity, they help explain societal reactions to homosexuality and bisexuality. In addition, the symbolic interaction perspective sheds light on the process of adopting a gay, lesbian, or bisexual identity.

Structural-Functionalist Perspective

Structural-functionalists, consistent with their emphasis on institutions and the functions they fulfil, emphasize the importance of monogamous hetero-sexual relationships for the reproduction, nurturance, and socialization of chil-dren. From a functionalist perspective, homosexual relations, as well as heterosexual nonmarital relations, are defined as "deviant" because they do not fulfil the family institution's main function of producing and rearing chil-dren. Clearly, this argument is less salient in a society in which other institu-tions, most notably schools, have supplemented the traditional functions of the family and in which reducing (rather than increasing) population is a soci-etal goal.

Some functionalists argue that antagonisms between heterosexuals and homosexuals may disrupt the natural state, or equilibrium, of society. Durkheim, however, recognized that deviation from society's norms might also be functional. As Durkheim observed, deviation "...may be useful as a prelude to reforms which daily become more necessary" ([1938] 1993: 66). Specifically, the gay rights movement has motivated many people to re-examine their treat-ment of sexual-orientation minorities and has produced a sense of cohesion and solidarity among members of the gay population (although bisexuals and the transgendered have often been excluded from gay and lesbian communi-ties and organizations). Gay activism has been instrumental in advocating for more research on HIV and AIDS, more and better health services for HIV and AIDS patients, protection of the rights of HIV-infected individuals, and

HIV/AIDS public education. Such HIV/AIDS prevention strategies and health services benefit the society as a whole.

The structural-functionalist perspective is concerned with how changes in one part of society affect other aspects. With this focus on the interconnectedness of society, we note that urbanization has contributed to the formation of strong social networks of gays and bisexuals. Cities "acted as magnets, drawing in gay migrants who felt isolated and threatened in smaller towns and rural areas" (Button et al. 1997: 15). Given the formation of gay communities in large cities, it is not surprising that the gay rights movement first emerged in large urban centres.

Conflict Perspective

Conflict theorists, particularly those who do not emphasize a purely economic perspective, note that the antagonisms between heterosexuals and nonheterosexuals represent a basic division in society between those with power and those without power. When one group has control of society's institutions and resources, as in the case of heterosexuals, they have the authority to dominate other groups. The recent battle over gay rights is just one example of the political struggle between those with power and those without it.

A classic example of the power struggle between gays and straights took place in 1973 when the American Psychiatric Association (APA) met to revise its classification scheme of mental disorders. Homosexual activists had been appealing to the APA for years to remove homosexuality from its list of mental illnesses but with little success. The view of homosexuals as mentally sick contributed to their low social prestige in the eyes of the heterosexual majority. In 1973, the APA's board of directors voted to remove homosexuality from its official list of mental disorders. The board's move encountered a great deal of resistance from conservative APA members and was put to a referendum, which reaffirmed the board's decision (Bayer 1987).

Recently, gays and lesbians have been waging a political battle to win human rights protections in the form of laws prohibiting discrimination based on sexual orientation (discussed later in this chapter). Conflict theory helps to explain why many business owners and corporate leaders oppose such rights protection for gays and lesbians. Employers fear that such protection would result in costly lawsuits if they refused to hire homosexuals, regardless of the reason for their decision. Business owners also fear that granting human rights protections to homosexual employees would undermine the economic health of a community by discouraging the development of new businesses and even driving out some established firms (Button et al. 1997).

However, some companies are recognizing that implementing antidiscrimination policies that include sexual orientation is good for the bottom line. A 1993 National Gay and Lesbian Task Force survey of Fortune 1000 companies found that 72 percent had a nondiscrimination policy that included sexual orientation (reported in Button et al. 1997). These companies realized that "many of their most talented employees might leave if they did not provide a more tolerant setting."

In summary, conflict theory frames the gay rights movement and the opposition to it as a struggle over power, prestige, and economic resources. Recent trends toward increased social acceptance of homosexuality may, in part, reflect the corporate world's competition over the gay and lesbian consumer dollar.

Symbolic Interactionist Perspective

Symbolic interactionism focuses on the meanings of heterosexuality, homosexuality, and bisexuality and how these meanings are socially constructed. The meanings we associate with same-sex relations are learned from society—from family, peers, religion, and the media. Freedman and D'Emilio (1990) observed that "...sexual meanings are subject to the forces of culture. Human beings learn how to express themselves sexually, and the content and outcome of that learning vary widely across cultures and across time" (p. 485). Historical and cross-cultural research on homosexuality reveals the socially constructed nature of homosexuality and its meaning. Although many North Americans may assume that same-sex romantic relationships have always been taboo in our society, during the nineteenth century, "romantic friendships" between women were encouraged and regarded as preparation for a successful marriage. The nature of these friendships bordered on lesbianism. President Grover Cleveland's sister Rose wrote to her friend Evangeline Whipple in 1890: "...It makes me heavy with emotion...all my whole being leans out to you....I dare not think of your arms" (Goode and Wagner 1993: 49).

The symbolic interactionist perspective also points to the effects of labelling on individuals. Once individuals become identified or labelled as lesbian, gay, or bisexual, that label tends to become their **master status**. In other words, the dominant heterosexual community tends to view "gay," "lesbian," and "bisexual" as the most socially significant statuses of individuals who are identified as such. Esterberg (1997) notes that "unlike heterosexuals, who are defined by their family structures, communities, occupations, or other aspects of their lives, lesbians, gay men, and bisexuals are often defined primarily by what they do in bed. Many lesbians, gay men, and bisexuals, however, view their identity as social and political as well as sexual" (p. 377).

CONSIDERATION

Because of the stigma of being labelled as lesbian, gay, or bisexual, many gays and bisexuals struggle through the process of developing a gay or bisexual identity, particularly those who are also members of a racial or ethnic minority group. However, others feel that they have always known and accepted their sexual orientation. One woman, for example, claimed: "I have never not felt that I was bisexual" (quoted in Esterberg 1997: 38). In addition, some bisexuals resist defining themselves with a sexual-orientation label. In interviews with bisexual women, Esterberg noted: "for a number of women, what was important was not taking on a label and an identity, but having the freedom to define themselves and live their lives as they please" (p. 157). This resistance to sexual-orientation labels may be analogous to the resistance among some individuals to using racial labels to describe themselves and who, instead, leave questions about their race blank or check "other."

HETEROSEXISM, HOMOPHOBIA, AND BIPHOBIA

Canada, along with many other countries throughout the world, is predominantly heterosexist. **Heterosexism** refers to "an ideological system that denies, denigrates, and stigmatizes any nonheterosexual form of behaviour, identity, relationship, or community" (Herek 1990: 316). Heterosexism is based on the belief that heterosexuality is superior to homosexuality, and it results in prejudice and discrimination against homosexuals and bisexuals. Prejudice refers to negative attitudes, whereas discrimination refers to behaviour that denies individuals or groups equality of treatment. Before reading further, you may wish to complete this chapter's Self and Society feature: The Homophobia Scale.

Homophobia

For Franklin Kameny (1972), a prominent gay rights leader who coined the phrase "gay is good," the homophile movement has two basic tenets: first, that homosexuals are the equals of heterosexuals and second, that homosexuality is fully the equal of heterosexuality. However, negative attitudes toward homosexuality and lesbianism persist, despite the passage of Bill C-33, which added "sexual orientation" to the *Canadian Human Rights Act* in 1996. In that year, a random sample survey of Canadians and Americans reported that just over one-third of Canadians (34 percent) and Americans (36 percent) agreed with the statement, "Gays should have the same rights as others" (*Maclean's* 1996). In 1999, a second survey, conducted by the Toronto-based Strategic Counsel and based on telephone interviews with a random sample of 1200 adult Canadians and 1000 adult Americans, reported that approximately 21 percent of Canadians and 32 percent of Americans surveyed disagreed with the statement, "It is acceptable to me for people who are gay to teach in the school system" (see Table 9.1).

The term **homophobia** is commonly used to refer to negative attitudes toward homosexuality. Other terms that refer to negative attitudes toward homosexuality include "homonegativity" and "antigay bias."

In general, certain categories of people are more likely to have negative attitudes toward homosexuals. Persons who are older, less educated, living in lightly populated rural areas, and Protestant are the most likely to have negative attitudes. In contrast, people who are younger, more educated, never married, living in the West, living in heavily populated urban areas, and Jewish are least likely to have antigay attitudes (Klassen et al. 1989). Public opinion surveys also indicate that men are more likely than women are to have negative attitudes toward gays (Moore 1993); however, many studies on attitudes toward homosexuality do not distinguish between attitudes toward gay men and attitudes toward lesbians (Kite and Whitley 1996). Research that has assessed attitudes toward male versus female homosexuality has found that heterosexual women and men hold similar attitudes toward lesbians, but men are more negative toward gay men (Louderback and Whitley 1997; Price and Dalecki 1998).

Table 9.1	Agreement with Gays Teaching School, Canada and the United States, 1999				
	Strongly Agree	**Somewhat Agree**	**Neither Agree/ Disagree**	**Somewhat Disagree**	**Strongly Disagree**
Canada	36	32	10	7	14
United States	28	28	9	10	22

SOURCE: *Maclean's* 1999b: 49

The Homophobia Scale

Directions: Indicate the extent to which you agree or disagree with each statement by placing a check mark on the appropriate line.

	Strongly agree	Agree	Undecided	Disagree	Strongly disagree
1. Homosexuals contribute positively to society.	____	____	____	____	____
2. Homosexuality is disgusting.	____	____	____	____	____
3. Homosexuals are just as moral as heterosexuals are.	____	____	____	____	____
4. Homosexuals should have equal civil rights.	____	____	____	____	____
5. Homosexuals corrupt young people.	____	____	____	____	____
6. Homosexuality is a sin.	____	____	____	____	____
7. Homosexuality should be against the law.	____	____	____	____	____

SCORING
Assign scores of 0, 1, 2, 3, and 4 to the five choices respectively ("strongly agree" through "strongly disagree") for items 1, 3, and 4. Assign scores of 0, 1, 2, 3, and 4 to the five choices in reverse order ("strongly disagree" through "strongly agree") for items 2, 5, 6, and 7. All items are summed for the total score. The possible range is 0 to 28; high scores indicate greater homophobia.

COMPARISON DATA
The Homophobia Scale was administered to 524 students enrolled in introductory psychology courses at the University of Texas. The mean score for men was 15.8; for women, it was 13.8. The difference was statistically significant.

From: Bouton, Richard A., P. E. Gallagher, P. A. Garlinghouse, T. Leal, et al. 1987. "Scales for Measuring Fear of AIDS and Homophobia." *Journal of Personality Assessment* 67(1): 609. Copyright © 1987 by Lawrence Erlbaum Associates, Inc. Reprinted by permission.

Based on a broad selection of undergraduates (101 men, 98 women) attending a Canadian university where the majority of students were of working-class or middle-class families of European descent, Schellenberg et al. (1999) report that attitudes toward gay men were more negative than toward lesbians. When compared to science or business students, students in the faculties of arts and social science had more positive attitudes toward gay men, and women were more positive than men were. Attitudes toward gay men improved with time spent at university but only for male students. Although attitudes toward lesbians also improved with time at university, this was not associated with students' gender or faculty of enrolment. Schellenberg et al. conclude that university education may encourage a reduction in antihomosexual prejudice among young people, particularly among young men. Positive contact with homosexuals or having homosexuals as friends is also associated with less homophobia (Simon 1995).

CONSIDERATION

The homophobic and heterosexist social climate of our society is often viewed in terms of how it victimizes the gay population. However, heterosexuals are also victimized by homophobia and heterosexism. Due to the antigay climate, heterosexuals, especially males, are hindered in their own self-expression and intimacy in same-sex relationships. "The threat of victimization (i.e., antigay violence) probably also causes many heterosexuals to conform to gender roles and to restrict their expressions of (nonsexual) physical affection for members of their own sex" (Garnets et al. 1990: 380).

Some sexual assaults are related to homophobia and compulsory heterosexuality. For example, some men who participate in gang rape, also known as "pulling train," entice each other into the act "by implying that those who do not participate are unmanly or homosexual" (Sanday 1995: 399). Homonegativity also encourages early sexual activity among adolescent men. Adolescent male virgins are often teased by their male peers, who say things like "You mean you don't do it with girls yet? What are you, a fag or something?" Not wanting to be labelled and stigmatized as a "fag," some adolescent boys "prove" their heterosexuality by having sex with girls.

Cultural Origins of Homophobia

Why is homosexuality viewed so negatively in North America? Antigay bias has its roots in various aspects of our culture.

1. *Religion.* Most individuals who view homosexuality as unacceptable say they object on religious grounds (Rosin and Morin 1999). Although some religious groups (such as the Quakers) accept homosexuality, many religions teach that homosexuality is sinful and prohibited by God. The Roman Catholic Church rejects all homosexual expression and resists any attempt to validate or sanction the homosexual orientation. Some fundamentalist churches have endorsed the death penalty for homosexual people and teach the view that AIDS is God's punishment for engaging in homosexual sex (Nugent and Gramick 1989). In June 1999, an American Baptist preacher from Topeka, Kansas. announced that he and a group of his followers would be leading a demonstration on the steps of the Supreme Court of Canada to protest its decision to extend the definition of "spouse" to same-sex couples. Mr. Phelps, who on previous occasions has picketed gay funerals, same-sex unions, and even Girl Scout meetings blandishing signs that read, "AIDS cures fags," had announced, "We're coming to spread the gospel to you Sinners." Phelps referred to Canada as the "sperm bank of Satan" and vowed that he and his supporters would burn Canadian flags in protest. In the end, Mr. Phelps did not appear and his group blamed the unwillingness of Canadian police, "who are as black-hearted as the perverts" to provide him with the level of protection he sought as the reason for the group's absence (Anderssen 1999).

   Some religions are divided on the issue of homosexuality. For example, while the official position of the United Methodist Church is one that condemns homosexuality, some Methodist ministers advocate acceptance of and equal rights for lesbians and gay men. The United Methodist Church has considered splitting into two organizations: one in favour of equal rights for gays and lesbians, and the other opposed (*The United Methodist Church and Homosexuality* 1999).

2. *Marital and procreative bias.* Many societies have traditionally condoned sex only when it occurs in a marital context that provides for the possibility of producing and rearing children. Although laws prohibiting same-sex marriages have been challenged in the courts (which we discuss later in this chapter), as of this writing, same-sex marriages are not legally recognized in Canada. Even though assisted reproductive technologies make it possible for gay individuals and couples to have children, many people believe that these advances should be used by heterosexual married couples only (Franklin 1993).

3. *Concern about HIV and AIDS.* Although most cases of HIV and AIDS worldwide are attributed to heterosexual transmission, the rates of HIV and AIDS in Canada are much higher among gay and bisexual men than among other groups. Because of this, many people associate HIV and AIDS with homosexuality and bisexuality. This association between AIDS and homosexuality has fuelled antigay sentiments. During a 1985 mayoral campaign in Houston, the challenging contender was asked what he would do about the AIDS problem. His answer: he would "shoot the queers" (Button et al. 1997: 70). Lesbians, incidentally, have a very low risk for sexually transmitted HIV—a lower risk than heterosexual women do.

4. *Threat to the power of the majority.* Like other minority groups, the gay minority threatens the power of the majority. Fearing loss of power, the majority group stigmatizes homosexuals as a way of limiting their power.

5. *Rigid gender roles.* Antigay sentiments also stem from rigid gender roles. When Cooper Thompson (1995) was asked to give a guest presentation on male roles at a suburban high school, male students told him that the most humiliating put-down was being called a "fag." The boys in this school gave Thompson the impression they were expected to conform to rigid, narrow standards of masculinity to avoid being labelled in this way.

   From a conflict perspective, heterosexual men's subordination and devaluation of gay men reinforces gender inequality. "By devaluing gay men...heterosexual men devalue the feminine and anything associated with it" (Price and Dalecki 1998: 155–6). Negative views toward lesbians also reinforce the patriarchal system of male dominance. Social disapproval of lesbians is a form of punishment for women who relinquish traditional female sexual and economic dependence on men. Not surprisingly, research findings suggest that individuals with traditional gender role attitudes tend to hold more negative views toward homosexuality (Louderback and Whitley 1997).

6. *Psychiatric labelling.* As noted earlier, before 1973 the APA defined homosexuality as a mental disorder. Treatments for the "illness" of homosexuality included lobotomies, aversive conditioning, and, in some cases, castration. The social label of mental illness by such a powerful labelling group as the APA contributed to heterosexuals' negative reactions to gays. Further, it created feelings of guilt, low self-esteem, anger, and depression for many homosexuals. Thus, the psychiatric care system is now busily treating the very conditions it, in part, created.

7. *Myths and negative stereotypes.* Prejudice toward homosexuals may also stem from some of the unsupported beliefs and negative stereotypes regarding homosexuality. One negative myth about homosexuals is that they are sexually promiscuous and lack "family values" such as monogamy and commitment to relationships. While some homosexuals do engage in

casual sex, as do some heterosexuals, many homosexual couples develop and maintain long-term committed relationships.

Another myth that is not supported by data is that homosexuals, as a group, are child molesters. The ratio of heterosexual to homosexual child molesters is approximately 11 to 1 (Moser 1992). Most often, the abuser is a father, stepfather, or heterosexual relative of the family. When a father sexually assaults his daughter, the media do not report that something is wrong with heterosexuality or with traditional families, but when a homosexual is reported to have molested a child, it is viewed as confirmation of "the way homosexuals are" (Mohr 1995: 404). "The Heterosexual Questionnaire" parodies the different ways in which we respond to heterosexual and homosexuals in our society.

The Heterosexual Questionnaire

1. What do you think caused your heterosexuality?
2. When and how did you decide you were a heterosexual?
3. Is it possible that your heterosexuality is just a phase you may grow out off?
4. Is it possible that your heterosexuality stems from a neurotic fear of others of the same sex?
5. If you have never slept with a person of the same sex, is it possible that all you need is a good gay lover?
6. Do you parents know that you are straight? Do you friends and/or roommate(s) know? How did they react?
7. Why do you insist on flaunting your heterosexuality? Can't you just be who you are and keep it quiet?
8. Why do heterosexuals place so much emphasis on sex?
9. Why do heterosexuals feel compelled to seduce others into their lifestyle?
10. A disproportionate majority of child molesters are heterosexual. Do you consider it safe to expose children to heterosexual teachers?
11. Just what do men and women do in bed together? How can they truly know how to please each other, being so anatomically different?
12. With all the societal support marriage receives, the divorce rate is spiralling. Why are there so few stable relationships among heterosexuals?
13. Statistics show that lesbians have the lowest incidence of sexually transmitted diseases. It is really safe for a woman to maintain a heterosexual lifestyle and run the risk of disease and pregnancy?
14. How can you become a whole person if you limit yourself to compulsive, exclusive heterosexuality?
15. Considering the menace of overpopulation, how could the human race survive if everyone were heterosexual?
16. Could you trust a heterosexual therapist to be objective? Don't you feel she or he might be inclined to influence you in the direction of his or her own leanings?
17. There seem to be very few happy heterosexuals. Techniques have been developed that might enable you to change if you really want to. Have you considered trying aversion therapy?
18. Would you want your child to be heterosexual, knowing the problems that she or he would face?

SOURCE: Rochlin, M. 1982. "The Heterosexual Questionnaire." *Changing Men* (Spring)

CHAPTER 9   SEXUAL ORIENTATION

Biphobia

Just as the term "homophobia" is used to refer to negative attitudes toward gay men and lesbians, **biphobia** refers to "the parallel set of negative beliefs about and stigmatization of bisexuality and those identified as bisexual" (Paul 1996: 449). Although both homosexual- and bisexual-identified individuals are often rejected by heterosexuals, bisexual-identified women and men also face rejection from many homosexual individuals. Thus, bisexuals experience "double discrimination."

Lesbians seem to exhibit greater levels of biphobia than do gay men, probably because many lesbian women associate their identity with a political stance against sexism and patriarchy. Some lesbians view heterosexual and bisexual women who "sleep with the enemy" as traitors to the feminist movement.

One negative stereotype that encourages biphobia is the belief that bisexuals are, by definition, nonmonogamous. However, many bisexual women and men prefer and have long-term committed monogamous relationships.

DISCRIMINATION AGAINST SEXUAL-ORIENTATION MINORITIES

Like other minority groups in Canadian society, homosexuals and bisexuals experience various forms of discrimination. Next, we look at sexual-orientation discrimination in the law, the workplace, in family matters, and in violent expressions of hate.

The Law

Historically, and in various ways, Canadian law has subject homosexuals to discrimination. From 1952 to 1977, immigration laws prohibited homosexuals from entering Canada and subjected those who were homosexual to the threat of deportation if their sexual orientation became known. From 1892 to 1969, Canadian criminal law made certain forms of sexual conduct engaged in by gay men illegal and rendered gay men vulnerable to indefinite incarceration as "dangerous sexual offenders."

Sodomy laws, sometimes referred to as "crimes against nature," prohibited what were considered "unnatural acts" such as oral and anal sex. However, Canadian criminal law has been historically uneven in its treatment of gay men and lesbians. The 1890 statute that introduced acts of "gross indecency" into the Code defined them as gender-specific offences that could only be committed by males. Indeed, Canadian law did not recognize the possibility of female acts of homosexuality until the 1953–54 simplification and expansion of the *Criminal Code*.

At present, under section 159 of the *Criminal Code*, Canadian law criminalizes anal intercourse with an exemption occurring for those acts engaged in between a husband and wife or by two consenting adults 18 years of age and over. In contrast, the age of consent for other forms of sexual expression, including vaginal intercourse, is 14. This section of the *Criminal Code* has been challenged in some provinces as discriminatory on the basis of age, sexual orientation, and marital status. For example, in the *Carmen M.* case, a 23-year-old man was charged with four criminal offences stemming from his having engaged, over a three-year period, in acts of oral, anal, and vaginal intercourse with a girl who was 13 at the time the sexual acts began. At his trial, the man was found guilty of sexual assault and sexual interference and given an 18-month prison sentence. However, the accused was found not guilty of anal intercourse after he challenged the higher age of consent for anal intercourse on the grounds that it violated the equality provisions of the Charter of Rights. In his efforts, he was buttressed by the support of the Canadian Foundation for Children, Youth, and the Law, which had received intervenor status in the case. It was argued that outlawing consensual anal intercourse by those under the age of 18 was discriminatory, particularly to gay teens. The judge in the case agreed. He noted that the girl had been 14 to 18 at the time the acts of anal sex had occurred and had consented to the acts. Despite the fact that the law prohibited such liaisons, the judge ruled that the law itself was unconstitutional because it denied the accused the defence of consent.

When the Crown appealed this decision, the children's foundation was joined by the Canadian AIDS Society and the Coalition for Lesbian and Gay Rights Organization. All maintained that the law discriminated against gay teens, exposed them to "unnecessary psychological detriment," made it difficult for them to benefit from health services that could reduce HIV transmission, and "denied [them] the liberty to make choices about their own bodies in respect to the sexual act impugned by the section." The Ontario Court of Appeal agreed, with two judges finding that a higher age of consent constituted age discrimination and one judge finding that it constituted discrimination on the bases of both age and sexual orientation. The court rejected the government's arguments that it was entitled to legislate morality. It also ruled that a higher age of consent impeded the efforts of safe-sex educators and held that the law "arbitrarily disadvantages gay men by denying to them until they are 18 a choice available at the age of 14 to those who are not gay, namely their choice of sexual expression with a consenting partner to whom they are not married" (Bell 1999). This ruling of the Ontario Court of Appeal is not binding on courts in other jurisdictions.

Discrimination in the Workplace

In recent years, the percentage of Canadians who express approval of equal employment rights for homosexuals has increased. An increasing amount of support for same-sex relationships is evident in the growing number of employers across Canada who have negotiated or voluntarily extended equal benefits to the partners of both gay and lesbian employees. Table 9.2 notes some of the major employers in Canada who recognize gay and lesbian relationships in their system of benefits.

Nevertheless, many gay people fear being fired, denied salary increases, or passed over for promotion. In the United States, where most states still do not offer protection against employment discrimination based on sexual orientation, there are numerous examples that this type of discrimination occurs. For example, the Cracker Barrel restaurant chain fired at least 11 openly gay and lesbian employees in 1991. Cracker Barrel stated that it would refuse employment to people "whose sexual preferences fail to demonstrate normal heterosexual values which have been the foundation of families in our society" (cited in Button et al. 1997: 126). In 1996, a manager at an Illinois Red Lobster fired Dale Hall after repeatedly ridiculing him for being gay. The Cook County Com-

Government
Government of Canada
Province of British Columbia
Province of Manitoba
Province of New Brunswick
Province of Nova Scotia
Province of Ontario
Province of Saskatchewan
Yukon
Northwest Territory

Labour Organizations
Alberta Federation of Labour
Canadian Auto Workers
Canadian Labour Congress
Canadian Union of Public Employees
Hospital Employees Union (B.C.)
Ontario College of Universities Faculty
     Associations
Public Service Alliance of Canada
Ontario Federation of Labour

Municipal
B.C. Transit
City of Barrie
City of Edmonton
City of Halifax
City of Kanaton
City of Kingston
City of Langley
City of New Westminster
City of North Vancouver
City of Ottawa
City of Port Moody
City of Regina
City of Prince Rupert
City of Richmond
City of Toronto
City of Vancouver
City of Winnipeg
Municipality of Delta
District of Burnaby
District of Coquitlam
Greater Vancouver Regional District
Regional Municipality of Kitchener-Waterloo
Regional Municipality of Ottawa-Carleton
Ville de Montréal

Education
Acadia University
Athabasca University
B.C. School District #43 (Coquitlam)
B.C. School District #44 (North Vancouver)

B.C. Institute of Technology
Brock University
Camosun College
Carleton Board of Education
Carleton University
Concordia University
Dalhousie University
East Kootenay Community College
London Board of Education
McGill University
Ontario Institute for Studies in Education
Ottawa Board of Education
Queen's University
Ryerson Polytechnic University
Toronto Board of Education
Trent University
University of Alberta
University of British Columbia
University of Calgary
University of Manitoba
University of New Brunswick
University of Ottawa
University of Saskatchewan
University of Toronto
University of Waterloo
University of Western Ontario
University of Windsor
Vancouver Community College
Wilfred Laurier University
Yellowknife Education District #4
York University

Health Sector
Alberta Health Care Association
Community Health Services Saskatoon
Centretown Community Health Centre
     (Toronto)
Health Labour Relations Association (B.C.)
Ontario Hospital Association
Riverdale Hospital (Toronto)
Toronto Hospital for Sick Children

Public Utilities
B.C. Hydro
Brampton Hydro Electric Commission
Hydro Hamilton-Wentworth
Northwest Territories Power Corporation
Ontario Hydro
Toronto Hydro

Community and Social Services
Canadian Hearing Society
Catholic Children's Aid Society of Manitoba

Catholic Social Services (Edmonton)
Children's Aid Society (Thunder Bay)
Corporation of the City of Toronto at
     519 Church Street
Elizabeth Fry Society (Ottawa)
Fort Nelson Women's Resource Centre
Guelph-Wellington Family and Children's
     Services
John Howard Society of North Island
     (Campbell River)
Law Society of Upper Canada
Legal Services of B.C.
Metro Toronto Children's Aid Society
Metropolitan Toronto Police
Pacific Legal Education Association
United Church of Canada
United Way of the Lower Mainland
Wellesley Hospital
York County Hospital
Young Men's Christian Association (Toronto)
Young Women's Christian Association
     (Toronto)
Youth Services Bureau of Ottawa

Libraries
Burnaby Public Library
Hamilton Public Library
North Vancouver Public Library Board
Toronto Public Library
Vancouver Public Library

Private Sector
3M
A and W Food Services of Canada
Air Canada
Air Ontario
Air Transit
Alcan Smelters and Chemicals Ltd.
Alfred l'Allaire
Amex
Anderson Consulting Canada
Art Gallery of Ontario
Bank of Montreal
Bank of Nova Scotia
B.C. Telecom
Bell Canada
Boeing of Canada
Britol Aerospace
Budd Automotive Company
Cablevision Videotron Limited
CAMI Automotive Inc.
Canada Post
Canadian Airlines

Canadian Broadcasting Corporation (CBC)	Hotel Beausejour	Princess Auto Ltd.
Canadian Offshore Financial Services S.A.	Hudson's Bay Company	Purolator Courier
Casino Windsor	IBM	Royal Bank Financial Group
Chrysler Canada	Jetware	St. James Hotel
CIBC	Levi Strauss (Canada)	Siemens Electric Ltd.
Cineplex Odeon Corporation	London Life Insurance Company	Swimware
C.N.	London Webmasters	Southam Publishing
Coldstream Products Corporation	Lotus Corporation	Star Aerospace
Falconbridge Mine	Maclean's magazine	Starbucks
Fulcrum Ltd.	MacMillan Bloedel Ltd.	Toronto Dominion Bank
GE Canada	Molson Brewery	Toronto Life Magazine/Key Publishing
The Globe and Mail	Nelvana Ltd.	Toronto Sun
General Motors of Canada	Nestle Enterprises Ltd.	Unitel
Green Shield	Newbridge Networks	VIA Rail
Hamilton Spectator	Nissan	Warner Brothers
Harbourfront Centre	North American Life Assurance	Windsor Star
Honda of Canada	Northern Telecom	
Honeywell Ltd.	Pinkerton's	

SOURCE: Abridged from EGALE 1999a

mission on Human Rights ruled that Red Lobster violated Chicago's antidiscrimination law and ordered Red Lobster to rehire Dale Hall and pay him $95 000 in back pay and damages (*Lawbriefs* 1999). In 1998, the company that owns Red Lobster filed a suit to have Chicago's antidiscrimination law overturned ("1998 in Review" 1999). Another publicized example of employment discrimination based on sexual orientation involves the case of a woman who was offered a job as a lawyer in the Georgia attorney general's office but lost the job offer after the state attorney general learned that she was planning a commitment ceremony with her lesbian partner. In January 1998, the Supreme Court decided not to hear her appeal (Greenhouse 1998). In 1998, Oklahoma passed a measure to ban homosexuals from working in public schools ("1998 in Review" 1999).

In Canada, reaction to gay and lesbian employees has shifted over time. Hostility toward gays in the workplace in the 1960s led to more than 8000 gay men being investigated by the RCMP; as a result, approximately 150 gay federal civil servants resigned or were dismissed from their employment positions without just cause. Until recently in Canada, lesbians and gays were not permitted to participate openly in the Armed Forces. In 1994, an Angus Reid and Southam News survey of 1504 Canadians reported that 81 percent believed that gays and lesbians were subject to discrimination in the workplace. Women, younger Canadians, and those who reported that they personally knew a gay man or a lesbian were particularly likely to report this belief. The survey also found that the same percentage of Canadians reported that they would either speak out in support of a lesbian or gay coworker who was facing discrimination or would be bothered by such a situation. Only 12 percent stated that they would neither be bothered nor speak out against this situation. Among those least likely to speak out or be bothered by this type of discrimination were those who claimed not to know anyone who was gay or lesbian and those who supported the Reform Party (EGALE 1994).

Table 9.3 notes the uneven protection gays and lesbians had across the Canadian provinces and territories as of November 1998. As of the time of writing, the governments of Nunavut and the Northwest Territories had yet to enact laws that protect gays and lesbians from discrimination and harassment because of sexual orientation.

Discrimination in Family Relationships

In addition to discrimination in the workplace, sexual-orientation minorities experience discrimination in policies concerning marriage, child custody and visitation, and adoption.

Same-Sex Marriage In June of 1999, the Canadian House of Commons voted overwhelmingly in favour of a motion, introduced by MP Eric Lowther, the Reform Party critic on "Children and Families," opposing same-sex marriages. The motion, which signalled the first time same-sex marriage was the subject of a vote in the House of Commons, affirmed the exclusion of gays and lesbians from the institution of marriage and committed Parliament to "take all necessary steps" to preserve legal marriage as an opposite-sex institution. Although passing the motion had no immediate legal impact, it might be presumed that as an official declaration of the Parliament's position on the matter, the "necessary steps" could include invoking the "notwithstanding" clause within the

Table 9.3	Protection of Gay and Lesbian Rights across Canada					
	Discrimination Prohibited[1]	Equal Workplace Benefits[2]	Equal Pension Benefits[3]	Medical Decisions[4]	Adoption[5]	Child/ Spousal Support Provision[6]
Federal	Yes	Yes	No	n.a.	n.a.	n.a.
Alberta	Yes	No	No	No	No	No
British Columbia	Yes	Yes	Yes	Yes	Yes	Yes
Manitoba	Yes	Yes	No	No	No	No
New Brunswick	Yes	Yes	No	No	No	No
Newfoundland	Yes	No	No	No	No	No
Nova Scotia	Yes	Yes	Yes	No	Yes	Yes
Ontario	Yes	Yes	Yes	Yes	Yes	Yes
Prince Edward Island	Yes	No	No	No	No	No
Quebec	Yes	Yes	Yes	Yes	Yes	Yes
Saskatchewan	Yes	Yes	No	No	No	No
Yukon	Yes	Yes	No	No	No	No
Northwest Territories	No	Yes	No	No	No	No

Notes: [1]Discrimination against gays and lesbians prohibited in human rights legislation

[2]Equal workplace benefits available to same-sex partners of government employees

[3]Equal pension benefits available to same-sex partners of lesbian and gay employees

[4]Medical decisions on behalf of same-sex partner who is incapacitated

[5]Adoption by same-sex couples allowed

[6]Child and spousal support provisions extended to same-sex couples

SOURCE: Adapted from EGALE. 1998. "Canada Watch: Who's Doing What? December 27 <www.egale.ca/features/watch.htm>.

Constitution that allows governments to opt out of the Charter of Rights and Freedom and to deny equality to some of their citizens, in this case, lesbians and gay men. In total, 216 MPs from all parties voted in favour of the motion, including the overwhelming majority of the Liberal caucus (all but 11), all Reform Party MPs, and a number of those from the New Democratic Party, Bloc Québécois, and Conservative Party. Only 55 MPS voted against the motion. Although it was expected that a "free vote" would be held, with MPs asked to "vote their conscience" rather than follow a party line, in the end the Liberal government adopted a government position that supported the Reform Party (EGALE 1999b).

In 1999, various provincial governments also grappled with the issues presented by same-sex marriages. In May 1999, the Supreme Court of Ontario ruled that an Ontario law that excluded gays and lesbians from a definition of common-law couples was unconstitutional. Shortly after, the Ontario government passed on omnibus bill that amended 67 of its laws to include same-sex couples. Although the Supreme Court's ruling was only binding on the Ontario government, several other provinces quickly announced plans to make similar changes. For example, in June of that year, when the Quebec National Assembly unanimously passed Bill 32, the Quebec government became the first Canadian province to ensure that same-sex couples would receive all the benefits and responsibilities of opposite-sex couples. Bill 32, which had been championed by such groups as the Coalition gaie et lesbienne du Québec, the Table de concertation des lesbiennes et des gais du Grand Montréal, and the Réseau des lesbiennes du Québec, changed the definition of "spouse" within that province and committed the Quebec government to making changes in 39 provincial laws and regulations. A month later, the British Columbia government introduced the "Definition of Spouse Amendment," which expanded the definition of "spouse" in that province to include "a person who has lived and cohabited with another person, for a period of at least 2 years immediately before the other person's death, in a 'marriage-like' relationship, including a marriage-like relationship between persons of the same gender." As in Quebec, this change sought to ensure that same-sex couples would be treated the same as opposite-sex couples in relation to such matters as, for example, wills, estates, and inheritance. In introducing the changes into law, B.C. Attorney General Ujjal Dosanjh stated that, "The legislation is proof that this government is committed to supporting stable family relationships, whether they involve traditional families, common law families, or same-sex relationships....All British Columbians deserve the same rights and benefits in life and death" (EGALE 1999d).

However, in Alberta, two laws were proposed in 1999 that gay rights groups viewed with dismay. The first, the *Constitutional Referendum Act*, would require the government to hold a province-wide referendum before it could use the notwithstanding clause that allows provinces to override the Charter of Rights and Freedoms, except in the case of same-sex marriage. The second proposed law, an amendment to the *Insurance Statute Amendment Act*, would change the definition of spouse to include common-law heterosexual couples but not gay couples (Mahoney 1999).

Advocates of same-sex marriage argue that banning same-sex marriages, or refusing to recognize same-sex marriages, denies same-sex couples the many legal and financial benefits that are granted to heterosexual married couples. For example, married couples have the right to inherit from a spouse who dies without a will; to avoid inheritance taxes between spouses; to make crucial medical decisions for a partner and take family leave to care for a partner in the event of the partner's critical injury or illness; to receive social security survivor benefits; and to include a partner in his or her health insurance coverage. Other rights bestowed to married (or once married) partners include assumption of a spouse's pension, bereavement leave, burial determination, domestic violence protection, reduced-rate memberships, divorce protections (such as equitable division of assets and visitation of children), automatic housing lease transfer, and immunity from testifying against a spouse.

Although advocates of same-sex marriage argue that as long as same-sex couples cannot be legally married, they will not be regarded as legitimate families by the larger society, opponents do not want to legitimize homosexuality as an acceptable, legitimate lifestyle. Opponents of same-sex marriage who view homosexuality as unnatural, sick, or immoral do not want their children to learn that homosexuality is an accepted "normal" lifestyle. The most common argument against same-sex marriage is that it subverts the stability and integrity of the heterosexual family. However, Sullivan (1997) suggests that homosexuals are already part of heterosexual families:

> [Homosexuals] are sons and daughters, brothers and sisters, even mothers and fathers, of heterosexuals. The distinction between "families" and "homosexuals" is, to begin with, empirically false; and the stability of existing families is closely linked to how homosexuals are treated within them. (p. 147)

Child Custody, Visitation, and Reproductive Rights Homosexual and bisexual individuals become involved in heterosexual relationships for a variety of reasons, including genuine love for a spouse, wanting to have children, family pressure to marry, and the desire to live a socially approved heterosexual lifestyle. Some individuals do not realize that they are homosexual or bisexual until after they are married.

Katherine Arnup (1995: vii), observing that an American study suggests that there are "between 3 and 8 million gay and lesbian parents in the United States, raising between 6 and 14 million children," argues that the proportions in Canada may be "equally high." Since the actual study referred to by Arnup is undated, we cannot easily or uncritically apply it to the Canadian context. In contrast to the upper-limit estimates cited by Arnup, American researchers Allen and Demo (1995: 115) note that "most researchers accept Schulenberg's (1983) estimate that at least 6 million children under age 18 have gay or lesbian parents." The editors of the *Harvard Law Review* (1990: 119) reported that "approximately three million gay men and lesbians in the United States are parents, and between eight and ten million children are raised in gay or lesbian households."

Knowing that the estimated total number of children under the age of 18 in 1985 was 62.6 million (Current Population Reports 1993: 47), the Schulenberg estimate (1985) leads to a conclusion that 9.6 percent of all children in the United States are raised in gay or lesbian households. With estimates for 1990 of a total of 64.2 million children under age 18 (Current Population Reports p. 47), the higher figures from the editors of the *Harvard Law Review* (1990) lead to a conclusion that between 12.5 and 15.6 percent of all children in the

National Data

Canadian Justice Minister Anne McLellan has repeatedly stated that Canadian law defines a marriage as a union between one man and one woman and that Ottawa has no plans to change that definition. However, when survey researchers asked a random sample of Canadians "Do you think gays and lesbians should or should not be entitled to spousal benefits?" 63 percent responded, "yes, they should," 35 percent stated, "no, they should not," and 2 percent said that they "didn't know."

SOURCE: McIlroy 1999

A 1999 Angus Reid survey of a national random sample of Canadians found that, when asked if gay couples should be able to legally married, younger Canadians were more likely to support the suggestion that older Canadians. Two-thirds of those 18 to 34 years of age versus just over half (52 percent) of those 35 to 54 and slightly less than a third (32 percent) of those 55 and older agreed with the idea of same-sex marriages. Support also varied with education; almost 6 out of 10 (59 percent) who possessed a university degree, versus 38 percent of those who had not completed high school, supported same-sex marriages.

SOURCE: EGALE 1999c

United States are raised in gay or lesbian households. With 1990 estimates of slightly over 32 million American family households with children under 18 years still living at home (Current Population Reports p. 50), the *Harvard Law Review* figure for parents suggests that 9.3 percent of all families with children are headed by gay or lesbian parents.

Census figures for 1991 indicate that we have slightly more than 6.8 million children under the age of 18 living in Canada (Statistics Canada 1992). Applying the proportional estimates derived from American data leads to a conclusion that either slightly more than 654 000 (based on the Schulenberg estimate) or between 852 000 and slightly more than one million (from the *Harvard Law Review* estimates) children in Canada are being raised in gay or lesbian households. Still assuming that we can directly apply the American estimates and knowing that approximately 4.8 million two-parent and lone-parent families in Canada have never-married sons and/or daughters of all ages still living at home (Statistics Canada 1992: 16), we could tentatively conclude that a little more than 444 000 families in our country have gay or lesbian parents.

We must stress that these estimates are tentative, based on questionable assumptions, and subject to debate. On the one hand, fear of negative repercussions may inhibit gay and lesbian couples from identifying themselves to either government or private research investigators and therefore estimates of the numbers of such couples may be too low. On the other hand, even though gays and lesbians cannot legally marry their domestic partners in Canada, nothing prevents a gay or lesbian couple from asserting on a census form that they are indeed a married couple with children. The census does not require proof of a wedding licence and creative manipulation of a domestic partner's name(s) can allow a submitted form to escape detection and challenge by the most skilled census checker. Our estimations for Canada must be based, therefore, on all married and cohabiting families, not just the seemingly more logical pool of cohabiting families only. Consequently, our estimates of the actual number of families headed by gay and lesbian parents in Canada may be too high, but they reflect the best estimates we can make today.

Estimates of the number of gays and lesbians currently raising children do not address issues such as whether currently being lesbian or gay is part of an enduring or a more recently adopted sexual orientation, nor which came first: the couple relationship and then the children, or one parent having children and then a gay or lesbian stepfamily relationship later on. It is likely that the number of lesbian parents raising children is significantly greater than the number of gay male parents for a number of reasons. On dissolution of a marriage or heterosexual cohabiting relationship, women are most likely to retain custody of any children (Laird 1993), although that custody award is by no means guaranteed if lesbianism is acknowledged.

Regardless of the actual numbers, little was known in the past about the nature of gay and lesbian family life. Until recently, most published accounts have been nonempirical and saturated with a heterosexist bias framing gay and lesbian families as thoroughly deviant or "pathological." Although publications on gay and lesbian families have expanded dramatically in the 1990s (e.g., Arnup 1995; Benkov 1994; Stone 1990; Weston 1991), generalizable information is still sparse due to nonrandom sampling, limited sample sizes, and the diversities of these families occasioned by ethnicity, class, age of parents and offspring, and circumstances leading to family formation. Of those writings that have emerged recently, Williams (1995: 98–9) notices a growing counter-tendency to "present fairy tale versions of our lives in which we are all happy individuals, partners and family members." The reality of the family lives of most gay and lesbian parents and their children presumably lies somewhere between the pathological and glowingly positive extremes depicted in current presentations.

Mainstream scholarly journals focusing on families have published virtually nothing on the family lives of gays and lesbians (Allen and Demo 1995). Since most nonempirical and empirical materials have been written with an intent to influence either public opinion or court and tribunal decision makers, authors and researchers tend to focus on and emphasize similarities between lesbian or gay families and families headed by heterosexuals (O'Brien and Weir 1995: 129). Little is known about whether sexual orientation has any meaningful impact on parenting behaviours.

At some point in their development, families with gay and lesbian parents have to deal with the stigma attached to the parents' sexual orientation by a homophobic society. Whether the strategies adopted by these parents are any different from those used by parents confronting their children with other disadvantaged statuses of ethnicity, social class, or disability is unclear. Williams (1995: 98–9) observes that for many lesbian parents, "the prospect of losing custody is never far from view" and that for all, "the threat of exposing our children to the profound homophobia that still permeates our society hovers over us" (p. ix).

In cases of divorce, openly gay, lesbian, and bisexual individuals experience discrimination in child custody and visitation rights. Judges are less apt to give a gay father sole or joint custody than to award it to a heterosexual father.

> The courts are homophobic, prejudiced, and biased against gay fathers. Two major cultural fears work against gay fathers who want full or joint custody of their children or a liberal visitation schedule. The first of these fears is that gay fathers will molest their children, and the second is that gay fathers will "recruit" their children into a gay lifestyle. (Knox 1998: 180)

Although Yogis et al. (1996: 56) have observed that "[n]othing in Canadian law stops a homosexual parent from applying for custody," they acknowledge that "the courts will often only take judicial notice (that is, recognize that it could easily be proved) of the fact that some harm might arise from living with a homosexual parent." Similarly, they note that Canadian case law suggests that "custody is awarded to discreet, non-militant homosexual parents who do not flaunt their sexual orientation" (p. 56). Thus, in *Case v. Case*, a 1974 custody case heard in Saskatchewan, the judge remarked that "I greatly fear that if these children are raised by the mother they will be too much in contact with people of abnormal tastes and proclivities." Similarly, in the 1989 case of *Saunders v. Saunders*, a judge in British Columbia denied a gay father overnight access to his child with the remark that, "Surely it cannot be argued that the exposure of a child to unnatural relationships is in the best interests of that child of tender years" (in Yogis et al. 1996: 57).

Lesbian or bisexual women may also be denied custody of their children on the sole basis of their sexual orientation, despite the fact that research shows that children of lesbian mothers are just as likely to be well-adjusted as those of heterosexual mothers (Patterson 1997; Tasker and Golombok 1997). Nevertheless,

Those Canadians who identify themselves as supporting the Bloc Québécois, the NDP, or the Liberal Party were more likely to say that gay marriages should be recognized by the state, while those who report that they are Reform and Conservative Party supporters are the least likely.

SOURCE: McIlroy 1999

In the United States, at least 21 states have granted second-parent adoptions to lesbian and gay couples to ensure that the children can enjoy the benefits of having two legal parents, especially if one parent dies or becomes incapacitated. In addition, at least 22 states allow lesbians and gay men to adopt children through state-run or private adoption agencies. Four states, New Hampshire, Florida, Colorado, and Connecticut, specifically ban gay and lesbian adoptions. In early 1998, New Jersey became the first state to set up a policy allowing same-sex (and unmarried) heterosexual couples to jointly adopt children under the same qualification standards as married couples.

SOURCES: ACLU Fact Sheet 1997; Beauvais-Godwin and Godwin 1997; "Idaho Court to Take Up First Case of Adoption by Same-Sex Couples" 1999

increasing numbers of lesbian mothers and gay fathers are fighting for and gaining custody of their children (up to 15 percent of custody awards in the United States by the mid-1980s); although formal statistics are unavailable, the same general pattern is assumed to exist in Canada (O'Brien and Weir 1995: 128).

It is also evident that although technological change may stimulate social change, the introduction of any device or set of procedures does not necessitate changed social attitudes or behaviours. For example, in 1993, a lesbian couple in Vancouver, B.C., sought treatment and were refused by the only doctor whose practice made available the artificial insemination of frozen sperm. The couple, a lawyer and a doctor, then complained to the B.C. College of Physicians and Surgeons. Their appeal was rejected in a letter stating that since "the service you sought was not urgent nor emergent" the doctor's refusal to take them as patients was justified. In drawing media attention to their experience, the couple stated that they sought to draw attention to discrimination against lesbians as potential users of the new reproductive technology. Their claims would seem valid. As the federal Royal Commission on New Reproductive Technologies reported in 1991 (p. 1081), in more than half of Canada's fertility programs (28 out of 49), "being a lesbian was probable or possible grounds for being refused artificial insemination."

Obtaining artificial insemination for one parent is by no means guaranteed in a lesbian relationship (Royal Commission on New Reproductive Technologies 1993). Gay male couples face additional difficulties finding a gestational or birth mother, and are probably less likely to be accepted as adoptive parents than are lesbian couples.

Hate Crimes against Sexual-Orientation Minorities

In eighteenth-century North America, where laws against homosexuality often included the death penalty, violence against gays and lesbians was widespread and included beatings, burnings, various kinds of torture, and execution (Button et al. 1997). Although such treatment of sexual-orientation minorities is no longer legally condoned, gays, lesbians, and bisexuals continue to be victimized by hate crimes. Surveys indicate that as many as one-fourth of lesbians and gay men report having been victims of physical attacks because of their sexual orientation (Herek 1989). A survey of more than 3000 high-school students found that students who reported having engaged in same-sex relations were more than three times as likely to report not going to school because they felt unsafe and more than twice as likely to report having been threatened or injured with a weapon at school (Faulkner and Cranston 1998). These students were also significantly more likely to report that their property was deliberately damaged or stolen at school.

Hate-motivated violence toward sexual-orientation minorities (also known as "gay-bashing") can be brutal. The following example is given in *Reaching Out: A Report on Lesbian, Gay, and Bisexual Youth Issues in Canada*, prepared for the United Church of Canada by John Fisher (1999), executive director of Equality for Gays and Lesbians Everywhere (EGALE).

> **When Christian Hernandez was 14 and a grade 9 student at Notre Dame College High School in Niagara Falls, Ontario, he screwed up his courage and told his best friend that he was gay. That was his first mistake. "He told me he couldn't accept it," recalls Hernandez. "And**

he began to spread it around." Over the next two years, Hernandez was teased and harassed almost daily. One day, a group of boys waited for him after school. Their leader had a knife, and, says Hernandez, "He told me he didn't accept faggots, that we brought AIDS into the world." The boy then cut Hernandez on the neck, putting him in the hospital for a week. When Hernandez told his parents about the attack, his father, who has since moved back to his native El Salvador, said he would "rather have a dead son than a queer son."

In recent years, the federal government has responded to such hate crimes with the passage of Bill C-41, which increased penalties for crimes motivated by hatred on certain grounds, including sexual orientation. It also launched a national initiative, the "Safe Spaces Project," funded by the federal Department of Health, to help produce educational materials for both heterosexual and lesbian and gay youth on lesbian, gay, and bisexual issues, and to create safe spaces for lesbian, gay, and bisexual youth. In Toronto, the Triangle Program offers gays who have been harassed at school an alternative place to study for up to 18 months and a curriculum that emphasizes the contributions of gays and lesbians in various fields.

CONSIDERATION

Not all victims of gay bashing are gay, lesbian, or bisexual. Victims are chosen not necessarily because they are lesbian, gay, or bisexual, but because the perpetrator perceives them to be. Therefore, "no one is safe from hate crimes and…it is in everyone's interest to stop this epidemic of hate" (National Coalition of Anti-Violence Programs 1998: 4).

STRATEGIES FOR ACTION: REDUCING ANTIGAY PREJUDICE AND DISCRIMINATION

Many of the efforts to change policies and attitudes regarding sexual-orientation minorities have been spearheaded by organizations such as the Equality for Gays and Lesbians Everywhere (EGALE), Canada's only national equality rights organization advocating for lesbians, gays, and bisexuals with members in every province and territory; Parents, Family, and Friends of Lesbians and Gays (PFLAG); the Foundation for Equal Families (FFEF); Victoria Youth Pride Society; Pink Triangle Services Youth Group in Ottawa; Lesbian and Gay Health Services in Saskatoon; and the British Columbia Civil Liberties Association. These organizations are politically active in their efforts to achieve equal rights for gays, lesbians, and bisexuals. For example, the mandate of the Foundation for Equal Families is to achieve equality and recognition of same-sex relationships and associated family rights through legal action and education. In January 1999, the Foundation launched an omnibus challenge of 58 federal laws affecting the rights of lesbian and gay couples. The omnibus challenge affected laws as diverse as the *Income Tax Act,* the *Canadian Pension Plan Act*, the *Criminal Code*, the *Immigration Act*, the *Evidence Act,* the *Judges' Act,* the *Old Age Security Act,* the *Veterans Allowance Act,* and the Royal Canadian Mounted Police's *Superannuation Act.* Under the current *Immigration Act,* for example, heterosexual couples could bring their spouses into Canada while

According to an independent survey conducted for the B.C. Teacher's Foundation, 73 percent of the parent respondents in British Columbia favoured the teaching of tolerance of homosexuality in schools.

SOURCE: Fisher 1999

same-sex couples could not, except when permission was obtained on "compassionate grounds."

The gay rights movement is also active in promoting HIV/AIDS research, adequate health care for AIDS victims, and the rights of HIV-infected individuals. Other target areas include providing programs and services for gay and lesbian students.

Next, we highlight some of the strategies for reducing and responding to prejudice and discrimination toward sexual-orientation minorities.

Politics and the Gay Rights Movement

Barney Frank (1997), an openly gay U.S. representative, emphasizes the importance of political participation in influencing social outcomes. He notes that demonstrative and cultural expressions of gay activism, such as "gay pride" celebrations, marches, demonstrations, or other cultural activities promoting gay rights are important in organizing gay activists. However, Frank notes:

> Too many people have seen the cultural activity as a substitute for democratic political participation. In too many cases over the past decades we have left the political arena to our most dedicated opponents [of gay rights], whose letter writing, phone calling, and lobbying have easily triumphed over our marching, demonstrating, and dancing. The most important lesson...is that politics—conventional, boring, but essential politics—will ultimately have a major impact on the extent to which we can rid our lives of prejudice. (1997: xi)

In Canada, the various political parties have shown different levels of support for gay rights issues. For example, despite a caucus of 175 members, no Member of Parliament who is a Liberal has identified himself or herself as gay, lesbian, or bisexual and some, such as Roseanne Stoke and Tom Wappel, have shown a willingness to consistently refer to homosexuality as "unnatural," "immoral," and a "perversion." The Prime Minister, in turn, when confronted with such reactions by members of his party has only seen fit to comment that, "We give our members the freedom to express themselves." In the Bloc Québécois, Réal Ménard is the only openly gay Member of Parliament but the party has, to date, voted consistently in favour of gay rights' issues. In the NDP, another openly gay MP, Svend Robinson, has also consistently demonstrated strong support for lesbian and gay equality, as has the leader of the federal New Democratic Party. In contrast, members of the Reform Party have almost invariably voted against bills seeking to advance the rights of lesbians and gays. Reform MP Bob Ringma has argued that it should be acceptable for businesses to fire gay (or Black) employees or relegate them "to the back of the shop" to placate bigoted customers—and his position was endorsed by other Reform MPs such as Myron Thompson and Leon Benoit. Reform MP Dave Chatters also maintains that "it's in the interest of society to have the right to discriminate against" gays and lesbians (*Toronto Star* 1996).

Although in the late 1990s Winnipeg elected its first openly gay mayor, Glen Murray, it would seem presumptuous to suppose that the issue of a candidate's sexual orientation is not considered relevant by at least some voters. It seems undeniable that the Christian right, religious and church groups, conservative family groups, and other conservative organizations and their political allies will continue to crusade against gay rights. Nevertheless, opposition groups are up against an increasingly powerful progay rights movement.

Educational Strategies: Policies and Programs in the Schools

In the United States, a survey of more than 3000 high-school students also found that students who reported having had same-sex relations were twice as likely to have attempted suicide at least once in the past year (Faulkner and Cranston 1998). Students reporting same-sex behaviour were also more likely to report heavy drinking and regular use of marijuana, cocaine, and other illegal drugs; to report being victimized by hate crimes; and more than three times as likely to report not going to school because they felt unsafe. To like effect, recent research conducted in Calgary reported that gay and bisexual males were "almost 14 times more likely to have made a serious suicide attempt at some point in their lives than their heterosexually oriented counterparts" and that lesbian, gay, and bisexual youth of colour were dramatically overrepresented in attempted suicide statistics. According to one of the authors of this research, Pierre Tremblay, "This is the fallout of living with no guidance and no support. It's a problem every teacher knows about, but too often the attitude is, 'we would like to help, but we don't want to promote homosexuality.' It is a total abdication" (in Fisher 1999).

All of these findings suggest that if schools are to promote the health and well-being of all students, they must address the needs of gay, lesbian, and bisexual youth and promote acceptance of sexual orientation diversity within the school setting. Otherwise, students will continue to experience the harassment and rejection—which can lead to violence, substance abuse, and suicide—reflected in the examples in this chapter's The Human Side feature. In Canada, it would seem that at least some schools are heading the message. For example, in February 1997, the Calgary board of education approved an "Action Plan on Gay/Lesbian/Bisexual Youth and Staff Safety" that requires guidance counsellors to provide "comprehensive information to students" when discussing sexual orientation and to "encourage students to discuss the issue with their parents." Several Canadian school boards and teaching institutes have adopted policies or initiatives that promote the equal treatment of gays and lesbians. For example, the Vancouver School Board's Statement of Mission and Beliefs states that, "We believe in equitable treatment for all individuals, regardless of race, culture, gender, religion, socioeconomic status, sexual orientation or physical or mental ability."

In December 1998, in a landmark case, a Canadian court was asked to rule for the first time on whether a school board could exclude from the curriculum books that have content depicting same-sex families. Controversy arose when three books were banned by the school board: *Asha's Mum*, because one character in the story tells a classmate that it is not wrong to have two mothers "if they're nice to you and you like them"; *One Dad, Two Dads, Brown Dads, Blue Dads*, because its dedication reads, "To Jacob who has only one mom and one dad" and, in small letters, "But don't feel sorry for him—They are both pretty great parents"; and *Belinda's Bouquet*, described as the "most neutral [of the three books] in its depiction of gays and lesbians" (Joyce 1998). None of the three books explicitly defines the relationship that exists between the two parental figures nor do the words "gays," "lesbian," "homosexual," or "sex" appear in them. However, while the school board did not object to housing the books within school libraries, they did ban them from classroom settings. In response, two homosexual teachers, supported by a group of parents, appealed the decision of the school board.

In her 44-page judgment that overturned the ban, Madam Justice Saunders of the B.C. Supreme Court ruled that the boards must reconsider the books it banned kindergarten and grade one students from reading and wrote that her decision was based "upon a very old provision of the *School Act* prohibiting religion or overt religious interference in the conduct of schools." The Act says, in part, "all schools and provincial schools must be constructed on strictly secular and non-sectarian principles." The decision of Madam Justice Saunders found that the school board in Surrey had given "significant weight" to "personal and parental concerns that the books would conflict with religious views, contrary to the Act." The Minister of Education in B.C., Paul Ramsey, said that the court's decision "sends a very positive signal to those in Surrey and throughout the province who want schools to be inclusive and tolerant places for all our children" (EGALE 1998).

One strategy for promoting tolerance for diversity among students involves establishing and enforcing a school policy prohibiting antigay behaviour. Another strategy for addressing the needs of homosexual and bisexual youth is having school-based support groups. Such groups can help students increase self-esteem, overcome their sense of isolation, provide information and resources, and provide a resource for parents.

In-service training for teachers and other staff is important and may include examining the effects of antigay bias, dispelling myths about homosexuality, and brainstorming ways to create a more inclusive environment (Mathison 1998). However, most public schools offer little to no support and education regarding sexual-orientation diversity. Most schools have no support groups or special counselling services for gay and lesbian youth, and the majority of schools do not have any policies prohibiting antigay harassment (Button et al. 1997).

Campus Policies Regarding Homosexuality

Student groups have been active in the gay liberation movement since the 1960s. Numerous gay student groups are organized in community colleges and universities across Canada.

D'Emilio (1990) suggests that colleges and universities have the ability and the responsibility to promote gay rights and social acceptance of homosexual people:

> For reasons that I cannot quite fathom, I still expect the academy to embrace higher standards of civility, decency, and justice than the society around it. Having been granted the extraordinary privilege of thinking critically as a way of life, we should be astute enough to recognize when a group of people is being systematically mistreated. We have the intelligence to devise solutions to problems that appear in our community. I expect us also to have the courage to lead rather than follow. (p. 18)

VOICES OF GAY AND LESBIAN YOUTH IN SCHOOL

The following excerpts describe the experiences of gay, lesbian, and bisexual youth in the school setting (cited in Button et al. 1997: 140–1; Mathison 1998: 3–4).

I was repeatedly tripped—everyday—in my classrooms. When students tripped me, they would call me "faggot," "pussy," etc. Nearly everyday, someone would push up against me. Out of eight teachers, I had only one teacher who would intervene in these antigay incidents. (16-year-old male)

I had a history teacher tell me that I couldn't come to class because I was gay....She wanted me out of there. Teachers would often gossip and make antigay hand motions....I expected teachers to help me out and to protect me—not to be the main ones to ridicule me. (17-year-old male)

One health teacher tells her students that homosexuality is wrong and evil. The other health teachers avoid the subject when teaching sex education. Almost all of my teachers have at one point in the year made some kind of joke about

homosexuals or have made a derogatory comment. Some do it on a regular basis. (female high-school student)

In my school, out of 2000 students, I only knew five other gay students. I felt very isolated, very alone, and I had no one I could turn to for support. (18-year-old female)

I felt like I didn't belong anymore. I felt like I was a small child in a sea of hate and that people didn't know me; they only knew of my sexual preference for women. (18-year-old female)

There were these junior bikers that just talked about how they were going to beat up fags whenever they found them...and I would just be listening to it and every now and then they would try to include me in their conversation. I would go "ah, well, you know, I just live and let live." And then they say, "I hear a wimp," and I hated being there because they would try to drag me down a road I didn't wanna go. If only they knew. (Juan)

Among the policies colleges and universities might adopt to meet this challenge are the following:

- develop outreach programs to provide support for victims of harassment and violence
- provide training of local law enforcement personnel in lesbian and gay issues
- create institutional policies that clearly affirm the unacceptability of discrimination on the basis of sexual orientation

As both functionalists and conflict theorists note, alternatives to a heterosexual lifestyle are threatening because for they challenge traditional definitions of family, childrearing, and gender roles. The result is economic, social, and legal discrimination by the majority. Gay, lesbian, and bisexual individuals are also victimized by hate crimes. In some countries, homosexuality is formally sanctioned, with penalties ranging from fines to imprisonment and even death.

In the past, homosexuality was thought to be a consequence of some psychological disturbance. More recently, some evidence suggests that homosexuality, like handedness, may have a biological component. The debate between biological and social explanations is commonly referred to as the "nature versus nurture" debate. Research indicates that both forces affect sexual orientation, although debate over which is dominant continues. Sociologists are interested in society's response to sexual-orientation diversity and how that response affects the quality of life of society's members. Because individuals' views toward homosexuality are related to their beliefs about what "causes" it, the question of the origins of sexual-orientation diversity has sociological significance.

Prejudice and discrimination toward sexual-orientation minorities are rooted in various aspects of culture, such as religious views, rigid gender roles, and negative myths and stereotypes. Hate crimes against homosexuals and bisexuals are blatant examples of the discrimination that sexual orientation minorities continue to experience.

The gay rights movement has made significant gains in the last few decades and has suffered losses and defeat due to gay rights opposition groups and politicians. Politicians, religious leaders, courts, and educators will continue to make decisions that either promote the well-being of sexual-orientation minorities or hinder it. Ultimately, however, each individual must decide to embrace either an inclusive or an exclusive ideology; collectively, those individual decisions will determine the future treatment of sexual-orientation minorities in Canada.

CRITICAL THINKING

1. How do you think the legalization of same-sex marriages in Canada would affect public attitudes toward homosexuals?
2. Through the use of the Internet, sexual-orientation minorities today can readily gain access to support organizations and networks. How do you think this use of the Internet has affected the gay rights movement?
3. How is the homosexual population similar to and different from other minority groups?
4. Do you think that social acceptance of homosexuality leads to the creation of laws that protect lesbians and gays? Or does the enactment of laws that protect lesbians and gays help to create more social acceptance of gays?

KEY TERMS

biphobia	heterosexuality	master status
bisexuality	homophobia	sexual orientation
heterosexism	homosexuality	sodomy laws

Section 3

Problems of Inequality and Power

The story of Harrison Bergeron is set in a futuristic society where absolute equality is rigidly enforced (Vonnegut 1968). If people can run faster, they must wear weights in their shoes; if they are brighter, disruptive transistors are implanted in their brains; if they have better vision, blinders are placed over their eyes. The point of the story is that equality, although a cultural ideal, in reality is not always the optimal way to live. The quality of life becomes so unbearable for Harrison Bergeron that he decides that it is better to commit one courageous act of grace and beauty and be killed than to live in a society where everyone is equal.

Differences between people in and of themselves are not what is meant by inequality as a social problem, for few would want to live in a society where everyone was the same. Rather, problems of inequality concern inequities in the quality of life—between the haves and the have-nots (Chapter 10).

Social inequality affects the opportunity to work and prosper (Chapter 11) and to attend quality schools (Chapter 12).

The chapters in Section 3—"The Haves and the Have-Nots," "Work and Unemployment" and "Problems in Education"—are highly interrelated and speak to the need for examining both the cultural and the structural underpinnings of the social problems described. Further, all three of the sociological perspectives, structural-functionalism, conflict theory, and symbolic interactionism, are used to understand various aspects of the three problem areas discussed.

CHAPTER TEN

The Haves and the Have-Nots

Is It True?

1. Canada has the lowest poverty rate of all industrialized nations.
2. About a quarter of the world's population live in dire poverty.
3. Unmarried teenagers make up most of the single-parent mothers on welfare.
4. Many single-parent mothers have many kids to boost their welfare cheques.
5. The age group with the highest poverty rate in Canada are individuals aged 65 and older.

Answers: 1 = F, 2 = T, 3 = F, 4 = F, 5 = F

T he blockbuster success of the 1997 film *Titanic* depicted how the luxury liner divided passengers into the "haves" and the "have-nots." Scenes of lower-deck passengers standing in water behind locked gates emphasized the fatal consequences of not having the resources to afford first-class passage and lifeboat access. Of the 1500 who died in the icy waters of the Atlantic, most were from the lower decks.

Despite the fact that Canada is a nation of wealth, our society is characterized by persistent economic inequalities that divide the population into haves and have-nots. This chapter examines the extent of poverty globally and in Canada, focusing on the consequences of poverty for individuals, families, and societies. Theories of poverty and economic inequality are presented and strategies for rectifying economic inequality and poverty are considered.

THE GLOBAL CONTEXT: POVERTY AND ECONOMIC INEQUALITY AROUND THE WORLD

Who are the poor? Are rates of world poverty increasing, decreasing, or remaining stable? The answers depend on how we define and measure poverty.

Defining and Measuring Poverty

Poverty can be loosely defined as lacking resources for an "adequate" standard of living. Some sociologists make a distinction between absolute poverty and relative poverty. **Absolute poverty** is characterized by the lack of the basic necessities of life, such as food, clean water, and housing. **Relative poverty** refers to having a deficiency in material and economic resources compared with some other population. However, even absolute poverty is, to some degree, relative, because standards for adequacy vary among and within societies and change across time. Thus, there is no universally accepted objective definition of poverty. Although starvation may be globally accepted as an indicator of poverty, other living conditions are not widely agreed on as indicators of poverty. For example, while living in a hut without indoor plumbing and electricity may be an indicator of poverty in Canada, such living conditions are considered normal and adequate among certain populations in less developed countries. In less developed countries where large segments of the population die of starvation and infectious diseases, poverty is equated with living on the brink of survival. Yet, the 19.8 percent of Canadians who were classified as living in poverty in 1997 did not face starvation, though many had inadequate diets. Similarly, if poverty is defined solely with reference to income, "Old Order Mennonites in southern Ontario or Hutterites in Western Canada may be called poor, even though their incomes reflect religious faith more than economics. Other Canadians have low taxable incomes only because they take full advantage of the tax guidelines" (Statistics Canada 1998a).

Various measures of poverty are used by governments, researchers, and organizations. Next, we discuss ways in which poverty is measured throughout the world and in Canada.

The World Bank sets a "poverty threshold" at $1 a day to compare poverty in most of the developing world, labelling population groups with a per capita income above $1 a day as "nonpoor."

A poverty line of $2 a day is often used for Latin America and the Caribbean; $4 a day in Eastern Europe and the Commonwealth of Independent States (CIS); and $14.40 a day in industrial countries. Another poverty measure used by the World Health Organization (WHO) is based on a household's ability to meet the minimum calorie requirements of its members. According to this poverty measure, a household is considered poor if it cannot meet 80 percent of the minimum calorie requirements (established by WHO), even when using 80 percent of its income to buy food.

In industrial countries, national poverty lines are sometimes based on the median household income of a country's population. According to this relative poverty measure, members of a household are considered poor if their household income is less than 50 percent of the median household income in that country.

In the *Human Development Report 1997*, the United Nations Development Programme proposes a new composite measure of poverty: the **Human Poverty Index (HPI).** Rather than measure poverty by income, three measures of deprivation are combined to yield the Human Poverty Index: (1) deprivation of life, which is measured by the percentage of people expected to die before the age of 40, (2) deprivation of knowledge, which is measured by the percentage of adults who are illiterate, and (3) deprivation in living standards, which is measured as a composite of three variables: the percentage of people without access to health services, the percentage of people without access to safe water, and the percentage of malnourished children under the age of five. The Human Poverty Index is a useful complement to income measures of poverty and "will serve as a strong reminder that eradicating poverty will always require more than increasing the income of the poorest" (*Human Development Report* 1997: 19).

Canadian Measures of Poverty

Statistics Canada developed the **low-income cutoff (LICO)** as a measure of poverty in 1968. Estimating that poor families or individuals spent approximately 34.7 percent or more of their pre-tax income on such basic needs as food, shelter, and clothing, they then added 20 percentage points to determine the cutoff. In consequence, it was arbitrarily established as a standard that families or individuals who spent 54.7 percent of their pre-tax income on food, clothing, and shelter would be in financial difficulty. Recognizing that the minimum income level necessary to avoid financial hardship also varies according to changes in the cost of living, family size, and place of residence, Statistics Canada calculates different low-income cutoffs for different communities and for families of varying sizes within these communities. For example, in 1997, the low-income cutoff for a family of four living in an urban area with a population of half a million or more was $33 063. For a family of four living in a rural area, it was $22 877. Table 10.1 provides the minimum income levels established by Statistics Canada to indicate low income in 1997.

Table 10.1 **Low Income in Canada, 1997[1]**

Family size[2]	< 30 000	Population 30 000 to 99 999	100 000 to 499 999	500 000+	Rural Areas
1 person	$13 924	$14 965	$15 070	$17 571	$12 142
2 persons	17 405	18 706	18 837	21 962	15 178
3 persons	21 647	23 264	23 429	27 315	18 877
4 persons	26 205	28 162	28 359	30 063	22 877
5 persons	29 293	31 481	31 701	36 958	25 542
6 persons	32 379	34 798	35 043	40 855	28 235
7+ persons	35 467	38 117	38 385	44 751	30 928

Notes:
[1] 1992 base
[2] Does not distinguish between adults and children as family members

SOURCE: Statistics Canada 1997

Poverty lines might be drawn in several other ways. For example, the poverty line established by a special Senate committee on poverty used posttax or disposable income. This method produces a poverty line that is set at approximately 56 percent of the level of average Canadian family income. If family needs were considered after taxes (Table 10.2), the poverty rate in 1997 would be 15.8 instead of 19.8. Another way of measuring poverty is by employing the "market basket measure"—a measure that Human Resources Development Canada has been developing at the request of the federal and provincial governments. This measure is based on the concept of "necessaries" as defined by the eighteenth-century economist Adam Smith: "Whatever the custom of the country renders it indecent for creditable people, even of the lowest order, to be without." While the market basket concept is used by the provinces to set welfare rates, defining what, exactly, are "necessaries" is not easy. The concept, as used by Smith, implies that necessaries are broader than what is needed for mere subsistence.

Another way of defining low income or the "poverty line" is to employ the **Low-Income Measure (LIM)**. To assess low income using this measure, Statistics Canada has established a figure for the needs of one adult and proceeded on the assumption that family needs increase in proportion to the size of the family, with each additional adult increasing the family needs by 40 percent of the first adult and each additional child increasing the family's needs by 30 percent. To calculate how many Canadians, individuals, or family members,

Table 10.2 **The Low-Income Cutoff, after Tax, 1997**

	Population 500 000+	100 000 to 499 999	30 000 to 99 999	<30 000	Rural areas
Two-person family	$17 542	$14 776	$14 547	$13 294	$11 501
Four-person family	$27 633	$23 277	$22 916	$20 941	$18 117

SOURCE: Statistics Canada 1997

lack sufficient income to cover their basic needs for food, clothing, shelter, and other necessities, Statistics Canada compares these income figures with the actual incomes of families and individuals.

It is evident that estimating the numbers of Canadians who are poor is no simple task. Consider as well that research conducted by the Survey of Labour and Income Dynamics reports that the poor are not a "static underclass of the permanently destitute" (Coyne 1997) and that there is considerable movement in and out of low income. For example, analysis of longitudinal data from the Survey of Labour and Income Dynamics (SLID) reveals that only a slight majority of those Canadians who experience low income remain below the low-income threshold for two years in a row. Of the 4.4 million Canadians who had incomes below the LICO in either 1993 or 1994, only 52 percent (2.3 million) had low incomes in both years. Although a second Canadian study did not use the LICO measurement of poverty and opted instead to use the Low Income Measure (LIM), it also reported that "roughly 60 percent of low income Canadians under age 65 are only temporarily living in straitened economic circumstances. They quickly exited the current spell of low income and were not likely to repeat it" (Laroche 1998: 24). However, as Coyne (1997) observes, the results of such research "prove" different things to different groups: "Aha, said the right, proof that the numbers of the poor have been grossly overstated....Aha, said the left, that means the poor are not trapped in their present state, either by their own sloth or by the welfare system. The whole campaign to reform social assistance has been a cruel waste of time."

The writings of Christopher Sarlo (1992, 1996) have repeatedly drawn attention to what he perceives to be the inadequacies of employing the LICO as a measure of poverty in Canada. For example, he notes that the LICO does not include benefits in kind, or capital gains, or, of course, unreported income. Sarlo additionally claims that "of all households below the LICO in 1990, almost one in five owned their homes, mortgage free...97 percent, had colour television...53 percent owned a car—the same rate as for those above the poverty line" (in Coyne 1997). According to Sarlo, "poverty, as it has been traditionally understood, has been virtually eliminated" (1992: 2). However, this claim is based on the assumptions that nonnutritious consumables such as coffee, ketchup, and jam are unnecessary, that $245 a year is sufficient to provide an individual with a year's supply of clothing and footwear, and that hairdressing services can be adequately performed by family members on each other. For those who experience trouble with their vision or experience toothaches, Sarlo "assumes that dental societies will provide free dental services to low-income families and that Lions Clubs will provide free eyeglasses" (Krahn 1994: 2.8).

Ross et al. (1994) emphasize that, in employing the LICO "Statistics Canada does not claim to measure poverty; rather, it defines a set of income cutoffs below which people may be said to live in straitened circumstances." However, as we have noted, the way in which poverty is defined does have serious practical consequences—it determines who will receive help and who will not and, what types of social policies and programs are thought necessary.

The Extent of Global Poverty and Economic Inequality

Economic and social progress in recent decades has eliminated mass poverty in economically advanced countries and significantly reduced poverty in many developing countries. The 1997 Report on the World Social Situation notes that "infant mortality has fallen almost steadily in all regions and life expectancy has risen all over the globe. Educational attainment is rising, health care and living conditions are improving in most countries, and the quantity, quality, and range of goods and services available to a large majority of the world's population is increasing" (*Human Development Report* 1997: 80). The report goes on to say that "not everyone has shared in this prosperity. Economic growth has been slow or non-existent in many of the world's poorest countries....The plight of the poor stands in stark contrast to the rising standards of living enjoyed by those favoured by growing abundance" (p. 80).

For those living in a wealthy nation such as Canada, it may be difficult to imagine the depth and scope of poverty in many less developed countries throughout the world. According to the *Human Development Report 1997*, about one-third of the population living in developing countries—1.3 billion people—live on incomes of less than $1 a day.

South Asia has the most people affected by poverty; sub-Saharan Africa has the highest proportion of people in poverty. In 2000, an estimated half of people in sub-Saharan Africa will be living in poverty. Eastern Europe and the countries of the Commonwealth of Independent States have experienced the greatest increase in poverty in the last decade. In that period, the proportion of people living in poverty grew from a small part of the population to about a third. Between 1992 and 1998, the average Russian household lost more than one-half of its income, and the male life expectancy dropped from 65.5 years to 57 years (Weisbrot 1998).

Poverty also affects industrial countries, where 100 million people live below the income poverty line (set at half the individual median income). More than 37 million are jobless, and more than five million people in industrialized countries are homeless (*Human Development Report* 1997).

Globally, income inequality has increased, widening the gap between the haves and the have-nots. In 1960, the ratio of the income of the richest 20 percent of the world to that of the poorest 20 percent was 30 to 1. In 1994, this ratio had increased to 78 to 1 (*Human Development Report* 1997).

SOCIOLOGICAL THEORIES OF POVERTY AND ECONOMIC INEQUALITY

The three main theoretical perspectives in sociology—structural-functionalism, conflict theory, and symbolic interactionism—offer insights into the nature, causes, and consequences of poverty and economic inequality.

Structural-Functionalist Perspective

According to the structural-functionalist perspective, poverty and economic inequality serve a number of positive functions for society. Decades ago, Davis and Moore (1945) argued that because the various occupational roles in society require different levels of ability, expertise, and knowledge, an unequal economic reward system helps to ensure that the person who performs a particular role is the most qualified. As people acquire certain levels of expertise (e.g., B.A., M.A., Ph.D., M.D.), they are progressively rewarded. Such a system, argued Davis and Moore, motivates people to achieve by offering higher rewards for

International Data

The World Bank estimates that about a quarter of the world's population live in dire poverty.

SOURCE: *Human Development Report* 1997

International Data

In 1997, the poorest 20 percent of the world's people accounted for a meagre 1.1 percent of global income, down from 1.4 percent in 1991 and 2.3 percent in 1960.

SOURCE: *Human Development Report* 1997

higher achievements. If physicians were not offered high salaries, for example, who would want to endure the arduous years of medical training and long, stressful hours at a hospital?

The structural-functionalist view of poverty suggests that a certain amount of poverty has positive functions for society. Although poor people are often viewed as a burden to society, having a pool of low-paid, impoverished workers ensures that there will be people willing to do dirty, dangerous, and difficult work that others refuse to do. Poverty also provides employment for those who work in the "poverty industry" (such as welfare workers) and supplies a market for inferior goods such as older, dilapidated homes and automobiles (Gans 1972).

The structural-functionalist view of poverty and economic inequality has received a great deal of criticism from contemporary sociologists, who point out that many important occupational roles (such as childcare workers) are poorly paid, whereas many individuals in nonessential roles (such as professional sports stars and entertainers) earn astronomical sums of money. Functionalism also accepts poverty as unavoidable and ignores the role of inheritance in the distribution of rewards.

Conflict Perspective

Conflict theorists regard economic inequality as resulting from the domination of the **bourgeoisie** (owners of the means of production) over the **proletariat** (workers). The bourgeoisie accumulate wealth as they profit from the labour of the proletariat, who earn wages far below the earnings of the bourgeoisie. The educational institution furthers the ideals of capitalism by perpetuating the belief in equal opportunity and the value of the work ethic. The proletariat, dependent on the capitalistic system, continue to be exploited by the wealthy and accept the belief that poverty is a consequence of personal failure rather than of a flawed economic structure.

Conflict theorists pay attention to how laws and policies benefit the wealthy and contribute to the gap between the haves and the have-nots. Laws and policies that favour the rich—sometimes referred to as **wealthfare** or **corporate welfare**—include low-interest government loans to failing businesses, special subsidies and tax breaks to corporations, and other laws and policies that benefit corporations and the wealthy. For example, Barlow and Campbell (1995: 174–5) point out that, according to a Department of Finance document, corporate "tax breaks" or "loopholes" that cost the Canadian treasury roughly $90 billion in 1993 alone have remained largely unplugged. "Businesses are still permitted to deduct from the money they owe in taxes 20 percent of their expenses for meals and entertainment—such as luxury boxes at the Skydome and escort services—from their taxable income." Closing this loophole, they observe, would generate as much as $500 million a year to the federal treasury. They also note that corporations are permitted to deduct one-quarter of all capital gains from their taxable income—a loophole that diverts over $400 million annually from government coffers—while "the same tax break for individuals costs another $700 million a year." In addition, "generous tax subsidies to oil and gas companies for their exploration and development costs" divert half a billion a year from Canada's treasury. As they observe,

> **So many tax loopholes are available to corporations that each year tens of thousands of profitable companies pay not a penny in income**

taxes. The result is that corporate income tax paid in Canada is in the bottom half of industrialized countries....Canada has the second worst record in the industrialized world (after Australia) for taxing wealth, making it a tax haven for wealthy individuals. (175–6)

A 1998 *Time* magazine series of special reports on corporate welfare also gave visibility to this issue. In one report, *Time* revealed that between 1990 and 1997, Seaboard Corporation, an agribusiness corporate giant, received at least $150 million in economic incentives from federal, state, and local governments to build and staff poultry- and hog-processing plants in the United States, support its operations in foreign countries, and sell its products (Barlett and Steele 1998). Taxpayers picked up the tab not just for the corporate welfare, but also for the costs of new classrooms and teachers (for schooling the children of Seaboard's employees, many of whom are immigrants), homelessness (due to the inability of Seaboard's low-paid employees to afford housing), and dwindling property values resulting from smells of hog waste and rotting hog carcasses in areas surrounding Seaboard's hog plants. Meanwhile, wealthy investors in Seaboard have earned millions in increased stock values.

Barlow and Campbell (1995: 175) also point out that corporations are able to exert political influence through the efforts of those who are paid to lobby on their behalf. "Lobbying," they observe, "has become a booming business in Ottawa—estimated at $100 million a year." Here again, Canada's tax laws function in a way that benefits the wealthy and increases economic inequality. Our current tax laws allow corporations "to deduct from their taxable income the costs for hiring lobbyists to influence policy to their advantage." Despite promises by the Liberal government to "restore integrity and democracy to government by reigning in the lobbyists...neither the budget nor subsequent legislation requires lobbyists to disclose their fees or eliminates this tax subsidy, which is costing the treasury at least $50 million a year."

In Canada, the *Lobbyists Registration Act* demands full disclosure from anyone who is employed by a company to try to influence policy or "the awarding of any grant, contribution or other benefit" from the government, and is intended to reveal who wields political influence. The registry, which identifies who lobbies for whom and on what subject, is open to public inspection. However, lax wording in the regulations allow at least some companies to remain invisible. For example, in 1998, of the 15 companies awarded more than $1 million from Technology Partnerships Canada—a $250-million-a-year federal subsidy fund that is largely geared to aerospace research and development—only seven were registered as employing lobbyists to secure TPC investments. Among those that did not register were "the Canadian branches of some global aerospace heavyweights...[such as] U.S. giant Raytheon's subsidiary in Waterloo, Ont., which got $3.3 million, and the Montreal operations of Europe's Sextant Avionique, awarded $9.9 million" (*Maclean's* 1999a). While negotiating for TPC is noted to be a "very time-consuming" process, companies can take advantage of a loophole in the law that states that only those full-time employees whose lobbying efforts occupy a "significant part" of their job are required to register. Companies claiming that such efforts on the part of their employees do not absorb a "significant part" of their employees' time are allowed to remain in the shadows.

Conflict theorists also note that throughout the world, "free-market" economic reform policies have been hailed as a solution to poverty. Yet, while such

National Data

According to the Canadian Centre for Policy Alternatives, between 1994 and 1999, federal handouts to businesses topped $14 billion.

SOURCE: Canadian Centre for Policy Alternatives Monitor 1999

economic reform has benefited many wealthy corporations and investors, it has also resulted in increasing levels of global poverty. As companies relocate to countries with abundant supplies of cheap labour, wages decline. Lower wages lead to decreased consumer spending, which leads to more industries closing plants, going bankrupt, or laying off workers (downsizing). This results in higher unemployment rates and a surplus of workers, enabling employers to lower wages even more. Chossudovsky (1998) suggests that "this new international economic order feeds on human poverty and cheap labour" (p. 299). Yet, the increasing levels of global poverty are masked by World Bank poverty statistics that, according to Chossudovsky, "blatantly misrepresent...the seriousness of global poverty" in order to portray a positive view of free-market reform policies (p. 298).

Symbolic Interactionist Perspective

Symbolic interactionism focuses on how meanings, labels, and definitions affect and are affected by social life. This view calls attention to ways in which wealth and poverty are defined and the consequences of being labelled as "poor." Individuals who are viewed as poor—especially those receiving public assistance (i.e., welfare)—are often stigmatized as lazy, irresponsible, and lacking in abilities, motivation, and moral values. Wealthy individuals tend to be viewed as capable, motivated, hard working, and deserving of their wealth.

Such stereotypes are potent. Consider, in this context, the formation of the United Council on Welfare Fraud (UCOWF), an international organization containing about 2000 individuals from the United States and Canada "who have combined their efforts to fight fraud, waste and abuse in social service programs" and whose primary focus is "the detection, elimination and prosecution of those who fraudulently obtain government benefits" (United Council on Welfare Fraud 2000). The phrase "poor but honest" in itself suggests that we view honesty and low income as an unlikely combination and must single out those who are both as exceptions to the rule.

However, the divide suggested by stereotypes of the wealthy and the poor may be far more apparent than real. For example, according to a 1996 *Financial Post* and COMPAS poll, 77 percent of Canadians say that they would cheat on their taxes if they could avoid detection (Fennell 1996). This chapter's The Human Side focuses on the tax-evading strategies of the wealthy. As you read, consider the different meanings associated with the actions of the wealthy and the poor in our society.

As noted earlier, definitions of wealth and poverty vary across societies and across time. For example, the Dinka are the largest ethnic group in the sub-Saharan African country of Sudan. By global standards, the Dinka are among the poorest of the poor, being among the least modernized peoples of the world. In the Dinka culture, wealth is measured in large part according to how many cattle a person owns. To the Dinka, cattle have a social, moral, and spiritual value, as well as an economic value. In Dinka culture, a man pays an average "bridewealth" of 50 cows to the family of his bride. Thus, men use cattle to obtain a wife to beget children, especially sons, to ensure the continuity of their ancestral lineage and, according to Dinka religious beliefs, their link with God. Although modernized populations might label the Dinka as poor, the Dinka view themselves as wealthy. As one Dinka elder explained, "It is for cattle that we are admired, we, the Dinka....All over the world, people

DODGING THE TAX MAN: CANADIANS AND TAX HAVENS

Although tax havens were once the sole preserve of the super-rich who transferred billions of dollars to off-shore jurisdictions, they have been democratized and [have] gone down-market. That may in part be due to the example set by famous expatriates who have settled in glamorous offshore tax havens: Grand Cayman boasts, among others, John Felderhoof of Bre-X infamy, while the Bahamas is home to Canadian fashion designer Peter Nygard and best-selling Canadian author Arthur Hailey. Now, average folks who have paid off their houses, maxed out their RRSPs, sold a small business or simply have some extra cash want in on the action. Among the favourite vehicles, or "structures," as they are known: offshore investment funds; hard-to-track companies known as IBCs (for international business corporation), which are usually used for trading stocks but camouflage ownership; and non-resident trusts, which shelter income and, on the face of it, are administered by an offshore trustee.

There is just one catch. While investing offshore is not in itself illegal, moving money for the purposes of generating tax-free profits, and hiding these profits from Revenue Canada, is. It can make for sleepless nights...but more and more Canadians appear to be living on the edge. Four years ago, when Vancouver lawyer Ken Finkelstein was laying the groundwork for his practice, he realized there were almost no small legal firms doing offshore work....Finkelstein, who recently wrote *The Tax Haven Guide Book*...says he advises all his clients about their Canadian tax obliga-

tions. "If they get a blank look in their eyes, I tell them again," he says. "But once they walk out the door you can't control them."

Neither, so far, can Revenue Canada. "Of the people that I know who are using the offshore, 99.99 percent are reporting squat," says Gordon Laight...author of *Offshore Advantage*, a primer on the complex world of international investments: "It's becoming out-and-out tax evasion. Period."...

Although federal government officials concede that the popularity of offshore investing is growing among Canadians, they will not offer an estimate as to how much is being lost in taxes. However, particularly worrisome is the threat that some of the $1 trillion estimated to be coming to Canadians might disappear offshore. As a result, in last February's budget, Finance Minister Paul Martin proposed a series of tough measures aimed at attacking the problem. They include stiff fines on lawyers, accountants, and financial planners who set up tax-evading offshore structures, and a crackdown on offshore investment funds and non-resident trusts....

Will the get-tough approach work? Some potential investors may be scared off. But the reality is that many Canadians will continue to try to cheat the system, and assets already generating income in tax havens as far-flung as Cyprus, Liechtenstein, or the British Virgin Islands are almost impossible—and prohibitively expensive—to chase down. Revenue Canada's job will become even more difficult when online banking and online stock trading take wider hold. The trend is already under way: the government

DODGING THE TAX MAN: CANADIANS AND TAX HAVENS *(continued)*

of the Caribbean island of Anguilla recently started a fully electronic, round-the-clock service that will allow customers to create and register offshore companies from home....In the Bahamas and the Cayman Islands, where dummy corporations shelter holding companies and shell companies are governed by mystery trusts, the veil of secrecy hangs over financial dealings. Conversations are in code....Offshore companies specialize in catering to their clients' desire for privacy. Some provide customers with 1-800 numbers, which do not show up on an itemized home phone bill. Others ask if clients want a "hold mail" account so correspondence will not arrive in Canada to give them away....

In this shadowy world discretion is mandatory. Under law in many tax havens, people can be thrown in jail or fined heavily for disclosing information about offshore activities. Tax evasion is not a crime in these jurisdictions. In Nassau, a French-Canadian banker laughs when asked how his Quebec clients will get around the finance department's tough new provisions. "That's not the right question," he said mischievously. "You should ask instead, what vehicles will be used to comply with the new laws." A meticulously dressed director of a private European bank in the Bahamas was more taciturn when asked about the type of services he provides, "I'm a private banker," he said. "Unfortunately, everything I say is private."

SOURCE: Abridged from O'Hara, Jane. 1999. "The Tax Dodgers." *Maclean's*, June 14: 18–22. Reprinted by permission.

look to us because of cattle...because of our great wealth; and our wealth is cattle" (Deng 1998: 107). Deng notes that many African peoples who are poor by North American standards resist being labelled as poor.

The symbolic interactionist perspective emphasizes that norms, values, and beliefs are learned through social interaction. Social interaction also influences the development of one's self-concept. Lewis (1966) argued that, over time, the poor develop norms, values, beliefs, and self-concepts that contribute to their own plight. According to Lewis, the **culture of poverty** is characterized by female-centred households, an emphasis on gratification in the present rather than in the future, and a relative lack of participation in society's major institutions. "The people in the culture of poverty have a strong feeling of marginality, of helplessness, of dependency, of not belonging....Along with this feeling of powerlessness is a widespread feeling of inferiority, of personal unworthiness" (Lewis 1998: 7). Early sexual activity, early marriage, and unmarried parenthood are considered normal and acceptable among individuals living in a culture of poverty. Certain groups, according to this view, remain poor over time as the culture of poverty is transmitted from one generation to the next. Critics of the culture of poverty approach argue that it blames the victim rather than the structure of society for poverty, justifies the status quo, and perpetuates inequality (Ryan 1992).

In an environment...where families with a steady, employed bread-winner have become the exception rather than the rule, the chance to contact families and institutions that represent conventional role models is small. Hence, people are not introduced into jobs, and they do not learn from experience about the behaviour and norms that belong to steady work and stable family life. Being surrounded by people who have to rely on other, often illegal strategies to survive, these strategies come to be seen as a way of life. (Van Kempen 1997: 434)

WEALTH, ECONOMIC INEQUALITY, AND POVERTY IN CANADA

Canada is a nation of tremendous economic variation ranging from the very rich to the very poor. Signs of this disparity are visible everywhere, from opulent mansions to squalid rooming houses, from those who drive or are driven in luxury cars to those who cannot afford the price of a monthly bus pass.

Wealth in Canada

Wealth refers to the total assets of an individual or household, minus liabilities (mortgages, loans, and debts). Wealth includes the value of a home; investment real estate; cars; an unincorporated business; life insurance (cash value); stocks, bonds, mutual funds, trusts; chequing and savings accounts; retirement savings plans; and valuable collectibles.

According to a 1998 *Forbes* magazine report, Bill Gates, chief of Microsoft Corporation, was the wealthiest North American for the fifth year in a row ("Bill Gates Tops Forbes Billionaires for 5th Year" 1998). Even after the 500-point stock market drop in August of 1998, Gates's net worth was $58.4 billion. Investor Warren Buffet was second at $29.4 billion. In September 1998, there were 189 billionaires in the United States, up from 170 in 1997. *Forbes* reported that of the richest 400 American individuals in 1998, only 58 were women. The United States also leads the world in countries with the greatest number of billionaires. It is followed, in order, by Germany, Japan, China–Hong Kong, France, Mexico, Saudi Arabia, Switzerland, the Philippines, and Taiwan. Consider that "[i]n 1994, the combined wealth of the world's 358 billionaires (including a handful of Canadians) equalled that of the lowest 45 percent of the population of the planet" (Barlow and Campbell 1995: 47). Canada's richest person is billionaire Kenneth R. Thomson, the owner of a major newspaper empire begun by his father. In 1995, dividends from Thomson's shareholding brought in over $330 million; in 1999, Thomson's assets topped U.S.$7.4 billion (Ash 1999: 218).

Economic Inequality in Canada

The three decades after the end of World War II were a time of unprecedented economic prosperity and stability in Canada. Throughout the 1950s and 1960s, unemployment and inflation were low and a steady increase in personal incomes financed the growth of the social safety net, including universal health care, the Canadian Pension Plan, unemployment insurance, and inex-

International Data

According to a UNICEF report, *Child Neglect in Rich Nations*, Canada's shrinking support to families is one of the major reasons why Canada's child poverty rates are far worse than are those of European countries. Using an international after-tax measure, UNICEF reported the rate of child poverty in Canada as 13.5 percent, compared to 9.9 percent in the United Kingdom, 6.8 percent in Germany, 6.5 percent in France, 6.2 percent in the Netherlands, and 2.7 percent in Sweden.

SOURCE: National Council of Welfare 1999c

pensive postsecondary education. By the 1970s however, "stagflation" had set in, with increases in both consumer prices and unemployment levels and a halt in the growth of real income. During this period, many Western countries, including Canada, were pushed into the steepest recession since the time of the Great Depression. Because of economic downturns, economic inequality—the gap between the haves and the have-nots—grew significantly. Since the 1970s, much has changed, beginning with the government's introduction of various tax measures and policy decisions, such as deregulation, privatization, free trade, and monetarism, which reflected a "corporate agenda." These measures have most obviously benefited corporations and those whom John Kenneth Galbraith has referred to as the "contented classes."

While the income gap between high- and low-income families was reduced during the recovery of the 1980s, the improvement was insufficient to eradicate the inequality increases associated with the 1981–82 recession. Barlow and Campbell (1995: 76) point out that income inequality in Canada has not only been growing in the past decades "but it has been picking up speed." While high-income families have reaped benefits from very high interest rates on their savings, and tax breaks, lower income tax rates, and an increase in both the numbers of those employed within professional and managerial groups and the level of executive earnings, others have fared more poorly. Declines in family income and median real wages, rising unemployment, increases in part-time, temporary, and low-paying jobs, and the accelerated pace of social cuts (designed to make Canada's system of social security more "affordable" and to level the free-trade playing field) have had a huge impact on Canada's poor. From 1973 to 1993, income inequality in Canada increased, with the top 30 percent of families gaining "an ever greater share of the [income] pie (from 49.6 percent to 52.3 percent)," the next 20 percent retaining their income share, and the bottom half of Canadian families dropping from 29.5 percent to 26.9 percent. Put in terms that are more concrete, Barlow and Campbell note, "in 1993 alone, the wealthiest 30 percent got $14 billion more of the income pie than they would have received had their share remained the same as it was in 1973. All of this extra income came at the expense of the poorest half of Canadian families." Since that time, cutbacks to government transfer payments have meant that taxes and government transfers are no longer able to offset pre-tax inequality. Indeed, since 1994, the gap in *after-tax inequality* has also grown, with Statistics Canada reporting that low-income families have been unable to benefit from the latest advances in earnings to the same degree that they did during the economic recovery of the late 1980s (Townson 1998). The gap in after-tax incomes between the richest and poorest families increased after 1995, when the federal government made drastic cuts in social program spending. Cuts to public programs at both the provincial and federal levels have hit poorest families the hardest (Daub and Young 1999).

Patterns of Poverty in Canada

Although poverty is not as widespread or severe in Canada as it is in many less developed countries, it nevertheless represents a significant social problem. Poverty is not equally distributed; certain demographic populations are more likely to experience poverty than are others. Poverty rates vary according to age, education, gender, family structure, disability, race/ethnicity, and labour force participation.

Age and Poverty

Despite a political landscape "littered with political rhetoric about children," Canada has had little success in reducing child poverty. Almost one in five Canadian children under the age of 18 live in low-income families, while almost one of every seven Canadian children under the age of 18 were on welfare as of March 1997 (National Council of Welfare 1999c). The federal, and provincial and territorial governments have negotiated a working arrangement known as the National Children's Agenda, which commits both levels of government to furthering the well-being of families with children. However, at the time of writing, it is too early to tell whether the federal government's 2000 budget will be, as hoped-for, a "children's budget," designed to assist children and their families.

Because of income security programs such as the Guaranteed Income Supplement, the Old Age Security pension, and the Spouse's Allowance, very few Canadian seniors have to rely on welfare (National Council of Welfare 1998). Between 1980 and 1996, the number of older Canadians who fell below Statistics Canada's low-income cutoff (LICO) dropped substantially. However, one in five seniors (mostly unattached women) is still likely to be living in a low-income situation.

Education and Poverty Education is one of the best insurance policies to protect against an individual living in poverty. In general, the higher a person's level of educational attainment, the less likely that person is to be poor (see also Chapter 12). However, as the National Council of Welfare (1998: 3) has noted, "Education does not offer absolute protection from welfare." In March 1997, 11 percent of those on welfare had some form of postsecondary education. In addition, immigrants from non-European countries may find that their educational qualifications are devalued or not recognized at all in Canada.

For example, a recent study, *Immigrant Success in the Knowledge Economy*, by University of Toronto sociologist Jeffrey Reitz, concluded that although today's immigrants are better educated, they are not as successful as were those who emigrated to Canada 15 to 20 years ago (in Drakes 1999). In the past, Reitz observes, "if immigrants had trouble, the reasons were racial discrimination or that their qualifications weren't recognized. Newly arriving immigrants 15 years ago would be skilled enough to have the top jobs in the country, but they would not get them—they would get the middle-level jobs. Today, more and more immigrants who are skilled enough to have the middle-level jobs are not getting them. They're getting the bottom ones." Reitz's research indicates that although European immigrants initially face the same problems as other immigrants, they are more likely than non-European immigrants are to find gainful employment. "The ones who are getting moved down to the bottom are the immigrants from places other than Europe, immigrants from other origins—the Caribbean, East and South Asia."

According to Reitz's research, a major reason many recent immigrants are not succeeding in the workforce is because employers and professional associations do not know how to judge their credentials and have no guidelines for comparing foreign degrees to Canadian-degrees. According to Reitz, "If somebody comes in with a degree from the University of X and it's far away and it's not well known to Canadian employers, they really almost have no value whatsoever." Reitz points out that institutions of higher learning are no better at assessing foreign degrees. "If you're from an Indian university, you get discounted one degree. If you have a master's degree and you want to come here,

International Data

Since 1960, the income gap between rich and poor countries has doubled. Countries that make up the richest 20 percent of the world's population now have an average per capita income that is 60 times that of the poorest one-fifth. When national borders are erased, the richest 20 percent of the world's population have average per capita incomes 160 times that of the poorest 20 percent.

SOURCE: Barlow and Campbell 1995

you have to do a master's degree over. It's the equivalent to a BA. That's just automatic—even from the best universities." Reitz's study of male immigrants arriving in Canada between 1981 and 1996 showed they earned $21 593 on average, while Canadian-born men earned $34 865. Recent female immigrants earned $14 208, while Canadian-born women earned $22 293 (Drakes 1999). Table 10.3 compares mean earnings of immigrants with Canadian-born men and women in each census year since 1981.

Gender and Poverty Women are more likely than men are to live below the poverty line—a phenomenon referred to as the **feminization of poverty.** As discussed in Chapter 7, women are less likely than men are to pursue advanced educational degrees in nontraditional areas of study. They also tend to be more heavily concentrated in a narrower range of jobs than men are, and within lower-paying jobs, such as service and clerical work. Women who are minorities or who are single mothers are at increased risk of being poor.

Family Structure and Poverty Poverty is much more prevalent among female-headed single-parent households than among other types of family structures. The relationship between family structure and poverty helps to explain why women and children have higher poverty rates than men. "Almost two-thirds of the families headed by single-parent mothers live below the poverty line, and the poorest of all are families with young single-parent mothers" (National Council of Welfare 1999a: 89). In Chapter 5, we noted the rising divorce rate and that following parental separation, the overwhelming majority of children live with their mothers. According to the National Children's Survey, following parental separation, about one-third of children have very little contact with their fathers (i.e., either irregular visits or no visits at all), with children born of common-law unions even less likely to see their fathers than are children born

Table 10.3 Earnings of Immigrants versus Canadian-Born Men and Women, Canada

	Men Arriving 0–5 Years before Census Year	Men Arriving 6–10 Years before Census Year	Canadian-Born Men
1981	$14 659	$18 005	$18 315
1986	16 583	24 050	24 806
1991	22 963	28 895	32 364
1996	21 593	28 178	34 865

	Women Arriving 0–5 Years before Census Year	Women Arriving 6–10 Years before Census Year	Canadian-Born Women
1981	$7 150	$9 780	$9 733
1986	9 624	13 061	14 067
1991	14 591	17 165	19 608
1996	14 208	18 960	22 293

All earnings figures are for persons aged 20 to 64 years and are adjusted for variations in specific year-of-arrival composition of immigrant groups.

SOURCE: Jeffrey G. Reitz, University of Toronto, based on data from the Canadian census

to married parents (Figure 10.1). "Since fathers who have low levels of contact with their children are least likely to pay child support, these findings indicate that many, many Canadian children are at a high risk of losing both the personal and financial support of their fathers when their parents separate" (National Council of Welfare 1999b: 5).

In addition, the National Council of Welfare (1999: 9b) has observed that, "For minimum-wage workers supporting dependent children, it is simply impossible to rise over the poverty line." They note that while the poverty line for a two-person family (for example, a mother and child) in a large Canadian city in 1998 was $22 452, a person working 40 hours a week for 52 weeks at Ontario's minimum hourly wage of $6.85 would only earn $14 248. Even when supplemented with the new Canada Child Tax Benefit of $1625 for one child and a GST refund of $503, the family would only receive a total of $16 376. In British Columbia, a person working full time at the provincial minimum wage of $7.15 would earn $14 872; with the Canada Child Tax Benefit, the GST refund, and the additional provincial family benefits available in that province, the family would only receive $17 937. In Newfoundland, an individual working full time at the minimum wage of $5.25 would earn $10 920 a year. With the Child Tax Benefit and the GST refund, the family's annual income would be $13 048.

CONSIDERATION

Levitan et al. (1998) note that "it is still an open question whether family structure is the cause or the victim of poverty. How many males disappear because they cannot support the children they have fathered? Are single-parent families poor because they are headed by a woman, or because the wage structure allows few mothers to earn their way out of poverty?" (p. 22). Although poverty is often seen as resulting from the rise of single female-headed families, Hernandez (1997) argues that low earnings for fathers continue to be a major determinant of childhood poverty, both because of their direct effect on family income and because of their indirect contribution to mother-only families.

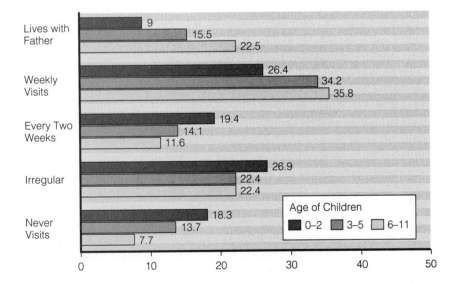

Figure 10.1
Contact with Father after Separation, by Age Group of Children

SOURCE: National Council of Welfare 1999b

Figure 10.2
**Poverty Rates for
Working-Age Women and
Men with and without
Disabilities, Canada, 1995**

SOURCE: Prepared by the Canadian Council on
Social Development using data from Statistics
Canada's 1996 census

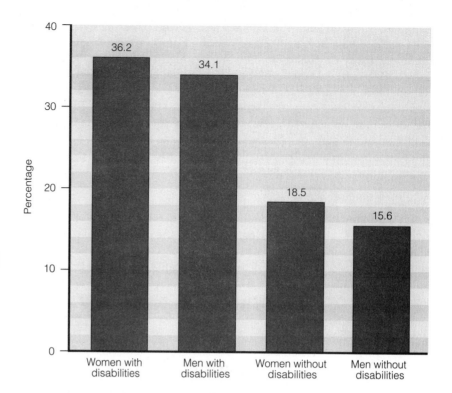

Disability and Poverty

According to data compiled by the Canadian Council on Social Development
(Fawcett 1999), disability is a strong indicator of poverty. In 1995, more than
one third (36.2 percent) of women with disabilities versus 18.5 percent of
Canadians without disabilities aged 15 to 64 were poor. This pattern also holds
for men with disabilities. In 1996, while the national poverty rate for men
without disabilities was 15.6 percent, among men with disabilities it was
34.1 percent (Figure 10.2). As one might expect, there are significant differences in the poverty rates between men with disabilities and particularly
women with disabilities who have full-time, full-year employment and those
who do not (Figure 10.3). However, a substantial proportion of people with disabilities do not participate in the paid labour force at all. Between 1993 and
1994, 56.8 percent of working-aged women and 46.3 percent of working-age
men with disabilities did not participate in the paid labour force for the entire
two-year period (compared to 15.3 percent of women without disabilities and
3.1 percent of men without disabilities).

Obtaining employment and remaining employed often poses a considerable
challenge to both men and women who have disabilities. First, among those
who were employed at some time between 1993 and 1994, almost 7 in 10 (69.3
percent) women with disabilities (compared with 42.3 percent of women
without disabilities) and 6 in 10 (59.5 percent) men with disabilities (compared
with 37 percent of men without disabilities) experienced a disruption in their
employment. According to Fawcett (1999), the reasons for these employment
discontinuities include: (1) the cyclical nature of some disabilities that requires
individuals to absent themselves from the labour force for some period of time,

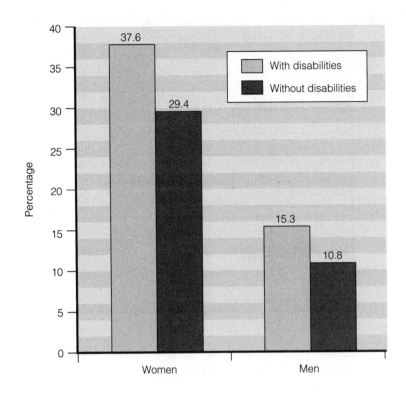

Figure 10.3
Women and Men Employed Full Year, with Earnings under $15 640, by Disability Status, Canada, 1996
SOURCE: Prepared by the Canadian Council on Social Development using Statistics Canada's Survey of Labour and Income Dynamics, 1993–94

and (2) a tendency for those with disabilities to be the "last hired and the first fired." Third, while many income support programs, including social assistance and disability pensions provide support for disability-related expenses (e.g., medication, transportation, and so on), such supports disappear when individuals with disabilities become employed. Accordingly, if one's employment income is insufficient to cover such expenses, one cannot truly "afford to work." As Fawcett points out, "persons with disabilities who look for work face a dilemma: in their attempts to convince potential employers that they are capable of working, they may disqualify themselves from the social assistance and disability supports they need in order to survive."

Compared to their counterparts without disabilities, both women and men with disabilities are more likely to be the sole providers of family income. However, the situation is particularly bleak among women with disabilities because they are more likely than other groups to live as lone parents. In 1996, almost 1 in 10 (9.7 percent) women with a disability was a lone parent (compared with 7.6 percent of women without disabilities, 2.8 percent of men with disabilities, and 1.1 percent of men without disabilities). Women with disabilities who obtain full-time, full-year employment typically earn less than either women without disabilities or men with disabilities (Figure 10.4). As Fawcett (1999) has observed, "with these earnings prospects, many women with disabilities would not be able to earn the 'premium' required to support themselves and their families, *and* pay the extra costs of disability-related supports. For many women with disabilities, the safest choice is to remain out of the labour market."

Race and Ethnicity and Poverty Based on the findings of the 1996 Canadian census, the incidence of low income is high among visible minorities in Canada and among its Aboriginal people (Figure 10.5). Canada's visible

Figure 10.4
**Poverty Rates for
Working-Age Women
and Men with and
without Disabilities,
by Employment
Activity, Canada, 1995**

SOURCE: Prepared by the Canadian
Council on Social Development using data
from Statistics Canada's 1996 census

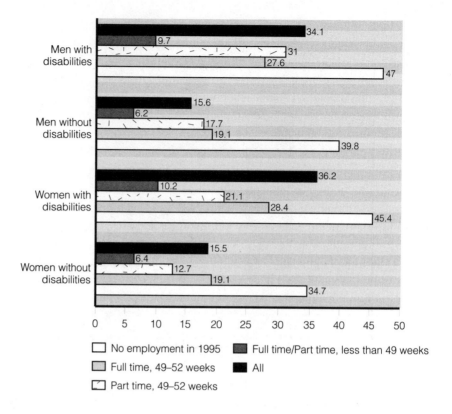

In 1995, the average
employment income of
those who were Canadian-
born visible minority
earners was almost 30 percent below the level
reported by all other
Canadian-born earners.

SOURCE: Statistics Canada 1998b

minority population, of which the largest proportion were recent immigrants, had below average employment incomes and an incidence of low income that was significantly above average (36 percent versus 20 percent). In that year, almost half (45 percent) of the children under the age of six in the visible minority population lived in low-income families (compared with 26 percent of all children). Among those who were 65 years of age or older, the incidence of low income was 32 percent (compared to a national average of 19 percent).

Excluding the Aboriginal population who lived on reserves, in the Yukon or Northwest Territories (where income is generally lower than for the Aboriginal population living off reserve), 44 percent of the Aboriginal population in 1995 was below Statistics Canada's low-income cutoffs. Among those who identified themselves as North American Indians, almost half (48 percent) were in a low-income situation. Among the Métis (the second largest group), almost 4 in 10 (39 percent) were in a low-income situation. In that year, three out of five Aboriginal children under the age of six were in low-income families. Among those aged 6 to 14, the incidence of low income was 48 percent, or more than twice the national rate of 22 percent (Statistics Canada 1998b).

Labour Force Participation and Poverty A common image of the poor is that they are jobless and unable or unwilling to work. Although the Canadian poor are primarily children and adults who are not in the labour force, many poor are classified as "**working poor**."

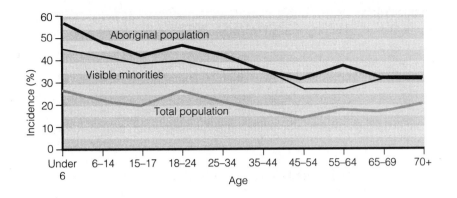

Figure 10.5
Incidence of Low Income by Age, Canada, 1995
SOURCE: Statistics Canada 1998b

CONSEQUENCES OF POVERTY AND ECONOMIC INEQUALITY

Poverty and economic inequality have enormous negative consequences for individuals, families, communities, and societies. These consequences include war and social conflict, health problems, problems in education, problems in families and parenting, substandard housing, and homelessness. In addition, poverty contributes to the perpetuation of poverty across generations, feeding a cycle of intergenerational poverty.

War and Social Conflict

Modern wars are fought mainly in poorer countries (see also Chapter 15). Poverty is often the root cause of conflict and war within and between nations, as "the desperation of the poor is never quiet for long" (Speth 1998: 281). Not only does poverty breed conflict and war, but also war contributes to poverty. For example, war contributes to homelessness as individuals and families are forced to flee from their homes. Military and weapons spending associated with war diverts resources away from economic development and social spending on health and education.

Briggs (1998) suggests that the widening inequalities between the haves and the have-nots present a threat to social order. He asks how long a country can maintain social order "when increasing numbers of persons are left out of the banquet while a few are allowed to gorge?" (p. 474). Although Karl Marx predicted that the have-nots would revolt against the haves, Briggs does not foresee a revival of Marxism; "the means of surveillance and the methods of suppression by the governments of industrialized states are far too great to offer any prospect of success for such endeavors" (p. 476). Instead, Briggs predicts that capitalism and its resulting economic inequalities will lead to social anarchy—a state of political disorder and weakening of political authority.

Health Problems and Poverty

In Chapter 2, we noted that poverty has been identified as the world's leading health problem. Persistent poverty is associated with higher rates of infant mortality and childhood deaths and lower life expectancies among adults. Poverty often causes chronic malnutrition, which can result in permanent brain damage, learning disabilities, and mental retardation in infants and

> **National Data**
>
> A 1999 study by Statistics Canada reported that women who worked part time, had irregular work hours, and had no maternity benefits were those most likely to be back at work within a month of giving birth.
>
> SOURCE: National Council of Welfare 1999b: 11

Regardless of age, sex, race, and place of residence, low-income Canadians are more likely to die earlier and to suffer more illnesses. "At each rung up the income ladder, Canadians have less sickness, longer life expectancies, and improved health."

SOURCE: Health Canada 1999: ix

International Data

Research conducted on a sample of 2145 men in the United States and published in 1997 in the *Annals of Internal Medicine* reported that social class plays a role in recovering from a heart attack and that educated men with good jobs are more likely to bounce back from heart attacks than their less fortunate peers. Using standards developed by the New York Heart Association, the study reported that upper-class male patients were 50 percent more likely to improve within a year than lower-class men were and 30 percent more likely to improve than middle-class men were. The study controlled for age, race, medical history, and other factors.

SOURCE: Associated Press 1997

children (Hill 1998). Although the United Nation's World Health Organization and the Breastfeeding Committee for Canada (whose membership includes the Canadian Medical Association, the Canadian Nurses Association, the Aboriginal Nurses Association, the Canadian Paediatric Society, the College of Family Physicians, the Society of Obstetricians and Gynaecologists of Canada, UNICEF Canada, and the federal health department) have recommended exclusive breastfeeding of infants for the first six months of life, babies born to poor mothers are more likely to be denied this important start to life. Research has shown that breastfeeding significantly reduces infections, the likelihood of Sudden Infant Death Syndrome (SIDS), and allergies. It also enhances cognitive development and the maintenance of acceptable infant growth rates. However, poor mothers often fail to breastfeed their babies because of a lack of adequate information and personal supports, or, because of a rushed return to work, they have to wean their babies prematurely (National Council of Welfare 1999b: 11).

Economic inequality also affects psychological and physical health. The National Longitudinal Survey of Children and Youth reports that the capacity of parents to care for children and their children's developmental outcomes are better at each step up the income ladder. Low social support, family dysfunction, and parental depression, all of which have significant negative effects on children, are all also more common in low-income households. According to this study, 18 percent of children living in low-income households (versus 8 percent of children in middle-income households and 5 percent of children in higher-income families) lived with parents who had many symptoms of depression (National Council of Welfare 1999c). Research also finds that "perceptions of inequality translate into psychological feelings of lack of security, lower self-esteem, envy and unhappiness, which, either directly or through their effects on life-styles, cause illness" (Streeten 1998: 5). People who live in areas with the greatest gap between the rich and the poor are much more likely to rate their own health as poor or fair than people who live in areas where income is more equitably distributed (Kennedy et al. 1998). This finding was true not only among poor people, but among middle-income adults as well.

Educational Problems and Poverty

The various adverse physical and mental outcomes of infant and childhood poverty combine to cause learning failure and to limit academic performance. Children from poor families score lower on tests of cognitive skill than children from affluent families (Mayer 1997a). Because school districts are determined by residential patterns, the poor often attend schools that are characterized by lower-quality facilities, overcrowded classrooms, and a higher teacher turnover rate (see also Chapter 12). Because poor parents have less schooling, on average, than do nonpoor parents, they may be less able to encourage and help their children succeed in school. However, research suggests that family income is a stronger predictor of ability and achievement outcomes than are measures of parental schooling or family structure (Duncan and Brooks-Gunn 1997). Poor parents have fewer resources to provide educational experiences (such as travel), private tutoring, books, and computers for their children. Not surprisingly, poor students are less likely to graduate from high school or go to college or university, creating a vicious cycle whereby subsequent generations remain poor.

Poverty also presents obstacles to educational advancement among poor adults. Women and men who want to further their education in order to escape poverty may have to work while attending school or may be unable to attend school because of unaffordable childcare, transportation, or tuition fees, or books.

Family and Parenting Problems Associated with Poverty

In some cases, family problems contribute to poverty. For example, domestic violence causes some women to flee from their homes and live in poverty without the economic support of their husbands. Poverty also contributes to family problems. The stresses associated with poverty contribute to substance abuse, domestic violence, child abuse, divorce, and questionable parenting practices. For example, poor parents unable to afford childcare expenses are more likely to leave children home without adult supervision. Poor parents are more likely than other parents are to use harsh disciplinary techniques, such as physical punishment, more likely to value obedience, and less likely to be supportive of their children (Mayer 1997a). While a 1999 report by the National Council of Welfare, *Preschool Children: Promises to Keep,* acknowledges that child abuse occurs in families of all incomes, it emphasizes that "it is a particularly great problem for children living in poverty" and that among families investigated by child welfare services, a disproportionate number are poor. For example, in 1993, between 38 and 50 percent of Ontario families investigated for child abuse were on welfare. It is stressed that "although some of these investigations may be biased on the basis of social class...strong evidence indicates that children are far more likely to be physically, sexually, and emotionally abused when they live in poor neighbourhoods. Concentrated neighbourhood poverty and child abuse are very closely linked, and abuse is more likely the more intense the poverty in the children's neighbourhood" (p. 23).

Another family problem associated with poverty is teenage pregnancy. Poor adolescent girls are more likely to have babies as teenagers or to become young single mothers. Early childbearing is associated with numerous problems, such as increased risk of premature or low birth-weight babies, dropping out of school, and lower future earning potential due to lack of academic achievement. Luker (1996) notes that "the high rate of early childbearing is a measure of how bleak life is for young people who are living in poor communities and who have no obvious arenas for success" (p. 189). For poor teenage women who have few employment opportunities and are disillusioned with education, "childbearing...is one of the few ways...such women feel they can make a change in their lives..." (p. 182).

> Having a baby is a lottery ticket for many teenagers: it brings with it at least the dream of something better, and if the dream fails, not much is lost....In a few cases it leads to marriage or a stable relationship; in many others it motivates a woman to push herself for her baby's sake; and in still other cases it enhances the woman's self-esteem, since it enables her to do something productive, something nurturing and socially responsible....To the extent that babies can be ill or impaired, mothers can be unhelpful or unavailable, and boyfriends can be unreli-

From 1991 to 1996, while the number of Canadians who owned a house increased by 10 percent, shelter became less afford- able for many Canadians. During this period, average shelters costs for owners decreased by approxi- mately 1 percent while average household incomes declined by 5 percent. Among renters, average shelter costs declined by 3 percent while average household incomes declined by 12 percent. Among those under 30, average household incomes declined by more than 17 percent while rent declined by less than 5 percent.

SOURCE: Health Canada 1999

According to the Canadian Real Estate Association, the cost of buying a home is expected to go up 2.3 per- cent in 2000, with the average Canadian home costing $161 020. The biggest jump is expected to occur in Edmonton, where the prices are projected to climb by 4.7 percent. The projected average house prices were $270 650 in Vancouver, $232 490 in Toronto, $168 949 in Cal- gary, and $122 580 in Montreal.

SOURCE: *Maclean's* 1999d

able or punitive, childbearing can be just another risk gone wrong in a life that is filled with failures and losses. (Luker 1996: 182)

Housing and Homelessness

According to the National Council of Welfare (1998: 53), finding decent and affordable housing that is suitable to a family's needs "is one of the biggest finan- cial burdens for people on welfare and for low-income people in general." The provision of housing for lower-income Canadians has been an area of continuing governmental concern since the first Canadian social-housing legislation, the 1938 *National Housing Act*, made provision for the construction of low-rent housing. In 1949, the NHA was broadened to include federal–provincial pro- grams (sometimes with municipal participation) to build publicly owned and provincially managed housing for low-income families, seniors, and people with disabilities. In 1974, the NHA was again amended; while existing public housing was to continue providing housing for those on low-income, additional rural and Native programs were added and new social housing was to be built by municipalities, nonprofit organizations, and cooperatives. From 1947 to 1986, 253 500 public housing units were built in Canada; Ontario has the largest share (43 percent), followed by Quebec (22 percent), British Columbia (8 percent), Manitoba (7 percent), and Alberta (5 percent) (McAfee 1999). However, Cana- dians continue to experience a housing affordability crisis. In 1996, 30 percent of families with children that rented had housing affordability problems. This figure increased to 58 percent among lone-parent families and to 76 percent among lone-parents under the age of 30 (Health Canada 1999).

The majority of low-income families and unattached individuals are renters rather than homeowners. For example, as of March 1997, 68.2 percent of all those living on welfare lived in rental housing; only a small portion lived in their own home (6.9 percent) or in subsidized housing (6.8 percent). Among couples with children, 71.3 percent were renters, 16.2 percent were home owners, 8.2 percent lived in subsidized housing, and 4.2 lived in other forms of housing (e.g., were boarding or living with relatives). Among single-parent families, 76.6 percent were renters, 6.3 percent lived in their own homes, 11 percent lived in subsidized housing, and 6.1 percent lived in other forms of housing. In general, single parents on welfare made proportionately more use of subsidized housing and were far less likely to board or to live with relatives.

Because different housing arrangements are promoted by welfare officials in various Canadian provinces and subsidized housing is not always available, vari- ations can be seen across Canada. For example, the Atlantic provinces have the highest proportion of homeowners among those on welfare with a percentage of renters that is well below the national average. In contrast, in both Alberta and British Columbia, the percentage of welfare recipients in rental housing was extremely high (84 percent and 86 percent, respectively). The percentage of those living with relatives is proportionately highest in Newfoundland (28 per- cent), Prince Edward Island (12 percent) and Quebec (13 percent). While only 12 percent of welfare recipients in Ontario lived in subsidized housing, 69 223 of the 96 996 in subsidized housing in March 1997 lived in Ontario.

While poor individuals are more likely than the nonpoor are to have spartan accommodations in high-crime neighbourhoods (Mayer 1997b), even substandard housing would be a blessing to many people who live without conventional housing—the homeless.

Homelessness is a growing problem in Canada. It is estimated that as many as 200 000 Canadians are homeless, including increasing numbers of women and children, Aboriginal people, adolescents, and people with mental illnesses (Health Canada 1999). Some homeless individuals have been forced out of their houses or apartments by rising rents or the inability to pay the mortgage. The homeless population also includes runaway or "throw away" youths, and individuals who have been released from mental hospitals because of the movement to deinstitutionalize individuals with psychiatric disorders. For these individuals, life is especially uncertain, danger-filled, and precarious.

According to an Environics public opinion survey conducted in March 1998, almost 95 percent of Canadians strongly or somewhat agreed with the statement that "dealing with the homeless should be a priority for governments and poli-cymakers." Almost 60 percent of Canadians strongly or somewhat agreed with the statement, "governments should spend more on preventing homelessness, even if the money must come out of other areas or possibly from increased taxes" (Canada Mortgage and Housing Corporation 1999).

Intergenerational Poverty

As we have seen, problems associated with poverty, such as health and educational problems, create a cycle of poverty from one generation to the next (see Table 10.4 and Figures 10.6a and 10.6b). Poverty that is transmitted from one generation to the next is called **intergenerational poverty**.

Using income tax information reported by a cohort of approximately 285 000 young men and women aged 28 in 31 in 1994, Corak (1998) related the total market income of these young adults to the incomes of their fathers and mothers in 1982 (when his participants were 16 to 19 years of age and still

Table 10.4	Adult Children's Increase in Income Based on Parent's Sources of Income	
Market Income of Adult Child Changed by $___		
	Sons	Daughters
Father's income if father reported income from		
Self-employment	1157	850
Assets	3107	2698
Unemployment Insurance	–1442	865
For every $1000 increase in father's income from		
Paid work	91	47
Self-employment	76	50
Assets	28	28
Unemployment Insurance	–10	–23
For every $1000 increase in		
Mother's income	90	82
Median income of neighbourhood	368	72

SOURCE: Corak 1988

Getting Ahead in Life: Does Your Parents' Income Count?

Parents hope their children will become successful and self-sufficient adults. But raising children is a complicated affair, and a child's fortune in life is determined not only by parenting strategies, but also by the support available in the community, the resources offered by the State, and sometimes just plain luck. That being said, a prime role in the eventual labour market outcomes of children is often attributed to money....But... a dollar is not a dollar is not a dollar...and...the sources of a parent's income influence the employment outcomes of their adult children....

The source of the father's income is strongly associated with the adult incomes of children. Children had significantly higher market incomes as adults if their fathers had self-employment income than if they did not—almost $1200 for sons and $850 for daughters in 1994. If fathers had received Unemployment Insurance (UI) benefits, the effect was just as dramatic but in the opposite direction: sons' incomes were $1400 and daughters' $870 lower than those of children whose fathers had not received UI.

A father with asset income [net income from interest and investments, real estate, dividends from Canadian corporations, and taxable capital gains or losses] provided the most significant advantages for his children. After accounting for all other factors, sons whose fathers had some income from assets earned over $3100 more than those whose fathers had no assets did, and daughters earned almost $2700 more.

These are very substantial amounts, but what may be even more significant is that the actual dollar amount of the father's asset income seems much less important than its presence. In fact, children's adult incomes rise by only an average $28 for every $1000 increase in their father's asset income; for example, someone whose father had $10 000 in asset income would enjoy a market income that was only $252 higher ($280 – $28) than a person whose father had $1000 in asset income....

Not only do varying sources of income have different effects on an adult child's labour market success, but so too does the parent who earns it. For every $1000 increase in the father's income, the adult child's market income increased by about $91 for sons and about $47 for daughters. In contrast, sons and daughters did equally well as the mother's income rose—about $80 to $90 per $1000 increase. There are two possible explanations for this finding. The first focuses on the father's role and suggests that a high-earner father has a stronger effect on sons than on daughters by encouraging the pursuit of income. The second keys on the mother's role and suggests that mothers may be more likely to treat children of each gender equally when making spending decisions, and if women have higher incomes, they probably have greater discretion over spending....

The affluence of the neighbourhood in which children, especially boys, spend their early teens is positively associated with their incomes as adults. For every $1000 increase in the median income of the neighbourhood, adult incomes increased by about $370 for sons, and by $72 for

daughters. There are a number of reasons why high-income neighbourhoods may improve the labour market outcomes of children. They may offer a more-developed physical infrastructure—higher quality schools, recreational facilities, and social institutions—as well as the kind of network or peer group effects sometimes called "social capital"—that is, the set of norms or standards that exist at the community level and help to reinforce the parents' goals for their children. An alternative interpretation is that parents will select a neighbourhood with the qualities they prefer if they can afford to choose the community where they raise their children. The type of neighbourhood may thus reflect the parents' choices and priorities for their children's future, rather than being a causal factor in its own right....

Clearly, different dollars produce different effects for the "average kid." Does the same hold true for low-income children?...In a world of equal opportunity, the labour market outcomes of adult children would not depend upon their family background. Ideally, a child with a very low-income father (bottom 10 percent of the income distribution) would have an equal chance of entering any income decile; that is, the child would be just as likely to become a very high-income earner (10 percent) as a very low-income earner (also 10 percent).

However, in fact, children of very low-income fathers were more likely to follow their father's example than to improve their own position in the income distribution. About 15 percent of sons also found themselves in the bottom decile, and another 14 percent moved up by only one decile. The figures for daughters were very similar, at 14 percent and 11 percent respectively. Only about 6 percent of sons and daughters of very low-income fathers managed to reach the top 10 percent of the income rankings (see Tables 10.6a and 10.6b). (In contrast, over 20 percent of sons and daughters born to fathers in the top decile also occupied the top decile, and less than 7 percent fell all the way to the bottom.) These patterns suggest that low-income in one generation is associated with low-income in the next, with children of very low-income families most likely to end up at the bottom of the income hierarchy.

A father's source of income had a clear effect on their adult children's incomes. Children were less likely (12 to 13 percent) to remain in the bottom income decile if their father had some self-employment income than if he did not (15 to 16 percent) while children whose father received UI benefits were more likely to remain there (15 to 16 percent) than if he did not (13 to 14 percent). However, the most striking result is the improvement in income mobility if a father reported some asset income: only 12 percent of sons remained in the bottom decile, compared with over 17 percent of those whose fathers had no income from assets. For daughters, the pattern was very similar, at 11 percent compared with 17 percent....

The community has as great an effect on a low-income child as on the average child. Children of very low-income fathers living in high-income neighbourhoods tended to do better. This was especially true in the case of sons; only 12 percent remained in the bottom income decile if they grew up in a high-income community, compared with 16 percent if they were raised in a low-income neighbourhood. For daughters, the difference was slight, at 14 percent and 15 percent respectively....

SOURCE: Abridged from Corak, Miles. 1998. "Getting Ahead in Life: Does Your Parent's Income Count?" *Canadian Social Trends*, Summer 49: 6–15.

living at home). Among his findings: the adult sons and daughters of very low-income fathers (i.e., those in the bottom 10 percent of income earners) were overrepresented in the lowest income decile. A detailed description of Corak's findings is contained within this chapter's Focus on Social Problems Research.

Intergenerational poverty creates a persistently poor and socially disadvantaged population sometimes referred to as the underclass. The term **underclass** usually refers to impoverished individuals who have low educational attainment, have criminal records, are unmarried mothers on welfare, or are ghetto residents. Although the underclass is stereotyped as being composed of minorities living in inner-city ghetto communities, the underclass is actually a far more heterogeneous population (Alex-Assensoh 1995).

Mead (1992) argues that intergenerational poverty may be caused by welfare dependency. According to Mead, when poor adults rely on welfare, the stigma of welfare fades, and welfare recipients develop poor work ethics that are passed on to their children. William Julius Wilson attributes intergenerational poverty and the underclass to a variety of social factors, including the decline in well-paid jobs and their movement out of urban areas, the resultant decline in the availability of marriageable males able to support a family, declining marriage rates and an increase in out-of-wedlock births, the migration of the middle class to the suburbs, and the impact of deteriorating neighbourhoods on children and youth (Wilson 1987, 1996).

STRATEGIES FOR ACTION: ANTIPOVERTY PROGRAMS, POLICIES, AND PROPOSALS

In Canada, federal, provincial, and local governments have devoted considerable attention and resources to antipoverty programs since the 1960s. In 1964, "the United States launched its 'war against poverty' and Canada began a more

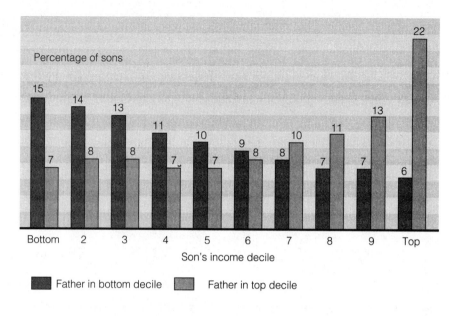

Figure 10.6a
One in Six Sons of Very Low-Income Fathers Also Had Incomes in the Lowest Decile

Figure 10.6b
Daughters of Very Low-Income Fathers Were Also Overrepresented in the Lowest Income Decile

SOURCE: Statistics Canada, Longitudinal Administrative Databank

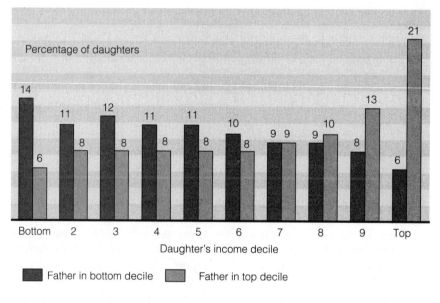

quiet campaign of study and legislation in an effort to understand better the causes of and remedies for poverty" (Ross and Lochhead 1999:1881). In the following year, the office of the federal Privy Council established a team of specialists to investigate and encourage greater federal–provincial cooperation in response to poverty. In addition, in 1965, the Company of Young Canadians (CYC) (a precursor of such federal government programs as Opportunities for Youth and Canada Works) was formed to help promote and coordinate local self-help efforts designed to reduce poverty.

The 1960s and 1970s saw the introduction of several significant pieces of antipoverty legislation. Recognition that the private pension system failed to provide adequate support for retired low-income workers and their families led to the introduction of the Canada and Quebec pension plans and to the Guaranteed

Income Supplement Program for those elderly individuals with little or no income other than Old Age Security. In 1966, the Canada Assistance Plan (CAP) was introduced. The CAP replaced the "many piecemeal cost-shared programs that the federal and provincial governments had begun entering into as far back as 1927" with a comprehensive social-assistance program that provided a major source of funds for people with disabilities who were unemployed, offered assistance to others in low-income circumstances, and brought a wide array of social services (e.g., daycare, family counselling, homemaker and child-welfare services) under federal cost sharing (Ross and Lochhead 1999: 1888). At least in theory, the CAP was designed not only to respond to the problem of poverty, but also to prevent it. In 1968, the *Medical Care Act* (Medicare) provided free access to basic health care for all Canadians. The *Unemployment Insurance Act* (1940), which had ushered in Canada's first national social-insurance program, was amended in 1971 to provide greater coverage to the unemployed as well as to the sick by extending its coverage and liberalizing its benefits. Such efforts are considered by many Canadians to distinguish us as a nation. Consider, for example, that in 1999, a *Maclean's* and CBC survey reported that almost 6 out of 10 Canadians believe that "the way we treat the poor and disadvantaged" is an important part of what makes us Canadian (Maclean's 1999e) (Table 10.5). At the same time, however, there is a growing awareness that, as a result of budget cuts to social security programs throughout the 1980s and 1990s, the gap between the rich and the poor is widening and that "the plight of those for whom prosperity is elusive" requires redress (Figure 10.7) (*Maclean's* 1999c: 29). In this section, we describe

Table 10.5	The Symbols of a Nation: Percentage of Respondents Who Think These Factors Are an Important Part of What Makes Us Canadian			
	Canada	Quebec	Men	Women
The flag	80	60	78	82
Achievements of prominent Canadians, such as artists and scientists, around the world	80	79	76	84
Our climate and geography	79	77	73	85
Our health care system	79	67	77	79
Our international role	77	76	73	80
Our multicultural and multiracial makeup	74	68	70	79
Canadian ownership of businesses operating in Canada	73	69	66	79
The traditional family	70	66	65	76
English- and French-speakers sharing one country	69	69	67	72
Hockey	67	46	66	67
Our Aboriginal peoples	63	48	58	69
Restrictions on gun ownership and use	63	58	56	70
Public broadcasting	63	62	54	72
The way we treat the poor and disadvantaged	59	54	55	63
A Christian heritage	54	47	45	63
Having the Queen as our monarch	41	20	34	48

SOURCE: *Maclean's* 1999e: 44

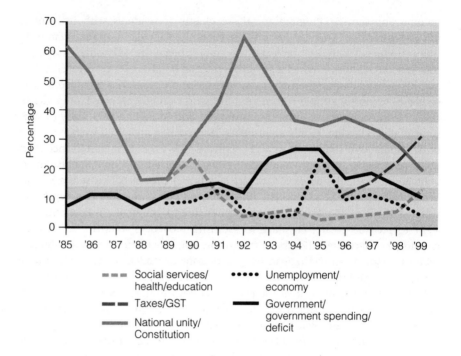

Figure 10.7
Shifting Priorities: Percentage Citing Various Topics as "The Most Important Problem Facing Canada" Over the Years
SOURCE: *Maclean's* 1999c: 29

both national and international responses to poverty and note the role of charity and the nonprofit sector in the alleviation of poverty.

Government Public Assistance and Welfare Programs in Canada

Under the *Constitution Act*, social and welfare services are the responsibility of the provincial and territorial governments. However, the federal government is also involved in the provision of these services through its cost-sharing agreements with the provinces and territories. Before April 1996, the federal government provided financial support for social services to the provinces and territories through a 50–50 cost-sharing scheme called the Canada Assistance Plan. The CAP was aimed at improving standards of provincial social-assistance programs ("welfare") and introduced national standards into public welfare for the first time. In place of "a confusing mix of program categories based on the poor law practice of separating the 'worthy' [e.g., the blind, people with disabilities, the elderly, and the single mother with children] from the 'unworthy' poor [e.g., people without disabilities who are unemployed]...one program [was to be established by each province and territory in exchange for federal funding] to meet financial need—provincial social assistance. An appeal procedure, a striking innovation in public assistance, was also a stipulation under the Canada Assistance Plan" (Guest 1999a: 2203).

However, beginning in the 1970s and in response to rising unemployment and inflation, claims were made that Canada's economic prosperity was best assured by decreasing government expenditures, particularly for social programs. Since that time, Moscovitch (1999: 2496) notes that both the federal and the provincial governments have used the following methods to control social expenditures: "changing eligibility and benefits, particularly under unemployment insurance and social assistance; 'privatizing' provincial social programs by contracting out responsibility for social services (particularly those relating to children and the aged); provincial attempts to raise revenues through Medicare premiums and user fees; decreasing social-program budgets relatively if not absolutely; imposing an eroding level of assistance benefits; and termination of some social programs—for example, the federal Family Allowance," which had, at its introduction in 1945, been Canada's first universal welfare program. In an attempt to reduce expenditures on social programs, between 1984 and 1993, the federal Conservative governments further reduced old-age security benefits at middle-income levels and above, decreased the range of workers who were covered by Unemployment Insurance and the benefits available to them, and imposed spending limits on Canada's three richest provinces, Ontario, British Columbia, and Alberta, effectively forcing these provinces to absorb up to 70 percent of the costs. In its 1997 report, *Another Look at Welfare Reform*, the National Council of Welfare noted that provincial and territorial governments also implemented cuts to most welfare programs with the most extreme example occurring in Ontario in 1995, with a 21.6 percent cut to welfare recipients. The depth of this cut, the report emphasizes, "was completely arbitrary, with no assessment of how people who depended on welfare would be able to afford adequate food, clothing and shelter, let alone the impact of these cuts on young children and their families." While those with disabilities were exempted from the cuts, families with children were not.

In February 1995, the federal budget introduced the *Canada Health and Social Transfer* (CHST) (which became effective in April of 1996) and eliminated two federal transfer programs: Established Programs Financing, which provided for the consolidation of hospital, Medicare, and postsecondary education funding, and the Canada Assistance Plan. The CHST combined federal transfer payments for social assistance (previously under the CAP) with those for Medicare and postsecondary education into a single "block" transfer made up of cash payments and tax points. As a result, Canada's social safety net was fundamentally altered. Among the changes: "the new arrangement included a significant cut in federal support for these programs and a significant change in the way the provinces and territories account for the money they receive" (National Council of Welfare 1999a: 79). The National Council of Welfare observes that while the federal government paid $29.4 billion to the provinces and territories (partly in cash and partly in taxing powers) during the 1994–95 fiscal year, total federal support fell by 14 percent to $25.2 billion by 1997–98.

Under the CHST, the provinces now have greater discretion in deciding how to apportion their share of the reduced federal transfer. At least theoretically, provincial and territorial governments could elect to use all of the federal money they receive for Medicare and devote none to the other areas. Guest (1999a: 2203) points out that "Some have already made the decision to cut social-assistance programs to Canada's poorest families and individuals— Ontario and Alberta— while British Columbia has imposed a residence requirement of three months on all new applications for social assistance." It is also evident that not all groups affected by spending cuts are equally vocal nor are all voices equally heard. As Guest additionally reports, "One concern by welfare advocates is that money will be siphoned from welfare to cool the anger of health and higher education supporters (p. 2203)."

Family Allowance and Child Benefits

Canada's first universal welfare program, introduced in 1945, was **family allowance**, a monthly allowance paid to families with children. The term "universal" here refers to the fact that such benefits flowed from the principle of entitlement and were available without reference to a recipient's income or assets. In contrast, when benefits are directed at particular groups within the population, they are termed **demogrants**.

According to Guest (1999b: 815), several factors led to the introduction of family allowances in Canada. First, research noting that poverty was related to family size concluded that a wage sufficient to maintain a single worker could be grossly inadequate for a worker with a family to support. Thus, "[f]amily allowances paid by the state (or less frequently by some form of payroll tax) were proposed as not only an attack on poverty but also to advance the principle of 'horizontal equity' between workers who were bearing the costs of raising the next generation and those without such responsibilities." Second, when Canada's plan for postwar reconstruction (the Marsh report) was released in 1943, it advanced the argument that if family allowances were set at a "defensible minimum they would replace all other allowances for children under a variety of income maintenance schemes" (e.g., workers' compensation, social assistance, unemployment insurance, and so on, etc.) and allow these other programs the administrative simplicity of calculating their benefit schedules with sole reference to the income needs of single persons or couples. Third, while the Marsh Report contained a comprehensive antipoverty proposal scheme that included a national health system, a large-scale national employment program, and a social insurance scheme supported by universal family allowances, this plan was considered too radical and too expensive by the government at that time. Implementing one facet of the proposal, however, allowed the government to attain a vote-getting device in a "bid to outflank the political left." In addition, because economists had predicted high unemployment at the war's end, "family allowances were also seen as a means of maintaining purchasing power." Although the introduction of family allowances in Canada was opposed by some as a waste of taxpayers' money and as an attempt to buy votes in Quebec (where large families were more common), the legislation introducing "baby bonuses" passed unanimously in the House of Commons in 1944. Although the average payment per child ($5.94) was less than what the Marsh Report had earlier recommended ($7.50 per child), family allowances provided tax-free payments that varied according to the age of a child. In 1961, the Quebec government instituted a similar scheme on its own.

Following a failed attempt by the federal government in 1972 to replace the universality of family allowances with selectivity related to income, the government introduced a new *Family Allowance Act* that made family allowances taxable. In 1978, further restructuring occurred with the government's establishment of a Refundable Child Tax Credit, which offered $200 per year for families with incomes under $18 000, and which taxed away benefits entirely for those whose incomes reached $26 000. The tax credit was financed through scaling back the amount of monthly family allowance payments (from an average of $28 per month to $20) and through the reduction or elimination of other tax exemptions for children. Beginning in 1985, family benefits were further restructured with the partial indexing of family allowances and child tax credits. As well, the number of families qualifying for the tax credit was reduced when the maximum income for receipt of the credit was decreased from \$26 300 to \$23 500. Guest (1999b: 815) reports that by 1991, these changes "represented a spending cut in family benefits [of] \$550 million…with only a token increase" in the net family benefits received by Canada's poorest families.

In 1989, the universality of family allowances disappeared with the federal government requiring parents with upper-incomes to repay all of their benefits at the time they paid their yearly taxes. In 1991, family allowances, the Refundable Child Tax Credit, and a nonrefundable child tax credit were consolidated into a new **Canada Child Tax Benefit** (CCTB). The CCTB is a tax-free monthly payment made to eligible families to help them with the cost of raising children under the age of 18. Benefits are calculated for a 12-month period based on the number of children in a family and their ages, the applicant's province or territory of residence, the family's net income, and the applicant's (or his or her spouse's) deduction for childcare expenses. Except in Alberta, the basic benefit is \$85 a month for each child under age 12 plus \$6.25 a month for a third or additional child, plus \$17.75 for each child under age 7. In Alberta, the basic monthly benefit rate is \$77.91 for children under 7, \$83.66 for children aged 7–11, \$94.91 for children 12–15 and \$100.41 for children 16–17. The CCTB is based on net family income reported on the tax return of the previous year and is gradually reduced as family income reaches an "income ceiling" (which in 1999 was \$25 921).

Beginning in July 1998, the federal government increased the Canada Child Tax Benefit for low-income families by adding the new **National Child Benefit Supplement** (NCBS). This change resulted in increased benefits for about 1.4 million Canadian families with 2.5 million children. This monthly benefit for low-income families with children is the federal government's contribution to the **National Child Benefit (NCB).** In 1999, the NCBS amounts were \$65.41 a month for a first child, \$48.75 for a second, and \$42.50 for each additional child. In July 2000, the supplement will increased by another \$170 per child per year. Since its inception, the scope of the NCBS has been broadened. Before July 1999, the National Child Benefit Supplement was paid to families with incomes up to \$25 921 (for families with up to three children). Currently, the NCBS is paid to families with incomes up to \$27 750 and, as of July 2000, is paid to families with incomes up to \$29 590. In most of Canada's provinces and territories, the NCBS is considered income and will affect the amount of social assistance families are eligible to receive.

The NCB, introduced in July 1998, is a joint initiative of federal, provincial, and territorial governments designed to help prevent and reduce the depth of child poverty and to promote parental attachment to the workforce by improving available benefits and services. According to the *National Child Benefit Progress Report 1999*, "key to the NCB is the effort to move child benefits out of the welfare system so that when parents leave social assistance for work, these benefits go with them, helping to ensure their children's well-being during this transition" (Government of Canada 1999). It is recognized that the transition from welfare to work may result in the loss of benefits provided through social assistance (e.g., dental and prescription drug coverage) and incur additional costs (e.g., for transportation, childcare, and clothing). To "lower the welfare wall" that forces many families to remain on social assistance, the NCB adopts two main approaches:

(1) *Government of Canada income support:* When families go off welfare to go to work, they retain the federal government's NCB Supplement, which, in

July 1999, provided up to $1370 per year for an eligible family with two children under the age of seven, the Canada Child Tax Benefit (CCTB) base benefit of $2040, and the under-seven supplement of up to $213 per child (when no childcare expenses are claimed). As of July 2000, the NCB Supplement will be raised by $170. For a family with two children under the age of seven, this would amount to a maximum of $4176 per year in government of Canada income benefits.

(2) *Provincial/territorial and First Nations reinvestment programs*: As part of the NCB, certain provinces and territories also provide complementary benefits and services for children in low-income families such as child benefits, earned income supplements, childcare, supplemental health benefits, and early prevention programs for children at risk. These include the Nova Scotia Benefit, the Saskatchewan Child Benefit and the Northwest Territories Benefit, as well as working income supplements such as the BC Earned Income Supplement and the Northwest Territories Workers' Supplement. The NCB also funds various programs for those on social assistance. For example, in British Columbia more than $2 million has been committed to Building Blocks, a community-based program aimed at improving the parenting skills of high-risk young parents and encouraging them to become self-sufficient. In Manitoba, the Women and Infant Nutrition program provides nutrition, information, and counselling to social assistance and low-income working families and offers a $65 monthly supplement to expectant mothers and mothers with infants on social assistance. The Samson Cree Nation (Alberta) has initiated the Happy Families project, a home-visiting initiative that ensures support, education, and links to existing community services for new parents. For working parents, a variety of other provincial and territorial programs exist, including the Ontario Child Care Supplement for Working Families, New Brunswick's Alternative Child Care Assistance, Prince Edward Island's Family Health Benefit, the Yukon Children's Drug and Optical Program, and Newfoundland and Labrador's Extended Drug Coverage.

Employment Insurance Benefits

In January 1997, the *Employment Insurance (EI) Act* was implemented in Canada, replacing the former Unemployment Insurance (UI) Program. Individuals may receive regular benefits if they lose a job through no fault of their own and cannot find work. Those who quit their job without just cause or who are fired for misconduct are ineligible to receive EI benefits. Similarly, those affected by a strike, lockout, or other forms of labour dispute are ineligible unless they are not taking part in the dispute, are not giving money to support the dispute, and are not directly interested in the dispute (i.e., their wages or working conditions are not affected by the outcome of the dispute).

To be eligible for EI benefits, individuals must apply; have paid into the EI account; have been without work and pay for at least seven consecutive days; have worked for the required number of hours based on where they live and the unemployment rate in their area; be available for work but unable to find it; and be in Canada. The current system is based on hours of paid work and responds to variations in work situations such as part time, extended hours, or compressed weeks. Whether one works full time, part time, or on a seasonal basis, the hours a person works for pay are accumulated toward eligibility for EI benefits. These hours include overtime (which is calculated on an hour for hour rate) and paid leave (which is insured for the number of hours that normally would be worked in that period).

To qualify for EI, most individuals will need to have worked between 420 and 700 hours during the last 52 weeks or since the start of their last claim, whichever is shorter. The specific number of hours of insurable employment in the past 52 week needed to qualify for EI depends on the unemployment rate in the region each person lives. For example, while in an area where the regional rate of unemployment is 0 percent to 6 percent, 700 hours of insurable employment are necessary, in an area with a regional unemployment rate of 9.1 percent to 10 percent, 560 hours are needed. In an area with a regional unemployment rate of 13.1 percent or higher, 420 hours are needed. In some instances, however, individuals will need a great number of insurable employment in the past 52 weeks to qualify. For example, among those who are in the workforce for the first time, a minimum of 910 hours of insurable work in the past 52 weeks is required. Those who apply for sickness, maternity, or parental benefits will need 700 hours of insurable work. Those who have previously committed EI violations may also face increases in the number of hours they are required to possess before qualifying for EI benefits.

The length of time for which benefits can be received depends on the regional unemployment rate and how long an individual has worked in the last 52 weeks or since their last claim (whichever is shorter). Depending on the amount of insurable hours, benefits can be received from 14 to a maximum of 45 weeks. The basic benefit rate is 55 percent of average insured earnings up to a maximum payment of $413 per week. However, those who have drawn regular benefits in the past may have their benefits adjusted and reduced under the "intensity rule." Under this rule, benefit rates are reduced by 1 percent for every 20 weeks of regular benefits claimed since June 30, 1996, to a maximum of 5 percent if that person has more than 100 weeks of benefits over that five-year period. Individuals receiving regular benefits can earn up to 25 percent of their weekly benefits or $50 (whichever is higher) without changing the weekly amount they receive. However, all earnings above this limit are deducted dollar for dollar on their weekly benefits. Other sources of money that can affect the amount of EI benefits include such things as Canada Pension Plan or Quebec Pension Plan retirement income, self-employment earnings, or monies received in damages for wrongful dismissal. Payment from private RRSPs, a disability pension, survivor's pension, or dependent's pensions do not affect the calculation of EI payments. Depending on net income and past-claim history, all or some of the EI benefits received may have to be repaid at income tax time.

Families with children in a low-income situation (i.e., having a family net income under $25 921 a year) who receive the Canada Child Tax Benefit (CCTB) automatically receive the **Family Supplement** with a rate based on family net income and the number and ages of children in the family. In 2000, the maximum Family Supplement will reach as much as 80 percent of average insurable earnings. If both spouses claim EI at the same time, only one can receive the Family Supplement. In most circumstances, it is most advantageous for the spouse with the lower EI benefit to receive the Family Supplement.

According to Statistics Canada, fewer Canadians are now obtaining EI benefits than ever. While more than one million Canadians received regular UI benefits in an average month in 1992, in 1996, an average 600 000 Canadians received such benefits. Fewer Canadians are now unemployed (with the unemployment rate of 6.9 percent in December 1999 Canada's lowest in almost 20 years), but there are other reasons for the reductions observed. First, since the 1970s, the federal government has steadily trimmed away the benefits available to unemployed workers. For example, while in the early 1970s, weekly benefits were as high as 75 percent of a person's maximum weekly insurable earnings while employed, they are now, as earlier noted, 55 percent. Similarly, while in the early 1970s, the maximum length available for regular benefits was 51 weeks, it is now 45 weeks. While some of those who are unemployed are able to locate and obtain employment quickly, for others, their unemployment will last far longer than the benefit coverage that EI provides. Over time, the percentage of unemployed Canadians who are eligible for UI or EI benefits has fallen. In 1989, the average annual number of people receiving regular UI benefits was almost three-quarters (74 percent) of the average number of unemployed Canadians; this fell to 41 percent in 1996.

Guest (1999a: 2203) emphasizes that the separation of claimants into "normal" and "frequent user" should also be considered significant. He notes that frequent users "may suffer benefit reductions and possibly be subject to an income test, and receipt of benefit might be contingent on the claimant's willingness to take part in community work projects or training programs." As a result, he argues, "This is no longer social insurance but a form of 'workfare.'"

Educational Assistance

In Canada, public education is free until the end of secondary school (or "high school"). However, the costs associated with higher education have long been recognized to pose special problems to those of low income. Until 1939 and the federal government's passage of the **Dominion Provincial Student Aid Program (DSAP),** economic assistance for low-income persons wanting to attend postsecondary institutions was limited to those high scholastic achievers who could obtain privately funded assistance from universities and colleges. The encroachment of the federal government into the area of education (which, under the *Constitution Act* of 1867, is the exclusive domain of provincial legislatures) was legitimated with reference to economic growth, labour training, and labour mobility—areas that fell under federal jurisdiction. From this vantage point, the DSAP was simply a subset of the *Youth Training Act* or another part of national economic policy. By 1944, all of Canada's provinces had joined the plan; however, in 1954, Quebec opted out of the arrangement, "citing constitutional reasons of provincial primacy and autonomy in higher education" (Orlikow 1999: 2265). DSAP was discontinued in 1967.

In 1964, the **Canada Student Loans Program (CSLP)** was established. Under this plan, the federal government guarantees loans to all full-time students demonstrating financial need to a provincial or territorial government. These loans must be repaid over a period that does not exceed 9.5 years at a rate of interest that is set annually. Students are not required to begin making payments until six months after they have ceased to be a full-time student, but interest on the monies owed begins to accrue as soon as they leave full-time studies. In 1994, the *Canada Student Financial Assistance Act* **(CSFA Act)** revised the CSLP. It (1) increased the amounts of the maximum loans available to full-time and part-time students, (2) established a national program of grants for students with permanent disabilities, part-time students with high financial need, students with dependents, and women in doctoral programs in certain

National Data

Canadians with limited educational attainment have the highest unemployment rates and the lowest participation rates in the wage economy. In 1985, only 26 percent of Canadians with less than a high-school education were active participants in the labour force, and 15 percent were unemployed. Among those with some school-high education, 51 percent participated in the labour force and 16 percent were unemployed. In contrast, 83 percent of Canadians with a university degree were active participants in the labour force and only 5 percent were unemployed.

SOURCE: Health Canada 1999

fields, and (3) expanded interest relief for unemployed borrowers and those of low income. More recently, in 1998, the government also introduced new measures to assist students in loan repayment. Nevertheless, the rising cost of tuition (up 115 percent since 1980) continues to make the costs of postsecondary education difficult for many and prohibitive for some (see also Chapter 12).

Childcare Assistance Many Western industrialized countries provide free, high-quality preschools for three- to five-year-olds, and many also subsidize childcare for infants and toddlers (Albelda and Tilly 1997). In France, for example, public nursery schools enrol almost all children between ages three and six and public childcare centres care for infants and toddlers. French law also assists women in caring for their own children in infancy; a woman giving birth to her first or second child is entitled to 16 weeks of paid maternity leave, and when she has a third child, she gets 26 weeks of paid leave (Bergmann 1996).

In Canada, maternity and parental leave is part of our federal employment insurance system. Under Canada's current EI rules, new mothers receive a maximum of 15 weeks (the first two of which are nonpayable) of pregnancy benefits *only* if they have worked at least 700 hours in the 52 weeks prior and then they only receive 55 percent of their normal weekly pay to a maximum of $413 a week. Pregnant workers can begin their maternity leave as early as eight weeks before the birth of a child. Although either parent (including adoptive parents) may apply for parental benefits for an additional 10-week period following the birth of the baby, existent provisions seem to encourage mothers, rather than fathers, to pursue primary parenting. That is, should the father decide to seek the 10-week parental benefits, he would not receive benefits for the first 2 of the 10 weeks. Parental leave can be extended a further five weeks in cases of adoptions with specific medical conditions. Nevertheless, according to the National Council of Welfare's pre-1999 budget report, *Children First*, "The EI program comes nowhere near meeting the needs of families with babies and nowhere near meeting the most basic of infant health needs."

Under provincial and territorial legislation, all Canadian provinces and territories provide either 17 or 18 weeks of unpaid maternity leave, with the province of Quebec providing the most generous parental leave benefits, including 34 weeks of unpaid leave for the mother, father, or adoptive parents, and guarantees that workers on maternity or parental leave have the right to return to the same job with the same benefits of any salary increases or rights (e.g., the accumulation of seniority, rights to apply for other jobs, participation in insurance and pension plans) that would have been given had they been at work. Both mothers and fathers in Quebec are also entitled to five days of leave at the time of their child's birth (or adoption) and a further five days of unpaid leave to take care of children in the event of emergencies. To fill in the gaps that exist under the federal EI benefit system, Quebec provides a maternity allowance that covers the two-week waiting period during which EI recipients do not receive benefits. The Quebec Workers' Compensation Plan also provides pregnant workers with safer work in the same workplace or leave with benefits worth 90 percent of their salaries for the full term of the pregnancy for those whose specific work poses potential hazards to either pregnancy or nursing. At the time of writing, Quebec was also negotiating with the federal government for an integrated system of parental leave that would combine federal EI with provincial programs. If successful, mothers in Quebec would be entitled to 18 weeks of maternity leave at 70 percent of gross earnings, fathers eligible for three weeks' leave, either parent could take seven weeks of parental leave, and adoptive parents would be eligible for 12 weeks, all at 70 percent of earnings (provided that the parent earned $2000 during the previous year). The two-week waiting period for benefits would also be eliminated. The National Council of Welfare has voiced its support for the recommendation that all parental leave be supported at 70 percent of earnings, and that benefits be at the same level for self-employed workers; currently, those who are self-employed are ineligible for maternity and parental benefits.

The National Council of Welfare has also recommended that all mothers be granted six-months maternity leave under the EI program and that a further six months of parental leave should be available for either the mother or the father of an infant to promote quality parenting. However, because of recent welfare reforms in various provinces, even single parents must re-enter the workforce when their children are very young. For example, while Alberta's old welfare policy exempted single parents from job-search requirements until their children were two years of age, as of 1993, single-parent welfare recipients must seek work or enter training once their children are six months old.

It is evident that lack of affordable quality childcare can also be a major obstacle to employment. It has been noted that "very little regulated child care even exists in Canada" and that "there are regulated child care spaces for only 8.4 percent of the children who need them" (National Council of Welfare 1999b: 17). While the costs of childcare in general, and for preschoolers in particular, are high and rising, the federal, provincial, and territorial governments have cut funding for social programs, cut or frozen fee subsidies to low-income families, and made eligibility criteria for subsidies more restrictive (Doherty et al. 1998). The National Council of Welfare (1999b) has noted that although parents who are able to do so may pay as much as $850 a month per child for high-quality care in downtown Toronto or Ottawa, most parents are forced to rely on unregulated care "where the quality of care is completely unpredictable." It is argued that this situation "creates unconscionable risks for children's health and safety, and unnecessary anxiety for their parents." For parents of children with special needs as well as those parents who work irregular hours or shift-work, "child care is often completely unavailable" (p. 17).

Observing that "[c]hild care is a fact of life for Canadian children and their families," the National Council of Welfare (1999b) maintains that a national childcare program that provides good quality, affordable care must be considered "the logical hub" for other family supports. In the United States, researchers evaluating the High/Scope Perry Preschool Program estimated that investing in intense preschool programs for "high-risk" children offered savings of $7.16 for every dollar spent. They calculated that while, on average, the program spent $12 356 in 1992 dollars for each child during two years of preschool, the program saved $6287 in elementary, secondary, and post-secondary education costs since these children were less likely to fail grades and have to repeat them or to use such extra services as special education. In addition, they reasoned that alumni of the program were less likely to become involved with the criminal justice system (as either victims or perpetrators) and calculated the savings to be $12 796 in savings to the justice system and $57 585 in reduced costs for victims of crimes. Savings to the welfare system were evaluated to be $2918 per person. A Canadian study that estimated the benefits of a high-quality, affordable universal system of childcare and early

According to the Canadian National Child Care Survey, if childcare costs rose by 10 percent, the employment rate of single-parent mothers would drop by about 6 percent. Nearly 40 percent of single-parent mothers who were working and paying for childcare reported that if their child-care costs were to rise by 25 percent, they would quit their jobs.

SOURCE: National Council of Welfare 1999b

childhood education costing $7.9 billion calculated that if such a system existed, the value of the increased employment of mothers would be worth $6.2 billion and the improvement in child development worth $4.3 billion (Cleveland and Krashinsky 1998).

In 1997, Quebec introduced a comprehensive family policy that attempts to integrate family benefits, paid parental leave, childcare, and kindergarten. Its childcare component heralds universally available, affordable childcare in that province. Its aim is that, by the year 2001, every child in Quebec will be able to get childcare for $5 a day and for as little as $2 a day for certain low-income families. This nominal fee will entitle a child to a maximum of 10 hours a day of childcare, one meal and two snacks, and use of all educational materials. As of September 1997, all five-year-olds in Quebec whose families want it became entitled to receive free full-time kindergarten with $5-a-day after-school care organized by the educational authorities. Similarly, all four-year-olds have part-time or full-time junior kindergarten or child care for $5 a day, with additional free early intervention services available for those whose parents receive welfare. As of September 1998, all three-year-olds became eligible for $5-a-day childcare. It is expected that childcare for every child under 12 will be available in Quebec by September 2001. However, the costs of providing such a comprehensive childcare system are significant. For the fiscal year 1998–99, the costs of all operating grants, subsidies, the development of new services, and the training of staff reached $427 million.

Although Quebec's family policy has been lauded as "a pioneering approach to family supports in North America," childcare in the rest of Canada "continues to be provided with no clear sense of direction" and "severely compromised on three fronts: the availability of spaces to meet the needs of children and their families, the affordability of care and the quality of services provided" (National Council of Welfare 1999c: 44).

Child Support Enforcement In February 1997, Bill C-41 received Royal assent and became law in May of that year. This legislation included amendments to the *Divorce Act* to establish a framework for the use of child support guidelines; amendments to the *Family Orders and Agreements Enforcement Assistance* Act (FOAEA) that added Revenue Canada to the list of federal departments whose databanks can be searched to locate persons who have breached family support orders; new provisions in the FOAEA Act to establish a new federal licence denial scheme that will also authorize the suspension of passports and certain federal transport licences when a payer of child support has persistently breached support obligations; amendments to the *Garnishment, Attachment and Pension Diversion Act* to expand access to federal public service employee pension benefits to satisfy support arrears, and amendments to the *Shipping Act* to allow the wages of a person working at sea to be garnished to support a family obligation. All Canadian provinces now have their own programs to protect against the nonpayment of child support (e.g., Alberta Maintenance, Ontario Family Responsibilities Office, Family Maintenance of B.C.). For example, under Ontario's Family Support Plan, all support payments are registered and paid to the Family Support office and then distributed to the receiving spouse— a system that allows the province to track and enforce payment. Other methods include "Friend of the Court," in which a division of the local courthouse works as a publicly supported collection system, maintaining vigilance

National Data

In Canada, the percentage of children in the three- to five-year age group who need childcare ranged from 52 percent in New Brunswick to 70 percent in Prince Edward Island.
SOURCE: National Council of Welfare 1999b

National Data

In public opinion polls conducted from the early 1980s onward, Canadians have consistently supported childcare services. A 1998 poll conducted by Environics for the Canadian Policy Research Networks reported that more than three-quarters (76 percent) of Canadians believe a childcare system should be available for all families with the costs shared by governments and the family themselves.
SOURCE: National Council of Welfare 1999b

National Data

According to statistics compiled by the National Council of Welfare, the number of unattached men on welfare is significantly higher than the number of unattached women on welfare.

SOURCE: National Council of Welfare 1998a

over parents responsible for child support payments, and the "Automatic Wage Deduction" in which the noncustodial parent has the legally declared monthly support payments deducted from his or her paycheque and the amount sent automatically to the custodial parent. The "Wage Withholding System" withholds the noncustodial parent's wages or other income if payments have been missed or are overdue. Under the *Divorce Act*, either spouse or former spouse may be ordered to pay child support; child support not is taxable for the parent who receives the support nor is it deductible for the parent who pays the support on agreements made after May 1, 1997. (Child support agreements made before this date are not affected by this ruling.) Child support is also completely protected against bankruptcy claims.

Despite such measures, the problem of "deadbeat parents" remains significant. Indeed, one Canadian organization, Families Against Deadbeats (FAD), which maintains a Web site featuring "Wanted Posters" of those who have never paid court-ordered child support or are seriously in arrears, along with personal information and possible whereabouts, has reported that "over 2 billion dollars in child support arrears is owed" in Canada (FAD 2000).

Welfare in Canada: Myths and Realities

Public attitudes toward welfare assistance and welfare recipients are generally negative. Rather than view poverty as the problem, many Canadians view welfare as the problem. What are some of the common myths about welfare that perpetuate negative images of the welfare and welfare recipients?

MYTH 1 People receiving welfare are lazy and have no work ethic.

Reality

First, single parents on welfare already do work—they do the work of parenting. Albelda and Tilly (1997) emphasize that "raising children is work. It requires time, skills, and commitment. While we as a society do not place a monetary value on it, it is work that is invaluable—and indeed, essential to the survival of our society" (p. 111). Single parents and people with disabilities tend to have longer spells on welfare and those who are *able to work* tend to have shorter spells. Second, it should be evident that not all persons who would prefer to work are able to find jobs, particularly those in low-skill job categories. For example, Newfoundland has long had very high rates of unemployment, a fact that helps to explain why its welfare caseload is heavily laden with long-term welfare recipients. The National Council of Welfare (1999a: 17) notes that "Canada has seen a decline in the number of secure, full-time, well-paying jobs and an increase in the number of short-term, part-time jobs with low wages, few benefits and little and no security." As they emphasize, "For those individuals with low levels of education, 'bad' jobs are often the only real possibilities of employment, yet they cannot eliminate child and family poverty, no matter how hard a parent works. When lay-offs come, parents fall still further behind." Some provinces, such as Ontario, have incorporated "workfare" into its welfare system, which requires able-bodied people to do specific jobs as a condition of welfare, but most of the workfare jobs created are menial, dead-end jobs that are unlikely to lead to permanent employment.

Rather than disparage the work ethic of those on welfare, the National Council of Welfare (1998a: 62) emphasizes that it might be well to recognize that "everyone is at risk of falling on welfare at some point in their lives. The numbers speak for themselves: the estimated 1 494 800 welfare cases as of March 1997 represent an estimated 2 774 900 individual children, women and men or nearly ten percent of Canada's population." As they observe, "Losing a job, losing a spouse, and losing good health are some of the reasons that people go on welfare. The biggest myth of all would be to assume that most of us are immune to any of these personal tragedies or the many other misfortunes that can lead to reliance on welfare."

MYTH 2 Welfare benefits are granted to many people who are not eligible to receive them and welfare fraud is rampant.

Reality

Although some people obtain welfare benefits through fraudulent means, it is much more common for people who are eligible to receive welfare to not receive benefits. A main reason for not receiving benefits is lack of information; people do not know they are eligible. Some people who are eligible for public assistance do not apply for it because they do not want to be stigmatized as lazy people who just want a "free ride" at the taxpayers' expense—their sense of personal pride prevents them from receiving public assistance. Others want to avoid the administrative and transportation hassles involved in obtaining it.

Nevertheless, the impression that welfare fraud is widespread is undoubtedly suggested by government statistics on welfare "fraud and misuse." For example, in December 1999, Ontario's Community and Social Service Minister John Baird boasted that $35 million in "fraud savings" had occurred because of increased government vigilance in policing welfare recipients. However, what the ministry figures show is not truly welfare "fraud" on the part of claimants at all but rather, overpayments resulting from administrative errors and a notable vigour in relation to the disqualification of vulnerable individuals from receiving assistance. While in 1997–98, 61 653 cases were investigated for "welfare fraud," in fewer than one in four cases (23.9 percent) did the Ministry reduce the amount of the benefit or terminate the benefit altogether; only 1.2 percent (or 1100) of the cases investigated resulted in a criminal conviction for fraud. In addition, in more than 90 percent of the 14 771 cases in which the Ministry reduced the amount of the benefit because of a previous overpayment or terminated the benefits altogether, such actions were the result of an administrative error, not fraud. Thus, reductions in benefits paid or termination of benefits can occur in the absence of any wrongdoing on the part of welfare recipients. For example, should the Consolidated Verification Project (CVP) investigation reveal that a document is missing from a welfare recipient's file, the recipient is required to provide the necessary paperwork (whether it is two days or 20 years old) or face termination of benefits.

MYTH 3 Most welfare parents are teenagers.

Reality

According to the National Council of Welfare (1998a), teenage single parents accounted for only 3 percent of single parents on welfare in March 1997. Parents in their 20s to 40s accounted for 87 percent of couples with children on welfare and 91 percent of single parents on welfare.

MYTH 4 Most welfare mothers have large families with many children.

Reality

Mothers receiving welfare have no more children, on average, than mothers in the general population. In March 1997, nearly half (49.2 percent) of all single-parent families on welfare had only one child and almost a third (31 percent) had only two children. In that year, only 13 percent of the single-parent families on welfare had three children and only 7 percent had four or more children. Despite the stereotype that suggests that single-parent welfare mothers have large families with many children, they are actually somewhat less likely than two-parent families on welfare to have many children (Figure 10.8) (National Council of Welfare 1998).

MYTH 5 Unmarried women have children so they can receive benefits. If single mothers already receive benefits, they have additional children to receive increased benefits.

Reality

Research consistently shows that receiving welfare does not significantly increase out-of-wedlock births (Albelda and Tilley 1997). In the United States, in states that had the lowest AFDC cash benefits to single mothers, the teenage birthrates were among the highest.

MYTH 6 Most people on welfare also have income from part-time work or Employment Insurance or government pensions.

Reality

According to the National Council of Welfare (1998a), only 29 percent of welfare cases in March 1997 had outside income from work, government pensions, support payments, Employment Insurance, or other sources. Among couples with children, wages were the most common form of outside income; among single parents with children, child support or alimony was the most common source of outside income, with wages a close second. While transfer payments and wages were the main sources of outside income both for couples without

Figure 10.8

Welfare Cases by Family Type and Number of Children, 95 Percent Sample, March 1997

SOURCE: National Council of Welfare 1999a

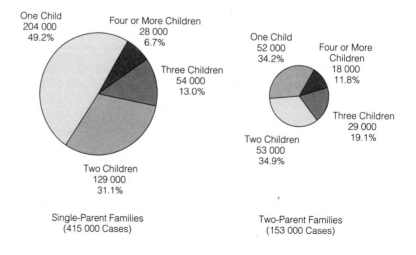

CHAPTER 10   THE HAVES AND THE HAVE-NOTS

children and for unattached persons, the percentage of unattached persons receiving either form of outside income was extremely low.

MYTH 7 Almost all the people on welfare are adults.

Reality
According to the National Council of Welfare (1998: 31), in March 1997, dependent children accounted for nearly 1.1 million of the people on welfare in Canada: 761 000 children in single-parent families and 329 000 children in two-parent families. However, they stress that any attempt to better the fortunes of Canadian children must acknowledge the poverty of their parents. "In reality, children are poor because their parents are poor" (National Council of Welfare 1999a: 8).

Despite the public perception that welfare benefits are too generous, cash and other forms of assistance to the poor do not meet the basic needs for many individuals and families who receive such benefits.

Minimum Wage Increase

As noted earlier, many families that leave welfare for work are still living in poverty because of involuntary part-time work and low wages. One strategy for improving the standard of living for low-income individuals and families is to increase the minimum wage. As the National Council of Welfare (1999a: 18) has noted, "Nowhere in Canada are minimum wages high enough to allow even full-time workers to escape poverty...[and] [t]he situation is much worse when a minimum wage worker has children to support."

> In Winnipeg in 1999, a single parent with one child had to work
> 80 hours a week simply to get to the poverty line. A two-parent
> family with two children in Winnipeg had to work 118 hours a week
> to reach the poverty line (and there are only 168 hours in a week). In
> Vancouver, where the minimum wage is the highest in the country, a
> single parent had to work 61 hours a week and a couple with two
> children had to work 89 hours a week to reach the poverty line.
> Clearly, minimum wages comes nowhere near to covering the costs
> of living.

For this reason, they argue that both the federal and provincial governments must ensure that minimum wages in their jurisdictions provide adequate incomes and that minimum wages must be indexed so that they rise each year with increases in the average industrial wage.

Those opposed to increasing the minimum wage argue that such an increase would result in higher unemployment and fewer benefits for low-wage workers; businesses would reduce wage costs by hiring fewer employees and providing fewer benefits. However, in a review of research on minimum wage increase, Card and Krueger (1995) found no evidence that employers reduced benefits to compensate for wage increases and employment actually increased slightly, rather than decreased.

In *Children First*, a report prepared in anticipation of the 2000 Canadian Budget, the National Council of Welfare included among its recommendations that:

Reasons for Contributing or Not Contributing to Charity

Directions: After reading each of the following reasons for contributing or not contributing to charity, indicate how important you think each reason is according to the following scale:

    1 = very or somewhat important   2 = not too important or not at all important

PART ONE: REASONS FOR CONTRIBUTING TO CHARITY

1. Being asked to give by someone you know well.
2. Because you volunteered at the organization.
3. Being asked by clergy to give.
4. Reading or hearing a news story.
5. Being asked at work to give.
6. Someone coming to the door asking you to give.
7. Being asked to give in a telethon/radiothon.
8. Receiving a letter asking you to give.
9. Receiving a phone call asking you to give.
10. Reading a newspaper or magazine advertisement.
11. Seeing a television commercial.

PART TWO: REASONS FOR NOT CONTRIBUTING TO CHARITY OR NOT CONTRIBUTING MORE

12. I could not afford to give money.
13. Because I already give as much as I can.
14. Because I am making less money this year than last.
15. Because I am unsure about having a job next year.
16. Because I lost my job.
17. I would rather spend my money in other ways.
18. Because no one I know personally asked me to give.
19. Because no charitable organization contacted me asking for a contribution.
20. Because I did not get around to it.

Comparison Data: You may compare your responses with those of a nationally representative sample of 2700 American adults. (Percentages are rounded and do not total 100 percent because some respondents did not respond to the item.)

	Percentage Who Said Reason Was Somewhat or Very Important	Percentage Who Said Reason Was Not Too Important or Not at All Important
1.	72	26
2.	61	36
3.	59	39
4.	43	55
5.	38	54
6.	36	61
7.	30	69
8.	29	70
9.	23	75
10.	17	81
11.	17	81
12.	56	43
13.	45	20
14.	40	40
15.	29	33
16.	29	37
17.	26	30
18.	17	26
19.	16	27
20.	15	29

SOURCE: Hodgkinson, Virginia A., and Murray S. Weitzman. 1996. *Giving and Volunteering in the United States, 1996.* <www.indepsec.org/media/reasons_for_contributing.html>. Reprinted by permission of Independent Sector.

- The federal government must provide wage supplements to parents in the labour force to cover the additional costs of raising children.
- Governments must provide job training that prepares workers for new jobs.
- Governments must ensure that postsecondary educational opportunities are open to everyone, not just students who are lucky enough to have families able to afford to pay their tuition fees and living expenses.
- Governments must ensure that legislation governing unpaid maternity and parental leave in their jurisdictions adequately covers the time parents require to care for young children. Existing parental leaves cover the first months of children's lives, but parents also need time to care for sick children and take them to medical appointments when their children are much older.
- Governments must ensure that employment and pay equity laws are strengthened and enforced.

Charity, Nonprofit Organizations, and Nongovernmental Organizations

Various types of aid to the poor are provided through individual and corporate donations to charities and nonprofit organizations. Before reading further, you may want to complete this chapter's Self and Society feature: "Reasons for Contributing or Not Contributing to Charity."

In 1996, the average charitable donation declared by tax filers was $730. Four billion dollars in donations was declared in that year. Those residing in Canada's richer provinces were not more likely to donate to charities nor were they the most generous donors. Rather, those residing in Manitoba and Prince Edward Island were the most likely to donate, and residents of Newfoundland, the province with the lowest total median income, made the highest median donation. Corporations also donate to charitable causes. In 1982, they contributed some $200 million; in 1995, they contributed $500 million to charities (Statistics Canada 1998a).

Charity involves giving not only money, but also time and effort in the form of volunteering. In Canada, those who reside in the Prairie provinces and the well educated are particularly likely to be volunteers. Women are slightly more likely than men are to be volunteers (6 out of 10) and rural and small-town residents more likely than city dwellers to be involved in volunteer activity. Nevertheless, high rates of volunteerism are found in cities such as Saskatoon (44 percent), Calgary (38 percent), and Edmonton (Statistics Canada 1998a).

Nongovernmental organizations (NGOs) play an important role in helping to reduce poverty and often collaborate with governmental poverty reduction efforts. In Thailand, for example, NGOs work with the government in such efforts as HIV/AIDS prevention and housing rights for slum dwellers. In Mumbai, Bombay, the nongovernmental organization YUVA—Youth for Unity and Voluntary Action—organizes youth and women for social action in housing, education, and health (*Human Development Report* 1997).

International Responses to Poverty

Alleviating worldwide poverty continues to be a major concern for both developing and developed countries. Approaches to poverty reduction include promoting economic growth and investing in "human capital." Conflict resolution and the promotion of peace are also important for reducing poverty worldwide.

Promoting Economic Growth Economic growth, over the long term, generally reduces poverty (*Human Development Report* 1997). An expanding economy creates new employment opportunities and increased goods and services. As employment prospects improve, individuals are able to buy more goods and services. The increased demand for goods and services, in turn, stimulates economic growth. As emphasized in Chapter 14, economic development requires controlling population growth and protecting the environment and natural resources, which are often destroyed and depleted in the process of economic growth.

However, economic growth does not always reduce poverty; in some cases, it increases it. For example, growth resulting from technological progress may reduce demand for unskilled workers. Growth does not help poverty reduction when public spending is diverted away from meeting the needs of the poor and instead is used to pay international debt or finance military operations. Thus, "economic growth, though essential for poverty reduction, is not enough. Growth must be pro-poor, expanding the opportunities and life choices of poor people" (*Human Development Report* 1997: 72–3). Because three-fourths of poor people in most developing countries depend on agriculture for their livelihoods, economic growth to reduce poverty must include raising the productivity of small-scale agriculture. Not only does improving the productivity of small-scale agriculture create employment, it also reduces food prices. The poor benefit the most because about 70 percent of their income is spent on food (*Human Development Report* 1997).

Investing in Human Capital Promoting economic development in a society requires having a productive workforce. Yet, in many poor countries, large segments of the population are illiterate and without job skills, or are malnourished and in poor health. Thus, a key feature of poverty reduction strategies involves investing in human capital. The term **human capital** refers to the skills, knowledge, and capabilities of the individual. Investments in human capital involve programs and policies that enhance the individual's health, skills, knowledge, and capabilities. Such programs and policies include those that provide adequate nutrition, sanitation, housing, health care (including reproductive health care and family planning), and educational and job training. Nobel Laureate Gary Becker has concluded that "the case is overwhelming that investments in human capital are one of the most effective ways to raise the poor to decent levels of income and health" (reported in Hill 1998: 279).

Poor health is both a consequence and a cause of poverty; improving the health status of a population is a significant step toward breaking the cycle of poverty. Increasing the educational levels of a population better prepares individuals for paid employment and for participation in political affairs that affect poverty and other economic and political issues. Improving the educational level and overall status of women in developing countries is also associated with lower birth rates, which in turn fosters economic development (see also Chapter 15).

One way to help poor countries invest in human capital and reduce poverty is to provide debt relief. If African countries were relieved of their national debts, they would have funds that would save the lives of millions of children and provide basic education to millions of girls and women. Providing debt relief to the 20 worst affected countries would cost between $5.5 billion and $7.7 billion— less than the cost of one Stealth bomber and roughly the cost of building the Euro-Disney theme park in France (*Human Development Report* 1997).

UNDERSTANDING THE HAVES AND THE HAVE-NOTS

As we have seen in this chapter, economic prosperity has not been evenly distributed; the rich have become richer, while the poor have become poorer. Meanwhile, Canada has implemented measures that essentially weaken the safety net for the impoverished segment of the population—largely, children. The decrease in assistance to the poor is a major reason poverty rates have remained high, despite the economic prosperity of the country. Many families leaving welfare report struggling to get food, shelter, medical care, childcare, and transportation. The effects of poverty on children perpetuate the cycle of poverty. Larin (1998) notes that "while it always has been possible for individuals to move up the economic ladder, the odds against it are high for individuals who suffer from the ill effects of poverty during childhood" (p. 26). Given the association between poverty and poor health and low educational attainment, poor children often grow up to be poor adults who are unable to escape poverty.

A common belief among Canadians is that the rich are deserving and the poor are failures. Blaming poverty on individuals rather than on structural and cultural factors implies not only that poor individuals are responsible for their plight, but also that they are responsible for improving their condition. If we hold individuals accountable for their poverty, we fail to make society accountable for making investments in human capital that are necessary to alleviate poverty. Such human capital investments include providing health care, adequate food and housing, education, childcare, and job training. Economist Lewis Hill (1998) believes that "the fundamental cause of perpetual poverty is the failure of...people to invest adequately in the human capital represented by impoverished children" (p. 299). Blaming the poor for their plight also fails to recognize that there are not enough jobs for those who want to work and that many jobs fail to pay wages that enable families to escape poverty. Lastly, blaming the poor for their condition diverts attention away from the recognition that the wealthy—individuals and corporations—receive far more benefits in the form of wealthfare or corporate welfare, without the stigma of welfare.

Ending or reducing poverty begins with the recognition that doing so is a worthy ideal and an attainable goal. Imagine a world where everyone had comfortable shelter, plentiful food, adequate medical care, and education. If this imaginary world were achieved, and absolute poverty were effectively eliminated, what would the effects be on such social problems as crime, drug abuse, family problems (such as domestic violence, child abuse, and divorce), health problems, prejudice and racism, and international conflict? It would be too costly to eliminate poverty—or would it? According to one source, the cost of eradicating poverty worldwide would be only about 1 percent of global income—and no more than 2 to 3 percent of national income in all but the poorest countries (*Human Development Report* 1997). Certainly the costs of allowing poverty to continue are much greater than that.

CRITICAL THINKING

1. Is it possible for a decline in Canada's "poverty rates" to be accompanied by an increase in the numbers of individuals experiencing economic hardships?
2. Should someone receiving welfare benefits be entitled to spend some of his or her money on "nonessentials" such as cigarettes, eating out, lottery tickets, and cable TV? Why or why not?
3. According to the National Council of Welfare (1999b: 8), "Many social programs support families but childcare is the backbone of them all." However, many groups that proclaim the need to promote and strengthen "family values" oppose the implementation of a national system of childcare and early childhood education. What reasons might underlie their opposition to this recommendation?
4. The poor have low rates of voting and thus have minimal influence on elected government officials and the policies they advocate. What strategies might be effective in increasing voter participation among the poor?
5. Oscar Lewis (1998) noted that "some see the poor as virtuous, upright, serene, independent, honest, secure, kind, simple and happy, while others see them as evil, mean, violent, sordid and criminal" (p. 9). Which view of the poor do you tend to hold? How have various social influences, such as parents, peers, media, social class, and education, shaped your views toward the poor?

KEY TERMS

absolute poverty
bourgeoisie
Canada Child Tax Benefit (CCTB)
Canada Student Financial Assistance Act (CSFA Act)
Canada Student Loans Program (CSLP)
corporate welfare
culture of poverty
demogrant

Dominion Provincial Student Aid Program (DSAP)
family allowance
Family Supplement
feminization of poverty
human capital
Human Poverty Index (HPI)
intergenerational poverty
low-income cutoff (LICO)
Low-Income Measure (LIM)

National Child Benefit (NCB)
National Child Benefit Supplement (NCBS)
poverty
proletariat
relative poverty
underclass
wealth
wealthfare
working poor

CHAPTER ELEVEN

Work and Unemployment

Is It True?

1. Child labour and sweatshops are virtually nonexistent worldwide.

2. Compared to male workers, Canadian women workers are more likely to be unionized.

3. The world's top two hundred corporations control more than one-fourth of all sales in the global economy but employ less than 1 percent of the world's workforce.

4. Women in Canada face a boom-and-bust job environment more so than do men.

5. As many people in Canada believe they could lose their jobs in the next few years as there are those who feel secure in their jobs.

Answers: 1 = F, 2 = F, 3 = T, 4 = F, 5 = T

On December 10, 1948, the General Assembly of the United Nations adopted and proclaimed the Universal Declaration of Human Rights. Among the articles of that declaration are the following:

> Article 23. Everyone has the right to work, to free choice of employment, to just and favourable conditions of work and to protection against unemployment.
>
> Everyone, without any discrimination, has the right to equal pay for equal work.
>
> Everyone who works has the right to just and favourable remuneration ensuring for himself and his family an existence worthy of human dignity, and supplemented, if necessary, by other means of social protection.
>
> Everyone has the right to form and to join trade unions for the protection of his interests.
>
> Article 24. Everyone has the right to rest and leisure, including reasonable limitation of working hours and periodic holidays with pay.

More than half a century later, workers around the world are still fighting for these basic rights. In this chapter, we examine problems of work and unemployment, including child labour, health and safety hazards in the workplace, job dissatisfaction and alienation, work–family concerns, and declining numbers of labour unions. We begin by looking at the global economy.

Before reading further, you may want to complete the "Attitudes toward Corporations" survey in the Self and Society feature of this chapter. It might be interesting to retake this survey after reading this chapter and see how your attitudes may have changed.

> *Promises of better things to come, repeated for years and years, are a cruel hoax on those who are hoping and waiting....*
>
> David Lewis, Politician, Key Architect of the New Democratic Party, labour lawyer, and university professor

THE GLOBAL CONTEXT: THE ECONOMY IN THE TWENTY-FIRST CENTURY

In January 1999, 11 of the 15 European Union nations began making the transition from their national currency to a new common currency—the euro—that will lock them together financially. The euro and national currencies will operate in parallel until 2002, after which German marks, French francs, and Italian lire will be replaced by single currency notes and coins. Some economists predict the euro could rival the U.S. dollar as the dominant international currency (Reed 1999). The adoption of the euro reflects the increasing globalization of economic institutions. The **economic institution** refers to the structure and means by which a society produces, distributes, and consumes goods and services.

In recent decades, innovations in communication and information technology have spawned the emergence of a **global economy**—an interconnected network of economic activity that transcends national borders and spans across the world. The globalization of economic activity means that increasingly our jobs, the products and services we buy, and our nation's political policies and agendas influence and are influenced by economic activities around the world. After summarizing the two main economic systems in the world—capitalism and socialism—we look at the emergence of corporate multinationalism. Then we describe how industrialization and postindustrialization have changed the nature of work.

Capitalism and Socialism

The principal economic systems in the world are capitalism and socialism. Under **capitalism,** private individuals or groups invest capital (money, technology, machines) to produce goods and services to sell for a profit in a competitive market. Capitalism is characterized by economic motivation through profit, the determination of prices and wages primarily through supply and demand, and the absence of governmental intervention in the economy. Critics of capitalism argue that it creates too many social evils, including alienated workers, poor working conditions, near-poverty wages, unemployment, a polluted and depleted environment, and world conflict over resources.

Pure capitalism (known as "hands off" capitalism) exists only when market forces can operate without interference from the government. However, in Canada, many restraints to the laissez-faire model have traditionally existed. State capitalism is a form of capitalism in which private citizens own the means of production and pursue profits but do so within a vast system of laws designed to protect the welfare of the population. In Canada, state capitalism also refers to public or state investment in sectors of the economy that could be private. Canada's economy was once described as "a strange mix of interventionism and free-market policies" (Hallsworth 1993: 445); however, since the 1980s, the state has begun to withdraw from the private sector by selling off public assets (e.g., Petro-Canada, Air Canada) and through an ongoing process of deregulation (e.g., the North American Free Trade Agreement, the reduction of interprovincial trade barriers, and the "open skies" agreement with the United States).

Socialism emphasizes public rather than private ownership. Theoretically, goods and services are equitably distributed according to the needs of the citizens. Whereas capitalism emphasizes individual freedom, socialism emphasizes social equality.

Advocates for capitalism and socialism claim that the one they support results in economic well-being for society and for its members. In reality, both capitalist and socialist countries have been unable to fulfil their promises. Although the overall standard of living is higher in capitalist countries, so is economic inequality. Some theorists suggest that capitalist countries will adopt elements of socialism and socialist countries will adopt elements of capitalism. This idea, known as the **convergence hypothesis**, is reflected in the economies of Germany, France, and Sweden, which are sometimes called "integrated economies" because they have elements of both capitalism and socialism.

CONSIDERATION

Panitch (1999: 2246) has observed that although "'free market' ideologies were not initially as pronounced in Canada as in the United States or Britain," economic crisis and the global restructuring of capital and labour have resulted in "a shift away from welfarist and regulatory criteria and towards more explicit free-market criteria in the making of Canadian state policy." He points out that free trade with the United States is an important aspect of this development in that "it removes some of the historical and material basis for a large role for the state in providing the infrastructure for and coordinating a specifically Canadian, albeit dependent, economic space north of the 49th parallel."

Corporate Multinationalism

Corporate multinationalism is the practice of corporations having their home base in one country and branches, or affiliates, in other countries. Corporate multinationalism allows businesses to avoid import tariffs and costs associated with transporting goods to another country. Access to raw materials, cheap foreign labour, and the avoidance of government regulations also drive corporate multinationalism. "By moving production plants abroad, business managers may be able to work foreign employees for long hours under dangerous conditions at low pay, pollute the environment with impunity, and pretty much have their way with local communities. Then the business may be able to ship its goods back to its home country at lower costs and bigger profits" (Caston 1998: 274–5).

Although multinationalization provides jobs for managers, secures profits for investors, and helps Canada compete in the global economy, it also has "far-reaching and detrimental consequences" (Epstein et al. 1993: 206). Corporate multinationalization must take its share of the blame for an array of social problems such as poverty resulting from fewer jobs, urban decline resulting from factories moving away, and racial and ethnic tensions resulting from competition for jobs. In addition, as Maule (1999: 1536) points out, "[l]ess developed countries argue that they have traded political independence for economic and cultural dependence. Politically, there remains concern over the extent to which multinational corporations are used as instruments of foreign policy by the governments of countries where parent companies are located. Culturally, the concern is over the loss of national identity." Noting that the rapid increase of foreign ownership in the Canadian economy after World War I was linked to the rise of multinational corporations, economic nationalists have also expressed concern over "the special problems created by this type of investment, particularly the stunted and distorted pattern of economic development" and the broader impact of multinationals on Canadian society, identity, and sovereignty (Rotstein 1999: 717). For example, Bellan (1999: 884–5) points out that

> **Huge and increasing amounts of money have to be remitted to U.S. owners in the form of dividends on their investment and contributions by branch plants toward head office costs of administration, research, product development and advertising. A large proportion of these payments must be made in U.S. dollars....The consequence is that a very large fraction of the U.S. dollars that Canada earns by its exports must be used to make interest and dividend payments and branch plant remittances to U.S. firms.**

Second, Bellan charges that multinational corporations have "carried on their Canadian operations to serve their own best interests, not those of

Canada," with industrial research and development that are "essential to industrial innovation and growth" generally conducted in their U.S. facilities rather than at their Canadian branch plants. Third, he notes that multinationals show no particular loyalty to Canada when the demand for their products falls or a cheaper source of supplies or labour is found in another country.

Industrialization, Postindustrialization, and the Changing Nature of Work

The nature of work has been shaped by the **Industrial Revolution**, the period between the mid–eighteenth century and the early nineteenth century when the factory system was introduced in England. Industrialization dramatically altered the nature of work: machines replaced hand tools; and steam, gasoline, and electric power replaced human or animal power. Industrialization also led to the development of the assembly line and an increased division of labour as goods began to be mass-produced. The development of factories contributed to the emergence of large cities where the earlier informal social interactions dominated by primary relationships were replaced by formal interactions centred on secondary groups. Instead of the family-centred economy characteristic of an agricultural society, people began to work outside the home for wages.

Postindustrialization refers to the shift from an industrial economy dominated by manufacturing jobs to an economy dominated by service-oriented, information-intensive occupations. Postindustrialization is characterized by a highly educated workforce, automated and computerized production methods, increased government involvement in economic issues, and a higher standard of living (Bell 1973). Like industrialization before it, postindustrialization has transformed the nature of work.

Three fundamental work sectors—primary, secondary, and tertiary—coexist. These work sectors reflect the major economic transformations in society—the Industrial Revolution and the Postindustrial Revolution. The **primary work sector** involves the production of raw materials and food goods. In developing countries with little industrialization, about 60 percent of the labour force works in agricultural activities; in Canada less than 3 percent of the workforce is in farming (Bracey 1995; *Report on the World Social Situation* 1997; Statistics Canada 1998a). The **secondary work sector** involves the production of manufactured goods from raw materials (e.g., paper from wood). The third sector is the **tertiary work sector**, which includes professional, managerial, technical support, and service jobs. In a postindustrial society, the highest proportion of jobs is in the tertiary sector.

In a postindustrial society, highly skilled and technological personnel are needed, but many workers, particularly women and minorities, are not educated and skilled enough for many of these positions (Koch 1998). In developing countries, many individuals with the highest level of skill and education leave the country in search of work abroad, leading to the phenomenon known as the **brain drain** (see also Chapter 12). Although employers in developed countries benefit, developing countries lose valuable labour.

SOCIOLOGICAL THEORIES OF WORK AND THE ECONOMY

Numerous theories in economics, political science, and history address the nature of work and the economy. In sociology, structural-functionalism, con-

Attitudes toward Corporations

PART ONE

How good a job do you think corporations are doing these days? Using letter grades like those in school, give corporations an A, B, C, D, or F in:

LETTER GRADE

1. Paying their employees good wages   _____
2. Being loyal to employees   _____
3. Making profits   _____
4. Keeping jobs in Canada   _____

PART TWO

Here are some things some large corporations are doing that some people think are serious problems, while others think they are not serious problems. For each of the following practices, indicate whether you think this is a serious problem or not.

	Serious Problem	Not a Problem	Don't Know
5. Not providing health care and pensions to employees	_____	_____	_____
6. Not paying employees enough so that they and their families can keep up with the cost of living	_____	_____	_____
7. Paying CEOs 200 times what their employees make	_____	_____	_____
8. Laying off large numbers of workers even when the company is profitable	_____	_____	_____

PART THREE

Which of the following statements comes closer to your view? (check one)

9A. Two major problems with the economy today are government waste and inefficiency. Excessive government spending and high taxes burden middle-class families and slow economic growth. Our government debt drives up interest rates, making it much harder for businesses to invest and create jobs.

9B. A major problem with the economy today is politicians catering to the interests of powerful corporations and wealthy campaign contributors at the expense of working families. That is why politicians are not doing anything to stop large corporations from laying off large numbers of employees, denying health benefits, moving jobs overseas, and raiding pension funds.

9A. _____ 9B. _____

10A. Wasteful and inefficient government is preventing the middle class from getting ahead and doing better. Excessive government spending and high taxes burden working families and slow economic growth. The budget deficit drives up interest rates and taxes, hurts consumers and business, and reduces job-creating investments. Red tape and excessive regulation are hurting business.

10B. Corporate greed is preventing the middle class from getting ahead and doing better. In the past, when people did their jobs well, they could earn a decent wage and provide a better life for their children. Now, corporate Canada is squeezing their employees—cutting wages, downsizing jobs, and eliminating pensions and health benefits. Companies say they cannot afford to treat employees better, but many have growing profits, record stock prices, and huge salaries for their executives.

10A. _____ 10B. _____

11A. Large corporations are laying people off, cutting benefits, and moving jobs overseas mainly because they have gotten greedy and are squeezing employees to maximize profits.

11B. Large corporations are laying people off, cutting benefits, and moving jobs overseas mainly because they have to stay in business and provide jobs.

                        11A. _____ 11B. _____

RESULTS OF A NATIONAL SAMPLE

You may want to compare your answers to this survey with responses from a national sample of American adults.

PART ONE (Percentages do not total 100 due to individuals who responded "Don't know.")

1.	A: 11%	2.	A: 10%	3.	A: 52%	4.	A: 12%
	B: 26%		B: 16%		B: 26%		B: 16%
	C: 36%		C: 28%		C: 9%		C: 31%
	D: 12%		D: 23%		D: 3%		D: 20%
	F: 7%		F: 19%		F: 2%		F: 18%

PART TWO

	Serious	Not Serious	Don't Know
5.	82%	15%	3%
6.	76%	19%	5%
7.	79%	14%	7%
8.	81%	14%	5%

PART THREE

9A.	33%	9B. 40%	(21% answered "both" and 6% answered "don't know")
10A.	28%	10B. 46%	(22% answered "both" and 4% answered "don't know")
11A.	70%	11B. 22%	(7% answered "don't know")

SOURCE: Adapted from "Corporate Irresponsibility: There Ought to be Laws." 1996. EDK Poll, Washington, D.C.: Preamble Center for Public Policy, December 12, 1998 <www.preamble.org/polledk.html>. Used by permission.

flict theory, and symbolic interactionism serve as theoretical lenses through which we may better understand work and economic issues and activities.

Structural-Functionalist Perspective

According to the structural-functionalist perspective, the economic institution is one of the most important of all social institutions. It provides the basic necessities common to all human societies, including food, clothing, and shelter. By providing for the basic survival needs of members of society, the economic institution contributes to social stability. After the basic survival needs of a society are met, surplus materials and wealth may be allocated to other social uses, such as maintaining military protection from enemies, supporting political and religious leaders, providing formal education, supporting an expanding population, and providing entertainment and recreational activities. Societal development is dependent on an economic surplus in a society (Lenski and Lenski 1987).

Although the economic institution is functional for society, elements of it may be dysfunctional. For example, before industrialization, agrarian societies had a low division of labour in which few work roles were available to members of society. Limited work roles meant that society's members shared similar roles and thus developed similar norms and values (Durkheim [1893] 1966). In contrast, industrial societies are characterized by many work roles, or a high division of labour, and cohesion is based not on the similarity of people and their roles but on their interdependence. People in industrial societies need the skills and services that others provide. The lack of common norms and values in industrialized societies may result in *anomie*—a state of normlessness—which is linked to a variety of social problems including crime, drug addiction, and violence (see Chapters 3 and 4).

Conflict Perspective

According to Karl Marx, capitalism is responsible for the inequality and conflict within and between societies. The ruling class controls the economic system for its own benefit and exploits and oppresses the working masses. While structural-functionalism views the economic institution as benefiting society as a whole, conflict theory holds that capitalism benefits an elite class that controls not only the economy but other aspects of society as well—the media, politics and law, education, and religion.

Corporate wealth and power have grown at the expense of workers. Between 1980 and 1992, the five hundred largest U.S. corporations increased their assets 227 percent, but during that same time, they cut jobs by 28 percent (Danaher 1998). As Nelson and Fleras (1998: 338) have observed, "[i]n a market-oriented climate that defines greed as good, General Motors Ltd. may have posted the largest profit of any private company in the history of Canada, but that did not deter it from slashing thousands of jobs in the process." Citing fears of another recession and competitive pressures from free trade and deregulation, GM recorded record profits of $1.39 billion but eliminated 2500 jobs. In like fashion, Petro-Canada, which employed approximately 6200 workers in 1990, downsized its workforce to 4800 in 1995 with warnings of additional cutbacks, despite healthy profits over this period.

Corporate power is also reflected in the policies of the International Monetary Fund (IMF) and the World Bank, which pressure developing countries to open their economies to foreign corporations, promoting export production at the expense of local consumption, encouraging the exploitation of labour as a means of attracting foreign investment, and hastening the degradation of natural resources as countries sell their forests and minerals to earn money to pay back loans. Ambrose (1998) asserts that "for some time now, the IMF has been the chief architect of the global economy, using debt leverage to force governments around the world to give big corporations and billionaires everything they want—low taxes, cheap labour, loose regulations—so they will locate in their countries" (p. 5). Treaties such as the North American Free Trade Agreement

(NAFTA), the General Agreement on Tariffs and Trade (GATT), and the Multilateral Agreement on Investments (MAI) also benefit corporations at the expense of workers by providing corporations with greater access to foreign markets. "These laws increasingly allow corporations to go anywhere and do anything they like, and prohibit workers and the governments that supposedly represent them from doing much about it" (Danaher 1998: 1).

According to the conflict perspective, work trends that benefit employees, such as work site health promotion programs and work–family policies (discussed later in this chapter) are not the result of altruistic or humanitarian concern for workers' well-being. Rather, corporate leaders recognize that these programs and policies result in higher job productivity and lower health care costs and are thus good for the bottom line.

Symbolic Interactionist Perspective

According to symbolic interactionism, the work role is a central part of a person's identity. When meeting someone new, one of the first questions we usually ask is, "What do you do?" The answer largely defines for us who that person is. For example, identifying a person as a truck driver provides a different social meaning than identifying someone as a physician. The title of a person's work status—maintenance supervisor or Prime Minister of Canada— also gives meaning and self-worth to the individual. People's jobs are one of their most important statuses; for many, it is a master status, that is, the most significant status in that person's social identity.

As symbolic interactionists note, definitions and meanings influence behaviour. Meanings and definitions of child labour (discussed later) contribute to its perpetuation. In some countries, children learn to regard working as a necessary and important responsibility and rite of passage, rather than an abuse of human rights. Some children look forward to becoming bonded to a master "in the same way that...children [in our society] look forward to a communion or getting a driver's license" (Silvers 1996: 83).

Symbolic interactionism emphasizes that attitudes and behaviours are influenced by interaction with others. The applications of symbolic interactionism in the workplace are numerous—employers and managers are concerned with using interpersonal interaction techniques that achieve the attitudes and behaviours they want from their employees; union organizers are concerned with using interpersonal interaction techniques that persuade workers to unionize; and job training programs are concerned with using interpersonal interaction techniques that are effective in motivating participants.

PROBLEMS OF WORK AND UNEMPLOYMENT

Next, we examine unemployment and other problems associated with work. The problem of discrimination in the workplace based on gender, race and ethnicity, and sexual orientation is addressed in other chapters. Minimum wage issues are discussed in Chapter 10. Here we discuss problems concerning child labour, health and safety hazards in the workplace, job dissatisfaction and alienation, work–family concerns, declining numbers of labour unions, and unemployment and underemployment.

Child Labour: A Global Problem

Employment can be a valuable experience for youth because it encourages psychosocial development and the acquisition of work skills, but for most working children around the world, work is an oppressive, dehumanizing way of life.

Child labour involves children performing work that is hazardous, that interferes with a child's education, or that harms a child's health or physical, mental, spiritual, or moral development (U.S. Department of Labor 1995). Even though virtually every country in the world has laws that limit or prohibit the extent to which children can be employed, child labour persists throughout the world.

Child labour is most prevalent in Africa, Asia, and Central and South America. India has the largest child labour force in the world, with between 20 and 80 million working children (Parker 1998). This chapter's The Human Side feature depicts child labour in Pakistan.

Child labourers work in factories, workshops, construction sites, mines, quarries, and fields, on deep-sea fishing boats, at home, and on the street. They make bricks, shoes, soccer balls, fireworks, matches, furniture, toys, rugs, and clothing. They pick crops and tend livestock. They work in the manufacturing of brass, leather goods, and glass. Children rummage through garbage searching for rags to sell or work in sweatshops. **Sweatshops** are work environments characterized by less than minimum wage pay, excessively long hours of work (often without overtime pay), unsafe or inhumane working conditions, abusive treatment of workers by employers, or the lack of worker organizations aimed at negotiating better work conditions. Adults—particularly immigrants and women—also work in sweatshops.

Extreme forms of child labour include bonded labour and commercial sexual exploitation. **Bonded labour** refers to the repayment of a debt through labour. Typically, an employer loans money to parents, who then give the employer their children as labourers to repay the debt. Sometimes the child is taken far away from the family to work; other times the child works in the same village and continues to live at home. The children are unable to work off the debt because of high interest rates, low wages, and wage deductions for meals, lodging, and mistakes made at work (U.S. Department of Labor 1995). Bonded labour is like slavery; a bonded worker is not free to leave the workplace. Between 10 and 20 million children in the world are forced to work as bonded labourers (Parker 1998). Bonded labour is most common in India, Nepal, Bangladesh, and Pakistan.

Child prostitution occurs throughout the world and is particularly prevalent in Asia and Central and South America. In poor societies, the sexual services of children are often sold by their families for the money. Some children are kidnapped or lured by traffickers with promises of employment, only to end up in a brothel. An estimated one-quarter of all visitors using child prostitutes in Asia are North American businessmen or military personnel (Kennedy 1996).

Causes of Child Labour Poverty, economic exploitation, social values, and lack of access to education are factors contributing to the persistence of child labour. One mother in Bangladesh whose 12-year-old daughter works up to 14 hours a day in a garment sweatshop explained, "Children shouldn't have to work....But if she didn't, we'd go hungry" (Parker 1998: 47). The economic advantages to industries that profit from child labour also perpetuate the

International Data

According to the International Labour Organization (ILO), nearly 250 million children around the world work. In less developed countries, nearly one-quarter of children aged 5 to 14 work.

SOURCE: Parker 1998

CHILD LABOUR IN PAKISTAN

Like most other countries, Pakistan has laws prohibiting child labour and indentured servitude. However, these laws are largely ignored, and about 11 million children aged 4 to 14 work under brutal and squalid conditions. Children make up about a quarter of the unskilled work force in Pakistan and can be found in virtually every factory, field, and workshop. They earn on average a third of the adult wage. Reading the following excerpts from an *Atlantic Monthly* report on child labour in Pakistan (Silvers 1996) will no doubt leave you outraged, sad, and shocked that such conditions persist in our modern world.

The median age of children now entering the Pakistani workforce is seven. Two years ago, it was eight. Two years from now, it may be six. In the lowest castes, children become labourers almost as soon as they can walk. Much of the nation's farmland is worked by toddlers, yoked teams of three-, four-, and five-year-olds who plough, seed, and glean fields from dawn to dusk....

In rural areas, children are raised without health care, sanitation, or education; many are as starved for affection as for food. As soon as they're old enough to have an elementary understanding of their circumstances, their parents teach them that they are expected to pay their way, to make sacrifices, and, if necessary, to travel far from home and live with strangers. "When my children were three, I told them they must be prepared to work for the good of the family," says Asthma, a Sheikhupura villager who bonded her five children to masters in distant villages....

Soon after I arrived in Pakistan, I arranged a trip to a town whose major factories were rumored to enslave very young children. I found myself hoping during the journey there that the children I saw working in fields, on the roads, at the marketplaces, would prepare me for the worst. They did not. No amount of preparation could have lessened the shock and revulsion I felt on entering a sporting-goods factory in the town of Sialkot, seventy miles from Lahore, where scores of children, most of them aged five to ten, produce soccer balls by hand for forty rupees, or about $1.20, a day. The children work eighty hours a week in near-total darkness and total silence. According to the foreman, the darkness is both an economy and a precautionary measure; child-rights activists have difficulty taking photographs and gathering evidence of wrongdoing if the lighting is poor. The silence is to ensure product quality: "If the children speak, they are not giving their complete attention to the product and are liable to make errors." The children are permitted one thirty-minute meal break each day; they are punished if they take longer. They are also punished if they fall asleep, if their workbenches are sloppy, if they waste material or miscut a pattern, if they com-

CHILD LABOUR IN PAKISTAN *(continued)*

plain of mistreatment to their parents or speak to strangers outside the factory....Punishments are doled out in a storage closet at the rear of the factory....Children are hung upside down by their knees, starved, caned, or lashed....The punishment room is a standard feature of a Pakistani factory, as common as a lunchroom at a Detroit assembly plant.

The town's other factories are no better, and many are worse. Here are brick kilns where five-year-olds work hip-deep in slurry pits, where adolescent girls stoke furnaces in 160-degree heat. Here are tanneries where nursing mothers mix vats of chemical dye, textile mills where eight-year-olds tend looms and breathe air thick with cotton dust....

A carpet workshop...was... about the size of a subway car, and about as appealing. The long, narrow room contained a dozen upright looms. On each rough-hewn workbench between the looms squatted a carpet weaver. The room was dark and airless. Such light as there was came from a single ceiling fixture, two of its four bulbs burned out. A thermometer read 105 degrees, and the mud walls were hot to the touch....

Of the twelve weavers, five were eleven to fourteen, and four were under ten. The two youngest were brothers named Akbar and Ashraf, aged eight and nine. They had been bonded to the carpet master at age five, and now worked six days a week at the shop. Their workday started at 6:00 a.m. and ended at 8:00 p.m., except, they said, when the master was behind on his quotas and forced them to work around the clock. They were small, thin, malnourished, their spines curved from lack of exercise and from squatting before the loom. Their hands were covered with calluses and scars, their fingers gnarled from repetitive work. Their breathing was laboured, suggestive of tuberculosis. Collectively these ailments, which pathologists call captive-child syndrome, kill half of Pakistan's working children by age twelve....

A hand-knotted carpet is made by tying short lengths of fine colored thread to a lattice of heavier white threads. The process is labour-intensive and tedious: a single four-by-six-foot carpet contains well over a million knots and takes an experienced weaver four to six months to complete....Each carpet Akbar completed would retail in the United States for about $2000—more than the boy would earn in ten years. Abkar revealed that, "the master screams at us all the time, and sometimes he beats us....We're slapped often. Once or twice he lashed us with a cane. I was beaten ten days ago after I made many errors of colour in a carpet. He struck me with his fist quite hard on the face....I was fined one thousand rupees and made to correct the

National Data

The majority of Canadian-made garments are produced by homeworkers earning less than minimum wage and working many unpaid hours of overtime. Homeworkers work on a piecework basis and even though they are legally entitled to the minimum wage plus 10 percent for overhead, violations of these standards are commonplace. The homeworker who sews the breezy summer shorts and top outfit that retails for $54.90 may earn merely $2.63 for sewing it. In Toronto alone, more than 5000 homeworkers produce goods for local subcontractors.

SOURCE: Yanz and Jeffcott 1997

CHILD LABOUR IN PAKISTAN *(continued)*

errors by working two days straight." The fine was added to Akbar's debt, and would extend his "apprenticeship" by several months....Akbar declared that "staying here longer fills me with dread. I know I must learn a trade. But my parents are so far away, and all my friends are in school. My brother and I would like to be with our family. We'd like to play with our friends. This is not the way children should live."

SOURCE: Silvers, Jonathan. 1996. From "Child Labour in Pakistan." © 1996 by Jonathan Silvers as first published in *The Atlantic Monthly*, February 1996. Reprinted by permission.

International Data

The majority of garments sold by Canadian retailers—particular in relation to women's and children's clothing—are made in Asia, with China as the world's largest garment producer and exporter. In 1996 there were approximately 44 000 garment factories in China employing four million workers—mostly women—with an annual output of 8.5 billion pieces.

SOURCE: Yanz and Jeffcott 1997

National Data

Two decades ago, the majority of garments in Canada were produced in large factories with a unionization rate of 80 percent. That rate has declined to 20 percent in recent years.

SOURCE: Yanz and Jeffcott 1997

practice. However, some employers and government officials in Eastern countries claim that child labour is not a violation of social values. In the words of one employer in Pakistan who uses child labour, "Child labour is a tradition the West cannot understand and must not attempt to change" (Silvers 1996: 86). Finally, child labour results from failure to provide education to all children. The education system in Pakistan, for example, can only accommodate about one-third of the country's school-age children, leaving the remainder to join the child labour pool.

Consequences of Child Labour Child labourers are at risk for a variety of health problems such as injuries, stunted growth, and many diseases. Child carpet weavers develop gnarled fingers from the repetitive work, and their spines are curved from sitting at looms all day. Young brickworkers breathe in dust from the dry bricks and sand, causing scarring of the lungs and early death. Child farmworkers are exposed to harmful pesticides. Child prostitutes are at high risk for acquiring HIV and suffer the emotional scars of their exploitation. Child labourers are fed inadequate diets and must endure harsh punishment from their employers. One girl who was forced into prostitution in Bangkok said, "One time I refused to sleep with a man and they slapped me, hit me with a cane and bashed my head against the wall. One of my friends tried to run away but unfortunately she was caught and very badly beaten" (Parker 1998: 42).

Child labour also has detrimental consequences for the larger society. Although poverty drives parents to send their children to work, child labour also increases poverty by depressing already low wages. Parker (1998) explains,

For every child who works, there may be an adult who cannot find a job. Children are usually paid less than adult workers—sometimes only one-third of what adults earn. As a result, adult workers' wages stay low or go down. When parents cannot find jobs, they are more likely to send their children to work. They have more children in the hope of increasing their income. Each generation of poor, uneducated child workers becomes the next genre of poor parents who must send their kids to work. Then the cycle of poverty and illiteracy continues. (Parker 1998: 48)

Although cheap child labour may fuel economic growth for some countries, it also hinders industrial development, especially in the use of advanced technologies. Rather than invest in labour-saving technology, manufacturers use a cheaper alternative: child labour.

Health and Safety Hazards in the Workplace

Accidents at work and hazardous working conditions contribute to illnesses, injuries, and deaths. The rate of reported time-loss work injuries has been decreasing steadily, from 49 injuries for every one thousand workers in 1987 to slightly less than 28 per one thousand workers in 1996. However, according to data collected by Statistics Canada on behalf of the Association of Workers' Compensation Boards of Canada, in 1996 there were still more than 377 000 time-loss work injuries in Canada. The definition of a "time-loss injury" is an injury that results in compensation for lost wages because of time off work or for a permanent disability, regardless of the time lost. In that year, men's rate of time-loss injury was more than two and a half times that of women (Figure 11.1). The rate of injuries per 1000 workers was highest among those aged 15 to 29; among this age cohort, the injury rate was 43.4 per 1000 (more than 57 percent above the average for all ages and both sexes). The rate of compensated injuries was far higher in forestry and logging than in any other industry, although rates in transportation, wholesale trade, manufacturing, and construction were also well above average (Figure 11.2) (Health Canada 1999). Among white-collar industries, government and the health care sectors had the two highest rates of time-loss injuries in 1996 (Health Canada 1999).

Common types of workplace illnesses are **cumulative trauma disorders**, which are muscle, tendon, vascular, and nerve injuries resulting from repeated or sustained actions or exertions of different body parts. Jobs that are associated with high rates of upper body cumulative trauma disorders include computer programming, manufacturing, meatpacking, poultry processing, and clerical or office work (National Safety Council 1997). Common medical conditions that have been related to cumulative trauma disorder include noise-induced hearing loss, tendonitis (inflammation of the tendons), epicondylitis ("tennis elbow"), and carpal tunnel syndrome (a wrist disorder that can cause numbness, tingling, and severe pain). Cumulative trauma disorders are classified as illnesses, not as injuries, because they are not sudden, instantaneous traumatic events.

Workplace Fatalities Unintentional work-related death rates have declined significantly over the past several decades. Although many workplaces are safer today than in generations past, fatal occupational injuries and illnesses still occur in troubling numbers.

In an average year in the 1970s, approximately 11 workers for every 100 000 workers died in the course of, or because of, their employment. In the 1990s, the fatality rate fell to seven deaths for every 100 000 workers. As we have noted elsewhere, the most dangerous occupations in Canada are, in order,

National Data

Provincial rates for time-loss injury are lowest in New Brunswick (12.5 per 1000) and highest in Prince Edward Island (40.6 per 1000). Quebec and British Columbia have very high rates of injuries as well as high total numbers of injuries.

SOURCE: Health Canada 1999

National Data

In 1994, there was one compensation claim resulting from injury for every 13 workers, amounting to direct medical costs of more than $250 per person and perhaps twice as much again in indirect costs.

SOURCE: Association of Workers' Compensation Boards of Canada 1995

Figure 11.1

Time-Loss Work Injuries, Employed Persons Aged 15+, Canada, 1992–96

SOURCE: Statistics Canada, Health Statistics Division, special tabulations of data from the Association of Workers' Compensation Boards of Canada (collected by Statistics Canada and the Labour Force Survey subdivision of Statistics Canada).

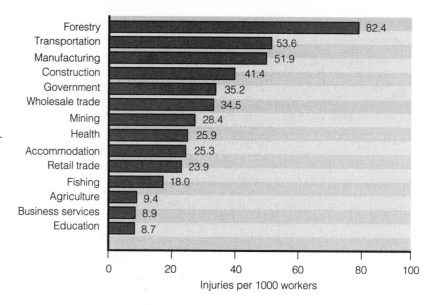

Figure 11.2

Time-Loss Work Injuries, by Industry, Employed Persons 15+, Canada, 1996

SOURCE: Statistics Canada, Health Statistics Division, special tabulations of data from the Association of Workers' Compensation Boards of Canada (collected by Statistics Canada) and the Labour Force Survey subdivision of Statistics Canada.

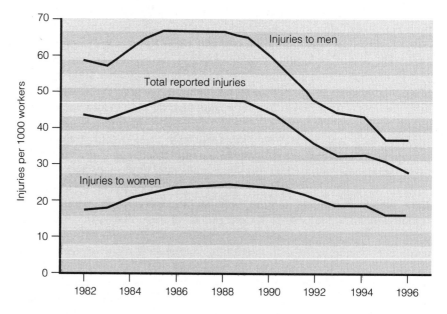

National Data

According to the 1996–97 *National Population Health Survey*, an estimated two million Canadians aged 12 and older suffered a repetitive strain injury during the past year. Injuries to the back or spine accounted for the greatest share of such injuries among men (20 percent), while injuries to the wrist, hand, or fingers were the most common among women (25 percent). For both sexes, the greatest proportion of these injuries occurred at work or school.

SOURCE: Health Canada 1999

the cutting and loading of rock, general mine labouring, and operating small engines (Statistics Canada 1998a).

The risk of fatal workplace injuries is much higher among men than among women, as men are more likely to work in jobs that have high fatal injury rates.

Many occupational health and safety hazards are attributed to company negligence or willful disregard of health and safety laws. For example, the dangers of asbestos were known as early as 1918, when insurance companies stopped selling life insurance policies to asbestos workers. Nevertheless, the asbestos industry took little action until the 1960s. Of the half-million workers exposed to "significant doses of asbestos," 100 000 will die from lung cancer, 35 000 from mesothelioma, and 35 000 from asbestosis (Coleman 1994: 79). In 1999, the Ontario Federation of Labour (OFL) launched a campaign to push the government for stricter limits on the exposure to toxic substances in workplaces and to demand that enough inspectors be put in place to ensure those limits are adhered to in all companies. In support of these demands, the OFL produced documents, obtained by the Canadian Auto Workers union through Freedom of Information requests, that showed a blatant disregard for the health and well-being of workers. For example, even though company and government officials knew that workers at the Holmes Insulation plant in Sarnia were being poisoned and exposed to amounts of asbestos that were far beyond the allowable limits, no one did anything to stop it. The OFL has compiled a top 12 dangerous workplace materials list that includes asbestos, benzene, cadmium, diesel exhaust emissions, fibreglass, formaldehyde, lead, metalworking fluids (used in coolants and lubricants in cutting, drilling, and machining metal), nickel, silica, styrene, and vinyl chloride (Simone 1999).

Another work-related health hazard is job stress and chronic fatigue. To measure work stress, the 1996–97 *National Population Health Survey* used a scale composed of 12 questions describing working conditions that were answered on a five-point scale of agree or disagree. The minimum score on the scale was 0 and the maximum was 45; "high stress" was defined as a score of 30 or higher. Using this scale, the survey found that more women reported high work stress levels than men did in every age category, with women aged 20 to 24 almost three times as likely to report high work stress than the average Canadian worker (Health Canada 1999). Notable differences in high work stress occurred among persons in different types of households. Single parents were twice as likely as Canadians in couple relationships without children were to report high work stress (Figure 11.3).

Prolonged job stress, also known as **job burnout**, can cause physical problems, such as high blood pressure, ulcers, and headaches, as well as psychological problems. In a survey of 1298 employees (Bond et al. 1997), nearly one-quarter of employees felt nervous or stressed often or very often in the three months before the survey; 13 percent had difficulty coping with the demands of everyday life often or very often. The survey also found that substantial numbers of employees felt burned out by their jobs. In the three months before the survey, 26 percent felt emotionally drained by their work often or very often, and 36 percent felt used up at the end of the workday often or very often. In Japan, as many as 10 000 workers each year perish from *karoshi*—literally translated as "death from overwork" (Bettelheim 1998). The Japanese government now recognizes *karoshi* as an industrial disease involving a blend of fatigue, high blood pressure, and hardening of the arteries.

Based on a survey of two thousand Canadian men and women 18 and older working at least 20 hours a week outside the home for an organization with at least 20 employees, about one-third of respondents agreed with the statement that "my job often is so stressful that I feel burned out," while an additional 23 percent reported that they sometimes felt that way. Women were more likely than men were to report feeling burned out, with 51.5 percent of men and 63.8 percent of women agreeing or somewhat agreeing with the statement. The survey also reported that susceptibility to burnout varied by industry, with those employed in government, education, and health care significantly more likely (44 percent) to say they often felt burned out, followed by those who worked in manufacturing and construction (35 percent), service industries (33 percent), and insurance and finance (32 percent). Those least likely to report feeling burned out worked in agriculture (15 percent). Those in

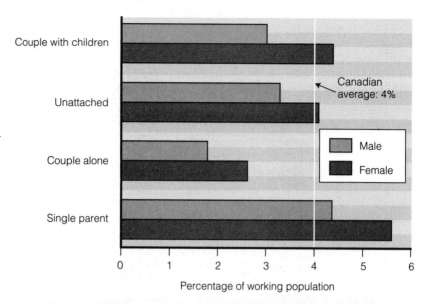

Figure 11.3
**High Work Stress, by
Household Type (Age-
Standardized), Employed
Persons Age 15+, Canada,
1994–95**

SOURCE: Statistics Canada, *National Population
Health Survey*, 1994–5, special tabulations.

Table 11.1	By Sector, the Perceptions of Workers						
By sector, the percentage who agreed with the following statements:	High tech	Finance/ insurance	Government/ health/ education	Service	Manufacturing/ construction	Transportation/ communication/ utilities	Agriculture
1. I have the resources I need to do my job well	61.1	64.2	50.7	62.4	71.2	62.7	66.7
2. My organization satisfies our customers' needs	68.6	68.8	60.8	71.1	75.9	71.3	76.9
3. My job often is so stressful that I feel burned out	29.6	31.8	43.8	33	35	30.2	15.4

SOURCE: Maclean's 1999c

National Data

In 1997, about 1 in 10
Canadian workers put in
overtime without being
reimbursed for it with
either extra pay or time off.
In that year, such unpaid
overtime was most
common for white-collar
workers, particularly those
who were teachers or man-
ufacturers.

SOURCE: Statistics Canada 1998a

occupations with high susceptibility to burnout (i.e., government, health, and education employees) were also likely to report that they lacked the resources they needed to perform their job well (Table 11.1).

Job stress, burnout, and chronic fatigue are related to the increasing demands of the workplace. That survey of 1298 employees found that employees are working longer hours today than employees 20 years ago worked. Among employees working 20 hours or more per week, hours worked at all jobs increased from 43.6 hours in 1977 to 47.1 hours in 1997 (Bond et al. 1997). The survey also found that nearly one in five employees are required to work paid or unpaid overtime hours at least once a week with little or no notice.

According to data obtained in the 1998 General Social Survey, Canadian men aged 25 to 44 averaged 48.6 hours of paid work and work-related activities per week, and women in this age group averaged 38.4 hours—an increase

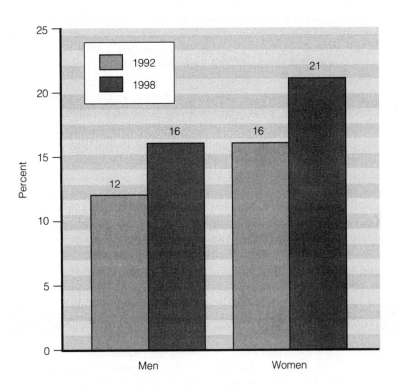

Figure 11.4
Time-Stress
SOURCE: Statistics Canada

of two hours per week for both men and women since 1992. The survey also found that 21 percent of women over 15 years of age complained about time stress in 1998, compared with 15 percent in 1992. The proportion of men complaining about time stress rose to 16 percent from 12 percent (Figure 11.4). It was also reported that time-stress levels were highest for married men and women aged 25 to 44 who were employed full-time with children at home (Canadian Press 1999).

Dissatisfaction and Alienation

If you read the classified ad section of any newspaper, you are likely to find job advertisements that entice applicants with claims such as "discover a rewarding and challenging career..." and "we offer opportunities for advancement and travel...." Unfortunately, most jobs do not allow workers to "be all that they can be." In reality, most employers want you to be all you can be for them, with limited concern for your career satisfaction.

Factors that contribute to job satisfaction include autonomy, income, prestige, congenial coworkers, pay and benefits, promotion opportunities, job security, a feeling of accomplishment, a sense of being challenged by the job, opportunities to be creative, and the feeling that one is making a contribution (Gordon 1996; Robie et al. 1998). These factors often overlap—for example, high-paying jobs tend to have more prestige, be more autonomous, provide more benefits, and permit greater creativity. However, many jobs lack these qualities, leaving workers dissatisfied. In Canada, fully one-third of Canada's workers believe that their jobs are not secure (Statistics Canada 1998a). Moreover, between 1991 and 1994–95, the proportion of the working population in Canada who were very satisfied with their work declined. According to the

National Data

Whether or not they are employed outside the home, Canadian women bear a disproportionate burden of unpaid housework. One in two fully employed women reported doing at least 15 hours per week of unpaid housework in the 1996 census, compared with one in four working men. Almost one in five working women performed 30 hours or more of housework per week, compared with fewer then one in 15 working men. The burden of housework increased substantially for both men and women when there were children in the household.
SOURCE: Health Canada 1999

1994–95 *National Population Health Survey*, only half of employed Canadians aged 15 and older reported that they were "very satisfied" with their work; 41 percent were "somewhat satisfied," and 9 percent said that they were "not satisfied" with their work. Overall, men are more likely than women are to be satisfied with their jobs. "Women are disadvantaged relative to men in terms of job satisfaction because they are more likely to work in situations affording them little control over the pace and content of their task" (Health Canada 1999: 64). Job satisfaction also increased with age, with those aged 15 to 24 the least likely to report that they were satisfied with their work. Marked variation also existed among the provinces in relation to job satisfaction. Those in the Atlantic provinces were more likely than Canadians in general to report high satisfaction with their jobs (e.g., 58 percent in New Brunswick), while those in Canada's three largest provinces were the least likely to do so (47 percent in Quebec, and 50 percent in both Ontario and British Columbia) (Health Canada 1999).

One form of job dissatisfaction is a feeling of **alienation**. Work in industrialized societies is characterized by a high division of labour and specialization of work roles. As a result, workers' tasks are repetitive and monotonous and often involve little or no creativity. Limited to specific tasks by their work roles, workers are unable to express and utilize their full potential—intellectual, emotional, and physical. According to Marx, when workers are merely cogs in a machine, they become estranged from their work, the product they create, other human beings, and themselves. Marx called this estrangement "alienation."

Alienation usually has four components: powerlessness, meaninglessness, normlessness, and self-estrangement. Powerlessness results from working in an environment in which workers have little or no control over the decisions that affect their work. Meaninglessness results when workers do not find fulfillment in their work. Workers may experience normlessness if workplace norms are unclear or conflicting. For example, many companies that have family leave policies informally discourage workers from using them, or workplaces that officially promote nondiscrimination in reality practise discrimination. Alienation also involves a feeling of self-estrangement, which stems from the workers' inability to realize their full human potential in their work roles and from a lack of connections to others. In general, traditional "women's work" is more alienating than "men's work" (Ross and Wright 1998). "Homemaking exposes women to routine, unfulfilling, isolated work; and part-time employment exposes them to routine, unfulfilling work, with little decision-making autonomy" (p. 343). This chapter's Focus on Social Problems Research feature examines job satisfaction among male and female lawyers.

Work–Family Concerns

As a result of a combination of social forces, including economic pressures, changing gender ideologies, improved contraception, increased life expectancy, and the marked trend toward smaller families, the dual-earner family has become the "new norm" in Canada.

Understandably, for many employed parents, balancing work and family demands is a daily challenge. When Hochschild (1997) asked a sample of employed parents, "Overall, how well do you feel you can balance the demands of your work and family?" only 9 percent said "very well" (pp. 199–200). (Work–family concerns are also discussed in Chapters 5, 7, and 10.)

CONSIDERATION

The demands of the workplace may also affect the amount of time and energy adults have to get involved in volunteer work and social activism. One employed mother said,

> I used to be an activist, leading the recycling movement [in my area]….I helped get out the vote for local environmental candidates. And I always thought when I had children, I'd work on a community garden with them planting, working in nature, and I'd throw out our TV. I wouldn't want them to be exposed to all that junk, ads, and violence. But now that I'm working these hours, Diane watches TV after school…and we're not doing a thing about recycling or gardening (Hochschild 1997: 220).

FOCUS ON SOCIAL PROBLEMS RESEARCH

What Determines Job Satisfaction among Male and Female Lawyers?

Researcher Charlotte Chiu (1998) wanted to investigate the effects of gender on job satisfaction. Despite women's often subordinate occupational statuses, most research suggests there is little difference in job satisfaction between men and women. The most commonly cited reasons for this finding include the following: (1) women have lower job expectations, thereby lower dissatisfaction levels, (2) women, due to traditional socialization, are less likely to voice discontent and thus appear to have higher job satisfaction rates, or (3) men and women value the variables that determine job satisfaction (for example, salary, job security) differently. The present study investigates the validity of the third explanation by examining gender and its relationship to job satisfaction in an oft-neglected sample of respondents—private practice attorneys.

Sample and Methods

The sample of respondents Chiu (1998) used was from the 1990 National Survey of Lawyers' Career Satisfaction sponsored by the American Bar Association. The survey was a self-administered questionnaire. To maximize homogeneity of the sample, respondents were restricted to full-time private practice attorneys who had graduated from law school within the 10 years before the survey date. The final sample included 326 lawyers; 27 percent of the sample were women and 12 percent other minorities. Statistics indicate that male and female respondents were similar to one another in terms of age, years since law school graduation, average number of hours worked per week, and law firm size. Men, however, were more likely to be married, to have children, and to be white.

Findings

Contrary to much of the literature, female attorneys reported overall lower rates of job satisfaction than their male counterparts. Specifically, women were significantly more likely to report dissatisfaction with (1) opportunities to succeed and influence decisions, (2) financial rewards, and (3) a competitive environment.

However, when respondents were asked to rank determinants of job satisfaction, there were no statistically significant gender differences. Both men and women ranked opportunity to succeed and influence decisions as the most important determinant, followed by a noncompetitive environment. For both men and women, financial rewards were relatively low on the list of what makes a job satisfying.

The research results thus led to several important conclusions. First, despite similarities in background characteristics (i.e., age, hours worked, etc.), female lawyers reported lower levels of job satisfaction than male lawyers did. Second, women's lower job satisfaction rate was predominantly a function of a stated lack of opportunity to succeed and influence decisions, and inadequate financial rewards. Third, and most important, women's lower job satisfaction rates were not a function of valuing job satisfaction determinants differently. There were no statistically significant gender differences in what makes a job satisfying.

What then explains the lowered job satisfaction rates of female versus male attorneys? Since both males and females ranked opportunity to succeed and influence decisions as the most important determinant of job satisfaction, and women were significantly more likely to express dissatisfaction on this variable, the author concludes that the "results support the discrimination thesis, and show that inequality in the workplace explains much more of women's dissatisfaction" than the traditional argument that men and women value job satisfaction determinants differently (p. 538). Chiu also suggests that future research examine whether the resulting relationship between gender and job satisfaction rates among lawyers is also true among other professional and nonprofessional occupational groups.

SOURCE: Chiu, Charlotte. 1998. "Do Professional Women Have Lower Job Satisfaction than Professional Men? Lawyers as a Case Study." *Sex Roles* 38: 521–38.

Unemployment and Underemployment

Measures of unemployment consider an individual to be unemployed if he or she is currently without employment, is actively seeking employment, and is available for employment. Unemployment figures do not include discouraged workers, who have given up on finding a job and are no longer looking for employment. Unemployment is a worldwide problem.

As of December 1999, Canada's unemployment rate was at its lowest level since 1981 due, in part to the creation of 89 000 full-time jobs in November of that year, which pushed the jobless rate down to 6.9 percent (*Maclean's* 1999b). Consider, for example, that in November of 1992, the unemployment rate stood at 11.9 and in December of 1997, at 8.6 percent.

However, although the Canadian economy witnessed the addition of 834 000 new jobs between 1992 and 1997, these figures pale in comparison to the boom years of the 1980s, when places were created for an average of 323 000 more workers each year. The unemployment rate in Canada varies by province, with, traditionally, the picture improving from east to west (Table 11.2).

Unemployment rates are based on the percentage of unemployed persons at any given time who are actively seeking work. Another measure of unemployment is the **work-experience unemployment rate**, or the percentage of persons who participated in the labour force in a given year and experienced some unemployment during that year. The unemployment rates in nine industrialized countries are given in Table 11.3.

Types and Causes of Unemployment There are two types of unemployment: discriminatory and structural. **Discriminatory unemployment** involves high rates of unemployment among particular social groups, such as racial and ethnic minorities and women (see Chapters 7 and 8). **Structural unemployment** exists when there are not enough jobs available for those who want them and is the result of social factors rather than personal inadequacies of the

Table 11.2   Canadian Labour Force by Province, 1998 (Thousands)

	Population 15 years & older	Labour Force[1]	Participation Rate[2]	Employed	Employed population ratio[3]	Unemployed[4]	% Unemployed[4]
Canada	23 993.9	15 631.5	65.1	14 326.4	59.7	1305.1	8.3
Newfoundland	446.0	241.0	54.1	197.9	44.4	43.1	17.9
Prince Edward Island	107.1	70.7	66.0	60.9	56.9	9.8	13.9
Nova Scotia	746.3	452.1	60.6	403.7	54.1	48.4	10.7
New Brunswick	605.6	368.9	60.9	324.2	53.5	44.7	12.1
Quebec	5968.2	3713.3	62.2	3327.5	55.8	385.8	10.4
Ontario	9118.8	6049.7	66.3	5612.9	61.6	436.8	7.2
Manitoba	862.6	578.9	67.1	546.1	63.3	32.8	5.7
Saskatchewan	763.8	508.6	66.6	478.6	62.7	30.0	5.9
Alberta	2225.1	1605.6	72.2	1514.0	68.0	91.6	5.7
British Columbia	3150.4	2042.6	64.8	1860.4	59.1	182.1	8.9

(1) The labour force consists of employed workers and those who are unemployed but actively seeking work. (2) Participation rate is the percent of the total population aged 15 and older that makes up the labour force. (3) The percent of the total population aged 15 and older that is employed. (4) The percent of the labour force that is unemployed.

SOURCE: Statistics Canada 1998

Table 11.3	Unemployment Rates in Nine Countries, 1999							
U.S.	Canada	Australia	Japan	France	Germany	Italy	Sweden	U.K.
4.4	8.3	8.1	4.5	12.4	12.8	12.2	6.2	4.6

SOURCE: Adapted from *Canadian Global Almanac* 2000

unemployed or discrimination. For example, unemployment can result from **corporate downsizing**—the corporate practice of discharging large numbers of employees. Simply put, the term "downsizing" is a euphemism for mass firing of employees (Caston 1998).

According to Brecher (1996), declining markets or sales are not the primary causes of downsizing. Brecher cites an annual survey conducted by the American Management Association that asked major U.S. firms to list one or more reasons for their downsizing. In 1995, only 6 percent of downsizing companies reported that an actual or anticipated business downswing was the sole cause of job cuts, although 38 percent listed business downturn as a contributing factor. Further, only 20 percent of all surveyed companies reporting layoffs had a net operating loss in the year of the cuts (Brecher 1996). More than half the companies that downsized in the survey created new positions at the same time, but these new positions were largely for low-wage part-time and temporary employees.

Another cause of unemployment is **job exportation,** the relocation of Canadian jobs to other countries where products can be produced more cheaply. Job exportation has had a particularly profound effect on garment workers and the Canadian garment industry over the past decade. One of the most significant changes has been the loss of full-time, standard jobs. Between 1988 and 1995, more than 3 of every 10 Canadian garment workers lost their job; in Toronto, 5 of every 10 jobs have been lost (Yanz and Jeffcott 1997).

Automation, or the replacement of human labour with machinery and equipment, is another feature of the work landscape that contributes to unemployment (see also Chapter 13). For example, recorded phone trees, automated teller machines (ATMs), and automatic car washes do jobs that otherwise would be performed by workers. By 1990, 32 percent of the painters and 17 percent of the welders in the auto industry had been replaced by robots (Hodson and Sullivan 1990).

In addition to the problem of unemployment, many individuals experience **underemployment**, which is employment in a job that is underpaid; is not commensurate with one's skills, experience, or education; or involves working fewer hours than desired. Many of those underemployed are **contingent workers** (also called "disposable workers")—involuntary part-time workers, temporary employees, and workers who do not perceive themselves as having an explicit or implicit contract for ongoing employment.

Effects of Unemployment and Underemployment The personal consequences of unemployment (and in some cases, underemployment) include anxiety, depression, alcohol abuse, and lowered self-esteem and confidence (Feather 1990; Liem and Liem 1990). Unemployment has consequences for families and communities as well, and has been linked to increased family violence (Straus 1980). Unemployment may also mean losing supplemental health care benefits for workers' and their families, and underemployed individuals rarely get health care benefits from their employers. Unemployment and underemployment result in a decline in an individual's standard of living.

National Data

Although the overall size of the Canadian labour force has grown significantly in the past three decades, much of the growth has been in part-time jobs and self-employment, neither of which provide benefits and pensions. In 1998, about 30 percent of adult women working part-time were doing so involuntarily because they could not obtain full-time employment. An additional 20 percent worked part-time so they care for their children.

SOURCE: Statistics Canada 1999

National Data

Despite a profit of $1.4 billion for the fiscal year 1999 (up 2.4 percent from 1998), the Bank of Montreal announced that it would cut 1450 jobs to boost profits. The bank also closed 62 neighbourhood branches in 1999, while opening 33 chapter branches in retail stores.

SOURCE: *Maclean's* 1999a

Because of the changing nature of work, displaced workers may find themselves unable to obtain satisfactory employment. For example, since 1989, the number of employed clerical workers in Canada dropped from 2.2 million to 1.9 million and the number of manufacturing jobs declined from 1.8 million to 1.7 million. Although more than 700 000 Canadians joined the managerial and administrative ranks between 1989 and 1997, it is evident that not all Canadians possess the credentials that are increasingly necessary to climb out of the ranks of the unemployed and underemployed (Statistics Canada 1998a).

STRATEGIES FOR ACTION: RESPONSES TO WORKERS' CONCERNS

Government, private business, human rights organizations, and labour organizations play important roles in responding to the concerns of workers. Next we look at responses to child labour, health and safety regulations, and work site programs, work–family policies and programs, efforts to strengthen labour, and workforce development programs.

Responses to Child Labour

In a global Agenda for Action, the 1997 International Conference on Child Labour urged all countries to eliminate child labour, giving urgent priority to the most extreme forms of child labour—slave or slavelike practices and forced or compulsory labour (including debt bondage), the use of children in the sex industry and drug trade, and other forms of dangerous or hazardous work that interfere with children's education (Child Labour 1997). Because child labour is often hidden, better methods of collecting evidence and monitoring child labour are needed. Two important strategies in the campaign against child labour include the provision of free and compulsory education for all children and the establishment and enforcement of laws prohibiting oppressive and harmful child labour practices (UNICEF 1997).

The United Nations Children's Fund also recommends that national and international corporations adopt codes of conduct guaranteeing that neither they nor their subcontractors will employ children in conditions that violate their rights (UNICEF 1997). Some industries, including rug and clothing manufacturers, use labels and logos to indicate that their products are not made by child labourers.

Human rights organizations such as the International Labour Organization, UNICEF, and the Child Labour Coalition, are active in the campaign against child labour. Another organization, the Bonded Labour Liberation Front (BLLF) has led the fight against bonded and child labour in Pakistan, freeing 30 000 adults and children from brick kilns, carpet factories, and farms, and placing 11 000 children in its own primary school system (Silvers 1996). However, employers in Pakistan have threatened workers with violence if they talk with "the abolitionists" or possess "illegal communist propaganda." Human rights activists campaigning against child labour have also been victims of threats and violence.

Efforts to eliminate child labour cannot succeed unless the impoverished conditions that contribute to its practice are alleviated. A living minimum wage must be established for adult workers so they will not need to send their children to work. One labour rights advocate said, "We will not end child labour merely by attacking it in the export sector in poor nations. If children's parents in all countries around the world are not earning a living wage..., children will be driven into working in dangerous informal sector jobs. Labour rights for adults are essential if we truly want to eliminate child labour" (Global March against Child Labor 1998).

Efforts to Strengthen Labour

Labour unions have played an important role in fighting for fair wages and benefits, healthy and safe work environments, and other forms of worker advocacy. In Canada, more than 3.5 million individuals belong to unions with workers in Newfoundland the most likely to be union members (approximately 40 percent), followed by workers in Quebec (38 percent). In contrast, workers in Alberta are the least likely to belong to a union (23 percent). In 1997, about one-third of Canada's white-collar workers, half of Canada's professional and managerial workers (e.g., nurses, teachers), and 4 in 10 blue-collar workers were union members (Statistics Canada 1998a).

The strength of unions to mobilize action in support of workers was evident when, in October 1996, 250 000 people in Metro Toronto turned out as part of seven city-wide one-day strikes (Metro Days of Action) to protest budget cuts by the Conservative government in Ontario. The strategy of combining mass mobilizations with one-day strikes was a new development in Canada. It required union leaders to convince their members to strike, lose a day's pay, and risk disciplinary measures by employers. Nevertheless, they were successful in their efforts and the political strike "shut down virtually all workplaces in Canada's largest city, including public transportation and all government and municipal services" (Flexner 1997).

Although efforts to strengthen labour are viewed as problematic by corporations and employers, such efforts have the potential to remedy many of the problems facing workers. In an effort to strengthen their power, labour unions are merging with one another. Labour union mergers result in higher membership numbers, thereby increasing the unions' financial resources, which are needed for successful recruiting and to withstand long strikes.

CONSIDERATION

In Canada and the United States, some workers, such as police and emergency service workers, are legally prohibited from striking. An alternative tactic called a "sickout" involves mass numbers of workers calling in sick and not showing up for work. In 1999, American Airlines pilots staged a sickout, resulting in the cancellation of more than 6000 flights. The travel plans of about 600 000 passengers were affected.

Compared to male workers, Canadian women workers are less likely to be unionized (31.2 percent of women versus 38.2 percent of men) (Statistics Canada 1998a). However, unions such as the Canadian Auto Workers (CAW) (which represents workers in such male-dominated workplaces as auto assembly, aerospace, auto parts, rail, mining, smelters, and marine workers and fishing) have shown attentiveness to the issues of sexism both within the workplace and within the union itself. For more than two decades, local union women's committees in the CAW have been mandatory under its national constitution. In addition, beginning in 1992, the CAW began running a two-week residential program for women activists, the Women Activists Course. A number of unions have been successful in bargaining for expanded family leave benefits, subsidized childcare, elder care, and pay equity.

Labour unions are not the only groups advocating for worker rights. Numerous national and international human rights groups support the labour agenda.

Workforce Development and Job-Creation Programs

Many workforce development programs have been implemented since the first major employment programs were instituted during the Great Depression in the 1930s. Workforce development programs provide a variety of services, including assessment to evaluate skills and needs, career counselling, job search assistance, basic education, occupational training (classroom and on-the-job), public employment, job placement, and stipends or other support services for childcare and transportation assistance (Levitan et al. 1998).

Numerous studies have looked at the effectiveness of workforce development programs. In general, "evaluations indicate that employment and training programs enhance the earnings and employment of participants, although the effects vary by service population, are often modest because of brief training durations and the inherent difficulty of alleviating long-term deficiencies, and are not always cost effective" (Levitan et al. 1998: 199).

Efforts to prepare high-school students for work include the establishment of technical and vocational high schools and high-school programs, and school-to-work programs. School-to-work programs involve partnerships among business, labour, government, education, and community organizations that help prepare high-school students for jobs. Although school-to-work programs vary, in general, they allow high-school students to explore different careers, and they provide job skill training and work-based learning experiences (Leonard 1996).

Unfortunately, funding for federal job training programs is insufficient to reach more than a small fraction of the workforce (Kenworthy 1995). Even those who complete the retraining do not always find new jobs at comparable wages. The rehiring of displaced workers also requires an improved economy that generates new jobs. Without job openings, the value of job retraining is limited.

Efforts to create jobs must consider where the jobs are being created. The Canadian economy can be described as a **split labour market** (or dual economy), because it is made up of two labour markets. The *primary labour market* refers to jobs that are stable, economically rewarding, and come with benefits. These jobs are usually occupied by the most educated and trained individuals (e.g., a corporate attorney, teacher, or accountant). The *secondary labour market* refers to jobs that involve low pay, no security, few benefits, and little chance for advancement. Domestic servants, clerks, and food servers are examples of these jobs. These workers often have no union to protect them and are more likely to be dissatisfied with their job than workers in the primary labour market.

Responses to Worker Health and Safety Concerns

Over the past few decades, health and safety conditions in the workplace have improved because of media attention, regulations, demands by unions for change, and more white-collar jobs. Canadian governments have expanded workplace protection through human rights laws, which prohibit discrimination in hiring, promotion, and working conditions, and workers' compensation programs, which pay partial lost wages to sick or injured workers. However, Lowe and Krahn (1993: 280–1) point out that "[t]he Canadian state's involvement in occupational health [actually] goes back to the *Factory Acts* of the 1800s..., [which] required fencing around machines, reasonable ventilation, lunchrooms, and lavatories." They note that "the first major initiative to involve workers directly in health and safety was the 1972 *Saskatchewan Occupational Health Act...*, [which] established workplace health and safety programs premised on the right of workers to participate in the identification and regulation of hazards" through their participation in joint health and safety committees. Since that time, they observe, "[o]ther provinces and the federal government have followed Saskatchewan's legislative lead, to varying degrees, and now most jurisdictions have elements of what is known as the "internal responsibility system" (IRS). The *Canada Labour Code*, in 1986, established the right of workers to be told about the potential hazards of workplace materials with this "right to know" buttressed by the national Workplace Hazardous Materials Information System. Worker health and safety committees are also a standard feature of companies in many industrialized countries and are mandatory in most of Europe. These committees are authorized to inspect workplaces and cite employers for violations of health and safety regulations.

Because of the increase in cumulative trauma disorders, **ergonomics**—the designing or redesigning of the workplace to prevent and reduce cumulative trauma disorders—is becoming an accepted health and safety strategy in the workplace. Table 11.4 lists recommendations for computer workstations that are designed to prevent cumulative trauma disorders associated with working on a computer. Does your workstation conform to these guidelines?

Maximizing the health and safety of workers involves more than implementing, monitoring, and enforcing regulations. Increasingly, businesses and corporations are attempting to maximize workers' health (and corporate profits) by offering work-site health promotion programs. Work-site health promotion consists of health education, screening, and interventions designed to achieve better health among workers. Programs range from single interventions

Table 11.4	Basic Ergonomic Recommendations for Computer Workstations

1. Keyboard and other input devices at elbow level
2. Video display screen 1 to 60 degrees below eye level
3. Screen display equipped or positioned to minimize glare
4. Rounded and/or padded hand, wrist, or forearm contact surfaces
5. Adequate space for performing tasks
6. Adequate legroom beneath work surface
7. Chair with appropriate back and arm support
8. Frequent short breaks or variation of tasks
9. Correct posture
10. Adjustments to work station to minimize awkward positions and applied force

SOURCE: Downs, Donald G. 1997. "Nonspecific Work-Related Upper Extremity Disorders." *American Family Physician* 55(4): 1296–1302.

(such as screening for high blood pressure) to comprehensive health and fitness programs, aerobic exercise and fitness, nutrition and weight control, stress management, smoking cessation, cancer-risk screening, drug and alcohol abuse prevention, accident prevention, and health information (Conrad 1999). Some workplaces have nap rooms, allowing workers to take naps (Bettelheim 1998). Many companies have employee assistance programs to help employees and their families with substance abuse, family discord, depression, and other mental health problems.

Health promotion programs benefit both employees and corporations. Corporations benefit because healthier employees have lower job absenteeism and turnover, file fewer health insurance claims (which results in lower health insurance costs for employers), file fewer workers' compensation claims, and exhibit higher morale and productivity. In addition, health promotion programs can enhance a company's image among workers and the community. Employees enjoy the wide range of physical, mental, and social benefits that are associated with health promotion programs.

Work–Family Policies and Programs

The influx of women into the workforce has been accompanied by an increase in government and company policies designed to help women and men balance their work and family roles. Fast and DaPont (1997) find that women in Canada are less likely to interrupt their paid work today and, when interruptions do occur, they return to gainful employment more quickly than women did in the past. This decrease in the length of work-history disruptions is partly because of the entrenchment of paid maternity leave policies. Currently, Employment Insurance allows women 15 weeks (the first two of which are unpaid) of pregnancy benefits. It also requires, however, that they have worked at least 700 hours during the previous year and only provides them with a percentage of their normal weekly pay. For those earning in excess of $375 a week, benefits are calculated at 55 percent of the individual's gross earnings over the past 26 weeks; for those earning less, benefits are calculated at 60 percent. Although either parent may apply for parental benefits following the birth of a baby for an additional 10-week period, existent provisions seem to encourage mothers rather than fathers to do so. That is, should the father decide to seek the 10-week parental benefits, he would not receive benefits for the first two of the 10 weeks. Similarly, if the couple decides to split the parental benefits, two of the five weeks during which the father assumes primary care of the child will be unpaid. In contrast, if the mother cares for the child continuously following its birth, she will receive payment for the entirety of the 10 weeks since she would have already satisfied the two-week unpaid period.

Corporations and employers have also begun to initiate policies and programs that address the family concerns of their employees. Employer-provided assistance with childcare, assistance with elder care, flexible work options, and job relocation assistance are becoming more common.

Offering employees more flexibility in their work hours helps parents balance their work and family demands. Flexible work arrangements, which benefit childfree workers as well as employed parents, include flextime, job sharing, a compressed workweek, and telecommuting. **Flextime** allows employees to begin and end the workday at different times as long as 40 hours per week are maintained. For example, workers may begin at 6 a.m. and leave

International Data

In Europe, women are granted five months' leave with full pay after giving birth. In addition, they are provided with prenatal and obstetrical care, generous hospital stays, and baby equipment subsidies.

SOURCE: Hewlett and West 1998

at 2 p.m. instead of the traditional 9 a.m. to 5 p.m. With **job sharing**, two workers share the responsibility of one job. In Canada, job-sharers are most likely to be well-educated individuals in good jobs. In 1995, about half had a college or university education and about 4 of 10 were professionals. In that year, about 171 000 Canadians shared their jobs with other workers with women in general and nurses and teachers in particular most likely to do so (Statistics Canada 1998a). A **compressed workweek** allows employees to condense their work into fewer days (e.g., four 10-hour days each week). **Telecommuting** allows employees to work part-time or full-time at home or at a satellite office. A study of U.S. companies found that the more women and minorities a company has in managerial positions, the more likely that company is to offer flexible work options (Galinsky and Bond 1998).

Work–family policies benefit both employees and their families and corporations. For example, Corning Glass Works found that its turnover rate for female employees was twice as high as the rate for male employees. This high turnover rate was costly—replacing each lost worker cost $40 000 (in search costs, on-the-job training costs, and the like). Corning conducted a survey and discovered that "family stress—particularly childcare problems—was the main reason so many women quit their jobs" (Hewlett 1992: 27). Corning decided to implement a family support package that included parenting leave, on-site childcare, part-time work options, job sharing, and a parent resource centre. The company's chairman, James P. Houghton, said that Corning's efforts "go way beyond simple justice; it's a matter of good business sense in a changing world...it's a matter of survival" (Hewlett 1992: 27).

Fran Rodgers, president of Work/Family Directions explains the need for work–family policies:

> For over 20 years we at Work/Family Directions have asked
> employees in all industries what it would take for them to contribute
> more at work. Every study found the same thing: They need aid with
> their dependent care, more flexibility and control over the hours and
> conditions of work, and a corporate culture in which they are not
> punished because they have families. These are fundamental needs of
> our society and of every worker. (Galinsky et al. 1993: 51)

UNDERSTANDING WORK AND UNEMPLOYMENT

To understand the social problems associated with work and unemployment, we must first recognize the power and influence of governments and corporations on the workplace. We must also be aware of the role that technological developments and postindustrialization have on what we produce, how we produce it, where we produce it, and who does the producing. Canada is moving away from producing manufactured goods toward producing services. The labour-intensive blue-collar assembly line is declining in importance, and information-intensive white-collar occupations are increasing. Because of increasing corporate multinationalization, Canadian jobs are being exported to foreign countries where labour is cheap, regulations are lax, and raw materials are available. Finally, the workforce is becoming more diverse in terms of gender and racial and ethnic background and is including more contingent workers than in the past.

Decisions made by Canadian corporations about what and where to invest influence the quantity and quality of jobs available in Canada. As conflict theorists argue, such investment decisions are motivated by profit, which is part of a capitalist system. Profit is also a driving factor in deciding how and when technological devices will be used to replace workers and increase productivity, but if goods and services are produced too efficiently, workers are laid off and high unemployment results. When people have no money to buy products, sales slump, a recession ensues, and social welfare programs are needed to support the unemployed. When the government increases spending to pay for its social programs, it expands the deficit and increases the national debt. Deficit spending and a large national debt make it difficult to recover from the recession, and the cycle continues (see Figure 11.5).

What can be done to break the cycle? Those adhering to the classic view of capitalism argue for limited government intervention on the premise that business will regulate itself via an "invisible hand" or "market forces." For example, if corporations produce a desired product at a low price, people will buy it, which means workers will be hired to produce the product, and so on.

Ironically, those who support limited government intervention also sometimes advocate that the government should intervene to bail out failed banks and lend money to troubled businesses (or hockey teams). Such government help benefits the powerful segments of our society. Yet, when economic policies hurt less powerful groups, such as minorities, there has been a collective hesitance to support or provide social welfare programs. It is also ironic that such bailout programs, which contradict the ideals of capitalism, are needed because of capitalism. For example, the profit motive leads to multinationalization, which leads to unemployment, which leads to the need for government programs. The answers are as complex as the problems. The various forces

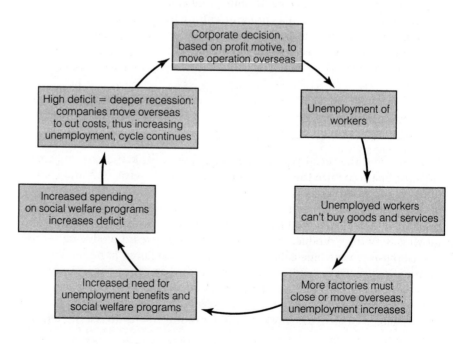

Figure 11.5

From Layoff to Layoff: A Cycle

transforming our economy are interrelated—technology, globalization, capital flight through multinationalization, and the movement toward a service economy (Eitzen and Zinn 1990). For the individual worker, the concepts of work, job, and career have changed forever.

CRITICAL THINKING

1. In 1999, 10 years after Canada and the United States signed a free trade accord that bound their economies ever more tightly, the C.D. Howe Institute released a study that argued the merits of Canada using the same currency as the United States. If Canadian nationalists reacted to the suggestion of a common currency with predictions of Canada's imminent demise, the issue of "dollarization"—instituting the American dollar for local currencies—has found considerable support in such countries as Argentina and Mexico. What would be the advantages and disadvantages of Canada establishing a currency union with the United States?

2. A considerable fraction of the Canadian economy is controlled by foreigners (chiefly Americans). Indeed, Bellan (1999: 884) notes that "[t]his large foreign presence in the economy [is] quite unparalleled elsewhere in the world [and] has deep historic roots." Identify some of the consequences of having a very large part of the Canadian economy controlled by American interests.

3. Compared with Canadian men, Canadian women are less likely to belong to unions. Why might this be so?

KEY TERMS

alienation
automation
bonded labour
brain drain
capitalism
child labour
compressed workweek
contingent workers
convergence hypothesis
corporate downsizing
corporate
    multinationalism

cumulative trauma
    disorders
discriminatory
    unemployment
economic institution
ergonomics
flextime
global economy
Industrial Revolution
job burnout
job exportation
job sharing
postindustrialization

socialism
split labour market
structural
    unemployment
sweatshops
telecommuting
underemployment
work-experience
    unemployment rate
work sectors (primary,
    secondary, tertiary)

CHAPTER TWELVE

Problems in Education

Is It True?

1. In 1996, more than half of Canada's population had less than a grade 9 education.

2. Among the 29 OECD countries, Canada has the highest percentage of humanities graduates and the second lowest percentage of graduates in science, mathematics, and engineering.

3. By 1997, almost all Canadian schools had Internet access.

4. More than half of the people living in developing nations are illiterate.

5. IQ is the best predictor of school success.

Answers: 1 = F, 2 = T, 3 = T, 4 = T, 5 = F

E

ducation is often claimed as a panacea—the cure-all for poverty and prejudice, drugs and violence, war and hatred—yet, daily, it seems, we are reminded of problems that exist in Canada's educational system. Some have charged that our educational system is encumbered by seniority and indifference to absolute educational outcomes, which hamper Canada's ability to compete. Others direct attention to the ravages of budget cuts and point out that between 1993 and 1998 governments cut $800 million from higher education in this country, that tuition costs have risen an average of 67 percent since 1993, and that student debt has soared. Others highlight funding reforms that have triggered dramatic cuts to special education programs and the allied services of speech pathologists and psychologists (Schofield 1999b, 1999c).

Anybody who cares about the matter knows that the intellect requires constant attention and renewal.

Robertson William Davies, Writer, Journalist, and Professor

Can one institution, riddled with obstacles, be a solution for other social problems? In this chapter, we focus on this question and what is being called one of the major sociopolitical issues of the next century—the educational crisis (Associated Press 1998). We begin with a look at education around the world.

THE GLOBAL CONTEXT: CROSS-CULTURAL VARIATION IN EDUCATION

Looking only at the Canadian educational system might lead to the conclusion that most societies have developed some method of formal instruction for their members. After all, there are almost 16 000 elementary and secondary schools in Canada employing a full-time teaching force of almost 300 000, and some 300 colleges and universities employing an additional 60 000 full-time educators (Statistics Canada 1998a). In reality, many societies have no formal mechanism for educating the masses. As a result, more than half of the people in developing nations are illiterate. In India alone, more than 400 million people cannot read or write, and nearly 35 million children do not attend school (*Hindustan Times* 1999).

At the other end of the continuum are societies that emphasize the importance of formal education. In Japan, students attend school on Saturday in addition to weekdays, and their lives at school are a fascinating cultural contradiction of cooperation, a core Japanese value, and intense competition. In grade school, children work as a group and teachers stress cooperation and respect for elders and for those in positions of authority. However, admission to university is intensely competitive and only the top scorers on a national test are admitted. Because of the monumental importance placed on winning a coveted place at university, children from affluent families attend cram schools (*juku*) in the evening. Those who are not successful academically may find themselves mercilessly bullied by their peers (*ijime*) or may even commit suicide in despair for bringing shame and disappointment to their families (Sakamaki 1996; Yee 1992).

Some countries also empower professionals to organize and operate their school systems. Japan, for example, hires professionals to develop and implement a national curriculum and to administer nationwide financing for its schools. In contrast, "Canada is unique among developed countries in having no federal office or ministry of education" (Orlikow and Peters 1999: 738) at either the public school level or postsecondary level. Our country lacks a coordinated education policy and, because of historical, cultural, and demographic differences between the various regions in Canada, we are unlikely to see the development of such a policy in the future.

Under the terms of the *British North America Act*, education is a provincial responsibility, and each province has the constitutional authority to develop its own educational organization. Although education in Yukon, the Northwest Territories, and Nunavut is funded by the federal government, it is governed by ordinances of the assemblies of these regions. In consequence, Canada has 13 unique school systems that fund and administer public, private, denominational, and linguistic schools somewhat differently. The issues of religion and language are two of the differences that exist within our system of education.

Consider, for example, that our Constitution, unlike that of the United States, protects denominational or "separate" schools. However, "[a]s each province joined Confederation, it brought its own approach to religious schools and Canadians are still dealing with the legacy of this process" (Statistics Canada 1998a: 146). In Canada, free public education in a nondenominational public school system is available for all Canadians. Separate schools, denominational schools operated by the Catholic Church, receive public support in Alberta, Ontario, Saskatchewan, Yukon, and the Northwest Territories; elsewhere, where available, separate schools are privately funded. Until 1997, Newfoundland had an entirely denominational system of education. However, in 1997, almost three-quarters (73 percent) of the citizenry of Newfoundland voted to abolish its 277-year-old system of church-run schools.

"In 1982, Canada's Charter of Rights and Freedoms gave English- and French-speaking minorities the right to educate their children in their mother tongue and the courts have consistently supported this right for these two minority groups across Canada" (Statistics Canada 1998a: 146). *Minority language education* is designed to offer the minority group in a province (anglophones in Quebec, francophones outside Quebec) education in their mother tongue. *Second language education* is designed to offer instruction in the minority language for children. In recognition of Canada's status as a multicultural society, heritage language programs now allow for education in the traditional languages of ethnic minorities where the numbers so warrant.

Although the BNA Act of 1867 made the federal government responsible for the education of Aboriginal people, over the past few decades, the growing demand that Aboriginal peoples be allowed to run their own schools has led to a reduction in the direct involvement of the Department of Indian Affairs. Because of agreements made between First Nations bands and the Department of Indian Affairs, the role of the federal government has increasingly been reduced to that of a funding source for programs controlled by the Native community. Generally, decisions regarding the distribution of resources, staffing, curriculum, language of instruction, and length of school year are now made by band education authorities in most areas.

Although Canadians hold a strong belief in the importance of education, we are increasingly likely to raise questions about its roles and central components. At present, it seems that we "have only a moderate level of confidence in the job being done by the public education sector as a whole" (Canadian Council on Social Development 1999) (see Figure 12.1). As indicated by Canadians' ratings of their province's elementary and secondary educational systems (Figure 12.2), many perceive there is considerable room—and need—for improvement.

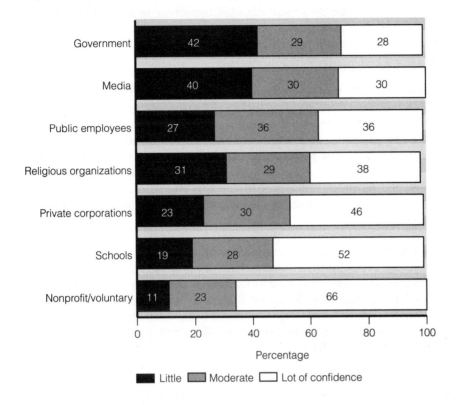

Figure 12.1
Canadians' Confidence in Their Institutions
SOURCE: EKOS Research Associates Inc. 1998. *Rethinking Government, 1998.*

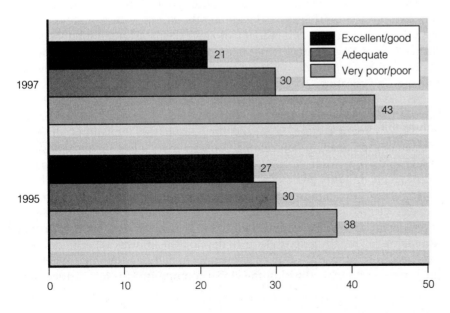

Figure 12.2
Canadians' Ratings of Their Province's Elementary and Secondary Educational Systems, 1995 and 1997
SOURCE: Environics Research Group Ltd. 1999. *Focus Canada 1997, Survey.*

SOCIOLOGICAL THEORIES OF EDUCATION

The three major sociological perspectives—structural-functionalism, conflict theory, and symbolic interactionism—are important in explaining different aspects of Canadian education.

Structural-Functionalist Perspective

According to structural-functionalism, the educational institution accomplishes important tasks for society, including instruction, socialization, the provision of custodial care, and the sorting of individuals into various statuses. Many social problems, such as unemployment, crime and delinquency, and poverty, may be linked to the failure of the educational institution to fulfil these basic functions (see Chapters 4, 10, and 11). Structural-functionalists also examine the reciprocal influences of the educational institution and other social institutions, including the family, political institution, and economic institution.

Instruction   A major function of education is to teach students the knowledge and skills necessary for future occupational roles, self-development, and social functioning. Although some parents teach their children basic knowledge and skills at home, most parents rely on schools to teach their children to read, spell, write, tell time, count money, and use computers. The failure of schools to instruct students in basic knowledge and skills both causes and results from many other social problems.

Socialization   The socialization function of education involves teaching students to respect authority—behaviour that is essential for social organization (Merton 1968). Students learn to respond to authority by asking permission to leave the classroom, sitting quietly at their desks, and raising their hands before asking a question. Students who do not learn to respect and obey teachers may later disrespect and disobey employers, police officers, and judges.

The educational institution also socializes youth into the dominant culture. Schools attempt to instil and maintain the norms, values, traditions, and symbols of the culture in a variety of ways, such as celebrating holidays (Remembrance Day, Thanksgiving); requiring students to speak and write in English and French; displaying the Canadian flag; and discouraging violence, drug use, and cheating.

As the number and size of racial and ethnic minority groups increase, Canadian schools are faced with a dilemma: should public schools promote only one common culture, or should they emphasize the cultural diversity reflected in the Canadian population? Consider that "[o]ver the next 20 years, an increasing proportion of children in schools will be immigrants and members of visible minority groups," and that of the 200 000 immigrants who enter Canada each year, almost 45 000 are school-aged children who enrol in Canada's elementary and secondary schools (Canadian Council on Social Development 1999). Banks and Banks (1993) suggest that **multicultural education** is vital to "help students to develop the knowledge, attitudes, and skills needed to function within their own micro cultures, the...macro culture, other micro cultures, and within the global community" (p. 25). Further, they

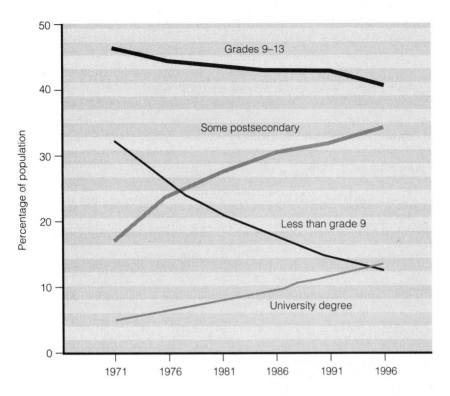

Figure 12.3
Highest Level of Schooling, Age 15+, Canada, 1971–96
SOURCE: Statistics Canada. 1996. 1996 Census: Education, *The Nation Series* (Statistics Canada Cat. No. 93F0028XDB96002).

argue that multicultural education is a necessary element in the battle against race, class, gender, and ethnic inequalities (Banks and Banks 1995).

CONSIDERATION

Recent research on fraternity members suggests that despite supporters who argue the benefits of the Greek system, the brotherhood has a negative effect on its participants. Several studies reported in Kuh et al.'s "The Questionable Value of Fraternities" (1996) conclude that fraternity membership is associated with (1) lower intellectual development, (2) higher alcohol use, and (3) a reduced respect for human differences (e.g., race, ethnicity, sexual orientation).

Sorting Individuals into Statuses Schools sort individuals into statuses by providing credentials for individuals who achieve various levels of education, at various schools, within the system. These credentials sort people into different statuses—for example, "high-school graduate," "Rhodes scholar," and "Ph.D." Further, schools sort individuals into professional statuses by awarding degrees in such fields as medicine, nursing, and law. The significance of such statuses lies in their association with occupational prestige and income.

Custodial Care The educational system also serves the function of providing custodial care (Merton 1968), which is particularly valuable to single-parent and dual-earner families, and the likely reason for the increase in enrolments of three- and four-year-olds. Kindergartens and nursery schools are not, however, a new development in Canada. Indeed, Canada's first public school kindergartens for the education of four- and five-year-old children were established in Kitchener (then called Berlin), Ontario, in 1882 and were formally incorpo-

National Data

In 1996, more than 14 million Canadians aged 15 and older (66 percent) had completed at least high school. Almost 7 of 10 Canadians aged 20 and older (69 percent) had completed at least high school. The 1996 census was the first census to record a higher number of university graduates than of people reporting less than a grade 9 education (see Figure 12.3).

SOURCE: Health Canada 1999

National Data

Approximately two-thirds of all school-aged immigrant children arrive in Canada speaking neither French nor English.

SOURCE: Canadian Council on Social Development 1999

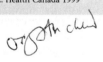

rated into the Ontario public school system in 1887. In Quebec, *salles d'asile* were run by nuns for the children of working parents and were attended by more than 10 000 children between 1898 and 1902.

In 1992–93, more than half a million Canadian children under the age of six were enrolled in kindergarten or preschool programs within schools, and almost 91 percent of five-year-olds attended kindergarten (with Newfoundland and Nova Scotia recording the highest proportions and Prince Edward Island, the lowest). In that period, Ontario was the only province in which the majority of four-year-olds (approximately 70 percent) attended kindergarten. In stark contrast, no four-year-olds in Newfoundland, Prince Edward Island, or British Columbia were enrolled, and less than 1 percent of four-year-olds in Nova Scotia were enrolled in public schools. Kindergarten is not mandatory, but local education authorities in all Canadian provinces and territories, with the exception of Prince Edward Island, provide programs for those too young to enter grade 1 (Statistics Canada 1998a).

The school system provides free supervision and care for children and adolescents until they complete secondary or "high school"—almost 13 000 hours per pupil! Some school districts are experimenting with offering classes year-round, offering Saturday classes, or having longer school days. Providing more hours of supervision for children and adolescents may reduce juvenile delinquency and teenage pregnancy. Indeed, "lack of parental supervision is one of the strongest predictors of the development of conduct problems and delinquency" (Sautter 1995: K8).

Conflict Perspective

Conflict theorists emphasize that the educational institution solidifies the class positions of groups and allows the elite to control the masses. Although the official goal of education in society is to provide a universal mechanism for achievement, in reality educational opportunities and the quality of education are not equally distributed.

Conflict theorists point out that the socialization function of education is really indoctrination into a capitalist ideology. In essence, students are socialized to value the interests of the state and to function to sustain it. Such indoctrination begins in kindergarten. Rosabeth Moss Kanter (1972) coined the term "the organization child" to refer to the child in nursery school who is most comfortable with supervision, guidance, and adult control. Teachers cultivate the organization child by providing daily routines and rewarding those who conform. In essence, teachers train future bureaucrats to be obedient to authority.

Further, to conflict theorists, education serves as a mechanism for cultural imperialism, or the indoctrination into the dominant culture of a society. When cultural imperialism exists, the norms, values, traditions, and languages of minorities are systematically ignored. For example, in his analysis of the development of the educational system in Ontario in the mid–nineteenth century, Neil McDonald emphasized how education was conceived of as crucial for maintaining dominant ideologies. He notes that the chief architect of the Ontario school system, Egerton Ryerson, purposefully set out to create a system in which "young people would remain loyal to the Crown...never participate in the kind of rebellion which had been put down in Upper Canada in 1837, and...cooperate with one another, regardless of their social class backgrounds."

Through education, the working class were to be persuaded that "their interests were also those of the middle and upper classes and that, as a collectivity, there was a 'common' or 'public good' towards which all must work" (McDonald, as cited in Curtis and Lambert 1994: 12). As Curtis and Lambert (1994: 12) remark, "In short, Ryerson's objective was social control, and he charged the schools with the responsibility of inculcating the beliefs and attitudes of mind that would accomplish it."

Traditionally, the school curriculum has not given voice to the perspective of minority groups, including women. Lessons in history, for example, are given from the perspective of the victors—not the vanquished. The cultural genocide promoted within the residential schools for Canada's Indigenous people must be recognized as one of the bleakest notes in the history of Canadian education (see this chapter's The Human Side). As only one example, those in Native schools who dared to speak their own language were routinely punished by having a sewing needle pushed through their tongue in a practice known as the "needle torture."

Finally, the conflict perspective focuses on what Kozol (1991) calls the "savage inequalities" in education that perpetuate racial inequality. As the Canadian Council of Social Development (1999) has emphasized, "[l]ower educational results among particular groups perpetuate their social exclusion and lower economic outcomes, raising serious doubts about how the educational system can be changed to serve the needs of these students."

For example, while comparisons between 1981 and 1996 indicate that Aboriginals are making educational progress, they remain less likely than non-Aboriginals to receive a high-school diploma and, in particular, a postsecondary degree or diploma (Figure 12.4). Tait (1999: 6) points out that "[b]etween 1986 and 1996, young Aboriginal adults improved their qualifications at every level of education....[However,] in 1996 there were still large gaps in relative attainment between Aboriginal and non-Aboriginal people aged 20 to 29." She additionally

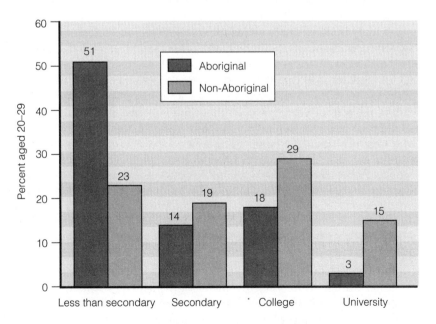

Figure 12.4
Educational Attainments of Aboriginals and Non-Aboriginals, Canada, 1996

SOURCE: Statistics Canada. 1996. *1996 Census of Population*.

Highest level of education completed

notes that the gap widened during this period for those without a high-school education. "While in 1986, Aboriginal people were 2.2 times more likely than their non-Aboriginal counterparts to have less than high school, by 1996 they were 2.6 times more likely to be without high school completion" (p. 7).

Symbolic Interactionist Perspective

Whereas structural-functionalism and conflict theory focus on macro-level issues such as institutional influences and power relations, symbolic interactionism examines education from a micro perspective. This perspective is concerned with individual and small group issues, such as teacher–student interactions, students' self-esteem, and the self-fulfilling prophecy.

Teacher–Student Interactions

Symbolic interactionists have examined the ways in which students and teachers view and relate to each other. For example, children from economically advantaged homes may be more likely to bring social and verbal skills into the classroom that elicit approval from teachers. From the teachers' point of view, middle-class children are easy and fun to teach: they grasp the material quickly, do their homework, and are more likely to value the educational process. Children from economically disadvantaged homes often bring fewer social and verbal skills to those same middle-class teachers, who may, inadvertently, hold up social mirrors of disapproval. Teacher disapproval contributes to the lower self-esteem of disadvantaged youth.

Self-Fulfilling Prophecy The **self-fulfilling prophecy** occurs when people act in a manner consistent with the expectations of others. For example, a teacher who defines a student as a slow learner may be less likely to call on that student or to encourage the student to pursue difficult subjects. Because of the teacher's behaviour, the student is more likely to perform at a lower level.

A study by Rosenthal and Jacobson (1968) provides empirical evidence of the self-fulfilling prophecy in the public school system. Five elementary-school students were selected at random and identified for their teachers as "spurters." Such a label implied that they had superior intelligence and academic ability. In reality, they were no different from the other students in their classes. At the end of the school year, however, these five students scored higher on their intelligence quotient (IQ) tests and made higher grades than their classmates who were not labelled as spurters. In addition, the teachers rated the spurters as more curious, interesting, and happy, and more likely to succeed than the "nonspurters." Because the teachers expected the spurters to do well, they treated the students in a way that encouraged better school performance.

WHO SUCCEEDS? THE INEQUALITY OF EDUCATIONAL ATTAINMENT

As noted earlier, conflict theory focuses on inequalities in the educational system. Educational inequality is based on social class and family background, race and ethnicity, and gender. Each of these factors influences who succeeds in school.

EDUCATION AS CULTURAL GENOCIDE

The province of Canada in 1847 published a report...[that] formed the basis for future directions in policy for Indian Education. Clearly expressed is the perception of the superiority of the European culture, the need "to raise [Aboriginal people] to the level of the Whites," and the ever-increasing pressure to take control of land out of Indian hands. At the same time, the contradictory need to isolate Indians from the evil influences of White society is acknowledged. The general recommendations of the report were that the Indians remain under the control of the Crown rather than the provincial authority, that efforts to Christianize the Indians and settle them in communities be continued, and finally that schools, preferably manual labour ones, be established under the guidance of missionaries....Cultural oppression was becoming written policy. Within the discussion of the recommendations is the following comment:

> Their education must consist not merely of the training of the mind, but of a weaning from the habits and feelings of their ancestors, and the acquirements of the language, arts and customs of civilized life.

What clearer statement of an effort to destroy a culture could exist?...

Following the establishment of the *Indian Act* of 1876, a consolidation of existing legislation, the government commissioned N.F. Davin to report on industrial schools established for native people in the United States. Out of his report came the strong recommendations...[that] resulted in the establishment of many residential schools across Canada....In the introduction to the report, Davin made references to President Grant's policy on the Indian question: "The industrial school is the principal feature of the policy known as aggressive civilization...." While positively endorsing the notion of residential schools for Indians in Canada, Davin's final comment is, "If anything is to be done with the Indian, we must catch him very young...."

By 1920 amendments to the *Indian Act* included compulsory school attendance of Indian children and industrial or boarding schools for Indians....It is interesting to note that in 1920 in the House of Commons discussion of changes to the *Indian Act*, Deputy Superintendent General Duncan Campbell Scott stated clearly the idea that Indian cultures as such were to be eliminated.

> Our object is to continue until there is not a single Indian in Canada that has not been absorbed into the body politic and there is no Indian question, and no Indian department, that is the whole object of the Bill.

Not until 1946 was there serious possibility for change in this attitude and in the expressed intent of Department of Indian Affairs policy....For the first time, and only after initial strong resistance by committee members, Native input was actually permitted. Andrew Paull, President of the North American Indian Brotherhood, appeared before the Special Joint Committee. He was highly critical of the committee's lack of Indian representation. He condemned the existing

EDUCATION AS CULTURAL GENOCIDE *(continued)*

Act as "an imposition, the carrying out of the most bureaucratic and autocratic system that were ever imposed upon any people in this world of ours." He spoke strongly of Indian self-government, and finally he commented that what was needed was

> to lift up the morale of the Indians in Canada. That is your first duty. There is no use in

passing legislation about this or that if you do not lift up the morale of the people. The only way you can lift up the morale of any people is to let the members look after themselves and look after their people.

His words fell upon deaf ears.

SOURCE: Abridged from Haig-Brown, Celia. 1993. *Resistance and Renewal: Surviving the Indian Residential School.* Vancouver: Arsenal Pulp Press.

National Data

Although average earnings declined in all education categories from 1990 to 1995, the largest downturns were felt by Canadians with less than a grade 9 education.

SOURCE: Statistics Canada 1998

Social Class and Family Background

The best predictor of educational success and attainment is socioeconomic status (Lam 1997). Children whose families are in middle and upper socioeconomic brackets are more likely to perform better in school and to complete more years of education than children from lower socioeconomic families are. In the United States, average SAT scores are positively correlated with family income—the higher the income, the higher the SAT score. On average, students who come from well-off families, those with incomes of $100 000 a year or more, score 257 points higher than students whose family incomes are under $10 000 a year (College Board 1997).

In Canada, Porter et al. (1982) note that students from a higher social class are four times more likely to pursue academic goals than those from a lower social class. If you rank families from the poorest to the richest, at each income level the likelihood increases that the children will receive postsecondary education (Guppy and Arai 1993; Manski 1993). It is also clear that the longer students stay in school, the more likely they are to get a job once they leave (Table 12.1). Among 1990 university graduates, about 8 in 10 who obtained a bachelor's

Table 12.1	Work for Graduates, Ontario's 1996 Graduates	
Employment rates, by program	Six months after graduation	Two years after graduation
Medicine	100.0	99.6
Business and commerce	94.1	97.7
Engineering	91.5	97.4
Humanities	91.8	96.1
Computer science	90.5	98.7

SOURCE: Council of Ontario Universities 1998

degree or a master's degree were working full time five years after graduation; among those with a doctorate, almost 9 in 10 (88 percent) had jobs. While those with a bachelor's degree earned a median income of $38 000, those with a master's degree earned a median income of $50 000, and those with doctorates earned a median income of $54 000 (Statistics Canada 1998a). In contrast, Canadians who did not complete high school reported earnings of merely $18 639 in 1995—a figure significantly below the Canadian average of $26 474 (Health Canada 1999). Because higher educational attainment generally leads to higher earnings, patterns of inequality reproduce themselves.

Families with low incomes have fewer resources to commit to educational purposes. Low-income families have less money to buy books and computers, hire tutors, enrol their children in activities such as dance and music, and are less likely to take their children to museums and zoos. Parents in low-income brackets are also less likely to expect their children to go to college or university, and their behaviour may lead to a self-fulfilling prophecy. Disproportionately, children from low-income families do not go on to institutions of higher learning.

Low-income parents are also less involved in their children's education, yet parental involvement is crucial to the academic success of the child. According to Barton (1992), the most powerful measure of school quality is a high parent–teacher ratio. Although working-class parents may value the education of their children, in contrast to middle- and upper-class parents, they are more likely to feel intimidated by their children's schools and teachers and to lack the time or job flexibility to attend teacher conferences (Lareau 1989).

Parental education is also strongly linked to the school readiness of children (Figure 12.5), which additionally helps to explain intergenerational patterns of poverty and unemployment (Health Canada 1999). Because low-income parents are often themselves low academic achievers, their children are exposed to parents who have limited language and academic skills. Children learn the limited language skills of their parents, which restrict their

National Data

According to the 1996 census, there is substantial provincial and territorial variation among Canadians who have not completed high school, ranging from a high of 45 percent in Newfoundland to a low of 31 percent in British Columbia. University degrees were most common in Ontario and the Yukon (17 percent), and least likely in Newfoundland (10 percent).

SOURCE: Health Canada 1999

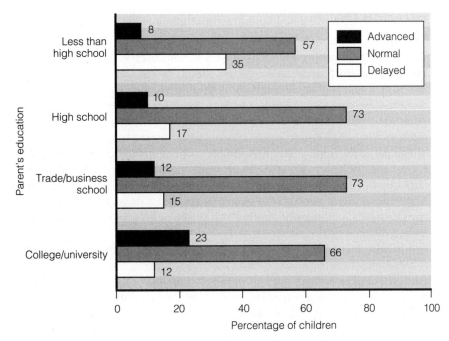

Figure 12.5

School Readiness, by Parents' Education,* Age 4–5, Canada, 1994–95

*Education of most-schooled parent.

SOURCE: Human Resources Development Canada and Statistics Canada. 1996. *Growing Up in Canada: National Longitudinal Survey of Children and Youth,* Ottawa: Statistics Canada, November 1996 (Statistics Canada Cat. No. 89-55-MPE, No. 1).

ability to do well academically. Low-income parents are often unable to help their children with their math, science, and English homework because they do not have the academic skills to do the assignments. Call et al. (1997) report that even among impoverished youths, parental education is one of the best predictors of a child's academic success.

Children from poor families also have more health problems and nutritional deficiencies. Children cannot learn when they are hungry, malnourished, sick, or in pain. Kozol (1991) observed:

> Bleeding gums, impacted teeth and rotting teeth are routine matters for the children I have interviewed....Children get used to feeling constant pain. They go to sleep with it....Children live for months with pain that grown-ups would find unendurable. The gradual attrition of accepted pain erodes their energy and aspiration. I have seen children...with teeth that look like brownish, broken sticks. I have also seen teenagers who were missing half their teeth....Many teachers in urban schools have seen this. It is almost commonplace. (pp. 20–1)

CONSIDERATION

According to the Canadian Council on Social Development (1999), "the gap in earnings and working conditions between postsecondary graduates and young people with a high-school education or less is widening, indicating that completing school is more critical than ever before." However, they note that Canada, like other countries, has been unable to provide jobs for educated elites and that higher levels of education do not always result in well-paid employment. As they point out, "A progressive economy in the twenty-first century will need citizens with higher levels of education, but there are many other 'supply-side' factors that are necessary if individuals are to realize the benefits that education has to offer."

Exceptional Children

The term "exceptional" refers to both remedial education to help children and young adults requiring special educational help because of "low intelligence, visual or auditory impairment, or emotional or specific learning difficulties, disabilities or problems" (Brown 1999: 741) and enrichment programs designed for those at the other end of the spectrum who are exceptionally gifted. It is evident that the educational needs of exceptional children may differ substantially. Gifted children, who are estimated to account for 5 percent of the population, may find the standard school curriculum for their chronological age unchallenging and benefit from "horizontal enrichment" or special enrichment programs at age-appropriate grade level or from acceleration into higher grades. However, classes geared to the needs of such children are often considered of low priority, leaving the brightest children bored and unchallenged in the regular classroom.

In other countries, identifying and developing programs for gifted children is considered to be of pivotal importance. For example, Singapore's ministry of education has established an office for gifted education and, as part of its mandate, is revising teacher training to include a course of identifying and nurturing highly intelligent children. In Germany, a long tradition exists for streaming children as young as 11 into separate schools leading to vocational, polytechnical, or university options. In Turkey, the mandate of the Inance Foundation of Istanbul is to educate the most academically able children from the country's impoverished and disadvantaged classes. However, Canada has shown concern that early streaming efforts seal a child's fate too early and are "elitist." In consequence, "Canadian public schools appear to be running headlong in the opposite direction—towards an increasingly uniform educational product" (Dwyer 1994: 38).

Although Ontario guarantees "that each school board provide special education programs and services for its gifted pupils," the Toronto Board of Education offers only 15 full-time enrichment classes at elementary schools and three such programs at the secondary level. The Calgary Public School Board, with 96 000 students, has only one school for gifted students; in Nova Scotia, two of 22 school districts offer formal gifted programs. While certain programs, such as the international baccalaureate program and advanced placement, are available to high-achieving high-school students, "many parents are giving up on the public school system altogether and turning to more costly, and exclusive alternatives" (Dwyer 1994: 17). However, for those parents who cannot afford the costs of educating their gifted child in such institutions as the semi-private University of Toronto Schools or the fully private Choice Learning Centre in Richmond, British Columbia, few options may be available.

In Canada, the field of special education has primarily focused on the 10 to 15 percent of the population who have a major or chronic disability. Until relatively recently, students with intellectual or other disabilities used to be isolated in special schools (often run by private agencies), kept at home, or warehoused in institutions. Although such institutions were not infrequently termed "training schools," the education and "training" provided within them was often minimal and their treatment of pupils not always humane.

For example, in Alberta, children and adults with disabilities and institutionalized at various training schools became unwitting candidates for sterilization under Alberta's *Sexual Sterilization Act*. This act, passed in 1928, had been "inspired by the philosophy of the eugenics movement, which believed mental retardation, criminality and much socially unacceptable behaviour (such as prostitution and poverty) were inherited." The Act permitted the provincial government's eugenics board to order sterilization where "procreation by the person under consideration (a) would result in the transmission of any mental disability or deficiency to his progeny, or (b) involves the risk of mental injury either to such person or his progeny." Of the 2844 people sterilized by order of the province's eugenics board, "a disproportionate number were eastern European, Catholic or native" (Daisley 1996: 7). Although Alberta and British Columbia were the only provinces to pass sterilization laws, it is believed that hundreds of such operations were also carried out in Ontario. In Alberta, the Act was finally repealed by the government in 1972.

Brown (1999: 741–2) observes that "The process of 'normalization' (now referred to as social role valorization), which is designed to assist a person with handicaps to develop as normal and valued a way of life as possible, took root in Canada in the early 1970s," encouraged by the efforts of the Canadian Association for the Mentally Retarded (now called the Canadian Association for Community Living). Educators increasingly recognized that specialized schools did injustice to special-needs students. In these settings, they learned only how to adjust to a world of people with disabilities; thus, they were ill prepared to cope with the dominant world. Today, while special education programs do include remediation of basic school subjects, they also emphasize social education or the learning of self-help and social skills as well as vocational preparation and training. "Mainstreaming" or incorporating special-needs children into regular schools wherever possible is now encouraged, from preschool on. **Inclusive education** stems from the belief that all children should be permitted to participate in society, regardless of their specific disability.

Winzer (1993: 78) emphasizes that mainstreaming does not "eliminate all special classes and special education teachers," dispense with special education support services, "indiscriminately dump all children from special classes back into regular classrooms," or end with the mere physical integration of special-needs children into regular classrooms. Rather, she stresses, mainstreaming attempts to integrate special-needs students with their peers as much as possible while recognizing that this effort requires modifications to regular classrooms, collaboration with special education professionals to develop suitable curricula, and the promotion of equal learning opportunities for all students.

Evidence suggests that many teachers are reluctant to integrate exceptional students into the classroom. In her review of research conducted on teachers' attitudes toward mainstreaming, Winzer (1993: 96–7) notes complaints that mainstreaming makes integration harder, that it dilutes the educational program for students without exceptionalities and diminishes teacher effectiveness. The perception exists that children with exceptionalities are potential sources of classroom disturbance and that they usurp too much of the teacher's energy.

At present, many Canadian children with disabilities continue to experience difficulties and disruptions in their education. According to Oderkirk (1993), children with disabilities are more likely than are others to experience emotional or behavioural problems, school failure, an extended disruption to their education, or a delay in entering their first year of school. In addition, "children with disabilities face restricted choices and unempowering environments compared with children without disabilities....These include fewer opportunities for friendship, making social and educational choices or simply controlling physical aspects of their environment" (Brown 1999: 741).

Racial and Ethnic Minorities

Socioeconomic status interacts with race and ethnicity. Because race and ethnicity are so closely tied to socioeconomic status, it appears that race or ethnicity alone can determine school success. While race and ethnicity also have independent effects on educational achievement (Bankston and Caldas 1997; Jencks and Phillips 1998), their relationship is largely due to the association between race and ethnicity, and socioeconomic status.

One reason some minority students have academic difficulty is that they did not learn English as their first language. As previously noted, the number of immigrant school-age children who do not speak either of Canada's official languages on arrival is growing—a fact that suggests the increasing importance of such programs as English as a second language (ESL).

Another factor that may have a negative impact on both immigrant and minority students is the use of tests to assess academic achievement and ability that are biased against minorities. For example, questions on standardized tests often require students to have knowledge that is specific to the White middle-class majority culture. For example, it has been noted that IQ tests measure not only intelligence but also culturally acquired knowledge. The cultural bias built into the IQ tests used in schools makes it more likely that children from some backgrounds—and not others—will have high scores. Consider as well that in 2000, it was reported that the Ontario Human Rights Commission had been asked to investigate the charge that the Law School Admission Test (LSAT), a test used by North American law schools to rank applicants, was biased against racial minorities (Humphreys 2000: A11).

In addition to being hindered by speaking a different language and by being from a different cultural background, minority students may also be disadvantaged by overt racism and discrimination. It has been noted, for example, that "[m]any visible minorities, such as native people and blacks, continue to have much greater school dropout rates" (Livingstone 1999: 743). While research conducted by the Toronto Board of Education (1993) suggests that immigrant children, in general, tend to do well at school after a period of acclimatization, a notable exception exists with respect to Black children "who experience lower rates of integration into the education system and have lower levels of educational attainment" (Figure 12.6).

Although the composition of Canada's student population is becoming increasingly multicultural, this is less true of Canada's teachers. According to the Canadian Council of Social Development (1999), "[r]esearch suggests that teachers will continue to be mainly white, middle-aged women." An ongoing debate in Canada is whether students, at all levels, would be better served by a faculty whose composition is less singular and that reflects the diversity of our population. Some have additionally suggested the need for a more inclusive curricula. For example, Ken Osborne (1988) maintains that, "[t]here can be no doubt that existing curricula are biased, both in what they include and in what

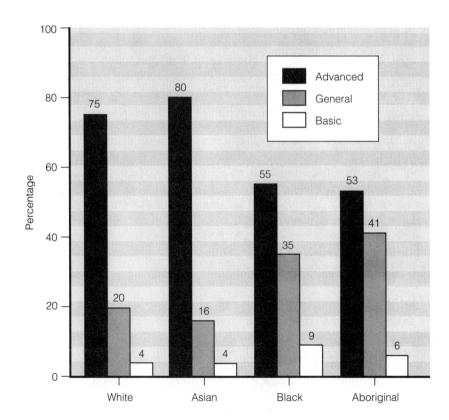

Figure 12.6
Education Program Level and Race
SOURCE: Toronto Board of Education. 1993.

they omit, nor that for many...students they have little appeal." In consequence, Gaskell et al. (1995: 104–5) argue that "the experiences of women (and of First Nations people, working-class people, visible minorities and other disadvantaged groups) must be incorporated into the curriculum....The purpose of schooling must be to "empower"...them, to give them the ability to participate fully in struggles, large and small, to gain respect, dignity and power."

Not all, however, agree with this position. For example, Thomas Sowell (1994) maintains that "most of the arguments" for an inclusive curriculum "are so flimsy, consistent, and downright silly that it is hard to imagine that they would have been taken seriously if they were not backed up by shrill rhetoric, character assassination, and the implied or open threat of organized disruption and violence on campus." In his opinion, the limited amount of class time available makes it impossible for educators to include the experiences of non-dominant groups. Those who would attempt to do so, he maintains, are "just kidding...[themselves] that...[they] are educating anybody....[A]ll you are really doing is teaching [students] to accept superficiality." Similarly, he maintains that the absence of information on the historic achievements and contributions of minority groups occurs for a reason:

> **[H]ow can a people's achievements be unaffected by their oppression? One of the many reasons to be against oppression is that it keeps people from achieving all that they could have had they been treated more decently...The past is many things, but one thing it is, is irrevocable. A past that is not to your liking is not an entitlement.**

In like fashion, some have argued that while educational authorities must censure teachers whose actions, both inside and outside the classroom, create a "chilly climate" for minority groups, others see the issue quite differently. For example, Fekete (1994) argues that on university campuses across Canada, freedom of speech is being curtailed by "thought police" and that "political correctness" has only served to create a "culture of forbidden questions" and a "new intolerance." Similarly, Roger Kimball argues that "[w]hat we are facing is nothing less than the destruction of the fundamental premises that underlie both our conception of liberal education and a liberal democratic policy" (as cited in D'Souza 1994: 90).

All these opposing viewpoints reflect the "**culture wars**" that surround education today. The field of education has "become increasingly politicized over issues involving curriculum, admission of minority students (and respect for minority cultures), women's rights, and other cultural debates" (Bender and Leone 1994: 72). However, as John K. Wilson suggests, the debates that have followed may well provide educators "with a unique opportunity to re-examine the ideals of colleges and universities, and to answer the questions of what should be taught and how we ought to teach" (as cited in Bender and Leone 1994: 13).

Gender

Worldwide, women receive less education than men do. Two-thirds of the world's 920 million illiterate people are women (United Nations Population Fund 1999).

International Data

According to data collected by the United Nations, Canada ties for 14th place among 125 countries in terms of the proportion of all students in postsecondary education who are women.

SOURCE: Neft and Levine 1997

Historically, schools have discriminated against women. When Martha Humm Lewis gained entrance to a training school for teachers in New Brunswick in 1849, the principal of the school cautioned her to "enter the classroom ten minutes before the male students, sit alone at the back of the room, always wear a veil, leave the classroom five minutes before the end of the lesson and leave the building without speaking to any of the young men" (MacLellan, 1972, in Schaefer et al. 1996: 282). Although Canadian schools are not typically segregated by sex any longer, a look at the elementary schools in any community that were built before 1960 will likely yield a large number with the designations "Girls" and "Boys" over separate entrances, reflecting past attempts to keep the sexes apart.

Since the 1960s, the women's movement has sought to end sexism in education. For example, the 1970 Canadian Royal Commission on the Status of Women made the following recommendations: "adoption of textbooks that portray both sexes in diversified roles and occupations; provision of career information about the broad field of occupational choice for girls; improved availability of sport programs for both sexes; development of educational programs to meet the special needs of rural and immigrant women and of Indian and Inuit girls and young women; and the continuing education of women with family responsibilities" (as cited in Mackie 1991: 158). Three decades later, textbooks using gender-neutral language and images are increasingly being adopted and there has been a trend toward a more integrated curriculum in which boys and girls learn, for example, both auto mechanics and cooking.

Traditional gender roles account for many of the differences in educational achievement and attainment between women and men. As noted in Chapter 7, schools, teachers, and educational materials reinforce traditional gender roles in several ways. Some evidence suggests, for example, that teachers provide less attention and encouragement to girls than to boys and that textbooks tend to stereotype females and males in traditional roles (Bailey 1993; Mensh and Lloyd 1997).

Studies of academic performance suggest that females tend to lag behind males in math and science. One explanation is that women experience workplace discrimination in these areas, which restricts their occupational and salary opportunities. The perception of restricted opportunities, in turn, negatively affects academic motivation and performance among girls and women (Baker and Jones 1993).

CONSIDERATION

Educational reformers have recently suggested a return to single-sex schools for both males and females. For males, the argument is that boys need the masculine environment provided by all-male academies where male teachers serve as positive adult role models. For females, the argument is that schools and teachers are consistently biased against girls, and that sex segregation minimizes the stereotyping and discrimination inherent in mixed sex classrooms. However, researcher Maggie Ford concludes that the evidence indicates "...that separating by sex is not the solution to gender inequity in education. When elements of good education are present, girls and boys succeed" (AAUW 1998).

Most research on gender inequality in the schools focuses on how female students are shortchanged in the educational system, but what about male students? For example, schools fail to provide boys with adequate numbers of

One of the most notable changes that occurred in Canada between 1971 and 1996 was the significant increase in the number of Canadian women obtaining university degrees. More than four times as many women over the age of 25 were university graduates in 1996 than in 1971, compared with twice as many men over the age of 25 who were university graduates. In 1996, women in their 20s were more likely to be college and university graduates than were men of the same age.

SOURCE: Health Canada 1999

male teachers to serve as positive role models. To remedy this, some school systems actively recruit male teachers, especially in the elementary grades, where female teachers dominate.

The problems that boys bring to school may indeed require schools to devote more resources and attention to them. More than 70 percent of students with learning disabilities such as dyslexia are male, as are about 75 percent of students identified as having serious emotional problems. Boys are also more likely than girls to have speech impairments and to be labelled as "mentally retarded." Lastly, boys are more likely than girls to exhibit discipline problems (Bushweller 1995; Goldberg 1999).

PROBLEMS IN THE CANADIAN EDUCATIONAL SYSTEM

Let us examine some of the major problems that have been identified within Canadian education today, and several potential solutions.

Low Levels of Academic Achievement

As Maude Barlow and Heather-Jane Robertson (1994: 35) wryly observe, "Everyone knows that every other country's kids know twice as much as our kids at half their age." They observe that the achievement of Canadian students on international tests has been bemoaned in *Maclean's* as "mediocre," lambasted in the *Financial Times* as "calamitously low," and depicted as representing a "crisis of mediocrity."

In mathematics tests administered in 1995, Canadian elementary-school students hovered near the middle of the scores for the 29 countries in the Organization for Economic Co-operation and Development (OECD), behind such nations as the Netherlands and Korea. However, it must be remembered that international testing that seeks to compare students from different countries is very difficult to carry out accurately. Interpreting the results produces many problems. For example, in some countries, such as Japan, the school authorities rather than the students decide who will or will not study a specific subject. They also exhort students to perform well to bring honour to their teachers, school, family, and country. In contrast, the range of abilities among Canadian students is much broader. Simply put, the Canadian sample on international tests generally represents a less select or elite body of students. Barlow and Robertson (1994: 38) emphasize that when "apples are compared to apples, Canadian students meet or exceed the...performance of students from other countries tested."

The performance of Canadian students on international tests can also be viewed as a sign that teachers are now doing a better—not worse—job. As Thomas Sowell (1993) suggests, the fact that students have a broad range of abilities need not be viewed as calamitous; it could just as likely be a good sign. Low test scores, he argues, are the result of teachers getting more students to stay in high school and go on to college and university. In the past, students with poorer academic backgrounds would have dropped out and not become part of the test results. Nevertheless, some claim that student achievement on tests reflects "dummied down" textbooks, low standards, "frill" courses, less homework, fewer term papers, grade inflation, and burned-out teachers who are more interested in collecting their paycheques than in educating their students.

Literacy

The first national survey in Canada to determine the degree of literacy of Canadians was conducted in 1987 and found that an estimated 24 percent of Canadians were illiterate. In 1989, the Canadian Survey of Literary Skills Used in Daily Activities, conducted by Statistics Canada, reported that 15 percent of Canadians aged 16 to 60 (about 2.7 million adult Canadians) had such limited reading abilities that they could not deal with most of the written material they were confronted with at home, at work, and in the community. A further 22 percent of Canadian adults could tackle simple texts but lacked sufficient reading skills to handle complex reading tasks. These problems were more likely to be reported among older Canadians, among immigrants, and among Canadians in central or Atlantic Canada. Although people with higher levels of education generally had adequate reading skills, "in 1989, 8% of people who had attended university, 15% of those who had been to community college, and 22% of high-school graduates could handle simple reading material [but] did not have the skills to cope with more complex contexts" (Montigny 1994: 322). The survey also reported that 14 percent of the population (2.4 million Canadians) had only limited quantitative literacy (or "numeracy") skills. At best, these individuals were able to recognize numbers but could not consistently perform numerical operations. Another 4.1 million Canadians (24 percent of the population), did not have the skills to manage "most everyday numeracy requirements" (p. 323).

Most recently, the *International Adult Literacy Survey*, conducted in 1994–95, investigated Canadians' prose literacy (i.e., ability to read and comprehend a passage of text), document literacy (i.e., ability to complete standard forms, such as job applications), and quantitative literacy (which requires basic computational skills). Five levels of each type of literacy were distinguished, with higher levels indicating greater competency. Respondents were generally between the ages of 16 and 65 (although there was no upper age limit on Canadians) and representative of the population of their countries. In Canada, 3130 respondents were tested in English and 1370 in French.

The results of this survey indicate that although the majority of Canadians (about 57 percent) possess sufficient skills to handle the printed materials they confront daily, a high proportion of Canadians (43 percent) have only marginal literacy skills. Fewer than 6 in 10 Canadians (57 to 58 percent) over the age of 16 attained Level 3 or higher in prose, document, and quantitative literacy (Table 12.2). About one in six Canadians has trouble using a weather chart to calculate temperature difference or deciphering a simple graph; one in four has difficulty using a bus schedule.

Among the findings of this survey:

- The literacy skills of Canadians older than 45 were markedly lower than were those of adults aged 16 to 45. Much of the difference was attributable to respondents' socioeconomic background, their years of education, and whether their first language was the test language.
- Women's scores in prose literacy were higher than the scores of men across the full age range of 16 to 90. However, no statistically significant differences existed between the sexes in document literacy scores. Men scored higher in quantitative literacy than did women; however, the differences were evident only for youth (16 to 25 years of age) and adults over age 65.

Table 12.2	Literacy on Prose, Documents, and Quantitative Material, by Country, Age 16–65, 1994–95			
	Level 1 (Lowest) (%)	Level 2 (%)	Level 3 (%)	Level 4/5 (Highest) (%)
Prose				
Australia	17	27	37	19
Belgium (Flanders)	18	28	39	14
Canada	**17**	**26**	**35**	**23**
Germany	14	34	38	13
Ireland	23	30	34	14
Netherlands	11	30	44	15
New Zealand	18	27	35	19
Sweden	8	20	40	32
Switzerland (French)	18	34	39	10
United Kingdom	22	30	31	17
United States	21	26	32	21
Documents				
Australia	17	28	38	17
Belgium (Flanders)	15	24	43	17
Canada	18	25	32	25
Germany	9	33	40	19
Ireland	25	32	32	12
Netherlands	10	26	44	20
New Zealand	21	29	32	18
Sweden	6	19	39	36
Switzerland (French)	16	29	39	16
United Kingdom	23	27	31	19
United States	24	26	31	19
Quantitative				
Australia	17	27	38	19
Belgium (Flanders)	17	23	38	23
Canada	17	26	35	22
Germany	7	27	43	24
Ireland	25	28	31	16
Netherlands	10	26	44	20
New Zealand	20	29	33	17
Sweden	7	19	39	36
Switzerland (French)	13	25	42	20
United Kingdom	23	28	30	19
United States	21	25	31	23

SOURCE: Organization for Economic Co-operation and Development and Human Resources Development Canada. 1997. *Literacy Skills for the Knowledge Society: Further Results from the International Adult Literacy Survey*. Ottawa: Human Resources Development Canada.

- Adults whose first language differed from the test language scored substantially lower than those whose first language matched the language of the test.
- Adults in rural communities scored slightly lower than those in urban areas (a difference of about five months of formal schooling); however, after

accounting for their background characteristics, rural adults scored higher, with a difference of about one full year of schooling.

- The 10 provinces varied substantially in their literacy scores. The unadjusted results for youth can be clustered into three groups with (1) Manitoba and Saskatchewan scoring more than one year of schooling above the national average, (2) British Columbia, Alberta, Nova Scotia, and Quebec scoring near the national average, and (3) Ontario, New Brunswick, Newfoundland, and Prince Edward Island scoring about one year of schooling below the national average. About three-eighths of the variation was attributable to differences in youths' socioeconomic background.

- The relationship between literacy skills and socioeconomic status varied dramatically among the provinces. The distribution of literacy skills along social class lines was considerably more equitable in Quebec and the three Prairie provinces. In Ontario, British Columbia, and the four Atlantic provinces, youth from less advantaged family backgrounds scored much lower than did youths with similar backgrounds in other provinces (Health Canada 1999: 31–2).

Perhaps most vexatiously, the survey reported that even a high-school education does not guarantee good results: about one in four high-school graduates aged 16 to 25 had low literacy skills and had difficulty reading and comprehending such basic texts as official forms and timetables.

For some social commentators, these findings suggest the inadequacy of our educational system and, in particular, the aftermath of **grade inflation** (the awarding of As to students whose work warrants lower grades) and **social promotion** (the practice of passing students from one grade to the next even thought they have not mastered the necessary grade-level skills). It is argued that, despite the higher educational attainments of Canadians, an alarmingly large proportion of our population remain **functional illiterates**: people who have difficulty with reading and writing despite their academic accomplishments.

CONSIDERATION

Education is not simply for the young; participation in adult education soared from about 4 percent in 1960 to around a third of the adult Canadian population in the 1990s. As Livingstone (1999: 743) observes, "In this context of accelerating economic and technological change, the watchword of educational opportunity has become 'lifelong learning.'" In 1993, almost six million Canadians 17 years of age and older participated in adult education or training, not including the more than one million Canadians who were pursuing diplomas, degrees, or certificates full-time. In that year, the majority of those who pursued adult education did so to upgrade their skills and enhance their chances of employment or career advancement; only one in eight were taking courses solely for personal interest. Generally, those who have high levels of education and full-time employment in the service sector are most likely to continue studying, to participate in employer-sponsored training, and to believe that they require additional training. In 1995–96, more than 350 260 people were registered in noncredit university-level continuing education courses (Statistics Canada 1998a). According to the National Survey of 1995 Graduates conducted in 1997, almost half (46 percent) of those who had earned a bachelor's degree in 1995 had gone back to school within two years of graduation and about 2 percent of bachelor's graduates had entered a college program in an attempt to improve their career prospects by learning more job-specific skills (Clark 1999).

About 80 percent of Canada's graduating high-school class of 1991 went on to take courses toward a postsecondary certificate, diploma, or degree. Among these students, just over 4 in 10 (42 percent) went on to university, almost 3 in 10 (29 percent) entered college or CEGEP (Collège d'enseignement général et professionnel), and about 1 in 10 (9 percent) enrolled in a trade school, an apprenticeship program, or a program offered by either the private sector or a professional association.

SOURCE: Health Canada 1999

In 1993, two-thirds of adult education and training opportunities were provided by employers, unions, community centres, and commercial suppliers such as business schools.

SOURCE: Statistics Canada 1998a

School Dropouts

In 1991, Canada's dropout rate was 18 percent, with Alberta having the highest retention rate (86 percent) and Prince Edward Island the lowest (75 percent) (Barlow and Robertson 1994: 28). However, by 1995, "about one in four of those who had left school in 1991 had found their way back and graduated" (Statistics Canada 1998a: 152). In 1995, approximately 85 percent of Canadians aged 22 to 24 had a graduated from high school. Aboriginal Canadians, however, continue to have a higher likelihood of leaving school early than non-Aboriginals. Although the proportion of young Aboriginal people (including current students) with less than a high-school diploma decreased from 60 percent in 1986 to 45 percent in 1996, in 1996, Aboriginal people were still 2.6 times more likely than non-Aboriginals to be without a high-school education. In 1996, more than half (54 percent) of the Aboriginal population 15 years and older (versus 35 percent of the non-Aboriginal population of the same age) had not received a high-school diploma.

The stereotype of the dropout as a poorly motivated underachiever who prefers to live on social assistance and use drugs is one that enjoys considerable popular appeal; however, a Statistics Canada survey presents a different picture. Indeed, recognizing the negative connotations associated with "drop-out," the study discarded this term and replaced it with the more neutral-sounding term, "school leaver."

In their summary of this research, Sid Gilbert and Bruce Orok (1993: 3) report that, in contrast to the stereotype, many school leavers come from intact, two-parent homes, were doing well at school, and were either not working or working only moderate hours. On leaving school, school leavers were generally employed, worked long hours, and planned to continue with further education or job training. "Among male school leavers aged 18 to 20, the two most important reasons for leaving were that they preferred work to school (28%) and boredom (19%)....Female leavers aged 18 to 20 cited boredom (22%) and problems with school work (13%) as the top two reasons for leaving school." The need to work for financial reasons was mentioned by 9 percent of male respondents, while problems with teachers were mentioned by 8 percent. Among female school leavers, 10 percent reported that they preferred work to school, while 9 percent reported that pregnancy was important in their leaving school.

According to survey research conducted by Paul Grayson and Michael Hall on the characteristics of dropouts,

> students who have the greatest probability of being dropouts are those who are disabled; have dependent children; have fathers who have not completed high school; have changed schools a number of times; live with friends or alone rather than with their families; work while attending high school; are male; are married, live common-law or have been separated or divorced; and, have parents and friends who do not consider completing high school to be important. (As summarized in Barlow and Robertson 1994: 30)

According to the School Leavers Survey, compared with graduates, more school leavers lived in lone-parent families or without a parent during their last year in school; had at least one parent with a low level of education; reported that they did not enjoy school; expressed dissatisfaction with the courses offered and their utility; reported that they had skipped school; did not get along with their teachers or felt they did not "fit in" at school; had experienced failure in elementary school; had grade averages of C or lower before leaving school; consumed alcohol on a regular basis; had experienced trouble with the law during the last year of school; and had worked long hours for paid employment.

A closer analysis of the relationships among school, work, and dropping out, conducted by the same survey, shows that although working moderate hours is associated with a reduced risk of dropping out for both male and female students, intensive work involvement appears to substantially increase the likelihood of dropping out among young men. In contrast, lack of employment is associated with the highest risk of dropping out for young women (Sunter 1993). It may be that such aspects of work as punctuality, initiative, and so on increase success-oriented behaviours as well as students' self-esteem. Since the bulk of working students are employed in low-skill, low-paying jobs, Sunter suggests that the work experiences of students "may convince many that high-school graduation is essential to gaining access to more interesting employment with greater earnings potential" (p. 51).

The economic and social consequences of dropping out of school are significant. School leavers are more likely than are those who complete high school to be unemployed and to earn less when they are employed. Individuals who do not complete high school are also more likely to engage in criminal activity, have poorer health and lower rates of political participation, and require more government services such as welfare and health care assistance (Natriello 1995; Rumberger 1987).

Student Violence

On April 28, 1999, just eight days after the shooting rampage at Columbine High School in Littleton, Colorado, where two students killed 13 people (12 students and one teacher) before taking their own lives, a 15-year-old boy in Taber, Alberta gunned down one teen and wounded another in a school hallway. Exactly one year after the Columbine massacre, a teenager in an Ottawa-area high school, who had been a victim of taunting, went on a rampage with a knife, stabbing four students and one staff member before his principal convinced him to surrender (*Maclean's* 2000: 20).

Although we might prefer to think of these situations as exceptional, Andrew Nikiforuk (1993: 189) reports that a survey of high schools published by the Calgary Board of Education found that "one in five students carried 'some sort of weapon' to class because they didn't feel safe in school." It seems that such fears may well be justified. Consider, as well, that at Cole Harbour High School in Nova Scotia, a snowball fight erupted into a racially charged incident in which Black and White students were fighting each other with chains. A few years later, the same school was closed for a week after another eruption of violence involving parents, teachers, and students left several students in hospital (Watson 1998).

Various attempts have been made to redress such situations. For example, following the week-long closing of Cole Harbour High School, the school made numerous changes to its systems of security and discipline: security cameras were installed, security guards were hired, the school days were shortened to eliminate free time, and troublemakers were expelled. In addition, the school introduced a "Student of the Week" program designed to encourage students to respect the cultures of others, and implemented a system of peer mediators—14 students, supervised by a staff person, who are given special training in mediation techniques and who work on the frontline in conflict between small numbers of students. As Watson (1998: 16) explains,

> **The rationale for the program has many parts: students develop a sense of responsibility for the condition of their school; they feel they have control over events in the school; and the program creates an environment where a minor conflict can be handled without the principal's intervention.**

In Ontario, the issue of school violence prompted the Metropolitan Toronto School Board and Ontario's Ministry of Education and Training to launch a $250 000 voluntary program for students who had been expelled from school because of violent behaviour. The program was to be tailored to meet "each students' educational, behavioural and social needs" with re-entry into regular classrooms contingent on demonstrated improvement in behaviour and attitude. However, in 1999, Premier Mike Harris announced a more punitive approach to high-school troublemakers and pledged to give teachers expanded powers to punish and expel disruptive students.

Although "zero-tolerance" policies attempt to discourage violence by making any misbehaviour grounds for immediate suspension, some have suggested that this approach is, at best, a half-measure. For example, at a national policy conference organized by the Canadian Institute for Advanced Research, Dan Offord, head of child psychiatry at McMaster University, argued that attempts to reduce violent behaviour must begin with screening programs directed at children in early grades who display antisocial behaviour. He suggested that as many as 20 percent of school-aged children and teens suffer "from some type of emotional disorder" and that "at least 12 percent" could benefit from individual attention. In addition, Offord argued that while many find a "get tough" approach appealing, "[t]here has to be a place for everyone in schools....[Y]ou can't just push kids out of the school system. Where do they go?"

The High Costs of Education

As Table 12.3 suggests, Canada compares favourably to many other countries in terms of various indicators of education. For example, about 40 percent of Canadians 15 years of age and older possess postsecondary credentials, with a third holding university degrees and the rest certificates or diplomas. Compared to most other Western countries, we also spend a higher proportion of our GDP on education. The salaries of our teachers additionally suggest the value we place on education. "Today…Canada's teachers average about $57 600 a year compared to the national income average for full-time workers of $36 235" (Statistics Canada 1998a: 145). Unlike the majority of countries worldwide, we also encourage those who are imprisoned in Canada's penitentiaries to enrol in secondary, vocational and postsecondary courses on site or through correspondence. In 1996–97, more than 22 000 inmates participated in some type of educational program.

Table 12.3   How We Compare: Education Spending, G-7 Countries, 1996

	Canada	U.S.	France	U.K.	Germany	Italy	Japan
Education spending as a percentage of total public expenditures	13.6	14.4	11.1	n.a.	9.5	9.0	9.8
Public spending as a percentage of GDP	5.8	5.0	5.8	4.6	4.5	4.5	3.6
Participation rate in formal education (percentage)[1]	68.2	68.8	64.5	66.8	61.8	53.8	57.0
Ratio of secondary school graduates to population (percentage)	73	72	85	n.a.	86	79	99
Ratio of first university degree to population (percentage)	32	35	n.a	34	n.a	1	23
Labour Force Participation by Education Attainment (Percentage)							
Secondary education							
– Men	89	88	90	89	85	80	n.a.
– Women	72	72	76	74	69	61	n.a.
University education							
– Men	92	93	92	94	93	92	n.a.
– Women	85	82	83	86	83	81	n.a.
Unemployment Rate by Level of Educational Attainment (Percentage)							
Upper secondary education							
– Men	9	6	8	8	8	6	n.a.
– Women	9	4	12	6	10	11	n.a.
University education							
– Men	5	2	6	4	5	5	n.a.
– Women	6	2	9	3	5	10	n.a.

[1] Total number of students enrolled in formal education as a percentage of the population aged 5–29. (n.a.) Not available.

SOURCE: Statistics Canada 1998a

At the same time, however, problems exist with Canada's educational funding. Reduced funding for public and postsecondary education and an increased reliance on student fees at the college and university level has led, in turn, to soaring increases in tuition costs for Canadian postsecondary students, demands for postsecondary institutions to accept more students (without additional funding), fewer academic hirings, rising student–faculty ratios, and dwindling resources. It is conservatively expected that university enrolment will increase by 20 percent by 2010. It is also expected, however, that more than 20 000 of Canada's 33 000 aging faculty will have retired or departed for greener vistas. As Johnston (1999b: 51) observes,

> the fallout has been huge. The number of lab assistants has been dwindling for years; lap equipment is outdated; library journals have been cancelled. And in many cases, what is known as the "physical plant"—the bricks and mortar—is crumbling. Two years ago, the administration at the University of Saskatchewan received an engineer's report, warning that the roof of their physical education building was in danger of collapsing.

Canada Study Grants are available to three categories of students: students with permanent disabilities; high-need part-time students, and students with children or other dependents. The amounts available vary depending on need; unlike Canada Student Loans, the monies awarded under the Canada Study Grants program do not have to be repaid. In addition, women who are full-time students in certain doctoral programs may also be eligible for a Canada Study Grant of up to $3000 per year for a maximum of three years.

SOURCE: Government of Canada 1999

In 1998, the government of Canada announced the creation of the Canada Millennium Scholarship Fund. Beginning in 2000, the Fund will award about 100 000 scholarships each year over the next 10 years based on financial need and merit to students of any age studying toward an undergraduate degree, diploma, or certificate at a Canadian postsecondary institution. It is expected that scholarships will average $3000 each year.

SOURCE: Government of Canada 1999

Would-be and current postsecondary students and their families are increasingly forced to confront the financial burdens posed by higher education. Clark (1999: 24) notes that although the cost of postsecondary education in Canada "has always been a responsibility shared by society through tax dollars, and by parents and children through personal savings," rising tuitions (up 115 percent since 1980) contrast sharply with the 1 percent rise in average family income (after adjusting for inflation).

Using data from the National Graduates Survey of 1995, Clark examined the extent of student debt and the impact of high debt on postsecondary graduates who had used government loans to finance their studies. He reports that both college and bachelor's degree graduates were most likely to finance their education through employment earnings (59 percent college, 69 bachelor's) and student loans (41 percent college, 42 percent bachelor's). Although parents ranked third as a funding source for those who acquired bachelor's degrees, neither college nor university students identified scholarships, fellowships, prizes, grants, or bursaries as a significant source of funding. Students from families with lower parental education (i.e., whose fathers had not completed high school) were more likely to use student loans than were those students with higher parental education. As well, students in their late 20s were more likely to borrow from government student loan programs and to borrow the most.

The financial burden assumed by the class of 1995 was often significant. Clark (1999: 25) notes:

> **Compared with the class of 1982, college and bachelor's graduates from the class of 1995 owed between 130% and 140% more to government student loan programs at graduation (after adjusting for inflation). On average, the 1995 graduates owed $9600 (college) and $13 000 (bachelor's) when they graduated.**

Among the class of 1995, 7 percent of college graduates and 22 percent of bachelor's graduates owned more than $20 000 at graduation. In Quebec, where undergraduate tuition fees for resident students are the lowest in Canada, graduates had one of the lowest debt levels at graduation ($11 600 in student loans). Students in Saskatchewan had the highest debt level at graduation ($16 200) (Clark 1999: 28).

It is not surprising, perhaps, that those who borrowed from student loans often faced difficulty in paying back the monies they had received. Clark reports that "during the two years following graduation, one-sixth of 1995 college and bachelor's borrowers indicated they were already having difficulty making payments on their government student loans." Women with bachelor's degrees with more likely to experience difficulty repaying their student loans; however, among college graduates, there were only marginal differences in repayment difficulties among women and men. Clark notes that "[b]ecause their earnings did not keep pace with these increasingly large loans, many graduates experienced repayment difficulties…[and w]ithin two years of graduation, one in 20 borrowers ended up defaulting on their loan" (p. 28).

STRATEGIES FOR ACTION: TRENDS AND INNOVATIONS IN CANADIAN EDUCATION

It is evident that education plays a critical role in Canadian society. Education has been referred to "as the one truly proactive public investment we make. It is not designed to address a problem, but rather to build the society we want for the future by investing in the creation of human and social capacity" (Canadian Council on Social Development 1999). Yet, at the same time, our educational system must be reactive and responsive to Canada's changing demography: changes in the age composition of our population, its ethno-racial mix, and family structures, as well as to trends in the labour market, economy, and the development of information and communications technology. To be sure, these are formidable challenges.

There is no shortage of suggestions about how we can improve our educational system. Here we review only a few.

Moral and Interpersonal Education

Violence, divorce, teen pregnancy, and drug abuse suggest that more attention needs to be placed on moral education. Most school curricula neglect the human side of education—the moral and interpersonal aspects of developing as an individual and as a member of society. Some educational reformers oppose the current emphasis on increasing academic standards and recommend that the main goal of education should be "to encourage the growth of competent, caring, loving and lovable people" (Noddings 1995: 366). To achieve this, Noddings suggests that students work together on school projects, help younger students, contribute to the care of buildings and grounds, and do supervised volunteer work in the community. Such activities would likely reduce the high rates of alienation experienced by many of today's students (see this chapter's Self and Society). She recommends that:

> All students should be engaged in a general education that guides them in caring for self, intimate others, global others, plants, animals, the environment, objects and instruments, and ideas. Moral life so defined should be frankly embraced as the main goal of education. (p. 368)

A moral and interpersonal emphasis in education implies that schools should prepare students not only for the world of work, but also for parenting and for civic responsibility. Noddings (1995) notes that:

> Almost all of us enter into intimate relationships, but schools largely ignore the centrality of such interests in our lives. And although most of us become parents, evidence suggests that we are not very good at parenting—and again the schools largely ignore this huge human task. (p. 367)

Moral and interpersonal education occurs to some extent in schools that have peer mediation and conflict resolution programs (discussed earlier and in Chapter 4). Such programs teach the value of nonviolence, collaboration, and helping others, as well as skills in interpersonal communication and conflict

National Data

Mount Royal Elementary School and Oliver School, both in Edmonton, are the first two Canadian schools to run the micro-society program.

resolution. Moral and interpersonal education also occur in micro-society schools.

Micro-Society Schools

A **micro-society school** is a simulation of the "real" or nonschool world. In a micro-society school, the students—with the help and guidance of their teachers—design and run their own democratic, free-market society within the school (Sommerfeld 1998). Micro-society schools were first created in 1967. At the City Magnet School in Lowell, Massachusetts, students set up their own government, complete with legislative, executive, and judicial branches. They wrote their own school constitution, and elected a legislature to make their own school laws. The school has its own courts and system of justice, as well as its own police force, called the City School Crime Stoppers. Students also devised and implemented a tax system operated by their own internal revenue service.

The school has an economic system with its own currency and banks in which every student has an account. Students have started numerous retail businesses that sell such things as pencils and stationery. They also set up their own publishing business within the language arts program.

All these micro-society activities are real jobs for which students are paid. To learn all the basic skills necessary to hold a job and participate in the micro-society, students go to the school within the school—the City School Academy. Students pay tuition from the money they earn by holding jobs in the rest of the micro-society.

Through participation in the micro-society school, both students and their teachers "constantly face moral dilemmas that they must solve as they strive to build a 'good' society" says reformer and founder George Richmond (1989: 232):

> Do you want a society with the extremes of poverty and wealth? Do you want a state of fear and violence? Should the microsociety's government assist or ignore children who may not be succeeding? Do you want a democracy or a totalitarian state? What liberties should children have? And what responsibilities should they shoulder? What kinds of activities should be taxed? When does one put the community's welfare ahead of the rights of the individual? What civil rights should children enjoy in their microsociety?

Computer Technology in Education

Computers in the classroom allow students to access large amounts of information (see this chapter's Focus on Technology). The proliferation of computers both in school and at home may mean that teachers will become facilitators and coaches rather than sole providers of information. Not only do computers enable students to access enormous amounts of information, including that from the World Wide Web, but they also allow students to progress at their own pace. Canada was one of the first countries to link its student body to the information superhighway. In 1995, Newfoundland became the first province with full Internet access in schools. By 1997, almost all Canadian schools had Internet access through the SchoolNet electronic network. In that year, Industry Canada's "Computers in the Schools" program had placed

Student Alienation Scale

Indicate your agreement to each statement by selecting one of the responses provided:

1. It is hard to know what is right and wrong because the world is changing so fast.

   Strongly agree — Agree — Disagree — Strongly disagree —

2. I am pretty sure my life will work out the way I want it to.

   Strongly agree — Agree — Disagree — Strongly disagree —

3. I like the rules of my school because I know what to expect.

   Strongly agree — Agree — Disagree — Strongly disagree —

4. School is important in building social relationships.

   Strongly agree — Agree — Disagree — Strongly disagree —

5. School will get me a good job.

   Strongly agree — Agree — Disagree — Strongly disagree —

6. It is all right to break the law as long as you are not caught.

   Strongly agree — Agree — Disagree — Strongly disagree —

7. I go to ball games and other sports activities at school.

   Always — Most of the time — Some of the time — Never —

8. School is teaching me what I want to learn.

   Strongly agree — Agree — Disagree — Strongly disagree —

9. I go to school parties, dances, and other school activities.

   Always — Most of the time — Some of the time — Never —

10. A student has the right to cheat if it will keep him or her from failing.

    Strongly agree — Agree — Disagree — Strongly disagree —

11. I feel like I do not have anyone to reach out to.

    Always — Most of the time — Some of the time — Never —

12. I feel that I am wasting my time in school.

    Always — Most of the time — Some of the time — Never —

13. I do not know anyone that I can confide in.

    Strongly agree — Agree — Disagree — Strongly disagree —

14. It is important to act and dress for the occasion.

    Always — Most of the time — Some of the time — Never —

15. It is no use to vote because one vote does not count very much.

    Strongly agree — Agree — Disagree — Strongly disagree —

16. When I am unhappy, there are people I can turn to for support.

    Always — Most of the time — Some of the time — Never —

17. School is helping me get ready for what I want to do after college or university.

    Strongly agree — Agree — Disagree — Strongly disagree —

18. When I am troubled, I keep things to myself.

    Always — Most of the time — Some of the time — Never —

19. I am not interested in adjusting to Canadian society.

    Strongly agree — Agree — Disagree — Strongly disagree —

20. I feel close to my family.

    Always — Most of the time — Some of the time — Never —

21. Everything is relative and there just aren't any rules to live by.

    Strongly agree — Agree — Disagree — Strongly disagree —

Student Alienation Scale (*continued*)

22. The problems of life are sometimes too big for me.

Always — Most of the time — Some of the time — Never —

23. I have lots of friends.

Strongly agree — Agree — Disagree — Strongly disagree —

24. I belong to different social groups.

Strongly agree — Agree — Disagree — Strongly disagree —

INTERPRETATION

This scale measures four aspects of alienation: *powerlessness*, or the sense that high goals (e.g., straight As are unattainable; *meaninglessness*, or lack of connectedness between the present (e.g., school) and the future (e.g., job); *normlessness*, or the feeling that socially disapproved behaviour (e.g., cheating) is necessary to achieve goals (e.g., high grades); and *social estrangement*, or lack of connectedness to others (e.g., being a "loner"). For items 1, 6, 10, 11, 12, 13, 15, 18, 19, 21, and 22, the response indicating the greatest degree of alienation is "strongly agree" or "always." For all other items, the response indicating the greatest degree of alienation is "strongly disagree" or "never."

SOURCE: Mau, Rosalind Y. 1992. "The Validity and Devolution of a Concept: Student Alienation." *Adolescence* 27 (107): 739–40. Used by permission of Libra Publishers, Inc., 3089 Clairemont Drive, Suite 383, San Diego, California 92117.

---

more than 20 000 computers and 40 000 pieces of software in Canadian schools and libraries (Canadian Council on Social Development 1999).

A downside has been noted. The conclusion of one of the largest studies of school computers found that students who use computers often scored lower on math tests than their low-use counterparts. The Educational Testing Service's study of 14 000 fourth and eighth graders concluded that how the computers were used—repetitive math drills versus real-life simulation—was responsible for the test variations. In addition, students in classrooms where teachers were trained in computer use did better than students in classrooms where teachers were less skilled. Minority and low-income students were the least likely to have teachers highly skilled in computer technology. Nevertheless, the Canadian government has evidenced its commitment to integrating computer technology into Canada's education system. In launching its "ThinkPad University" program, Acadia University (in partnership with IBM Canada) became the first Canadian university to require that each of its students purchase a computer as a condition of enrolment (Bergman 1999).

Alternative School Choices

Traditionally, children have gone to school in the district where they live. However, alternative schools, charter schools, home schooling, and private schools provide parents with alternative school choices for their children. With their origins in the reports of the Hall-Dennis Committee on Aims and Objectives of Education (Ontario) and the Worth Commission on Educational Planning (Alberta), **alternative schools** began in Canada in the 1970s. According to Chernos (1998: 13), "[p]erhaps the one element that unifies alternative schools is their diversity. Each operates within school board and education ministry guidelines yet maintains a unique character. Like snowflakes, no two are exactly alike." However, this diversity may encourage students who might oth-

---

National Data

In 1995, British Columbia announced a five-year plan that would see one computer for every three secondary students and every six elementary students. By 2000, Alberta had spent $85 million making computer equipment available to students and promoting the classroom use of technology.

SOURCE: Canadian Council on Social Development 1999

DISTANCE LEARNING AND THE NEW EDUCATION

Imagine never having an eight o'clock class or walking into the lecture room late. Imagine no room and board bills, or having to eat your roommate's cooking one more time. Imagine going to class when you want, even three o'clock in the morning. Imagine not worrying about parking! The future of higher education? Maybe. It's possible that the World Wide Web and other information technologies have so revolutionized education that the above scenarios are a *fait accompli*. What is distance learning? Distance learning separates, by time or place, the teacher from the student. They are, however, linked by some communication technology: videoconferencing, satellites, computers, audiotapes or videotapes, real-time chat rooms, closed-circuit televisions, electronic mail, or the like.

Examples of distance learning abound. "In 1997, New Brunswick's TeleEducation NB launched TeleCampus—one of the world's first virtual campuses—on the World Wide Web" (Statistics Canada 1998a: 159), an electronic school that allows students to enrol, study, and pay for courses via the Internet. By the end of 2000, TeleCampus anticipates that 10 000 students will be taking courses online. Athabasca University in northern Alberta is Canada's leading open university and considered a leader in developing electronic courseware. It offers students access to courses through teleconferencing, videoconferencing, and electronic means and offers many courses over the World Wide Web. Wasja, run by the Northern Nishnawbe Education Council, uses radio to provide educational opportunities to students in the Sioux Lookout area in Ontario. Kayas Cultural College runs the Little Red River Cree Nation in northeast Alberta and uses videoconferencing to provide acad-

emic upgrading and college courses. The University of Waterloo offers more than 270 distance education courses and has approximately 10 000 registrants (Haughey 1999: 672).

Distance education has been available in Canada for more than a century. It was first used in 1889 "to provide opportunities for teachers who were unable to attend McGill University in the winter months to study for their degree" (Haughey 1999: 672). However, since that time, the scope and clientele of distance education have vastly expanded. At present, a minimum of half a million people in Canada study through distance education and programs. The available courses range from those at the elementary level through to university level.

> Across Canada, over 65% of colleges offer at least one distance education course with over 60 000 students enrolled. Over 35 universities offer distance education courses. Many government departments and over 35% of large companies in Canada are already using some form of distance education. Commercial suppliers as well as industrial, trade and professional organizations are also providing distance learning courses and resources (Haughey 1999: 672).

With access to the World Wide Web, schools no longer carry a flag and attending a "foreign university" is increasingly possible (Figure 12.7).

Have a bachelor's degree? Looking for a graduate degree? Graduate and professional degrees can also be completed via the net. Kaplan Education Centers, known for their test preparation courses, opened the Internet's first law school in December 1998, the Concord School of Law.

Although the school is not accredited by either the Canadian or the American Bar Association, students who complete the four-year, $17 000 program can sit for

the bar examination in California—and only California thus far (Bulkeley 1998).

The benefits of distance learning are clear. It provides a less expensive, accessible, and often more convenient way to complete a degree. There are even pedagogical benefits. Research suggests that "students of all ages learn better when they are actively engaged in a process, whether that process comes in the form of a sophisticated multimedia package or a low-tech classroom debate on current events" (Carvin 1997). Distance education also benefits those who have historically been disadvantaged in the classroom. A review of research on gender differences suggests that females outperform males in distance learning environments (Koch 1998).

However, all that glitters is not gold. Evidence exists that students feel more estranged from their distance learning instructors than from teachers in conventional classrooms. The results of a study by Freitas et al. (1998) indicate that students in distance learning classes perceive significantly lower levels of teacher nonverbal immediacy (e.g., eye contact) when compared with students in conventional classes.

Additionally problematic is the proliferation of "virtual degrees." An elementary-school teacher enrolled in an online university to complete a master's degree in special education. After paying $800 of a total $2000 bill, she was sent a book to summarize as part of her degree requirements. Shortly after returning her summary, she was sent not only a master's degree, but a Ph.D. and transcripts of courses she had never taken with a recorded 3.9 grade point average (GPA) (Koeppel 1998). Although "degree mills" are not a new problem, there is the concern that the Internet lends itself to such fraudulent practices.

Further, teachers, particularly in higher education, are concerned about the quality of distance education. Several regulatory bodies, including the Council of Graduate Schools, are presently establishing quality standards and guidelines (Guernsey 1998). Although a committee of the American Association of University Professors acknowledged that distance learning may be a "valuable pedagogical tool," it also questioned whether "academic quality, academic freedom, intellectual property rights and instructor's workloads and compensation" will be compromised (Arenson 1998: A14).

Over the objections of many, distance education continues to expand. More than 100 colleges and universities have joined the Internet2 project, which promises to deliver information from 100 to 1000 times faster than the Internet (Rudich 1998). Its expansion may, in part, reflect the fact that distance education is a moneymaker—a $225 billion industry (Bulkeley 1998). New York University, for example, is planning to market an Internet subsidiary that is likely to earn millions of dollars for the university through private investors and stock offerings (Arenson 1998).

Although some would say that distance learning is only a fad, the growth of such private sector ventures would suggest otherwise. Thus, speed, availability, and accessibility are likely to increase as a response to market demands and, with them, use. Will distance learning solve all the problems facing education today? The answer is clearly no. While not the technological fix some are looking for, distance education, from digital libraries to cutting-edge technologies, does provide a provocative and financially lucrative alternative to traditional education providers.

erwise fall through the cracks of the educational system to remain in school or to re-enter the mainstream system at some later time.

For example, in London, Ontario, Richmond Centre and Dundas Centre Schools "are intended as an interim measure for students experiencing social, emotional, psychological, behavioral or academic troubles"(Chernos 1998: 15). The London school board also maintains other alternative schools for Native youth, Annishnabe and Wiingashk, both of which incorporate Native culture and traditions within a core curriculum of basic grade 9 to 12 subjects. In Toronto, the focus of Horizon Alternative Senior School "is on creating a caring community" that "balances core subjects...with an outward world-view that emphasizes self-expression, debate, role playing dialogue and conflict resolution" (Chernos 1998: 13). In Ontario alone, several dozen elementary and secondary schools bill themselves as alternative schools.

Alternative schools typically offer a variety of innovative and experimental programs. They generally have small student populations ranging from 70 to 250, with small, informal classes, and they place emphasis on close interaction between students and teachers. In many alternative high schools, student representatives join teachers, parents, and, sometimes, community members on the school's board of directors. According to Levin (1999: 732) alternative schools can be distinguished by "the sense of ownership, autonomy and control that teachers, parents, and students feel towards their school," and he suggests that "alternative schools may be forerunners of a more decentralized, pluralistic, community-based education system."

In complementary fashion, **charter schools** are public schools that function as semiautonomous units but derive their special character from a charter that declares the school's specialized purpose and reason for being. Currently, Alberta is the only province in Canada with charter schools. In that province, charter schools were established to provide students and their parents with greater choice and to encourage educational innovation. "Some of the specific characteristics of these schools are that they cannot deny access to students as long as space is available, they must require students to write provincial exam-

National Data

Data on home schoolers in Canada are limited. Currently, the only provinces with available data on the grade level of home schoolers are Alberta, Ontario, Nova Scotia, and Saskatchewan. These data report that more than 60 percent of children studying at home were elementary-school students.

SOURCE: Luffman 2000

Figure 12.7

**Western Governors
University Homepage**

SOURCE: Western Governors University Homepage. 1999. Homepage. <www.wgu.edu>. Used
by permission.

WGU Home | About WGU | Academics | Catalog | Admission | Library | Bookstore | Union

ABOUT WGU

Welcome to WGU

What We Are

Who's Involved

**Vision, History
& Mission**

Press Releases

Newsletters

Administration

About Your Privacy

Glossary

FAQs

Western Governors University offers a totally new way of looking at higher education. We're a new type of university centered around you, the student.

What makes WGU so different and exciting is that we know that not everyone who wants a college degree or courses can live on, or near, the campus of their choice. We offer distance learning courses from dozens of colleges, universities, and corporations across the United States (and soon the world!). Courses offered through WGU (you'll find them in the Catalog) will come to you, wherever you are, not the other way around. These courses use both high-tech and low-tech ways — from the Internet to satellite to the Postal Service — to provide you with real options.

Through WGU, you will also be able to earn degrees by focusing only on the skills and knowledge areas that you need. We call this "competency-based" education, since it is not based on the number of credits you may have accumulated. We won't make you relearn what you already know. You can count skills and knowledge you've gained at other universities, on the job, or just through life, toward your WGU degree.

Our students have online access to our Catalog, directory of programs, advising services, and important resources, like our online library with over 60 full-text and comprehensive citation databases.

Come in, tour our online campus and resources, and discover the WGU advantage. You can be part of WGU as a student, an education provider, or a corporate partner. If you still have questions about WGU, call us at 877-HELP-WGU (877-435-7948). Wondering if distance education is right for you? Take this quiz and find out!

Finally! Real options for higher education.

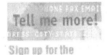

Tell me more!

Sign up for the
WGU mailing list

WGU Home | About WGU | Academics | Catalog | Admission | Library | Bookstore | Union
Guide | Students | Educators | Corporate | Site Map | Contact

Determining the number of children who are home schooled is problematic. In 1996–97, provincial ministries of education registered approximately 17 500 children as home schoolers. However, home schooling organizations, such as the Canadian Alliance of Home Schoolers, have placed the number of home schoolers between 30 000 and 40 000.

SOURCE: Arnott 1997; Luffman 2000

Canada's first nonreligious private university is scheduled to open in Squamish, British Columbia, in 2002. The yet-to-be named university promises major international figures as guest faculty, a 10 to 1 faculty–student ratio, and a maximum of 1000 students, half of whom will be drawn from other countries. The school will operate year-round and all graduates will be required to master three languages: one Asian, one European, and English. The school will charge an estimated $25 000 a year in tuition.

SOURCE: Johnston 1999a

inations, they may exist in present school buildings, they must employ certified teachers, and they are subject to annual audits" (Brown 1999: 440).

Some parents are choosing not to send their children to school at all but to teach them at home. For some parents, **home schooling** is part of a fundamentalist movement to protect children from perceived non-Christian values in the public schools. Other parents are concerned about the quality of their children's education and about their safety. How does being schooled at home instead of attending public school affect children? Webb (1989) found that children educated at home, either partly or completely, were equally successful in going to college and securing employment as those who were educated in the public school system.

Another choice parents may make is to send their children to private schools. The primary reason parents send their children to private schools is for religious instruction. The second most frequent reason is the belief that private schools are superior to public schools in terms of academic achievement. Research suggests, however, that when controlling for parents' education and income, there are few differences in private and public school educational outcomes (Ascher et al. 1997; Cohen 1998; Shanker 1996). Parents also choose private schools for their children to have greater control over school policy, or to obtain a specific course of instruction such as dance or music. Concern with the quality of education has also led to a boom in private tutoring schools. For example, since 1988, the Toronto-based Kumon Educational Institute of Canada Inc. has opened 215 franchises and attracted more than 20 000 students hoping to improve their math skills. Founded in 1958 in Japan, Kumon now operates in 28 countries worldwide. Sylvan Learning Systems, an American company specializing in math and language, sold its first Canadian franchise in 1985 and now has more than 40 operations across the country. Other smaller tutoring schools include the Canada Home Tutoring Ltd. in Edmonton and the nonprofit Vancouver-based Teacher's Tutoring Service whose 600 certified teachers work with 2000 students a year (Jenish 1994).

UNDERSTANDING PROBLEMS IN EDUCATION

What can we conclude about the educational crisis in Canada? Any criticism of education must take into account that a century ago, many children did not receive even a primary school education. Instead, they worked in factories and on farms to help support their families. Whatever education they received came from the family or the religious institution. It is evident that Canada has come a long way since that time. From humble beginnings, education in Canada has grown into a massive industry with expenditures for elementary and secondary education of about $35 billion; for postsecondary education, approximately $16 billion; and for vocational education and training, almost $5 billion. The educational service industry employs a million people in Canada, and in 1996, education generated more than $40 billion of our GDP (Statistics Canada 1998a: 144–5).

At the same time, it is evident that problems exist. Public schools are supposed to provide all Canadian children with the academic and social foundations necessary to participate in society in a productive and meaningful way, but some students remain marginalized and do not enjoy the benefits as well as others. As conflict theorists note, the educational institution can perpetuate a downward cycle of failure, alienation, and hopelessness.

Although education requires adequate funding for teachers, school building, equipment, and educational materials, education alone cannot bear the burden of improving the lives of Canadians. Jobs must be provided for those who successfully complete their education. Students with little hope of school success will continue to experience low motivation as long as job prospects are bleak and earnings in available jobs are low. Ray and Mickelson (1993) explain:

> ...School reforms of any kind are unlikely to succeed if...students
> cannot anticipate opportunity structures that reward diligent efforts
> in school. Employers are not apt to find highly disciplined and moti-
> vated young employees for jobs that are unstable and low paying.
> (pp. 14–5)

Canada's "brain drain" demonstrates the lack of career opportunities that exist in our country. A Statistics Canada study that tracked 43 000 individuals who graduated from Canadian postsecondary institutions in 1995 reported that although relatively few (only 1.5 percent of the total graduating class) had moved to the United States after graduation, nearly half of those who did relocate ranked near the top of their graduating class in their field of study, and that those who left were more likely to have received scholarships or other academic awards than their counterparts. The group that left also included a disproportionate number of Ph.D. holders and master's graduates. Fifteen percent of those who moved had a master's degree and 8 percent had a doctorate. Among graduates who stayed in Canada, 7 percent had a master's degree and 1 percent had a doctorate. About one-third of those who immigrated to the United States were either nurses or doctors; the next largest occupation categories were engineers and computer specialists.

The research reported that the most common reason these individuals gave for leaving Canada was career opportunity. More than half of those who moved to the United States did so for career opportunity; few moved to take advantage of the lower taxes. Although approximately 18 percent of the graduates who had left in 1995 had returned to Canada by March 1999 (mostly to advance their careers or for personal reasons), the majority of those who remained in the United States indicated that they planned to remain there (Waldie 1999).

Finally, "if we are to improve the skills and attitudes of future generations of workers, we must also focus attention and resources on the quality of the lives children lead outside the school" (Murnane 1994: 290). We must provide support to families so that children grow up in healthy, safe, and nurturing environments. Children are the future of our nation and of the world. Whatever resources we provide to improve the lives and education of children are sure to be wise investments in our collective future.

CRITICAL THINKING

1. Clearly, micro-society schools have both advantages and disadvantages. After making a list of each, would you want your child to attend a micro-society school? Why or why not?

2. As discussed in Chapter 6, the proportion of elderly in Canada is increasing dramatically as we move into the twenty-first century. Since the elderly are unlikely to have children in public schools, how will the allocation of needed school funds be affected by this demographic trend?

3. One response to school violence is primarily defensive, that is, expelling students, installing metal detectors, and so on. Other than such defensive tactics, what violence prevention techniques could be instituted?

4. Students who drop out of school are often blamed for their lack of motivation. How may a teenager's dropping out of high school be explained as a failure of the educational system rather than as a "motivation" problem?

KEY TERMS

alternative schools
charter schools
culture wars
functional illiterates

grade inflation
home schooling
inclusive education
micro-society school

multicultural education
self-fulfilling prophecy
social promotion

Section 4

Problems of Modernization

Section 4 focuses on problems of modernization—the cultural and structural changes that occur as a consequence of society changing from traditional to modern. Both Durkheim and Marx were concerned with the impact of modernization. Each theorized that as societies moved from "mechanical" to "organic solidarity" (in Durkheimian terms) or from "production for use" to "production for exchange" (in Marxian terms), fundamental changes in social organization would lead to increased social problems. Although modernization has contributed to many of the social problems we have already discussed, it is more directly related to the four problems we examine in this section—technology, population, the environment, and global conflict.

One of the difficulties in understanding social problems involves sorting out the numerous social forces that contribute to social problems. Every social problem is related, in some way, to many other social problems. Nowhere is this more apparent than in these final three chapters. For example, even though scientific and technological advances are designed and implemented to enhance the quality and conditions of social life, they contribute to other social problems. Science and technology (Chapter 13) have extended life through various medical advances and have successfully lowered the infant mortality rate in many developing nations. However, these two "successes" (fewer babies dying and an increased life expectancy), when coupled with a relatively high fertility rate, lead to expanding populations. Many nations struggle to feed, clothe, house, or provide safe drinking water and medical care for their increased numbers. Further, in responding to problems created by overpopulation, science and technology have contributed to the growing environmental crisis. For example, many developing countries use hazardous pesticides to increase food production for their growing populations; overuse land, which leads to desertification; and, out of economic necessity, agree to deforestation by foreign investors.

Developed countries also contribute to the environmental crisis. Modernization itself, independent of population problems, exacerbates environmental concerns as the fragile ecosystem is overburdened with the by-products of affluent societies and scientific and technological triumphs: air pollution from the burning of fossil fuels, groundwater contamination from chemical runoff, nuclear waste disposal, and destruction of the ozone layer by chlorofluorocarbons. Thus, science and technology, and population and the environment (Chapter 14), are inextricably related.

While population patterns and the resultant increased scarcity of resources provide a motivation for global conflict (Chapter 15), science and technology provide more efficient means for worldwide destruction. Global conflict has devastating effects on the environment (e.g., nuclear winter) and has inspired much scientific and technological research and development such as laser-based and nuclear technologies. Thus, each of the chapter topics that follow is both an independent and a dependent variable in a complex web of cause and effect.

CHAPTER THIRTEEN

Science and Technology

Is It True?

1. Although the birth control pill has been commonly used in the West for the past three decades, it was not until 1999 that women in Japan won the right to use it.

2. Since 1998, the amount of time that the average Internet user spends online each week has risen from 4.4 hours to 7.6 hours.

3. More than 30 million people in 160 countries use the Internet.

4. The clock was invented by capitalistic industrialists as a means of controlling the time workers spent on the job.

5. In Canada, it is estimated that between $20 billion to $30 billion was spent on preparing for Y2K.

Answers: 1 = T, 2 = T, 3 = T, 4 = F, 5 = T

Virtual reality, cloning, and teleportation are no longer just the stuff of popular sci-fi shows such as *Star Trek*, *Millennium*, and *The X-Files*. Virtual reality is now used to train workers in occupations as diverse as medicine, engineering, and professional football.

The ability to genetically replicate embryos has sparked worldwide debate over the ethics of reproduction, and California Institute of Technology scientists have beamed a ray of light from one location to another (Fox 1998). Just as the telephone, the automobile, the television, and countless other technological innovations have forever altered social life, so will more recent technologies.

Science and technology go hand in hand. **Science** is the process of discovering, explaining, and predicting natural or social phenomena. A scientific approach to understanding AIDS, for example, might include investigating the molecular structure of the virus, the means by which it is transmitted, and public attitudes about AIDS. **Technology,** "the skills, tools and machines used by members of a society to convert material objects (e.g., natural resources) into products useful to themselves" (Richardson 1999: 2297), is intended to accomplish a specific task—in this example, the development of an AIDS vaccine.

Societies differ in their level of technological sophistication and development. In agricultural societies, which emphasize the production of raw materials, **mechanization**, or the use of tools to accomplish tasks previously done by hand, dominates. As societies move toward industrialization and become more concerned with the mass production of goods, automation prevails. **Automation** involves the use of self-operating machines, as in an automated factory where autonomous robots assemble automobiles. Finally, as a society moves toward postindustrialization, it emphasizes service and information professions (Bell 1973). At this stage, technology shifts toward **cybernation**, whereby machines control machines—making production decisions, programming robots, and monitoring assembly performance.

What are the effects of science and technology on humans and their social world? How do science and technology help to remedy social problems and how do they contribute to social problems? Is technology, as Postman (1992) suggests, both a friend and a foe to humankind? This chapter addresses each of these questions.

> Most of the consequences of technology that are causing concern at the present time—pollution of the environment, potential damage to the ecology of the planet, occupational and social dislocations, threats to the privacy and political significance of the individual, social and psychological malaise...are with us in large measure because it has not been anybody's explicit business to foresee and anticipate them.
>
> Emmanuel Mesthene,
> Former Director
> of the Harvard
> Program on
> Technology
> and Society

International Data

According to a Commerce Department report, it took 38 years for radio use to reach 50 million people; it took television only 13 years to reach the same number; the Internet reached 50 million people in four years.

SOURCE: Leslie 1998

THE GLOBAL CONTEXT: THE TECHNOLOGICAL REVOLUTION

Fifty years ago, travelling across Canada was an arduous task, a long-distance phone call was a memorable event, and mail carriers brought belated news of friends and relatives from far away. Today, travellers journey between continents in a matter of hours, and for many, e-mail, faxes, videoconferencing, and electronic fund transfers have replaced conventional means of communication.

The world is a much smaller place than it used to be, and it will become even smaller as the technological revolution continues. The Internet is projected to have a quarter of a billion users in more than 100 countries by the year 2000 (GIP 1998a). In the past two years, the amount of time the average

Internet user spends online each week has risen from 4.4 hours to 7.6 hours (Wright 2000). Although more than half of Internet users speak English, non-English speakers constitute the fastest growing language group on the Internet. Of the 67 million non–English-speaking Internet users, 20 percent speak Spanish, 20 percent German, 18 percent Japanese, 9 percent French, and 6 percent Chinese (Global Statistics 1998). The Global Internet Project, begun by software and computer industry executives, "believes that the Internet must be viewed as a global medium transcending geographical differences that is transforming not only how commerce is conducted, but education, health care, and society in general" (GIP 1998b).

The movement toward the globalization of technology is, of course, not limited to the use and expansion of the Internet. The world robot market continues to expand (IFR 1997); Latin America's computer industry is dominated by Texas-based manufacturer Compaq; 60 percent of Microsoft's Internet platform and support products are sold overseas (GIP 1998c); and "globe-trotting scientists" collect skin and blood samples from remote islanders for genetic research (Shand 1998).

To achieve such scientific and technological innovations, sometimes called research and development (R&D), countries need material and economic resources. Research entails the pursuit of knowledge; development refers to the production of needed materials, systems, processes, or devices directed toward the solution of a practical problem. In Canada, the amount spent on R&D as a percentage of the economy (Table 13.1) puts Canada at the bottom of the industrialized Group of Seven nations. With our government spending $2.9 billion on research and development, Canada lags behind Sweden, Finland, and Norway.

Despite the fact that R&D incentives are the most generous among the 29 nations of the OECD, Canada's R&D record is poor. Many Canadian businesses, and in particular small and midsize businesses, are comparatively slow to innovate. "Proportionately, in 1995, Canada had the lowest level of private sector spending on R&D among the Group of Seven industrialized countries. And Canada's high-tech industry is the smallest in the G-7 as a proportion of the overall manufacturing sector" (Janigan 1999).

Scientific discoveries and technological developments require the support of a country's citizens and political leaders. For example, although abortion has been technically possible for years, 24 percent of the world's population live in countries where abortion is either prohibited or permitted only when the life of the mother is in danger (United Nations Population Fund 1991). In like fashion, although the birth control pill has been available in most countries in

Table 13.1	Research and Development Spending as a Percentage of GDP	
Japan	2.98%
United States	2.55
Finland	2.37
Germany	2.3
United Kingdom	2.05
Canada	**1.65**
Italy	1.14

the West for more than three decades, it was only in the summer of 1999 that Japan's national pharmaceutical regulatory board recommended approval of the pill to the government's ministry of health. Critics of the birth control pill had long claimed that its use would damage the nation's morals and cause a variety of social ills, including environmental harm from the hormones of women who took it. Nevertheless, women's groups in Japan intensified their campaign for the pill's approval after the Japanese government gave their swift approval to Viagra, the male anti-impotence pill, in January of 1999 (*Maclean's* 1999b: 53). It is evident that the degree to which science and technology are considered good or bad, desirable or undesirable, is largely socially constructed.

Postmodernism and the Technological Fix

Many people believe that social problems can be resolved through a **technological fix** (Weinberg 1966) rather than through social engineering. For example, a social engineer might approach the problem of water shortages by persuading people to change their lifestyle: use less water, take shorter showers, and wear clothes more than once before washing. A technologist would avoid the challenge of changing people's habits and motivations and instead concentrate on the development of new technologies that would increase the water supply. Social problems may be tackled through both social engineering and technological fixes. In recent years, for example, social engineering efforts to reduce drunk driving have included imposing stiffer penalties for drunk driving and disseminating public service announcements such as "Friends Don't Let Friends Drive Drunk." An example of a technological fix for the same problem is the development of car air bags, which reduce injuries and deaths from car accidents.

Not everyone, however, agrees that science and technology are good for society. **Postmodernism**, an emerging worldview, holds that rational thinking and the scientific perspective have fallen short in providing the "truths" they were once presumed to hold. During the industrial era, science, rationality, and technological innovations were thought to pave the way to a better, safer, and more humane world. Today, postmodernists question the validity of the scientific enterprise, often pointing to the unforeseen and unwanted consequences of resulting technologies. Automobiles, for example, began to be mass-produced in the 1930s in response to consumer demands. However, the proliferation of automobiles also led to increased air pollution and the deterioration of cities as suburbs developed, and today, traffic fatalities are the number one cause of death from all accidents. Examine Table 13.2 and consider the positive and negative consequences of each of these modern-day technologies.

CONSIDERATION

Postman (1992) suggests that technology is both a friend and an enemy:

Technology…makes life easier, cleaner, and longer. Can anyone ask more of a friend?…It is the kind of friend that asks for trust and obedience, which most people are inclined to give because its gifts are truly bountiful. But of course, there is a dark side to this friend. Its gifts are not without a heavy cost.... The uncontrolled growth of technology destroys the vital sources of our humanity. It creates a culture without a moral foundation. It undermines certain mental processes and social relations that make human life worth living. Technology, in sum, is both friend and enemy. (p. xii)

SOCIOLOGICAL THEORIES OF SCIENCE AND TECHNOLOGY

International Data

Worldwide, the number of scientists and engineers per million population varies dramatically: 3548 in Japan, 2685 in the United States, 1632 in Europe, 209 in the Arab states, and 53 in Africa.

SOURCE: Kennedy 1998

Each of the three major sociological frameworks helps us to better understand the nature of science and technology in society.

Structural-Functionalist Perspective

Functionalists view science and technology as emerging in response to societal needs—that "[science] was born indicates that society needed it" (Durkheim [1925] 1973). As societies become more complex and heterogeneous, finding a common and agreed-on knowledge base becomes more difficult. Science fills the need for an assumed objective measure of "truth" and provides a basis for

Table 13.2	Home Electronics and Appliances Owned by Canadians, Selected Years, 1965–98				
	1965	**1975**	**1985**	**1996**	**1998**
Air conditioners	2.2	12.4	18.0	29.3	29.1*
Automobiles	75.0	78.9	77.3	73.9	79.0
Camcorders	n.a.	n.a.	n.a.	16.1	17.7
Cellular phones	n.a.	n.a.	n.a.	14.1	26.0
Clothes dryers	25.2	48.1	68.4	76.5	79.0
Compact disc players	n.a.	n.a.	n.a.	53.4	67.0
Computer modems	n.a.	n.a.	n.a.	15.5	32.0
Dishwashers	2.7	15.2	37.1	47.7	51.0
Electric stoves	69.0	85.1	92.3	93.7	93.5*
Electric washers	86.2	76.9	77.3	79.6	80.0*
Freezers	22.6	41.8	57.0	57.1	53.9*
Gas barbecues	n.a.	n.a.	19.9	57.1	59.0
Home computers	n.a.	n.a.	n.a.	31.6	45.0
Microwave ovens	n.a.	0.8	23.0	85.2	89.0
Radios	96.1	98.3	98.7	98.6	98.7*
Refrigerators	95.8	99.3	99.2	99.6	99.8*
Smoke detectors	n.a.	n.a.	n.a.	95.7	98.6*
Telephones	89.4	96.4	98.2	98.7	98.6*
Television, cable	n.a.	40.4	62.5	74.0	73.0
Television	92.6	96.8	98.3	99.1	99.0
Television, colour	n.a.	53.4	91.4	98.5	99.0
Videocassette recorders	n.a.	n.a.	23.5	83.5	88.0

*1997 figure.

SOURCE: based on *Canadian Global Almanac* 2000; Statistics Canada 1999

making intelligent and rational decisions. In this regard, science and the resulting technologies are functional for society.

If society changes too rapidly because of science and technology, however, problems may emerge. When the material part of culture (i.e., its physical elements) changes at a faster rate than the nonmaterial (i.e., its beliefs and values), a **cultural lag** may develop (Ogburn 1957). For example, the typewriter, the conveyor belt, and the computer expanded opportunities for women to work outside the home. With the potential for economic independence, women were able to remain single or to leave unsatisfactory relationships or establish careers. But although new technologies have created new opportunities for women, beliefs about women's roles, expectations of female behaviour, and values concerning equality, marriage, and divorce have "lagged" behind.

Robert Merton (1973), a functionalist and founder of the subdiscipline sociology of science, also argued that scientific discoveries or technological innovations may be dysfunctional for society and create instability in the social system. For example, the development of timesaving machines increases production, but also displaces workers and contributes to higher rates of employee alienation. Defective technology can have disastrous effects on society. In 1994, a defective Pentium chip was discovered to exist in more than two million computers in aerospace, medical, scientific, and financial institutions, as well as schools and government agencies. Replacing the defective chip was a massive undertaking, but was necessary to avoid thousands of inaccurate computations and organizational catastrophes.

Conflict Perspective

Conflict theorists, in general, emphasize that science and technology benefit a select few. For some conflict theorists, technological advances occur primarily as a response to capitalist needs for increased efficiency and productivity and thus are motivated by profit. As McDermott (1993) notes, most decisions to increase technology are made by "the immediate practitioners of technology, their managerial cronies, and for the profits accruing to their corporations" (p. 93). The Dalkon Shield and silicone breast implants are examples of technological advances that promised millions of dollars in profits for their developers. However, the rush to market took precedence over thorough testing of the products' safety. Subsequent lawsuits filed by consumers who argued that both products had compromised the physical well-being of women resulted in large damage awards for the plaintiffs.

Science and technology also further the interests of dominant groups to the detriment of others. The need for scientific research on AIDS was evident in the early 1980s, but the required large-scale funding was not made available as long as the virus was thought to be specific to homosexuals and intravenous drug users. Only when the virus became a threat to all North Americans were millions of dollars made available for AIDS research. Hence, conflict theorists argue that granting agencies act as gatekeepers to scientific discoveries and technological innovations. These agencies are influenced by powerful interest groups and the marketability of the product rather than by the needs of society.

CONSIDERATION

Some feminists argue that technology is an extension of the patriarchal nature of society that promotes the interest of men and ignores the needs and interests of women. For example, washing machines, although time-saving devices, disrupted the communal telling of stories and the resulting friendships among women who gathered together to do their chores. Bush (1993) observes:

> Technology always enters into the present culture,
> accepting and exacerbating the existing norms and values.
> In a society characterized by a sex-role division of labour,
> any tool or technique…will have dramatically different
> effects on men than on women. (p. 204)

Other feminists acknowledge that technological innovations have improved the lives of women by balancing employment opportunities, especially in new, skilled, blue-collar and technical jobs such as computer repair specialist and telecommunications operator. Walshok (1993) studied women in these occupations and found that they reported high levels of job satisfaction and a strong sense of job security.

Symbolic Interactionist Perspective

Knowledge is relative. It changes over time, over circumstances, and between societies. We no longer believe that the world is flat or that the earth is the centre of the universe, but such beliefs once determined behaviour as individuals responded to what they thought to be true. The scientific process is a social process in that "truths"—socially constructed "truths"—result from the interactions between scientists, researchers, and the lay public.

Kuhn (1973) argues that the process of scientific discovery begins with assumptions about a particular phenomenon (e.g., the world is flat). Since unanswered questions about a topic always exist (e.g., why don't the oceans drain?), science works to fill these gaps. When new information suggests that the initial assumptions were incorrect (e.g., the world is not flat), a new set of assumptions or a framework emerges to replace the old one (e.g., the world is round). It then becomes the dominant belief or paradigm.

Symbolic interactionists emphasize the importance of this process and the impact social forces have on it. Conrad (1997), for example, describes the media's contribution to framing societal beliefs that alcoholism, homosexuality, and racial inequality are genetically determined. Technological innovations are also affected by social forces, and their success is, in part, dependent on the social meaning assigned to any particular product. If a product is defined as impractical, cumbersome, inefficient, or immoral, it is unlikely to gain public acceptance. Consider, for example, that when Segolene Royal, the French deputy education minister, announced that, beginning in 2000, schoolgirls in France would be provided with the morning-after contraceptive pill in "cases of distress and extreme urgency," he also noted that this decision was likely to "cause uproar among conservative church groups." However, he emphasized that teen pregnancies caused a "huge problem of distress amid adolescents in France," with 6700 of 10 000 pregnancies ending in abortion, and he justified this move as an "emergency" measure (*National Post* 1999: A11).

Not only are technological innovations subject to social meaning, but who becomes involved in what aspects of science and technology is also socially defined. As we note in Chapter 7, men outnumber women in earning computer

The Social Construction of the Hacking Community

Sample and Methods

Jordan and Taylor (1998) researched computer hackers and the hacking community through 80 semistructured interviews, 200 questionnaires, and an examination of existing data on the topic. As is often the case in crime, illicit drug use, and other similarly difficult research areas, a random sample of hackers was not possible. Nonetheless, the authors lend insight into this increasingly costly social problem and the symbolic interactionist notion of "social construction"—in this case, of an online community.

Findings

Computer hacking, or "unauthorized computer intrusion," is an increasingly serious problem, particularly in a society dominated by information technologies. Unlawful entry into computer networks or databases can be achieved by several means including (1) guessing someone's password, (2) tricking a computer about the identity of another computer (called "IP spoofing"), or (3) "social engineering," a slang term referring to getting important access information by stealing documents, looking over someone's shoulder, going through their garbage, and so on.

Hacking carries with it certain norms and values because, according to Jordan and Taylor, the hacking community can be thought of as a culture within a culture. The two researchers identify six elements of this socially constructed community:

- *Technology*. The core of the hacking community is the technology that allows it to occur. As one professor interviewed stated, the young today have "…lived with computers virtually from the cradle, and therefore have no trace of fear, not even a trace of reverence."

- *Secrecy*. The hacking community must, on the one hand, commit secret acts since their "hacks" are illegal. On the other hand, much of the motivation for hacking requires publicity to achieve the notoriety often sought. Further, hacking is often a group activity that bonds members together. As one hacker stated, hacking "can give you a real kick some time. But it can give you a lot more satisfaction and recognition if you share your experiences with others.…"

- *Anonymity*. While secrecy refers to the hacking act, anonymity refers to the importance of the hacker's identity remaining anonymous. Thus, for example, hackers and hacking groups take on names such as Legion of Doom, the Inner Circle I, Mercury, and Kaos, Inc.

- *Membership Fluidity*. Membership is fluid rather than static, often characterized by high turnover rates, in part, as a response to law enforcement pressures. Unlike more structured organizations, there are no formal rules or regulations.

- *Male Dominance*. Hacking is defined as a male activity and, consequently, there are few female hackers. Jordan and Taylor also note, after recounting an incidence of sexual harassment, that "…the collective identity hackers share and construct…is in part misogynist" (p. 768).

- *Motivation*. Contributing to the articulation of the hacking communities' boundaries are the agreed on definitions of acceptable hacking motivations, including: (1) addiction to computers, (2) curiosity, (3) excitement, (4) power, (5) acceptance and recognition, and (6) community service through the identification of security risks.

Finally, Jordan and Taylor note that hackers also maintain group boundaries by distinguishing between their community and other social groups, including "an antagonistic bond to the computer security industry (CSI)" (p. 770). Ironically, hackers admit a desire to be hired by the CSI, which would not only legitimize their activities but give them a steady income as well.

The authors conclude that the general fear of computers and of those who understand them underlies the common although inaccurate portrayal of hackers as pathological, obsessed computer "geeks." When journalist Jon Littman asked hacker Kevin Mitnick if he was being demonized because of increased dependence on and fear of information technologies, Mitnick replied, "Yeah.…That's why they're instilling fear of the unknown. That's why they're scared of me. Not because of what I've done, but because I have the capability to wreak havoc" (Jordan and Taylor 1998: 776).

SOURCE: Jordan, Tim, and Paul Taylor. 1998. "A Sociology of Hackers." *Sociological Review* (November): 757–78.

science degrees. Men also score higher on measures of computer aptitude and report higher computer use than do women (Lewin 1998). Societal definitions of men as being rational, mathematical, scientifically minded, and having greater mechanical aptitude than women are, in part, responsible for these differences. This chapter's Focus on Social Problems Research highlights one of the consequences of the masculinization of technology, as well as the ways in which computer hacker identities and communities are socially constructed.

TECHNOLOGY AND THE TRANSFORMATION OF SOCIETY

A number of modern technologies are considerably more sophisticated than technological innovations of the past. Nevertheless, older technologies have influenced the social world as profoundly as the most astonishing modern inventions. Indeed, without older technological innovations, such as the clock and printing press, most modern technology would not have been possible.

Technology has far-reaching effects on every aspect of social life. As noted earlier, technology has altered the very concept of society. New transportation and communication systems have created interconnections between previously separated societies and thus led to the development of a global society. The following sections discuss other societal transformations resulting from various modern technologies, including workplace technology, computers, the information highway, and science and biotechnology.

Technology in the Workplace

All workplaces, from doctors' offices to factories and from supermarkets to real estate corporations, have felt the impact of technology. Technology can make workers more accountable by gathering information about their performance. Through such timesaving devices as personal digital assistants and battery-powered store shelf labels, technology can enhance workers' efficiency. Technology is also changing the location of work and allowing some employees to work from home (Carey 1998).

Information technologies are also changing the nature of work. Lilly Pharmaceutical employees communicate via their own intranet on which all work-related notices are posted. Federal Express not only created a FedEx network for their 30 000 employees, but allowed customers to enter their package-tracking database, saving that company $2 million a year. It is estimated that one-fifth of all corporations are now using such telecommunication devices, offering the potential of a paperless workplace (GIP 1998c).

Robotic technology, sometimes called computer-aided manufacturing (CAM), has also revolutionized work, particularly in heavy industry such as automobile manufacturing. An employer's decision to use robotics depends on direct (e.g., initial investment) and indirect (e.g., unemployment compensation) costs, the feasibility and availability of robots performing the desired tasks, and the increased rate of productivity. Use of robotics may also depend on whether there is union resistance to the replacement of workers by machines.

CONSIDERATION

Postman (1992) describes how the clock—a relatively simple innovation that is taken for granted in today's world—profoundly influenced not only the workplace but the larger economic institution:

The clock had its origin in the Benedictine monasteries of the twelfth and thirteenth centuries. The impetus behind the invention was to provide a more or less precise regularity to the routines of the monasteries, which required, among other things, seven periods of devotion during the course of the day. The bells of the monastery were to be rung to signal the canonical hours; the mechanical clock was the technology that could provide precision to these rituals of devotion....What the monks did not foresee was that the clock is a means not merely of keeping track of the hours but also of synchronizing and controlling the actions of men. And thus, by the middle of the fourteenth century, the clock had moved outside the walls of the monastery, and brought a new and precise regularity to the life of the workman and the merchant....In short, without the clock, capitalism would have been quite impossible. The paradox...[is] that the clock was invented by men who wanted to devote themselves more rigorously to God; it ended as the technology of greatest use to men who wished to devote themselves to the accumulation of money. (pp. 14–5)

The Computer Revolution

Early computers were much larger than the small machines we have today, and they were thought to have only esoteric uses among members of the scientific and military communities. In 1951, only about half a dozen computers existed (Ceruzzi 1993). The development of the silicon chip and sophisticated microelectronic technology allowed tens of thousands of components to be imprinted on a single chip that was smaller than a dime. The silicon chip led to the development of laptop computers, mini-television sets, cellular phones, electronic keyboards, and singing birthday cards. The silicon chip also made computers affordable. Although the first personal computer (PC) was developed only 20 years ago, by 1998, almost half (45 percent) of Canadian households had a computer (Statistics Canada 1999).

Today, computers form the backbone of universities, government agencies, corporations, and businesses. Statistics Canada (1998) notes that the federal, provincial, and municipal governments in Canada are the "prime customers for services" and account for 17 percent of computer and computer-related services (closely followed by the finance and insurance sector). In addition, employment in computer and computer-related services has climbed in Canada. Between 1986 and 1996, employment in these areas more than doubled from 40 000 to 83 700 positions. Compared to others providing business services, those employed in computer and computer-related services tend to earn higher-than-average salaries. For example, in 1996, those employed in computer and computer-related services earned average weekly salaries of $830 (versus an average of $652 for others employed in all business services). While in the 1970s, there were only 50 000 computers worldwide, "[t]oday, that many are being installed every day" (Statistics Canada 1998). In 1994, approximately

International Data

The successful implementation of the SchoolNet program has made Canada the first nation in the world to connect its schools and libraries to the information superhighway.

SOURCE: Fenna 1999

International Data

A survey of 6000 companies in 47 countries reported that half would not have critical computer systems fixed in time for the year 2000.

SOURCE: Bajak 1998

International Data

According to Statistics Canada, 99.5 percent of Canadian organizations with more than 250 employees reported making fixes to their systems in anticipation of the Y2K problem.

SOURCE: Oh 1999

6.2 million Canadians, the majority of them professionals, managers, and clerical workers, used computers on the job.

Computers are also big business. The United States is one of the most successful producers of computer technology, boasting the three top-selling desktops in the world—Packard Bell, Compaq, and Gateway. Ranked by revenues, IBM Canada Ltd. is the fourth largest foreign-owned company in Canada, with revenues of $8 700 000; it is also the 16th largest corporation in Canada with 17.2 employees (*Canadian Global Almanac* 2000). Retail sales of computers exceeded $18 billion in 1997, with an average home computer cost of $1745 (Scout Report 1998). By the year 2006, spending on home computers is predicted to grow tenfold as consumers increasingly define PCs as a necessity rather than a luxury (Klein 1998).

On the eve of the twenty-first century, concern raged that computers programmed with double-digit years (i.e., 97, 98, 99) would interpret 00 as 1900, 01 as 1901, and so forth, rather than the years 2000, 2001, and so on. Known as the **year 2000 (Y2K)** problem, countries varied dramatically in their preparation for this event. While some countries (e.g., the United States, Canada) invested billions of dollars preparing for the glitch, many other nations virtually ignored the problem. For example, according to a U.S. State Department survey of 113 countries, telecommunication companies in 33 countries were working on the problem but with little success, and 29 countries were unaware of the problem or had not begun to address it (Bajak 1998). It is estimated that Canada spent an estimated $20 to $30 billion in its efforts to combat the "millennium computer bug." However, given the global economy, it was feared that some Y2K effects would be felt regardless of the efforts of individual countries. Some social commentators predicted that telecommunications would be disrupted, affecting global fund transfers; that international airlines would be grounded as a result of computer-guided air traffic jams; that payrolls around the world would not be met; and that the provision of many taken-for-granted goods (e.g., electricity) and services (e.g., medical care) to millions of people would be disrupted. Computer experts were themselves divided about the impact of the Y2K problem, with some predicting doom and gloom and others suggesting that, at most, the problems posed would result in relatively mild inconveniences. The predictions of the latter seem to have been correct.

The Information Highway

Information technology, or **IT** for short, refers to any technology that carries information. Most information technologies were developed within a hundred-year span: photography and telegraphy (1830s), rotary power printing (1840s), typewriter (1860s), transatlantic cable (1866), telephone (1876), motion pictures (1894), wireless telegraphy (1895), magnetic tape recording (1899), radio (1906), and television (1923) (Beniger 1993). The concept of an "information society" dates back to the 1950s when an economist identified a work sector he called "the production and distribution of knowledge." Today, demand far exceeds supply in this particular work sector. Consider, for example, that "the number of information technology jobs vacant in Canada tops 16 000 and in the United States, it is more in the neighbourhood of 190 000" (Statistics Canada 1998).

The **Internet** is an international information infrastructure—a network of networks—available through universities, research institutes, government agencies, and businesses. Between 1996 and 1997 alone, Internet access in Canadian workplaces more than doubled; one in four Canadian workers now uses a wide variety of cyberspace tools (Statistics Canada 1998).

With a personal computer, a modem, and a telephone line, users log onto locations around the world to access information, transfer files, and send and receive e-mail. The Internet also provides access to thousands of discussion groups, databases, bulletin boards, videos, and reservation systems from around the globe. Commercial access to the Internet is available through such services as Rogers, Prodigy, America Online, and CompuServe.

As Internet use has expanded, so has **e-commerce**, or the buying and selling of goods and services over the Internet. For example, France expects 10 percent of all retail revenues to be "Internet generated" by the year 2001; Great Britain expects 12 percent, and the Scandinavian countries 15 percent. Not surprisingly, advertising on the Internet has increased dramatically over the past several years, as has "spam," the slang term for Internet junk mail.

Science and Biotechnology

While recent computer innovations and the establishment of an information highway have led to significant cultural and structural changes, science and its resulting biotechnologies have led to not only dramatic changes, but also hotly contested issues. Here we will look at some of the issues raised by developments in genetics and reproductive technology.

Genetics Molecular biology has led to a greater understanding of the genetic material found in all cells—DNA (deoxyribonucleic acid)—and with it the ability for **genetic screening**. Currently, researchers are trying to complete genetic maps that will link DNA to particular traits (Lemonick 1999). Already, specific strands of DNA have been identified as carrying such physical traits as eye colour and height, as well as such diseases as breast cancer, cystic fibrosis, prostate cancer, and Alzheimer's. In the year 2000, "routine tests will detect predispositions to dozens of diseases as well as indicate a wide range of normal human traits" (Weinberg 1993: 319).

The Human Genome Project, a 15-year effort to map human DNA, "will have decoded all 3 billion chemical letters that spell out our 70 000 or so genes" by the year 2003 (Begley 1998: 62). In a 1999 move that gave Canada a key role in the global effort to decode and understand the function of genes, Toronto's Hospital for Sick Children took over the management of a database that is the world's main repository of gene-mapping information. Funding from an anonymous donor and a $2.7 million grant from IBM enabled the hospital to take on the Genome Database from Baltimore's Johns Hopkins University after the U.S. government withdrew support. While the international Human Genome Project unravels the genetic code, the database is the major resource in determining the location of genes and other information that is of crucial importance to medical research. The hope is that if a defective or missing gene can be identified, it may be possible to get a healthy duplicate and transplant it to the affected cell. This is known as **gene therapy.** Alternatively, viruses have their own genes that can be targeted for removal. Experiments are now under way to accomplish these biotechnological feats.

Genetic engineering is the ability to manipulate the genes of an organism in such a way that the natural outcome is altered. Genetic engineering is accomplished by splicing the DNA from one organism into the genes of another. Often, however, there are unwanted consequences. For example, through genetic engineering some plants are now self-insecticiding, that is, the plant itself produces an insect-repelling substance. Ironically, the continual plant production of the insecticide, in contrast to only sporadic application by farmers, is leading to insecticide-resistant pests (Ehrenfeld 1998).

CONSIDERATION

Gregory Carey, a geneticist, poses an interesting question. Suppose scientists discovered a genetic marker that would permit accurate prediction of violent behaviour before a child's birth. If we knew that this child was, say, nine times more likely to be arrested and convicted of a violent act, should that child be aborted? What if the child had Down's syndrome or a physical disability, was an alcoholic, or was gay? What if the child had a known life expectancy of 35? Which, if any, of these fetuses should be aborted? Carey reminds us that we have already identified the gene that predicts violent behaviour—males are nine times more likely to be arrested and convicted of a violent crime than females (Elmer-Dewitt 1994).

Reproductive Technologies The evolution of "reproductive science" has been furthered by scientific developments in biology, medicine, and agriculture. At the same time, however, its development has been hindered by the stigma associated with sexuality and reproduction, its link with unpopular social movements (e.g., contraception), and the feeling that such innovations challenge the natural order (Clarke 1990). Nevertheless, new reproductive technologies have been and continue to be developed.

In **in-vitro fertilization (IVF),** an egg and a sperm are united in an artificial setting such as a laboratory dish or test tube. Although the first successful attempt at IVF occurred in 1944, it was not until 1978 that the first test-tube baby, Louise Brown, was born. In Canada, 23 clinics from Halifax to Vancouver offer IVF, which, reportedly, is responsible for thousands of pregnancies a year (Geddes 1999). In the United States, more than 300 fertility clinics provide this procedure, resulting in about 10 000 live births a year.

Criticisms of IVF are often based on traditional definitions of the family and the legal complications created when a child can have as many as five potential parental ties—egg donor, sperm donor, surrogate mother, and the one or two people who raise the child (depending on the situation, IVF may not involve donors or a surrogate). Litigation over who are the "real" parents has already occurred. As well, while IVF fees are in the $25 000 range in Canada (only Ontario's health insurance plan covers IVF, and only then in limited circumstances), such procedures are not very effective. According to Professor Patricia Baird, who chaired the 1989–93 Royal Commission on New Reproductive Technologies, only about 14 percent of couples succeed in having a child over a single cycle (compared with approximately 20 percent for fertile couples having sex without birth control) (Chisholm 1999). Consider as well that in 1999, Health Canada ordered approximately 35 of Canada's 49 sperm banks to quarantine some or all of their sperm stocks after federal officials discovered that some clinics were not meeting federal testing rules. Health Canada's investigation revealed deficiencies in some clinics' testing for chlamydia and gonorrhea pathogens and that one clinic had failed to test sperm donors for HIV-II, a form of the AIDS virus that is rare in North America. As a result, clinics were advised to notify women who had been artificially inseminated with donated sperm so that they could be tested for a number of disease-causing bacteria and viruses, including those causing AIDS and hepatitis B and C (*Maclean's* 1999c: 51).

Perhaps more than any other biotechnology, **abortion** epitomizes the potentially explosive consequences of new technologies. Abortion is the removal of an embryo or fetus from a woman's uterus before it can survive on its own. After amendments to Canada's abortion laws were made in 1969, which allowed for "therapeutic abortions" in hospitals, both the numbers and rates of therapeutic abortions rose significantly, then began to drop and stabilize beginning in 1983 and continuing for some years (Figure 13.1). The number and rate of abortions began to rise substantially again after 1989, when the Supreme Court struck down the 1969 abortion law. Before 1989, abortion clinics operated only in Quebec; by 1995, abortion clinics outside hospitals operated in all Canadian provinces except Prince Edward Island and

International Data

Globally, Canadian abortion rates are low at 10.3 per 1000 women aged 15 to 44. Countries with higher rates include the United States (21 per 1000 women), Cuba (57), Bulgaria (77), Vietnam (84), Russian Federation (119), and Romania (172).

SOURCE: Health Canada 1999; "World Abortion Policies 1994" 1997

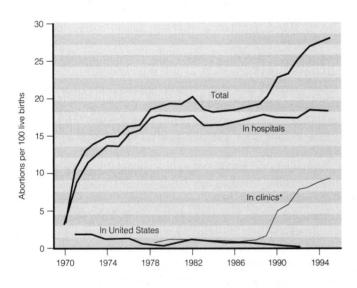

Figure 13.1

Therapeutic Abortions, Canadian Residents, 1970–95

* For 1978–89, information pertains to Quebec only. For 1990, clinics in Newfoundland, Nova Scotia, Quebec, Ontario, Manitoba, and British Columbia are included. Alberta clinics are added in 1991–95 data, and New Brunswick clinics are included in 1994 and 1995.

SOURCE: Statistics Canada 1995. *Therapeutic Abortions*, 1995 (Statistics Canada Cat. No. 82-219-XPB), Table 11.

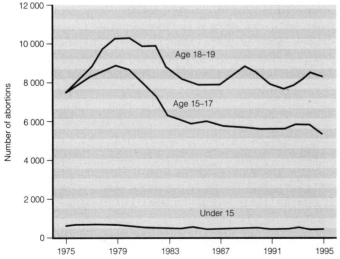

Figure 13.2

Therapeutic Teenage Abortions in Hospitals, by Age,* Canada, 1975–95

* Includes redistribution where the age of women was unknown.

SOURCE: Statistics Canada 1995. *Therapeutic Abortions*, 1995 (Statistics Canada Cat No. 82-219-XPB), Table 5.

Saskatchewan. In 1995, abortions performed in clinics in the eight Canadian provinces housing them accounted for almost one-third of all Canadian abortions. In Canada, both the total number of abortions and the abortion rate reached all-time highs in 1995 and have since declined. As a proportion of all abortions in Canada, the number of teenage abortions decreased significantly from 1975 to 1995 (Figure 13.2) (Health Canada 1999).

Most recent debates concern intact dilation and extraction (D&X) abortions. Opponents refer to such abortions as partial birth abortions because the limbs and the torso are typically delivered before the fetus has expired. D&X abortions are performed because the fetus has a serious defect, the woman's health is jeopardized by the pregnancy, or both.

Abortion is a complex issue for everyone, but especially for women, whose lives are most affected by pregnancy and childbearing. On a global level, women who have abortions are disproportionately poor, unmarried minority members who say they intend to have children in the future. Abortion is also a complex issue for societies, which must respond to the pressures of conflicting attitudes toward abortion and the reality of high rates of unintended and unwanted pregnancy. Figure 13.3 portrays the percentage of countries allowing abortions on various grounds.

Attitudes toward abortion tend to be polarized between two opposing groups of abortion activists—prochoice and prolife. Advocates of the prochoice movement hold that freedom of choice is a central human value, that procreation choices must be free of government interference, and that since the woman must bear the burden of moral choices, she should have the right to make such decisions. Alternatively, prolifers hold that the unborn fetus has a right to live and be protected, that abortion is immoral, and that alternative means of resolving an unwanted pregnancy should be found.

In July 1996, Scottish scientist Ian Wilmut successfully cloned an adult sheep named Dolly. He did so by placing an udder cell from a six-year-old sheep with an immature egg cell from another sheep and implanting the resulting embryo in a third sheep. This technological breakthrough has caused worldwide concern about the possibility of human cloning, which prompted quick European action banning human cloning. In England, the Human Fertilisation and Embryology Authority (HFEA), one of the few national statutory bodies of its kind in the world, has ruled that while cloning a sheep is acceptable research, human cloning is not. At the time this book went to press, Health Minister Allan Rock's law on reproductive technology was still in the process of being drafted. However, it was expected that the law would establish a new agency, modelled after the HFEA, that would regulate what types of embryo research would be permitted in Canada (Geddes 1999).

Figure 13.3
Percentages of Countries Permitting Abortions on Specified Grounds

SOURCE: "World Abortion Policies 1994" 1997

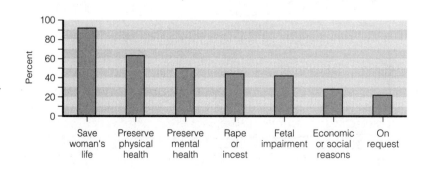

One argument in favour of developing human cloning technology is its medical value: it may potentially allow everyone to have "their own reserve of therapeutic cells that would increase their chance of being cured of various diseases, such as cancer, degenerative disorders and viral or inflammatory diseases" (Kahn 1997: 54). Human cloning could also provide an alternative reproductive route for couples who are infertile and for those in which one partner is at risk for transmitting a genetic disease.

Arguments against cloning are largely based on moral and ethical considerations. Critics of human cloning suggest that, whether used for medical therapeutic purposes or as a means of reproduction, human cloning is a threat to human dignity. For example, cloned humans would be deprived of their individuality and, as Kahn (1997: 119) points out, "creating human life for the sole purpose of preparing therapeutic material would clearly not be for the dignity of the life created." Despite the current moratorium on human cloning, according to Arthur Caplan, director of the Center on Bioethics at the University of Pennsylvania, the first infant clone could be created within the next seven years (Kluger 1997).

Despite what appears to be a universal race to the future and the indisputable benefits of such scientific discoveries as the workings of DNA and the technology of IVF, some people are concerned about the duality of science and technology. Science and the resulting technological innovations are often life assisting and life giving; they are also potentially destructive and life threatening. The same scientific knowledge that led to the discovery of nuclear fission, for example, led to the development of both nuclear power plants and the potential for nuclear destruction. Thus, we now turn our attention to the problems associated with science and technology.

SOCIETAL CONSEQUENCES OF SCIENCE AND TECHNOLOGY

Scientific discoveries and technological innovations have implications for all social actors and social groups. As such, they also have consequences for society as a whole.

Alienation, Deskilling, and Upskilling

As technology continues to play an important role in the workplace, workers may feel there is no creativity in what they do—they feel alienated (see Chapter 11). The movement from mechanization to automation to cybernation increasingly removes individuals from the production process, often relegating them to flipping a switch, staring at a computer monitor, or entering data at a keyboard. For example, many low-paid employees, often women, sit at computer terminals for hours entering data and keeping records for thousands of businesses, corporations, and agencies. The work is monotonous and solitary and provides little autonomy.

Not only are these activities routine and boring, they promote **deskilling**, that is, "labour requires less thought than before and gives them [workers] fewer decisions to make" (Perrolle 1990: 338). Deskilling stifles development of alternative skills and limits opportunities for advancement and creativity as old skill sets become obsolete. To conflict theorists, deskilling also provides the

International Data

It is estimated that 2.5 billion people know of Dolly because of the "Dollymania" that ensued.

SOURCE: "Dollymania" 1999

International Data

Although investment in biotechnological research has been strong in Canada—$985 million in 1997—the United States invested $48 billion in this field in the same year with $12 billion invested in American labs for research and development.

SOURCE: McClelland 1999

Abortion Attitude Scale

This is not a test. There are no wrong or right answers to any of the statements, so just answer as honestly as you can. The statements ask you to tell how you feel about abortion (the voluntary removal of a human fetus from the mother) during the first three months of pregnancy by a qualified medical person. Indicate how you feel about each statement by circling one of the choices beside each sentence. Respond to each statement and circle only one response.

Strongly agree = 5; Agree = 4; Slightly agree = 3; Slightly disagree = 2; Disagree = 1; Strongly disagree = 0

	5	4	3	2	1	0
1. Abortion is a good way of solving an unwanted pregnancy.	5	4	3	2	1	0
2. A mother should feel obligated to bear a child she has conceived.	5	4	3	2	1	0
3. Abortion is wrong no matter what the circumstances are.	5	4	3	2	1	0
4. A fetus is not a person until it can live outside its mother's body.	5	4	3	2	1	0
5. The decision to have an abortion should be the pregnant mother's.	5	4	3	2	1	0
6. Every conceived child has the right to be born.	5	4	3	2	1	0
7. A pregnant female not wanting to have a child should be encouraged to have an abortion.	5	4	3	2	1	0
8. Abortion should be considered killing a person.	5	4	3	2	1	0
9. People should not look down on those who choose to have an abortion.	5	4	3	2	1	0
10. Abortion should be an available alternative for unmarried, pregnant teenagers.	5	4	3	2	1	0
11. Persons should not have the power over the life or death of a fetus.	5	4	3	2	1	0
12. Unwanted children should not be brought into the world.	5	4	3	2	1	0
13. A fetus should be considered a person at the moment of conception.	5	4	3	2	1	0

SCORING AND INTERPRETATION

As its name indicates, this scale was developed to measure attitudes toward abortion. It was developed by Sloan (1983) for use with high-school and college students. To compute your score, first reverse the point scale for items 2, 5, 8, 10, and 13. Total the point responses for all items. Sloan provided the following categories for interpreting the results:

65–51 Strong proabortion
50–39 Moderate proabortion
38–22 Unsure
21–11 Moderate prolife
10–0 Strong prolife

Abortion Attitude Scale (*continued*)

RELIABILITY AND VALIDITY

An unmodified Abortion Attitude Scale was administered to high-school and college students, Right to Life group members, and abortion service personnel. Sloan reported a high total test estimate of reliability (0.92). Construct validity was supported in that Right to Life members' mean scores were 16.2; abortion service personnel mean scores were 55.6, and other groups' scores fell between these values.

SOURCE: Adapted from "Abortion Attitude Scale" by L.A. Sloan. Reprinted with permission from the *Journal of Health Education* Vol. 14, No. 3, May/June 1983. The *Journal of Health Education* is a publication of the American Allegiance for Health, Physical Education, Recreation and Dance. 1900 Association Drive, Reston, Virginia 20191.

basis for increased inequality because "throughout the world, those who control the means of producing information products are also able to determine the social organization of the 'mental labour' which produces them" (Perrolle 1990: 337).

Technology in some work environments, however, may lead to **upskilling**. Unlike deskilling, upskilling reduces alienation as employees find their work more rather than less meaningful, and have greater decision-making powers as information becomes decentralized. Futurists argue that upskilling in the workplace could lead to a "horizontal" work environment where "employees do not so much what they are told to do, but what their expansive knowledge of the entire enterprise suggests to them needs doing" (GIP 1998c).

Social Relationships and Social Interaction

Technology affects social relationships and the nature of social interaction. The development of telephones has led to fewer visits with friends and relatives; with the coming of VCRs and cable television, the number of places where social life occurs (e.g., movie theatres) has declined. Even the nature of dating has changed as computer networks facilitate cyberdates and private chat rooms. As technology increases, social relationships and human interaction are transformed.

Technology also makes it easier for individuals to live in a cocoon—to be self-sufficient in terms of finances (e.g., Quicken), entertainment (e.g., pay-per-view movies), work (e.g., telecommuting), recreation (e.g., virtual reality), shopping (e.g., amazon.com), communication (e.g., Internet), and many other aspects of social life. Ironically, although technology can bring people together, it can also isolate them from each other, leading the Amish to ban any technology that "is seen as a threat to the cohesion of the community or might contaminate the culture's values" (Hafner 1999: 1). For example, some technological innovations replace social roles—an answering machine may replace a secretary, a computer-operated vending machine may replace a waitperson, an automatic teller machine may replace a banker, and closed circuit television, a teacher (Johnson 1988; Winner 1993). These technologies may improve efficiency, but they also reduce human contact.

Loss of Privacy and Security

When Massachusetts Institute of Technology (MIT) professor of media technology Nicholas Negroponte was asked "what do you fear most in thinking about the digital future?" his response was "privacy and security."

> When I send you a message in the future, I want you to be sure it is from me; that when that message goes from me to you, nobody is listening in; and when it lives on your desk, nobody is snooping later. (Negroponte 1995: 88)

Schools, employers, and the government are increasingly using technology to monitor individuals' performance and behaviour. Today, through cybernation, machines monitor behaviour by counting a telephone operator's minutes on-line, videotaping a citizen walking down a city street, or tracking the whereabouts of a needed employee (Quick 1998).

Through computers, individuals can obtain access to phone bills, tax returns, medical reports, credit histories, bank account balances, and driving records. Some companies sell such personal information. Unauthorized disclosure is potentially devastating. In response to the possibility of such consequences Brin (1998), author of *The Transparent Society*, argues that since it is impossible to prevent such intrusions, "reciprocal transparency," or complete openness, should prevail. If organizations can collect the information, then citizens should have access to it and to its uses.

Technology has created threats not only to the privacy of individuals, but also to the security of entire nations. Computers and modems can be used (or misused) in terrorism and warfare to cripple the infrastructure of a society and tamper with military information and communication operations.

To protect unauthorized access to information stored in or transmitted through computers and communication technologies, groups, organizations, and corporations may code information using a technique called encryption. Information that is encrypted is unintelligible without the code or "keys" to unscramble it.

In August of 1999, a Montreal-based company, Zero-Knowledge Systems Inc., announced that it was about to launch a product, Freedom software, designed to conceal all cyber-wanderings. According to Beiser (1999),

> [i]t works by stripping all data leaving a user's computer for identifying information—be it e-mail, chat-room gossip or requests for Web pages—then wrapping it in several layers of 128-bit encryption, currently considered unbreakable. The data is then routed through a series of randomly chosen servers, each of which unwraps one of the encryption envelopes to find where to send the packet next. That means no single server knows both the origin and destination of the packet.

Although encryption services have been hailed by cyber-rights groups such as Electronic Frontier Canada as necessary to ensure privacy and freedom of speech, such software also makes it difficult for law-enforcement agencies to monitor what appears on the Internet. The president of Zero-Knowledge, for example, notes that even his own company will not know which data packets connect to which users. Consider as well, that users of Freedom software are allowed to create up to five pseudonymous identities.

Unemployment

Some technologies replace human workers—robots replace factory workers, word processors displace secretaries and typists, and computer-assisted diagnostics reduce the need for automobile mechanics. It is estimated, for example, that thousands of bank branches will be replaced by automatic teller machines in the next decade. The cost of a teller transaction is $1.07; an electronic transaction, 7¢ (Fix 1994). In Canada, there are currently more than 34 million debit cards in use and more than 400 000 merchant terminals and automatic teller machines (*Maclean's* 1999d: 56).

Increases in unemployment due to technology are likely to be worldwide according to activist Jeremy Rifkin, whose book *The End of Work* (1996) predicts a global reduction in service-sector employees. Unlike previous decades, according to Rifkin, when uprooted workers moved from farms to factories to offices, today's technologically displaced workers have no place to go. Today's low unemployment rates seem to contradict Rifkin's dire forecasts.

Technology changes the nature of work and the types of jobs available. For example, fewer semiskilled workers are needed since many of these jobs have been replaced by machines. The jobs that remain, often white-collar jobs, require more education and technological skills. Technology thereby contributes to the split labour market as the pay gulf between skilled and unskilled workers continues to grow (Pascal 1996).

The Haves and the Have-Nots

One of the most significant social problems associated with science and technology is the increased division between the classes. As Welter (1997: 2) notes,

> ...it is a fundamental truth that people who ultimately gain access to, and who can manipulate, the prevalent technology are enfranchised and flourish. Those individuals (or cultures) that are denied access to the new technologies, or can not master and pass them on to the largest number of their offspring, suffer and perish.

The fear that technology will produce a "virtual elite" (Levy 1997) is not uncommon. Several theorists hypothesize that as technology displaces workers, most notably the unskilled and uneducated, certain classes of people will be irreparably disadvantaged—the poor, minorities, and women (Hayes 1998; Welter 1997). Concern exists that biotechnologies will lead to a "genetic stratification," whereby genetic screening, gene therapy, and other types of genetic enhancements are available only to the rich (Mehlman and Botkin 1998).

The wealthier the family, for example, the more likely the family is to have a computer. According to Statistics Canada, in 1998, the 20 percent of households with the highest incomes were four times more likely to have a computer than those in the lower income group. In that year, almost three in four (74 percent) of those in the highest income group versus fewer than one in five (18 percent) in the lowest income group had a computer. Internet access was six times more common in households in the highest income group (48 per-

Although factory work in the clothing industry has traditionally furnished employment for the poorly uneducated and unskilled, between 1989 and 1994, the clothing industry lost 32 000 jobs, in part because of the introduction of advanced technologies.

SOURCE: Statistics Canada 1998

In the United States, inner-city neighbourhoods, disproportionately populated by racial and ethnic minorities, are simply less likely to be "wired," that
is, to have the telecommunications hardware necessary for schools to access
online services. In fact, cable and telephone companies are less likely to lay
fibre optics in these areas—a practice called "information apartheid" or "electronic redlining." Students who live in such neighbourhoods are technologically disadvantaged and may never catch up to their middle-class counterparts
(Welter 1997).

The cost of equalizing such differences is enormous, but the cost of not
equalizing them may be even greater. Technological disparities exacerbate the
structural inequities perpetuated by the split labour force and the existence of
primary and secondary labour markets (see Chapter 11).

CONSIDERATION

As symbolic interactionists note, language itself perpetuates inequality. Until the mid-1980s,
biologists described human conception in terms of gender-specific qualities. Such words as
"velocity" and "penetrating" were used in reference to the male's sperm. The female egg, however, was described as docile, passively wandering about, as the determined sperm
approaches. More recently, scientists, in part motivated by feminist thinking, conducted further
research that revealed that sperm are not quite the swimmers once thought. It appears that
sperm are rather inefficient swimmers, often losing direction as they approach the egg. It also
appears that, contrary to traditional theorizing, the egg plays a more active role in conception,
moving closer to the sperm as it nears (Begley 1997).

Mental and Physical Health

Some new technologies have unknown risks. Biotechnology, for example, has
promised and, to some extent, has delivered everything from life-saving drugs
to heartier pest-free tomatoes. Biotechnologies have also, however, created
technology-induced diseases such as those experienced by Chellis
Glendinning (1990). Glendinning, after using the pill and, later, the Dalkon
Shield IUD, became seriously ill.

> Despite my efforts to get help, medical professionals did not seem to
> know the root of my condition lay in immune dysfunction caused
> by ingesting artificial hormones and worsened by chronic inflamma-
> tion. In all, my life was disrupted by illness for twenty years,
> including six years spent in bed....For most of the years of illness,
> I lived in isolation with my problem. Doctors and manufacturers of
> birth control technologies never acknowledged it or its sources.

Other technologies that pose a clear risk to a large number of people
include nuclear power plants, DDT, automobiles, x-rays, food colouring, and
breast implants.

The production of new technologies may also place manufacturing
employees in jeopardy. For example, the electronics industry uses thousands of
hazardous chemicals, including freon, acetone, and sulphuric and nitric acids:

National Data

In 1999, the Calgary Board
of Education introduced
into its 220 schools a Web-
blocker called *Bess*, reportedly the most efficient
software it was able to find
in an attempt to block the
viewing of hate or porno-
graphic sites by student
searchers. This measure was
undertaken after a series of
incidents in which stu-
dents sent passages from
hate sites on the Web
(which numbered more
than 800 in that year) or
other e-mail threats to
fellow students.

SOURCE: Sheppard 1999

[Semiconductor] workers are expected to dip wafer-thin silicon that has been painted with photoresist into acid baths. The wafers are then heated in gas-filled ovens, where the gas chemically reacts with the photosensitive chemicals. After drying, the chips are then bonded to ceramic frames, wires are attached to contacts and the chip is encapsulated with epoxy. These integrated circuits are then soldered onto boards, and the whole device is cleaned with solvents. Gases and silicon lead to respiratory and lung diseases, acids to burning and blood vessel damage, and solvents to liver damage. (Hosmer 1986: 2)

Finally, technological innovations are, for many, a cause of anguish and stress. Nearly 60 percent of workers report being "technophobes," that is, fearful of technology (Boles and Sunoo 1998). Says Dr. Michelle Weil, a clinical psychologist, the key to dealing with technophobia is to decide "which tools make sense in a person's life and will give them more control, and, ultimately, more enjoyment" (Kelly 1997: 4). This chapter's The Human Side, "Data Smog Removal Techniques," deals directly with this issue.

The Challenge to Traditional Values and Beliefs

Technological innovations and scientific discoveries often challenge traditionally held values and beliefs, in part because they enable people to achieve goals that were previously unobtainable. Before recent advances in reproductive technology, for example, women could not conceive and give birth after menopause. Technology that allows postmenopausal women to give birth challenges societal beliefs about childbearing and about the role of older women. Macklin (1991) notes that the techniques of egg retrieval, in-vitro fertilization, and gamete intrafallopian transfer (GIFT) make it possible for two different women to each make a biological contribution to the creation of a new life. Such technology requires society to re-examine its beliefs about what a family is and what a mother is. Should family be defined by custom, law, or the intentions of the parties involved?

Medical technologies that sustain life lead us to rethink the issue of when life should end. The increasing use of computers throughout society challenges the traditional value of privacy. New weapons systems challenge the traditional idea of war as something that can be survived and even won. Cloning challenges our traditional notions of family, parenthood, and individuality. Toffler (1970) coined the term **future shock** to describe the confusion resulting from rapid scientific and technological changes that unravel our traditional values and beliefs.

Finally, if the information superhighway allows us to increasingly live in a global village, some have expressed concern that, in the process, we may lose our national identity as Canadians (Wallace 1999b). According to the *Maclean's* 1999 year-end poll, after noting the pervasiveness of the American media and the impact of U.S. investment and takeovers of Canadian businesses, "more respondents think the Internet now has a greater impact on drawing us closer to Americans. Only 23 percent of those who think we are becoming more like Americans attribute it to free trade, while 34 percent finger the Internet" (Wallace 1999a) (Table 13.3).

DATA SMOG REMOVAL TECHNIQUES

The following excerpt from David Shenk's Data Smog: Surviving the Information Glut *(1997), outlines techniques for simplifying your life and reducing the stress associated with a "high-tech" lifestyle.*

Most of us have excess information in our lives, distracting us, pulling us away from our priorities and from a much-desired tranquility. If we stop just for a moment to look (and listen) around us, we will begin to notice a series of data streams that we'd be better off without, including some distractions we pay handsomely for.

Turn the television off. There is no quicker way to regain control of the pace of your life, the peace of your home, and the content of your thinking than to turn off the appliance that supplies for all-too-many of us the ambiance of our lives....

...It is not enough to simply turn the TV off; one must also make it somewhat difficult to turn it on again. Many TV-free participants have liked the results so much that they have gotten rid of their televisions altogether. My own alternative to this radical gesture has been to move the offending item from our kitchen/living room into the closet. There it stays except for a few select hours per week, when I lug it out, plug it in, and turn it on.

Leave the pager and cell-phone behind. It is thrilling to be in touch with the world at all times, but it's also draining and interfering. Are wireless communicators instruments of liberation, freeing people to be more mobile with their lives— or are they more like electronic leashes, keeping people more plugged-into their work and their info-glutted lives than is necessary and healthy?

Limit your e-mail. As one spends more and more time online, e-mail quickly changes from being a stimulating novelty to a time-consuming burden, with dozens of messages to read and answer every day from colleagues, friends, family, news group posts, and unsolicited sales pitches....

...If we're spending too much time each day reading and answering e-mail that has virtually no value, we must take steps to control it. Ask people (nicely) not to forward trivia indiscriminately. "Unsubscribe" to the news groups that you're no longer really interested in. Tell spammers that you have no interest in their product, and ask them to remove you from their customer list.

Say no to dataveillance. With some determination and a small amount of effort, one can also greatly reduce the amount of junk mail and unsolicited sales phone calls. It involves writing just a few letters, requesting to have your name put on "do-not-disturb" lists, which some 75 percent of direct marketers honour.

Resist advertising. We read, watch, and listen to advertisements all day. Must we also wear them on our clothes?

Resist upgrade mania. Remember: Upgrades are designed to be sales tools, not to give customers what they've been clamoring for.

Be your own "smart agent." A new class of robotic "smart agent"

DATA SMOG REMOVAL TECHNIQUES *(continued)*

help consumers automate their information–
filtering needs—software such as IBM's InfoSage...delivers a custom set of news stories according to programmed preferences. Other programs weed out e-mail not written by a select list of people.

But...smart agents are not the answer to the information glut. Regardless of how efficient they become, they will never be adequate substitutes for our own manual filtering. Instead, we must become our own smart agents.

Cleanse your system with "data-fasts." As your own smart agent, you are also your own data dietitian. Take some time to examine your daily intake and con-

sider whether or not your info diet needs some fine-tuning. Take some data naps in the afternoon, during which you stay away from electronic information for a prescribed period. You could also consider limiting yourself to no more than a certain number of hours on the Internet each week, or at least balancing the amount of time spent online with an equal amount of time reading books....

[P]eriodic fasts of a week or month have a remarkably rejuvenating effect. One sure way to gauge the value of something, after all, is to go without it for a while.

SOURCE: Shenk, David. 1997. *Data Smog: Surviving the Information Glut.* pp. 184–9. San Francisco: HarperEdge. Reprinted by permission.

Table 13.3 | **How Much of an Impact Has Each of the Following Had on Making Us More Like Americans?**

Asked of those who thought that Canadians were becoming more like Americans.

	Major impact	Some impact	Neutral	Not too much impact	No Impact at all
American media like TV, magazines, and film	48	36	7	7	2
U.S. investment and takeovers of Canadian businesses	35	44	9	8	4
The Internet and information economy	34	41	11	6	4
The North American Free Trade Agreement	23	42	14	10	4
Canadian government adopting the same kinds of policies as the U.S. government	20	42	18	14	4
Changes in our social programs	15	39	21	18	6

SOURCE: Wallace 1999a

More than 30 public and private livestock centres in Japan have received $2.2 million from the Japanese government to conduct cattle cloning research; thus far, 400 cows have been cloned and sent to market.

SOURCE: Associated Press 1998

In 1998, the Swiss pharmaceutical company Roche Holding paid Decode Genetics $200 million for research in Iceland; with a homogeneous population of 270 000, Icelanders provide a much-needed "narrow gene pool" for the identification of genes carrying diseases.

SOURCE: Marshall 1998

STRATEGIES FOR ACTION: CONTROLLING SCIENCE AND TECHNOLOGY

As technology increases, so does the need for social responsibility. Nuclear power, genetic engineering, cloning, and computer surveillance all increase the need for social responsibility: "...technological change has the effect of enhancing the importance of public decision making in society, because technology is continually creating new possibilities for social action as well as new problems that have to be dealt with" (Mesthene 1993: 85). In the following section, we address various aspects of the public debate, including science, ethics, the law, and the role of corporations and government policy.

Science, Ethics, and the Law

Science and its resulting technologies alter the culture of society by challenging traditional values. Public debate and ethical controversies, however, have led to structural alterations in society as the legal system responds to calls for action. The Institute of Science, Law and Technology at the Illinois Institute of Technology, for example, recently recommended that minimum standards for fertility treatments be set. In an effort to reduce the number of multiple births, the group called for a legal limit of four transferred embryos for each IVF attempt. Ethicist George Annas also called for states to pass laws "defining legal parentage to avoid confusion when disputes occur among the parties who helped create a child...." ("Group Seeks Standards for Infertility Services" 1998: 12).

Are such regulations necessary? In a society characterized by rapid technological and thus social change—a society where custody of frozen embryos is part of the divorce agreement—many would say yes. Cloning, for example, is one of the most hotly debated technologies in recent years. Bioethicists and the public vehemently debate the various costs and benefits of this scientific technique. Ironically, the Internet provides numerous sites that discuss the benefits and disadvantages of cloning, with one high-tech innovation providing a forum for discussion for another.

Should the choices that we make, as a society, be dependent on what we can do or what we *should* do? While scientists and the agencies and corporations who fund them often determine the former, who should determine the latter? Although such decisions are likely to have a strong legal component, that is, they must be consistent with the rule of law and the right of scientific inquiry (Eibert 1998), legality or the lack thereof often fails to answer the question, what *should* be done? Thus, it is likely that the issues surrounding the most controversial of technologies will continue into the twenty-first century and with no easy answers.

Technology and the Corporate World

As philosopher Jean-François Lyotard notes, knowledge is increasingly produced to be sold (Powers 1998). The development of genetically altered crops, the commodification of women as egg donors, and the harvesting of regenerated organ tissues are all examples of potentially market-driven technologies. Like the corporate pursuit of computer technology, profit-motivated biotechnology creates several concerns.

Foremost is the concern that only the rich will have access to such life-saving technologies as genetic screening and cloned organs. Such fears are justified. Several "companies with enigmatic names such as Progenitor, Millennium Pharmaceuticals, and Darwin Molecular have been pinpointing and patenting human life with the help of $4.5 billion in investments from pharmaceuticals companies" (Shand 1998: 46). Millennium Pharmaceutical holds the patent on the melanoma gene and the obesity gene; Darwin Molecular controls the premature aging gene, and Progenitor the gene for schizophrenia.

These patents result in **gene monopolies**, which could lead to astronomical patient costs for genetic screening and treatment. One company's corporate literature candidly states that its patent of the breast cancer gene will limit competition and lead to huge profits (Shand 1998: 47). The biotechnology industry argues that such patents are the only way to recoup research costs, which, in turn, lead to further innovations.

The commercialization of technology causes several other concerns, including the tendency for discoveries to remain closely guarded secrets rather than collaborative efforts, and issues of quality control (Lemonick and Thompson 1999; Rabino 1998). Finally, although there is little doubt that profit acts as a catalyst for some scientific discoveries, other less commercially profitable but equally important projects may be ignored. As biologist Isaac Rabino states, "imagine if early chemists had thrown their energies into developing profitable household products before the periodic table was discovered…" (1998: 112).

Runaway Science and Government Policy

Science and technology raise many public policy issues. Policy decisions, for example, address concerns about the safety of nuclear power plants, the privacy of electronic mail, the hazards of chemical warfare, and the legality of surrogacy. In creating science and technology, have we created a monster that has begun to control us rather than the reverse? What controls, if any, should be placed on science and technology?

The government, through regulatory agencies and departments, prohibits the use of some technologies (e.g., assisted-suicide devices) and requires others (e.g., seat belts). To instil consumer trust in Internet commerce, the federal government has engaged in several efforts designed to complement the technological and management security solutions developed by industry. For example, the federal government introduced Bill C-54, the *Personal Information and Electronic Documents Act,* to facilitate e-commerce in Canada by enabling the use of electronic documents and electronic signatures. The proposed legislation seeks to accommodate a wide array of authentication technologies to protect e-transactions with the federal government. In addition, the Organization for Economic Cooperation and Development (OECD) Working Party on Information Security and Privacy, comprises government and private sector representatives from OECD member countries. To date it has issued a number of reports and policies related to authentication, including the 1992 *OECD Guidelines for the Security of Information Systems*, the 1997 *OECD Guidelines on Cryptography Policy*, and the 1998 *Declaration on Authentication for Electronic Commerce*.

National Data

In Canada, the unprecedented boom in biotech and pharmaceutical companies is so great that, in 1998, one-fifth of the available Canadian positions in this country's $1-billion biotechnology industry were unfilled.

SOURCE: McClelland 1999

Evidence suggests that the Canadian government wants to establish control over both research into human reproduction and the ways in which private fertility clinics and public hospitals employ the results. In 1996, the Liberal government introduced Bill C-47, legislation designed to ban 14 practices, including the creation of embryos for research and the sale of human sperm and eggs. However, after the medical community strongly opposed the legislation, the bill did not pass. A new bill, anticipated to be introduced sometime in 2000, is expected to include the establishment of an agency that will operate at arm's length from the government rather than as part of Health Canada. It is anticipated that, akin to the earlier failed legislation, the new bill will forbid the buying and selling of both human sperm and eggs, the hiring of surrogate mothers, the practice of cloning humans, and the selection of children according to sex or appearance. It is additionally believed that the proposed new agency would be given power to regulate what types of embryo research would be permitted, establish a registry of sperm and egg donors that would allow information to be retained on their medical histories and genetic information, and seek to regulate research into human reproduction and fertility. The thorny issue of whether or not children produced by donor sperm or eggs would be eligible to obtain information on the identities of their genetic parents will also, reportedly, be dealt with by the proposed agency (Geddes 1999).

UNDERSTANDING SCIENCE AND TECHNOLOGY

What are we to understand about science and technology from this chapter? As functionalists argue, science and technology evolve as a social process and are a natural part of the evolution of society. As society's needs change, scientific discoveries and technological innovations emerge to meet these needs, thereby serving the functions of the whole. Consistent with conflict theory, however, science and technology also meet the needs of select groups and are characterized by political components. As Winner (1993) notes, the structure of science and technology conveys political messages including "power is centralized," "there are barriers between social classes," "the world is hierarchically structured," and "the good things are distributed unequally" (Winner 1993: 288).

The scientific discoveries and technological innovations that are embraced by society as truth itself are socially determined. Research indicates that science and the resulting technologies have both negative and positive consequences—a technological dualism. Technology saves lives, time, and money; it also leads to death, unemployment, alienation, and estrangement. Weighing the costs and benefits of technology poses ethical dilemmas as does science itself. Ethics, however, "is not only concerned with individual choices and acts. It is also and, perhaps, above all concerned with the cultural shifts and trends of which acts are but the symptoms" (McCormick 1994: 16).

Thus, society makes a choice by the very direction it follows. Such choices should be made based on guiding principles that are both fair and just (Eibert 1998; Goodman 1993; Winner 1993):

1. Scientists and those working in technology should be prudent. Adequate testing, safeguards, and impact studies are essential. Impact assessment should include an evaluation of the social, political, environmental, and economic factors.

2. No technology should be developed unless all groups, and particularly those who will be most affected by the technology, have at least some representation "at a very early stage in defining what that technology will be" (Winner 1993: 291). Traditionally, the structure of the scientific process and the development of technologies has been centralized (that is, decisions have been in the hands of a few scientists and engineers); decentralization of the process would increase representation.

3. There should be no means without ends. Each innovation should be directed toward fulfilling a societal need rather than the more typical pattern in which a technology is developed first (e.g., high-definition television) and then a market is created (e.g., "you'll never watch regular TV again!"). Indeed, from the space program to research on artificial intelligence, the vested interests of scientists and engineers, whose discoveries and innovations build careers, should be tempered by the demands of society.

What the twenty-first century will hold, as the technological transformation continues, may be beyond the imagination of most of society's members. Technology empowers; it increases efficiency and productivity, extends life, controls the environment, and expands individual capabilities. But, as Steven Levy (1995) notes, there is a question as to whether society can accommodate such empowerment (p. 26).

Now that we have entered the first computational millennium, one of the great concerns of civilization is the attempt to reorder society, culture, and government in a manner that exploits the digital bonanza, yet prevents it from running roughshod over the checks and balances so delicately constructed in those simpler precomputer years.

CRITICAL THINKING

1. Use of the Internet by neo-Nazi and White supremacist groups has recently increased. Should such groups have the right to disseminate information about their organizations and recruit members through the Internet?

2. A Canadian student at the University of Waterloo developed the "V-chip"—a technological device designed to prevent children from watching programs their parents find objectionable. Hollywood executives opposed the V-chip on the grounds that it is intrusive and violates guarantees of freedom of expression. Others have also been critical, pointing to the difficulty of establishing a universal definition of violence, and the impact on advertising revenues (Makris 1996). How might a conflict theorist explain opposition to the V-chip?

3. What currently existing technologies have had more negative than positive consequences for individuals and for society?

4. Some research suggests that productivity actually declines with the use of computers (Rosenberg 1998). Assuming this "paradox of productivity" is accurate, what do you think causes the reduction in efficiency?

KEY TERMS

abortion
automation
cultural lag
cybernation
deskilling
e-commerce
future shock
gene monopolies

gene therapy
genetic engineering
genetic screening
information technology
Internet
in-vitro fertilization
mechanization
postmodernism

science
technological fix
technology
technology-induced
    diseases
upskilling
year 2000 (Y2K)

CHAPTER FOURTEEN

Population and Environmental Problems

Is It True?

1. In some countries, a woman must obtain her husband's consent to obtain contraception.

2. Most of the growth in the world population is occurring in wealthy, industrialized countries.

3. Evidence of global warming includes the fact that 1998 was the hottest year on record in the world.

4. At least one thousand plant and animal species are lost each year to extinction.

5. Approximately one-quarter of Canadians reported voting for, or against, political candidates or parties based on their stand on environmental issues.

Answers: 1 = T, 2 = F, 3 = T, 4 = T, 5 = T

I f all the people in the world stood shoulder to shoulder, they would fill

a. the island of Bali, Indonesia
b. the province of Manitoba
c. all of Canada
d. all of Asia

One defining characteristic of a civilized society is a sense of responsibility to the next generation. If we do not assume that responsibility, environmental deterioration leading to economic decline and social disintegration could threaten the survival of civilization as we know it.

Lester R. Brown
and Jennifer
Mitchell
of the World Watch
Institute

You may be surprised that the answer is (a)—all the people on Earth (as of 1998) could fit on the small island of Bali, with each person occupying less than one square metre—about the size of half a bathtub (Stiefel 1998). Does this mean that there is plenty of room for the world's growing population? The real question, according to Professor Joel Cohen, is not how many people can the Earth support, but how many people can the Earth support with what quality of life (Livernash and Rodenburg 1998)? In 1992, the U.S. National Academy of Sciences and the Royal Society of London issued a report that warned:

> If current predictions of population growth prove accurate and patterns of human activity on the planet remain unchanged, science and technology may not be able to prevent either irreversible degradation of the environment or continued poverty for much of the world. (cited in Brown 1995: 411)

In this chapter, we discuss population growth and the concomitant environmental implications. These concerns reflect two branches of social science: demography and human ecology. **Demography** is the study of the size, distribution, movement, and composition of human populations. **Human ecology** is the study of the relationship between human populations and their natural environment. After discussing population growth in the world and in Canada, we view population and environmental problems through the lens of structural-functionalism, conflict theory, and symbolic interactionism. We also explore how population growth contributes to a variety of social problems and examine strategies for limiting population growth. The second half of the chapter examines the extent of, social causes of, and solutions to environmental problems. Before reading further, you may want to take the "Eco-Quiz" in this chapter's Self and Society feature.

THE GLOBAL CONTEXT: A WORLD VIEW OF POPULATION GROWTH

For thousands of years, the world's population grew at a relatively slow rate. During 99 percent of human history, the size of hunting and gathering societies was restricted by disease and limited food supplies. Around 8000 B.C., the development of agriculture and the domestication of animals led to increased food supplies and population growth, but even then harsh living conditions and disease still put limits on the rate of growth. This pattern continued until the mid-eighteenth century when the Industrial Revolution improved the standard of living for much of the world's population. The improvements included better food, cleaner drinking water, and improved housing, as well as advances

This quiz is designed to see how environmentally conscious you are. For each question, select the correct answer from the choices provided. When complete, calculate the number of correct answers you have and check your level of eco-awareness.

1. In Peninsular Malaysia, more tree species are found in _____ acres of tropical forest than in the entirety of North America.

   a. 125   b. 1000   c. 1 000 000

2. _____ of the world's rainforests are found in Brazil.

   a. one-sixteenth   b. one-fourth   c. one-half

3. Leaves alone account for _____ of our solid wastes in the fall season.

   a. 25 percent   b. 75 percent   c. 90 percent

4. Every ton of recycled office paper saves _____ gallons of oil.

   a. 12   b. 135   c. 380

5. Energy saved from one recycled aluminum can will operate a TV set for _____.

   a. 3 hours   b. 5 hours   c. 5 days

6. Toxic chemicals that you dump down the storm drain may end up in _____.

   a. a water treatment plant   b. your dishwasher   c. the ocean

7. Insulating your attic reduces the amount of energy loss in most houses by up to _____.

   a. 5 percent   b. 20 percent   c. 50 percent

8. Every day, _____ children die from preventable diseases somewhere in the world.

   a. 40 000   b. 4 000   c. 400

9. The human population of the world is expected to have nearly _____ by the year 2100.

   a. doubled   b. tripled   c. quadrupled

10. The uncontrolled fishing that is allowed has reduced the amount of some commercial species to _____ of their original population.

    a. one-tenth   b. one-half   c. three-fourths

11. Every day, _____ species of plants and animals become extinct as their habitat and human influences destroy them.

    a. 10 to 25   b. 25 to 50   c. 50 to 100

12. A study has shown that there are possibly more than _____ species of insects dwelling in the canopies of tropical forests.

    a. 3 million   b. 30 million   c. 300 000

13. _____ square miles of rainforests are being destroyed each year.

    a. 13 000   b. 43 000   c. 63 000

14. Medicine produced in tropical forests brings in _____ dollars a year commercially.

    a. 30 000 b. 3 million c. 300 billion

15. Grasslands cover _____ of the land on Earth.

    a. one-sixteenth b. one-eighth c. one-fifth

16. Every year approximately _____ tons of carbon accumulates in the air.

    a. 400 billion b. 400 million c. 400 000

17. Batteries contain heavy metals, which cause contamination in dumpsites and in the air when incinerated. This is why you should _____ your batteries.

    a. throw away b. recharge c. recycle

18. Life in the oceans provides the earth with most of our _____, a most precious chemical.

    a. oxygen b. nitrogen c. fresh water

19. Instead of using an incandescent light bulb, use a _____ light bulb, which uses one-fourth of the energy and lasts longer. It still gives off the same amount of light.

    a. fluorescent b. burnt-out c. black

20. Releasing helium balloons into the air may result in animals such as a whale or sea turtle swallowing them and _____.

    a. floating into the sky b. dying c. talking in a high-pitched voice

ANSWERS

Question 1:   The correct answer is (a); imagine the biodiversity within that one small area!

Question 2:   The correct answer is (b); with nearly 25 percent of the world's rainforests being located in this country, it is so sad they are being destroyed so rapidly.

Question 3:   The correct answer is (b); nearly three-quarters of our waste during the autumn is made up of leaves, which should be composted.

Question 4:   The correct answer is (c); that's a lot of oil!

Question 5:   The correct answer is (a); now you see why recycling can save a lot of energy.

Question 6:   The correct answer is (c); if you don't want to swim in it, don't dump it!

Question 7:   The correct answer is (b); you should insulate your attic to save energy and save money.

Question 8:   The correct answer is (a); isn't it sad that so many children die unnecessarily? The cost of medical treatment for these children is equal to just 2 percent of the Third World's expenditure on weapons!

Question 9:   The correct answer is (b); just imagine how crowded the earth will be if our population triples.

Question 10: The correct answer is (a); uncontrolled fishing is wreaking havoc upon marine ecosystems and has resulted in the reduction of our commercial species.

Question 11: The correct answer is (c); that's a lot of lost plants and animals!

Question 12: The correct answer is (c); insects have been one of the most successful organisms to conquer this planet.

Question 13: The correct answer is (c); our rainforests are rapidly disappearing, and this needs to stop!

Question 14: The correct answer is (c); rainforest destruction not only harms the environment, but also eliminates possible cures for deadly diseases.

Question 15: The correct answer is (c); this biome sure covers a lot of our planet!
Question 16: The correct answer is (a); ever since the Industrial Revolution began, we have been dumping tons of carbon dioxide into the atmosphere.
Question 17: The correct answer is (b); batteries contain hazardous chemicals, so it is best to use rechargeable batteries.
Question 18: The correct answer is (a); due to the high amounts of seaweed and phytoplankton, our oceans release most of the world's oxygen.
Question 19: The correct answer is (a); fluorescent lights save energy and money.
Question 20: The correct answer is (b); helium balloons are deadly to wild animals.

SCORE	RATING
20	EcoNaut
17–19	Eco-whiz
15–16	Eco-star
12–14	Eco-conscious
9–11	Eco-disaster
6–8	Eco-calamity
0–5	Eco-hazard

SOURCE: Adapted from "Eco-Quiz." 1999. *Save Our Earth and Make a Difference*. Think Quest. <library.advanced.org/11353/text/quiz.html>. Used by permission.

in medical technology such as vaccinations against infectious diseases; all contributed to rapid increases in population.

World Population Growth

In the year A.D. 1, the world's population was about 250 million. The **doubling time**—or time it takes for a population to double in size from any base year—decreases as the population grows. Although the population in A.D. 1 took 1650 years to double, the second doubling took only 200 years, the third 80 years, and the fourth 45 years. In 1998, the doubling time for the world's population was 49 years (Population Reference Bureau 1998). Figure 14.1 illustrates world population growth from 1950 projected until 2050.

International Data

Sixty-five countries are expected to double their populations in 30 years or fewer, and 14 countries will triple or nearly triple their populations by 2050.

SOURCE: Population Institute 1998

CONSIDERATION

If you were born before 1950, you are a member of the first generation ever to witness a doubling of the world's population. There has been more growth in population since 1950 than during the four million years since our early ancestors first walked on earth (Brown, Gardner, and Halweil 1998).

More than 90 percent of population growth is occurring in less developed countries (Livernash and Rodenburg 1998). Compared to the developed countries, these nations are characterized by greater illiteracy, higher infant mortality rates, less industrialization, shorter life expectancies, more poverty, lower-quality health care, and higher **fertility rates**, or average number of births per woman.

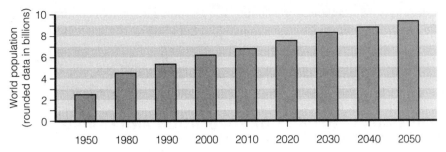

Figure 14.1

World Population Growth and Projections, 1950–2050

SOURCES: Brown, Lester R., Gary Gardner, and Brian Halweil. 1998. *Beyond Malthus: Sixteen Dimensions of the Population Problem*. World Watch Paper 143. Washington, D.C.: World Watch Institute; *Statistical Abstract of the United States: 1998*, 118th ed. U.S. Bureau of the Census. Washington, D.C.: U.S. Government Printing Office, Table 1340.

Falling Fertility Rates and the "Birth Dearth"

While many countries, especially in the developing world, are experiencing continued population growth, other countries are declining in population. In a growing number of countries, births are falling below 2.1 children per woman—the **replacement level** below which the population begins to decline. Declining birthrates in some countries are thought to result from high unemployment and a high cost of living.

Spain has the lowest birthrate in the world: each woman has an average of 1.15 children in her lifetime. Falling population levels are also a concern in France, Germany, Greece, Italy, Russia, and Japan. According to Steve Mosher, president of the Population Research Institute, "humanity's long-term problem is not too many children being born but too few....Over time, the demographic collapse will extinguish entire cultures" (Cooper 1998: 612).

International Data

As many as 58 countries—43 of them in Africa and 12 in Asia—have fertility rates of five or more children per woman. Half of these countries, 29, have fertility rates of six or more children per woman.

SOURCE: Population Institute 1998

Canadian Population Growth

Based on the census of 1851, the population of Canada was estimated to be 2 436 000, largely (80 percent) concentrated in Ontario and Quebec. Following Confederation, the total combined population of the four provinces (Ontario, Quebec, Nova Scotia, and New Brunswick) reached 3 486 000. However, as Canada's boundaries expanded to the Hudson's Bay Company territories of Rupert's Land and the North-Western Territory, Manitoba, and British Columbia, its population increased to 3 595 000 in 1871. With the addition of Prince Edward Island in 1873 and the establishment of the provinces of Alberta and Saskatchewan in 1905, Canada continued to increase in population size. Between 1901 and 1931 (and particularly between 1901 and 1911), large-scale immigration helped to almost double the population from 5 371 000 to 10 377 000. However, the 1930s and the years of the Great Depression saw our lowest rate of growth (McVey and Kalbach 1995). Although Canada experienced a high fertility rate during the period of the baby boom (which is generally considered to have occurred in Canada from 1946 to 1959), the birth rate in Canada has been declining since the 1970s with the fertility rate remaining around 1.6 children per woman for several years. Reasons for this decline include (1) fewer children born to women of child-bearing age following the baby boom (the "baby bust" years), (2) the decline in the size of large families, (3) the increase in the average age of women giving birth for the first time, (4) and the increasing popularity of sterilization as a method of contraception (*Canadian Global Almanac* 2000).

In 1995, all Canadian provinces reported figures below the replacement rate of 2.1 children that is theoretically necessary to ensure the renewal of gen-

International Data

In about 61 countries the average number of children born to each woman has fallen below 2.1—the replacement level required to maintain the population.

SOURCE: United Nations 1999

Compared to other Western countries, Canada has a high rate of sterilization. According to the General Social Survey, approximately 46 percent of all couples in their reproductive years were sterile for either natural, medical, or contraceptive reasons. Couples with two children are more likely than couples with one child to undergo sterilization (47 percent versus 14 percent, respectively).

SOURCE: *Canadian Global Almanac* 2000

For most of the century after Confederation, Quebec was home to about one-third of our nation's population. However, its slice of the Canadian population has been shrinking. Although Quebec has tried to aggressively reverse its plunging birth rate through baby bonuses and, more recently, family-friendly policies, total births in Quebec have decreased 25 percent since 1990. In 1999, the birth rate in Quebec was its lowest since 1908. The drop in the birth rate is particularly abrupt among women aged 20 to 29.

SOURCE: Peritz 1999

erations. In Newfoundland, for example, the reported rate of 1.25 children per woman was the lowest level ever reported by any Canadian province (Statistics Canada 1998). It has been estimated that as the death rate rises, Canada's natural growth in the population will approach zero by 2020 (Figure 14.2). Accordingly, population growth in Canada now depends on immigration.

SOCIOLOGICAL THEORIES OF POPULATION AND ENVIRONMENTAL PROBLEMS

The three main sociological perspectives—structural-functionalism, conflict theory, and symbolic interactionism—may be applied to the study of population and environmental problems.

Structural-Functionalist Perspective

Structural-functionalism focuses on how changes in one aspect of the social system affect other aspects of society. For example, the **demographic transition theory** of population describes how industrialization has affected population growth. According to this theory, in traditional agricultural societies, high fertility rates are viewed as necessary to offset high mortality rates and to ensure continued survival of the population. As a society becomes industrialized and urbanized, improved sanitation, health, and education lead to a decline in mortality. The increased survival rate of infants and children, along with the declining economic value of children, leads to a decline in fertility rates.

Other changes in social structure and culture that affect population include the shift in values toward individualism and self-fulfillment. The availability and cultural acceptability of postnatal forms of family size limitation also affect fertility rates (Mason 1997). In some countries, traditional values permit parents to control family size postnatally by "returning" children at birth (i.e., killing them), selling them to families in need of a child, sending them into bonded labour or prostitution, or marrying them off in early childhood.

Structural-functionalism emphasizes the interdependence between human beings and the physical environment. From this perspective, human actions, social arrangements, and cultural values contribute to environmental problems, which in turn affect social life. For example, war, industrialization, urbanization, and materialistic values contribute to the destruction of the environment and the depletion of natural resources. Population growth also affects the environment; however, its impact varies tremendously according to a society's lifestyle and economic activities (Livernash and Rodenburg 1998).

Conflict Perspective

The conflict perspective focuses on how wealth and power, or the lack thereof affects population and environmental problems. In 1798, Thomas Malthus predicted that the population would grow faster than the food supply and that masses of people were destined to be poor and hungry. According to **Malthusian theory**, food shortages would lead to war, disease, and starvation that would eventually slow population growth. However, conflict theorists argue that food shortages result primarily from inequitable distribution of power and resources. The world's farmers produce enough food for the world's nearly six

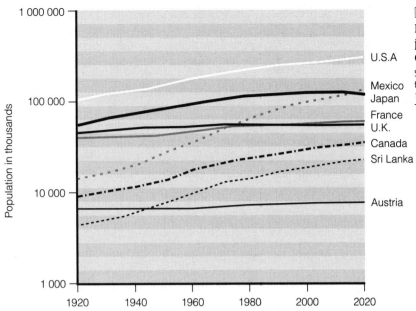

Figure 14.2

Population Trends and Projections, Canada and Selected Countries: 1920–2020

SOURCE: Medium variant estimates and projections from United Nations World Population Projections, 1992.

billion people, yet about 800 million people are malnourished, primarily in sub-Saharan Africa and South Asia. "Poverty and the lack of political power are the primary causes of their hunger, not insufficient food" (Livernash and Rodenburg 1998: 4).

Conflict theorists also note that population growth results from pervasive poverty and the subordinate position of women in many less developed countries. Poor countries have high infant and child mortality rates. Hence, women in many poor countries feel compelled to have many children to increase the chances that some will survive into adulthood. The subordinate position of women prevents many women from limiting their fertility. For example, in 14 countries around the world, a woman must get her husband's consent before she can receive any contraceptive services (United Nations Population Fund 1997). Thus, according to conflict theorists, population problems result from continued inequality within and between nations.

The conflict perspective also emphasizes how wealth, power, and the pursuit of profit underlie many environmental problems. Wealth is related to consumption patterns that cause environmental problems. Wealthy nations have higher per capita consumption of petroleum, wood, metals, cement, and other commodities that deplete the earth's resources, emit pollutants, and generate large volumes of waste.

The capitalistic pursuit of profit encourages making money from industry regardless of the damage done to the environment. Further, to maximize sales, manufacturers design products intended to become obsolete. Because of this **planned obsolescence**, consumers continually throw away used products and purchase replacements. Industry profits at the expense of the environment, which must sustain the constant production and absorb ever-increasing amounts of waste. Industries also use their power and wealth to resist environmental policies that would hurt the industries' profits. For example, there is growing consensus among scientists that global warming is occurring and that the burning of fossil fuels is a major cause of the problem. To fight the attack on fossil-fuel use, petroleum, automobile, coal, and other industries that profit from fossil-fuel consumption created and fund the Global Climate Coalition, an industry-front group that proclaims global warming a myth and characterizes hard evidence of global climate change as "junk science"(Jensen 1999).

Symbolic Interactionist Perspective

The symbolic interaction perspective focuses on how meanings, labels, and definitions learned through interaction affect population and environmental problems. For example, in some societies, women learn through interaction with others that deliberate control of fertility is defined as deviant and socially unacceptable. Once some women learn new definitions of fertility control, they become role models and influence the attitudes and behaviours of others in their personal networks (Bongaarts and Watkins 1996). The level of development of a country is relevant in that it facilitates or hinders social interaction. The more developed a country is, the more likely women will be exposed to new meanings of fertility control through interaction in educational settings and through media and information technologies.

Meanings, labels, and definitions learned through interaction and the media also affect environmental problems. Whether an individual recycles, carpools, or joins an environmental activist group is influenced by the meanings and definitions of these behaviours that the individual learns through interaction with others.

Increasingly, businesses and industries are attempting to increase profits through a strategy called **greenwashing**, which essentially involves redefining their corporate image and products as being "environmentally friendly" or socially responsible. For example, many companies publicly emphasize the steps they have taken to help the environment. Another greenwashing strategy is to retool, repackage, or relabel a company's product. For example, in 1990, McDonald's announced it was phasing out foam packaging and switching to a new, paper-based packaging that is partially degradable. Many products have labels that indicate the packaging is made from recycled material. Proctor and Gamble reformulated its liquid detergent, changing from a 64-ounce bottle to a 50-ounce concentrated formula that can be refilled from another container made from 50 percent recycled plastic. ACX Technologies, a subsidiary of Adolph Coors Co., has patented Heplon, a plastic polymer made from plant sources such as corn and beets ("A New Way to Make a Six-Pack Disappear" 1998). Beer cans made from this plastic are biodegradable and can be thrown in a compost pile.

Switzer (1997) explains that greenwashing is commonly used by public relations firms that specialize in damage control for clients whose reputations and profits have been hurt by poor environmental practices. DuPont, the biggest private generator of toxic waste in the United States, attempted to project a "green" image by producing a TV ad showing seals clapping, whales and dolphins jumping, and flamingos flying. In an Earth Day event at the National Mall in Washington, D.C., the National Association of Manufacturers (NAM) highlighted renewable and energy-efficient technologies, however, members of NAM have spent millions of dollars lobbying against use of these very same technologies (Karliner 1998). In another greenwashing attempt, a leading ant-killing and roach-killing product included a label that read: "Made with Pyrethrins: Pyrethrin Insecticide Is Made from Flowers." The fine print reveals that pyrethrins make up only 0.08 percent of the product, while the neurotoxic pesticide Dursban makes up three times as much of the product (0.24 percent). Although greenwashing often involves manipulation of public perception to maximize profits, some firms do make genuine and legitimate efforts to improve their operations, packaging, or overall sense of corporate responsibility toward the environment (Switzer 1997).

SOCIAL PROBLEMS RELATED TO POPULATION GROWTH

Some of the most urgent social problems today are related to population growth. They include poor maternal and infant health, shortages of food and water, environmental degradation, overcrowded cities, and conflict within and between countries.

Poor Maternal and Infant Health

As noted in Chapter 2, maternal deaths (deaths due to causes related to pregnancy and childbirth) are the leading cause of mortality for reproductive-age women in the developing world. Having several children at short intervals increases the chances of premature birth, infectious disease, and death for the mother or the baby. Childbearing at young ages has been associated with anemia and hemorrhage, obstructed and prolonged labour, infection, and higher rates of infant mortality (Zabin and Kiragu 1998). In developing countries, one in four children are born unwanted, increasing the risk of neglect and abuse. In addition, the more children a woman has, the fewer parental resources (parental income, time, and maternal nutrition) and social resources (health care and education) are available to each child (Catley-Carlson and Outlaw 1998). The adverse health effects of high fertility on women and children are, in themselves, compelling reasons for providing women with family planning services. "Reproductive health and choice are often the key to a woman's ability to stay alive, to protect the health of her children and to provide for herself and her family" (p. 241).

Food Shortages, Malnourishment, and Disease

Countries with large populations, few resources, and limited land are particularly vulnerable to food shortages. Food shortages lead to malnourishment, disease, and premature death.

In 1950, 500 million people (20 percent of the world's population) were considered malnourished; in the late 1990s, more than three billion people (one-half of the world's population) suffered from malnutrition (Pimentel et al. 1998). In many countries, shortages of vitamin A cause blindness and death. Deficiencies of iron cause anemia and death, and iodine deficiencies cause iodine-deficiency disease—a leading cause of brain damage in children and infants.

CONSIDERATION

Another factor contributing to food shortages is the increase in meat consumption in affluent countries. Reid (1998) explains that "a meat-centered diet is an inefficient use of resources because you have to feed the animal before it's fed to people" (p. 74). For example, a pig consumes about 600 pounds [272 kg] of corn and 100 pounds [45 kg] of soybean meal before it is sent to slaughter at 240 pounds [109 kg]. The meat from that pig would provide a person with a minimum daily caloric intake for 49 days. Eating the corn and soybean meal directly would provide the same person with enough food for more than 500 days.

Water Shortages and Depletion of Other Natural Resources

International Data

The World Health Organization estimates that half the people in the world do not have access to a decent toilet. Unsanitary disposal of human waste contaminates water supplies. Half the people in the developing world suffer from disease caused by poor sanitation. One of these diseases, diarrhea, is the leading killer of children today.

SOURCE: Gardner 1998

The authors of the *State of the World 1998* suggest that "one of the most underrated issues facing the world as it enters the third millennium is spreading water scarcity" (Brown, Flavin, and French 1998: 5). About 40 percent of the world population faces water shortages at some time during the year (Zwingle 1998). Because 70 percent of all water pumped from underground or drawn from rivers is used for irrigation, water scarcity also threatens food supplies.

Water shortages are exacerbating international conflict. Jordan, Israel, and Syria compete for the waters of the Jordan River basin. Jordan's King Hussein declared that water was the only issue that could lead him to declare war on Israel (Mitchell 1998). Speaking of the water shortage, General Federico Mayor, director of UNESCO, warned that, "[a]s it becomes increasingly rare, it becomes coveted, capable of unleashing conflicts. More than petrol or land, it is over water that the most bitter conflicts of the near future may be fought" ("Water Wars Forecast if Solutions Not Found" 1999).

Population growth also contributes to the depletion of other natural resources such as forests, oil, gas, coal, and certain minerals. Whether our planet will be able to sustain the world's population depends not only on how many people there are to sustain, but also on how these people make use of the resources that sustain them.

International Data

In developing countries, at least 120 million married women—and a large number of unmarried women—want more control over their pregnancies but cannot obtain family planning services.

SOURCE: Mitchell 1998

Urban Crowding and High Population Density

Population growth contributes to urban crowding and high population density. Without economic and material resources to provide for basic living needs, urban populations in developing countries often live in severe poverty. Urban poverty in turn produces environmental problems such as the unsanitary disposal of waste. In Nigerian urban ghettos, for example, the "mounds of refuse (including human wastes) that litter everywhere—gutters, schools, roads, market places and town squares—have been accepted as part of the way of life" (Nzeako, quoted in Agbese 1995). Urbanization also diverts water from irrigation and food production to industrial and residential uses.

Densely populated urban areas facilitate the spread of disease among people. Infectious diseases cause more than one-third of all deaths worldwide. Crowded conditions in urban areas provide the ideal environment for the culture and spread of diseases such as cholera and tuberculosis (Pimentel et al. 1998).

CONSIDERATION

The world's most crowded spot is Macau, the Portuguese colony on China's coast, with 23 194 people per square kilometre. In contrast, in Mexico there are 40 people for every square kilometre, and in Canada, only 3 (Figure 14.3). The population density in Tokyo is approximately 17 000 people per square kilometre; in Toronto it is 6729, and in Whitehorse, slightly more than 40 (Statistics Canada 1998).

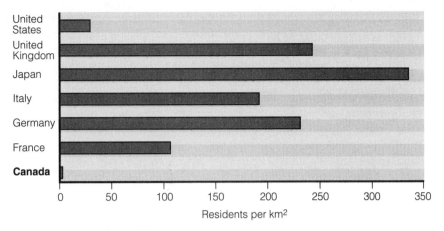

Figure 14.3
**Population Densities,
Group of Seven Countries**
SOURCE: *Labour Force Statistics*, 1975–1995,
Organization for Economic Co-operation and
Development.

STRATEGIES FOR ACTION: SLOWING POPULATION GROWTH

Both governments and nongovernmental organizations (NGOs) have attempted to slow world population growth by reducing fertility levels. Strategies for slowing population growth include providing access to birth control methods, improving the status of women, increasing economic development, improving health status, and imposing governmental regulations and policies.

CONSIDERATION

In some European countries with below-replacement-level birthrates, government policies have attempted to encourage rather than discourage childbearing. For example, Italy, Germany, and France have implemented generous child subsidies, in the form of tax credits for every child born, extended maternal leave with full pay, guaranteed employment on returning to work, and free childcare (Cooper 1998). Over the past 30 years, the global percentage of couples using some form of contraception has increased dramatically—from less than 10 to more than 50 percent.

Provide Access to Birth Control Methods

Although researchers have developed a wide range of contraceptives, many of these methods are not widely available or are prohibitively expensive for individuals with few economic resources. In some countries, methods of birth control are provided only to married women. Family planning personnel often refuse, or are forbidden by law or policy, to make referrals for contraceptive and abortion services for unmarried women. Finally, many women throughout the world do not have access to legal, safe abortion. Without access to contraceptives, many women who experience unwanted pregnancy resort to abortion—even under illegal and unsafe conditions (see also Chapter 2).

Contraceptive use has increased in many countries throughout the world. Nevertheless, many countries still have low rates of contraceptive use. In Ethiopia, less than 5 percent of women use contraception; in Niger and Chad, only 4 percent use contraception. In Nigeria and Pakistan, the figures are 15 percent and 18 percent (Population Institute 1998).

> **International Data**
>
> Over the past 30 years, the global percentage of couples using some form of contraception has increased dramatically—from less than 10 to more than 50 percent.
>
> SOURCE: Mitchell 1998

> **International Data**
>
> The amount of money needed each year to provide reproductive health care for all women in developing countries is $12 billion—the same amount that is spent annually on perfumes in England and the United States.
>
> SOURCE: "Matters of Scale" 1999

In 1994, delegates from 180 countries met in Cairo, Egypt, for the International Conference on Population and Development and adopted a 20-year Program of Action aimed at reducing population growth. The Cairo conference determined that about $17 billion would be needed annually to meet global family planning programs—and industrialized countries pledged to provide one-third of this amount. However, family planning assistance funds from developed countries have fallen far short of the amount promised. According to the United Nations Population Fund, funding cuts in international family planning programs means that "870 000 women will be deprived of effective contraception that would cost only $29 per woman. This will result in 500 000 unwanted pregnancies and 200 000 abortions" (Population Institute 1998: 10).

CONSIDERATION

Making contraceptives available does not reduce fertility unless women and men want to use birth control methods to prevent childbearing. In many societies, **pronatalism**—a cultural value that promotes having children—contributes to high fertility rates. In traditional Chinese culture, having many children was considered a blessing and a way of honouring one's ancestors. Confucius, the ancient Chinese philosopher, said that the greatest sin is to die without an heir. Throughout history, many religions have worshipped fertility and recognized it as being necessary for the continuation of the human race. In many countries, religions prohibit or discourage birth control, contraceptives, and abortion.

Improve the Status of Women

Throughout the developing world, the status of women is primarily restricted to that of wife and mother. Women in developing countries traditionally have not been encouraged to seek education or employment, but rather to marry early and have children. In some countries, a woman must obtain the consent of her husband before she can receive contraceptive services. Women who are never-married, divorced, widowed, or who cannot persuade their husbands to grant them permission to use contraceptives are denied family planning services.

Improving the status of women is vital to curbing population growth. Nafis Sadik, executive director of the United Nations Population Fund, argues that population growth cannot be slowed without gender equality and the social empowerment of women to control their lives, especially their reproductive lives. Education plays a key role in improving the status of women and in reducing fertility rates. Educated women are more likely to delay their first pregnancies, to use safe and effective contraception, and to limit and space their children (United Nations Population Fund 1997).

Increase Economic Development and Health Status

Although fertility reduction may be achieved without industrialization, economic development may play an important role in slowing population growth. Families in poor countries often rely on having many children to provide needed labour and income to support the family. Economic development decreases the economic value of children. Economic development is also associated with more education for women and greater gender equality. As previously noted, women's education and status are related to fertility levels. Finally, economic development tends to improve the health status of populations. Reductions in infant and child mortality are important for fertility decline, as couples no longer need to have many pregnancies to ensure that some children survive into adulthood.

Impose Government Regulations and Policies

Some countries have imposed strict governmental regulations on reproduction. In the 1970s, India established mass sterilization camps and made the salaries of public servants contingent on their recruiting a quota of citizens who would accept sterilization. The Indian state of Maharashtra enacted compulsory sterilization legislation and in a six-month period sterilized millions of people, many of them against their will (Boland et al. 1994). This policy has since been rescinded.

Governmental population regulations in China are less extreme, but still controversial. In 1979, China developed a one-child family policy whereby parents get special privileges for limiting their family size. Specifically, parents who pledge to have only one child receive an allowance for health care for five years that effectively increases their annual income by 10 percent. Parents who have only one child also have priority access to hospitals and receive a pension when they reach old age. In addition, their only child is given priority enrolment in nursery school and is exempted from school tuition. Chinese couples who have three or more children lose these privileges and must pay a special tax that effectively lowers their income for the first 14 years of the child's life (Zhang and Strum 1994).

China also implemented mandatory gynecologic exams. Twice each year health care workers visit each village and, theoretically, check every woman of reproductive age. Under the guise of reproductive health care, each woman is checked for gynecologic problems, has an IUD inserted if she has already had a child, and is subjected to an abortion if she already has a child and her new pregnancy has not been approved by her village. The Chinese government also promotes sterilization (Greenhalgh et al. 1994).

Critics of China's population policy argue that government policies that are intended to directly influence fertility are coercive and abusive of women's right to choose the number and timing of their children (McIntosh and Finkle 1995). The 1994 International Conference on Population Development advanced the agenda to replace coercive population programs with those that empower women, improve their health, and raise their status in the family and community.

CONSIDERATION

Even if countries around the world achieved replacement-level fertility rates (an average of 2.1 births per woman), populations would continue to grow for several decades because of the large numbers of people now entering their reproductive years. This population momentum is expected to account for up to two-thirds of the projected growth of the world population (United Nations Population Fund 1997).

ENVIRONMENTAL PROBLEMS

An expanding population is one of many factors that contribute to environmental problems such as land, water, and air pollution and depletion of natural resources. Each of these environmental problems poses a growing threat to the physical, economic, and social well-being of all people throughout the world. As Table 14.1 suggests, the majority of Canadians believe that environmental problems demand attention and redress.

Air Pollution

Transportation vehicles, fuel combustion, industrial processes (such as the burning of coal and wood), and solid waste disposal have contributed to the growing levels of air pollutants, including carbon monoxide, sulphur dioxide, nitrogen dioxides, and lead. Air pollution levels are highest in areas with both heavy industry and traffic congestion, such as Los Angeles and Mexico City. In China, heavy reliance on coal has resulted in some of the world's most polluted air. In 1996, the National Environmental Protection Agency of China reported three million deaths in cities during the preceding two years from chronic bronchitis resulting from urban air pollution (Brown 1998).

In Canada, the latest craze of boomers—minivans, sport utility vehicles (SUVs), and other light trucks—has alarmed environmentalists. They note that these vehicles, when compared with the standard passenger car, not only guzzle one-third more gas, but also spew out one-third more pollution out their tailpipes (Figures 14.4 and 14.5). Nevertheless, in 1999, sales of light trucks accounted for more than 50 percent of the passenger vehicle market. According to the David Suzuki Foundation, "[t]his light truck category is a moving disaster" (Speirs 2000: A24).

A poll of 2000 Canadians conducted by Maritz Automotive Research and Ernst and Young in October 1999 indicated that 80 percent would consider environmental issues before buying a new car or truck (with many also reporting their willingness to pay $2000 more for a "green vehicle"); however,

---

Table 14.1	What Canadians Are Saying

- **78%** of Canadians believe that their children will experience greater health difficulties because of a worsening environment (POLLARA INC., November 1997).
- **80%** of Canadians say they are just as concerned about the global impact of pollution and global warming as they are about its effect in their neighbourhood (Environics International, April 1997).
- **61%** of Canadians want government action to eliminate climate change (Environics International, April 1997).
- **59%** of Canadians feel that their health has been affected by environmental problems (Environics and Synergistics Consulting, March 1997).
- **75%** of Canadians want tougher legal measures to protect endangered species in Canada including extending protection to the habitats of species at risk (Canadian Endangered Species Coalition, November 1996).

SOURCE: CELA 1999

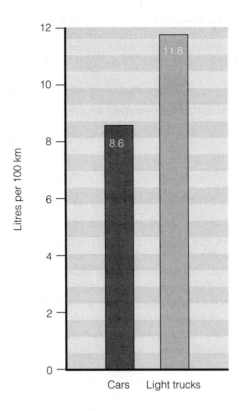

Figure 1 4.4
Fuel Efficiency Compared
SOURCE: Speirs 2000: A1

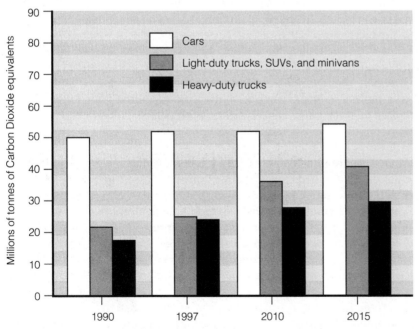

Figure 1 4.5
Greenhouse Gas Emissions
SOURCE: Speirs 2000: A24

their purchasing habits suggest otherwise. According to Mark Nantais, president of the Canadian Vehicle Manufacturers' Association, industry surveys of customer preferences suggest that such vehicle amenities as coffee-cup holders outrank green concerns, and that "[f]uel efficiency is not at the top of consumers' lists in terms of purchasing requirements. It ranks 9th to 15th on their list of criteria, depending on the study. Coffee cups rank higher. Stereos rank higher" (as cited in Speirs 2000: A24).

Indoor Air Pollution When we hear the phrase "air pollution," we typically think of smokestacks and vehicle exhausts pouring grey streams of chemical matter into the air. However, much air pollution is invisible to the eye and exists where we least expect it—in our homes, schools, workplaces, and public buildings.

Sick building syndrome (SBS) is a situation in which occupants of a building experience symptoms that seem to be linked to time spent in a building, but no specific illness or cause can be identified (Lindauer 1999). Building occupants complain of symptoms such as headaches; eye, nose, and throat irritation; a dry cough; dry or itchy skin; dizziness and nausea; difficulty concentrating; fatigue; and sensitivity to odours. While specific causes of SBS remain unknown, contributing factors may include polluted outdoor air that enters a building through poorly located air intake vents, windows, and other openings. Most indoor air pollution comes from sources inside the building, such as adhesives, upholstery, carpeting, copy machines, manufactured wood products, cleaning agents, and pesticides.

In poor countries, fumes from cooking and heating are major contributors to indoor air pollution. Globally, four million people die each year from acute respiratory problems caused by breathing fumes from cooking and heating (Kemps 1998).

In developed countries, common household, personal, and commercial products contribute to indoor pollution. For some individuals, exposure to these products can result in a variety of temporary acute symptoms such as drowsiness, disorientation, headaches, dizziness, nausea, fatigue, shortness of breath, cramps, diarrhea, and irritation of the eyes, nose, throat, and lungs. Long-term exposure can affect the nervous system, reproductive system, liver, kidneys, heart, and blood. Some solvents found in household, commercial, and workplace products cause cancer; others, birth defects ("The Delicate Balance" 1994). Some of the most common indoor pollutants include carpeting (which emits nearly 100 different chemical gases), mattresses (which may emit formaldehyde and aldehydes), drain cleaners, oven cleaners, spot removers, shoe polish, dry-cleaned clothes, paints, varnishes, furniture polish, potpourri, mothballs, fabric softener, and caulking compounds. Air fresheners, deodorizers, and disinfectants emit the pesticide paradichlorobenzene. Potentially harmful organic solvents are present in numerous office supplies, including glue, correction fluid, printing ink, carbonless paper, and felt-tip markers.

Many consumer products contain fragrances. The air in public and commercial buildings often contains deodorizers, disinfectants, and fragrances that are emitted through the building's heating, ventilation, and air conditioning system. Some fragrance fumes produce various combinations of sensory irritation, pulmonary irritation, decreases in expiratory airflow velocity, and possible neurotoxic effects (Fisher 1998). Fragrance products can cause skin sensitivity, rashes, headaches, sneezing, watery eyes, sinus problems, nausea, wheezing, shortness of breath, inability to concentrate, dizziness, sore throat, cough, hyperactivity, fatigue, and drowsiness (DesJardins 1997). Increasingly, businesses are voluntarily limiting fragrances in the workplace or banning them altogether to accommodate employees who experience ill effects from them.

Indoor air pollution is particularly problematic for sufferers of a controversial condition known as **multiple chemical sensitivity (MCS)**. People suffering from MCS say that after one or more acute or traumatic exposures to a chemical or group of chemicals, they began to experience adverse effects from low levels of chemical exposure that do not produce symptoms in most people. Even individuals who are not diagnosed as having MCS may experience adverse health effects from indoor air pollution.

Destruction of the Ozone Layer The use of human-made chlorofluorocarbons (CFCs), which are used in refrigerators, computer chips, hospital sterilization, solvents, dry cleaning, and aerosols, has damaged the ozone layer of the earth's atmosphere. The depletion of the ozone layer allows hazardous levels of ultraviolet rays to reach the earth's surface. Ultraviolet light has been linked to increases in skin cancer and cataracts, declining food crops, rising sea levels, and global warming.

Greenhouse Effect and Global Warming Various gases collect in the atmosphere and act like the glass in a greenhouse, holding heat from the sun close to the earth and preventing it from rising back into space. Greenhouse gases include carbon dioxide, CFCs, and methane. The most prevalent, carbon dioxide, results from energy production, transportation, and deforestation (World Resources Institute 1998b). Evidence for the greenhouse effect lies in the increasing temperatures recorded around the world. Heat and drought caused by the greenhouse effect threaten crops and food supplies and accelerate the extinction of numerous plant and animal species.

The greenhouse effect also threatens to melt polar ice caps and other glaciers, resulting in a rise in sea level. Some island countries would become uninhabitable. Low-lying deltas, such as in Egypt and Bangladesh, would be flooded, displacing millions of people. Brown (1995) warns that "rising seas in a warming world would be not only economically costly, but politically disruptive as well" (p. 415).

Acid Rain Air pollutants, such as sulphur dioxide and nitrogen oxide, mix with precipitation to form acid rain. Polluted rain, snow, and fog contaminate crops, forests, lakes, and rivers.

Acid rain is a particular threat in Ontario, New Brunswick, Nova Scotia, and Quebec because these provinces are directly in the path of much of the continent's SO_2 and NOx emissions, and the nonporous granite that composes the majority of the Canadian Shield is less able to absorb acid rain. Roughly 40 percent of Canada's total land area (approximately four million square kilometres) is extremely sensitive to acid rain (Statistics Canada 1998).

Land Pollution

About 30 percent of the world's surface is land, which provides soil to grow the food we eat. Increasingly, humans are polluting the land with toxic and radioactive waste, solid waste, and pesticides.

Toxic and Radioactive Waste The global community generates more than a million tons of hazardous waste each day (Brown 1995).

Decades of nuclear weapons production has polluted more than 2.3 million acres of land in at least 24 U.S. states; cleanup will extend well into the twenty-first century at a cost of more than $200 billion (Black 1999). Radioactive waste from nuclear power plants and major weapons production sites is associated with cancer and genetic defects. Radioactive plutonium, used in both nuclear power and weapons production, has a half-life (the time it takes for its radioactivity to be reduced by half) of 24 000 years (Mead 1998). The disposal of nuclear waste is particularly problematic. The U.S. Nuclear Regulatory Commission licenses nuclear reactors for 40 years. When nuclear reactors reach the end of their 40-year licences, the radioactive waste must be stored somewhere. About 28 000 metric tons of nuclear waste are already stored around the United States. This figure is expected to grow to 48 000 metric tons by 2003 and 87 000 metric tons by 2030 (not including waste from military nuclear operations) (Stover 1995). The United States has also promised to accept nuclear waste from about 40 nations with nuclear research reactors.

In Canada, radioactive waste has been produced since the early 1930s when the first uranium mine began operating in the Northwest Territories at Port Radium. Radium was refined for medical use and uranium was later processed at Port Hope, Ontario. In the 1940s, research and development on the application of nuclear energy to produce electricity began at the Chalk River Laboratories (CRL) of Atomic Energy of Canada Limited (AECL). Currently, radioactive waste is produced from uranium mining, milling, refining and conversion; nuclear fuel fabrication; nuclear reactor operations; and nuclear research and radioisotope manufacture and use (Figure 14.6). Under Canada's Radioactive Waste Policy Framework, producers and owners of radioactive waste are responsible for the funding, organization, management, and operation of disposal and other facilities required for their waste. Radioactive wastes are grouped into three categories: nuclear fuel waste, low-level radioactive waste, and uranium mine and mill tailings. Table 14.2 provides a summary of the quantity of radioactive waste produced in Canada in 1998 and the cumulative inventory to the end of 1998. Table 14.3 provides a projection of the inventory in Canada to the end of 1999 and 2035.

The cost of storing radioactive waste and cleaning other hazardous waste sites is immense, but not cleaning these sites is also costly. Brown (1995) remarks that "one way or another, society will pay—either in clean up bills or in rising health care costs" (p. 416). Scientists have proposed several options for disposing of nuclear waste, including burying it in rock formations deep below the Earth's surface or under Antarctic ice, injecting it into the ocean floor, or hurling it into outer space. Each of these options is risky and costly.

In Canada, the Atomic Energy Control Board (AECB), established in 1946, regulates the Canadian nuclear industry, including the use of nuclear energy and certain uses of ionizing radical and prescribed substances. Its mandate is "to ensure that the use of nuclear energy in Canada does not pose undue risk to health, safety, security and the environment." The AECB has two advisory committees, the members of which come from industry, universities, and other institutions. The AECB maintains all nuclear power policy, regulates power and research reactors, nuclear fuel fabrication plants, heavy water plants, radioactive waste management facilities, and uranium mines, mills, and refineries. Its regulations cover all aspects of the development, production, and application of nuclear energy and uranium mining, and extend to the import and

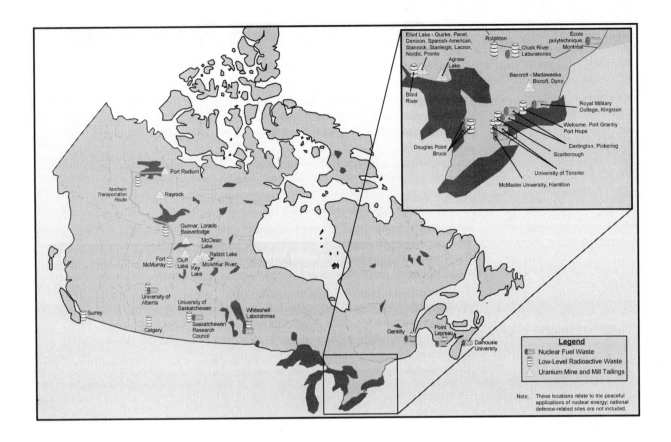

Within the map image:

Elliot Lake - Quirke, Panel, Denison, Spanish-American, Stanrock, Stanleigh, Lacnor, Nordic, Pronto

Rolphton

École polytechnique, Montréal

Chalk River Laboratories

Agnew Lake

Bancroft - Madawaska Bicroft, Dyno

Blind River

Royal Military College, Kingston

Welcome, Port Granby Port Hope

Douglas Point Bruce

Darlington, Pickering

Scarborough

University of Toronto

McMaster University, Hamilton

Port Radium

Northern Transportation Route

Rayrock

Gunnar, Lorado Beaverlodge

McClean Lake

Fort McMurray

Cluff Lake

Rabbit Lake

McArthur River

Key Lake

Surrey

University of Alberta

University of Saskatchewan

Whiteshell Laboratories

Calgary

Saskatchewan Research Council

Gentilly

Point Lepreau

Dalhousie University

Legend
- Nuclear Fuel Waste
- Low-Level Radioactive Waste
- Uranium Mine and Mill Tailings

Note: These locations relate to the peaceful applications of nuclear energy; national defence-related sites are not included.

Figure 14.6

Radioactive Waste Sites in Canada as of December 31, 1998

Note: These locations relate to the peaceful applications of nuclear energy; national defence-related sites are not included.

SOURCE: Duke Engineering and Services (Canada), Inc. 1999. "Executive Summary." *Inventory of Radioactive Waste in Canada: A Report Prepared for the Low-Level Radioactive Waste Management Office*. Gloucester, Ontario. Low-Level Radioactive Waste Management Office, November.

Table 14.2 **Waste Data to 1998**

Waste Category	Waste Produced in 1998	Waste Inventory to End of 1998
Nuclear fuel waste	320 m³	5600 m³
Low-level radioactive waste	4300m³	1.8 million m³
Uranium mine and mill tailings	1 million tons	210 million tons

SOURCE: Duke Engineering and Services (Canada), Inc. 1999. "Executive Summary." *Inventory of Radioactive Waste in Canada: A Report Prepared for the Low-Level Radioactive Waste Management Office*. Gloucester, Ontario: Low-Level Radioactive Waste Management Office, November, p. 1.

Table 14.3 **Projection of the Waste Inventory in Canada to the end of 1999 and 2035**

Waste Category	Waste Inventory to End of 1999	Waste Inventory to End of 2035
Nuclear fuel waste	5900 m³	14 500 m³
Low-level radioactive waste	1.8 million m³	2.1 million m³
Uranium mine and mill tailings	211 million tons	248 million tons

SOURCE: Duke Engineering and Services (Canada), Inc. 1999. "Executive Summary." *Inventory of Radioactive Waste in Canada: A Report Prepared for the Low-Level Radioactive Waste Management Office*. Gloucester, Ontario: Low-Level Radioactive Waste Management Office, November, p. ii.

export of nuclear materials, equipment, and technology. The AECB also administers the *Nuclear Liability Act* and is involved in international activities related to Canada's participation in the Treaty on the Non-Proliferation of Nuclear Weapons and the International Atomic Energy Agency. Although scheduled to become, at some point in 1999, the Canadian Nuclear Safety Commission under new legislation that provided for a more modern and effective framework for regulating the nuclear industry, this change had not yet occurred by the time this book went to press.

Solid Waste According to the Canadian Waste Management Industry Survey, governments and businesses disposed of 20.6 million tons of waste in 1996, the equivalent of approximately 620 kilograms of waste for each Canadian (Statistics Canada 1999). Some of this waste is converted into energy by incinerators; more than half is taken to landfills. However, it has been reported that no less than a trillion litres of raw and partially treated sewage are dumped into Canada's waters every year (CELA 1999b).

Pesticides Pesticides are used worldwide in the growing of crops and gardens; outdoor mosquito control; the care of lawns, parks, and golf courses; and indoor pest control.

Pesticides contaminate food, water, and air and can be absorbed through the skin, swallowed, or inhaled. Many common pesticides are considered potential carcinogens and neurotoxins. Even when a pesticide is found to be hazardous and is banned in one country, other countries may continue to use it. In this chapter's Focus on Social Problems Research, we highlight a 1999 study conducted by the Ontario College of Family Physicians (Environmental Health Committee) and the Canadian Environmental Law Association (CELA), which provides an urgent warning about the health dangers pesticide use poses to children.

Water Pollution

Our water is being polluted by many harmful substances, including pesticides, industrial waste, acid rain, and oil spills. Although Canada is home to approximately one-seventh of the world's accessible fresh water, we cannot afford to become complacent. Our experience in relation to the Great Lakes illustrates this point well. The Great Lakes are a major source of fresh water, but they are bordered on the Canadian side by land that is both densely populated and heavily farmed. "By the late 1950s, fertilizers from farms and phosphates from household detergents had leached into the lake," encouraging abnormal growth of algae, which in turn choked other life forms out of the lakes (Statistics Canada 1998). Fish that survived the algae problem were poisoned by various substances, particularly PCB (polychlorinated biphenyl). These substances can harm those who eat the contaminated fish. One study reported that pregnant women who had consumed 12 kilograms or more of the contaminated fish from the Great Lakes over a six-year period were more likely than those who had not to give birth prematurely and to smaller babies (Statistics Canada 1998). In the 1970s, substance controls brought the algae problem within the Great Lakes under control and, currently, the federal government and the provincial government of Ontario are working with the United States to clean up the Great Lakes. This effort includes the federal government's Great Lakes Clean-up Fund, which, since 1994, has seen the investment of more than $35 million in more than 150 projects designed to develop solutions to the problems of pollutions, the development of new technologies, and the rehabilitation of wildlife habitat (Statistics Canada 1998).

However, worldwide, more diseases and deaths are caused by water contaminated by feces, not by chemicals (Kemps 1998). About 1.2 billion people lack access to clean water. In developing nations, as much as 95 percent of untreated sewage is dumped directly into rivers, lakes, and seas that are used for drinking and bathing (Pimentel et al. 1998).

Depletion of Natural Resources

Overpopulation contributes to the depletion of natural resources, such as coal, oil, and forests. The demand for new land, fuel, and raw materials has resulted in **deforestation**—the destruction of the earth's rainforests. The major cause of deforestation is commercial logging.

Trees naturally absorb carbon dioxide—one of the main gases that contribute to the "greenhouse effect" and global warming—from the air. Deforestation is responsible for about 30 percent of the atmospheric build-up of carbon dioxide (World Resources Institute 1998b). Deforestation also displaces people and wild species from their lands. About half of the world's approximately 14 million species live in tropical forests (World Resources Institute 1998b). Once the trees are gone, these species disappear forever. Finally, soil erosion caused by deforestation may lead to flooding.

At Risk: Canadian Children and Environmental Toxins

In December 1999, a study by the Ontario College of Physicians (Environmental Health Committee) and the Canadian Environmental Law Association (CELA) concluded that the health of Canadian children was being jeopardized by weaknesses within Canada's regulatory system that governs pesticides and their use and by the failure of the Canadian government to enforce existing laws and policies. The study focused on children because of their particular susceptibility to pesticides. Compared to adults, children are relatively more frequently exposed to pesticides. Exposure to pesticide may come through everyday applications in homes and yards, residues from agricultural applications of pesticides, and through diet.

For example, a 1997 study on toxic chemicals in food and on bio-engineered food available in Canada noted that "from paint stripper to pesticides to urinal deodorizers and wood preservatives, the variety of toxic chemicals in food is truly amazing. From conception on, a Canadian child is exposed to toxins in food through the womb, the breast-milk, and the first peanut butter sandwich; children get more toxins from their food than any other way." Pork, for example, was found to contain lindane, dioxins and furans, butyl benzyl phthala pentachlorophenol, lead, selenium, cadmium, di-2-ethythexyl phtalate, PCBs, arsenic, and octochlorodibenzode. Based on data contained in dozens of government reports, databases, and scientific studies, this study also directed attention to the possible risks posed by foods bio-engineered for antibiotic resistance, pest resistance, herbicide resistance, delayed ripening, and other traits. In Canada, bio-engineered food does not have to be labelled as such and, in consequence, Canadians may unknowingly purchase some 18 federally approved engineered foods from supermarket shelves

without even knowing that they are doing so. Bio-engineered crops include, corn, potatoes, soybean, canola (for oil and margarine), and tomatoes. As Paul Burkhard, a lawyer with CELA has remarked, "[t]he government says the food is safe to eat but they generally only look at one compound at a time. Braised pork, for example, can be full of different toxins. What happens when you add them up? Are they still safe? These questions are not asked, nor studies rarely done, and the answers remain unclear."

Dr. Loren Vanderlinden, a co-author of the 1999 study, voiced some additional concerns. "Our study warns that every parent should be concerned about exposure of their children to pesticides. The potential for children's health to be affected by pesticides is undeniable. Although more research needs to be done, this does not exonerate pesticides as human toxins, especially when one considers that children are far more vulnerable to pesticides than are adults. Not only is there potential for harm, but in all likelihood some Canadian children are now enduring the negative effects of pesticides."

The 1999 research noted that, in particular, the immune systems of Inuit children were being jeopardized by exposure to many persistent chemicals, including DDE (a by-product of the pesticide DDT) through their mothers' breast-milk and through their traditional diet, which relies heavily on marine mammals, which have relatively high levels of contaminants. Children in agricultural areas may also face heightened risk of cognitive defects (i.e., damage to their nervous systems) without obvious clinical symptoms of pesticide exposure. Children from poorer families, those who live in older housing, and children with chemical sensitivities or immune system problems are also believed to have a heightened vulnerability to the effects of pesticide exposure.

The study noted that many commonly used pesticides can be detected in our

food supply and frequently at levels that would be unsafe for children. As well, pesticide use in the home puts children, pregnant women, and their potential offspring at risk of such health problems as cancer and reproductive problems in later life. "The sad message is that children's health is being impacted because of our inadequate regulatory system, a system that the federal government promised to fix as far back as 1994. Our study finds that the great majority of prior commitments remain unfulfilled. Canadians do not really have a regulator. Rather, industry has a customer services department," said Kathleen Cooper, co-author of the 1999 study.

Of the 45 recommendations made by authors of the study, many suggested changes to Canada's regulatory system. These included: (1) changes to the *Pest Control Products Act* to ensure a precautionary approach when the weight of evidence suggests a potentially unacceptable risk of harm; (2) implementation of a Federal Toxic Substances Management Policy to allow for immediate bans on pesticides that stay in the environment for a long time or accumulate in fat cells; (3) revision of the registration process for new products to ensure that their impact on children is taken into account; (4) improved inspection and enforcement by the Pest Management Regulatory Agency (PMRA) to ensure appropriate pesticide use; (5) development and application by PMRA of a sustainable pest management policy to reduce overall pesticide use; and (6) improvements to public access to information that is essential to understanding the risks posed by pesticide exposure. As Cooper observed, "[t]he message is not only that children are being impacted by pesticides but that the federal government is knowingly refusing to act to make legislative changes and spend the necessary resources. What can be more important than the health of young Canadians?"

SOURCE: Adapted from CELA 1997, 1999

A related concern is **desertification,** which occurs when semiarid land on the margins of deserts is overused. Overgrazing by cattle and other herd animals and the cutting of brush and trees for firewood leave the land denuded of vegetation and allow the desert to expand. By the year 2000, the world will have lost 25 million acres of cultivated land.

Environmental Injustice

Although environmental pollution and degradation and depletion of natural resources affect us all, some groups are more affected than others. **Environmental injustice**, also referred to as **environmental racism**, refers to the tendency for socially and politically marginalized groups to endure the worst of environmental ills. For example, in the United States, polluting industries, industrial and waste facilities, and transportation arteries (which generate vehicle emissions pollution) are often located in minority communities (Bullard 1996; Bullard and Johnson 1997). U.S. communities that are predominantly Black, Hispanic, or Native American are disproportionately affected by industrial toxins, contaminated air and drinking water, and the location of hazardous waste treatment and storage facilities. One study found, for example, that hog industries—and the associated environmental and health risks associated with hog waste—in eastern North Carolina tend to be located in communities with high Black populations, low voter registration, and low incomes (Edwards and Ladd 1998). Not only are minority communities more likely to be polluted than others are, but environmental regulations are also less likely to be enforced in these areas (Stephens 1998).

Environmental injustice affects marginalized populations around the world, including minority groups, Indigenous peoples, and other vulnerable and impoverished communities such as peasants and nomadic tribes (Renner 1996). These groups are often powerless to fight against government and corporate powers that sustain environmentally damaging industries. For example, in the early 1970s, a huge copper mine began operations on the South Pacific island of Bougainville. While profits of the copper mine benefited the central government and foreign investors, the lives of the island's inhabitants were being destroyed. Farming and traditional hunting and gathering suffered as mine pollutants covered vast areas of land, destroying local crops of cocoa and bananas, and contaminating rivers and their fish. Indigenous groups in Nigeria, such as the Urhobo, Isoko, Kalabare, and Ogoni, are facing environmental threats caused by oil production operations run by multinational corporations. Oil spills, natural gas fires, and leaks from toxic waste pits have polluted the soil, water, and air and compromised the health of various local tribes. "Formerly lush agricultural land is now covered by oil slicks, and much vegetation and wildlife has been destroyed. Many Ogoni suffer from respiratory diseases and cancer, and birth defects are frequent" (Renner 1996: 57). The environmental injustices experienced by Bougainville and the Ogoni are only the tip of the iceberg. Renner warns that "minority populations and Indigenous peoples around the globe are facing massive degradation of their environments that threatens to irreversibly alter, indeed destroy, their ways of life and cultures" (p. 59).

Environmental Illness

Exposure to pollution, toxic substances, and other environmental hazards is associated with numerous illnesses and health problems. The smoke of cooking fires fuelled by wood, coal, and other organic material contains harmful particulate matter as well as carcinogenic chemicals (such as benzene and formaldehyde). According to one World Bank study, fuel-wood cooking smoke causes the death of approximately four million children worldwide each year (Pimentel et al. 1998).

By one estimate, every 1 percent decrease in the ozone layer increases ultraviolet B (UVB) radiation by 1.4 percent, and the incidence of skin cancer is increasing accordingly. Since 1969, the rates of melanoma, a serious form of skin cancer, have increased fourfold for men and almost doubled for women in Canada. Despite public education messages alerting Canadians to the risks of sun damage, in 1996 less than half of Canadians used sunscreen, avoided the sun, or wore a sunhat or other protective clothing (Statistics Canada 1998). Destruction of the ozone layer also results in increased exposure of the eyes to radiation in sunlight, which increases the risk of cataracts (Bergman 1998).

Environmental illness also results from exposure to toxic chemicals, such as benzene, lead, pesticides, and cyanides. Of the approximately 80 000 chemicals in use today, 10 percent are recognized as carcinogens (cancer causing) (Pimentel et al. 1998). Between 1988 and 1993, one in five work-related deaths was caused by exposure to harmful substances including poisons, chemicals, radiation, and asbestos. Jobs classified under the category of "insulating occupations" collectively rank as the seventh most dangerous occupations in Canada—not because of day-to-day hazards, but because of the long-term cumulative effects of exposure to asbestos. "For those aged 65 and over, work-related exposure to harmful substances accounts for 55% of all work fatalities, even though most have already retired from the work force. For those under age 65, exposure to harmful substances accounts for 13% of all work fatalities" (Statistics Canada 1998).

Persistent organic pollutants (POPs) accumulate in the food chain, and persist in the environment, taking centuries to degrade. Although the effects of POPs on human health are unclear, many researchers believe that long-term exposure contributes to increasing rates of birth defects, fertility problems, greater susceptibility to disease, diminished intelligence, and certain cancers (Fisher 1999). The United Nations Environment Programme has identified 12 POPs that require urgent regulatory attention, nine of which are pesticides.

Threats to Biodiversity

Biodiversity refers to the great variety of life forms on Earth. In recent decades, we have witnessed mass extinction rates of diverse life forms. Most estimates suggest that at least one thousand species of life are lost per year (Tuxill 1998). Unlike the extinction of the dinosaurs millions of years ago, humans are the primary cause of disappearing species today. Air, water, and land pollution; deforestation; disruption of native habitats, and overexploitation of species for their meat, hides, horns, or medicinal or entertainment value threaten bio-diversity and the delicate balance of nature. Table 14.4 lists the percentages of various species that are currently classified as threatened.

Table 14.4	Threatened Species Worldwide

Species	Percentage of Species Threatened with Extinction
Birds	11
Mammals	25
Reptiles	20
Amphibians	25
Fish	34

SOURCE: Brown, Lester R., Gary Gardner, and Brian Halweil. 1998. *Beyond Malthus: Sixteen Dimensions of the Population Problem.* World Watch Paper 143. Washington, D.C.: Worth Watch Institute. Used by permission.

The loss of biodiversity affects everyone. The diverse forms of life on Earth provide humanity with food, fibres, and many other products and "natural services." Insects, birds, and bats provide pollination services that enable us to feed ourselves. Frogs, fish, and birds provide natural pest control. Various aquatic organisms filter and cleanse our water and plants and microorganisms enrich and renew our soil.

SOCIAL CAUSES OF ENVIRONMENTAL PROBLEMS

In addition to population growth, various other structural and cultural factors have also played a role in environmental problems.

Industrialization and Economic Development

Many of the environmental problems confronting the world have been caused by industrialization and economic development. Industrialized countries, for example, consume more energy and natural resources than developing countries. Environmental problems of developed countries are caused by industrialization, overconsumption of natural resources, and the demand for increasing quantities of goods and services. Industrialization and economic development have been the primary cause of global environmental problems such as the ozone hole and global warming (Koenig 1995). Conflict theorists argue that governments pursue economic development and industrialization at the expense of environmental conditions. In less developed countries, environmental problems are largely due to poverty and the priority of economic survival over environmental concerns. Vajpeyi (1995) explains:

> Policymakers in the Third World are often in conflict with the ever-increasing demands to satisfy basic human needs—clean air, water, adequate food, shelter, education—and to safeguard the environmental quality. Given the scarce economic and technical resources at their disposal, most of these policymakers have ignored long-range environmental concerns and opted for short-range economic and political gains. (p. 24)

International Data

Every time we turn on our air conditioners, we may be releasing CFCs into the environment. However, our consumption of CFCs and halons (another ozone-depleting substance) is slightly lower than that of most other OECD countries. In 1990, we consumed 0.6 kilograms per capita, the same amount as Spain and Denmark. On the other hand, France, Germany, the Netherlands, and the United Kingdom all consumed more than one kilogram of these substances per capita.

SOURCE: Statistics Canada 1998

Cultural Values and Attitudes

Cultural values and attitudes that contribute to environmental problems include individualism, capitalism, and materialism. Individualism puts individual interests over collective welfare. Even though recycling is good for our collective environment, many individuals do not recycle because of the personal inconvenience involved in washing and sorting recyclable items. Similarly, individuals often indulge in countless behaviours that provide enjoyment and convenience at the expense of the environment: long showers, use of dishwashing machines, recreational boating, meat eating, and use of air conditioning, to name just a few.

Finally, the influence of materialism, or the emphasis on worldly possessions, also encourages individuals to continually purchase new items and throw away old ones. The media bombard us daily with advertisements that tell us life will be better if we purchase a particular product. Materialism contributes to pollution and environmental degradation by supporting industry and contributing to garbage and waste.

The cultural value of militarism also contributes to environmental degradation. This issue is discussed in detail in Chapter 15.

STRATEGIES FOR ACTION: RESPONDING TO ENVIRONMENTAL PROBLEMS

Solving environmental problems is difficult and costly. Lowering fertility, as discussed earlier, helps reduce population pressure on the environment. Environmentalist groups, modifications in consumer behaviour, government regulations, and the development of alternative sources of energy can also alleviate environmental problems.

Environmentalist Groups

Environmentalist groups exert pressure on the government to initiate or intensify actions related to environmental protection. They also design and implement their own projects, and disseminate information to the public about environmental issues.

In North America, environmentalist groups date back to 1892 with the establishment of the Sierra Club, followed by the Audubon Society in 1905. Other environmental groups include the National Wildlife Federation, World Wildlife Fund, Environmental Defense Fund, Friends of the Earth, Union of Concerned Scientists, Canadian Environmental Law Association, Canadian Environmental Defence Fund, Canadian Environmental Network, Great Lakes United, Common Frontiers, Greenpeace, Environmental Action, Natural Resources Defense Council, World Watch Institute, National Recycling Coalition, Campaign for Nuclear Phase-Out, the New Brunswick Environmental Network, World Resources Institute, Rainforest Alliance, Global Climate Coalition, and Mothers and Others, to name a few. A recent development in the environmental movement is the emergence of **ecofeminism**—a synthesis of feminism, environmentalism, and antimilitarism.

In the mid-1980s, membership in the 10 largest environmental organizations was about four million. That figure had doubled by 1990, when it began a gradual decline (Switzer 1997).

Modifications in Consumer Behaviour

According to surveys conducted in Canada by Environics Research Group in late 1997 and early 1998, many Canadians are engaging in actions designed to preserve their physical environment or to protect their health against perceived environmental hazards, or both (Figure 14.7). In addition to those activities mentioned, smaller but still significant proportions of Canadians report either belonging to environmental groups or supporting them financially (28 percent) or voting for, or against, political candidates or parties because of their stand on environmental issues (27 percent) (Environics Research Group Ltd. 1998).

Increasingly, consumers are making choices in their behaviour and in purchases that reflect environmental awareness. For example, between 1988 and 1997, global sales of energy-efficient compact fluorescent bulbs increased eightfold (O'Meara 1998b). The estimated 980 million compact fluorescent bulbs in use today save the equivalent of roughly 100 coal-fired power plants. Recycling has also increased. In the 1970s and early 1980s, between 22 and 27 percent of wastepaper was recycled, increasing to 45 percent by 1995 (Mattoon 1998). Table 14.5 notes the household environmental practices of Canadians in 1994.

Sales of organic foods (foods on which pesticides are not used) have increased, as have other environmentally friendly products and services. From using credit card and long-distance telephone companies that donate a percentage of their profits to environmental causes to socially responsible investment services, consumers are increasingly voting with their dollars to support environmentally responsible practices. This chapter's The Human Side offers examples of how consumers can resist materialistic urges and reduce waste and overconsumption.

Alternative Sources of Energy

Generating energy from coal and oil contributes to the world's growing level of pollution. In addition, the earth's supplies of coal and oil are finite and are being depleted. Nuclear power produces harmful radioactive wastes and involves potential harm caused by accidents, such as the 1986 explosion at the Chernobyl nuclear reactor in the Soviet Ukraine. One solution to the problems associated with the use of coal and oil for energy is to use alternative sources of energy, such as solar power, geothermal power, wind power, ocean thermal power, nuclear power, tidal power, and power from converting corn, wood, or garbage.

The fastest developing alternative source of energy is wind power (see Table 14.6). While new energy technologies are promising, the World Resources Institute (1998a) suggests that "technology alone is not a panacea, and changes in consumer behaviour would be necessary to achieve rapid rates of improvement in the energy intensity of the global economy" (p. 15).

Figure 14.7

Environmentally Inspired Actions in the Past Year, Age 18+, Canada, 1997–98

SOURCES: Environics Research Group Ltd. 1997. *The Environmental Monitor, 1997, Cycle 4,* Toronto: Environics; Environics Research Group Ltd. 1998. *The Environmental Monitor, 1998, Cycle 1.* Toronto: Environics.

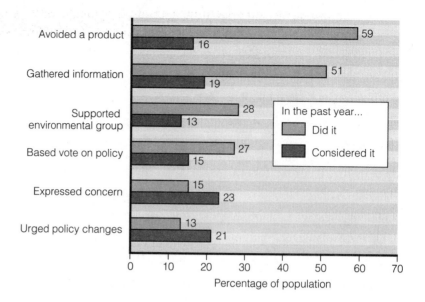

Government Regulations and Funding

Through regulations and the provision of funds, governments play a vital role in protecting and restoring the environment. Governments have responded to concerns related to air and water pollution, ozone depletion, and global warming by imposing regulations affecting the production of pollutants. Governments have also been involved in the preservation of deserts, forests, reefs, wetlands, and endangered plant and animal species.

For example, in 1985, the seven provinces east of Ontario formed the Canadian Acid Rain Control Program, agreeing to cut their total SO_2 emissions to 2.3 million tons a year by 1994. By 1993, SO_2 emissions were 1.7 million tons, a figure that was half the 1980 level. Between 1986 and 1994, the amount spent by the Canadian federal government on measures to prevent and control pollution doubled. Municipal governments, which typically have the primary responsibility for tasks such as sewage and garbage collection, have spent the greatest amount of monies on pollution controls. In 1993 alone, municipal governments spent $3.2 billion to prevent and control pollution (Statistics Canada 1998).

CONSIDERATION

Some environmentalists advocate using taxes to discourage polluting practices. Governments now rely on personal and corporate income taxes for revenue, while taxes on environmentally destructive activities are either negligible or nonexistent. Environmentalists argue that if governments heavily taxed destructive activities such as carbon emissions, sulphur emission, the generation of toxic waste, the use of pesticides, and the use of virgin raw material, these activities would decrease.

Brown and Mitchell note that "not only are we not taxing many environmentally destructive activities, some of these efforts are actually being subsidized" (p. 182). For example, more than $600 billion a year of taxpayers' money is spent to subsidize deforestation, overfishing, the burning of fossil fuels, the use of virgin raw materials, and other environmentally destructive activities. The Earth Council remarked, "There's something unbelievable about the world spending hundreds of billions of dollars annually to subsidize its own destruction."

Table 14.5   Household Environmental Practices, 1994

	Canada	Nfld.	P.E.I.	N.S.	N.B.	Que.	Ont.	Man.	Sask.	Alta.	B.C.
					% of households						
Access to recycling programs											
Paper	69.6	19.7	20.8	50.3	46.7	57.2	83.5	61.0	69.3	71.2	74.5
Metal cans	67.2	21.3	16.7	47.6	69.8	48.9	82.3	61.0	77.3	72.2	69.6
Glass bottles	67.4	12.0	18.8	47.3	72.9	50.1	82.0	58.9	74.8	72.6	70.7
Plastics	62.8	18.6	16.7	42.5	61.2	49.5	77.7	61.0	73.7	66.2	55.7
Special disposal	40.2	3.3	10.4	12.0	12.2	41.8	45.9	29.0	34.9	56.9	32.2
Use of recycling programs[1]											
Paper	83.1	44.4	70.0	72.5	58.8	74.0	92.9	48.3	73.2	75.8	88.2
Metal cans	83.5	48.7	62.5	69.6	81.5	70.0	93.3	51.2	81.0	78.7	86.0
Glass bottles	83.5	40.9	66.7	68.8	82.8	70.9	93.3	46.2	81.1	78.8	86.1
Plastics	81.7	47.1	62.5	67.4	77.6	71.4	92.2	51.2	80.8	70.8	82.4
Special disposal	57.1	66.7	80.0	65.0	64.5	54.5	60.1	48.7	46.8	53.8	59.1
Use of disposable diapers[2]											
All of the time	76.9	92.3	100.0	68.2	82.4	81.9	79.0	70.4	62.5	67.1	73.2
Most of the time	9.5	7.7	–	13.6	5.9	10.2	7.6	7.4	12.5	11.8	13.4
Sometimes	11.1	–	–	–	–	–	11.3		25.0	19.7	12.2
Never	2.0	–	–	4.5	5.9	1.7	2.1	–	–	–	–
Regularly purchase paper towels or toilet paper made from recycled paper											
	58.3	68.3	56.3	65.7	66.3	60.7	59.9	48.6	49.3	51.5	53.9
Regularly take their own bag when shopping											
	24.4	4.4	12.5	14.8	22.7	17.6	25.4	35.0	32.7	31.3	31.1
Use a compost heap, compost container, or composting service											
	22.7	9.3	16.7	19.0	16.1	7.9	30.3	18.1	21.6	21.2	37.9
Use chemical pesticide[3]											
	31.1	9.4	11.6	18.7	19.7	29.8	34.3	30.1	37.2	36.1	29.6
Use chemical fertilizer[3]											
	46.8	26.4	23.3	35.3	35.8	41.4	50.7	38.5	57.0	58.1	47.2
Have programmable thermostat[4]											
	16.0	5.6	6.7	9.4	9.1	9.7	23.6	14.9	10.2	15.1	15.3
Regularly lower temperature[5]											
	71.1	82.1	87.8	82.4	75.3	70.5	64.4	65.9	77.0	72.0	81.0

	Canada	Nfld.	P.E.I.	N.S.	N.B.	Que.	Ont.	Man.	Sask.	Alta.	B.C.
					% of households						
Use energy-efficient compact fluorescent light bulbs											
	18.9	8.2	20.8	13.3	17.6	14.2	24.6	13.1	14.1	15.9	20.0
Have water-saving, low-flow, or modified showerhead											
	42.3	27.9	33.3	40.7	42.4	46.0	44.9	34.0	26.6	32.2	43.4
Have water-saving, low-volume toilet											
	14.8	6.0	6.3	12.7	11.4	8.7	18.0	19.4	12.5	20.6	15.9
Have water filter or purifier for drinking water											
	19.5	9.8	2.1	16.3	14.2	9.7	24.9	18.4	22.7	16.4	29.1
Purchase bottled water											
	21.9	8.7	6.3	18.1	16.9	33.4	19.6	13.4	8.9	15.3	19.9
Principal method of travel to work[6]											
Public transit	13.7	–	–	6.7	2.7	14.9	16.3	10.1	3.7	11.2	14.4
Motor vehicle (driver)	78.8	79.3	85.7	80.0	82.7	76.6	79.7	78.5	80.4	80.3	77.8
Motor vehicle (passenger)	10.6	18.5	17.9	16.9	17.3	9.6	10.0	13.4	11.0	9.5	10.7
Bicycle	2.3	–	–	–	–	2.0	1.9	5.3	4.1	2.4	3.7
Walk only	7.8	12.0	–	8.7	6.7	8.5	6.3	11.3	11.4	7.4	8.7
Other	0.3	–	–	–	–	–	–	–	–	–	–
Not ascertained	5.8	5.4	–	6.7	6.7	6.2	5.5	5.3	7.3	6.3	5.2

1. Percentage calculated among households with access to each type of program.
2. Percentage calculated among households with children under two years old.
3. Percentage calculated among households with a lawn, yard, or garden.
4. Percentage calculated among households with thermostats.
5. Percentage calculated among households with thermostats, excluding households with programmable thermostats.
6. Percentage calculated among households where at least one member worked outside the home.

SOURCE: Canadian Global Almanac 2000

Table 14.6   **Trends in Energy Use, by Source, 1990–97**

Energy Source	Annual Rate of Growth
Wind power	25.7
Solar power	16.8
Geothermal power	3.0
Natural gas	2.1
Hydroelectric power	1.6
Oil	1.4
Coal	1.2
Nuclear power	0.6

SOURCE: Lester R. Brown, Gary Gardner, and Brian Halweil. 1998. *Beyond Malthus: Sixteen Dimensions of the Population Problem*. World Watch Paper 143. Washington, D.C.: World Watch Institute. Used by permission.

ESCAPE FROM AFFLUENZA

A 1997 PBS television program, *Affluenza*, explored "the high social and environmental costs of materialism and overconsumption." In a 1998 sequel, *Escape from Affluenza*, people working to reduce waste and overconsumption and live their lives in balance with the environment are profiled. Below is a partial list, by category, of some of the ways you can *Escape from Affluenza*.

Shopping
- Biggest shopping trap—it was on sale. If it was not something you identified as a need, you did not save money, you spent money. Learn this mantra: It is not a bargain if I don't need it.
- Mail-order shopping is a great way to save time, fuel, and money. But avoid the companies that make up the cost of glossy catalogues by charging twice as much. About 94 percent of these catalogues go unused into the waste stream: don't be one of the 6 percent who pay more to make this practice profitable!
- The average family of four spends an estimated 10 percent of its annual income on clothing. Using principles you already know (only buying what you need, buying secondhand items that are as good as new, for instance), you can easily cut your clothing expenditures in half.

Waste and Clutter
- A poorly insulated house can easily waste 30 to 50 percent of the energy poured into it... Simple changes around the house: run the dishwasher half as often as you do now, and save 50 percent in water, energy and time. Wash only full loads of clothing, and, since 90 percent of the cost of washing clothes is to heat the water, avoid using hot water.
- Half of the average family's household energy goes to heating and cooling, at a cost of about $450 a year. Put a 15 percent dent in this expense by keeping the thermostat set at 65°F [14°C] in the daytime, and 55°F or 60°F [13°C to 16°C] at night.
- Planting a large tree to shade your home can save you an estimated $73 a year in air-conditioning bills. If every household did this, the country would save more than $4 billion in energy costs.
- An estimated 50 percent of the waste stream is discarded packaging. Be very aware of packaging excess, and when all else is equal, choose the least-packaged. Help raise awareness of this issue by being a packaging activist: ask your grocers to phase out pre-wrapped fruits and vegetables.

Home and Hearth
- When home-hunting, pick the smallest amount of space in which you are comfortable. This will limit the amount of stuff you can accumulate, and take far less of your time and resources to furnish, clean, maintain, insure, and pay for.
- Eighty percent of the dirt in your home is brought in on shoes. Save time and cleaning expenses by starting a no-shoes policy.
- Start a neighbourhood swap of seldom-used tools. Why should a street of 10 houses have 10 lawn-mowers, 10 paint-sprayers, and 10 band saws (or 55 Disney videos, for that matter)?

THE HUMAN SIDE

ESCAPE FROM AFFLUENZA (continued)

Food

- Eat a local diet as much as possible. This creates jobs in the region, reduces transportation costs and energy consumption, ensures higher nutritional value and encourages local small-scale agriculture that protects land from development. Ask your grocers to mark foods local. Hint—If it's out of season (e.g., strawberries in December in Manitoba), you know it's not local.
- To dramatically reduce your ecological footprint, save about 50 percent in food costs and maximize your prospects for a longer, healthier life—become a vegetarian.

Health and Happiness

- Prevention is the cheapest and best health insurance. Get an annual checkup. Take care of your body by eating and sleeping right, and stop smoking.
- Stop equating the amount of fun and pleasure you get with the amount of money you spend to get it. Sit down and make a list of 25 things you like to do that cost little or no money, and keep it where you can see it every day.
- Instead of spending your time and energy buying and taking care of stuff, volunteer to feed the hungry, care for the suffering, visit the lonely, or mentor a child.
- Be happy with what you have. If you make a habit of thinking in terms of what you have, rather than what you don't, you may well find that you have enough.

SOURCE: Adapted from *100 Ways to Escape from Affluenza* as appears on <www.pbs.org/kcts/affluenza/escape> by Vivia Boe. Reprinted by permission. Films are available from bullfrog films, 800-543-FROG or <www.bullfrogfilms.com>.

International Cooperation

Global environmental concerns such as global warming and climate change require international governmental cooperation. In 1997, delegates from 160 nations met in Kyoto, Japan, and forged the Kyoto Protocol—the first international agreement to place legally binding limits on greenhouse gas emissions from developed countries. As part of this protocol, Canada has promised to reduce its emissions to 6 percent below its 1990 levels by 2008 to 2012. To date, however, Canada has had limited success. In 1995, Canada ranked fourth (behind the United States, Australia, and Luxembourg) among OECD in carbon dioxide output per capita (Statistics Canada 1998).

The 1972 Stockholm Conference on the Human Environment, the United Nations Environment Programme (UNEP) since the 1970s, and the 1983 World Commission on Environment and Development all represent efforts to address environmental concerns at the international level. The 1992 Earth Summit in Rio de Janeiro—a 12-day event—brought together heads of states, delegates from more than 170 nations, representatives from nongovernmental organizations, representatives of Indigenous people, and members of the media to discuss an international agenda for both economic development and the environment. International cooperative efforts have resulted in, for example, the Global Environmental Facility (GEF), located at the World Bank in Washington, and the United Nations' International Environmental Technology Center in Osaka and Shiga, Japan. The United Nations Development Programme supports countries in environmental management. The 1992 Earth Summit in Rio resulted in the Rio Declaration—"a nonbinding statement of broad principles to guide environmental policy, vaguely committing its signatories not to damage the environment of other nations by activities within their borders and to acknowledge environmental protection as an integral part of development" (Koenig 1995: 15).

Another example of international cooperation on environmental issues is the agreement made by 70 nations to curb the production of CFCs, which contribute to ozone depletion and global warming. The largest consumers of CFCs have established a fund to help developing countries acquire alternatives to CFCs (Koenig 1995).

Because industrialized countries have more economic and technological resources, they bear primary responsibility for leading the nations of the world toward environmental cooperation. Jan (1995) emphasizes the importance of international environmental cooperation and the role of developed countries in this endeavour:

> Advanced countries must be willing to sacrifice their own economic well-being to help improve the environment of the poor, developing countries. Failing to do this will lead to irreparable damage to our global environment. Environmental protection is no longer the affair of any one country. It has become an urgent global issue. Environmental pollution recognizes no national boundaries. No country, especially a poor country, can solve this problem alone. (pp. 82–3)

Sustainable Economic Development: An International Agenda

Achieving global cooperation on environmental issues is difficult, in part, because developed countries (primarily in the Northern Hemisphere) have different economic agendas from developing countries (primarily in the Southern Hemisphere). The northern agenda emphasizes preserving wealth, affluent lifestyles, and the welfare state while the southern agenda focuses on overcoming mass poverty and achieving a higher quality of life (Koenig 1995). Southern countries are concerned that northern industrialized countries—having already achieved economic wealth—will impose international environmental policies that restrict the economic growth of developing countries just as they are beginning to industrialize. Global strategies to preserve the environment must address both wasteful lifestyles in some nations and the need to overcome overpopulation and widespread poverty in others.

Development involves more than economic growth, it involves sustainability—the long-term environmental, social, and economic health of societies. **Sustainable development** involves meeting the needs of the present world without endangering the ability of future generations to meet their own needs. Achieving sustainable development has become a primary goal of governments throughout the world.

Because population increases exponentially, the size of the world's population has grown and will continue to grow at a staggering rate. Given the problems associated with population growth—deteriorating socioeconomic conditions, depletion of natural resources, and urban crowding—most governments recognize the value of controlling population size. Efforts to control population must go beyond providing safe, effective, and affordable methods of birth control. Slowing population growth necessitates interventions that change the cultural and structural bases for high fertility rates. These interventions include increasing economic development and improving the status of women, which includes raising their levels of education, their economic position, and their (and their children's) health.

Many countries have reported declining fertility rates in recent years: Bangladesh, from 6.2 children per woman to 3.4; India, from 4.5 to 3.4; Pakistan from 6.5 to 5.5; Turkey, from 4.1 to 2.7; Syria from 7.4 to 4.7, and Kenya, from 7.5 to 5.4 ("Fertility Declines Reported" 1997). Such accomplishments have helped to slow population growth. Unfortunately, high mortality rates from HIV/AIDS and war have also contributed to the slowing of population growth. Although birthrates have decreased in most countries throughout the world, population continues to grow; because of past high fertility rates, more young women than ever are currently entering their childbearing years. In addition, low contraception use and high fertility rates persist in many less developed countries. These factors combined—population momentum and continued high fertility rates in some countries—contribute to escalating world population. As noted earlier, 65 countries are expected to double their populations in 30 years or less, and 14 countries will triple or nearly triple their populations by 2050. "The impact of population growth in these fast-growing countries will more than offset the gains of low fertility in 80 other countries" (Population Institute 1998: 3).

Rapid and dramatic population growth, along with expanding world industrialization and patterns of consumption, has contributed to environmental problems. The greater numbers of people make increased demands on natural resources and generate excessive levels of pollutants. Environmental problems are due not only to large populations, but also to the ways in which these populations live and work. As conflict theorists argue, individuals, private enterprises, and governments have tended to choose economic and political interests over environmental concerns.

Many believe in a technological fix for the environment—that science and technology will solve environmental problems. Paradoxically, the same environmental problems that have been caused by technological progress may be solved by technological innovations designed to clean up pollution and preserve natural resources. While technological innovation is important in resolving environmental concerns, other social changes are needed as well. Addressing the values that guide choices, the economic contexts in which the choices are made, and the governmental policies that encourage various choices are critical to resolving environmental and population problems.

Global cooperation is also vital to resolving environmental concerns, but is difficult to achieve because rich and poor countries have different economic development agendas: poor developing countries struggle to survive and provide for the basic needs of their citizens; wealthy developed countries struggle to maintain their wealth and relatively high standard of living. Can both agendas be achieved without further pollution and destruction of the environment? Is sustainable economic development an attainable goal? The answer must be yes.

CRITICAL THINKING

1. One writer observed that "on a certain November Day an obscure woman in Iowa gives birth to seven babies; we marvel and rejoice. On the same day an obscure woman in Nigeria gives birth to her seventh child in a row; we are distressed and appalled" (Zwingle 1998: 38). Why might reactions to these two events be so different?

2. In many developing countries that have strict laws against abortion, the use of child labour is common. Do you think there may a connection between laws prohibiting abortion and child labour in developing countries? How could you find out if there is a connection?

3. Do you think governments should regulate reproductive behaviour to control population growth? If so, how?

4. Babies eat more, drink more, and breathe more, proportionally, than adults—which means babies are more susceptible to environmental toxins than are adults (Dionis 1999). Yet, federal environmental standards are largely set at levels designed to protect adults. What social forces do you think discourage the government from setting environmental standards based on what is safe for infants and young children?

KEY TERMS

acid rain
biodiversity
deforestation
demographic transition
   theory
demography
desertification
doubling time

ecofeminism
environmental injustice
environmental racism
fertility rate
greenwashing
human ecology
Malthusian theory

multiple chemical
   sensitivity (MCS)
planned obsolescence
pronatalism
replacement level
sick building syndrome
   (SBS)
sustainable development

CHAPTER FIFTEEN

Conflict around the World

Is It True?

1. In Canada, the defence budget grew by nearly 50 percent during the last decade.

2. The resolution of conflict between nations also tends to result in the resolution of conflict within nations.

3. Although the military causes a great deal of environmental damage during wartime, during times of peace, military forces are geared to help clean up the environment.

4. Military spending in the world as a whole has far exceeded spending for health care and education, especially in poor countries.

5. In 1998, the combined total of U.S. and Russian warheads was estimated to be 34 000. Only five hundred to two thousand are needed to induce a nuclear winter and destroy most of life on earth.

Answers: 1 = F, 2 = F, 3 = F, 4 = T, 5 = T

The history of the world is a history of conflict. Never in recorded history has there been a time when conflict did not exist between and within groups. The most violent form of conflict—**war**—refers to organized armed violence aimed at a social group in pursuit of an objective. Wars have existed throughout human history and continue in the contemporary world (see Figure 15.1)

War is one of the great paradoxes of human history. It both protects and annihilates. It creates and defends nations but also destroys them. Whether war is just or unjust, defensive or offensive, it involves the most horrendous atrocities known to humankind. This chapter focuses on the causes and consequences of global conflict and war. Along with population and environmental problems, war and global conflict are among the most serious of all social problems in their threat to the human race and life on earth.

> What a power is there for good in the world, what a power to right many wrongs, to solve many problems, in amity, without recourse to arms.
>
> Georges Vanier,
> Former Governor
> General of Canada
> (1959–67)

THE GLOBAL CONTEXT: CONFLICT IN A CHANGING WORLD

As societies have evolved and changed throughout history, the nature of war has also changed. Before industrialization and the sophisticated technology that resulted, war occurred primarily between neighbouring groups on a relatively small scale. In the modern world, war can be waged between nations that are separated by thousands of miles, as well as between neighbouring nations. In the following sections, we examine how war has changed our social world and how our changing social world has affected the nature of war in the industrial and postindustrial information age.

Figure 15.1

As of 1999, conflict existed in the world at more than 33 different locations.

SOURCE: Map design by Aaron Bradley, <www.cfcsc.dnd.ca/links/wars/index.html>. Copyright © 1996–1998, Information Resource Centre, Canadian Forces College. Reprinted by permission.

War and the Development of Civilization

The very act that now threatens modern civilization—war—is largely responsible for creating the advanced civilization in which we live. Before large political states existed, people lived in small groups and villages. War broke the barriers of autonomy between local groups and permitted small villages to be incorporated into larger political units known as "chiefdoms." Centuries of warfare between chiefdoms culminated in the development of the state. The **state** is "an apparatus of power, a set of institutions—the central government, the armed forces, the regulatory and police agencies—whose most important functions involve the use of force, the control of territory and the maintenance of internal order" (Porter 1994: 5–6). The creation of the state in turn led to other profound social and cultural changes:

> And once the state emerged, the gates were flung open to enormous cultural advances, advances undreamed of during—and impossible under—a regimen of small autonomous villages....Only in large political units, far removed in structure from the small autonomous communities from which they sprang, was it possible for great advances to be made in the arts and sciences, in economics and technology, and indeed in every field of culture central to the great industrial civilizations of the world. (Carneiro 1994: 14–5)

Thus, war, in a sense, gave rise to the state. Interestingly, the development of the state reduced the amount of lethal conflict (i.e., death through war, execution, homicide, or rebellion) in a society by providing alternative means of dispute resolution (Cooney 1997).

The Influence of Industrialization on War

Industrialization and technology could not have developed in the small social groups that existed before military action consolidated them into larger states. Thus, war contributed indirectly to the industrialization and technological sophistication that characterize the modern world.

Industrialization, in turn, has had two major influences on war. Cohen (1986) calculated the number of wars fought per decade in industrial and pre-industrial nations and concluded that "as societies become more industrialized, their proneness to warfare decreases" (p. 265). Cohen summarized the evidence for this conclusion: the preindustrial nations had an overall mean of 10.6 wars per decade, while the industrial nations averaged 2.7 wars per decade. Perhaps industrialized nations have more to lose, so they avoid war and the risk of defeat. Consider, in this context, Gentry's (1998) observation that U.S. leaders "are increasingly reluctant to use [military forces] in roles that could lead to casualties in combat." The result—a "national aversion to danger" (pp. 179–80). Similarly, in Canada, Joel Sokolsky, a professor at the Royal Military College in Kingston, has commented that "[r]ealism in foreign policy begins at home. And, realistically, neither the government nor the people will support the type of defence spending [that]...would allow us to meet a wide range of contingencies abroad. We should step away from the plate for a little while" (in Thompson 1999).

Although industrialization may decrease a society's propensity to war, it also increases the potential destruction of war. With industrialization, military technology became more sophisticated and more lethal. Rifles and cannons replaced the clubs, arrows, and swords used in more primitive warfare and in turn were replaced by tanks, bombers, and nuclear warheads. This chapter's Focus on Technology looks at how modern computers and information technology are transforming warfare capabilities.

The Economics of Military Spending

The increasing sophistication of military technology has commanded a large share of resources totalling, worldwide, $740 billion in 1997. Military spending has, however, declined in recent years, averaging a 4.5 percent decrease in the past decade. Military spending includes expenditures for salaries of military personnel, research and development, weapons, veterans' benefits, and other defence-related expenses. The largest cuts have occurred in Russia, the United States, Africa, and Central America (SIPRI 1998). In Canada, the defence budget has been cut by nearly 25 percent in the last decade. Between 1994 and 1999, Canada's defence budget also fell from $12 billion to $9.25 billion. Although proposed capital spending on defence projects totalled about $11 billion in 1999, merely $6.5 billion was available under existing budgets. Consider as well that our regular force strength of approximately 60 000 members (47 000 non-commissioned members and the rest officers) is 28 800 less than it was in 1989. In 1999, Alain Pellerin, the executive director of the Conference of Defence Association, a promilitary lobby group, argued before the Commons finance committee that, because of massive budget cuts that have affected virtually every aspect of Canada's military, "parts of the Canadian Forces, especially the army, are on the verge of collapse" (in Thompson 1999).

The **Cold War,** the state of political tension and military rivalry that existed between the United States and the former Soviet Union, provided justification for large expenditures on military preparedness. The end of the Cold War, along with concerns about our national debt, has resulted in cutbacks in the military budget.

The economic impact of defence cutbacks around the world has been mixed. On the negative side, defence cutbacks result in job losses and the closure of military bases, facilities, factories, and plants in defence industries. Certain industries and the countries, regions, and states where they are located suffer disproportionately because of defence cutbacks. Worldwide, 8.3 million jobs were lost in the defence industry between 1987 and 1996—47 percent of the 1987 total (BICC 1998).

On the positive side, defence cutbacks provide a **peace dividend**, in that resources previously spent on military purposes can be used for private or public investment or consumption. For example, the peace dividend could be used for new manufacturing plants and machinery (private investment) or for public education, transportation, housing, health, or the environment. The peace dividend could also be used to lower the national debt or taxes.

Achieving a peace dividend requires the reallocation of resources from military forces and defence industries to other sectors of the economy—a process referred to as **economic conversion**. For example, military bases could be converted to civil airports, prisons, housing developments, or shopping centres, and workers in the defence industry could be employed in the civil sector.

Information Warfare

In the postindustrial information age, computer technology has revolutionized the nature of warfare and future warfare capabilities. Today, a "whole range of new technologies are offered for the next generations of weapons and military operations" (BICC 1998: 3), including the use of high-performance sensors, information processors, directed-energy technologies, and precision-guided munitions (BICC 1998; O'Prey 1995). With the increasing proliferation and power of computer technology, military strategists and political leaders are exploring the horizons of "information warfare," or **infowar**. Essentially, infowar uses technology to attack or manipulate the military and civilian infrastructure and information systems of an enemy. Infowar capabilities include the following (Waller 1995):

- Breaking into the communications equipment of the enemy army and disseminating incorrect information to enemy military leaders.
- Inserting computer viruses into the computer systems that control the phone system, electrical power, banking, stock exchanges, and air-traffic control of an enemy country.
- Jamming signals on the enemy's government television station and inserting a contrived TV program that depicts enemy leaders making unpopular statements that will alienate their people.
- Incapacitating the enemy's military computer systems, such as the one that operates the weapons system.

For example, by 2010, the U.S. army hopes to digitize the battlefield by linking every soldier and weapons system electronically. Further, a prototype of the equipment to be used by the infantry in the twenty-first century is currently being developed:

> His helmet will be fitted with microphones and earphones for communications, night-vision goggles and thermal-imaging sensors to see in the dark, along with a heads-up display in front of his eyes to show him where he is on the ground and give him constant intelligence reports. (Waller 1995: 41)

The U.S. army, navy, and air force are setting up infowar offices. In 1995, the first 16 infowar officers graduated from the National Defense University in Washington after being specially trained in everything from defending against computer attacks to using virtual reality computer technology to plan battle manoeuvres.

Two concerns exist with the use of infowar technologies. The first is who will become infowar leaders? Currently, the United States is the world leader but other countries are challenging their dominant position (Bernstein and Libicki 1998). For example, France now leads in digitizing three-dimensional battles, a process in which information technologies are used to "acquire, exchange and employ timely information throughout the battlespace." (Cook 1996: 602).

A second problem is that infowar is relatively inexpensive and readily available. With a computer, a modem, and some rudimentary knowledge of computers, anyone could initiate an information attack (Broder 1999). Nation-states are not the only entities to be feared. Any individual or group with a cause could potentially become an "infowarrior."

It was the United States's concern with vulnerability to infowar that led, in 1999, to new regulations that severely curtailed Canada's once-favoured status for cross-border defence, satellite, and aerospace contracts. For almost six decades, Canadian contractors were treated essentially the same as Americans in bidding on U.S. military work; no other country had such a special relationship. However, the fear that sensitive military expertise might be diverted through Canada to unfriendly places was acted on. On April 12, 1999, the U.S. State Department removed Canada's exemption under the U.S. International Trafficking in Arms Regulations, or ITAR, which governs the sale of American weaponry and defence technology. In consequence, Canadian companies must now follow cumbersome approval procedures before doing defence-related work for the U.S. government—including work as subcontractors to U.S. firms.

This development was of no small concern to Canada. Cross-border trade in defence products is worth about $1 billion a year to Canadian companies, and the industry reports that up to a third of its 50 000 jobs are at risk, many of them high-tech engineering and computer positions. Related work in aerospace and satellite technology may also be affected. Canadian firms must now wait 100 days, or more than 14 weeks, to get technical specifications for sensitive contract work, even though bids typically close in six to eight weeks—effectively excluding them from the competition.

SOURCES: Bernstein Alvin, and Martin Libicki. 1998. "High-Tech: The Future of War." *Commentary* 105: 28–37; BICC (Bonn International Center for Conversion). 1998. "Chapter Six." *Conversion Survey, 1998.* Bonn, Germany: BICC; Broder, John. 1999. "President Steps up War on New Terrorism." *New York Times,* January 23: 14; Cook, Nick. 1996. "Battlespace 2000." *Interavia Business and Technology* 51: 43–4; O'Prey, Kevin P. 1995. *The Arms Export Challenge: Cooperative Approaches to Export Management and Defense Conversion.* Washington, D.C.: The Brookings Institute; Waller, Douglas. 1995. "Onward Cyber Soldiers." *Time,* August 21: 38–44.

SOCIOLOGICAL THEORIES OF CONFLICT AND WAR

Sociological perspectives can help us understand various aspects of war. In this section, we describe how structural-functionalism, conflict theory, and symbolic interactionism may be applied to the study of conflict and war.

Structural-Functionalist Perspective

Structural-functionalism focuses on the functions war serves and suggests that war would not exist unless it had positive outcomes for society. It has already been noted that war has served to consolidate small autonomous social groups into larger political states. An estimated 600 000 autonomous political units existed in the world around the year 1000 B.C. Today, that number has dwindled to fewer than 200 (Carneiro 1994).

Another major function of war is that it produces social cohesion and unity among societal members by giving them a common cause and a common enemy. Unless a war is extremely unpopular, military conflict promotes economic and political cooperation. Internal domestic conflicts between political parties, minority groups, and special interest groups dissolve as they unite to fight the common enemy. During World War II, Canadian citizens worked together as a nation to help defeat Germany and Japan.

In the short term, war also increases employment and stimulates the economy. For example, in the United States, the increased production needed to fight World War II helped pull the United States out of the Great Depression. Investments in the manufacturing sector during World War II also had a long-term affect on the U.S. economy. Hooks and Bloomquist (1992) studied the effect of the war on the U.S. economy between 1947 and 1972 and concluded that the U.S. government "directed, and in large measure, paid for a 65% expansion of the total investment in plant and equipment" (p. 304). The Canadian economy also boomed during World War II and the gross national product doubled. WWII promoted development in industry (which continued to expand in peacetime); consumer spending, which had increased dramatically during the war years, continued to rise with the postwar baby boom. In consequence, the years following World War II saw Canadians enjoying a standard of living that was in stark contrast to the years of the Depression (*Canadian Global Almanac* 2000).

Another function of war is the inspiration of scientific and technological developments that are useful to civilians. Research on laser-based defence systems led to laser surgery, for example, and research in nuclear fission and fusion facilitated the development of nuclear power. The airline industry owes much of its technology to the development of air power by the U.S. Department of Defense, and the Internet was created by the Pentagon for military purposes. Presently, researchers are developing insect-like robots that will act as scouts in detecting the presence of enemy forces. The five-centimetre tall spies will also be made available to police SWAT teams and other emergency personnel (Koerner 1998).

Finally, war serves to encourage social reform. After a major war, members of society have a sense of shared sacrifice and a desire to heal wounds and rebuild normal patterns of life. They put political pressure on the state to care for war victims, improve social and political conditions, and reward those who have sacrificed lives, family members, and property in battle. As Porter (1994) explains:

> Only the promise of a better world can give meaning to a terrible conflict. Since...the lower economic strata usually contribute more of their blood in battle than the wealthier classes, war often gives impetus to social welfare reforms. (p. 19)

Conflict Perspective

Conflict theorists emphasize that the roots of war often stem from antagonisms that emerge whenever two or more ethnic groups (e.g., Bosnians and Serbs), countries (United States and Vietnam), or regions within countries (the U.S. North and South) struggle for control of resources or have different political, economic, or religious ideologies. Further, conflict theory suggests that war benefits the corporate, military, and political elites. Corporate elites benefit because war often results in the victor taking control of the raw materials of the losing nations, thereby creating a bigger supply of raw materials for its own industries. Indeed, many corporations profit from defence spending. In the United States, under the Pentagon's bid and proposal program, for example, corporations can charge the cost of preparing proposals for new weapons as overhead on their Defense Department contracts. In addition, Pentagon contracts often guarantee a profit to the developing corporations. Even if the project's cost exceeds initial estimates, called a cost overrun, the corporation still receives the agreed on profit. In the late 1950s, President Dwight D. Eisenhower referred to this close association between the military and the defence industry as the **military-industrial complex**.

The military elite benefit because war and the preparations for it provide prestige and employment for military officials. For example, Military Professional Resources, Inc. (MPRI), in Virginia, is described in its brochure as "a corporation of former military leaders organized to provide a wide range of professional and technical services" (Harris 1996: 12). The company employs more than 2000 retired military professionals, has clients around the world, and represents a movement toward the privatization of the military.

War also benefits the political elite by giving government officials more power. Porter (1994) observed that "throughout modern history, war has been the lever by which...governments have imposed increasingly larger tax burdens on increasingly broader segments of society, thus enabling ever-higher levels of spending to be sustained, even in peacetime" (p. 14). Political leaders who lead their country to a military victory also benefit from the prestige and hero status conferred on them.

Symbolic Interactionist Perspective

The symbolic interactionist perspective focuses on how meanings and definitions influence attitudes and behaviours regarding conflict and war. The development of attitudes and behaviours that support war begins in childhood. Movies romanticize war, children play war games with toy weapons (or GI Joe action figures), and various video and computer games glorify heroes conquering villains. Indeed, from 1938 to 1942 a series of "Horrors of Wars" cards were manufactured and distributed in the United States and collected by millions of American youth much like baseball cards (Nelson 1999). When compared to the United States, Canada has been called an "unmilitary community," but children may still be encouraged to view belonging to groups such as the Junior Canadian Rangers or cadets as a symbol of patriotism. Each year, programs affiliated with Canada's Department of National Defence provide employment or training to approximately 75 000 young Canadians—more than any other organization in Canada. Nationwide sea, army, and air cadet programs are designed as youth development programs in which cadets, aged 12 to 19, are taught citizenship, physical fitness, leadership, and activities related to their environment. For young Canadians who live in isolated communities, Junior Canadian Rangers provides similar programs.

CONSIDERATION

Arguing that "political cultures operate as historical systems of meaning," Olick and Levy (1997: 934) investigated the impact of collective definitions of the Holocaust on German political claims-making. The authors, using official records of the Federal Republic of Germany, traced post–World War II efforts to redefine Germany's negative image as a function of evolving definitions of the causes and consequences of the Nazi regime. Consistent with a symbolic interactionist perspective, the authors conclude that Germany's "ongoing work to define who it is, what it can do, and what it should do" is dependent on a "continuous negotiation between past and present" (p. 934).

Symbolic interactionism helps to explain how military recruits and civilians develop a mind-set for war by defining war and its consequences as acceptable and necessary. The word "war" has achieved a positive connotation through its use in various phrases—the "war on drugs," the "war on poverty," and the "war on crime." Positive labels and favourable definitions of military personnel facilitate military recruitment and public support of armed forces. Military personnel wear uniforms that command public respect and earn badges and medals that convey their status as heroes.

Many government and military officials convince the masses that the way to ensure world peace is to be prepared for war. Most world governments preach peace through strength rather than strength through peace. Governments may use propaganda and appeals to patriotism to generate support for war efforts and motivate individuals to join armed forces.

To legitimize war, the act of killing in war is not regarded as "murder." Deaths that result from war are referred to as "casualties." Bombing military and civilian targets appears more acceptable when nuclear missiles are "peacekeepers" that are equipped with multiple "peace heads." Killing the enemy is more acceptable when derogatory and dehumanizing labels such as Gook, Jap, Chink, and Kraut convey the attitude that the enemy is less than human.

CAUSES OF WAR

The causes of war are numerous and complex. Most wars involve more than one cause. The immediate cause of a war may be a border dispute, for example, but religious tensions that have existed between the two countries for decades may also contribute to the war. The following section reviews various causes of war.

Conflict over Land and Other Natural Resources

Nations often go to war in an attempt to acquire or maintain control over natural resources, such as land, water, and oil. Disputed borders are one of the most common motives for war. Conflicts are most likely to arise when borders are physically easy to cross and are not clearly delineated by natural boundaries, such as major rivers, oceans, or mountain ranges.

Water is another valuable resource that has led to wars. At various times the empires of Egypt, Mesopotamia, India, and China all went to war over irrigation rights. Recently, Serbia's desire for access to the Adriatic Sea has contributed to the conflict between the Bosnian Serbs and the Muslims of Bosnia and Herzegovina.

Not only do the oil-rich countries in the Middle East present a tempting target in themselves, but war in the region can also threaten other nations that are dependent on Middle Eastern oil. Thus, when Iraq seized Kuwait and threatened the supply of oil from the Persian Gulf, many nations reacted militarily in the Gulf War. In a document prepared for the Center for Strategic and International Studies, Starr and Stoll (1989) warned that

> By the year 2000, water, not oil will be the dominant resource issue of the Middle East. According to World Watch Institute, "despite modern technology and feats of engineering, a secure water future for much of the world remains elusive." The prognosis for Egypt, Jordan, Israel, the West Bank, the Gaza Strip, Syria, and Iraq is especially alarming. If present consumption patterns continue, emerging water shortages, combined with a deterioration in water quality, will lead to more competition and conflict. (p. 1)

Conflict over Values and Ideologies

Many countries initiate war not over resources, but over beliefs. World War II was largely a war over differing political ideologies: democracy versus fascism. The Cold War involved the clashing of opposing economic ideologies: capitalism versus communism. Wars over differing religious beliefs have led to some of the worst episodes of bloodshed in history, in part, because some religions are partial to martyrdom—the idea that dying for one's beliefs leads to eternal salvation. The Shiites (one of the two main sects within Islam) in the Middle East represent a classic example of holy warriors who feel divine inspiration to kill the enemy.

Conflicts over values or ideologies are not easily resolved. The conflict between secularism and Islam has lasted for 14 centuries (Lewis 1990). According to Brown (1994), wars fought over values and ideologies are less likely to end in compromise or negotiation because they are fuelled by people's convictions and their desire to spread their way of life.

If ideological differences can contribute to war, do ideological similarities discourage war? The answer seems to be yes; generally, countries with similar ideologies are less likely to engage in war with each other than are countries with differing ideological values (Dixon 1994). Democratic nations are particularly disinclined to wage war against one another (Doyle 1986).

Racial and Ethnic Hostilities

Ethnic groups vary in their cultural and religious beliefs, values, and traditions. Thus, conflicts between ethnic groups often stem from conflicting values and ideologies. Racial and ethnic hostilities are also fuelled by competition over land and other natural and economic resources. Gioseffi (1993) notes that "experts agree that the depleted world economy, wasted on war efforts, is in great measure the reason for renewed ethnic and religious strife. 'Haves' fight with 'have-nots' for the smaller piece of the pie that must go around" (xviii). As noted in Chapter 8, racial and ethnic hostilities are also perpetuated by the wealthy majority to divert attention away from their exploitations and to maintain their own position of power.

Gioseffi (1993) conveys the idiocy and irony of racial and ethnic hostilities:

> At this dangerous juncture, as we near the year 2000, after more than eighty centuries of art and human creativity, philosophy, music, poetry, social and biological science—we humans, considered the paragon of animals in our ability to think, named *Homo sapiens*, meaning wise or knowing animal, persist, brutishly, in hating and killing each other for the colours of our skin, the shapes of our features, our places of origin on our common terra firma, our styles of culture or language, and most ironically of all our "religious" beliefs—despite the fact that all the great religions of the Earth teach the same basic golden rule: "Do unto others as you would have them do unto you." (xlix)

International Data

Following the 1998 Northern Ireland–United Kingdom peace plan, a car bomb exploded in Omagh, Northern Ireland, killing 29 people and wounding more than 200.

SOURCE: "Light of Day in Bloody Eire" 1998

CONSIDERATION

As described by Paul (1998), sociologist Daniel Chirot argues that the recent worldwide increase in ethnic hostilities is a consequence of "retribalization," that is, the tendency for groups, lost in a globalized culture, to seek solace in the "extended family of an ethnic group" (p. 56). Chirot identifies five levels of ethnic conflict: (1) multiethnic societies without serious conflict (e.g., Switzerland), (2) multiethnic societies with controlled conflict (e.g., United States, Canada), (3) societies with ethnic conflict that has been resolved (e.g., South Africa), (4) societies with serious ethnic conflict leading to warfare (e.g., Sri Lanka), and (5) societies with genocidal ethnic conflict, including "ethnic cleansing" (e.g., Germany, Yugoslavia).

Defence against Hostile Attacks

The threat or fear of being attacked may cause the leaders of a country to declare war on the nation that poses the threat. The threat may come from a foreign country or from a group within the country. After Germany invaded Poland in 1939, Britain and France declared war on Germany out of fear that they would be Germany's next victims. Germany attacked Russia in World War I, in part out of fear that Russia had entered the arms race and would use its weapons against Germany. Japan bombed Pearl Harbor hoping to avoid a later confrontation with the U.S. Pacific Fleet, which posed a threat to the Japanese military. In 1981, the Israelis conducted an air raid against Iraq's nuclear facilities in an attempt to disarm Iraq and remove its threat to Israel (Brown 1994).

Revolution

Revolutions involve citizens warring against their own government. A revolution may occur when a government is not responsive to the concerns and demands of its citizens and when there are strong leaders willing to mount opposition to the government (Brown 1994).

The birth of the United States resulted from colonists revolting against British control. Contemporary examples of civil war include Sri Lanka, where the Tamils, a separatist group living in the northern region of the country, have been at war with the Sri Lankan government for more than 10 years. According to Mylvaganam (1998), the Liberation of Tamil Tigers (LTTE) has successfully fought off the better-prepared Sri Lankan government army through the "use of paramilitary and guerrilla warfare, coupled with their expert knowledge of the terrain..." (p. 1). Additionally, civil wars have erupted in newly independent republics created by the collapse of communism in Eastern Europe, as well as in Rwanda, Liberia, Guatemala, Chile, and Uganda.

Nationalism

Some countries engage in war in an effort to maintain or restore their national pride. For example, Scheff (1994) argues that "Hitler's rise to power was laid by the treatment Germany received at the end of World War I at the hands of the victors" (p. 121). Excluded from the League of Nations, punished by the Treaty of Versailles, and ostracized by the world community, Germany turned to nationalism as a reaction to material and symbolic exclusion.

In the late 1970s, Iranian fundamentalist groups took hostages from the American Embassy in Iran. U.S. President Carter's attempt to use military forces to free the hostages was not successful. That failure intensified doubts about America's ability to effectively use military power to achieve its goals. The hostages in Iran were eventually released after President Reagan took office. Doubts about the strength and effectiveness of America's military still called into question America's status as a world power. Subsequently, U.S. military forces invaded the small island of Grenada because the government of Grenada was building an airfield large enough to accommodate major military armaments. U.S. officials feared that this airfield would be used by countries in hostile attacks on the United States. From one point of view, the large scale and "successful" attack on Grenada functioned to restore faith in the power and effectiveness of the American military.

SOCIAL PROBLEMS ASSOCIATED WITH WAR AND MILITARISM

Social problems associated with war and militarism include death and disability; rape, forced prostitution, and displacement of women and children; disruption of social-psychological comfort; diversion of economic resources; and destruction of the environment.

Death and Disability

War in the twentieth century took the lives of more than 100 million persons—more than the total number of deaths in all previous wars or massacres in human history combined (Porter 1994). Inscribed in the Books of Remembrance in Ottawa's Parliament buildings are the names of the almost 67 000 Canadians who died in action or of their war wounds between 1914 and 1918, the nearly 45 000 who died in World War II, the 516 killed in the Korean conflict, and those who died in the Nile Expedition and the South African War (Statistics Canada 1998). This chapter's *The Human Side* features John McCrae's poignant poem, "In Flanders Field."

In our modern world, sophisticated weapons technology combined with increased population density has made it easier to kill large numbers of people in a short time. When the atomic bomb was dropped on the Japanese cities of Hiroshima and Nagasaki during World War II, 250 000 civilians were killed. More recently, in the civil war in Rwanda, more than half a million people died within three months (Gibbs 1994).

War's impact extends far beyond those who are killed. Many of those who survive war incur disabling injuries as well as diseases. For example, Gulf War syndrome, a mysterious disease of unknown origin, affects an estimated 80 000 to 100 000 U.S. veterans (National Gulf War Resource Center 1997). In Canada, about 150 of the 2500 Canadians deployed in the Gulf for the 42-day war to expel Iraqi forces from Kuwait have since reported problems with virtually every bodily system—immune, reproductive, and musculoskeletal included. Most of these Canadians served in field hospitals or were attached to U.S. units in Saudi Arabia. Many possible causes have been suggested, including smoke from burning oilfields in Kuwait; pyridostigmine bromide, a drug used experimentally to combat the effects of nerve gas; heavy doses of bug repellents; anthrax vaccinations; or a toxic cocktail of many such ingredients. For its part, the Department of National Defence (DND) in Ottawa emphasized, in July 1998, that the symptoms of Gulf War syndrome were related to the psychological stresses of war. However, in 1999, the U.S. media reported that a doctor had found traces of depleted uranium in the bones of a former U.S. military policeman. Depleted uranium, a by-product of the manufacture of enriched uranium for nuclear fuel, was used for the first time in the Gulf War to harden tips of missiles and shells and to armour-plate military vehicles. Although the DND had ruled out depleted uranium as an explanation for the Gulf War illnesses and claimed that few Canadians were stationed where they could have been exposed to any of its radioactive dust created by an explosion, only two Canadian Gulf War veterans had been tested for depleted uranium prior to February 2000 (the urine tests of both were negative). Although in February 2000 the DND announced that any soldiers who believe that they may be victims of depleted uranium will be tested, the official position of the DND remains that wartime stress caused the mysterious Gulf War illness (*Maclean's* 2000a).

War-related deaths and disabilities also deplete the labour force, create orphans and single-parent families, and burden taxpayers who must pay for the care of orphans and disabled war veterans.

Persons who participate in experiments for military research may also suffer physical harm. Representative Edward Markey of Massachusetts identified 31 experiments dating back to 1945 in which U.S. citizens were subjected to harm from participation in military experiments. Markey charged that many

IN FLANDERS FIELDS

"In April 1915 Canada's ill-trained army faced its first real battle of the First World War. Led by a massive bombardment and clouds of poison gas, the Germans were determined to capture the old Flemish city of Ypres. At a cost of six thousand men—half of its infantry—the Canadian line held" (Morton and Weinfeld 1998). One of those caught up in the battle was John McCrae (1872–1908), a Canadian physician, soldier, and poet.

Born in Guelph, Ontario, McCrae graduated from the University of Toronto and, in 1900, became a pathologist at McGill University and at Montreal General Hospital. As the chief medical officer at a general hospital in Boulogne, France, in World War I, McCrae witnessed the suffering and death he wrote about; almost 67 000 Canadians died in action or of their war wounds between 1914 and 1918.

Although McCrae had contributed verses to various Canadian magazines, he did not become famous until 1915 when he published "In Flanders Fields" in *Punch*, an English magazine. This poem has been interpreted in various ways. To some, it epitomizes a pacifist message. To others, it carries forth "an appeal from the dead to avenge them" and reflects "the mood that held half a million Canadians to volunteer for the struggle, most of them after the terrible battle at Ypres had shattered the easy patriotic illusions about war" (Morton and Weinfeld 1998).

McCrae died in France of pneumonia 10 months before the end of World War I. His poems were published after his death under the title *In Flanders Fields and Other Poems* (1919). The title poem in this collection "helped to make the red Flanders poppy a symbol of remembrance for the most terrible war western civilization could remember. Probably no Canadian poem is better known to the world" (Morton and Weinfeld 1998).

In Flanders fields the poppies
  blow
Between the crosses, row on
  row,
That mark our place; and in the
  sky
The larks, still bravely singing,
  fly
Scarce heard amid the guns
  below.
We are the Dead. Short days ago
We lived, felt dawn, saw sunset
  glow,
Loved and were loved, and now
  we lie
In Flanders fields.
Take up our quarrel with the
  foe:
To you from failing hands we
  throw
The torch; be yours to hold it
  high.
If ye break faith with us who die
We shall not sleep, though poppies grow
In Flanders fields.

SOURCE: Morton, Desmond, and Morton Weinfeld. 1998. *Who Speaks for Canada? Words That Shape a Country*. p. 88–9. Toronto: McClelland & Stewart, Inc.

of the experiments used human subjects who were captive audiences or populations considered "expendable," such as the elderly, prisoners, and hospital patients. Eda Charlton of New York was injected with plutonium in 1945. She and 17 other patients did not learn of their poisoning until 30 years later. Her son, Fred Shultz, said of his deceased mother:

> I was over there fighting the Germans who were conducting these horrific medical experiments...at the same time my own country was conducting them on my own mother. (Miller 1993: 17)

In the 1950s and early 1960s, the Allan Memorial Institute in Montreal, affiliated with both McGill University and the Royal Victoria Hospital, served as one of a number of sites for a CIA-funded series of mind control experiments, code-named "MK-Ultra." The experiments were designed as a "defensive response" to the Chinese "brainwashing" of American prisoners during the Korean War. In the 1980s, nine Canadians who had sought therapy at the Institute and unwittingly become research "participants" in these experiments successfully sued the CIA for a million dollars each, claiming that they had suffered emotional and psychological damage. As involuntary guinea pigs for the CIA, patients at the Allan Memorial Institute underwent radiation, electrode implants, microwaves, massive electroshock treatments, and were given LSD without being told what to expect. In the "sleep room,...people were drugged into sleep for days and days...[They were] given ECT [electro convulsive therapy] until they didn't know who they were or where they were or how to feed themselves, until they lost control of their bladders and bowels" (in Collins 1988: 235–6). According to the institute's files, between May 1 and September 12, 1963, one Vancouver woman received more than 100 electroshock treatments, 86 days of drugged sleep, and intensive "psychic driving"—which attempted to change behaviour through extended repetitions of cue statements. She emerged "completely disoriented and [needing] complete nursing assistance." She could not remember the first 26 years of her life, the births of her five children, and "had to be taught how to eat, to dress, to read, to write, to cook, and to love her parents, husband, and children, none of whom she recognized" (Collins 1988: 235–6).

The Canadian government was later to provide financial compensation to those who had suffered psychological or physical harm because of their unwitting participation in the experiment. However, it is surely ironic to note that the director of the Institute at the time, Dr. Ewan Cameron, had, in addition to serving at various times as president of the Quebec, Canadian, and American Psychiatric Associations and as co-founder and first president of the World Psychiatric Association, been one of the psychiatrists who examined Rudolf Hess in preparation for the Nuremberg trials. Part of his role, on that occasion, was to ensure that the horrors of the medical "research" that had been conducted at Auschwitz and other concentration camps would never be repeated, and to draft a code of ethics for medical conduct. It declared that research must only be conducted on willing participants and that no research warranted the infliction of serious injury or death. It would seem that when, after the war, Cameron resumed his directorship of the Allan Institute, he choose to ignore these lofty ideals.

Rape, Forced Prostitution, and Displacement of Women and Children

Half a century ago, the Geneva Conventions prohibited rape and forced prostitution in war. Nevertheless, both continue to occur in modern conflicts.

Before and during World War II, the Japanese military forced an estimated 100 000 to 200 000 women and teenage girls into prostitution as military "comfort women" (Amnesty International 1995). These women were forced to have sex with dozens of soldiers every day in "comfort stations." Many of the women died from untreated sexually transmitted disease, harsh punishment, or indiscriminate acts of torture.

More recently, armed forces in Bosnia-Herzegovina raped women civilians and prisoners. Most of the victims were Muslim women raped by Bosnian Serbian soldiers:

> In one such case, a 17-year-old Muslim girl was taken by Serbs from her village to huts in woods nearby....She was held there for three months....She was among 12 women who were raped repeatedly in the hut in front of the other women—when they tried to defend her they were beaten off by the soldiers. (Amnesty International 1995: 19)

In 1994, militia forces roamed through the town of Kibuye, Rwanda, burning houses and killing civilians. "Women found sheltering in the parish church were raped, then pieces of wood were thrust into their vaginas, and they were left to die slowly" (Amnesty International 1995: 17). Feminist analysis of wartime rape emphasizes that the practice reflects not only a military strategy, but ethnic and gender dominance as well (Card 1997).

War also displaces women and children from their homes, forcing them to flee to other countries or other regions of their homeland. Refugee women and female children are particularly vulnerable to sexual abuse and exploitation by locals, members of security forces, border guards, or other refugees. In refugee camps, women and children may also be subjected to sexual violence from officials and other refugees.

Disruption of Social-Psychological Comfort

War or living under the threat of war interferes with social-psychological well-being. In a study of 269 Israeli adolescents, Klingman and Goldstein (1994) found a significant level of anxiety and fear, particularly among younger females, regarding the possibility of nuclear and chemical warfare. Similarly, female scientists when compared to their male counterparts perceived significantly higher nuclear-related risks (Barke et al. 1997).

Civilians who are victimized by war and military personnel who engage in combat may experience a form of psychological distress known as **posttraumatic stress disorder (PTSD)**, a clinical term referring to a set of symptoms that may result from any traumatic experience, including crime victimization, rape, or war. Symptoms of PTSD include sleep disturbances, recurring nightmares, flashbacks, and poor concentration (Novac 1998). Research on PTSD in children reveals that females are generally more symptomatic than males and that PTSD may disrupt the normal functioning and psychological development of children (Cauffman et al. 1998; Pfefferbaum 1997). PTSD is also associated with other personal problems, such as alcoholism, family violence, divorce, and suicide.

One study estimates that about 30 percent of male veterans of the Vietnam War have experienced PTSD, and about 15 percent continue to experience it

(Hayman and Scaturo 1993). In another study of 215 Army National Guard and Army Reserve troops who served in the Gulf War and who did not seek mental health services on returning to the United States, 16 to 24 percent exhibited symptoms of PTSD (Sutker et al. 1993). In a study of 1300 returning Canadian peacekeepers, military psychiatrist Lieutenant-Colonel Greg Passey found that almost one in five suffered from posttraumatic stress disorder and that the rate of depression among these soldiers was three times the rate found in the general population. In various ways, keeping peace can be particularly stressful. While success in war may be calculated by "counting hills or towns captured" against a clearly defined enemy, "in Croatia and Bosnia, for example, the peacekeepers themselves are viewed as the enemy, standing in the way of settling accounts. Locals spit in their faces, and they are regularly shelled and shot at by both sides." Many Canadian peacekeepers returning from places such as Rwanda and Yugoslavia were reportedly "haunted by scenes of ethnic cleansing: fetuses cut from the womb, young girls who were gang-raped then set ablaze, entire churches full of people hacked to death with machetes," and by the requirement that they not intervene (Picard 1995).

The label of posttraumatic stress disorder is relatively new, but the phenomena it describes are not. According to historians Terry Cobb and Bill McAndrew (1990), soldiers during World War I suffering from "battle fatigue" (as it was then termed) were executed; 25 Canadians were shot to death for this form of "cowardice." Although a psychiatric corps had been set up by World War II, the reception of the military had not improved; Canadian soldiers experiencing psychological problems were labelled LMFs ("lack of moral fibre") and often jailed. Although counselling services for Canadian troops and their families before and after tours of duty have been dramatically improved, especially in recent years (prompted, in part, by the suicide of a corporal recently returned from a peacekeeping tour in Croatia), only a few soldiers make use of these facilities. As the father of one commando commented: "We spend a lot of time and money teaching them how to fight, but no effort is made to teach them [how] to grieve. So why should anyone be surprised when the only way they can think of solving their problems is with a bullet to the head?" (Picard 1995).

Diversion of Economic Resources

As discussed earlier, maintaining the military and engaging in warfare require enormous financial capital and human support. In 1997, an estimated $740 billion was spent worldwide on military research and development (SIPRI 1998). This amount exceeds the combined government research expenditures on developing new energy technologies, improving human health, raising agricultural productivity, and controlling pollution.

Money that is spent for military purposes could be allocated for social programs. The decision to spend $1.4 billion for one Trident submarine, equal in cost to a five-year immunization program that would prevent nearly one million childhood deaths annually (Renner 1993b), is a political choice. Similarly, world leaders could choose to allocate the $774 billion needed to reverse environmental damage in four priority areas: reforesting the earth, raising energy efficiency, protecting croplands from erosion of topsoil, and developing renewable sources of energy (Renner 1993a).

Destruction of the Environment

Traditional definitions of and approaches to national security have assumed that political states or groups constitute the principal threat to national security and welfare. This assumption implies that national defence and security are best served by being prepared for war against other states. The environmental costs of military preparedness are often overlooked or minimized in such discussions, but environmental security is also vital to national and global security, and achieving one at the expense of the other is like taking one step forward and two steps back.

Destruction of the Environment during War The environmental damage that occurs during war continues to devastate human populations long after war ceases. In Vietnam, 13 million tons of bombs left 25 million bomb craters. Nineteen million gallons of herbicides, including Agent Orange, were spread over the countryside. An estimated 80 percent of Vietnam's forests and swamplands were destroyed by bulldozing or bombing (Funke 1994).

The Gulf War also illustrates how war destroys the environment (Funke 1994; Renner 1993a). In six weeks, one thousand air missions were flown, dropping six million bombs. In 1991, Iraqi troops set 650 oil wells on fire, releasing oil, which still covers the surface of the Kuwaiti desert and seeps into the ground, threatening to poison underground water supplies. The estimated six to eight million barrels of oil that spilled into the Gulf waters are threatening marine life. This spill is by far the largest in history—25 to 30 times the size of the 1989 *Exxon Valdez* oil spill in Alaska.

The clouds of smoke that hung over the Gulf region for eight months contained soot, sulphur dioxide, and nitrogen oxides—the major components of acid rain—and a variety of toxic and potentially carcinogenic chemicals and heavy metals. The U.S. Environmental Protection Agency estimates that in March 1991 about 10 times as much air pollution was being emitted in Kuwait as by all U.S. industrial and power-generating plants combined. Acid rain destroys forests and harms crops; it also activates several dangerous metals normally found in soil, including aluminum, cadmium, and mercury.

The ultimate environmental catastrophe facing the planet is a massive exchange thermonuclear war. Aside from the immediate human casualties, poisoned air, poisoned crops, and radioactive rain, many scientists agree that the dust storms and concentrations of particles would block vital sunlight and lower temperatures in the Northern Hemisphere, creating a **nuclear winter.** In the event of large-scale nuclear war, most living things on earth would die. The fear of nuclear war has greatly contributed to the military and arms build-up, which, ironically, also causes environmental destruction even in times of peace.

CONSIDERATION

Several researchers argue that the continued high-alert status of U.S. and Russian missiles is conducive to accidental nuclear war (Forrow et al. 1998). Of particular concern is the strategy of "launch on warning"–the policy that allows only minutes for detection of an approaching nuclear warhead, decision making, authorization of a launch, and a response. A launch response based on a false warning is the most likely scenario leading to an accidental nuclear war.

In assessing the consequences of such an event, Forrow et al. (1998) conclude that eight U.S. urban areas (Atlanta, Boston, Chicago, New York, Pittsburgh, San Francisco, Seattle, and

Washington, D.C.)—with four hit with four warheads and four hit with eight warheads—would, conservatively, result in more than six million immediate deaths. The number of secondary deaths, that is, those not as a direct consequence of the bombing, would likely exceed that number. The authors also acknowledge that destruction of health infrastructures would be so great that medical care of the injured would be nearly impossible.

Destruction of the Environment in Peacetime Even when military forces are not engaged in active warfare, military activities assault the environment. For example, modern military manoeuvres require large amounts of land. The use of land for military purposes prevents other uses, such as agriculture, habitat protection, recreation, and housing. More important, military use of land often harms the land. In practising military manoeuvres, the armed forces demolish natural vegetation, disturb wildlife habitats, erode soil, silt up streams, and cause flooding. Military bombing and shooting ranges leave the land pock-marked with craters and contaminate the soil and groundwater with lead and other toxic residues.

Further, the production, maintenance, and storage of weapons and military equipment poison the environment and its human, plant, and animal inhabitants. As Calhoun (1996) notes, "decades of improper and unsafe handling, storage and disposal of hazardous materials while building and maintaining the world's most powerful fighting force have severely polluted America's air, water and soil" (p. 60). In the United States, the military is the largest producer of hazardous material (Calhoun 1996).

Bombs exploded during peacetime leak radiation into the atmosphere and groundwater. From 1945 to 1990, 1908 bombs were tested—that is, exploded—at more than 35 sites around the world. Although underground testing has reduced radiation, some still escapes into the atmosphere and is suspected of seeping into groundwater (Renner 1993a).

Finally, although arms-control and disarmament treaties of the last decade have called for the disposal of huge stockpiles of weapons, there are no completely safe means of disposing of weapons and ammunition. Greenpeace has called for placing weapons in storage until safe disposal methods are found (Renner 1993b), but the longer weapons are stored, the more they deteriorate, increasing the likelihood of dangerous leakage.

CONFLICT AND POLITICS IN THE POST–COLD WAR ERA

One of the most significant recent events affecting global conflict has been the end of the Cold War due to the collapse of the communist regime of the former Soviet Union. Prospects for world peace in the post–Cold War era are examined next.

Internal Conflict in the Post–Cold War Era

In the discussion of the structural-functionalist view of global conflict and war, we noted that war functions as a catalyst for social cohesion. The corollary to the cohesive effect of war is that without a common enemy to fight, internal strife is likely to occur. Porter (1994) identifies a historical pattern in which "the end of an era of international rivalry and conflict has marked the beginning of internal conflict and disarray almost everywhere" (p. 300). According to Porter, the post–Cold War era is likely to be an era of political turmoil and divisiveness among social, racial, religious, and class groups.

Terrorism and Guerrilla Warfare: A Growing Threat

Terrorism is the premeditated use, or threatened use, of violence by an individual or group to gain a political or social objective (INTERPOL 1998). Terrorism may be used to publicize a cause, promote an ideology, achieve religious freedom, attain the release of a political prisoner, or rebel against a government. Terrorists use a variety of tactics, including assassinations, skyjackings, armed attacks, kidnapping and hostage taking, threats, and various forms of bombing. According to Laqueur (1998), terrorism has become "far more indiscriminate in its choice of targets" (p. 169).

Terrorism can be either domestic or transnational. Transnational terrorism occurs when a terrorist act in one country involves victims, targets, institutions, governments, or citizens of another country. The 1993 bombing of the World Trade Center in New York exemplifies transnational terrorism. Four Muslim extremists were convicted of the bombing, which killed six people and injured a thousand. In 1998, Ramzi Ahmed Yousef, one of the convicted, was sentenced to 240 years in solitary confinement for his role in the bombing (USIS 1998). Domestic terrorism is exemplified by the 1995 truck bombing of a nine-story federal office building in Oklahoma City, resulting in 168 deaths and more than 200 people injured. Gulf War veteran Timothy McVeigh, who, along with Terry Nichols, was convicted of the crime, is reported to have been a member of a paramilitary group that opposes the U.S. government.

Another example of terrorism occurred in 1995, when the prime minister of Israel, Yitzhak Rabin, was assassinated by Yigal Amir. Amir was part of an extremist Jewish group that insisted that lands seized by Israel during the Six-Day War in 1967 (the Sinai, West Bank, and Gaza Strip) must remain as part of Israel's biblical birthright. Amir and other extremists opposed Rabin's plan to trade land for peace with the Palestinians. Amir assassinated Rabin in an attempt to thwart the peace process.

A government can use both defensive and offensive strategies to fight terrorism. Defensive strategies include using metal detectors at airports and strengthening security at potential targets, such as embassies and military command posts. Offensive strategies include retaliatory raids (such as the U.S. bombing of terrorists facilities in Afghanistan), group infiltration, and preemptive strikes. Unfortunately, efforts to stop one kind of terrorism may result in an increase in other types of terrorist acts. For example, after the use of metal detectors in airports increased, the incidence of skyjackings decreased, but the incidence of assassinations increased (Enders and Sandler 1993).

Unlike terrorist activity, which targets civilians and may be committed by lone individuals, **guerrilla warfare** is committed by organized groups opposing a domestic or foreign government and its military forces. Guerrilla warfare often involves small groups who use elaborate camouflage and underground tunnels to hide until they are ready to execute a surprise attack. Since 1945, more than 120 armed guerrilla conflicts have occurred, resulting in the death of more than 20 million people (Perdue 1993). Most of these conflicts occurred in developing countries. Fidel Castro's guerrillas in Cuba and the Vietcong guerrillas in Vietnam are examples.

International Data

In 1999, escalating violence in the civil war in Kosovo, a province of Yugoslavia, led to the mass murder of 45 ethnic Albanians.

SOURCE: Eddy 1999

Two theories have been advanced to explain why guerrilla warfare occurs most often in less developed countries (Moaddel 1994). First, as societies change from traditional to modern industrialized societies, they experience institutional instability, which leads to conflict as various groups compete for control and resources. A second theory holds that the conflicts arise from external international relations. Less developed countries are dependent on more developed countries, which exploit their labour forces and resources. The growing inequality between less developed and more developed countries creates conflict.

This chapter's Self and Society focuses on the World Values Survey and attitudes toward how social change is best accomplished.

Politics in the Post–Cold War Era: Three Possible Scenarios

Porter (1994) outlines three possible scenarios for the future of global security. In the first scenario, civil strife grows out of the extreme dissatisfaction of ethnic communities living in a state dominated by other ethnic groups. Conflict between ethnic groups may ultimately result in each group forming its own independent political community. In Europe, which currently consists of at least one thousand possible political communities, this scenario would result in the devolution of state structures. Small independent polities would replace centralized states, and Europe would essentially be remedievalized. "Post-modernity," suggests Porter, "would loom as a return to the past" (p. 301).

In the second scenario, terrorism, low-intensity conflict, and street-level violence replace state-centred, large-scale warfare. As the tools of war slip out of the control of central states and fall into the hands of guerrilla militia forces and terrorist groups, the state will become increasingly powerless.

The third scenario Porter (1994) envisions is entirely different. In this view, independent states are threatened by a return of empire. "In a complex world of economic interdependence and mass communications, large-scale organizations that transcend national borders are growing in importance....By the year 2000 or 2010, it is conceivable that Western Europe will again be a unified empire"(p. 301.)

STRATEGIES FOR ACTION: IN SEARCH OF GLOBAL PEACE

Various strategies and policies are aimed at creating and maintaining global peace. These include the redistribution of economic resources, the creation of a world government, peacekeeping activities of the United Nations, mediation and arbitration, and arms control.

Redistribution of Economic Resources

Inequality in economic resources contributes to conflict and war as the increasing disparity in wealth and resources between rich and poor nations fuels hostilities and resentment. Any measures that result in an equal distribution of economic resources are likely to prevent conflict. For example, John J. Shanahan (1995), retired U.S. navy vice admiral and director of the Center for Defense Information, suggests that wealthy nations can help reduce social and economic roots of conflict by providing economic assistance to poorer countries. Despite

National Data

In the "October Crisis" of October 1970, separatist extremists belonging to the FLQ (Front de liberation du Québec) kidnapped British Trade Commissioner James Cross, and killed Quebec cabinet minister Pierre Laporte. In response, Prime Minister Pierre Trudeau invoked the *War Measures Act* to apply emergency measures of arrest, detention, and martial law. Under the emergency regulations, the FLQ was banned, normal liberties were suspended, and arrests and detentions authorized without charge. Of the 467 individuals arrested under the provision of this Act and related public orders, 61 were eventually charged and 13 convicted; only 1 of the 13 was found to have been associated with the Laporte case.

SOURCE: *Canadian Global Almanac* 2000; Corrado 1992

Strategies of Social Change

The World Values Survey, conducted by Ronald Inglehart and his colleagues, has been conducted several times in 19 industrialized countries. Two of the questions posed by Inglehart et al. have especial relevancy for this chapter. The first asked respondents to respond to the following question:

> On this card are three basic kinds of attitudes on the society we live in. Please choose the one that best describes your own opinion: (1) The entire way our society is organized must be radically changed by revolutionary action; (2) Our society should be gradually improved by reforms; (3) Our present society should be valiantly defended against all subversive forces.

The results they obtained in various countries are given in Table 15.1.

Table 15.1   Percentages with Various Views on the Need for Social Change

Country	Want Radical Change	Want Gradual Change	Defend Status Quo	Undecided
Canada	5	67	19	9
Australia	4	69	21	6
Belgium	6	57	16	21
Britain	5	67	21	7
Denmark	4	61	22	13
France	8	68	18	6
Iceland	3	82	14	1
Ireland	4	67	18	11
Italy	7	69	18	6
Japan	2	42	15	41
Mexico	10	68	9	13
Netherlands	3	61	23	13
N. Ireland	1	68	23	8
Norway	2	48	44	6
Sweden	4	72	15	9
S. Africa	12	45	17	26
Spain	7	75	9	9
United States	4	66	20	10
West Germany	2	52	34	12

SOURCE: Inglehart, Ronald. 1990. World Values Survey Datafile. Ann Arbor, Mich.: Ann Arbor Institute for Social Research, University of Michigan.

The second question they posed was:

> I'm going to read out some different forms of political action that people can take, and I'd like you to tell me, for each one, whether you have actually done any of these things, whether you would do it, or would never do.

The social protest strategies identified to respondents were: (1) signing a petition, (2) joining a boycott, (3) participating in a demonstration, (4) joining a strike, and (5) personal violence.

Inglehart et al. reported that the mild forms of lawful protest such as signing one's name to a petition or joining a boycott were the most common. Confrontation activities, such as demonstrating and participating in an informal strike came next, with the use of personal violence far behind. At 60 percent, the Canadian sample was among the top four countries with the highest levels of involvement in signing petitions. Only the United States surpassed Canada in joining boycotts, with 14 percent of Canadians doing so. Canada ranked seventh in strike involvement at 5 percent, and 11th in participation with demonstrations (13 percent). There were only two countries, Italy and the United States, where more than 1 percent of the national samples reported the use of personal violence. In both of these cases, these levels were at 2 percent. In all the countries surveyed, more than 90 percent of each national sample indicated that, under no circumstances, would they use personal violence in the future.

SOURCE: Adapted from Curtis, James E., and Ronald D. Lambert. 1994. "Ideology, Elites and Social Change." In *Sociology*, edited by Lorne Tepperman, James E. Curtis and James Richardson, pp. 717–8. Toronto: McGraw-Hill Primis.

this advice, however, it is notable that U.S. military expenditures for national defence far outweigh U.S. economic assistance to foreign countries.

As we discussed in Chapter 14, strategies that reduce population growth are likely to result in higher levels of economic well-being. Conversely, unrestrained population growth contributes to economic hardship of impoverished countries. Funke (1994) explains that "rapidly increasing populations in poorer countries will lead to environmental overload and resource depletion in the next century, which will most likely result in political upheaval and violence as well as mass starvation" (p. 326). Although achieving worldwide economic well-being is important for minimizing global conflict, it is important that economic development does not occur at the expense of the environment.

World Government

Some analysts have suggested that world peace might be attained through the establishment of a world government. The idea of a single world government is not new. In 1693, William Penn advocated a political union of all European monarchs, and in 1712, Jacques-Henri Bernardin de Saint-Pierre of France suggested an all-European Union with a "Senate of Peace." Proposals such as these have been made throughout history. In the United States, President Bush spoke of a new world order that would become possible after the fall of communism in Eastern Europe.

While some commentators are pessimistic about the likelihood of a new world order, Lloyd (1998) identifies three global trends that, he contends, signify the "ghost of a world government yet to come" (p. 28). First, there is the increasing tendency for countries to engage in "ecological good behaviour," indicating a concern for a global rather than national well-being. Second, despite several economic crises worldwide, major world players such as the United States and Great Britain have supported rather than abandoned nations in need. Finally, an International Criminal Court has been created with "powers to pursue, arraign, and condemn those found guilty of war and other crimes against humanity" (p. 28). Based on these three trends, Lloyd concludes, "global justice, a wraith pursued by peace campaigners for over a century, suddenly seems achievable" (p. 28).

The United Nations

The United Nations (UN), whose charter begins, "We the people of the United Nations—Determined to save succeeding generations from the scourge of war...," has engaged in more than 40 peacekeeping operations since 1948 (United Nations 1998). UN peacekeeping efforts designed to maintain or restore peace may involve military personnel from many countries. They are meant to be temporary measures and such missions have generally been formed to monitor ceasefires, observe troop withdrawals, or to provide a buffer between warring forces. In some cases, unarmed peacekeepers may be deployed on observer missions where their task is simply to observe and report on what they have witnessed. In cases in which they are required to act as the buffer between opposing forces, they may carry weapons for the purpose of self-defence. However, "peacemaking" missions that attempt to restore order and peace may also consist of operations that very much resemble conventional warfare.

United Nations peacekeeping began with an observer mission in the Middle East in 1948 when the UN Truce Supervision Organization was established to oversee the ceasefire between Israel and its Arab neighbours. However, the first peacekeeping force was established when fighting broke out after Egypt seized the Suez Canal from its British and French owners in 1956. The UN accepted the suggestion of Lester Pearson, Canada's Secretary of State for External Affairs (who would later serve as Canada's Prime Minister from 1963 to 1968) that an emergency military force be established to end the fighting and supervise a ceasefire. As a result, the United Nations Emergency Force (UNEF) was to keep the peace on the Israeli–Egyptian border for the next decade. For his settlement of the Suez crisis, Pearson received the Nobel Peace Prize in 1957, the first time a Canadian had ever received this distinction.

Since that time, Canada has continued to play a leading role in UN peacekeeping efforts. Its troops have served in such places as Kashmir (1949–79), West New Guinea (1962–63), and Yemen (1963–64), have helped secure peace in the Congo (1960–64) and in the Sinai (1956–67, 1973–9), and have assisted Namibia's transition to independence (1989–90). In recent years, Canadian Forces have formed part of the UN Protection Force (UNPROFOR) in the former Yugoslavia (1992–95), been involved in the Sarajevo airlift (1992–96) and the UN Assistance Mission in Rwanda (UNAMR) (1993–96), and assisted the UN in the demining of Mozambique (Table 15.2). Canadian Forces have also participated in various non–UN peacekeeping in Indochina (1954–74), as part of the Multinational Force and Observers (MFO) in the Sinai (since 1981) and the European Community Monitoring Mission (EUMM) in the former Yugoslavia.

Recently, the UN has been involved in overseeing multinational peacekeeping forces in Angola, Lebanon, Bosnia-Herzegovina, and Kosovo. One of its most challenging missions to date is the inspection of weapons facilities in Iraq. When, in December 1998, UN inspectors were refused entry to certain military installations, the United States and Great Britain initiated Operation Desert Fox—four days of air strikes on Iraqi military targets—at an estimated cost of $450 million.

A major problem with the concept of the UN is that its members represent individual nations, not a region or the world. Because nations tend to act in their own best economic and security interests, UN actions performed in the name of world peace may be motivated by nations acting in their own interests. Nevertheless, as the UN celebrates more than 50 years of operation, it remains an international agency dedicated to keeping, making, and enforcing peace.

Mediation and Arbitration

Mediation and arbitration are nonviolent strategies used to resolve conflicts and stop or prevent war. In mediation, a neutral third party intervenes and facilitates negotiation between representatives or leaders of conflicting groups. Mediators do not impose solutions, but rather help disputing parties generate options for resolving the conflict. Ideally, a mediated resolution to a conflict meets at least some of the concerns and interests of each party to the conflict. In other words, mediation attempts to find "win-win" solutions in which each side is satisfied with the solution. Although mediation is used to resolve conflict between individuals, it is also a valuable tool for resolving international conflicts. For example, Irish prime minister Bertie Ahern helped to successfully

Table 15.2 **Canadian Participation in UN Peacekeeping Missions 1947–99**

Location	Year	Mission (Canadian participation)
Korea	1947–48	Supervision of elections (2)
India-Pakistan	1949–96	Supervision of ceasefire between India and Pakistan (39)
Korea	1950–53	Supervision of Armistice Agreement (6146)
Korea	1953–	Supervise armistice agreement between North and South Korea (1)
Cambodia, Laos, Vietnam	1954–74	Supervision of withdrawal of French forces (133)
Middle East	1954–	UN Truce Supervision of 1949 armistice between Israel and Egypt, Lebanon, Jordan, and Syria (11)
Egypt (Sinai)	1956–67	Supervision of withdrawal of French, British, and Israeli forces (1007)
Lebanon	1958	Ensure no infiltration across Lebanese borders (77)
Congo	1960–64	Assist in maintaining law and order (421)
West New Guinea (now West Iran)	1962–63	Maintain peace and security (13)
Yemen	1963–64	Observe withdrawal of Egyptian troops (36)
Cyprus	1964, 1974–	Maintain 1974 ceasefire, preserve peace (2)
Dominican Republic	1965–66	Observe withdrawal of OAS forces (1)
India-Pakistan border	1965–66	Supervise ceasefire (112)
Nigeria	1968–70	Observation of ceasefire (2)
Egypt (Sinai)	1973–79	Supervise redeployment of Israeli and Egyptian forces (1145)
South Vietnam	1973	Truce supervision (248)
Syria, Israel	1974–	Supervise ceasefire on Golan Heights (185)
Southern Lebanon	1978	Confirm withdrawal of Israeli forces (117)
Sinai, Egypt	1986–	Supervise 1979 peace treaty between Israel, Egypt, and U.S. (Camp David Accord) (25)
Afghanistan	1988–90	Confirm withdrawal of Soviet forces (5)
Iran/Iraq	1988–91	Supervise ceasefire and withdrawal of forces (525)
Namibia	1989–90	Assist in transition to independence (301)
Central America	1989–92	Verify compliance with Esquipulas Agreement (174)
Afghanistan, Pakistan	1990–92	Military advisory unit (1)
Haiti	1990–91	Observe 1990 elections (11)
Persian Gulf	1990–91	Air, naval, infantry units to help secure liberation of Kuwait
Iraq-Kuwait	1991	Monitor demilitarized pre-war boundary at end of Persian Gulf War (5)
Iraq	1991–	Supervision of destruction of Iraq's nuclear, biological, and chemical weapons (12); periodic enforcement of UN restrictions on Iraq's oil trade; periodic monitoring of no-fly zones over Iraq
Western Sahara	1991–94	Monitor ceasefire; supervise referendum (34)
Angola	1991–93	Monitor ceasefire (15)
El Salvador	1991–94	Investigate human rights violations and monitor progress leading to military reform (55)
Former Yugoslavia & neighbouring states	1991–4	Monitor and report on the implementation of ceasefire (15); report on breaches of Geneva Convention (7)
Red Sea	1992	Naval participation in post–Gulf War embargo of Iraq (250)
Cambodia	1992–93	Monitor ceasefire, establish mine awareness, and monitor disarmament (240)
Yugoslavia	1992–95	Observation patrols, mine clearance, and construction and maintenance of shelters (2400)
El Salvador	1992–95	Investigate human rights violations; develop process for military reform and elections (55)

Somalia	1992–93	Headquarters personnel (12)
Somalia, Kenya	1992–93	Distribution of relief supplies (1250)
Mozambique	1993–95	Security, monitor de-mining operations, ceasefire verification (4)
Cambodia	1993–	Assist Cambodian Mine Action Centre in demining the country (7)
Somalia	1993–95	Assist in provision of relief, economic rehabilitation, and political reconciliation (9)
Uganda, Rwanda	1993–94	Monitor border to enforce military embargo (3)
Haiti	1993–94	Embargo enforcement (250)
Rwanda	1993–96	Provide security and protection for refugees and civilians, distribution of relief supplies (112)
Yugoslavia	1993–95	Enforce no-fly zone (13)
Dominican Republic	1994	Monitor DR–Haitian border, provide technical advice to UN re: enforcement of Haitian trade embargo (15)
Haiti	1994–96	Provide secure and stable environment for training of Haitian armed forces and police and for legislative elections (500)
Haiti	1996, 1997–	Assist government of Haiti in professionalizing the Haitian National Police Force (5)
Bosnia-Herzegovina	1995–	Participate in stabilization force to allow for consolidation of peace as set out in Dayton peace agreement (1350)
Guatemala	1997–	Verify implementation of Comprehensive Agreement on Human Rights and strengthen institutions for the protection of human rights (1)
Central African Republic	1998–	Maintain and improve security and stability following a series of mutinies, disarmament, police training, advice, and technical support (55)
Central Europe	1998–99	Participate in Organization for Security and Cooperation in Europe military inspections in Macedonia and Slovakia and military evaluations in Estonia and Moldova
Kosovo	1999	Support CF-18 fighter jets in Italy (260); support NATO land forces in Macedonia (800); coordinate humanitarian aid in Albania (10)
Mozambique	1999	Assist UN in demining the country (3)

SOURCE: Department of National Defence 1999

mediate between opposing groups leading to the Good Friday peace agreement in Northern Ireland (Burns 1998).

Arbitration also involves a neutral third party who listens to evidence and arguments presented by conflicting groups. Unlike mediation, however, in arbitration the neutral third party arrives at a decision or outcome that the two conflicting parties agree to accept. As Sweet and Brunell (1998) note, **triad dispute resolution**, that is, resolution that involves two disputants and a negotiator—performs "profoundly political functions including the construction, consolidation, and maintenance of political regimes" (p. 64).

Arms Control

In the 1960s, the United States and the Soviet Union led the world in an arms race, each competing to build a more powerful military arsenal than that of its adversary. If either superpower were to initiate a full-scale war, the retaliatory powers of the other nation would result in the destruction of both nations. Thus, the principle of **mutually assured destruction (MAD)** that developed from nuclear weapons capabilities transformed war from a win-lose proposition to a lose-lose scenario. If both sides would lose in a war, the theory goes, neither side would initiate war.

Due to the end of the Cold War and the growing realization that current levels of weapons literally represented "overkill," governments have moved in the direction of arms control, which involves reducing or limiting defence spending, weapons production, and armed forces. Recent arms-control initiatives include SALT (Strategic Arms Limitation Treaty), START (Strategic Arms Reduction Treaty), NPT (Nuclear Nonproliferation Treaty), and the CTBT (Comprehensive Test Ban Treaty).

Strategic Arms Limitation Treaty Under the 1972 SALT agreement (SALT I), the United States and the Soviet Union agreed to limit both their defensive weapons and their land-based and submarine-based offensive weapons. Also in 1972, Henry Kissinger drafted the Declaration of Principles, known as **detente**, which means "negotiation rather than confrontation." A further arms limitation agreement (SALT II) was reached in 1979, but was never ratified by the U.S. Congress because of the Soviet invasion of Afghanistan. Subsequently, the arms race continued with the development of new technologies and an increase in the number of nuclear warheads.

Strategic Arms Reduction Treaty Strategic arms talks resumed in 1982, but made relatively little progress for several years. During this period, President Reagan proposed the Strategic Defense Initiative (SDI), more commonly known as "Star Wars," which purportedly would be able to block missiles launched by another country against the United States (Brown 1994). Although some research was conducted on the system, Star Wars was never actually built. However, in 1999, President Clinton proposed spending $6.6 billion on further development of a "national missile-defense shield by 2005" (M. Thompson 1999: 1).

By 1991, the international situation had changed. The communist regime in the Soviet Union had fallen, the Berlin Wall had been dismantled, and many Eastern European and Baltic countries were under self-rule. SALT was renamed START (Strategic Arms Reduction Treaty) and was signed in 1991. A second START agreement, signed in 1993 and ratified by the U.S. Senate, signalled the end of the Cold War. START II calls for the reduction of nuclear warheads to 3500 by the year 2003, a significant reduction from present levels (Zimmerman 1997). To date, START II awaits ratification by the Russian Parliament, thereby delaying any official negotiations on START III.

Nuclear Nonproliferation Treaty The Nuclear Nonproliferation Treaty (NPT) was signed by 156 countries in 1970. The agreement held that countries without nuclear weapons would not to try to get them; in exchange, the nuclear-capable countries (the United States, United Kingdom, France, China, Russia, and India) agreed they would not provide nuclear weapons to countries that did not have them. The 1994 *Nuclear Proliferation Act* requires that the United States impose economic sanctions on any country that violates the NPT (McGeary 1998).

International Data

The combined total of U.S. and Russian warheads is estimated to be 34 000. Only five hundred to two thousand are needed to induce a nuclear winter and destroy most life on Earth.

SOURCES: McGeary 1998; Sagan 1990

However, even if military superpowers honour agreements to limit arms, the availability of black market nuclear weapons and materials presents a threat to global security. For example, Kyl and Halperin (1997) note that U.S. security is threatened more by nuclear weapons falling into the hands of a terrorist group than by a nuclear attack from an established government such as Russia. The authors further conclude that if Russia were to launch missiles directed at the United States "the odds are overwhelming that it [would] be a Russian missile fired by accident or without authority" (p. 28).

Comprehensive Test Ban Treaty On September 10, 1996, the UN General Assembly passed the Comprehensive Test Ban Treaty (CTBT) by a vote of 158 to 3. The treaty, a "prime disarmament goal for more than forty years" (UCS 1998: 1), would put an end to underground nuclear testing. President Clinton, the first world leader to sign the ban, submitted it to the U.S. Senate for ratification in September 1997. Britain and France have already ratified the agreement. For the CTBT to be enforced, it must be ratified by the 44 members of the Conference on Disarmament. Both India and Pakistan, which tested nuclear devices in 1998, are members of the Conference (UCS 1998).

UNDERSTANDING CONFLICT AROUND THE WORLD

As we come to the close of this chapter, how might we have an informed understanding of conflict around the world? Each of the three theoretical positions discussed in this chapter reflects the realities of war. As functionalists argue, war offers societal benefits—social cohesion, economic prosperity, scientific and technological developments, and social change. Further, as conflict theorists contend, wars often occur for economic reasons as corporate elites and political leaders benefit from the spoils of war—land and water resources and raw materials. The symbolic interactionist perspective emphasizes the role that meanings, labels, and definitions play in creating conflict and contributing to acts of war.

Ultimately, we are all members of one community—Earth—and have a vested interest in staying alive and protecting the resources of our environment for our own and future generations. Nevertheless, conflict between groups is a feature of social life and human existence that is not likely to disappear. What is at stake—human lives and the ability of our planet to sustain life—merits serious attention. Traditionally, nations have sought to protect themselves by maintaining large military forces and massive weapons systems. These strategies have serious costs. In diverting resources away from other social concerns, militarism undermines a society's ability to improve the overall security and well-being of its citizens. Conversely, defence-spending cutbacks can potentially free up resources for other social agendas, including lowering taxes, reducing the national debt, addressing environmental concerns, eradicating hunger and poverty, improving health care, upgrading educational services, and improving housing and transportation. Therein lies the promise of a "peace dividend."

It is hoped that future dialogue on the problem of global conflict and war will redefine national and international security to encompass social, economic, and environmental concerns. These other concerns play a vital role in the security of nations and the world. The World Commission on Environment and Development (1990) concluded:

> **The deepening and widening environmental crisis presents a threat to national security—and even survival—that may be greater than well-armed, ill-disposed neighbours and unfriendly alliances....The arms race in all parts of the world—pre-empts resources that might be used more productively to diminish the security threats created by environmental conflict and the resentments that are fueled by widespread poverty....There are no military solutions to environmental insecurity.**

National and global policies aimed at reducing poverty and ensuring the health of our planet and its present and future inhabitants are important aspects of world peace, but as long as we define national and global security in military terms, we will likely ignore the importance of nonmilitary social policies in achieving world peace. According to Funke (1994), changing the definition of national security "is the first step to changing policy" (p. 342).

CRITICAL THINKING

1. Certain actions constitute "war crimes." Such actions include the use of forbidden munitions such as biological weapons, purposeless destruction, killing of civilians, poisoning of waterways, and violation of surrender terms. In addition to those listed above, what other actions should constitute "war crimes"?
2. Describe countries that have the highest probability of going to war in terms of their economic, social, and psychological makeup. Now, describe countries that are the least likely to go to war. Does history confirm your hypotheses?
3. Selecting each of the five major institutions in society, what part could each play in attaining global peace?
4. Make a list of famous war movies (e.g., *Saving Private Ryan*, *Apocalypse Now*, *Platoon*). With specific movies in mind, list media sounds and images of war. Has the portrayal of war in movies changed over time? If so, how and why?

KEY TERMS

Cold War
detente
economic conversion
guerrilla warfare
infowar

military-industrial
  complex
mutually assured destruction (MAD)
nuclear winter
peace dividend

posttraumatic stress disorder (PTSD)
state
terrorism
triad dispute resolution
war

abortion The intentional termination of a pregnancy.

absolute poverty The chronic absence of the basic necessities of life, including food, clean water, and housing.

acculturation Learning the culture of a group different from the one in which a person was originally raised.

achieved status A status assigned on the basis of some characteristic or behaviour over which the individual has some control.

acid rain The mixture of precipitation with air pollutants, such as sulphur dioxide and nitrogen oxide.

acquaintance rape Rape that is committed by someone known by the victim.

activity theory A theory that emphasizes that the elderly disengage, in part, because they are structurally segregated and isolated with few opportunities to engage in active roles.

acute condition A health condition that can last no more than three months.

adaptive discrimination Discrimination that is based on the prejudice of others.

age grading The assignment of social roles to given chronological ages.

age pyramids Graphlike presentations that show the percentage of a population in various age groups.

ageism The belief that age is associated with certain psychological, behavioural, or intellectual traits.

alienation The concept used by Karl Marx to describe the condition when workers feel powerlessness and meaninglessness as a result of performing repetitive, isolated work tasks. Alienation involves becoming estranged from one's work, the products one creates, other human beings, or one's self; it also refers to powerlessness and meaninglessness experienced by students in traditional, restrictive educational institutions.

alternative schools Alternative schools, which began in Canada in the 1970s. Each operates within school board and education ministry guidelines but is unique in its character.

amalgamation The physical blending of different racial or ethnic groups, resulting in a new and distinct genetic and cultural population; results from the intermarriage of racial and ethnic groups over generations.

anomie A state of normlessness in which norms and values are weak or unclear; results from rapid social change and is linked to many social problems, including crime, drug addiction, and violence.

anorexia nervosa An eating disorder characterized by weight loss, excessive exercise, food aversion, distorted body image, and an intense and irrational fear of body fat and weight gain.

Antabuse A prescribed medication that, when combined with alcohol, produces severe nausea.

ascribed status A status that society assigns to an individual on the basis of factors over which the individual has no control.

assimilation The process by which minority groups gradually adopt the cultural patterns of the dominant majority group.

automation A type of technology in which self-operated machines accomplish tasks formerly done by workers; develops as a society moves toward industrialization and becomes more concerned with the mass production of goods.

beliefs Definitions and explanations about what is assumed to be true.

biodiversity The variability of living organisms on earth.

biphobia Negative attitudes toward bisexuality and people who identify as bisexual.

bisexuality A sexual orientation that involves cognitive, emotional, and sexual attraction to members of both sexes.

blended family A family that consists of remarried spouses with at least one of the spouses having a child from a previous relationship.

bonded labour The repayment of a debt through labour.

bourgeoisie The owners of the means of production.

brain drain The phenomenon whereby many individuals with the highest level of skill and education leave the country in search of work abroad.

bulimia nervosa An eating disorder characterized by cycles of binge-eating and purging (self-induced vomiting, use of laxatives, or use of diuretics).

burden of disease The number of deaths in a population combined with the impact of premature death and disability on that population.

Canada Child Tax Benefit (CCTB) A tax-free monthly payment made to eligible families to help them with the cost of raising children under the age of 18. Benefits are calculated for a 12-month period based on the number of children in a family and their ages, the applicant's province or territory of residence, the family's net income and the applicant's (or the applicant's spouse's) deduction for childcare expenses.

***Canada Student Financial Assistance Act* (CSFA Act)** The CSFA Act of 1994 revised the Canada Student Loans Plan and increased the amounts of the maximum loans available for full-time and part-time students.

Canada Student Loans Program (CSLP) A plan that permits eligible Canadian citizens and permanent residents to finance their postsecondary education with government-sponsored loans. Full-time students, enrolled in a program that lasts for at least 12 weeks, may qualify for a loan that is based on the costs of their program and on the financial resources available to them.

capitalism An economic system in which private individuals or groups invest capital to produce goods and services, for a profit, in a competitive market.

charter groups A term that has been traditionally used in Canada to refer to the English-speaking people and French-speaking people and that reflects the historical importance of these groups in Canada's history.

charter schools Public schools founded by parents, teachers, and communities, and maintained by school tax dollars.

chemical dependency A condition in which drug use is compulsive, and users are unable to stop because of physical or psychological dependency or both.

child abuse The physical or mental injury, sexual abuse, negligent treatment, or maltreatment of a child under the age of 18 by a person who is responsible for the child's welfare.

child labour Children performing work that is hazardous, that interferes with a child's education, or that harms a child's health or physical, mental, spiritual, or moral development.

chronic condition A long-term health problem, such as a disease or impairment.

classic rape A rape committed by a stranger with the use of a weapon resulting in serious bodily injury.

Cold War The state of political tension and military rivalry that existed between the United States and the former Soviet Union from the 1950s through the late 1980s.

colonialism When a racial or ethnic group from one society takes over and dominates the racial or ethnic group(s) of another society.

compressed workweek Workplace option in which employees work a full week, full-time, but in four rather than five days.

computer crime Any violation of the law in which a computer is the target or means of criminal activity.

conflict perspective A sociological perspective that views society as comprising different groups and interests competing for power and resources.

contingent workers Also called "disposable workers"; involuntary part-time workers, temporary employees, and workers who do not perceive themselves as having an explicit or implicit contract for ongoing employment.

control theory A theory that argues that a strong social bond between a person and society constrains some individuals from violating norms.

conventional crimes Traditional illegal behaviours that most people think of as crimes, including such offences as murder, sexual assault, assault, armed robbery, break and enter, and theft.

convergence hypothesis The argument that capitalist countries will adopt elements of socialism and socialist countries will adopt elements of capitalism; that is, they will converge.

corporate downsizing The corporate practice of discharging large numbers of employees. Simply put, the term "downsizing" is a euphemism for mass firing of employees.

corporate murder The label for deaths as a result of unsafe consumer products.

corporate multinationalism The practice of corporations to have their home base in one country and branches, or affiliates, in other countries.

corporate violence The production of unsafe products and the failure of corporations to provide a safe working environment for their employees.

corporate welfare Laws and policies that favour corporations, such as low-interest government loans to failing businesses and special subsidies and tax breaks to corporations.

covenant marriage A type of marriage offered in Louisiana that permits divorce only under condition of fault or after a marital separation of more than two years.

crime The violation of norms that are written into law.

crude divorce rate The number of divorces per 100 000 population.

cultural lag A condition in which the material part of the culture changes at a faster rate than the nonmaterial part.

cultural sexism The ways in which the culture of society perpetuates the subordination of individuals based on their sex classification.

culture of poverty The set of norms, values, and beliefs and self-concepts that contribute to the persistence of poverty among the underclass.

culture wars The modern use of this term originates in late nineteenth-century Germany, where the statesman Otto Von Bismarck engaged in a *Kultur-kreig*—a bitter struggle to restrict the political power and authority of the Catholic Church. More recently, culture wars have sometimes occurred around religious issues, but more broadly, the phrase is used in reference to controversies over censorship, obscenity, and the definition of cultural standards.

cumulative trauma disorders The most common type of workplace injury; it includes muscle, tendon, vascular, and nerve injuries that result from repeated or sustained actions or exertions of different body parts. Jobs that are associated with high rates of upper body cumulative stress disorders include computer programming, manufacturing, meat packing, poultry processing, and clerical or office work.

cybernation The use of machines that control other machines in the production process; characteristic of postindustrial societies that emphasize service and information professions.

de facto segregation Segregation that is not required by law, but exists "in fact," often as a result of housing and socio-economic patterns.

de jure segregation Segregation that is required by law.

decriminalization The removal of criminal penalties for a behaviour, as in the decriminalization of drug use.

deforestation The destruction of the earth's rainforests.

deindustrialization The loss or relocation of manufacturing industries.

deinstitutionalization The removal of individuals with psychiatric disorders from mental hospitals and large residential institutions and into outpatient community mental health centres.

demogrant A benefit directed at a particular group within the population.

demographic transition theory A theory that attributes population growth patterns to changes in birthrates and death rates associated with the process of industrialization. In preindustrial societies, the population remains stable because, although the birthrate is high, the death rate is also high. As a society becomes industrialized, the birthrate remains high, but the death rate declines, causing rapid population growth. In societies with advanced industrialization, the birthrate declines, and this decline, in conjunction with the low death rate, slows population growth.

demography The study of the size, distribution, movement, and composition of human populations.

dependent variable The variable that the researcher wants to explain. *See also* independent variable.

deregulation The reduction of government control of, for example, certain drugs.

desertification The expansion of deserts and the loss of usable land due to the overuse of semiarid land on the desert margins for animal grazing and obtaining firewood.

deskilling The tendency for workers in a postindustrial society to make fewer decisions and for labour to require less thought.

detente The philosophy of "negotiation rather than confrontation" in reference to relations between the United States and the former Soviet Union; put forth by Henry Kissinger's Declaration of Principles in 1972.

deterrence The use of harm or the threat of harm to prevent unwanted behaviours.

devaluation hypothesis The hypothesis that argues that women are paid less because the work they perform is socially defined as less valuable than the work performed by men.

differential association A theory developed by Edwin Sutherland that holds that through interaction with others, individuals learn the values, attitudes, techniques, and motives for criminal behaviour.

disability-adjusted life year (DALY) Years lost to premature death and years lived with illness or disability. More simply, one DALY equals one year of healthy life.

discrimination Differential treatment of individuals based on their group membership.

discriminatory unemployment High rates of unemployment among particular social groups such as racial and ethnic minorities and women.

disengagement theory A theory claiming that the elderly disengage from productive social roles to relinquish these roles to younger members of society. As this process continues, each new group moves up and replaces another, which,

according to disengagement theory, benefits society and all of its members.

diversity training Workplace training programs designed to increase employees' awareness of cultural differences in the workplace and how these differences may affect job performance.

divorce law reform Policies and proposals designed to change divorce law. Usually, divorce law reform measures attempt to make divorce more difficult to obtain.

divorce mediation A process in which divorcing couples meet with a neutral third party (mediator) who assists the individuals in resolving such issues as property division, child custody, child support, and spousal support in a way that minimizes conflict and encourages cooperation.

Dominion Provincial Student Aid Program (DSAP) An act passed by the federal government in 1939. Under DSAP, the federal government contributed to each participating province and the province was expected to provide an equal amount of assistance to students.

double jeopardy *See* multiple jeopardy.

doubling time The time it takes for a population to double in size from any base year.

dowry deaths In some countries, the killing of a woman if she brings an insufficient dowry into the marriage.

drug Any substance other than food that alters the structure and functioning of a living organism when it enters the bloodstream.

drug abuse The violation of social standards of acceptable drug use, resulting in adverse physiological, psychological, or social consequences.

ecofeminism A synthesis of feminism, environmentalism, and antimilitarism.

e-commerce The buying and selling of goods and services over the Internet.

economic conversion The reallocation of resources from military forces and defence industries to other sectors of the economy.

economic family For the purposes of the Canadian census, an economic family is a group of individuals sharing a common dwelling unit who are related by blood, marriage (including common-law relationships) or adoption.

economic institution The structure and means by which a society produces, distributes, and consumes goods and services.

employment equity An attempt to ensure that there is a proportional number of designated target groups (e.g., women, visible minorities, Aboriginal peoples, and people with disabilities) throughout all income and occupational levels at ratios that are consistent with the proportion of these groups within the local or regional workforce.

endogamy The social norm that influences people to marry within their social group and discourages interracial and interethnic marriages.

environmental injustice *See also* environmental racism. The tendency for socially and politically marginalized groups to bear the brunt of environmental ills.

environmental racism The tendency for hazardous waste sites and polluting industries to be located in areas where the surrounding residential population is an ethnic or racial minority.

epidemiological transition The shift from a society characterized by low life expectancy and parasitic and infectious diseases to one characterized by high life expectancy and chronic and degenerative diseases.

epidemiologist A scientist who studies the social origins and distribution of health problems in a population and how patterns of illness and disease vary between and within societies.

epidemiology The study of the distribution of disease within a population.

ergonomics The designing or redesigning of the workplace to prevent and reduce cumulative stress disorders.

ethnicity A shared cultural heritage or national origin.

euthanasia The deliberate taking of an individual's life at her or his request.

experiment A research method that involves manipulating the independent variable to determine how it affects the dependent variable.

expulsion When a dominant group forces a subordinate group to leave the country or to live only in designated areas of the country.

familicide A form of spousal homicide in which the offender not only kills a spouse but also kills one or more of the couple's children at the same time.

familism A value system that encourages family members to put their family's well-being above their individual and personal needs.

family allowance Canada's first universal welfare program, introduced in 1945, which promised a monthly allowance paid to families with children. The term "universal" here refers to the fact that the benefit flowed from the principle of entitlement and were available without reference to a recipient's income or assets.

Family Supplement Those families with children in a low-income situation (i.e., having a family net income under $25 921 a year) and who receive the Canada Child Tax Benefit automatically receive the Family Supplement with a rate based on family net income and the number and ages of children in the family.

famulus The Latin word for "servant."

feminization of poverty The disproportionate distribution of poverty among women.

fertility rate The average number of births per woman.

field research A method of research that involves observing and studying social behaviour in settings in which it naturally occurs; includes participant observation and nonparticipant observation.

flextime An option in work scheduling that allows employees to begin and end the workday at different times as long as they perform 40 hours of work per week.

folkway The customs and manners of society.

functional illiterates High-school graduates who have difficulty with basic reading and math skills.

future shock The state of confusion resulting from rapid scientific and technological changes that challenge traditional values and beliefs.

gateway drug A drug (e.g., marijuana) that is believed to lead to the use of other drugs (such as cocaine and heroin).

gender The social definitions and expectations associated with being male or female.

gene monopolies Exclusive control over a particular gene as a result of government patents.

gene therapy The transplantation of a healthy duplicate gene to replace a defective or missing gene.

genetic engineering The manipulation of an organism's genes in such a way that the natural outcome is altered.

genetic screening The use of genetic maps to detect predispositions to human traits or diseases.

genocide The systematic annihilation of one racial or ethnic group by another.

gerontophobia Fear or dread of the elderly.

glass ceiling An invisible, socially created barrier that prevents some women and other minorities from being promoted into top corporate positions.

global economy An interconnected network of economic activity that transcends national borders.

grade inflation Higher grades given for the same work; a general increase in student grades without a corresponding increase in learning.

greenwashing The corporate practice of displaying a sense of corporate responsibility for the environment. For example, many companies publicly emphasize the steps they have taken to help the environment. Another greenwashing strategy is to retool, repackage, or relabel a company's product.

guerrilla warfare Warfare in which organized groups oppose domestic or foreign governments and their military forces; often involves small groups of individuals who use camouflage and underground tunnels to hide until they are ready to execute a surprise attack.

hate crime An act of violence motivated by prejudice against different racial, ethnic, religious, gender, or sexual-orientation groups.

health A state of complete physical, mental, and social well-being.

health expectancy Number of years an individual can expect to live in good health.

heterosexism The belief that heterosexuality is the superior sexual orientation; it results in prejudice and discrimination against homosexuals and bisexuals.

heterosexuality The predominance of cognitive, emotional, and sexual attraction to persons of the other sex.

home schooling The education of children at home instead of in a public or private school; often part of a fundamentalist movement to protect children from perceived non-Christian values in the public schools.

homophobia Negative attitudes toward homosexuality.

homosexuality The predominance of cognitive, emotional, and sexual attraction to persons of the same sex.

honour murder The practice of wife murder that occurs in some countries when a man suspects his wife of being unfaithful.

human capital The skills, knowledge, and capabilities of the individual.

human capital hypothesis The hypothesis that female–male pay differences are a function of differences in women's and men's levels of education, skills, training, and work experience.

human ecology The study of the relationship between populations and their natural environment.

Human Poverty Index (HPI) A composite measure of poverty based on three measures of deprivation: (1) deprivation of life, which is measured by the percentage of people expected to die before age 40; (2) deprivation of knowledge, which is measured by the percentage of adults who are illiterate; and (3) deprivation in living standards, which is measured as a composite of three variables—the percentage of people without access to health services, the percentage of people without access to safe water, and the percentage of malnourished children under five.

hypothesis A prediction or educated guess about how one variable is related to another variable.

incapacitation A criminal justice philosophy that views the primary purpose of the criminal justice system as preventing criminal offenders from committing further crimes against the public by putting them in prison.

incidence The number of new cases of a specific health problem within a given population during a specified period.

inclusive education Educational efforts premised on the belief that all children should be encouraged to participate in society, regardless of having any specific disability.

independent variable The variable that is expected to explain change in the dependent variable.

individual discrimination Discriminatory acts by individuals that are based on prejudicial attitudes.

individualism A value system that stresses the importance of individual happiness.

Industrial Revolution The period between the mid-eighteenth and the early nineteenth century when machines and factories became the primary means for producing goods. The Industrial Revolution led to profound social and economic changes.

infant mortality rate The number of deaths of infants under one year of age per one thousand live births in a calendar year.

infantilizing elders The portrayal of the elderly in the media as childlike in terms of clothes, facial expression, temperament, and activities.

information technology (IT) Any technology that carries information.

infowar The utilization of technology to manipulate or attack an enemy's military and civilian infrastructure and information systems.

institution An established and enduring pattern of social relationships. The five traditional social institutions are family, religion, politics, economics, and education. Institutions are the largest elements of social structure.

institutional discrimination Discrimination in which the normal operations and procedures of social institutions result in unequal treatment of minorities.

intergenerational poverty Poverty that is transmitted from one generation to the next.

Internet An international information infrastructure available through many universities, research institutes, government agencies, and businesses; developed in the 1970s as a U.S. Defense Department experiment.

in-vitro fertilization (IVF) The union of an egg and a sperm in an artificial setting such as a laboratory dish.

job burnout Prolonged job stress; it can cause physical problems, such as high blood pressure, ulcers, and headaches, as well as psychological problems.

job exportation The relocation of jobs to other countries where products can be produced more cheaply.

job sharing A work option in which two people share and are paid for one job.

labelling theory A symbolic interactionist theory that is concerned with the effects of labelling on the definition of a social problem (e.g., a social condition or group is viewed as problematic if it is labelled as such) and with the effects of labelling on the self-concept and behaviour of individuals (e.g., the label "juvenile delinquent" may contribute to the development of a self-concept and behaviour consistent with the label).

latent functions Consequences that are unintended and often hidden or unrecognized; for example, a latent function of education is to provide schools that function as babysitters for employed parents.

law Norms that are formalized and backed by political authority.

legalization Making prohibited behaviour legal; for example, legalizing marijuana or prostitution.

life expectancy The average number of years that a person born in a given year can expect to live.

living will An advance care directive in which people declare whether they want all possible medical intervention or limits placed on treatment should they become incapacitated.

low-income cutoff line (LICO) Developed by Statistics Canada as a measure of poverty in 1968. Estimating that poor families or individuals spend approximately 34.7 percent or more of their pre-tax income on such basic needs as food, shelter, and clothing, 20 percentage points were added to this figure to determine the cutoff. This standard suggests that individuals or families who spent 54.7 percent of their pre-tax income on food, clothing, and shelter would experience financial difficulty. Different low-income cutoff lines are established by Statistics Canada for different communities as well as for families of varying sizes within these communities.

low-income measure (LIM) For the purposes of assessing low income using this measure, Statistics Canada has established a figure for the needs of one adult and proceeded on the assumption that family needs increase in proportion to the size of the family, with each additional adult increasing the family needs by 40 percent of the first adult and each additional child increasing the family's needs by 30 percent.

macro sociology The study of large aspects of society, such as institutions and large social groups.

MADD Mothers Against Drunk Driving. A social action group committed to reducing drunk driving.

Malthusian theory The theory proposed by Thomas Malthus in which he predicted that the population would grow faster than the food supply and that masses of people were destined to be poor and hungry. According to Malthus, food shortages would lead to war, disease, and starvation that would eventually slow population growth.

manifest function A consequence that is intended and commonly recognized; for example, a manifest function of education is to transmit knowledge and skills to youth.

marital assimilation Assimilation that occurs when different ethnic or racial groups become married or pair-bonded and produce children.

master status The status that is considered the most significant in a person's social identity.

mater familias An archaic term used to refer to the "woman of the house" in the sense of the person who directed its domestic affairs.

maternal mortality rate The numbers of death that result from complications associated with pregnancy or childbirth per one thousand pregnant women.

mechanization The use of tools to accomplish tasks previously done by workers; characteristic of agricultural societies that emphasize the production of raw materials.

medicalization The tendency to define negatively evaluated behaviours or conditions as medical problems in need of medical intervention.

Medicare Canada's health care system, which provides access to universal comprehensive coverage for medically necessary inpatient and outpatient physician services.

melting pot The product of different groups coming together and contributing equally to a new common culture.

mental disorder A behavioural or psychological syndrome or pattern that occurs in an individual and that is associated with present distress or disability, or with a significantly increased risk of suffering, death, pain, disability, or loss of freedom.

micro society school A simulation of the "real" or nonschool world where students design and run their own democratic free-market society within the school.

micro sociology The study of the social psychological dynamics of individuals interacting in small groups.

military-industrial complex A term used by Dwight D. Eisenhower to connote the close association between the military and defence industries.

minority A category of people who are denied equal access to positions of power, prestige, and wealth because of their group membership.

modern racism A subtle and complex form of racism in which individuals are not explicitly racist but tend to hold negative views of racial minorities and blame minorities for their social disadvantages.

modernization theory A theory claiming that as society becomes more technologically advanced, the position of the elderly declines.

morbidity The amount of disease, impairment, and accidents in a population.

mores Norms that have a moral basis.

mortality Death.

multicultural education Education that includes all racial and ethnic groups in the school curriculum and promotes awareness and appreciation for cultural diversity.

multiculturalism A philosophy that argues that the culture of a society should represent and embrace all racial and ethnic groups in that society.

multiple chemical sensitivity (MCS) A controversial health condition in which, after one or more acute or traumatic exposures to a chemical or group of chemicals, people experience adverse effects from low levels of chemical exposure that do not produce symptoms in the general public.

multiple jeopardy The disadvantages associated with being a member of two or more minority groups.

mutually assured destruction (MAD) A perspective that argues that if both sides in a conflict were to lose in a war, neither would initiate war.

National Child Benefit (NCB) Introduced in July 1998, NCB is a joint initiative of federal, provincial, and territorial governments designed to help prevent and reduce the depth of child poverty and to promote parental attachment to the workforce.

National Child Benefit Supplement (NCBS) A monthly benefit for low-income families with children that is the federal government's contribution to the National Child Benefit (NCB).

neglect A form of abuse involving the failure to provide adequate attention, supervision, nutrition, hygiene, health care, and a safe and clean living environment for a minor child or a dependent elderly individual.

new ageism The belief that the elderly are a burden on the economy and, specifically, on the youth of Canada.

no-fault divorce A divorce that is granted based on the claim that there are irreconcilable differences within a marriage (as opposed to one spouse being legally at fault for the marital breakup).

norms Socially defined rules of behaviour, including folkways, mores, and laws.

nuclear winter The predicted result of a thermonuclear war whereby dust storms and concentrations of particles would block out vital sunlight, lower temperatures in the Northern Hemisphere, and lead to the death of most living things on Earth.

objective element of a social problem Awareness of social conditions through one's own life experience and through reports in the media.

occupational sex segregation The concentration of women in certain occupations and of men in other occupations.

one drop of blood rule A rule that specified that even one drop of Negroid blood defined a person as Black and, therefore, eligible for slavery.

operational definition In research, a definition of a variable that specifies how that variable is to be measured (or was measured) in the research.

organized crime Criminal activity conducted by members of a hierarchically arranged structure devoted primarily to making money through illegal means.

overt discrimination Discrimination that occurs because of an individual's own prejudicial attitudes.

pater familias An archaic term used to refer to the "householder" that took on the connotation of "an ordinary citizen."

patriarchy A tradition in which families are male-dominated.

peace dividend Resources that are diverted from military spending and channelled into private or public investment or consumption, used to reduce the deficit, or used to lower taxes.

phased retirement Retirement in which the older worker can withdraw from the workforce gradually.

pink-collar jobs Jobs that offer few benefits, often have low prestige, and are disproportionately held by women.

planned obsolescence The manufacturing of products that are intended to become inoperative or outdated in a fairly short time.

pluralism A state in which racial or ethnic groups maintain their distinctness but respect each other and have equal access to social resources.

population The word scientists who reject the race concept now use when referring to groups that most people would call races.

population transfer *See* expulsion.

postindustrialization The shift from an industrial economy dominated by manufacturing jobs to an economy dominated by service-oriented, information-intensive occupations.

postmodernism A world view that questions the validity of rational thinking and the scientific enterprise.

posttraumatic stress disorder (PTSD) A set of symptoms that may result from any traumatic experience, including crime victimization, war, natural disasters, or abuse.

poverty Lacking resources for an "adequate" standard of living (*see also* absolute poverty and relative poverty).

prejudice An attitude or judgment, usually negative, about an entire category of people based on their group membership.

prevalence The total number of cases of a condition within a population that exist at a given time.

primary aging Biological changes associated with aging that are due to physiological variables such as cellular and molecular variation (e.g., grey hair).

primary assimilation The integration of different groups in personal, intimate associations such as friends, family, and spouses.

primary group A small group characterized by intimate and informal interaction.

primary prevention strategies Family violence prevention strategies that target the general population.

proletariat Workers who were often exploited by the bourgeoisie.

pronatalism A cultural value that promotes having children.

race A category of people who are believed to share distinct physical characteristics that are deemed socially significant.

racism The belief that certain groups of people are innately inferior to other groups of people based on their racial classification. Racism serves to justify discrimination against groups that are perceived as inferior.

refugees Immigrants who apply for admission on the basis of persecution or fear of persecution for their political or religious beliefs.

rehabilitation A criminal justice philosophy that views the primary purpose of the criminal justice system as changing the criminal offender through such programs as education and job training, individual and group therapy, substance abuse counselling, and behaviour modification.

relative poverty A deficiency in material and economic resources compared with some other population.

replacement level The average number of births per woman (2.1) in a population below which the population begins to decline.

reverse discrimination The unfair treatment of members of the majority group (i.e., white males) that, according to some, results from employment equity.

role A set of rights, obligations, and expectations associated with a status.

sample In survey research, the portion of the population selected to be questioned.

sanctions Social consequences for conforming to or violating norms. Types of sanctions include positive, negative, formal, and informal.

sandwich generation The generation that has the responsibility of simultaneously caring for their children and their aging parents.

science The process of discovering, explaining, and predicting natural or social phenomena.

secondary aging Biological changes associated with aging that can be attributed to poor diet, lack of exercise, and increased stress.

secondary assimilation The integration of different groups in public areas and in social institutions, such as in government, neighbourhoods, schools, and the workplace.

secondary group A group characterized by impersonal and formal interaction.

secondary prevention strategies Prevention strategies that target groups that are thought to be at high risk for family violence.

segregation The physical and social separation of categories of individuals, such as racial or ethnic groups.

self-fulfilling prophecy A concept referring to the tendency for people to act in a manner consistent with the expectations of others.

senescence The biology of aging.

senilicide The killing of the elderly.

sex A person's biological classification as male or female.

sexism The belief that there are innate psychological, behavioural, or intellectual differences between females and males and that these differences connote the superiority of one group and the inferiority of another.

sexual harassment When an employer requires sexual favours in exchange for a promotion, salary increase, or any other employee benefit, or the existence of a hostile environment that unreasonably interferes with job performance, as in the case of sexually explicit remarks or insults being made to an employee.

sexual orientation The identification of individuals as heterosexual, bisexual, or homosexual based on their emotional and sexual attractions, relationships, self-identity, and lifestyle.

sick building syndrome (SBS) A situation in which occupants of a building experience symptoms that seem to be linked to time spent in a building but for which no specific illness or cause can be identified.

slavery A condition in which one social group treats another group as property to exploit for financial gain.

social group Two or more people who have a common identity and who interact and form a social relationship; institutions are made up of social groups.

social problem A social condition that a segment of society views as harmful to members of society and in need of remedy.

social promotion The passing of students from grade to grade even if they are failing.

socialism An economic ideology that emphasizes public rather than private ownership. Theoretically, goods and services are equitably distributed according to the needs of the citizens.

sociological imagination A term coined by C. Wright Mills to refer to the ability to see the connections between our personal lives and the social world in which we live.

sociological mindfulness A term used by sociologist Michael Schwalbe to refer to the practice of seeing the many ways in which social conditions shape and are shaped by individuals and groups.

sodomy laws Laws that prohibit anal sex.

special education Remedial education designed to help children and adults who are exceptional in some way, including but not limited to, low intelligence, visual or auditory disabilities, and emotional or specific learning difficulties.

split labour market The existence of primary and secondary labour markets. A primary labour market refers to jobs that are stable and economically rewarding and have many benefits; a secondary labour market refers to jobs that offer little pay, no security, few benefits, and little chance for advancement.

state The organization of the central government and government agencies such as the armed forces, police force, and regulatory agencies.

status A position a person occupies within a social group.

stereotype An oversimplified or exaggerated generalization about a category of individuals. Stereotypes are either untrue or are gross distortions of reality.

strain theory A theory that argues that when legitimate means of acquiring culturally defined goals are limited by the structure of society, the resulting strain may lead to crime or other deviance.

street crime Also known as "conventional crime"; those traditional illegal behaviours that most people think of as crime, such as sexual assault, assault, armed robbery, break and enter, and so on.

structural-functionalism A sociological perspective that views society as a system of interconnected parts that work together in harmony to maintain a state of balance and social equilibrium for the whole; focuses on how each part of society influences and is influenced by other parts.

structural sexism The ways in which the organization of society, and specifically its institutions, subordinate individuals and groups based on their sex classification.

structural unemployment Exists when there are not enough jobs available for those who want them; unemployment that results from structural variables such as government and business downsizing, job exportation, automation, a reduction in the number of new and existing businesses, an increase in the number of people looking for jobs, and a recessionary economy where fewer goods are purchased and, therefore, fewer employees are needed.

subcultural theory A theory that argues that certain groups or subcultures in society have values and attitudes that are conducive to crime and violence.

subjective element of a social problem The belief that a particular social condition is harmful to society, or to a segment of society, and that it should and can be changed.

subsidized housing The leasing of private housing units by local housing authorities or direct payments of rent supplements to low-income families.

suburbs The urbanlike areas surrounding central cities.

survey research A method of research that involves eliciting information from respondents through questions; includes interviews (telephone or face-to-face) and written questionnaires.

sustainable development Societal development that meets the needs of current generations without threatening the future of subsequent generations.

sweatshop A work environment characterized by less than minimum wage pay, excessively long hours of work often without overtime pay, unsafe or inhumane working conditions, abusive treatment of workers by employers, or the lack of worker organizations aimed at negotiating better work conditions.

symbol Something that represents something else.

symbolic interactionism A sociological perspective that emphasizes that human behaviour is influenced by definitions and meanings that are created and maintained through symbolic interaction with others.

technological fix The use of scientific principles and technology to solve social problems.

technology Activities that apply the principles of science and mechanics to the solution of specific problems.

technology-induced diseases Diseases that result from the use of technological devices, products, or chemicals.

telecommuting A work option in which workers complete all or part of their work at home with the use of information technology.

telemedicine Using information and communication technologies to deliver a wide range of health care services, including diagnosis, treatment, prevention, health support and information, and education of health care workers.

telepathology Transmitting images of tissue samples to a pathologist in another location, who can look at the image on a monitor and offer an interpretation.

teleradiology The transmission of radiological images from one location to another for the purpose of interpretation or consultation.

terrorism The premeditated use or threatened use of violence by an indi-

vidual or group to gain a political objective.

tertiary prevention strategies Prevention strategies that target families who have experienced family violence.

therapeutic communities Organizations in which 35 to 100 individuals reside for up to 15 months to abstain from drugs, develop marketable skills, and receive counselling.

triad dispute resolution Dispute resolution that involves two disputants and a negotiator.

triple jeopardy *See* multiple jeopardy.

underclass A persistently poor and socially disadvantaged group that disproportionately experiences joblessness, welfare dependency, involvement in criminal activity, dysfunctional families, and low educational attainment.

underemployment Employment in a job that is underpaid; is not commensurate with one's skills, experience, or education; or involves working fewer hours than desired.

under-five mortality rate The rate of deaths among children under age five.

upskilling The opposite of deskilling; upskilling reduces employee alienation and increases decision-making powers.

values Social agreements about what is considered good and bad, right and wrong, desirable and undesirable.

variable Any measurable event, characteristic, or property that varies or is subject to change.

victimless crimes Illegal activities, such as prostitution or drug use, that have no

complaining party; also called "vice crimes."

war Organized armed violence aimed at a social group in pursuit of an objective.

wealth The total assets of an individual or household minus liabilities.

wealthfare Governmental policies and regulations that economically favour the wealthy.

white-collar crime Includes both occupational crime, where individuals commit crimes in the course of their employment, and corporate crime, where corporations violate the law in the interest of maximizing profit.

work-experience unemployment rate The percentage of persons who participated in the labour force in a given year and experienced some unemployment during that year.

working poor Individuals who spend at least 27 weeks a year in the labour force (working or looking for work), who nevertheless live in poverty.

work sectors The division of the labour force into distinct categories (primary, secondary, and tertiary) based on the types of goods or services produced.

***Young Offenders Act* (YOA)** An act that governs the conduct of Canadian youths between the ages of 12 and 18.

Y2K (year 2000) Sometimes called the millennium bug, it was the concern that computers programmed with double-digit years only (e.g., 97, 98, 99) would interpret 00 as 1900, 01 as 1901, and so forth rather than the years 2000, 2001, and so on.

Preface

Safransky, Sy. 1990. *Sunbeams: A Book of Quotations*. Berkeley, Calif.: North Atlantic Books.

Chapter 1

Bibby, Reginald W. 1995. *The Bibby Report: Social Trends Canadian Style*. Toronto: Stoddart.

Blumberg, Paul. 1989. *The Predatory Society: Deception in the American Market Place*. New York: Oxford University Press.

Blumer, Herbert. 1971. "Social Problems as Collective Behavior." *Social Problems* 8(3): 298–306.

Catania, Joseph A., David R. Gibson, Dale D. Chitwook, and Thomas J. Coates. 1990. "Methodological Problems in AIDS Behavioral Research: Influences on Measurement Error and Participation Bias in Studies of Sexual Behavior." *Psychological Bulletin* 108: 339–62.

Coleman, John R. 1990. "Diary of a Homeless Man." In *Social Problems*, pp. 160–9. Englewood Cliffs, N.J.: Prentice-Hall.

Corak, Miles. 1998. "Getting Ahead in Life: Does Your Parents' Income Count?" *Canadian Social Trends* 49: 6–15.

Curtis, James, and Edward Grabb. 1999. "Social Status and Beliefs about What's Important for Getting Ahead." In *Social Inequality in Canada: Patterns, Problems, Policies*, 3rd ed., edited by James Curtis, Edward Grabb and Neil Guppy, pp. 330–46. Scarborough, Ont.: Prentice Hall Allyn and Bacon Canada Inc.

Dordick, Gwendolyn A. 1997. *Something Left to Lose: Personal Relations and Survival Among New York's Homeless*. Philadelphia: Temple University Press.

Frank, James G. 1991. "Risk Factors for Rape: Empirical Confirmation and Preventive Implications." Poster session presented at the 99th Annual Convention of the American Psychological Association, San Francisco, August 16.

Hewlett, Sylvia Ann. 1992. *When the Bough Breaks: The Cost of Neglecting Our Children*. New York: Harper Perennial.

Hills, Stuart L. 1987. *Corporate Violence: Injury and Death for Profit*, edited by Stuart L. Mills. Lanham, Minn.: Rowman and Littlefield.

Human Development Report 1997. United Nations Development Programme. New York: Oxford University Press, Inc.

Jekielek, Susan M. 1998. "Parental Conflict, Marital Disruption and Children's Emotional Well-Being." *Social Forces* 76: 905–35.

Maclean's. 1999. "What Makes a Canadian?" December 20: 45–8.

Manis, Jerome G. 1974. "Assessing the Seriousness of Social Problems." *Social Problems* 22: 1–15.

Merton, Robert K. 1968. *Social Theory and Social Structure*. New York: Free Press.

Mills, C. Wright. 1959. *The Sociological Imagination*. London: Oxford University Press.

Nader, Ralph, Nadia Milleron, and Duff Conacher. 1993. *Canada Firsts*. Toronto: McClelland and Stewart Inc.

Nyden, Philip, Anne Figert, Mark Shibley, and Darryl Burrows. 1997. "University–Community Collaborative Research. In *Building Community: Social Science in Action*, edited by P. Nyden, A. Figert, M. Shibley, and D. Burrows, pp. 3–13. Thousand Oaks, Calif.: Pine Forge Press.

Picard, Andre. 1999. "Lack of Charity Hurts Quebec Society." *The Globe and Mail*, October 4.

Rodgers, Karen. 1994. "Wife Assault: The Findings of a National Survey." *Juristat Service Bulletin*, 14, 9, Cat. 85-002. Ottawa: Minister of Industry, Science and Technology.

Romer, D., R. Hornik, B. Stanton, M. Black, X. Li, I. Ricardo, and S. Feigelman. 1997. "'Talking Computers': A Reliable and Private Method to Conduct Interviews on Sensitive Topics with Children." *Journal of Sex Research* 34: 3–9.

Rubington, Earl, and Martin S. Weinberg. 1995. *The Study of Social Problems*,

5th ed. New York: Oxford University Press.

Schwalbe, Michael. 1998. *The Sociologically Examined Life: Pieces of the Conversation*. Mountain View, Calif: Mayfield Publishing Company.

Skeen, Dick. 1991. *Different Sexual Worlds: Contemporary Case Studies of Sexuality*. Lexington, Mass.: Lexington Books.

Statistics Canada. 1998. *Canada Yearbook 1999*. Ottawa: Ministry of Industry.

Thomas, W. I. [1931] 1966. "The Relation of Research to the Social Process." In *W.I. Thomas on Social Organization and Social Personality*, edited by Morris Janowitz, pp. 289–305. Chicago: University of Chicago Press.

Troyer, Ronald J., and Gerald E. Markle. 1984. "Coffee Drinking: An Emerging Social Problem." *Social Problems* 31: 403–16.

Ukers, William H. 1935. *All About Tea*, Vol. 1. The Tea and Coffee Trade Journal Co.

Wilson, John. 1983. *Social Theory*. Englewood Cliffs, N.J.: Prentice-Hall.

Chapter 2

Abeysinghe, Devinka. 1998. "First Lady Stresses Family Planning on World Health Day." *Popline* (March–April): 3–4.

Academy for Eating Disorders. 1997. September 13, 1998 <www.acadeatdis.org/>.

Alderman, Tracy. 1997. *The Scarred Soul: Understanding and Ending Self-Inflicted Violence*. New York: New Harbinger Publications.

American Psychiatric Association. 1994. *Diagnostic and Statistical Manual of Mental Disorders*, 4th ed. (DSM-IV). Washington, D.C.: American Psychiatric Association.

Antezana, Fernando S., Claire M. Chollat-Traquet, and Derik Yach. 1998. "Health for All in the 21st Century." *World Health Statistics Quarterly* 51: 3–6.

Armstrong, Pat, Hugh Armstrong, and Claudia Fegan. 1998. *Universal Health Care: What the United States Can Learn from the Canadian Experience*. New York: The New Press.

Barnes, John A. 1990. "Canadians Cross Border to Save Their Lives." *Wall Street Journal*, December 12: A14.

Bergman, Brian. 2000. "Paramedics: Pride and Frustration." *Maclean's*, February 7: 48–50.

Blinick, Abraham. 1992. "Socialized Medicine is No Cure All." *Wall Street Journal*, January 17: A1.

Blumenthal, Heather. 1999. "AIDS Harm Reduction: More Complicated than Previously Thought." *Let's Talk* 24(4): 17–8.

Boroditsky, R., W. A. Fisher, and M. Sand. 1996. "Condoms: Attitudes and Practices of Canadian Women: The 1995 Canadian Contraception Study." *Journal of the Society of Obstetrics and Gynaecology*, special supplement, December.

Canadian Centre on Substance Abuse. 1991. *Canadian Profile: Alcohol, Tobacco, and Other Drugs, 1999*. Ottawa: Canadian Centre on Substance Abuse and Centre for Addiction and Mental Health.

Canadian Coalition for the Rights of the Child. 1999. *How Does Canada Measure Up?* Ottawa: Canadian Coalition for the Rights of the Child.

Canadian Medical Association. 1999. *Access to Health Care in Canada Report*. <www.cma.ca/advocacy/access/index.asp>.

Cockerham, William C. 1998. *Medical Sociology*, 7th ed. Upper Saddle River, N.J.: Prentice Hall.

Conlon, R. T. 1997. "Introducing Technology into the Public STD Clinic." *Health Education and Behavior* 24(1): 12–19.

Cooper, M., R. Corrado, A.M. Karlberg, and L.P. Adams. 1992. "Aboriginal Suicide in British Columbia: An Overview." *Canada's Mental Health* (September) 19–23.

Creese, Andrew L., John D. Martin, and Jan H.M. Visschedijk. 1998. "Health Systems for the Twenty-First Century." *World Health Statistics Quarterly* 51: 21–27.

"Economic Growth Unnecessary for Reducing Fertility." 1998. *Popline* 20: 4.

Everett, Sherry A., Rae L. Schnuth, and Joanne L. Tribble. 1998. "Tobacco and Alcohol Use in Top-Grossing American Films." *Journal of Community Health* 23: 317–24.

Favazzo, Armando R. 1998. *Bodies Under Siege: Self-Mutilation and Body Modification in Culture and Psychiatry*, 2nd ed. Chicago: John Hopkins University Press.

Gfellner, B.M., and J.D. Hundelby. 1995. "Patterns of Drug Use among Native and White Adolescents: 1990–1995." *Canadian Journal of Public Health* 86: 95–7.

Gittens, Margaret, David P. Cole, May Tam, Toni Williams, Ed Ratushy, and Sri-Guggan Sri-Skanda-Rajah. 1994. *Racism Behind Bars: The Treatment of Black and Other Minority Prisoners in Ontario Prisons*. Interim Report of the Commission on Systemic Racism in the Ontario Criminal Justice System. Ottawa: Queen's Printer.

Goldstein, Michael S. 1999. "The Origins of the Health Movement." In *Health, Illness, and Healing: Society, Social Context, and Self*, edited by Kathy Charmaz and Deborah A. Paterniti, pp. 31–41. Los Angeles: Roxbury Publishing Co.

Graham, Mel. 1999. "Budget 2000 and People with Disabilities." *Abilities: Canadian Lifestyle Magazine for People with Disabilities* 41, Winter: 48.

Grant, Karen R. 1993. "Health and Health Care." In *Contemporary Sociology: Critical Perspectives*, edited by Peter S. Li and B. Singh Bolaria, pp. 394–409. Toronto: Copp-Clark Pitman.

Harper, Elijah (with Pauline Comeau). 1993. *Elijah: No Ordinary Hero*. Vancouver: Douglas and McIntyre.

Health Canada. 1999a. *Toward a Healthy Future: Second Report on the Health of Canadians*. Prepared by the Federal, Provincial, and Territorial Advisory Committee on Population Health for the Meeting of Ministers of Health, Charlottetown, PEI, September.

———. 1999b. *Statistical Report on the Health of Canadians*. December 25, 1999 <www.hc-sc.gc.ca/hppb/phdd/report/state/englover.html>.

———. 2000. "The AIDS/HIV Files." April 28, 2000 <www.hc-sc.gc.ca/real/aids/state.html>

———. n.d.(a) "Diabetes." December 28, 1999 <www.hc-sc.gc.ca/msb/Inhp.diabet_e.htm>.

———. n.d.(b). "HIV/AIDS and Aboriginal People in Canada." December 28, 1999 <www.hc-sc.gc.ca/hppb/hiv_aids/programs/aboriginal.html>.

Inciardi, James A., and Lana D. Harrison. 1997. "HIV, AIDS, and Drug Abuse in the International Sector." *Journal of Drug Issues* 27: 1–8.

Isaacs, S., S. Keogh, C. Menard, et al. 1998. "Suicide in the Northwest Territories: A Descriptive Review." *Chronic Diseases in Canada* 19(4): 152–6.

Johnson, Elmer Hubert, and Benjamin Britt. 1967. *Self-Mutilations in Prison: Interaction of Stress and Social Structure.* Carbondale, Ill: University of Chicago Press.

Johnson, Tracy L., and Elizabeth Fee. 1997. "Women's Health Research: An Introduction." In *Women's Health Research: A Medical and Policy Primer,* edited by Florence P. Haseltine, and Beverly Greenberg Jacobson, pp. 3–26. Washington, D.C.: Health Press International.

Kennedy, Mark. 1999. "Doctors Warn Ottawa to Heed Physician Shortages Right Away." *National Post,* August 3: A6.

Kerzner, Lana, and David Baker. 1999. *A Canadians with Disability Act?* May 14 <www.hc-sc.gc.ca>.

Kessler, Ronald C., Katherine A. McGonagle, Shanyang Zhao, Christopher B. Nelson, Michael Hughes, Suzann Eshleman, Hans-Ulrich Wittchen, and Kenneth S. Kendler. 1994. "Lifetime and 12-Month Prevalence of DSM-III-R Psychiatric Disorders in the United States." *Archives of General Psychiatry* 51: 8–19.

KW Record. 1999. "What's up with Viagra Decision?" November 25: A16.

Lantz, Paula M., James S. House, James M. Lepkowski, David R. Williams, Richard P. Mero, and Jieming Chen. 1998. "Socioeconomic Factors, Health Behaviors, and Mortality: Results from a Nationally Representative Prospective Study of U.S. Adults." *Journal of the American Medical Association* 279: 1703–8.

LaPorte, Ronald E. 1997. "Improving Public Health via the Information Superhighway." June 8, 1998 <www.the-scientist.library.upenn.edu/yr1997/august/opin_970 18.html>.

Leiss, William. 1997. "Tobacco Control Policy in Canada: Shadow-Boxing with Risk." *Policy Options,* June 18(5): 3–6.

Lerer, Leonard B., Alan D. Lopez, Tord Kjellstrom, and Derek Yach. 1998. "Health for All: Analyzing Health Status and Determinants." *World Health Statistics Quarterly* 51: 7–20.

Levenkron, Steven. 1997. *The Luckiest Girl in the World.* New York: Penguin.

———. 1998. *Cutting: Understanding and Overcoming Self-Mutilation.* New York: W.W. Norton.

Lorber, Judith. 1997. *Gender and the Social Construction of Illness.* Thousand Oaks, Calif.: Sage Publications.

Maclean's. 2000. "Provinces Struggle to Keep up with Demands for Senior Care." January 17: 19.

"Maternal Mortality: A Preventable Tragedy." 1998. *Popline* 20: 4.

McClelland, Susan. 1999. "Users Beware." *Maclean's,* June 21: 58–9.

Miller, Dusty. 1995. *Women Who Hurt Themselves: A Book of Hope and Understanding.* New York: Basic Books.

Miller, K., and A. Rosenfield. 1996. "Population and Women's Reproductive Health: An International Perspective." *Annual Review of Public Health* 17: 359–82.

Mitchell, Alana. 1995. "Down's Transplant Bid Poses Dilemma." *The Globe and Mail,* April 28: A1, A10.

Moore, R., Y. Mao, and J. Zhang. 1997. *Economic Burden of Illness in Canada, 1993.* Ottawa: Health Canada, Laboratory Centre for Disease Control. Cat. H21-13611993E.

Morse, Minna. 1998. "The Killer Mosquitoes." *Utne Reader* (May–June): 14–5.

Morton, Desmond, and Morton Weinfeld (eds.). 1998. *Who Speaks for Canada? Words That Shape a Country.* Toronto: McClelland and Stewart Inc.

Murray, C., and A. Lopez (eds.). 1996. *The Global Burden of Disease.* Boston: Harvard University Press.

Nader, Ralph, Nadia Millerton, and Conacher Duff. 1993. *Canada Firsts.* Toronto: McClelland and Stewart.

National Center for Health Statistics. 1998. *Health, United States, 1998: With Socioeconomic Status and Health Chartbook.* Hyattsville, Minn.: U.S. Government Printing Office.

National Forum on Health. n.d. *The Need for An Aboriginal Health Institute in Canada.* Synthesis Reports and Issues Paper, Final Report, Vol. II <www.hc-sc.gc.ca/publicat/involv2/aborig/idsabo/html>.

"Older Populations Expanding Rapidly." 1998. *Popline* 20 (September–October): 1–2.

Ostrof, Paul. 1998. "Readers Write: My Chair." *Sun* (August): 33–40.

Parsons, Talcott. 1951. *The Social System.* New York: The Free Press.

Pate, Russell R., Michael Pratt, Steven N. Blair, William L. Haskell, Caroline A. Macera, Claude Bouchard, David Buchner, Walter Ettiger, Gregory W. Health, Abby C. King, Andrea Kriska, Arthur L. Leon, Bess H. Marcus, Jeremy Morris, Ralph S. Paffenbarger, Kevin Patrick, Michael L. Pollock, James M. Rippe, James Sallis, and Jack H. Wilmore. 1995. "Physical Activity and Public Health: A Recommendation from the Centers for Disease Control and Prevention and the American College of Sports Medicine." *Journal of the American Medical Association* 273(5): 402–6.

"Poverty Threatens Crisis." 1998. *Popline* 20 (May–June): 3.

Ross, Robert R., and Hugh B. McKay. 1979. *Self-Mutilation.* Toronto: Lexington Books.

Roth, J.A. 1991. *Psychoactive Substances and Violence.* Rockville: National Institute of Justice, U.S. Department of Justice.

Royal Commission on Aboriginal Peoples. 1996. *Looking Forward, Looking Back: Report of the Royal Commission on Aboriginal Peoples,* Vol. 1. Ottawa: Supply and Services Canada.

Safe Motherhood Initiative. 1998. "Fact and Figures." September 24 <www.safemotherhood.org/init_facts.htm>.

Scott, K. 1997. "Indigenous Canadians." In *Canadian Profile: Alcohol, Tobacco and Other Drugs, 1997,* edited by D. McKenzie, R. William, and E. Single. Ottawa: Canadian Centre on Substance Abuse.

Shkilnyk, Anastasia. 1985. *A Poison Stronger Than Love.* New Haven, Conn: Yale University Press.

Statistical Abstract of the United States: 1998. 118th ed. U.S. Bureau of the Census, Washington, D.C.: U.S. Government Printing Office.

Statistics Canada. 1998a. *Canada Yearbook 1999.* Ottawa: Ministry of Industry.

———. 1998b. *The Daily.* October 29 <www.statcan.ca:80/Daily/English/981029/d981029.htm>.

———. 1999. *The Daily,* March 13 <www.statcan.ca/Daily/English/990313/d990313.htm>.

Stephens, T. 1994. *Smoking among Aboriginal People in Canada 1991.* Ottawa: Health Canada.

Strong, Marilee. 1998. *A Bright Red Line: Self-Mutilation and the Language of Pain.* New York: Viking Press.

Szasz, Thomas. 1970 (orig. 1961). *The Myth of Mental Illness: Foundations of a Theory of Personal Conduct.* New York: Harper and Row.

Thirunarayanapuram, Desikan. 1998. "'Population Explosion' Is Far from Over." *Popline* 20 (January–February): 1, 4.

"Using Computers to Advance Health Care." 1996. July 28, 1998 <www.ahcpr.gov/research/computer.htm>.

Verbrugge, Lois M. 1999. "Pathways of Health and Death." In *Health, Illness, and Healing: Society, Social Context, and Self,* edited by Kathy Charmaz and Deborah A. Paterniti, pp. 377–94. Los Angeles: Roxbury Publishing Co.

Visschedijk, Jan, and Silvere Simeant. 1998. "Targets for Health for All in the Twenty-First Century." *World Health Statistics Quarterly* 51: 56–67.

Walsh, Barent W., and Paul R. Rosen (eds.). 1999. *Self-Mutilation: Theory, Research and Treatment.* New York: Guilford Press.

Weitz, Rose. 1996. *The Sociology of Health, Illness, and Health Care: A Critical Approach.* Belmont, Calif.: Wadsworth Publishing Co.

Wilkins, R. 1998. "Mortality by Neighbourhood Income in Canada, 1986 to 1991." Paper presented at the Conference of the Canadian Society for Epidemiology and Biostatistics, St. John's, Newfoundland, August.

Williams, David R., and Chiquita Collins. 1999. "U.S. Socioeconomic and Racial Differences in Health: Patterns and Explanations." In *Health, Illness, and Healing: Society, Social Context, and Self,* edited by Kathy Charmaz and Deborah A. Paterniti, pp. 349–76. Los Angeles: Roxbury Publishing Co.

World Health Organization. 1946. *Constitution of the World Health Organization.* New York: World Health Organization Interim Commission.

———. 1997a. Fact Sheet No. 178: Reducing Mortality from Major Childhood Killer Diseases. July 28, 1998 <www.cdc.gov/ogh/frames.htm>.

———. 1997b. The World Health Report 1997. July 28, 1998 <www.who.org/whr/1997/exsum97e.htm>.

———. 1998. "Fifty Facts from the World Health Report 1998." August 8 <www.who.int/whr/1998/factse/htm>.

World Health Organization and United Nations Joint Programme on HIV/AIDS. 1998. "Report on the Global HIV/AIDS Epidemic—June 1998." August 8 <www.who.int/emchiv/global_report/data/globrep_e/pdf>.

"Youth Suicide Prevention: Warning Signs and How to Respond." 1998. *Every Teen Counts.* Washington State PTA. 2003 65th Ave., West Tacoma, Wash. 98466-6215. <www.wastatepta.org>. Reprinted by permission.

Chapter 3

AADAC (Alberta Alcohol and Drug Abuse Commission). 1992. *Substance Use and the Alberta Workplace: The Prevalence of Alcohol and Other Drugs: Final Report.* Edmonton: AADAC.

AAP (Australian Associated Press). 1998. "Genetics of Alcoholism." *Institute of Alcohol Studies Update.* London: IAS Publications.

Adlaf, E.M., Y.M. Zdanowicz, and R.G. Smart. 1996. "Alcohol and Other Drug Use among Street-Involved Youth in Toronto." *Addiction Research* 4(1): 11–24.

American Heart Association. 1997. "Tobacco Industry's Targeting of Youth, Minorities, and Women." AHA Advocacy Position. American Heart Association. <www.americanheart.org>.

Becker, H.S. 1966. *Outsiders: Studies in the Sociology of Deviance.* New York: Free Press.

Bennett, William. 1993. "Should Drugs Be Legalized?" In *Social Problems: A Critical Thinking Approach,* 2nd ed., edited by Paul J. Baker, Louise E. Anderson, and Dean S. Dorn, pp. 246–48. Belmont, Calif.: Wadsworth.

Boyle, Theresa. 1999. "Forcing Welfare Drug Tests Could be Discriminatory." *KW Record,* October 29: A5.

Bureau of Justice Statistics. 1992. "Drugs, Crime, and the Justice System: A National Report from the Bureau of Justice Statistics." U.S. Department of Justice, Office of Justice Programs. Washington, D.C.: U.S. Government Printing Office, Superintendent of Documents.

Canadian Cancer Society. 1999. <www.cancer.ca/tobacco/index.htm>.

CCSA (Canadian Centre on Substance Abuse and Centre for Addiction and Mental Health). 1999. *Canadian Profile 1999: Alcohol, Tobacco and Other Drugs.* Ottawa: Centre on Substance Abuse and Centre for Addiction and Mental Health.

Clark, Campbell. 1999. "Vezana Says Sorry, But Not for Taking Banned Substances." *National Post,* August 3: B14.

Clark, Wayne. 1996. "Youth Smoking in Canada." *Canadian Social Trends* Winter 43: 2–7.

Clinton, William. 1998. "The President's Message to the Congress of the United States." ONDCP. <www.whitehousedrugpolicy/gov/policy/98ndcs/message.html>.

Cooper, M., R. Corrado, A.M. Karlberg, and L.P. Adams. 1992. "Aboriginal Suicide in British Columbia: An Overview." *Canada's Mental Health* (September): 19–23.

DATOS (Drug Abuse Treatment Outcome Study). 1998. "Representative Drug Treatment Research." ONDCP. <www.whitehousedrugpolicy.gov/drugfact/research.html>.

De Guia, N., J. Cohen, and M. Ashley. 1996–97. *How Provincial and Territorial Legislators View Tobacco and Tobacco Control: Findings From a Canadian Study*. Toronto: Ontario Tobacco Research Unit.

Dembo, Richard, Linda Williams, Jeffrey Fagan, and James Schmeidler. 1994. "Development and Assessment of a Classification of High Risk Youths." *Journal of Drug Issues* 24: 25–53.

Dennis, Richard J. 1993. "The Economics of Legalizing Drugs." In *Social Problems: A Critical Thinking Approach*, 2nd ed., edited by Paul J. Baker, Louise E. Anderson, and Dean S. Dorn, pp. 249–55. Belmont, Calif.: Wadsworth.

Department of Justice. 1998. "How Do Canadian Crime Rates Compare to Those of Other Countries?" *Justice Research Notes* 5 (April): 17–8.

Duke, Steven, and Albert C. Gross. 1994. *America's Longest War: Rethinking Our Tragic Crusade against Drugs*. New York: G.P. Putnam and Sons.

Duster, Troy. 1995. "The New Crisis of Legitimacy in Controls, Prisons, and Legal Structures." *American Sociologist* 26: 20–9.

Easley, Margaret, and Norman Epstein. 1991. "Coping with Stress in a Family with an Alcoholic Parent." *Family Relations* 40: 218–24.

Eliany, M. 1994. "Alcohol and Drug Consumption among Canadian Youth." *Canadian Social Trends* 26 (Autumn): 10–3.

Feagin, Joe R., and C.B. Feagin. 1994. *Social Problems*. Englewood Cliffs, N.J.: Prentice-Hall.

Fennell, Tom. 2000. "Truth and Consequences." *Maclean's*, January 31: 66–7.

Fife, R. 1999. "Police Chiefs Get through to the Top." *National Post*, April 22.

Foster, Burk, Craig J. Forsyth, and Stasia Herbert. 1994. "The Cycle of Family Violence among Criminal Offenders: A Study of Inmates in One Louisiana Jail." *Free Inquiry in Creative Sociology* 22: 133–7.

Gentry, Cynthia. 1995. "Crime Control through Drug Control." In *Criminology*, 2nd ed., edited by Joseph F. Sheley, pp. 477–93. Belmont, Calif.: Wadsworth.

Gfellner, B.M., and J.D. Hundelby. 1995. "Patterns of Drug Use among Native and White Adolescents: 1990–1993." *Canadian Journal of Public Health* 86: 95–7.

Giffen, P.J., S. Endicott, and S. Lambert. 1991. *Panic and Indifference: The Politics of Canada's Drug Laws*. Ottawa: Canadian Centre on Substance Abuse.

Green, Melvyn. 1986. "The History of Canadian Narcotics Control: The Formative Years." In *The Social Dimensions of Law*, edited by Neil Boyd, pp. 24–40. Scarborough, Ont.: Prentice Hall.

Gusfield, Joseph. 1963. *Contested Meanings: The Construction of Alcohol Problems*. Madison: University of Wisconsin Press.

Hackler, James C. 2000. *Canadian Criminology: Strategies and Perspectives*, 2nd ed. Scarborough, Ont.: Prentice Hall Allyn and Bacon Canada.

Hagan, J., and McCarthy, B. 1997. *Mean Streets: Youth Crime and Homelessness*. Cambridge: Cambridge University Press.

Health Canada. 1999. *Statistical Report on the Health of Canadians*. <www.hc-sc.gc.ca/hppb/phdd/report/stat/eng/over.html>.

HHS (U.S. Department of Health and Human Services). 1998. "Tobacco Use Continues to Rise among High School Students in the U.S." *Substance Abuse and Mental Health Service Administration* Press Release (April 2). Washington, D.C.

Institute of Alcohol Studies. 1997. "Alcohol and Crime Fact Sheet." <www.ias.org.uk/factsheets/crime/html>.

Jarvik, M. 1990. "The Drug Dilemma: Manipulating the Demand." *Science* 250: 387–92.

Johnson, Holly. 1996. *Dangerous Domains: Violence Against Women in Canada*. Scarborough, Ont.: Nelson.

Join Together. 1998. "Inhalant Abuse." *Hot Issues*, July 11 <www.jointogether.org/sa/issues/hot_issues/inhalants/default.html>.

Klonoff-Cohen, Sandra H., S.L. Edelstein, E.S. Lefkowitz, Indu Sriwirasan, David Kaegi, Jae Chun Chang, and Karen Wiley. 1995. "The Effect of Passive Smoking and Tobacco Exposure through Breast Milk on Sudden Infant Death Syndrome." *Journal of the American Medical Association* 273: 795–98.

Kort, Marcel de. 1994. "The Dutch Cannabis Debate, 1968–1976." *Journal of Drug Issues* 24: 417–27.

KW Record. 1997. "Price Cut Boosts Youth Smoking." July 10: 172.

Leonard, K.E., and H.T. Blane. 1992. "Alcohol and Marital Aggression in a National Sample of Young Men." *Journal of Interpersonal Violence* 7: 19–30.

Lipton, Douglas S. 1994. "The Correctional Opportunity: Pathways to Drug Treatment for Offenders." *Journal of Drug Issues* 24: 331–48.

Maclean's. 1995. Untitled. August 28: 23.
———. 2000. "Butting Out." January 10: 35.

Mauro, Tony. 1998. "Fla. Jury Awards Biggest Tobacco Verdict Ever." *Nationline*. Daily Reflector wire service, June 11.

McMillan, D. 1991. *Winning the Battle Against Drugs*. New York: Franklin Watts.

Morgan, Patricia A. 1978. "The Legislation of Drug Law: Economic Crisis and Social Control." *Journal of Drug Issues* 8: 53–62.

Murphy, Judge Emily. 1922. *The Black Candle*. Toronto: Thomas Allen.

Nuwer, H. 1990. *Steroids*. New York: Franklin Watts.

Nylander, Albert, Tuk-Ying Tung, and Xiaohe Xu. 1996. "The Effect of Religion on Adolescent Drug Use in America: An Assessment of Change." American Sociological Association Meetings, San Francisco, Calif., August.

ONDCP (Office of National Drug Control Policy). 1998a. "Focus on the Drug

Problem." <www.whitehousedrug-policy.gov/drugfact/drugprob.html>.

———. 1998b. "Trends in Drug Use: Part II: Cocaine." *Pulse Check* (Winter) <www.health.org/pulse98/trend2.html>.

Perkins, Louise. 1997. *Slaughter of the Innocents*. Unpublished manuscript. Lambton Families in Action for Drug Education Inc., January.

Pickens, R.W., and D.S. Svikis. 1988. "Biological Vulnerability in Drug Abuse." National Institute on Drug Abuse (NIDA) Research Monograph No. 88. Washington, D.C.: NIDA.

Rorabaugh, W.J. 1979. *The Alcoholic Republic: An American Tradition*. New York: Oxford University Press.

Roth, J.A. 1994. *Psychoactive Substances and Violence*. Rockville: National Institute of Justice, U.S. Department of Justice.

Scott, K. 1997. "Indigenous Canadians." *Canadian Profile: Alcohol, Tobacco and Other Drugs, 1997*, edited by D. McKenzie, R. Williams, and E. Single, pp. 133–64. Ottawa: Canadian Centre on Substance Abuse.

Sheppard, Robert. 1999. "Ottawa Butts up against Big Brother." *Maclean's*, December 6: 20–4.

Single, E. 1997. "Public Opinion on Alcohol and Other Drug Issues." In *Canada's Alcohol and Other Drug Survey 1994: A Discussion of the Findings*, edited by P. MacNeil, and I. Webster. Cat. H39-336/1-1994E. Ottawa: Ministry of Public Works and Government Services Canada.

Solomon, Robert. 1999. "Alcohol and Drug Law." In *Canadian Profile 1999: Alcohol, Tobacco and Other Drugs*, pp. 295–315. Ottawa: Centre on Substance Abuse and Centre for Addiction and Mental Health.

Statistics Canada. 1998. *Canada Yearbook 2000*. Ottawa: Ministry of Industry.

———. 1999a. *The Daily*, March 9 <www.statcan.ca/Daily/English/990309/d990309.htm>.

———. 1999b. *The Daily*, November 17 <www.statca.ca/Daily/English/991113/d991113.htm>.

———. 2000. *The Daily*, February 16 <www.statcan.ca/Daily/English/000216/d000216c.htm>.

Sullivan, Thomas, and Kenrick S. Thompson. 1994. *Social Problems*. New York: Macmillan.

Tubman, J. 1993. "Family Risk Factors, Parental Alcohol Use, and Problem Behaviors among School-Aged Children." *Family Relations* 42: 81–6.

Van Dyck, C., and R. Byck. 1982. "Cocaine." *Scientific American* 246: 128–41.

Van Kammen, Welmoet B., and Rolf Loeber. 1994. "Are Fluctuations in Delinquent Activities Related to the Onset and Offset in Juvenile Illegal Drug Use and Drug Dealing?" *Journal of Drug Issues* 24: 9–24.

Waldorf, D., C. Reinarman, and S. Murphy. 1991. *Cocaine Changes: The Experience of Using and Quitting*. Philadelphia: Temple University Press.

Wechsler, Henry, George Dowdall, Andrea Davenport, and William Dejong. 1998. "Binge Drinking on Campus: Results of a National Study." Higher Education Center. <www.edc.org/hes/pubs/binge.html>.

White, Helene Raskin, and Erich W. Labouvie. 1994. "Generality versus Specificity of Problem Behavior: Psychological and Functional Differences." *Journal of Drug Issues* 24: 55–74.

Witters, Weldon, Peter Venturelli, and Glen Hanson. 1992. *Drugs and Society*, 3rd ed. Boston: Jones and Bartlett.

World Drug Report. 1997. "Report Highlights." United Nations International Drug Control Program. New York: United Nations.

Wysong, Earl, Richard Aniskiewicz, and David Wright. 1994. "Truth and Dare: Tracking Drug Education to Graduation and as Symbolic Politics." *Social Problems* 41: 448–68.

Chapter 4

Albanese, Jay, and Robert D. Pursley. 1993. *Crime in America: Some Existing and Emerging Problems*. Englewood Cliffs, N.J.: Prentice-Hall.

Anderson, Elijah. 1994. "The Code of the Streets: Sociology of Urban Violence." *Atlantic* 273(5): 80–91.

AP (Associated Press). 1998. "Safety Groups Renew Recall against GM Pickups." *USA Today*, Money Section. May 15 <www.usatoday.com/money/consumer/autos/mauto126.html>.

Bailey, Ian. 1999. "Having Child Porn Not a Crime, Judge Rules." *KW Record*, January 16: A4.

Barkan, Steven. 1997. *Criminology: A Sociological Understanding*. Englewood Cliffs, N.J.: Prentice-Hall.

Barlow, Hugh. 1993. *Introduction to Criminology*. New York: Harper Collins.

Becker, Howard S. 1963. *Outsiders: Studies in the Sociology of Deviance*. New York: Free Press.

Besserer, Sandra. 1999. "Criminal Victimization: An International Perspective." Canadian Centre for Justice Statistics, *The Juristat Reader: A Statistical Overview of the Canadian Justice System*, pp. 103–15. Toronto: Thompson Educational Publishing, Inc.

Bibby, Reginald W. 1995. *The Bibby Report: Social Trends Canadian Style*. Toronto: Stoddart.

Brantingham, Paul J., Shihong Mu, and Arvind Verma. 1995. "Patterns in Canadian Crime." In *Canadian Criminology: Perspectives on Crime and Criminality*, 2nd ed., edited by Margaret A. Jackson, and Curt T. Griffiths, pp. 187–246. Toronto: Harcourt Brace and Company, Canada.

Brookbank, Candace, and Bob Kingsley. 1999. "Adult Criminal Court Statistics, 1997–98." In *Canadian Centre for Justice Statistics, The Juristat Reader: A Statistical Overview of the Canadian Justice System*, pp. 69–84. Toronto: Thompson Educational Publishing, Inc.

Canadian Associated Press. 1999. "Teen hookers oppose child protection law." *KW Record*, November 17: B11.

Canadian Centre for Justice Statistics. 1999. "Overview of the National Justice Statistics Initiative and the Canadian Centre for Justice Statistics." In *Canadian Centre for Justice Statistics, The Juristat Reader: A Statistical Overview of the Canadian Justice System*, pp. v–vi. Toronto: Thompson Educational Publishing, Inc.

CATW (Coalition Against Trafficking in Women). 1997. "Promoting Sex Work in the Netherlands." *Coalition Report* 4(1) <www.uri.edu/artsci/wms/hughes/catw>.

Chesney-Lind, Meda. 1996. "Girls, Crime, and Women's Place: Toward a Feminist Model of Female Delinquency." In *Social Deviance: Readings in Theory and Research*, edited by Henry Pontell, pp. 166–80. Englewood Cliffs: N.J.: Prentice-Hall.

Chua-Eoan, Howard, and Tim Latimer. 1999. "Beware of the PokéMania." *Time*, Canadian edition, November 22: 60–7.

Comstock, George. 1993. "The Medium and the Society: The Role of Television in American Life." In *Children and Television: Images in a Changing Sociocultural World*, edited by Gordon L. Berry and Joy Keiko Asamen, pp. 117–31. Newbury Park, Calif.: Sage Publications.

COPS. 1998. "About the Office of Community Oriented Policing Services (COPS)." <communitypolicing.org/copspage.html>.

DeJong, William. 1994. "School-Based Violence Prevention: From the Peaceable School to the Peaceable Neighborhood." *Forum*, pp. 8–14. Washington, D.C.: National Institute for Dispute Resolution.

DiIulio, John. 1999. "Federal Crime Policy: Time for a Moratorium." *Brookings Review* 17(1): 17.

Duchesne, Doreen. 1999. "Street Prostitution in Canada." In *Canadian Centre for Justice Statistics, The Juristat Reader: A Statistical Overview of the Canadian Justice System*, pp. 241–52. Toronto: Thompson Educational Publishing, Inc.

Erikson, Kai T. 1966. *Wayward Puritans*. New York: John Wiley and Sons.

Evans, John, and Alexander Himelfarb. 2000. "Counting Crime." In *Criminology: A Canadian Perspective*, 4th ed., edited by Rick Linden, pp. 60–93. Toronto: Harcourt Brace and Company.

Faison, Seth. 1996. "Copyright Pirates Prosper in China Despite Promises." *New York Times*, February 20: A1, A6.

Farhi, Paul. 1996. "Researchers Link Psychological Harm to Violence on TV." *Boston Globe*, February 7: D3.

Fattah, Ezzat A. 1991. *Understanding Criminal Victimization: An Introduction to Theoretical Victimology*. Scarborough, Ont.: Prentice Hall.

Fedorowycz, Orest. 1999. "Homicide in Canada, 1998." *Juristat* 19(10), October, Canadian Centre for Justice Statistics, Cat. 85-002-XIE.

Felson, Marcus. 1998. *Crime and Everyday Life*, 2nd ed. Thousand Oaks, Calif.: Pine Forge Press.

Fitzgerald, Robin. 1999. "Assaults Against Children and Youth in the Family, 1996." In *Canadian Centre for Justice Statistics, The Juristat Reader: A Statistical Overview of the Canadian Justice System*, pp. 185–96. Toronto: Thompson Educational Publishing, Inc.

Garey, M. 1985. "The Cost of Taking a Life: Dollars and Sense of the Death Penalty." *U.C. Davis Law Review* 18: 1221–73.

Gest, Ted, and Dorian Friedman. 1994. "The New Crime Wave." *U.S. News and World Report*, August 29, 26–8.

Gorelick, David A. 1992. "Pathophysiological Effects of Cocaine in Humans: Review of Scientific Issues." *Journal of Addictive Diseases* 11(4): 97–110.

Griffiths, C.T., D.S. Wood, E. Zellerer, and J. Simon. 1994. *Aboriginal Policing in British Columbia*. Victoria: Ministry of Attorney General.

Hackler, James C. 2000. *Canadian Criminology: Strategies and Perspectives*, 2nd ed. Scarborough, Ont.: Prentice Hall Allyn and Bacon Canada.

Hagan, John. 2000. "White-Collar and Corporate Crime." In *Criminology: A Canadian Perspective*, 4th ed., edited by Rick Linden, pp. 459–82. Toronto: Harcourt Brace and Company.

Hagan, John, and Ruth Peterson. 1995. "Criminal Inequality in America: Patterns and Consequences." In *Crime and Inequality*, ed. John Hagan and Ruth Peterson, pp. 14–36. Stanford, Calif.: Stanford University Press.

Hartnagel, Timothy F. 2000. "Correlates of Criminal Behaviour." In *Criminology:*

A Canadian Perspective, 4th ed., edited by Rick Linden, pp. 94–136. Toronto: Harcourt Brace and Company.

Hendrick, Dianne. 1999. "Youth Court Statistics 1997–98 Highlights." In *Canadian Centre for Justice Statistics, The Juristat Reader: A Statistical Overview of the Canadian Justice System*, pp. 85–100. Toronto: Thompson Educational Publishing, Inc.

Hills, Stuart. 1987. "Introduction." In *Corporate Violence: Injury and Death for Profit*, edited by Stuart Hills, pp. 1–7. Lanham, Minn.: Rowman Publishing Co.

Hirschi, Travis. 1969. *Causes of Delinquency*. Berkeley: University of California Press.

Hochstetler, Andrew, and Neal Shover. 1997. "Street Crime, Labor Surplus, and Criminal Punishment, 1980–1990." *Social Problems* 44(3): 358–67.

Hughes, Donna M. 1997. "Trafficking in Women on the Internet." *CATW: Coalition Report* 4(1) <www.uri.edu/artsci/wms/hughes/catw>.

INTERPOL. 1998. "INTERPOL Warning: Nigerian Crime Syndicate's Letter Scheme Fraud Takes on New Dimension." Press Releases. <www.kenpubs.co.uk/INTERPOL.COM/English/pres/nig.html>.

Jacobs, David. 1988. "Corporate Economic Power and the State: A Longitudinal Assessment of Two Explanations." *American Journal of Sociology* 93: 852–81.

Janoff-Bulman, Ronnie, C. Timko, and L. Carli. 1985. "Cognitive Biases in Blaming the Victim." *Journal of Experimental Social Psychology* 23: 161–77.

Johnstone, Rebecca, and Jennifer Thomas. 1999. "Legal Aid in Canada: 1996–97." In *Canadian Centre for Justice Statistics, The Juristat Reader: A Statistical Overview of the Canadian Justice System*, pp. 27–36. Toronto: Thompson Educational Publishing, Inc.

Kluger, Jeffrey. 1999. "DNA Detectives." *Time*, Canadian edition, January 11: 46–7.

Koenig, Daniel J. 2000. "Conventional or 'Street' Crime." In *Criminology: A Canadian Perspective,* 4th ed., edited by Rick Linden, pp. 396–429. Toronto: Harcourt Brace and Company.

Kong, Rebecca. 1999. "Canadian Crime Statistics, 1997." In *Canadian Centre for Justice Statistics, The Juristat Reader: A Statistical Overview of the Canadian Justice System,* pp. 117–37. Toronto: Thompson Educational Publishing, Inc.

Kurtz, Howard. 1997. "U.S. Television News Distorts Reality of Homicide Rates." *Edmonton Journal,* August 13: A5.

Lagan, Bernard. 1997. "$3 Billion Cost of White Collar Criminals." *Sydney Morning Herald,* August 13 <www.smh.com.au>.

LaPrairie, Carol. 1996. *Examining Aborginal Correction in Canada.* Ottawa: Supply and Services Canada.

Laub, John, Daniel S. Nagan, and Robert Sampson. 1998. "Trajectories of Change in Criminal Offending: Good Marriages and the Desistance Process." *American Sociological Review* 63 (April): 225–38.

Leesti, Tracey. 1999. "Weapons and Violent Crime." In *Canadian Centre for Justice Statistics, The Juristat Reader: A Statistical Overview of the Canadian Justice System,* pp. 165–74. Toronto: Thompson Educational Publishing, Inc.

Lehrur, Eli. 1999. "Communities and Cops Join Forces." *Insight on the News* 15(3): 16.

Leidholdt, Dorchen. 1997. "A Fact-Finding Trip to Thailand." *CATW: Coalition Report* 4(1) <www.uri.edu/artsci/wms/hughes/catw>.

Leonard, Tim. 1999. "Crime in Major Metropolitan Areas, 1991–1995." In *Canadian Centre for Justice Statistics, The Juristat Reader: A Statistical Overview of the Canadian Justice System,* pp. 139–50. Toronto: Thompson Educational Publishing, Inc.

Lewis, Peter H. 1998. "Threat to Corporate Computers Is Often the Enemy Within." *New York Times,* March 2: 1–5.

Maclean's. 1999. "Rounding up Suspects for their DNA." December 13: 13.
———. 2000. "Child Porn Hearing." January 31: 39.

Mauer, Marc. 1997. *Americans behind Bars: The International Use of Incarceration.* Washington D.C.: The Sentencing Project <www.sproject.com/press-1.htm>.

Merton, Robert. 1957. "Social Structure and Anomie." In *Social Theory and Social Structure.* Glencoe, Ill.: Free Press.

Meyer, Michael, and Anne Underwood. 1994. "Crimes of the 'Net.'" *Newsweek,* November 14, 46–7.

Moore, Elizabeth, and Michael Mills. 1990. "The Neglected Victims and Unexamined Costs of White Collar Crime." *Crime and Delinquency* 36: 408–18.

Murray, John P. 1993. "The Developing Child in a Multimedia Society." In *Children and Television: Images in a Changing Sociocultural World,* edited by Gordon L. Berry and Joy Keiko Asamen, pp. 9–22. Newbury Park, Calif.: Sage Publications.

Murray, Mary E., Nancy Guerra, and Kirk Williams. 1997. "Violence Prevention for the Twenty-First Century." In *Enhancing Children's Awareness,* edited by Roger P. Weissberg, Thomas Gullota, Robert L. Hampton, Bruce Ryan, and Gerald Adams, pp. 105–28. Thousand Oaks, Calif: Sage Publications.

Myths and Facts about the Death Penalty. 1998. "Death Penalty: Focus on California." <members.aol.com/Dpfocus/facts.htm>.

National Research Council. 1994. *Violence in Urban America: Mobilizing a Response.* Washington, D.C.: National Academy Press.

(NCVS) National Crime Victimization Survey. 1997. "Crime and Victim Statistics." Bureau of Justice Statistics. Washington, D.C.: U.S. Department of Justice.

(OJP) Office of Justice Programs. 1998. "Gallery 37." Innovations in American Government: Award Winners in the Field of Criminal Justice. <wwwojp/usdoj/nij/innvprog>.

Olmsted, A.D. 1988. "Morally Controversial Leisure." *Symbolic Interaction* 11: 277–87.

Parker, Laura. 1998. "Tests Point to Sheppard's Innocence." *USA Today,* March 5: A3.

Radelet, M.L., H.A. Bedeau, and C.E. Putnam. 1992. *In Spite of Innocence: Erroneous Convictions in Capital Cases.* Boston: Northeastern University Press.

Randall, Melanie, and Lori Haskell. 1995. "Sexual Violence in Women's Lives." *Violence against Women* 1: 6–31.

Reed, Micheline, and Julian Roberts. 1999. "Adult Correctional Services in Canada, 1997–98." Pp. 39–51 in Canadian Centre for Justice Statistics, *The Juristat Reader: A Statistical Overview of the Canadian Justice System.* Toronto: Thompson Educational Publishing, Inc.

Rideau, William. 1994. "Why Prisons Don't Work." *Time,* March 21: 80.

Robinson, David, Frank J. Porporino, William A. Millson. 1999. "A One-Day Snapshot of Inmates in Canada's Adult Correctional Facilities." In *Canadian Centre for Justice Statistics, The Juristat Reader: A Statistical Overview of the Canadian Justice System,* pp. 53–66. Toronto: Thompson Educational Publishing, Inc.

Russell, Cheryl. 1995. "Murder Is All American." *American Demographics* (September). <www.demographics.com>.

Sanday, P.R. 1981. "The Sociocultural Context of Rape: A Cross-Cultural Study." *Journal of Social Issues* 37: 5–27.

Schofield, John. 1996. "In the Fickle Hands of Lady Luck." *Maclean's,* November 4: 53.

Seagrave, J. 1997. *Introduction to Policing in Canada.* Scarborough, Ont.: Prentice Hall.

Shabad, Steven. 1999. "A Himalayan Mafia." *World Press Review* 46(2): 20.

Shabalin, Victor, J.J. Albini, and R.E. Rogers. 1995. "The New Stage of the Fight against Organized Crime in Russia." *IASOC: Criminal Organization* 10(1): 19–21.

Stamler, Rodney T. 2000. "Organized Crime." In *Criminology: A Canadian*

Perspective, 4th ed., edited by Rick Linden, pp. 429–58. Toronto: Harcourt Brace and Company.

Statistical Abstract of the United States: 1998, 118th ed. U.S. Bureau of the Census. Washington, D.C.: U.S. Government Printing Office.

Statistics Canada. 1998a. *Canada Yearbook 2000*. Ottawa: Ministry of Industry.

———. 1998b. "The Gambling Industry: Raising the Stakes." *The Daily*, December 9.

———. 1999. *National Population Health Survey*, 1996–97. Ottawa: Ministry of Industry. Cat. 82-567-XPB.

Steffensmeier, Darrell, and Emilie Allan. 1995. "Criminal Behavior: Gender and Age." In *Criminology: A Contemporary Handbook*, 2nd ed., edited by Joseph F. Sheley, pp. 83–113. Belmont, Calif.: Wadsworth.

Sutherland, Edwin H. 1939. *Criminology*. Philadelphia: Lippincott.

Swartz, Joel. 1978. "Silent Killers at Work." In *Corporate and Governmental Deviance*, edited by M. David Ermann and Richard Lundman, pp. 114–28. New York: Oxford University Press.

Swol, Karen. 1999. "Private Security and Public Policing in Canada." In *Canadian Centre for Justice Statistics, The Juristat Reader: A Statistical Overview of the Canadian Justice System*, pp. 15–25. Toronto: Thompson Educational Publishing, Inc.

Tibbets, Janice. 1999. "DNA Evidence Goes on Trial." *National Post*, December 15: A20.

United Nations. 1997. "Crime Goes Global." Document No. DPI/1518/ SOC/CON/ 30M. New York: United Nations.

U.S. Department of Justice. 1998. "International Crime Statistics." Bureau of Justice Statistics. Washington, D.C. <www.ojp.usdoj.gov/bjs/pub>.

Warner, Barbara, and Pamela Wilcox Rountree. 1997. "Local Social Ties in a Community and Crime Model." *Social Problems* 4(4): 520–36.

White, Michael, 1999. "GM Ordered to Pay Accident Victims $49 B." *National Post*, July 10: A1.

Williams, Linda. 1984. "The Classic Rape: When Do Victims Report?" *Social Problems* 31: 459–67.

Willing, Richard. 1997. "Tests Exonerate One in Four Suspects." *USA Today*, November 28: A3.

Zagaroli, Lisa. 1997. "Consumer Groups Call Side-Mounted GM Truck Fuel Tanks 'Lethal.'" *Detroit News*, October 14 <www.detnews.com>.

Zimring, F.E., and G. Hawkins. 1997. *Crime Is Not the Problem: Lethal Violence in America*. New York: Oxford University Press.

Chapter 5

Adams, Michael. 1997. *Sex in the Snow*. Toronto: Viking Press.

Amato, Paul R., and Bruce Keith. 1991. "Parental Divorce and Adult Well-Being: A Meta-Analysis." *Journal of Marriage and the Family* 53: 43–58.

Anderson, Kristin L. 1997. "Gender, Status, and Domestic Violence: An Integration of Feminist and Family Violence Approaches." *Journal of Marriage and the Family* 59: 655–9.

Arendell, Terry. 1995. *Fathers and Divorce*. Thousand Oaks, Calif.: Sage Publications.

Balakrishnan, T.R., K. Krotki, and E. Lapierre-Adamcyk. 1985. "Contraceptive Use in Canada." *Family Planning Perspectives* 17: 209–15.

Berne, L.A., and B.K. Huberman. 1996. "Sexuality Education Works: Here's Proof." *Education Digest* (February): 25–9.

Bibby, Reginald W. 1995. *The Bibby Report: Social Trends Canadian Style*. Toronto: Stoddart.

Blankenhorn, David. 1995. *Fatherless America: Confronting Our Most Urgent Social Problem*. New York: Basic Books.

Braithwaite, John. 1989. *Crime, Shame, and Reintegration*. Melbourne: Cambridge University Press.

Brienza, Julie. 1996. "At the Fault Line: Divorce Laws Divide Reformers." *Trial* 32(2): 12–4.

Brinkerhoff, M.B., and E. Lupri. 1988. "Interpersonal Violence." *Canadian Journal of Sociology* 31(4): 407–34.

Browning, Christopher R., and Edward O. Laumann. 1997. "Sexual Contact between Children and Adults: A Life Course Perspective." *American Sociological Review* 62: 540–60.

Busby, Dean M. 1991. "Violence in the Family." In *Family Research: A Sixty-Year Review* Vol. 1, edited by S. J. Bahr, pp. 335–85. New York: Lexington Books.

Carney, James. 1989. "Can a driver be too old?" *Time*, January 16: 28.

Chesley, L., D. MacAulay, and J.L. Ristock. 1991. *Abuse in Lesbian Relationships: A Handbook of Information and Resources*. Toronto: Counselling Centre for Lesbians and Gays.

Clark, Charles. 1996. "Marriage and Divorce." *CQ Researcher* 6(18): 409–32.

Clark, L., and D. Lewis. 1977. *Rape: The Price of Coercive Sexuality*. Toronto: Women's Educational Press.

Conway, J.F. 1990. *The Canadian Family in Crisis*. Toronto: James Lorimer.

Crawford, Maria, Rosemary Gartner, and Myrna Dawson. 1997. *Intimate Femicide in Ontario*. Toronto: Ontario Women's Directorate.

Demo, David H. 1992. "Parent-Child Relations: Assessing Recent Changes." *Journal of Marriage and the Family* 54: 104–17.

———. 1993. "The Relentless Search for Effects of Divorce: Forging New Trails or Tumbling Down the Beaten Path?" *Journal of Marriage and the Family* 55: 42–5.

Dobash, R.E., and R.P. Dobash. 1992. *Women, Violence and Social Change*. New York: Routledge.

———. 1995. "Reflections on Findings from the Violence Against Women Survey." *Canadian Journal of Criminology* 37(3): 457–84.

"Domestic Violence and Homelessness." 1998. *NCH Fact Sheet No. 8*. National Coalition for the Homeless.

Elliott, D.M., and J. Briere. 1992. "The Sexually Abused Boy: Problems in Manhood." *Medical Aspects of Human Sexuality* 26: 68–71.

Fedorowycz, Orest. 1999. "Homicide in Canada: 1998." *Juristat* 19(10), Canadian Centre for Justice Statistics, Cat. 85-002-XIE.

Fleras, A., and J.L. Elliott. 1996. *Unequal Relations: An Introduction to Race, Ethnicity, and Indigeneity in Canada*, 2nd ed. Scarborough, Ont.: Prentice Hall.

Frederick, Judith A., and Jason Hamel. 1998. "Canadian Attitudes to Divorce." *Canadian Social Trends* (Spring) 48: 6–10.

Gairdner, W. 1991. *The War against the Family: A Parent Speaks Out.* Toronto: Stoddart.

Geile, Janet Z. 1996. "Decline of the Family: Conservative, Liberal, and Feminist Views." In *Promises to Keep: Decline and Renewal of Marriage in America*, edited by D. Popenoe, J.B. Elshtain, and D. Blankenhorn, pp. 89–115. Lanham, Minn.: Rowman and Littlefield.

Gelles, Richard. 1980. "The Myth of Battered Husbands and New Facts About Family Violence." In *Social Problems,* edited by Robert L. David, pp. 80–1. Guilford, Conn.: Dushkin.

———. 1993. "Family Violence." In *Family Violence: Prevention and Treatment*, edited by Robert L. Hampton, Thomas P. Gullotta, Gerald R. Adams, Earl H. Potter III, and Roger P. Weissberg, pp. 1–24. Newbury Park, Calif.: Sage Publications.

Gelles, Richard J., and Jon R. Conte. 1991. "Domestic Violence and Sexual Abuse of Children: A Review of Research in the Eighties." In *Contemporary Families: Looking Forward, Looking Back*, edited by Alan Booth, pp. 327–40. Minneapolis: National Council on Family Relations.

Global Study of Family Values. 1998. The Gallup Organization. April 13, 1998 <198.175.140.8/Special_Reports/family.htm>.

Gottlieb, Beatrice. 1993. *The Family in the Western World: From the Black Death to the Industrial Age.* New York: Oxford University Press.

Groenveld, J., and M. Shain. 1989. *Drug Abuse among Victims of Physical and Sexual Abuse: A Preliminary Report.* Toronto: Addiction Research Foundation.

Hacker, S.S. 1992. "The Transition from the Old World to the New: Sexual values for the 1990s." In *Human Sex-*

uality 92/93, edited by Ollie Pocs, pp. 22–9. Guildford, Conn.: Dushkin.

Harrington, Donna, and Howard Dubowitz. 1993. "What Can Be Done to Prevent Child Maltreatment?" In *Family Violence: Prevention and Treatment*, edited by Robert L. Hampton, Thomas P. Gullotta, Gerald R. Adams, Earl H. Potter III, and Roger P. Weissberg, pp. 258–80. Newbury Park, Calif.: Sage Publications.

Health Canada. 1999. *Statistical Report in the Health of Canadians.* <www.hc-sc.gc.ca/hppb/phdd/report/stat/eng/over.html>.

Heim, Susan C., and Douglas K. Snyder. 1991. "Predicting Depression from Marital Distress and Attributional Processes." *Journal of Marital and Family Therapy* 17: 67–72.

Hewlett, Sylvia Ann, and Cornel West. 1998. *The War against Parents: What We Can Do for Beleaguered Moms and Dads.* Boston: Houghton Mifflin Company.

Hochschild, Arlie Russell. 1997. *The Time Bind: When Work Becomes Home and Home Becomes Work.* New York: Henry Holt and Company.

Ingrassia, Michelle. 1993. "Daughters of Murphy Brown." *Newsweek*, August 2: 58–9.

"In the News." 1998. Family Violence Prevention Fund. May 16, 1998 <www. igc.org/fund/materials/speakup/02_13_98.htm>.

Jacobs, C.D., and E.M. Wolf. 1995. "School Sexuality Education and Adolescent Risk-Taking Behavior." *Journal of School Health* 65: 91–5.

Jekielek, Susan M. 1998. "Parental Conflict, Marital Disruption and Children's Emotional Well-Being." *Social Forces* 76: 905–35.

Johnson, Holly. 1996. *Dangerous Domains: Violence Against Women in Canada.* Scarborough, Ont.: Nelson.

Kaufman, Joan, and Edward Zigler. 1992. "The Prevention of Child Maltreatment: Programming, Research, and Policy." In *Prevention of Child Maltreatment: Developmental and Ecological Perspectives*, edited by Diane J. Willis, E. Wayne Holden, and Mindy

Rosenberg, pp. 269–95. New York: John Wiley and Sons.

Kitson, Gay C., and Leslie A. Morgan. 1991. "The Multiple Consequences of Divorce: A Decade Review." In *Contemporary Families: Looking Forward, Looking Back*, edited by Alan Booth, pp. 150–91. Minneapolis: National Council on Family Relations.

Knox, David (with Kermit Leggett). 1998. *The Divorced Dad's Survival Book: How to Stay Connected with Your Kids.* New York: Insight Books.

Kong, R. 1997. "Criminal Harassment in Canada." *Canadian Social Trends* 45 (Autumn): 29–33.

Krug, Ronald S. 1989. "Adult Male Report of Childhood Sexual Abuse by Mothers: Case Description, Motivations, and Long-Term Consequences." *Child Abuse and Neglect* 13: 111–9.

Le Bourdais, C., and N. Marcil-Gratton. 1996. "Family Transformations across the Canadian-American Border: When the Laggard becomes the Leader." *Journal of Comparative Family Studies* 27(2): 415–36.

Lindgren, April. 1999. "Gamblers drop $2-billion at Ontario Casinos." *National Post*, July 14: A12.

Lloyd, S.A., and B.C. Emery. 1993. "Abuse in the Family: An Ecological, Life-Cycle Perspective." In *Family Relations: Challenges for the Future*, edited by T.H. Brubaker, pp. 129–52. Newbury Park, Calif.: Sage Publications.

Louisiana Divorce. 1997. Women's Connection Online, Inc. July 21, 1998 <www.womenconnect.com>.

Luker, Kristin. 1996. *Dubious Conceptions: The Politics of Teenage Pregnancy.* Cambridge, Mass.: Harvard University Press.

Marlow, L., and S.R. Sauber. 1990. *The Handbook of Divorce Mediation.* New York: Plenum.

Masheter, C. 1991. "Post-Divorce Relationships between Ex-Spouses: The Roles of Attachment and Interpersonal Conflict." *Journal of Marriage and the Family* 53: 103–10.

McEvoy, Maureen. 1990. *Let the Healing Begin: Breaking the Cycle of Child Sexual Abuse in Our Communities.*

Merritt, B.C.: Nicola Valley Institute of Technology.

Morrison, N. 1987. "Separation and Divorce." In *The Canadian Woman's Legal Guide*, edited by M. J. Dymond, pp. 125–43. Toronto: Doubleday.

Morrow, R.B., and G.T. Sorrell. 1989. "Factors Affecting Self-Esteem, Depression, and Negative Behaviors in Sexually Abused Female Adolescents." *Journal of Marriage and the Family* 51: 677–86.

Morton, M. 1990. "Controversies within Family Law." In *Families: Changing Trends in Canada*, edited by M. Baker, pp. 211–40. Toronto: McGraw-Hill Ryerson.

Mugford, Jane, and Stephen Mugford. 1991. "Shame and Reintegration in the Punishment and Deterrence of Spouse Assault." Paper Presented at the Annual Meeting of the American Society of Criminology, San Francisco.

Nault, F. 1996. "Twenty Years of Marriages." *Health Reports* 8(2): 39–46.

Nelson, E.D., and B.W. Robinson. 1999. *Gender in Canada*. Scarborough: Prentice Hall Allyn and Bacon Canada.

North Carolina Coalition Against Domestic Violence. 1991. Domestic Violence Fact Sheet. (Spring). P.O. Box 51875, Durham, NC 27717–1875.

Novac, S., J. Brown, and C. Bourbonnais. 1996. *No Room of Her Own: A Literature Review on Women and Homelessness*. Canadian Mortgage and Housing Corporation. May 1, 2000 <www.cmhc-schl.gc.ca/cmhc.html>.

O'Keefe, Maura. 1997. "Predictors of Dating Violence among High School Students." *Journal of Interpersonal Violence* 12: 546–68.

O'Leary, K.D., J. Barling, I. Arias, A. Rosenbaum, K. Malone, and A. Tyree. 1989. "Prevalence and Stability of Physical Aggression between Spouses: A Longitudinal Analysis." *Journal of Consulting and Clinical Psychology* 57: 263–8.

Oderkirk, J. 1994. "Marriage in Canada: Changing Beliefs and Behaviours 1600–1990." *Canadian Social Trends* (Summer): 2–7.

Oderkirk, J., and C. Lochhead. 1992. "Lone Parenthood: Gender Differences." *Canadian Social Trends* 27 (Winter): 16–9.

Pagelow, M. 1992. "Adult Victims of Domestic Violence." *Journal of Interpersonal Violence* 7(1): 87–120.

Peterson, Karen S. 1997. "States Flirt with Ways to Reduce Divorce Rate." *USA Today*, April 10: D1–D2.

Popenoe, David. 1993. "Point of View: Scholars Should Worry about the Disintegration of the American Family." *Chronicle of Higher Education*, April 14: A48.

———. 1996. *Life without Father*. New York: Free Press.

Ram, B. 1990. *New Trends in the Family: Demographic Facts and Features*. Current Demographic Analysis Series. Cat. 91-535E. Ottawa: Minister of Supply and Services.

Razack, Sherene. 1994. "What Is to Be Gained by Looking White People in the Eye? Culture, Race, and Gender in Cases of Sexual Violence." *Signs* 19(4): 894–923.

Reform Watch. 1997. "Hitting Kids." <www.vcn.bc.ca/refwatch/>.

Resnick, Michael, Peter S. Bearman, Robert W. Blum, Karl E. Bauman, Kathleen M. Harris, Jo Jones, Joyce Tabor, Trish Beubring, Renee E. Sieving, Marcia Shew, Marjore Ireland, Linda H. Berringer, and J. Richard Udry. 1997. "Protecting Adolescents from Harm." *Journal of the American Medical Association* 278(10): 823–32.

Riddington, Jill. 1989. *Beating the Odds: Violence and Women with Disabilities*. Vancouver: DAWN Canada.

Ristock, J.L. 1991. "Beyond Ideologies: Understanding Violence in Lesbian Relationships." *Canadian Woman Studies* 12(1): 74–9.

Russell, D.E. 1990. *Rape in Marriage*. Bloomington: Indiana University Press.

Sacco, V.L., and L.W. Kennedy. 1994. *The Criminal Event*. Scarborough, Ont.: Nelson.

Sapiro, Virginia. 1990. *Women in American Society*, 2nd ed. Mountain View, Calif.: Mayfield.

Shapiro, Joseph P., and Joanna M. Schrof. 1995. "Honor Thy Children." *U.S.-News and World Report*, February 27, 39–49.

Silverman, R., and L. Kennedy. 1993. *Deadly Deeds: Murder in Canada*. Scarborough, Ont.: Nelson.

Song, Young I. 1991. "Single Asian American Women as a Result of Divorce: Depressive Affect and Changes in Social Support." *Journal of Divorce and Remarriage* 14: 219–30.

Stanley, Scott M., Howard J. Markman, Michelle St. Peters, and B. Douglas Leber. 1995. "Strengthening Marriage and Preventing Divorce: New Directions in Prevention Research." *Family Relations* 44: 392–401.

Statistics Canada. 1996. *The Daily*, October 14 <www.statcan.ca/ Daily/English/961014/d961014.htm>.

———. 1997a. *Age, Sex, Marital Status and Common Law, Canada, Provinces and Territories, 1996*. Electronic Media Release. 14 October.

———. 1997b. *Divorce, 1995*. Cat. 84-213-XMB. Ottawa: Minister of Industry.

———. 1997c. *The Daily*, October 14 <www.statcan.ca/Daily/English/ 971014/d971014.htm>.

———. 1998a. *Canada Yearbook 1999*. Ottawa: Minister of Industry.

———. 1998b. *The Daily*, March 28 <www.statcan.ca/Daily/English/ 980328/d980328.htm>.

———. 1999. *The Daily*, September 1 <www.statcan.ca/Daily/English/ 990901/d990901.htm>.

Stets, J. 1991. "Cohabiting and Marital Aggression: The Role of Social Isolation." *Journal of Marriage and the Family* 53: 669–80.

Stets, J., and M.A. Straus. 1989. "The Marriage License as a Hitting License: A Comparison of Assaults in Dating, Cohabiting and Married Couples." *Journal of Family Violence* 4 (June): 161–80.

Stock, J.L., M.A. Bell, D.K. Boyer, and F.A. Connell. 1997. "Adolescent Pregnancy and Sexual Risk-Taking among Sexually Abused Girls." *Family Planning Perspectives* 29: 200–3.

Stout, James W., and Fredrick P. Rivara. 1989. "Schools and Sex Education: Does It Work?" *Pediatrics* 83: 375–9.

Straus, M.A. 1992. "Explaining Family Violence." In *Marriage and Family in a Changing Society*, 4th ed., edited by J. M. Henslin, pp. 344–56. New York: Free Press.

Straus, M.A., and R. Gelles. 1990. *Physical Violence in American Families: Risk Factors and Adaptations to Violence in 8, 145 Families*. New Brunswick, N.J.: Transaction.

Trevethan, S., and T. Samagh. 1993. "Gender Differences among Violent Crime Victims." *Juristat*, 12 (Winter), Cat. 85-992. Ottawa: Ministry of Industry, Science and Technology.

U.S. Department of Justice. 1998. (March 16). "Murder by Intimates Declined 36 Percent since 1976, Decrease Greater for Male than for Female Victims." Washington, D.C. <www.ojp.usdoj.gov/bjs/pub/press.vi.pr>.

Viano, C. Emilio. 1992. "Violence among Intimates: Major Issues and Approaches." In *Intimate Violence: Interdisciplinary Perspectives*, edited by C.E. Viano, pp. 3–12. Washington, D.C.: Hemisphere.

Waite, L.J. 1995. "Does Marriage Matter?" *Demography* 32: 483–507.

Waterman, C., L. Dawson, and M. Bologna. 1989. "Sexual Coercion in Gay and Lesbian Relationships: Predictors and Implications for Support Services." *Journal of Sex Research* 26: 118–24.

Willis, Diane J., E. Wayne Holden, and Mindy Rosenberg. 1992. "Child Maltreatment Prevention: Introduction and Historical Overview." In *Prevention of Child Maltreatment: Developmental and Ecological Perspectives*, edited by Diane J. Willis, E. Wayne Holden, and Mindy Rosenberg, pp. 1–14. New York: John Wiley and Sons.

Wilson, M., and M. Daly. 1994. "Spousal Homicide." *Juristat* 14, 8. Cat. 85-992. Ottawa: Minister of Industry, Science and Technology.

Chapter 6

Adler, Jerry. 1994. "Kids Growing up Scared." *Newsweek*, January 10: 43–50.

Anetzberger, Georgia J., Jill E. Korbin, and Craig Austin. 1994. "Alcoholism and Elder Abuse." *Journal of Interpersonal Violence* 9: 184–93.

Arluke, Arnold, and Jack Levin. 1990. "'Second Childhood': Old Age in Popular Culture." In *Readings on Social Problems*, edited by W. Feigelman, pp. 261–5. Fort Worth: Holt, Rinehart and Winston.

Arnold, Tom. 1999. "Older Heart-Attack Patients Less Likely to Get Vital Drugs." *National Post*, November 30: A5.

Boudreau, François A. 1993. "Elder Abuse." In *Family Violence: Prevention and Treatment*, edited by R.L. Hampton, T.P. Gullota, G. R. Adams, E.H. Potter III, and R.P. Weissberg, pp. 142–58. Newbury Park, Calif.: Sage Publications.

Bradshaw, York, Rita Noonan, Laura Gash, and Claudia Buchmann Sershen. 1992. "Borrowing against the Future: Children and Third World Indebtedness." *Social Forces* 71(3): 629–56.

Brazzini, D.G., W.D. McIntosh, S.M. Smith, S. Cook, and C. Harris. 1997. "The Aging Woman in Popular Film: Underrepresented, Unattractive, Unfriendly, and Unintelligent." *Sex Roles* 36: 531–43.

Brooks-Gunn, Jeanne, and Greg Duncan. 1997. "The Effects of Poverty on Children." *Future of Children* 7(2): 55–70.

Cahill, Spenser. 1993. "Childhood and Public Life: Reaffirming Biographical Divisions." *Social Problems* 37(3): 390–400.

Canadian Press. 1999. "Older Drivers More at Risk." *KW Record*, November 17: B11.

CARP (Canadian Association of Retired Persons). 2000. <www.fifty-plus.net/join/index.cfm>.

"Children's Legal Rights." 1993. *Congressional Quarterly*, April 23: 339–54.

Clements, Mark. 1993. "What We Say about Aging." *Parade Magazine*, December 12, 4–5.

Cowgill, Donald, and Lowell Holmes. 1972. *Aging and Modernization*. New York: Appleton-Century-Crofts.

Cummings, Elaine, and William Henry. 1961. *Growing Old: The Process of Disengagement*. New York: Basic Books.

DeAngelis, Tori. 1997. "Elderly May Be Less Depressed Than the Young." *APA Monitor*. October <www.apa.org/monitor/oct97/elderly.html>.

DHHS (Department of Health and Human Services). 1998. "Statement of Jeanette Takamura." U.S. Department of Health and Human Services, Administration on Aging. June 8 <www.aoa.dhhs.gov/pr/graying.html>.

Duncan, Greg, W. Jean Yeung, Jeanne Brooks-Gunn, and Judith Smith. 1998. "How Much Does Childhood Poverty Affect the Life Chance of Children?" *American Sociological Review* 63: 402–23.

Fields, Jason, and Kristin Smith. 1998. "Poverty, Family Structure, and Child Well-Being." Population Division. Washington, D.C.: U.S. Bureau of Census.

Fine, Sean. 1999a. "Child Development More Affected by Parenting than Social Class." *The Globe and Mail*, October 4: A4.

———. 1999b. "How Canada Broke Its Pledge to Poor Children." *The Globe and Mail*, November 24: A14.

Friedan, Betty. 1993. *The Fountain of Age*. New York: Simon and Schuster.

Gee, E.M. 1995. "Families in Later Life." In *Families over the Life Course*, edited by R. Beaujot, E.M. Gee, F. Rajulton, and Z.R. Ravenera, pp. 77–113. Current Demographic Analysis Series. Ottawa: Statistics Canada.

George, M.V., M.J. Norris , F. Nault, S. Loh, and S.Y. Dai. 1994. *Population Projections for Canada: Provinces and Territories, 1993–2016*. Ottawa: Minister of Industry, Science and Technology.

GLARP (Gay and Lesbian Association of Retiring Person). 2000. <www.gaylesbianretiring.org/about.htm>.

Harrigan, Anthony. 1992. "A Lost Civilization." *Modern Age: A Quarterly Review* (Fall): 3–12.

Harris, Kathleen, and Jeremy Marmer. 1996. "Poverty, Paternal Involvement and Adolescent Well-Being." *Journal of Family Issues* 17(5): 614–40.

Health Canada. 1999. *Statistical Report in the Health of Canadians* <www.hc-sc.gc.ca/hppb/phdd/report/stat/eng/over.html>.

Huuhtanen, P., and M. Piispa. 1996. "Attitudes toward Work and Retirement among Elderly Workers." Helsinki, Finland: Finnish Institute of Occupational Health.

Ingrassia, Michelle. 1993. "Growing up Fast and Frightened." *Newsweek*, November 22: 52–3.

Jorgensen, Brithe. 1986. *Crime Against the Elderly in Institutional Care*. Report Produced through an Independent Research Grant from the Solicitor General with permission from Concerned Friends.

Kinsella, K. and C.M. Taeuber. 1993. *An Aging World*. Washington, D.C.: U.S. Bureau of the Census.

Knoke, David, and Arne L. Kalleberg. 1994. "Job Training in U.S. Organizations." *American Sociological Review* 59: 537–46.

Kolland, Franz. 1994. "Contrasting Cultural Profiles between Generations: Interests and Common Activities in Three Intrafamilial Generations." *Aging and Society* 14: 319–40.

Krahn, H.K., and Lowe, G.S. 1993. *Women, Industry and Canadian Society*, 2nd ed. Scarborough, Ont.: Nelson.

Maclean's. 1999a. "Taking It to the Streets." November 15: 41.

———. 1999b. "New Moves to Curb Kids." December 20: 91.

———. 2000. "Provinces Struggle to Keep up with Senior Care." January 17: 19.

Matras, Judah. 1990. *Dependency, Obligations, and Entitlements: A New Sociology of Aging, the Life Course, and the Elderly*. Englewood Cliffs, N.J.: Prentice-Hall.

McVey, Wayne W. Jr., and Warren E. Kalbach. 1995. *Canadian Population*. Scarborough, Ont.: Nelson.

Miner, Sonia, John Logan, and Glenna Spitze. 1993. "Predicting Frequency of Senior Center Attendance." *Gerontologist* 33: 650–7.

Minkler, Meredith. 1989. "Gold Is Gray: Reflections on Business' Discovery of the Elderly Market." *Gerontologist* 29(1): 17–23.

National Council of Welfare. 1995. *Profiles of Welfare: Myths and Realities*. Spring <www.ncwcnbes.net/htmdocument/reportprowelfare/repprowelfare.htm>.

Nikiforuk, Andrew. 1999. "A Question of Style." *Time*, May 31: 58–9.

Novak, Mark. 1997. *Aging and Society: A Canadian Perspective*, 3rd ed. Scarborough, Ont.: Nelson.

Peterson, Peter. 1997. "Will America Grow Up before It Grows Old? In *Social Problems: Annual Editions,* ed. Harold A. Widdison, p. 74. Guilford, Conn: Dushkin.

Pillemer, Karl, and Beth Hudson. 1993. "A Model Abuse Prevention Program for Nursing Assistants." *Gerontologist* 33(1): 128–31.

Plouffe, L. 1991. *Consumer Fraud and Seniors*. Ottawa: NACA.

Purvis, Andrew. 1999. "Tapestry." *Time*, May 31: 33–4.

Regoli, Robert, and John Hewitt. 1997. *Delinquency in Society*. New York: McGraw-Hill.

Riley, Matilda White. 1987. "On the Significance of Age in Sociology." *American Sociological Review* 52 (February): 1–14.

Riley, Matilda W., and John W. Riley. 1992. "The Lives of Older People and Changing Social Roles." In *Issues in Society*, edited by Hugh Lena, William Helmreich, and William McCord, pp. 220–31. New York: McGraw-Hill.

Ross, D.P., S.K. Kelly, and M. A. Scott. 1996. "Overview: Children in Canada in the 1990s." In *Human Resources Development Canada and Statistics Canada, Growing up in Canada: National Longitudinal Survey of Children and Youth*, November 1996. Statistics Canada Cat. 89-55-MPE, No.1.

Russell, Charles. 1989. *Good News about Aging*. New York: Wiley.

Seeman, Teresa E., and Nancy Adler. 1998. "Older Americans: Who Will They Be?" *National Forum* (Spring): 22–5.

Simon-Rusinowitz, Lori, Constance Krach, Lori Marks, Diane Piktialis, and Laura Wilson. 1996. "Grandparents in the Workplace: the Effects of Economic and Labor Trends." *Generations* 20(1): 41–4.

Statistics Canada. 1998a. *Canada Yearbook*. Ottawa: Ministry of Industry.

———. 1998b. *The Daily*. March 28 <www.statcan.ca/Daily/English/980328/d980328.htm>.

———. 1998c. *The Daily*. May 12 <www.statcan.ca/Daily/English/980512/d980512.htm>.

Thurow, Lester C. 1996. "The Birth of a Revolutionary Class." *New York Times Magazine*, May 19: 46–7.

Townson, Monica. 1995. *Financial Futures: Mid-Life Prospects for a Secure Retirement*. Ottawa: Canadian Advisory Council on the Status of Women.

UNICEF (United Nations Children's Fund). 1994. "The Progress of Nations." United Nations.

Vanier Institute of the Family. 1994. *Profiling Canada's Families*. Ottawa: Vanier Institute of the Family.

Weissberg, Roger P., and Carol Kuster. 1997. "Introduction and Overview: Let's Make Healthy Children 2010 a National Priority." In *Enhancing Children's Well-Being*, edited by Roger Weissberg, Thomas Gullotta, Robert Hampton, Bruce Ryan, and Gerald Adams, pp. 1–16. Thousand Oaks, Calif.: Sage Publications.

World Congress Against Commercial Sexual Exploitation of Children. 1998. "Regional Profiles." <wwwusis.usemb.se/children/csec/226e.html>.

Chapter 7

Adamson, N., L. Briskin, and M. McPhail. 1988. *Feminists Organizing for Change: The Contemporary Women's Movement in Canada*. Don Mills, Ont.: Oxford University Press.

American Association of University Women. 1992. *How Schools Shortchange Girls*. Washington, D.C.: American Association of University Women.

Andersen, Margaret L. 1997. *Thinking about Women*, 4th ed. New York: Macmillan.

Anderson, John, and Molly Moore. 1998. "The Burden of Womanhood." In *Global Issues 98/99*, edited by Robert Jackson, pp. 170–5. Guilford, Conn: Dushkin/McGraw-Hill.

Atcheson, E., M. Eberts, E. Symes, and J. Stoddart. 1984. *Women and Legal Action*. Ottawa: Canadian Advisory Council on the Status of Women.

Attwood, Lynne. 1996. "Young People's Attitudes towards Sex Roles and Sexuality." In *Gender, Generation and Identity in Contemporary Russia*, edited by Hilary Pilkington, pp. 132–51. London: Routledge.

Bacchi, C.L. 1983. *Liberation Deferred? The Ideas of the English-Canadian Suffragists, 1877–1918*. Toronto: University of Toronto Press.

Baker, Robin, Gary Kriger, and Pamela Riley. 1996. "Time, Dirt and Money: The Effects of Gender, Gender Ideology, and Type of Earner Marriage on Time, Household Task, and Economic Satisfaction among Couples with Children." *Journal of Social Behavior and Personality* 11: 161–77.

Basow, Susan A. 1992. *Gender: Stereotypes and Roles*, 3rd ed. Pacific Grove, Calif.: Brooks/Cole.

Beatty, C., A. McKeen, and C. Kurdyak. 1993. "Generation X: The Changing Career Values and Expectations of Recent Business Graduates." Paper Presented at the 1994 Meetings of the Administrative Sciences Association of Canada, Lake Louise, June.

Best, P. 1995. "Women, Men, and Work." *Canadian Social Trends* 36: 30–3.

Beutel, Ann M., and Margaret Mooney Marini. 1995. "Gender and Values." *American Sociological Review* 60: 436–8.

Bibby, Reginald W. 1995. *The Bibby Report: Social Trends Canadian Style*. Toronto: Stoddart.

Burger, Jerry M., and Cecilia H. Solano. 1994. "Changes in Desire for Control over Time: Gender Differences in a Ten-Year Longitudinal Study." *Sex Roles* 31: 465–72.

Burke, R.J. 1994. "Canadian Business Students' Attitudes Towards Women as Managers." *Psychological Reports* 75: 1123–9.

Calasanti, Toni, and Carol A. Bailey. 1991. "Gender Inequality and the Division of Labor in the United States and Sweden: A Socialist-Feminist Approach." *Social Problems* 38(1): 34–53.

Cassidy, B., R. Lord, and N. Mandell. 1998. "Silenced and Forgotten Women: Race, Poverty, and Disability." In *Feminist Issues: Race, Class and Sexuality*, 2nd ed, edited by N. Mandell, pp. 26–54. Scarborough: Prentice Hall Allyn and Bacon Canada.

CEDAW (Convention to Eliminate All Forms of Discrimination against Women). 1998. <www.feminist.org/research/cedawhist.html>.

Das Gupta, T. 1996. *Racism and Paid Work*. Toronto: Garamond Press.

DeStefano, Linda, and Diane Colasanto. 1990. "Unlike 1975, Today Most Americans Think Men Have It Better." *Gallup Poll Monthly* 293: 25–36.

Dhooma, Rashida. 1997. "A Growing Wave of Surfer Girls." *Toronto Sun*, April 7: 49.

Driedger, D. 1993. "Discovering Disabled Women's History." In *And Still We Rise*, edited by L. Carty, pp. 173–88. Toronto: Women's Press.

Educational Indicators. 1998. "Indicator 18: Gender Differences in Earnings." National Center for Educational Statistics. Washington, D.C.: U.S. Department of Education.

Errington, J. 1993. "Pioneers and Suffragists." In *Changing Patterns: Women in Canada*. 2nd ed., edited by S. Burt, L. Code, and L. Dorney, pp. 59–91. Toronto: McClelland and Stewart.

Fiebert, Martin S., and Mark W. Meyer. 1997. "Gender Stereotypes: A Bias against Men." *Journal of Psychology* 131(4): 407–10.

Fitzgerald, Louise F., and Sandra L. Shullman. 1993. "Sexual Harassment: A Research Analysis and Agenda for the '90s." *Journal of Vocational Behavior* 40: 5–27.

Frank, J. 1994. "Voting and Contributing: Political participation in Canada." In *Canadian Social Trends: A Canadian Studies Reader*, Vol. 2, pp. 333–57. Toronto: Thompson Educational Publishing.

Gaskell, J., and J. Willinsky. 1995. *Gender Informs Curriculum*. Toronto: OISE Press.

Ghalam, N.Z. 1997. "Attitudes towards Women, Work, and Family." *Canadian Social Trends* 46: 13–7.

Gilligan, C., N.P. Lyons, and T.J. Harimer. 1990. *Making Connections*. London: Cambridge University Press.

Goldberg, Stephanie. 1997. "Making Room for Daddy." *American Bar Association Journal* 83: 48–52.

Hagan, J. 1990. "The Gender Stratification of Income Inequality Among Lawyers." *Social Forces* 68(3): 835–55.

Henslin, J., and A. Nelson. 1997. *Essentials of Sociology*. Scarborough, Ont.: Allyn and Bacon.

Hochschild, Arlie. 1989. *The Second Shift: Working Patterns and the Revolution at Home*. New York: Viking Penguin.

Hoy, C. 1995. *The Truth About Breast Cancer*. Toronto: Stoddart.

Human Development Report. 1997. United Nations Development Programme. New York: Oxford University Press.

Hunter, A., and M. Denton. 1984. "Do Female Candidates 'Lose' Votes?" *Canadian Review of Sociology and Anthropology* 2: 395–406.

Kantrowitz, B. 1994. "Men, Women, and Computers." *Newsweek*, May 16: 48–55.

Kelly, K.L., L. Howatson, and W. Clark. 1997. "I Feel Overqualified for My Job..." *Canadian Social Trends* 47: 11–6.

Kilbourne, Barbara S., George Farkas, Kurt Beron, Dorothea Weir, and Paula England. 1994. "Returns to Skill, Compensating Differentials, and Gender Bias: Effects of Occupational Characteristics on the Wages of White Women and Men." *American Journal of Sociology* 100: 689–719.

Klein, Matthew. 1998. "Women's Trip to the Top." *American Demographics*, February: 22.

Kopelman, Lotetta M. 1994. "Female Circumcision/Genital Mutilation and Ethical Relativism." *Second Opinion* 20: 55–71.

Larkin, J. 1994. *Sexual Harassment: High-School Girls Speak Out*. Toronto: Second Story Press.

Laroche, M. 1998. "In and Out of Low Income." *Canadian Social Trends* 40: 20–4.

Leo, John. 1997. "Fairness? Promises, Promises." *U.S. News and World Report* 123(4): 18.

Long, J. Scott, Paul D. Allison, and Robert McGinnis. 1993. "Rank Advancement in Academic Careers: Sex Differences and the Effects of Productivity." *American Sociological Review* 58: 703–22.

Lorber, Judith. 1998. "Night to His Day." In *Reading Between the Lines*, edited by Amanda Konradi and Martha Schmidt, pp. 213–20. Mountain View, Calif.: Mayfield Publishing.

Luo, Tsun Yin. 1996. "Sexual Harassment in the Chinese Workplace." *Violence Against Women* 2(3): 284–301.

Macklin, A. 1992. "*Symes v. M.N.R.*: Where Sex Meets Class." *Canadian Journal of Women and the Law* 5: 498.

Mandell, N. 1995. "Introduction." *Feminist Issues: Race, Class and Sexuality*, pp. vii–xxi. Scarborough, Ont.: Prentice Hall Allyn and Bacon Canada.

———. 1998. *Feminist Issues: Race, Class and Sexuality*, 2nd ed. Scarborough, Ont.: Prentice Hall Allyn and Bacon Canada.

Marini, Margaret Mooney, and Pi-Ling Fan. 1997. "The Gender Gap in Earnings at Career Entry. *American Sociological Review* 62: 588–604.

Martin, Patricia Yancey. 1992. "Gender, Interaction, and Inequality in Organizations." In *Gender, Interaction, and Inequality*, edited by Cecilia Ridgeway, pp. 208–31. New York: Springer-Verlag.

McCammon, Susan, David Knox, and Caroline Schacht. 1998. *Making Choices in Sexuality*. Pacific Grove, Calif.: Brooks/Cole Publishing Co.

McDaniel, S.A., and E. Roosmalen. 1992. "Sexual Harassment in Canadian Academe: Explorations of Power and Privilege." *Atlantis* 17(1): 3–19.

McVey, W.J. Jr., and W. Kalbach. 1995. *Canadian Population*. Scarborough, Ont.: Nelson.

Mensh, Barbara, and Cynthia Lloyd. 1997. "Gender Differences in the Schooling of Adolescents in Low-Income Countries: The Case of Kenya." *Policy Research Working Paper* no. 95. New York: Population Council.

Merida, Kevin, and Barbara Vobejda. 1998. "Role Shift Causes Conflict on the Home Front." *Washington Post*, April 27: D1.

Mirowsky, John, and Catherine E. Ross. 1995. "Sex Differences in Distress: Real or Artifact?" *American Sociological Review* 60: 449–68.

Moreau, J. 1991. "Employment Equity." *Canadian Social Trends* 22 (Autumn): 26–8.

Mossman, M.J. 1998. "The Paradox of Feminist Engagement with Law." In *Feminist Issues: Race, Class, and Sexuality*, edited by N. Mandell, pp. 180–207. Scarborough, Ont.: Prentice Hall Allyn and Bacon Canada.

National Post. 1999. "Job Ad Seeking Only Women Draws Criticism." August 6: A4.

NCFM (National Coalition of Free Men). 1998. "Historical." Manhasset, NY: NCFM. <ncfm.org>.

Neft, N., and A.D. Levine. 1997. *Where Women Stand: An International Report on the Status of Women in 140 Countries, 1997–1998*. New York: Random House.

Nichols-Casebolt, Ann, and Judy Krysik. 1997. "The Economic Well-Being of Never and Ever-Married Mother Families." *Journal of Social Service Research* 23(1): 19–40.

Normand, J. 1995. "Education of Women in Canada." *Canadian Social Trends* 39: 17–21.

O'Kelly, Charlotte G., and Larry S. Carney. 1992. "Women in Socialist Societies." In *Issues in Society*, edited by Hugh F. Lena, William B. Helmreich, and William McCord, pp. 195–204. New York: McGraw-Hill.

Olson, Josephine E., Irene H. Frieze, and Ellen G. Detlefsen. 1990. "Having It All? Combining Work and Family in a Male and a Female Profession." *Sex Roles* 23: 515–34.

Peterson, Sharyl B., and Tracie Kroner. 1992. "Gender Biases in Textbooks for Introductory Psychology and Human Development." *Psychology of Women Quarterly* 16: 17–36.

Purcell, Piper, and Lara Stewart. 1990. "Dick and Jane in 1989." *Sex Roles* 22: 177–85.

Reid, Pamela T., and Lillian Comas-Diaz. 1990. "Gender and Ethnicity: Perspectives on Dual Status." *Sex Roles* 22: 397–408.

Rheingold, Harriet L., and Kaye V. Cook. 1975. "The Content of Boys' and Girls' Rooms as an Index of Parent's Behavior." *Child Development* 46: 459–63.

Robinson, John P., and Suzanne Bianchi. 1997. "The Children's Hours." *American Demographics* (December): 1–6.

Rosenberg, Janet, Harry Perlstadt, and William Phillips. 1997. "Now That We Are Here: Discrimination, Disparagement, and Harassment at Work and the Experience of Women Lawyers." In *Workplace/Women's Place*, edited by Dana Dunn, pp. 247–59. Los Angeles: Roxbury.

Rubenstein, Carin. 1990. "A Brave New World." *New Woman* 20(10): 158–64.

Sadker, Myra, and David Sadker. 1990. "Confronting Sexism in the College Classroom." In *Gender in the Classroom: Power and Pedagogy*, edited by S. L. Gabriel, and I. Smithson, pp. 176–87. Chicago: University of Illinois Press.

Sapiro, Virginia. 1994. *Women in American Society*. Mountain View, Calif.: Mayfield.

Schneider, Margaret, and Susan Phillips. 1997. "A Qualitative Study of Sexual Harassment of Female Doctors by Patients." *Social Science and Medicine* 45: 669–76.

Schroeder, K.A., L.L. Blood, and D. Maluso. 1993. "Gender Differences and Similarities between Male and Female Undergraduate Students regarding Expectations for Career and Family Roles." *College Student Journal* 27: 237–49.

Schur, Edwin. 1984. *Labeling Women Deviant: Gender, Stigma, and Social Control*. New York: Random House.

Schwalbe, Michael. 1996. *Unlocking the Iron Cage: The Men's Movement, Gender Politics, and American Culture*. New York: Oxford University Press.

Shain, A. 1995. "Employment of People with Disabilities." *Canadian Social Trends* 38: 8–13.

Signorielli, Nancy. 1998. "Reflections of Girls in the Media: a Content Analysis across Six Media."

Overview. <http://childrennow.org/media/mc97/ReflectSummary.html>.

Sommers, Christina Hoff. 2000. *The War Against Boys: How Misguided Feminism Is Harming Young Men.* New York: Simon and Schuster.

Spurr, S. J. 1990. "Sex Discrimination in the Legal Profession: A Study of Promotion." *Industrial and Labor Relations Review* 43(4): 406–17.

Stark, R. 1992. *Sociology*, 4th ed. Belmont, Calif.: Wadsworth.

Statistics Canada. 1994. *Characteristics of Dual-Earner Families.* Catalogue 13-215. Ottawa: Ministry of Industry, Science and Technology.

———. 1997a. *The Daily.* January 27 <www.statcan.ca/Daily/English/972701/d972701.htm>.

———. 1997b. *Earning of Men and Women.* Annual. Cat. No. 13-217-XPB.

———. 1998a. *Canada Yearbook 2000.* Ottawa: Minister of Industry.

———. 1998b. *The Daily.* March 17 <www.statcan.ca/Daily/English/980317/d980317.htm>.

———. 1998c. *The Daily.* April 16 <www.statcan.ca/Daily/English/980416/d980416.htm>.

———. 1998d. *The Daily.* May 12 <www.statcan.ca/Daily/English/980512/d980512.htm>.

———. 1998e. *The Daily.* June 17 <www.statcan.ca/Daily/English/980617/d980617.htm>.

———. 1998f. "What Is Happening to Earnings Inequality in the 1990s?" <www.statcan.ca>.

———. 1999a. *Income After Tax, Distribution by Size in Canada.* Annual. Cat. 13-217XPB.

———. 1999b. *The Daily.* January 22 <www.statcan.ca/Daily/English/990122/d990122.htm>.

———. 1999c. *The Daily.* March 25 <www.statcan.ca/Daily/English/990325/d990325.htm>.

———. 1999d. *The Daily.* April 14 <www.statcan.ca/Daily/English/990417/d990417.htm>.

———. 1999e. *The Daily.* December 20 <www.statcan.ca/Daily/English/991220/d991220.htm>.

———. 1999f. *The Daily.* September 1 <www.statcan.ca/Daily/English/990901/d990001.htm>.

Stoneman, Z., G.H. Brody, and C.E. MacKinnon. 1986. "Same-Sex and Cross-Sex Siblings: Activity Choices, Behavior and Gender Stereotypes." *Sex Roles* 15: 495–511.

Tait, H. 1999. "Educational Achievement of Young Aboriginal Adults." *Canadian Social Trends* 52: 6–10.

Tam, Tony. 1997. "Sex Segregation and Occupational Gender Inequality in the United States: Devaluation or Specialized Training?" *American Journal of Sociology* 102(6): 1652–92.

Tannen, Deborah. 1990. *You Just Don't Understand: Women and Men in Conversation.* New York: Ballantine Books.

Tomaskovic-Devey, Donald. 1993. "The Gender and Race Composition of Jobs and the Male/Female, White/Black Pay Gap." *Social Forces* 72(1): 45–76.

Tserkonivnitska, Marina. 1997. "Where Have All the Women Gone?" *Gender and Global Change Newsletter* (Spring): 1–4.

United Nations. 1997. "Report on the World Social Situation: 1997." Department for Economic and Social Information and Public Analysis. New York: United Nations.

United Nations Development Programme. 1995. *Human Development Report, 1995.* New York: Oxford University Press.

———. 1997. *Human Development Report, 1997.* New York: Oxford University Press.

———. 1999. *Human Development Report, 1999.* New York: Oxford University Press.

UP (University of Philippines). 1997. "Teachers, Textbooks Reinforce Gender Bias—UP Study." *University of Philippines Newsletter* 21(4): <www.icpd.edu.ph/newsletter>.

Van Willigen, Marieke, and Patricia Drentea. 1997. "Benefits of Equitable Relationships: The Impact of Sense of Failure, Household Division of Labor, and Decision-Making Power on Social Support." Presented at the Meeting of the American Sociological Association, Toronto, Ontario, August.

Vanin, S. 1997. "Nutritional Intervention in Eating Disorders." Workshop Presented at the 17th Annual Saskatchewan Psychiatric Association of Continuing Education Conference: Eating Disorders, Past, Present, and Future: A Multi-Disciplinary Approach. Saskatoon, Sask.

White, L. 1996. "No Boys Allowed in This Class." *Oshawa Whitby This Week.* November 17: 3.

Whitla, W. 1995. "A Chronology of Women in Canada." In *Feminist Issues: Race, Class and Sexuality,* edited by N. Mandell, pp. 315–53. Scarborough, Ont.: Prentice Hall Canada.

Wilkins, K. 1996. "Causes of Death: How the Sexes Differ." *Canadian Social Trends* 41: 11–7.

Williams, Christine L. 1995. *Still a Man's World: Men Who Do Women's Work.* Berkeley: University of California Press.

Williams, John E., and Deborah L. Best. 1990a. *Measuring Sex Stereotypes: A Multination Study.* London: Sage Publications.

———. 1990b. *Sex and Psyche: Gender and Self Viewed Cross-Culturally.* London: Sage Publications.

Wine, J.D., and J.L. Ristock (eds.). 1991. "Introduction: Feminist Activism in Canada." In *Women and Social Change: Feminist Activism in Canada,* pp. 1–18. Toronto: James Lorimer.

WOC Alert. 1998. "Tell the Senate to Join the World; Good News." Women Leaders Online. <wlo.org/alert/021398.html>.

Wootton, Barbara. 1997. "Gender Differences in Occupational Employment." *Monthly Labor Review* (April): 15–24.

Wright, Erik Olin, Janeen Baxter, with Gunn Elisabeth Birkelund. 1995. "The Gender-Gap in Workplace Authority: A Cross-National Study." *American Sociological Review* 60: 407–35.

Zimmerman, Marc A., Laurel Copeland, Jean Shope, and T.E. Dielman. 1997. "A Longitudinal Study of Self-Esteem: Implications for Adolescent Development." *Journal of Youth and Adolescence* 26(2): 117–41.

Zuckerman, H., J.R. Cole, and J.T. Bruer. 1991. *The Outer Circle: Women in the Scientific Community*. New York: Norton.

Chapter 8

Abella, Irving. 1999. "Anti-Semitism." In *The Canadian Encyclopedia: Year 2000 Edition*, edited by James H. Marsh, p. 90. Toronto: McClelland and Stewart, Inc.

Abella, Irving, and H. Troper. 1998. *None Is Too Many: Canada and the Jews of Europe, 1933–1948*. Toronto: Lester Publishing.

Association of Multiethnic Americans (AMEA). 2000. <www.ameasite.org>.

Barlow, Melissa. 1998. "Race and the Problem of Crime in *Time* and *Newsweek* Cover Stories, 1946 to 1995." *Social Justice* 25(2): 149–83.

Beaudoin, Gerald A. 1999. "Keegstra Case." In *The Canadian Encyclopedia: Year 2000 Edition*, edited by James H. Marsh, pp. 1237. Toronto: McClelland and Stewart, Inc.

Behiels, M.D. 1999. "Francophone-Anglophone Relations." In *The Canadian Encyclopedia: Year 2000 Edition*, edited by James H. Marsh, pp. 909–13. Toronto: McClelland and Stewart.

Bibby, Reginald W. 1995. *The Bibby Report: Social Trends Canadian Style*. Toronto: Stoddart.

Bobo, Lawrence, and James R. Kluegel. 1993. "Opposition to Race-Targeting: Self Interest, Stratification Ideology, or Racial Attitudes?" *American Sociological Review* 58(4): 443–64.

Bogardus, Emory. 1968. "Comparing Racial Distance in Ethiopia, South Africa, and the United States." *Sociology and Social Research* 52(January): 149–56.

Bowd, A., and P. Brady. 1998. "Note on Preferred Use of Ethnic Identity Labels by Aboriginal and Non-Aboriginal Canadians." *Psychological Reports* 82: 1153–4.

Boyd, Monica. 2000. "Canada's Refugees Flows: Gender Inequality." *Canadian Social Trends*, Vol. 3, pp. 84–7. Toronto: Thompson Educational Publishing.

Breton, R. 1988. "French-English Relations." In *Understanding Canadian Society*, edited by J.E. Curtis and L. Tepperman, pp. 557–85. Toronto: McGraw-Hill Ryerson Limited.

Burnet, Jean. 1999. "Multiculturalism." In *The Canadian Encyclopedia*, edited by James H. Marsh, p. 1535. Toronto: McClelland and Stewart, Inc.

Canadian Press. 1996. "Premier Not Sold on Racism Report." *KW Record*, January 18: A3.

Chow, Henry P. 1997. *In Search of a Land Flowing with Milk and Honey: The Adaptation Experiences of Uprooted Chinese and Black Immigrant Students in a Multicultural Society*. Ph.D. Thesis, University of Toronto.

Claxton-Oldfield, Stephen, and Sheila M. Keefe. 1999. "Assessing Stereotypes about the Innu of Davis Inlet, Labrador." *Canadian Journal of Behavioural Sciences* 31(2): 86–91.

Coates, L. 1999. "International Indigenous Symposium on Corrections." *Let's Talk* 24(4): 2–6.

Cohen, Mark Nathan. 1998. "Culture, Not Race, Explains Human Diversity." *Chronicle of Higher Education* 44(32): B4–B5.

Columbo, J.R. 1986. *1001 Questions About Canada*. Toronto: Doubleday.

Crauford-Lewis, M. 1999. "Nunavut." In *The Canadian Encyclopedia Year 2000 Edition*, edited by James H. Marsh, p. 1686. Toronto: McClelland and Stewart, Inc.

DeMont, John. 1999. "Building New Bridges." *Maclean's*, September 27: 24–30.

Doerr, A. 1999. "Royal Commission on Aboriginal Peoples." In *The Canadian Encyclopedia Year 2000 Edition*, edited by James H. Marsh, pp. 3–4. Toronto: McClelland and Stewart, Inc.

Donakowski, D.W., and V.M. Esses. 1996. "Native Canadians, First Nations, or Aboriginals: The Effects of Labels on Attitudes toward Native Peoples." *Canadian Journal of Behavioural Science* 28: 86–91.

Dovidio, John F., and Samuel L. Gaertner. 1991. "Changes in the Expression and Assessment of Racial Prejudice." In *Opening Doors: Perspectives on Race Relations in Contemporary America*, edited by Harry J. Knopke, Robert J. Norrell, and Ronald W. Rogers, pp. 119–48. Tuscaloosa: University of Alabama Press.

Dreidger, L. 1999. "Prejudice and Discrimination." In *The Canadian Encyclopedia Year 2000 Edition*, edited by James H. Marsh, pp. 1888–92. Toronto: McClelland and Stewart, Inc.

Etzioni, Amitai. 1997. "New Issues: Rethinking Race." *Public Perspective* (June–July): 39–40. May 11, 1998 <www.ropercenter.unconn.edu/pubper/pdf/!84b.htm>.

Fitzhugh, T.V. 1991. *The Dictionary of Geneology*, 3rd ed. London: A. and C. Black.

Frideres, J.S. 1993. "Health Promotion and Indian Communities: Social Support or Social Disorganization." In *Racial Minorities, Medicine and Health*, edited by B. Singh Bolaria, and R. Bolaria, pp. 269–95. Halifax, NS: Fernwood.

Goldstein, Joseph. 1999 (January). "Sunbeams." *Sun* 277: 48.

Guinier, Lani. 1998. Interview with Paula Zahn. *CBS Evening News*, July 18.

Healey, Joseph F. 1997. *Race, Ethnicity, and Gender in the United States: Inequality, Group Conflict, and Power*. Thousand Oaks, Calif.: Pine Forge Press.

Health Canada. 1999. *Toward a Healthy Future: Second Report on the Health of Canadians*. Prepared by the Federal, Provincial, and Territorial Advisory Committee of Population Health for the Meeting of Ministers of Health, Charlottetown, PEI, September.

Henry, Frances, and Carol Tator. 1985. "Racism in Canada: Social Myths and Strategies for Change." In *Ethnicity and Ethnic Relations in Canada*, 2nd ed., edited by Rita M. Bienvenue, and Jay E. Goldstein, pp. 321–35. Toronto: Butterworths.

Henry, Frances, Carol Tator, Winston Mattis, and Tim Rees. 1995. *The Colour of Democracy*. Toronto: Harcourt Brace.

Horwood, Harold. 1969. *Newfoundland*. Toronto: Macmillan.

Infantry, A. 2000. "This Is What A Canadian Looks Like." *Toronto Star*, March 11: A1, A2.

"In Our Own Words." 1996. *Teaching Tolerance* (Fall). Montgomery, Ala.: Southern Poverty Law Center.

Intelligence Report. 1998. *Teaching Tolerance* (Winter) 89. Montgomery, Ala.: Southern Poverty Law Center.

Jain, Harish. 1988. *Employment Discrimination Against Visible Minorities and Employment Equity*. Ottawa: Department of Secretary of State, Multiculturalism Sector, Policy and Research.

Kawakami, K., K.L. Dion, and J.F. Dovidio. 1998. "Racial Prejudice and Stereotype Activation." *Personality and Social Psychology Quarterly* 24(4): 407–16.

Keita, S.O.Y., and Rick A. Kittles. 1997. "The Persistence of Racial Thinking and the Myth of Racial Divergence." *American Anthropologist* 99(3): 534–44.

Kleg, Milton. 1993. *Hate, Prejudice, and Racism*. Albany: State University of New York Press.

Landau, Elaine. 1993. *The White Power Movement: America's Racist Hate Groups*. Brookfield, Conn.: Millbrook Press.

Levin, Jack, and Jack McDevitt. 1995. "Landmark Study Reveals Hate Crimes Vary Significantly by Offender Motivation." *Klanwatch Intelligence Report* August: 7–9.

Lian, J.Z. 1996. *Ethnic Earnings Inequality in Canada*. Ph.D. Dissertation. McMaster University.

Lieberman, Leonard. 1997. "Gender and the Deconstruction of the Race Concept." *American Anthropologist* 99(3): 545–58.

Lofthus, Kai R. 1998. "Swedish Biz Decries Racist Music." *Billboard*, January 24: 71, 73.

Maclean's. 1996. "How Very Different Are We?" November 4: 36–40.

———. 1999a. "Building New Bridges." September 27: 24–30.

———. 1999b. "Skinheads Sentenced." November 29: 33.

———. 1999c. "What Makes a Canadian?" December 20: 45–8.

———. 1999d. "Untitled." December 29: 45.

———. 2000. "A New Wave of Chinese Migrants." January 17: 42.

Mann, Coramae, and Marjarorie S. Zatz Richey. (eds). 1993. *Unequal Justice: A Question of Color*. Bloomington: Indiana University Press.

Mendelberg, Tali. 1997. "Executing Horizons: Racial Crime in the 1988 Presidential Campaign." *Public Opinion Quarterly* 61: 134–57.

Molnar, Stephen. 1983. *Human Variation: Races, Types, and Ethnic Groups*, 2nd ed. Englewood Cliffs, N.J.: Prentice-Hall.

Mosher, Clayton J. 1998. *Discrimination and Denial: Systemic Racism in Ontario's Legal and Criminal Justice System, 1892–1961*. Toronto: University of Toronto Press.

Nash, Manning. 1962. "Race and the Ideology of Race." *Current Anthropology* 3: 258–88.

National Post. 1999a. "StatsCan Debates: How Canadian Are We?" November 30: A1.

———. 1999b. "Conditions Curtail Quebec's Right to Self-Determination." December 11: A11.

———. 1999c. "Clarity Act Fails to Arouse Separatist Sentiments." December 15: A7.

Noh, S., and M. Belser. 1999. "Perceived Racial Discrimination, Depression, and Coping: A Study of Southeast Asian Refugees in Canada." *Journal of Health and Social Behavior* 40(3): 193–207.

Oliver, Mary Beth. 1994. "Portrayals of Crime, Race, and Aggression in "Reality-Based" Police Shows: A Content Analysis." *Journal of Broadcasting and Electronic Media* (Spring): 179–92.

Pardo, P.A. 1996. *Working for Change from Within: The Independent Living Movement in Canada Reflects on Multiculturalism*, Ph.D. Dissertation. University of Calgary.

Pascarella, Ernest T., Marcia Edison, Amaury Nora, Linda Serra Hagedorn, and Patrick T. Terenzini. 1996. "Influences on Students' Openness to Diversity and Challenge in the First Year of College." *Journal of Higher Education* 67(2): 174–93.

Pescosolido, Bernice A., Elizabeth Grauerholz, and Melissa A. Milkie. 1997. "Culture and Conflict: The Portrayal of Blacks in U.S. Children's Picture Books Through the Mid- and Late-Twentieth Century." *American Sociological Review* 62: 443–64.

Reitz, Jeffrey C., and Raymond Breton. 1994. *The Illusion of Difference: Realities of Ethnicity in Canada and the United States*. Toronto: C.D. Howe Institute.

Rice, G., Anderson, C., Risch, N., and Ebers, G. 1999. "Male Homosexuality: Absence of Linkage to Microsatellite Markers at Xq28." *Science*, 23 April, 284 (5414): 665–667.

Roberts, J. 1995. "Disproportionate Harm: Hate Crime in Canada." <ftp.nizkor.org/hweb/orgs/Canadian/canada/justice/disproportionate-harm>.

Rowe, Frederick W. 1977. *Extinction: The Beothuks of Newfoundland*. Toronto: McGraw-Hill Ryerson.

Schaefer, Richard T. 1998. *Racial and Ethnic Groups*, 7th ed. New York: HarperCollins.

Schwartz, Herman. 1992. "In Defense of Affirmative Action." In *Taking Sides*, 7th ed., pp. 189–94. Guilford, Conn.: Dushkin Publishing Co.

Sher, J. 1983. *White Hoods: Canada's Klu Klux Klan*. Vancouver: New Star Books.

Solomon, R.P., and C. Levine-Rasky. 1996. "When Principle Meets Practice: Teachers' Contradictory Responses to Antiracist Education." *Alberta Journal of Educational Research* 42(1): 19–33.

Spencer, Jon Michael. 1997. *The Mixed-Race Movement in America*. New York: New York University Press.

Statistics Canada. 1998a. *Canada Yearbook 2000*. Ottawa: Minister of Industry.

———. 1998b. "1996 Census: Ethnic Origin, Visible Minorities." *The Daily*. February 17 <www.Statcan.ca/Daily/English/980217/d980217/d980217.htm>.

———. 1998c. "1996 Census: Sources of Income, Earnings, and Total Income, and Family Income." *The Daily*. May 12 <www.statscan.ca:80/Daily/English/980512/d980512.htm>.

Stodolska, M., and E.L. Jackson. 1998. "Discrimination in Leisure and Work Experience by a White Ethnic Minority Group." *Journal of Leisure Research* 30(1): 23–41.

Such, P. 1978. *The Vanished People: The Beothuk People of Newfoundland.* Toronto: NC Press.

Time. 1999. "A Changing People." May 31: 30–4.

Troper, H. 1999. "Immigration." In *The Canadian Encyclopedia Year 2000 Edition,* edited by James H. Marsh, pp. 1139–41. Toronto: McClelland and Stewart Inc.

Wheeler, Michael L. 1994. *Diversity Training: A Research Report.* New York: The Conference Board.

Williams, Eddie N., and Milton D. Morris. 1993. "Racism and Our Future." In *Race in America: The Struggle for Equality,* edited by Herbert Hill and James E. Jones Jr., pp. 417–24. Madison: University of Wisconsin Press.

Wilson, William J. 1987. *The Truly Disadvantaged: The Inner City, the Underclass, and Public Policy.* Chicago: University of Chicago Press.

Winks, Robin W. 1999. "Slavery." In *The Canadian Encyclopedia Year 2000 Edition,* edited by James H. Marsh, p. 2174. Toronto: McClelland and Stewart, Inc.

Zack, Naomi. 1998. *Thinking about Race.* Belmont, Calif.: Wadsworth Publishing Co.

Zinn, Howard. 1993. "Columbus and the Doctrine of Discovery." In *Systemic Crisis: Problems in Society, Politics, and World Order,* edited by William D. Perdue, pp. 351–7. Fort Worth, Tex.: Harcourt Brace Jovanovich.

Chapter 9

"1998 in Review." 1999. *Out* (January): 6.

Allen, K.R., and D.H. Demo. 1995. "The Families of Lesbians and Gay Men: A New Frontier in Family Research." *Journal of Marriage and the Family* 57: 111–27.

Anderssen, Erin. 1999. "Gay-Bashing Preacher Calls Off Protest." *The Globe and Mail,* June 29 <www.egale.ca/archives/press/9906299gm.htm>.

Arnup, Katherine (ed.). 1995. *Lesbian Parenting: Living with Pride and Prejudice.* Charlottetown, PEI: gynergy books.

Bayer, Ronald. 1987. *Homosexuality and American Psychiatry: The Politics of Diagnosis,* 2nd ed. Princeton, N.J.: Princeton University Press.

Beauvais-Godwin, Laura, and Raymond Godwin. 1997. *The Complete Adoption Book.* Holbrook, Mass.: Adams Media Corporation.

Bell, M. 1999. "Child Advocacy Group Fought for Teens' Right to Sodomy." *National Post,* December 15: A1.

Benkov, Laura. 1994. *Reinventing the Family: The Emerging Story of Gay and Lesbian Parents.* New York: Crown Publishers.

Bibby, R.W., and D.G. Posterski. 1992. *Teen Trends: A Nation in Motion.* Toronto: Stoddart.

Brannock, J.C., and B.E. Chapman. 1990. "Negative Sexual Experiences with Men among Heterosexual Women and Lesbians." *Journal of Homosexuality* 19: 105–10.

Button, James W., Barbara A. Rienzo, and Kenneth D. Wald. 1997. *Private Lives, Public Conflicts: Battles over Gay Rights in American Communities.* Washington, D.C.: CQ Press.

Cipriaso, Jon Christian. 1999. "The Wages of Hate." *Out* (February): 28.

"Comparative Survey of the Legal Situation for Homosexuals in Europe." 1998. *Gay and Lesbian International Lobby.* <inet.uni2.dk/~steff/ghl.htm>.

"Constitutional Protection." 1999. GayLawNet. February 14 <www.nexus.net.au/~dba/news.html#top>.

Culbert, Lori. 1999. "Gays' Manhood Surpasses that of Straight Men: Study." *National Post,* September 28: A1, A10.

Current Population Reports. 1993. *Population Profile of the United States, 1993.* Special Studies Series, 23-185. Washington: U.S. Government Printing Office.

D'Emilio, John. 1990. "The Campus Environment for Gay and Lesbian Life." *Academe* 76(1): 16–9.

De Cecco, John P., and D.A. Parker. 1995. "The Biology of Homosexuality: Sexual Orientation or Sexual Preference?" *Journal of Homosexuality* 28: 1–28.

Doell, R.G. 1995. "Sexuality in the Brain." *Journal of Homosexuality* 28: 345–56.

Durkheim, Emile. 1993. "The Normal and the Pathological." Originally published in *The Rules of Sociological Method, 1938.* In *Social Deviance,* edited by Henry N. Pontell, pp. 33–63. Englewood Cliffs, N.J.: Prentice-Hall.

EGALE. 1994. "Polls." <www.egale.ca.features/polls/htm>.

———. 1998. "Press release." December 27 <www.egale.ca>.

———. 1999a. "Employers Offering Same-Sex Benefits." April 10 <www.egale.ca/features/employers.htm>.

———. 1999b. "Press Release." June 7 <www.egale.ca/politics.motion.htm>.

———. 1999c. "Press Release." June 10 <www.egale.ca/archives/press/990610poll.htm>.

———. 1999d. "BC Introduces New Same-Sex Laws, Commits to Omnibus Legislation." July 9 <www.egale.ca/pressrel/990709.htm>.

Esterberg, K. 1997. *Lesbian and Bisexual Identities: Constructing Communities, Constructing Selves.* Philadelphia: Temple University Press.

Faulkner, Anne H., and Kevin Cranston. 1998. "Correlates of Same-Sex Sexual Behavior in a Random Sample of Massachusetts High School Students." *Journal of Public Health* 88 (February): 262–6.

Fisher, John. 1999. *A Report on Lesbian, Gay and Bisexual Youth Issues in Canada.* Ottawa: EGALE.

Frank, Barney. 1997. Foreword to *Private Lives, Public Conflicts: Battles over Gay Rights in American Communities,* by J.W. Button, B.A. Rienzo, and K.D. Wald. Washington D.C.: CQ Press.

Franklin, Sarah. 1993. "Essentialism, Which Essentialism? Some Implications of Reproductive and Genetic Techno-Science." *Journal of Homosexuality* 24: 27–39.

Freedman, Estelle B., and John D'Emilio. 1990. "Problems Encountered in Writing the History of Sexuality:

Sources, Theory, and Interpretation." *Journal of Sex Research* 27: 481–95.

Garnets, L., G.M. Herek, and B. Levy. 1990. "Violence and Victimization of Lesbians and Gay Men: Mental Health Consequences." *Journal of Interpersonal Violence* 5: 366–83.

Goode, Erica E., and Betsy Wagner. 1993. "Intimate Friendships." *U.S. News and World Report*, July 5: 49–52.

Greenhouse, Linda. 1998. "Gay Rights Case Fails in Bid for Supreme Court Hearing." *New York Times*, January 13, 15, late edition, East Coast.

Hamer, D., P.F. Copeland, S. Hu, V.L. Magnuson, N. Hu, and A.M.L. Pattatucci. 1993. "A Linkage Between DNA Markers on the X Chromosome and Male Sexual Orientation." *Science* 261: 321–7.

Harvard Law Review. 1990. *Sexual Orientation and the Law*. Cambridge: Harvard University Press.

Herek, Gregory M. 1989. "Hate Crimes against Lesbians and Gay Men." *American Psychologist* 44: 948–55.

———. 1990. "The Context of Anti-Gay Violence: Notes on Cultural and Psychological Heterosexism." *Journal of Interpersonal Violence* 5: 316–33.

"Idaho Court to Take Up First Case of Adoption by Same-Sex Couple." 1999. GayLawNet, January 16 <www.labyrinth.net.au/~dba/ch1999.html#supreme_court_rules>.

ILGA Annual Report. 1996/1997. February 14 <www.pangea.org/org/cgl/ilga/repilga97e.html>.

Jackson, E., and S. Persky. 1982. *Flaunting It: A Decade of Gay Journalism from the Body Politic.* Toronto: Pink Triangle Press.

Joyce, Gregg. 1998 "Court Overturns School Board Ban on Same-Sex Books." *Canadian Press*, December 16 <www.egale.ca/archives/press/9812cp.htm>.

Kameny, Franklin. 1972. "Gay Liberation and Psychiatry." In *The Homosexual Dialectic*, edited by J. A. McCaffrey, pp. 182–94. Englewood Cliffs, N.J.: Prentice Hall.

Kite, M.E., and B.E. Whitley, Jr. 1996. "Sex Differences in Attitudes toward Homosexual Persons, Behavior and Civil Rights: A Meta-analysis." *Personality and Social Psychology Bulletin* 22: 336–52.

Klassen, Albert D., Colin J. Williams, and Eugene E. Levitt. 1989. *Sex and Morality in the United States.* Middletown, Conn.: Wesleyan University Press.

Knox, David. 1998. *The Divorced Dad's Survival Book.* New York: Insight Publishing Co.

Laird, J. 1993. "Lesbian and Gay Families." In *Normal Family Processes*, 2nd ed., edited by F. Walsh, pp. 282–328. New York: Guilford.

Lawbriefs. 1999. Human Rights Campaign, Winter, Vol. 2(1). February 16 <www.hrc.org/pubs/lawb0201.html>.

Lever, J. 1994. "The 1994 Advocate Survey of Sexuality and Relationships: The Men." *Advocate,* August 23: 16–24.

Louderback, L.A., and B.E. Whitley. 1997. "Perceived Erotic Value of Homosexuality and Sex-Role Attitudes as Mediators of Sex Differences in Heterosexual College Students' Attitudes toward Lesbians and Gay Men." *Journal of Sex Research* 34: 175–82.

Maclean's. 1996. "Untitled." November 4.

Maclean's. 1999a. "Marriage Vows." June 21: 25.

———. 1999b. "Peering Inward and Outward." December 20: 49.

Mahoney, Jill. 1999. "Alberta Gays Want Laws Amended." *The Globe and Mail*, November 24: A3.

Mathison, Carla. 1998. "The Invisible Minority: Preparing Teachers to Meet the Needs of Gay and Lesbian Youth." *Journal of Teacher Education* 49: 151–5.

McIlroy, Anne. 1999. "Most in Poll Want Gay Marriages Legalized." *The Globe and Mail*, June 10 <www.egale.ca/archives/press/190610poll.htm>.

Michael, Robert T., John H. Gagnon, Edward O. Laumann, and Gina Kolata. 1994. *Sex in America: A Definitive Survey.* Boston: Little, Brown.

Mohr, Richard D. 1995. "Anti-Gay Stereotypes." In *Race, Class, and Gender in the United States*, 3rd ed., edited by P.S. Rothenberg, pp. 402–8. New York: St. Martin's Press.

Moore, David W. 1993. "Public Polarized on Gay Issue." *Gallup Poll Monthly* 331 (April): 30–4.

Moser, Charles. 1992. "Lust, Lack of Desire, and Paraphilias: Some Thoughts and Possible Connections." *Journal of Sex and Marital Therapy* 18: 65–9.

National Coalition of Anti-Violence Programs. 1998. *Anti-Lesbian, Gay, Bisexual and Transgendered Violence in 1997.* New York: The New York City Gay and Lesbian Anti-Violence Project (March 4).

Nugent, Robert, and Jeannine Gramick. 1989. "Homosexuality: Protestant, Catholic, and Jewish Issues: A Fishbone Tale." *Journal of Homosexuality* 18: 7–46.

O'Brien, C.A., and L. Weir. 1995. "Lesbians and Gay Men Inside and Outside Families." In *Canadian Families: Diversity, Conflict and Change*, pp. 111–39. Toronto: Harcourt Brace Canada.

Patterson, Charlotte. 1997. "Children of Lesbian and Gay Parents: Summary of Research Findings." In *Same-Sex Marriage: Pro and Con*, edited A. Sullivan, pp. 146–54. New York: Vintage Books.

Paul, J.P. 1996. "Bisexuality: Exploring/Exploding the Boundaries." In *The Lives of Lesbians, Gays, and Bisexuals: Children to Adults*, edited by R. Savin-Williams, and K.M. Cohen, pp. 436–61. Fort Worth, Tex.: Harcourt Brace.

Peele, S., and R. DeGrandpre. 1995. "My Genes Made Me Do It." *Psychology Today*, 28(4), July/August: 50–3.

Pillard, Richard C., and J. Michael Bailey. 1998. "Human Sexuality Has a Heritable Component." *Human Biology* 70 (April): 347–65.

"Poll Supports Gay Marriages." 1999. *The Globe and Mail*, June 10 <www.egale.ca/pressrel/990611.htm>.

Price, Jammie, and Michael G. Dalecki. 1998. "The Social Basis of Homophobia: An Empirical Illustration." *Sociological Spectrum* 18: 143–59.

Rice, G. Anderson, C., Risch, N., and Ebers, G. 1999. "Male Homosexuality: Absence of Linkage to Microsatellite Markets at Xq28." *Science*, 23 April, 284 (5415): 665–667.

Rosin, Hanna, and Richard Morin. 1999. "In One Area, Americans Still Draw a Line on Acceptability." *Washington*

Post, National Weekly Edition (January 11), 16(11): 8.

Royal Commission on New Reproductive Technologies. 1993. Patricia Baird, Chairperson, 1993. *Proceed With Caution: Final Report of the Royal Commission on New Reproductive Technologies.* Ottawa: Canadian Communications Group.

Saad, Lydia. 1996. "Americans Growing More Tolerant of Gays." *Gallup Poll Archives,* Princeton, N.J.: The Gallup Organization. <98.175.140.8/POLL-ARCHIVES/961214.htm>.

Sanday, Peggy R. 1995. "Pulling Train." In *Race, Class, and Gender in the United States,* 3rd ed., edited by P.S. Rothenberg, pp. 396–402. New York: St. Martin's Press.

Sarda, Alejandra. 1998. "Lesbians and the Gay Movement in Argentina." *NACL A Report on the Americas* 31(4): 40–1.

Schellenberg, E. Glenn, Jessie Hirt, and Alan Sears. 1999. "Attitudes Toward Homosexuals Among Students at a Canadian University." *Sex Roles* 40 (1/2): 139–52.

Schulenberg, J. 1983. *Gay Parenting.* New York: Doubleday.

Simon, A. 1995. "Some Correlates of Individuals' Attitudes toward Lesbians." *Journal of Homosexuality* 29: 89–103.

Statistics Canada. 1992. *Families: Number, Type and Structure, The Nation, 1991 Census.* Cat. No. 93-912. Ottawa: Minister of Industry, Science and Technology.

Stone, Sharon D. (ed.). 1990. "Lesbian Mothers: Organizing." In *Lesbians in Canada,* pp. 191–205. Toronto: Between the Lines.

Sullivan, A. 1997. "The Conservative Case." In *Same-Sex Marriage: Pro and Con,* edited by A. Sullivan, pp. 146–54. New York: Vintage Books.

Tasker, Fiona L., and Susan Golombok. 1997. *Growing Up in a Lesbian Family: Effects on Child Development.* New York: Guilford.

Thompson, Cooper. 1995. "A New Vision of Masculinity." In *Race, Class, and Gender in the United States,* 3rd ed., edited by P. S. Rothenberg, pp. 475–81. New York: St. Martin's Press.

Toronto Star. 1996. "The Changing Family." May 10: A1, A14, A26.

United Methodist Church and Homosexuality. 1999. February 16 <religioustolerance.org/hom_umc.htm>.

Weston, Kath. 1991. *Families We Choose: Lesbians, Gays, Kinship.* New York: Columbia University Press.

Williams, Karen. 1995. "The Good Mother." In *Lesbian Parenting: Living with Pride and Prejudice,* edited by Katherine Arnup, pp. 98–110. Charlottetown, PEI: gynergy books.

Yogis, J.A., R.R. Duplak, and J.R. Trainor. 1996. *Sexual Orientation and Canadian Law: An Assessment of the Law Affecting Lesbian and Gay Persons.* Toronto: Emond Montgomery Publications Limited.

Chapter 10

Albelda, Randy, and Chris Tilly. 1997. *Glass Ceilings and Bottomless Pits: Women's Work, Women's Poverty.* Boston, Mass.: South End Press.

Alex-Assensoh, Yvette. 1995. "Myths about Race and the Underclass." *Urban Affairs Review* 31: 3–19.

Ash, Russell. 1999. *The Top 10 of Everything 2000.* Montreal: Reader's Digest Association (Canada) Ltd.

Associated Press. 1997. "Class Plays Role in Heart-Attack Recovery." *Toronto Sun,* October 13: 24.

Barlett, Donald L., and James B. Steele. 1998. "The Empire of the Pigs." *Time,* November 30, 52–64.

Barlow, Maude, and Bruce Campbell. 1995. *Straight through the Heart.* Toronto: HarperCollins Publishers Ltd.

Bergmann, Barbara R. 1996. *Saving Our Children from Poverty: What the United States Can Learn from France.* New York: Russell Sage Foundation.

"Bill Gates Tops Forbes Billionaires for 5th Year." 1998 (September 28). *Point-Cast Network* (Online News Channel).

Briggs, Vernon M. Jr. 1998. "American-Style Capitalism and Income Disparity: The Challenge of Social Anarchy." *Journal of Economic Issues* 32(2): 473–81.

Canada Mortgage and Housing Corporation (CMHC). 1999. "Survey of Canadians' Attitudes towards Homelessness, June 1996, March 1997, and March 1998 Survey Results." May 10, 2000 <www.cmhc-schl.gc.ca/>.

Canadian Centre for Policy Alternatives Monitor. 1999. September <www.policyalternatives.ca>.

Canadian Press. 2000. "Attitudes Need Adjusting." *KW Record,* May 2: A3.

Card, David, and Alan Krueger. 1995. *Myth and Measurement: The New Economics of the Minimum Wage.* Princeton, N.J.: Princeton University Press.

Chossudovsky, Michel. 1998. "Global Poverty in the Late Twentieth Century." *Journal of International Affairs* 52(1): 293–303.

Clark, Warren. 1998. "Paying off Student Loans." *Canadian Social Trends* 51(Winter): 24–8.

Cleveland, Gordon, and Michael Krashinsky. 1998. *The Benefits and Costs of Good Child Care: The Economic Rationale for Public Investment in Young Children.* Toronto: University of Toronto.

Corak, Miles. 1998. "Getting Ahead in Life: Does Your Parents' Income Count?" *Canadian Social Trends* 49(Summer): 6–15.

Coyne, Andrew. 1997. "Poverty Study Raises Questions." *KW Record,* July 17: A7.

Daub, Shannon and Margaret Young. 1999. "Families Need More than Tax Fairness." <www.policyalternatives.ca>.

Davis, Kingsley, and Wilbert Moore. 1945. "Some Principles of Stratification." *American Sociological Review* 10: 242–49.

Deng, Francis M. 1998. "The Cow and the Thing Called 'What': Dinka Cultural Perspectives on Wealth and Poverty." *Journal of International Affairs* 52(1): 101–15.

Doherty, Gillian, Martha Friendly, and Mab Oloman. 1998. *Women's Support, Women's Work: Child Care in an Era of Deficit Reduction, Downsizing and Deregulation.* Ottawa: Status of Women Canada.

Drakes, Shellene. 1999. "Recent Immigrants Have Tougher Time Finding

Good Jobs." *Toronto Star*, November 24: A1.

Duncan, Greg J., and Jeanne Brooks-Gunn. 1997. "Income Effects across the Life Span: Integration and Interpretation." In *Consequences of Growing Up Poor*, edited by Greg J. Duncan, and Jeanne Brooks-Gunn, pp. 596–610. New York: Russell Sage Foundation.

FAD (Families Against Deadbeats). 2000. <www.wantedposters.com>.

Fawcett, 1999. "Disability in the Labour Market: Barriers and Solutions." *Perception*, 23(3), December. Canadian Council on Social Development. <www.ccsd.ca/perception/233 /disab.htm>.

Fennell, Tom. 1996. "How Very Different Are We?" *Maclean's*, November 4: 36–40.

Gans, Herbert J. 1972. "The Positive Functions of Poverty." *American Journal of Sociology* 78 (September): 275–388.

Government of Canada. 1999. <www.socialunion.gc.ca/ NCB-99/html>.

Guest, Dennis. 1999a. "Social Security." In *The Canadian Encyclopedia: Year 2000 Edition*, edited by James H. Marsh, pp. 2200–4. Toronto: McClelland and Stewart, Inc.

———. 1999b. "Family Allowance. *The Canadian Encyclopedia: Year 2000 Edition*, edited by James H. Marsh, pp. 1815–6. Toronto: McClelland and Stewart, Inc.

Health Canada. 1999. *Toward a Healthy Future: Second Report on the Health of Canadians*. Prepared by the Federal, Provincial, and Territorial Advisory Committee on Population Health for the Meeting of Ministers of Health, Charlottetown, PEI, September 1999.

Hernandez, Donald J. 1997. "Poverty Trends." In *Consequences of Growing up Poor*, edited by Greg J. Duncan, and Jeanne Brooks-Gunn, pp. 18–34. New York: Russell Sage Foundation.

Hill, Lewis E. 1998. "The Institutional Economics of Poverty: An Inquiry into the Causes and Effects of Poverty." *Journal of Economic Issues* 32(2): 279–86.

Human Development Report 1997. 1997. United Nations Development Programme. New York: Oxford University Press.

Kennedy, Bruce P., Ichiro Kawachi, Roberta Glass, and Deborah Prothrow-Stith. 1998. "Income Distribution, Socioeconomic Status, and Self-Rated Health in the U.S.: Multilevel Analysis." *British Medical Journal* 317(7163): 917–22.

Krahn, Harvey. 1994. "Social Stratification." In *New Society Brief Edition: Sociology for the Twenty-First Century*, edited by Robert Brym, pp. 2.1–2.31. Toronto: Harcourt Brace Jovanovich.

Larin, Kathryn. 1998. "Should We Be Worried about the Widening Gap between the Rich and the Poor?" *Insight on the News* 14(5): 24–8.

Laroche, M. 1998. "In and Out of Low Income." *Canadian Social Trends* 40: 20–4.

Levitan, Sar A., Garth L. Mangum, and Stephen L. Mangum. 1998. *Programs in Aid of the Poor*, 7th ed. Baltimore: Johns Hopkins University Press.

Lewis, Oscar. 1966. "The Culture of Poverty." *Scientific American* 2(5): 19–25.

———. 1998. "The Culture of Poverty: Resolving Common Social Problems." *Society* 35(2): 7–10.

Luker, Kristin. 1996. *Dubious Conceptions: The Politics of Teenage Pregnancy*. Cambridge, Mass.: Harvard University Press.

Maclean's. 1999a. "No Title." January 11: 16.

———. 1999b. "No Title." December 6: 33.

———. 1999c. "Shifting Priorities." December 20: 29.

———. 1999d. "Forecast: Housing Prices." December 13: 56.

———. 1999e. "What Makes a Canadian?" December 20: 44–8.

Mayer, Susan E. 1997a. *What Money Can't Buy: Family Income and Children's Life Chances*. Cambridge, Mass.: Harvard University Press.

———. 1997b. "Trends in the Economic Well-Being and Life Chances of America's Children." In *Consequences of Growing Up Poor*, eds. Greg J.

Duncan and Jeanne Brooks-Gunn, pp. 46–99. New York: Russell Sage Foundation.

McAfee, A. 1999. "Housing and Housing Policy." *The Canadian Encyclopedia: Year 2000 Edition*, edited by James H. Marsh, pp. 1107–8. Toronto: McClelland and Stewart, Inc.

Mead, L. 1992. *The New Politics of Poverty: The Non-Working Poor in America*. New York: Basic Books.

Moscovitch, Allan. 1999. "Welfare State." In *The Canadian Encyclopedia: Year 2000 Edition*, edited by James H. Marsh, pp. 2493–6. Toronto: McClelland and Stewart, Inc.

National Child Benefit Progress Report. 1999. <www/socialunion.gc.ca/ NCB-99/html>.

National Council of Welfare. 1997. "Canada Welfare Incomes." <csf.colorado.edu/lists/psn/dec97/ 0071.html>.

———. 1998. *Profiles of Welfare: Myths and Realities: A Report by the National Council of Welfare*. Spring <www. ncwcnbes.net/htmdocument/ reportprowelfare.repprowelfare. htm>.

———. 1999a. "No Such Thing as a 'Typical' Welfare Case, Says National Council of Welfare Report." <www. ncwcnbes.net/htmdocument/ reportprowelfare/PRESSPROWELFARE. htm>.

———. 1999b. *Preschool Children: Promises to Keep*. Spring <www.ncwcnbes. net/htmdocument/reportpromise/ firstpag.html>.

———. 1999c. *Children First: A Pre-Budget Report by the National Council of Welfare*. Autumn <www.ncwcnbes.net/ htmdocument/reportchildfirst/ repchildfirst.htm>.

Orlikow, Lionel. 1999. "Students, Financial Aid." In *The Canadian Encyclopedia: Year 2000 Edition*, edited by James H. Marsh, pp. 2264–5. Toronto: McClelland and Stewart, Inc.

Ross, David P., and Clarence Lochhead. 1999. "Poverty." In *The Canadian Encyclopedia: Year 2000 Edition*, edited by James H. Marsh, pp. 1880–2. Toronto: McClelland and Stewart, Inc.

Ross, David P., E. Richard Shillington, and Clarence Lochhead. 1994. *The Canadian Fact Book on Poverty*. Ottawa: Canadian Council on Social Development.

Ryan, William. 1992. "Blaming the Victim." In *Taking Sides*, 7th ed., edited by Kurt Finsterbusch, and George McKenna, pp. 155–62. Guilford, Conn.: Dushkin Publishing Group.

Sarlo, Christopher. 1992. *Poverty in Canada*. Vancouver: The Fraser Institute.

———. 1996. *Poverty in Canada*. Vancouver: The Fraser Institute.

Speth, James Gustave. 1998. "Poverty: A Denial of Human Rights." *Journal of International Affairs* 52(1): 277–86.

Statistics Canada. 1998a. *Canada Yearbook 1999*. Ottawa: Minister of Industry.

———. 1998b. *The Daily*. May 12

Streeten, Paul. 1998. "Beyond the Six Veils: Conceptualizing and Measuring Poverty." *Journal of International Affairs* 52(1): 1–8.

Toronto Star. 1999. "A Picture of Poverty." January 15: B3.

Townson, Monica. 1998. "Canada's Record." *CCPA Monitor* (October) <www.policyalternatives.ca>.

Trainor, C. 1999. "Canada's Shelters." *Canadian Social Trends* 57 (Winter): 20–3.

United Council on Welfare Fraud. 2000. <www.cowf.org>.

Van Kempen, Eva T. 1997. "Poverty Pockets and Life Chances: On the Role of Place in Shaping Social Inequality." *American Behavioural Scientist* 41(3): 430–50.

Weisbrot, Mark. 1998. "Globalization for Whom? Preamble Center. <www.preamble.org/Globalization.html> (October 22, 1998).

Wilson, William J. 1996. *When Work Disappears: The World of the New Urban Poor*. New York: Knopf.

Yalnizyan, A. 1998. *The Growing Gap*. Toronto: Centre for Social Justice.

Chapter 11

Ambrose, Soren. 1998. "The Case against the IMF." *Campaign for Human Rights Newsletter* No. 12, December 8 <www. summersault.co....wsletter/news12.html>.

Association of Workers' Compensation Boards of Canada. 1995. *Canadian Workers' Compensation: Basic Statistical and Financial Information 1990–93*. Edmonton: Association of Workers' Compensation Boards of Canada.

Bell, Daniel. 1973. *The Coming of Post-Industrial Society*. New York: Basic Books.

Bellan, Ruben C. 1999. "Foreign Investment." In *The Canadian Encyclopedia: Year 2000 Edition*, edited by James H. Marsh, pp. 884–5. Toronto: McClelland and Stewart, Inc.

Best, P. 1995. "Women, Men, and Work." *Canadian Social Trends* 36(Spring): 30–3.

Bettelheim, Adriel. 1998. "Sleep Deprivation." *CQ Researcher* 8(24): 553–76.

Bond, James T., Ellen Galinsky, and Jennifer E. Swanberg. 1997. *The 1997 National Study of the Changing Workforce*. New York: Families and Work Institute.

Bracey, Gerald W. 1995. "The Fifth Bracey Report on the Condition of Public Education." *Phi Delta Kappan* (October): 149–62.

Brecher, Jeremy. 1996. "Countering Corporate Downsizing: A Survey of Proposals to Halt Layoffs and Job Degradation." The Preamble Collaborative Center. December 8, 1998 <www.preamble.org/intro.html>.

Canadian Global Almanac. 2000. Edited by Susan Girvan. Toronto: Macmillan Canada.

Canadian Press. 1999. "Many Canadians Admit They're Workaholics." *KW Record*, November 10: A3.

Caston, Richard J. 1998. *Life in a Business-Oriented Society: A Sociological Perspective*. Boston: Allyn and Bacon.

Child Labour. 1997. *UN Chronicle* 4: 52.

Chisholm, Patricia. 2000. "All in the Family." *Maclean's*, January 17: 16–26.

Chossudovsky, Michel. 1998. "Global Poverty in the Late Twentieth Century." *Journal of International Affairs* 52(1): 293–303.

Coleman, James. 1994. *The Criminal Elite: The Sociology of White Collar Crime*, 3rd ed. New York: St. Martins Press.

Conrad, Peter. 1999. "Wellness in the Work Place: Potentials and Pitfalls of Work-Site Health Promotion." In *Health, Illness, and Healing: Society, Social Context, and Self*, edited by K. Charmaz, and D.A. Paterniti, pp. 263–75. Los Angeles: Roxbury Publishing Company.

Danaher, Kevin. 1998. "Are Workers Waking Up?" Global Exchange: Education for Action. December 17 <www.globalexchange.org/education/econnomy/laborday.html>.

Durkheim, Emile. [1893] 1966. *On the Division of Labor in Society*, trans. G. Simpson. New York: Free Press.

Eitzen, Stanley, and Maxine Baca Zinn (eds.) 1990. *The Reshaping of America: Social Consequences of the Changing Economy*. Englewood Cliffs, N.J.: Prentice-Hall.

EKOS Research Associates. 1995. *What Does Workplace Change Mean for Different Segments of the Canadian Labour Market?* Toronto: EKOS.

Epstein, Gerald, Julie Graham, and Jessica Nembhard (eds.). 1993. "Third World Socialism and the Demise of COMECON." In *Creating a New World Economy: Forces of Change and Plans of Action*, pp. 405–20. Philadelphia: Temple University Press.

Fast, J., and DaPont, M. 1997. "Changes in Women's Work Continuity." *Canadian Social Trends* 46(Autumn): 2–7.

Feather, Norman T. 1990. *The Psychological Impact of Unemployment*. New York: Springer-Verlag.

Flexner, Joe. 1997. "The Ontario Fightback Movement in Crisis; Days of Action or DOA?" *Canadian Dimension*, October 31(5): 7–11.

Galinsky, Ellen, and James T. Bond. 1998. *The 1998 Business Work-Life Study*. New York: Families and Work Institute.

Galinsky, Ellen, James E. Riesbeck, Fran S. Rodgers, and Faith A. Wohl. 1993. "Business Economics and the Work-Family Response." In *Work-Family Needs: Leading Corporations Respond*, pp. 51–4. New York: The Conference Board.

Global March against Child Labor. 1998. "Global March against Child Labor." 1998. December 12, 1998 <children.globalmarch-us.org>.

Gordon, David M. 1996. *Fat and Mean: The Corporate Squeeze of Working Americans and the Myth of Managerial "Downsizing."* New York: The Free Press.

Hallsworth, Alan. 1993. "The External Trade of Canada." In *The U.S.A. and Canada*, pp. 432–9. London, U.K.: Europa Publications.

Health Canada. 1999. *Statistical Report on the Health of Canadians.* December 25 <www.hc-sc.gc.ca/hppb/phdd/report/state/englover.html>.

Hewlett, Sylvia Ann. 1992. *When the Bough Breaks: The Cost of Neglecting Our Children.* New York: Harper-Collins.

Hewlett, Sylvia Ann, and Cornell West. 1998. *The War against Parents: What We Can Do for America's Beleaguered Moms and Dads.* Boston: Houghton Mifflin Company.

Hochschild, Arlie Russell. 1997. *The Time Bind: When Work Becomes Home and Home Becomes Work.* New York: Henry Holt and Company.

Hodson, Randy, and Teresa A. Sullivan. 1990. *The Social Organization of Work.* Belmont, Calif.: Wadsworth.

Kennedy, Joseph II. 1996. "Keynote Address." In *Forced Labor: The Prostitution of Children*, pp. 1–6, Washington, D.C.: U.S. Department of Labor, Bureau of International Labor Affairs.

Kenworthy, Lane. 1995. *In Search of National Economic Success.* Thousand Oaks, Calif.: Sage Publications.

Koch, Kathy. 1998. "High-Tech Labor Shortage." *CQ Researcher* 8(16): 361–84.

Lee, C., L. Duxbury, and C. Higgins. 1994. *Employed Mothers: Balancing Work and Family Life.* Ottawa: Canadian Centre for Management Development.

Lenski, Gerard, and J. Lenski. 1987. *Human Societies: An Introduction to Macrosociology*, 5th ed. New York: McGraw-Hill.

Leonard, Bill. 1996. "From School to Work: Partnerships Smooth the Transition." *HR Magazine (Society for Human Resource Management).* December 8, 1998 <www.shrm.org/hrmag...articles/0796cov.htm>.

Levitan, Sar A., Garth L. Mangum, and Stephen L. Mangum. 1998. *Programs in Aid of the Poor*, 7th ed. Baltimore: Johns Hopkins University Press.

Liem, Joan H., and G. Ramsey Liem. 1990. "Understanding the Individual and Family Effects of Unemployment." In *Stress between Work and Family*, edited by J. Eckenrode, and S. Gore, pp. 175–204. New York: Plenum Press.

Lowe, Graham, and Harvey Krahn. 1993. *Work, Industry and Canadian Society.* Scarborough, Ont.: Nelson Canada.

Maclean's. 1999a. "Making Babies." December 6: 53–6.

———. 1999b. "Deciphering Debit-Card Dilemmas." December 13: 56.

———. 1999c. "The Best and Worst Jobs." May 31: 18–23.

Maule, C.J. 1999. "Multinational Corporation." In *The Canadian Encyclopedia: Year 2000 Edition*, edited by James H. Marsh, pp. 1536. Toronto: McClelland and Stewart Inc.

Messing, K. 1994. "Women's Occupational Health: A Critical Review and Discussion of Issues." *Women and Health* 25(4): 39–69.

Mishel, Lawrence, Jared Bernstein, and John Schmitt. 1999. *The State of Working America, 1998–99.* Economic Policy Institute Series. Ithaca, N.Y.: Cornell University Press.

National Safety Council. 1997. *Accident Facts 1997 Edition.* Itasca, Ill.: National Safety Council.

Nelson, A., and A. Fleras. 1998. *Social Problems in Canada*, 2nd ed. Scarborough, Ont.: Prentice Hall Allyn and Bacon Canada.

Panitch, Leo. 1999. "State." In *The Canadian Encyclopedia, Year 2000 Edition*, edited by James H. Marsh, pp. 2245–6. Toronto: McClelland and Stewart, Inc.

Parker, David L. (with Lee Engfer and Robert Conrow). 1998. *Stolen Dreams: Portraits of Working Children.* Minneapolis: Lerner Publications Company.

Reed, Stanley. 1999. "Now the Dollar Has a Co-Star on the World Stage." *Business Week*, January 18: 36–7.

Report on the World Social Situation. 1997. New York: United Nations.

Robie, Chet, Ann Marie Ryan, Robert A. Schmieder, Luis Fernando Parra, and Patricia C. Smith. 1998. "The Relation between Job Level and Job Satisfaction." *Group and Organizational Management* 23(4): 470–86.

Ross, Catherine E., and Marylyn P. Wright. 1998. "Women's Work, Men's Work, and the Sense of Control." *Work and Occupations* 25(3): 333–55.

Rotstein, Abraham. 1999. "Economic Nationalism." In *The Canadian Encyclopedia, Year 2000 Edition*, edited by James H. Marsh, pp. 716–7. Toronto: McClelland and Stewart, Inc.

Silvers, Jonathan. 1996. "Child Labor in Pakistan." *Atlantic Monthly* 277(2): 79–92.

Simone, Rose. 1999. "Couple Speak out about Dangers of Toxic Substances in Workplace." *KW Record*, November 10: B7.

Statistics Canada. 1998a. *Canadian Profile 2000.* Ottawa: Ministry of Industry.

———. 1998b. *Canada Yearbook 1999.* Ottawa: Ministry of Industry.

———. 1999. "Labour Force Update: An Overview of the Labour Market." *The Daily.* January 27, 1999.

Straus, Murray A. 1980. "A Sociological Perspective on the Prevention of Wife-Beating." *The Social Causes of Husband-Wife Violence*, edited by M.A. Straus, and G.T. Hotaling, pp. 211–32. Minneapolis: University of Minnesota Press.

UNICEF. 1997. *State of the World's Children, 1997.* New York: United Nations.

U.S. Department of Labor. 1995. "By the Sweat and Toil of Children," Vol. 2, *The Use of Child Labor in U.S. Agricultural Imports and Forced and Bonded Child Labor.* Washington, D.C.: U.S. Department of Labor, Bureau of International Labor Affairs.

Yanz, Lynda, and Bob Jeffcott. 1997. "Fighting Sweatshops/Building Solidarity: Exposing the Gap." *Canadian Dimensions*, October, 31(4): 25–9.

Chapter 12

AAUW (American Association of University Women). 1998. "Report Finds Separating by Sex Not the Solution to Gender Inequity in School." *Press Release* (2300) <aauw.org>.

Arenson, Laren W. 1998. "More Colleges Plunging into the Unchartered Waters of On-Line Courses." *New York Times*, November 2: A14.

Arnott, Kim. 1997. "Home and School." *Education Today* Spring, 9(2): 16–21.

Ascher, Carol, Norm Fruchter, and Robert Berne. 1997. *Hard Lessons: Public Schools and Privatization.* New York: Twentieth Century Fund.

Associated Press. 1998. "Education Becomes Major Political Issue as Candidates Listen to Voters." *New York Times*, September 20: A5.

Bailey, Susan M. 1993. "The Current Status of Gender Equity Research in American Schools." *Educational Psychologist* 28: 321–40.

Baker, David P., and Deborah P. Jones. 1993. "Creating Gender Equality: Cross-National Gender Stratification and Mathematical Performance." *Sociology of Education* 66: 91–103.

Banks, James A., and Cherry A. Banks (eds.). 1993. *Multicultural Education*, 2nd ed. Boston: Allyn and Bacon.

———. 1995. *Handbook of Multicultural Education.* New York: MacMillan.

Bankston, Carl, and Stephen Caldas. 1997. "The American School Dilemma: Race and Scholastic Performance." *Sociological Quarterly* 38(3): 423–29.

Barlow, Maude, and Heather-Jane Robertson. 1994. *Class Warfare: The Assault on Canada's Schools.* Toronto: Key Porter Books.

Barnett, Steven. 1995. "Long Term Effects of Early Childhood Programs on Cognitive and School Outcomes." *Future of Children* 5: 25–50.

Barton, Paul. 1992. *America's Smallest School: The Family.* Princeton, N.J.: Educational Testing Service.

Bender, David, and Bruno Leone (eds.). 1994. *Culture Wars: Opposing Viewpoints.* San Diego, Calif: Greenhaven Press Inc.

Bergman, Brian. 1999. "First-Year Confidential." *Maclean's*, January 17: 86–9.

Brown, Roy J. 1999. "Special Education." In *The Canadian Encyclopedia: Year 2000 Edition*, edited by James H. Marsh, pp. 741–2. Toronto: McClelland and Stewart, Inc.

Bulkeley, William M. 1998. "Education: Kaplan Plans a Law School via the Web." *Wall Street Journal*, September 16: B1.

Bushweller, Kevin. 1995. "Turning Our Backs on Boys." *Education Digest* (January): 9–12.

Call, Kathleen, Lorie Grabowski, Jeylan Mortimer, Katherine Nash, and Chaimun Lee. 1997. "Impoverished Youth and the Attainment Process." Presented at the Annual Meeting of the American Sociological Association, Toronto, Ontario. August.

Canadian Council on Social Development. 1999. *Thinking Ahead: Trends Affecting Public Education in the Future.* Ottawa: Canadian Council on Social Development.

Canadian Global Almanac. 2000. Edited by Susan Girvan. Toronto: Macmillan Canada.

Carvin, Andy. 1997. *EdWeb: Exploring Technology and School Reform.* <edweb.gsn.org>.

Celis, William. 1993. "10 Years after a Scathing Report, Schools Show Uneven Progress." New York Times, April 28.

Chernos, Saul. 1998. "Alternative Route." *Education Today*, 10(1), Winter: 12-5.

Clark, Warren. 1999. "Paying off Student Loans." *Canadian Social Trends* 51(Winter): 24–8.

Cohen, Warren. 1998. "Vouchers for Good and 111." *U.S. News and World Report*, April 27, 46.

College Board. 1997. "1997 Profile of College Bound Seniors." In *Fair Test Examiner: SAT/ACT Scores 1996.* <fairtest.org>.

Curtis, James E., and Ronald D. Lambert. 1994. "Ideology and Social Change." In *The Social World*, 3rd ed., edited by Lorne Tepperman, James E. Curtis, and R. Jack Richardson, pp. 710–58. Toronto: McGraw-Hill.

D'Souza, Dinesh. 1994. "Political Correctness is Harmful." In *Culture Wars: Opposing Viewpoints*, edited by David Bender, and Bruno Leone, pp. 84–91. San Diego, Calif.: Greenhaven Press, Inc.

Daisley, B. 1996. "Foreign Domestic Wins Sexual Harassment Suit against Boss." *The Lawyers' Weekly* 15(47), April: 21.

Dwyer, Victor. 1994. "Bright Kids, Bright Futures?" *Maclean's*, August 29: 36–40.

Fekete, John. 1994. *Moral Panic: Biopolitics Rising.* Toronto: Robert Davies.

Fichten, Catherine S., Maria Barile, and Evelyn Reid. 1999. "Computer Technologies and Women with Disabilities: Is There Common Ground?" *1999 SWC Supplement.* Ottawa: CAUT: 5, 10.

Freitas, Frances Anne, Scott Meyers, and Theodore Avtgis. 1998. "Student Perceptions of Instructor Immediacy in Conventional and Distributed Learning Classrooms." *Communication Education* 47(4): 366–72.

Gaskell, Jane, Arlene McLaren, and Myra Novogrodsky. 1995. "What's Worth Knowing." In *Gender in the 1990s*, edited by E.D. Nelson, and B.W. Robinson, pp. 100–18. Scarborough, Ont.: Nelson.

Gilbert, Sid, and Bruce Orok. 1993. "School Leavers." *Canadian Social Trends* (Winter): 2–7.

Goldberg, Carey. 1999. "After Girls Get Attention, Focus is on Boys' Woes." In *Themes of the Times: New York Times*, p. 6. Upper Saddle River, N.J.: Prentice-Hall.

Government of Canada. 1999. "Learning Technologies." <www.hrdc-drhc.gc.ca>.

Guernsey, Lisa. 1998. "An Unusual Graduate Program Requires Students to Find and Pay Their Professors." *Chronicle of Higher Education* 44: A14–A16.

Guppy, Neil, and Bruce Arai. 1993. "Who Benefits from Higher Education? Differences by Sex, Social Class, and Ethnic Background." In *Social Inequality in Canada: Patterns, Problems, Policies*, 2nd ed., edited by James E. Curtis, Edward Grabb, and Neil Guppy, pp. 214–32. Scarborough, Ont.: Prentice-Hall.

Harrington. 1999: A4.

Haughey, Margaret. 1999. "Distance Learning." In *The Canadian Encyclopedia: Year 2000 Edition*, edited by James H. Marsh, pp. 672–3. Toronto: McClelland and Stewart, Inc.

Health Canada. 1999. *Statistical Report on the Health of Canadians*. December 25 <www.hc-sc.gc.ca/hppb/phdd/report/state/englover.html>.

Hindustan Times. 1999. "40% Men and 60% Women Illiterate in India." September 19 <www.hindutimes.com>.

Janigan, Mary. 1999. "What's Right—and Wrong—with Canada." *Maclean's*, August 16: 30–5.

Jencks, Christopher, and Meredith Phillips. 1998. "America's Next Achievement Test: Closing the Black-White Test Score Gap." *The American Prospect* (September/October): 44–53.

Jenish, D'Arcy. 1994. "The Tutoring Boom." *Maclean's*, August 29: 42–3.

Johnston, Ann Dowsett. 1999a. *Maclean's*, November 15: 31

———. 1999b. "Measuring Excellence." *Maclean's*, November 15: 49–52.

Kanter, Rosabeth Moss. 1972. "The Organization Child: Experience Management in a Nursery School." *Sociology of Education* 45: 186–211.

Koch, James V. 1998. "How Women Actually Perform in Distance Education." *Chronicle of Higher Education* 45: A60.

Koeppel, David. 1998. "Easy Degrees Proliferate on the Web." *New York Times*, August 2: 17.

Kozol, Jonathan. 1991. *Savage Inequalities: Children in America's Schools*. New York: Crown Publishers.

Kuh, George, Ernest Pascarella, and Henry Wechsler. 1996. "The Questionable Value of Fraternities." *Chronicle of Higher Education*, April 19: A68.

Lam, Julia. 1997. "The Employment Activity of Chinese-American High-School Students and Its Relationship to Academic Achievement." Presented at the Annual Meeting of the American Sociological Association, Toronto, Ontario, August.

Lan, K.S. 1992. *Cultural Identity: A Case Study of the Chinese Heritage Language Schools in Calgary*. Ph.D. Thesis. University of Calgary.

Lareau, Annette. 1989. *Home Advantage: Social Class and Parental Intervention in Elementary Education*. Philadelphia: Falmer Press.

Levin, Macolm. 1999. "Alternative Education." In *The Canadian Encyclopedia: Year 2000 Edition*, edited by James H. Marsh, p. 732. Toronto: McClelland and Stewart, Inc.

Livingstone, D.N. 1999. "Educational Opportunity." In *The Canadian Encyclopedia: Year 2000 Edition*, edited by James H. Marsh, pp. 743–744. Toronto: McClelland and Stewart, Inc.

Luffman, Jacqueline. 2000. "When Parents Replace Teachers: The Home-Schooling Option." In *Canadian Social Trends: Volume 3*, pp. 148–50. Toronto: Thompson Educational Publishing.

Mackie, Marlene. 1991. *Gender Explorations in Canada: Further Explorations*. Toronto: Butterworths.

Maclean's. 1999. "Sterilization Deal." November 15: 41.

———. 2000. "Echoes of the Columbine Massacre." May 1: 20.

Manski, Charles F. 1993. "Income and Higher Education." *Focus* 14(3), Winter: 14–9.

Mensh, Barbara, and Cynthia Lloyd. 1997. "Gender Differences in the School Experiences of Adolescents in Low-income Countries." Policy Research Working Paper No. 95. New York: Population Council.

Merton, Robert K. 1968. *Social Theory and Social Structure*. New York: Free Press.

Montigny, Gilles. 1994. "Reading Skills." In *Canadian Social Trends: A Canadian Studies Reader* Vol. 2, pp. 321–4. Toronto: Thompson Educational Press.

Murnane, Richard J. 1994. "Education and the Well-Being of the Next Generation." In *Confronting Poverty: Prescriptions for Change*, edited by Sheldon H. Danziger, Gary D. Sandefur, and Daniel H. Weinberg, pp. 289–307. New York: Russell Sage Foundation.

Natriello, Gary. 1995. "Dropouts: Definitions, Causes, Consequences, and Remedies." In *Transforming Schools*, edited by Peter W. Cookson Jr., and Barbara Schneider, pp. 107–28. New York: Garland Publishing Co.

Neft, N., and A.D. Levine. 1997. *Where Women Stand: An International Report on the Status of Women in 140 Countries, 1997–1998*. New York: Random House.

Nikiforuk, Andrew. 1993. *School's Out: The Catastrophe in Public Education and What We Can Do About It*. Toronto: Macfarlane Walter and Ross.

Noddings, Nel. 1995. "A Morally Defensible Mission for Schools in the Twenty-First Century." *Phi Delta Kappan* (January): 365–8.

Oderkirk, Jillian. 1993. "Disabilities among children." *Canadian Social Trends* (Winter): 22–5.

Orlikow, Lionel, and Frank Peters. 1999. "Educational Organization." In *The Canadian Encyclopedia: Year 2000 Edition*, edited by James H. Marsh, pp. 736–9. Toronto: McClelland and Stewart, Inc.

Osborne, Ken. 1988. *Educating Citizens: A Democratic Socialist Agenda for Canadian Education*. Toronto: Our Schools/Our Selves.

Porter, John, Marion Porter, and Bernard Blishen. 1982. *Stations and Callings*. Toronto: Methuen.

Ray, Carol A., and Roslyn A. Mickelson. 1993. "Restructuring Students for Restructured Work: The Economy, School Reform, and Non-College-Bound Youths." *Sociology of Education* 66: 1–20.

Richmond, George. 1989. "The Future School: Is Lowell Pointing Us toward a Revolution in Education?" *Phi Delta Kappan* (November): 232–6.

Rosenthal, Robert, and Lenore Jacobson. 1968. *Pygmalion in the Classroom: Teacher Expectations and Pupils' Intellectual Development*. New York: Holt, Rinehart and Winston.

Rudich, Joe. 1998. "Internet Learning." *Link-Up* 15: 23–5.

Rumberger, Russell W. 1987. "High School Dropouts: A Review of Issues and Evidence." *Review of Educational Research* 57: 101–21.

Sakamaki, Sachiko. 1996. "Fates Worse than Death." *Far East Economic Review* 29(February): 38–40.

Sautter, R. Craig. 1995. "Standing Up to Violence: Kappan Special Report." *Phi Delta Kappan* (January): K1–K12.

Schaefer, Richard T., Robert P. Lamm, Penny Biles, and Susannah J. Wilson. 1996. *Sociology: An Introduction*. Toronto: McGraw-Hill Ryerson.

Schofield, John. 1999a. "Learning on the Front Lines." *Maclean's*, January 15: 90–4.

———. 1999b. "Classroom Crunch." *Maclean's*, June 14: 57–8.

———. 1999c. "Days of Discontent." *Maclean's*, September 20: 53–4.

———. 1999d. "Reach for the Top." *Maclean's*, December 13: 90–4.

Shanker, Albert. 1996. "Mythical Choice and Real Standards." In *Reducing Poverty in America*, edited by Michael Darby, pp. 154–72. Thousand Oaks, Calif.: Sage.

Sommerfeld, Meg. 1998. "Micro-Society Schools Tackle Real World Woes." *Teacher Magazine* Vol. 12, December 2 <www.teachermag.org>.

Sowell, Thomas. 1993. *Inside American Education: The Decline, the Deception, the Dogmas*. Toronto: Maxwell Macmillan.

———. 1994. "Multicultural Education Is Harmful." In *Culture Wars: Opposing Viewpoints*, edited by David Bender, and Bruno Leone, pp. 104–8. San Diego, Calif.: Greenhaven Press, Inc.

Statistics Canada. 1998a. *Canada Yearbook 1999*. Ottawa: Minister of Industry.

———. 1998b. "1996 Census: Education." *The Daily*. September 14.

Sunter, S. 1993. "Juggling School and Work." *Perspectives on Labour and Income* (Spring): 15–21.

Tait, Heather. 1999. "Educational Achievement of Young Aboriginal Adults." *Canadian Social Trends* (Spring): 7–10.

Toronto Board of Education. 1993. *The 1991 Every Secondary Student Survey, Part II: Detailed Profiles of Toronto's Secondary School Students*. Toronto: Toronto Board of Education Research Services.

United Nations Population Fund. 1999. "Campaign Issues: Facing the Facts." *Face to Face*. <www.facecampaign. org>.

U.S. Department of Education. 1998. "Help Meet the Technology Chal-

lenge." <www.ed.gov/ Technology/challenge>.

Waldie, Paul. 1999. "Best Brains Likely to Leave Canada." *National Post*, August 28: A1, A2.

Watson, Catherine. 1998. "Cole Harbour: A School Facing Challenges." *Education Today* 11(1): 16–7.

Webb, Julie. 1989. "The Outcomes of Home-Based Education: Employment and Other Issues." *Educational Review* 41: 121–33.

Winzer, Margaret. 1993. *Children With Exceptionalities: A Canadian Perspective*. Scarborough, Ont.: Prentice Hall Canada, Inc.

Yee, M. 1992. "Finding the Way Home through Issues of Gender, Race, and Class." In *Returning the Gaze: Essays on Racism, Feminism, and Politics*, edited by H. Bannerji, pp. 3–44. Toronto: Star Vision Press.

Chapter 13

Associated Press. 1998. "Japanese Pushing Cloning Efforts." *Greensboro News Record*, November 9: A5.

Bajak, Frank. 1998. "Brace Yourself for Year 2000 Glitches: Much of the World Hasn't." *Associated Press*, July 5.

Begley, S. 1997. "The Science Wars." *Newsweek*, April 21: 54–7.

———. 1998. "Designer Babies." *Newsweek*, November 9: 61–2.

Beiser, B. 1999. "Hiding Web Trails." *Maclean's*, August 16: 35.

Bell, Daniel. 1973. *The Coming of Post-Industrial Society: A Venture in Social Forecasting*. New York: Basic Books.

Boles, Margaret, and Brenda Sunoo. 1998. "Do Your Employees Suffer from Technophobia?" *Workforce* 77(1): 21.

Brin, David. 1998. *The Transparent Society: Will Technology Force Us to Choose between Privacy and Freedom?* Reading, Mass.: Addison Wesley.

Buckler, Grant. 1999. "Electronics Industry." In *The Canadian Encyclopedia: Year 2000 Edition*, edited by James H. Marsh, pp. 754–5. Toronto: McClelland and Stewart, Inc.

Bush, Corlann G. 1993. "Women and the Assessment of Technology." In *Technology and the Future*, edited by

Albert H. Teich, pp. 192–214. New York: St. Martin's Press.

Came, Barry. 1999. "Under the Microscope." *Maclean's*, December 6: 62.

Canadian Global Almanac. 2000. Edited by Susan Girvan. Toronto: Macmillan Canada.

Carey, Patricia M. 1998. "Sticking It Out in the Sticks." *Home Office Computing* 16: 64–9.

Ceruzzi, Paul. 1993. "An Unforeseen Revolution: Computers and Expectations, 1935–1985." In *Technology and the Future*, edited by Albert H. Teich, pp. 160–74. New York: St. Martin's Press.

Chisholm, Patricia. 1999. "For Infertile Couples, Heartache and Hope." *Maclean's*, December 6: 58–60.

Clarke, Adele E. 1990. "Controversy and the Development of Reproductive Sciences." *Social Problems* 37(1): 18–37.

Clayton, Gary. 1998. "Manager's Journal: Eurocrats Try to Stop Data at the Border." *Wall Street Journal*, November 2: A34.

Conrad, Peter. 1997. "Public Eyes and Private Genes: Historical Frames, New Constructions, and Social Problems." *Social Problems* 44: 139–54.

"Dollymania." 1999. <www2.r1.bb.src.ac. urk/library/research/cloning/cloning. html>.

Durkheim, Emile. [1925] 1973. *Moral Education*. New York: Free Press.

Ehrenfeld, David. 1998. "A Techno-Pox upon the Land." *Harper's*, October: 13–7.

Eibert, Mark D. 1998. "Clone Wars." *Reason* 30(2): 52–4.

Elmer-Dewitt, Philip. 1994. "The Genetic Revolution." *Time*, January 17: 46–53.

Executive Summary. 1998. "Public Perceptions of Genetic Engineering." *International Social Science Survey*. Sydney, Australia: Australian National University.

Facts in Brief: Induced Abortion. 1996. New York: Alan Guttmacher Institute.

Fang, Bay. 1998. "Chinese 'Hacktivists' Spin a Web of Trouble: The Regime is Unable to Control the Net." *U.S. News and World Report*, September 28: 47.

Fenna, Donald. 1999. "Internet." In *The Canadian Encyclopedia, Year 2000 Edi-*

tion, edited by James H. Marsh, pp. 1181–2. Toronto: McClelland and Stewart, Inc.

Find/SVP. 1997. "The Market for Gene Therapy." April <www.findsvp.com/tocs/ML0497.htm>.

Fix, Janet L. 1994. "Automation Makes Bank Branches a Liability." *USA Today,* November 28: B1.

Fox, Maggie. 1998. "Spooky Teleportation Study Brings Future Closer." *Reuters: The PointCast Network*, October 23.

Geddes, John. 1999. "Making Babies." *Maclean's*, December 6: 53–6.

GIP (Global Internet Project). 1998a. "Introduction: The Internet Today and Tomorrow." <www.gip.org/gip2a.html>.

———. 1998b. "Press Alert." <www.gip.org>.

———. 1998c. "The Workplace." <www.gip.org/gip2g.html>.

Glendinning, Chellis. 1990. *When Technology Wounds: The Human Consequences of Progress*. New York: William Morrow.

Glickman, Leonard, and Sarah Robertson. 1999. "Internet Law." In *The Canadian Encyclopedia, Year 2000 Edition*, edited by James H. Marsh, pp. 1182–3. Toronto: McClelland and Stewart, Inc.

Global Statistics. 1998. "Global Internet Statistics by Language." <www.euromktg.com/globalstats/>.

Goodman, Paul. 1993. "Can Technology Be Humane?" In *Technology and the Future*, edited by Albert H. Teich, pp. 239–55. New York: St. Martin's Press.

"Group Seeks Standards for Infertility Services." 1998. *American Medical News* 21(40): 12.

Hafner, Katie. 1999. "Horse and Blender, Car and Crockpot." In *Themes of the Times: N.Y. Times*, p. 1. Upper Saddle River, N.J.: Prentice Hall.

Hayes, Frank. 1998. "Age Bias an IT Reality." *Computerworld* 32(46): 12.

Health Canada. 1999. *Statistical Report on the Health of Canadians*. <www.hc-sc.gc.ca/hppb/phdd/report/stat/eng/over.html>.

Hosmer, Ellen. 1986. "High Tech Hazards: Chipping Away at Workers' Health." *Multinational Monitor* 7 (January 31): 1–5.

IFR (International Federation of Robotics). 1997. "1997 Key Data for the World Robot Market." <www.ifr.org>.

Janigan, Mary. 1999. "What's Right—and Wrong—with Canada." *Maclean's*, Maugust 16: 305.

Johnson, Jim. 1988. "Mixing Humans and Nonhumans Together: The Sociology of a Door-Closer." *Social Problems* 35: 298–310.

Kahn, A. 1997. "Clone Mammals…Clone Man." *Nature*, March 13: 119.

Kelly, Jason. 1997. "Technophobia." *Atlanta Business Chronicle*, August 18 <www.amcity.com/atlanta/stories/1997/08/18/focus1.html>.

Kennedy, Paul. 1998. "Preparing for the Twenty-First Century: Winners and Losers." In *Global Issues*, edited by Robert Jackson, pp. 10–26. Guilford, Conn.: Dushkin/McGraw Hill.

Klein, Matthew. 1998. "From Luxury to Necessity." *American Demographics* 20(8): 8–12.

Kluger, J. 1997. "Will We Follow the Sheep?" *Time*, March 10: 67, 70–2.

Kuhn, Thomas. 1973. *The Structure of Scientific Revolutions*. Chicago: Chicago University Press.

Lemonick, Michael D. 1999. "Smart Genes?" *Time*, September 13: 40–4.

Lemonick, Michael, and Dick Thompson. 1999. "Racing to Map Our DNA." *Time Daily*, 153: 1–6. <www.time.com>.

Leslie, Jacques. 1998. "Computer Visions." *Modern Maturity*, November–December, 36–9.

Levy, Pierre. 1997. "Cyberculture in Question: A Critique of the Critique." *Revue-du-Mauss* 9: 111–26.

Levy, Steven. 1995. "TechnoMania." *Newsweek*, February 27: 25–9.

Lewin, Tamar. 1998. "Serious Gender Gap Remains in Technology." *N.Y. Times News Service*. October 18.

Lewis, Robert. 2000. "R and D: A Home for Global Leaders." *Maclean's*, May 1: 2.

Macklin, Ruth. 1991. "Artificial Means of Reproduction and Our Understanding of the Family." *Hastings Center Report*, January/February: 5–11.

Maclean's. 1999a. "Hands off the Net." May 31: 51.

———. 1999b. "The Pill, Finally." June 14: 53.

———. 1999c. "Sperm Bank Caution." July 19: 51.

———. 1999d. "Deciphering Debit-Card Dilemmas." December 13: 56.

Makris, Greg. 1996. "The Myth of a Technological Solution to Television Violence." *Journal of Communication Inquiry* 20: 72–91.

Marshall, Eliot. 1998. "Iceland's Blond Ambition." *Mother Jones*, May/June: 53–6.

McClelland, Susan. 1999. "Wanted: Biotech Brains." *Maclean's*, August 16: 61–2.

McCormick, S.J., and Richard A. 1994. "Blastomere Separation." *Hastings Center Report*, March/April: 14–6.

McDermott, John. 1993. "Technology: The Opiate of the Intellectuals." In *Technology and the Future*, edited by Albert H. Teich, pp. 89–107. New York: St. Martin's Press.

McNicholl, Martin K. 1999. "Research, Provincial Organization." In *The Canadian Encyclopedia: Year 2000 Edition*, edited by James H. Marsh, pp. 2004. Toronto: McClelland and Stewart Inc.

McVey, Wayne Jr., and Warren Kalbach. 1995. *Canadian Population*. Scarborough, Ont.: Nelson Canada.

Mehlman, Maxwell H., and Jeffery R. Botkin. 1998. *Access to the Genome: The Challenge to Equality*. Washington, D.C.: Georgetown University Press.

Merton, Robert K. 1973. "The Normative Structure of Science." In *The Sociology of Science*, edited by Robert K. Merton. Chicago: University of Chicago Press.

Mesthene, Emmanuel G. 1993. "The Role of Technology in Society." In *Technology and the Future*, edited by Albert H. Teich, pp. 73–88. New York: St. Martin's Press.

National Post. 1999. "French Schools to Hand out Morning-After Pills." November 30: A11.

Negroponte, Nicholas. 1995. "Nicholas Negroponte: The Multimedia Today Interview." *Multimedia Today*, July–September: 86–8.

Ogburn, William F. 1957. "Cultural Lag as Theory." *Sociology and Social Research* 41: 167–74.

Oh, Susan. 1999. "What's in a Glitch?" *Maclean's*, September 26: 41.

Pascal, Zachary G. 1996. "The Outlook: High Tech Explains Widening Wage Gap." *Wall Street Journal*, April 22: A1.

Perrolle, Judith A. 1990. "Computers and Capitalism." In *Social Problems Today*, edited by James M. Henslin, pp. 336–42. Englewood Cliffs, N.J.: Prentice-Hall.

Postman, Neil. 1992. *Technopoly: The Surrender of Culture to Technology.* New York: Alfred A. Knopf.

Powers, Richard. 1998. "Too Many Breakthroughs." Op-Ed. *New York Times*, November 19: 35.

Quick, Rebecca. 1998. "Technology: Pieces of the Puzzle—Not So Private Lives: Will We Have Any Secrets in the Future?" *Wall Street Journal*, November 13: R27.

Rabino, Isaac. 1998. "The Biotech Future." *American Scientist* 86(2): 110–2.

Richardson, W.G. "Technology." In *The Canadian Encyclopedia: Year 2000 Edition,* edited by James H. Marsh, pp. 2297–301. Toronto: McClelland and Stewart, Inc.

Rifkin, Jeremy. 1996. *The End of Work: The Decline of the Global Labor Force and the Dawn of Post-Market Era.* Berkeley, Calif.: Putnam.

Rosenberg, Jim. 1998. "Troubles and Technologies." *Editor and Publisher* 131(6): 4.

Scout Report. 1998. "PC Sales Heat up in First Quarter of 1998." *RetailVision* 12(Fall): 102.

Shand, Hope. 1998. "An Owner's Guide." *Mother Jones*, May/June: 46.

Sheppard, Robert. 1999. "Patrolling for Hate on the Net." *Macleans*, January 11: 64.

Statistics Canada. 1998. *Canada Yearbook 1999.* Ottawa: Minister of Industry.

———. 1999. *The Daily.* <www.statca.ca/Daily/English/991212/d991213.htm>. December 13.

Toffler, Alvin. 1970. *Future Shock.* New York: Random House.

United Nations Population Fund. 1991. *Population Policies and Programmes: Lessons Learned from Two Decades of Experience,* edited by Nafis Sadik. New York: New York University Press.

Wallace, Bruce. 1999a. "Say It Ain't So. *Maclean's*, July 5: 14–9.

———. 1999b. "Move Over." *Maclean's*, September 27: 20–3.

Walshok, Mary Lindenstein. 1993. "Blue Collar Women." In *Technology and the Future*, edited by Albert H. Teich, pp. 256–64. New York: St. Martin's Press.

Weinberg, Alvin. 1966. "Can Technology Replace Social Engineering?" *University of Chicago Magazine* 59 (October): 6–10.

Weinberg, Robert A. 1993. "The Dark Side of Genome." In *Technology and the Future*, edited by Albert H. Teich, pp. 318–28. New York: St. Martin's Press.

Welter, Cole H. 1997. "Technological Segregation: A Peek through the Looking Glass at the Rich and Poor in an Information Age." *Arts Education Policy Review* 99(2): 1–6.

Winner, Langdon. 1993. "Artifact/Ideas as Political Culture." In *Technology and the Future*, edited by Albert H. Teich, pp. 283–94. New York: St. Martin's Press.

"World Abortion Policies 1994." 1997. United Nations Department for Economic and Social Information and Policy Analysis. <gopher//gopher.undp.org:70/00/~ungophers/popin/wdtrends/charts>.

Chapter 14

Agbese, Pita Ogaba. 1995. "Nigeria's Environment: Crises, Consequences, and Responses." In *Environmental Policies in the Third World: A Comparative Analysis,* edited by O.P. Dwivedi, and Dhirendra K. Vajpeyi, pp. 125–44. Westport, Conn.: Greenwood Press.

Beniger, James R. 1993. "The Control Revolution." In *Technology and the Future*, ed. Albert H. Teich, pp. 40–65. New York: St. Martin's Press.

Bergman, Lester V. 1998 (December). "Cataract Development: It's Cumulative." *Environmental Health Perspectives* 106(12). February 1, 1999 <ehpnet1.niehs.gov/docs/1998/06-12/forum.html>.

Black, Harvey Karl. 1999. "Complex Cleanup." *Environmental Health Perspectives* 107(2). February 1 <ehpnet1.niehs.nih.gov/docs/1999/07-2/focus-abs.html>.

Boland, Reed, Sudhakar Rao, and George Zeidenstein. 1994. "Honoring Human Rights in Population Policies: From Declaration to Action." In *Population Policies Reconsidered: Health, Empowerment, and Rights,* edited by Gita Sen, Adrienne Germain, and Lincoln C. Chen, pp. 89–105. Boston: Harvard School of Public Health.

Bongaarts, John, and Susan Cotts Watkins. 1996. "Social Interactions and Contemporary Fertility Transitions." *Population and Development Review* 22(4): 639–82.

Brown, Lester R. 1995. "The State of the World's Natural Environment." In *Seeing Ourselves: Classic, Contemporary, and Cross-Cultural Readings in Sociology*, 3rd ed., edited by John J. Macionis, and Nijole V. Benokraitis, pp. 411–16. Englewood Cliffs, N.J.: Prentice-Hall.

———. 1998. "Overview: New Records, New Stresses." In *Vital Signs 1998*, edited by Lester R. Brown, Michael Renner, and Christopher Flavin, pp. 15–24. New York: W. W. Norton and Co.

Brown, Lester R., and Jennifer Mitchell. 1998. "Building a New Economy." In *State of the World 1998*, edited by Lester R. Brown, Christopher Flavin, and Hilary French pp. 168–87. New York: W. W. Norton and Co.

Brown, Lester R., Christopher Flavin, and Hilary French. 1998. Foreword. In *State of the World 1998*, edited by Lester R. Brown, Christopher Flavin, and Hilary French, pp. xvii–xix. New York: W.W. Norton and Co.

Brown, Lester R., Gary Gardner, and Brian Halweil. 1998. *Beyond Malthus: Sixteen Dimensions of the Population Problem.* World Watch Paper 143. Washington, D.C.: World Watch Institute.

Bullard, Robert D. 1996. *Unequal Protection.* Sierra Club Books.

Bullard, Robert D., and Glenn S. Johnson. 1997. "Just Transportation." In *Just Transportation: Dismantling Race and Class Barriers to Mobility*, edited by Robert D. Bullard and Glenn S. Johnson, pp. 1–21. Stony Creek, Conn.: New Society Publishers.

Canadian Global Almanac 2000. Edited by Susan Girvan. Toronto: Macmillan Canada.

Catley-Carlson, Margaret, and Judith A. M. Outlaw. 1998. "Poverty and Population Issues: Clarifying the Connections." *Journal of International Affairs* 52(1): 233–43.

CELA. Canadian Environmental Law Association. 1997. "A Taste of Canada: Toxins in Our Food and Bio-engineering on Supermarket Shelves." *Media Release*, April 2 <www.web.net/~cela/mr970402.htm>.

———. 1998. "What's On the Hill Menu?" *Media Release*, October 20 <www.web.net/~cela/mr981020.htm>.

———. 1999a. "Polls." <www.web.net/~cela/polls.htm>.

———. 1999b. "Water Watch Summit a Huge Success." Media Release. September 19 <www.web.net/~cela/mr990919.htm>.

———. 1999c. "New Study Warns of Children's Health Risks from Pesticides and Calls for Urgent Changes to Pesticide Regulatory Systems." Media Release. December 1 <www.web.net/~cela/mr991201.htm>.

Cooper, Mary H. 1998. "Population and the Environment." *CQ Researcher* 8(26): 601–24.

"The Delicate Balance." 1994. *The National Center for Environmental Health Strategies* Vol. 5, Nos. 3–4. 1100 Rural Avenue, Voorhees, N.J. 08043.

DesJardins, Andrea. 1997. "Sweet Poison: What Your Nose Can't Tell You about the Dangers of Perfume." January 20, 1999 <members.aol.com/enviroknow/ perfume/sweet_poison.htm>.

Dionis, Joanna. 1999. "Handle with Care." *Mother Jones*, January–February: 25.

Edwards, Bob, and Anthony Ladd. 1998. "Where the Hogs Are '97: Environmental Justice and Farm Loss in North Carolina, 1980–1997." Paper Presented at the Second National Black Land Loss Summit in Tillery, N.C., February 1998.

Environics Research Group Ltd. 1998. *The Environmental Monitor, 1998, Cycle 1.* Toronto: Environics.

"Fertility Declines Reported." 1997. *Popline*, May–June: 3.

Fisher, Brandy E. 1998. "Scents and Sensitivity." *Environmental Health Perspectives* 106(12). February 1, 1999 <ehpnet1.niehs.nih.gov/docs/1998/106-12/focus-abs.html>.

———. 1999. "Focus: Most Unwanted." *Environmental Health Perspectives* 107(1). February 1, 1999 <ehpnet1.niehs.nih.gov/docs/1999/107-1/focus-abs.html>.

Gardner, Gary. 1998. "Sanitation Access Lacking." In *Vital Signs* 1998, edited by Lester R. Brown, Michael Renner, and Christopher Flavin, pp. 70–1. New York: W.W. Norton and Co.

Greenhalgh, Susan, Zhu Chujuzhu, and Li Nan. 1994. "Restraining Population Growth in Three Chinese Villages, 1988–93." *Population and Development Review* 20: 365–95.

Jan, George P. 1995. "Environmental Protection in China." *Environmental Policies in the Third World: A Comparative Analysis*, edited by O.P. Dwivedi, and Dhirendra K. Vajpeyi, pp. 71–84. Westport, Conn.: Greenwood Press.

Jensen, Derrick. 1999. "The War on Truth: The Secret Battle for the American Mind: An Interview with John Stauber." *Sun* 279(March): 6–15.

Karliner, Joshua. 1997. *The Corporate Planet: Ecology and Politics in the Age of Globalization.* Sierra Club Books.

———. 1998. "Corporate Greenwashing." *Green Guide* 58 (August): 1–3.

Kemps, Dominic. 1998. "Deaths, Diseases Traced to Environment." *Popline* 20 (May–June): 3.

Koenig, Dieter. 1995. "Sustainable Development: Linking Global Environmental Change to Technology Cooperation." *Environmental Policies in the Third World: A Comparative Analysis*, edited O.P. Dwivedi, and Dhirendra K. Vajpeyi, pp. 1–21. Westport, Conn.: Greenwood Press.

Lindauer, Wendy. 1999. "Fact Sheet: Sick Building Syndrome." *Environmental Health Center.* February 1, 1999 <www.nsc.org/ehc/indoor/sbs.htm>.

Livernash, Robert, and Eric Rodenburg. 1998. "Population Change, Resources, and the Environment." *Population Bulletin* 53(1): 1–36.

Maclean's. 1999. "Plutonium Shipments Set." November 29: 41.

———. 2000. "On Canadian Soil." January 24: 24.

Mason, Karen Oppenheim. 1997. "Explaining Fertility Transition." *Demography* 34(4): 443–54.

"Matters of Scale." 1999. "Spending Priorities." *World Watch.* January 29 <www.worldwatch.org/mag/1999/99-1b.html>.

Mattoon, Ashley T. 1998. "Paper Recycling Climbs Higher." In *Vital Signs 1998*, edited by Lester R. Brown, Michael Renner, and Christopher Flavin, pp. 144–5. New York: W. W. Norton and Co.

McIntosh, C. Alison, and Jason L. Finkle. 1995. "The Cairo Conference on Population and Development: A New Paradigm?" *Population and Development Review* 21: 223–60.

McVey, Wayne Jr., and Warren Kalbach. 1995. *Canadian Population.* Scarborough, Ont.: Nelson Canada.

Mead, Leila. 1998. "Radioactive Wastelands." *The Green Guide* 53 (April 14): 1–3.

Mitchell, Jennifer D. 1998. "Before the Next Doubling." *World Watch* 11(1): 21–9.

Murray, C.J.L., and A.D. Lopez. 1996. *The Global Burden of Disease.* Geneva: World Health Organization.

"A New Way to Make a Six-Pack Disappear." 1998. *Utne Reader*, May–June: 18.

National Oceanic and Atmospheric Administration (NOAA). 1999. "1998 Warmest Year on Record, NOAA Announces." January 29, 1999 <www.publicaffairs.noaa.gov/stories/sir45.html>.

O'Meara, Molly. 1998a. "CFC Production Continues to Plummet." In *Vital Signs 1998*, edited by Lester R. Brown, Michael Renner, and

Christopher Flavin, pp. 70–1. New York: W.W. Norton and Co.

——. 1998b. "Sales of Compact Fluorescents Surge." In *Vital Signs 1998*, edited by Lester R. Brown, Michael Renner, and Christopher Flavin, pp. 62–3. New York: W.W. Norton and Co.

Peritz, Ingrid. 1999. "Birth Rate in Quebec Lowest Since 1908." *The Globe and Mail*, October 4: A1.

Pimentel, David, and Anthony Greiner. 1997. "Environmental and Socio-Economic Costs of Pesticide Use." In *Techniques for Reducing Pesticide Use*, edited by D. Pimentel, pp. 50–78. New York: John Wiley and Sons.

Pimentel, David, Maria Tort, Linda D'Anna, Anne Krawic, Joshua Berger, Jessica Rossman, Fridah Mugo, Nancy Doon, Michael Shriberg, Erica Howard, Susan Lee, and Jonathan Talbot. 1998. "Ecology of Increasing Disease: Population Growth and Environmental Degradation." *BioScience* 48(October): 817–27.

Population Institute. 1998. "1998 World Population Overview and Outlook 1999." January 29, 1999 <www.populationinstitute.org/overview98.html>.

Population Reference Bureau. 1998. "World and Regional Population." *1998 World Population Data Sheet*. January 28, 1999 <www.prb.org/prb/>.

Reid, T.R. 1998. "Feeding the Planet." *National Geographic*, October: 56–74.

Renner, Michael. 1996. *Fighting for Survival: Environmental Decline, Social Conflict, and the New Age of Insecurity*. New York: W. W. Norton and Co.

Roodman, David Malin. 1998. "Taxation Shifting in Europe." In *Vital Signs 1998*, edited by Lester R. Brown, Michael Renner, and Christopher Flavin, pp. 140–1. New York: W. W. Norton and Co.

Speirs, Rosemary. 2000. "For Boomers, Minivans are Still a Big Gas." *Toronto Star*, March 11: A24.

Statistical Abstract of the United States: 1998, 118th ed. U.S. Bureau of the Census. Washington, D.C.: U.S. Government Printing Office.

Statistics Canada. 1998. *Canada Yearbook 2000*. Ottawa: Ministry of Industry.

——. 1999. *The Daily*. October 5. <www.statca.ca/Daily/English/991005/d991005.htm>.

Stephens, Sharon. 1998. "Reflections on Environmental Justice: Children as Victims and Actors." In *Environmental Victims*, edited by Christopher Williams, pp. 48–71. London: Earthscan Publications.

Stiefel, Chana. 1998. "Population Puzzle: Is the World Big Enough?" *Science World* 54(13): 17–20.

Stover, Dawn. 1995. "The Nuclear Legacy." *Popular Science*, August: 52–83.

Switzer, Jacqueline Vaughn. 1997. *Green Backlash: The History and Politics of Environmental Opposition in the U.S.* Boulder, Colo.: Lynne Rienner Publishers.

Tuxill, John. 1996. *1996 State of the World Population*. New York: United Nations.

——. 1998. *Losing Strands in the Web of Life: Vertebrate Declines and the Conservation of Biological Diversity*. Worldwatch Paper 141. Washington, D.C.: Worldwatch Institute.

United Nations. 1999. "Below-Replacement Fertility." March 1, 1999 <www.popin.org/pop1998/7.htm>.

United Nations Population Fund. 1997. *1997 State of the World Population*. New York: United Nations.

Vajpeyi, Dhirendra K. 1995. "External Factors Influencing Environmental Policy-making: Role of Multilateral Development Aid Agencies." *Environmental Policies in the Third World: A Comparative Analysis*, edited by O.P. Dwivedi, and Dhirendra K. Vajpeyi, pp. 24–45. Westport, Conn.: Greenwood Press.

"Water Wars Forecast if Solutions Not Found." 1999 (January 1). *Environment News Service*. January 8, 1999 <ens.lycos.com/ens/jan99/1999L-01-01-02.html>.

World Health Organization. 1997. "Health and Environment in Sustainable Development." July 28, 1998 <www.cdc.gov/ogh/frames.htm>.

World Resources Institute. 1998a. *Building a Safe Climate, Sound Business Future*. Baltimore, Minn.: World Resource.

——. 1998b. *Climate, Biodiversity, and Forests: Issues and Opportunities Emerging from the Kyoto Protocol*. Baltimore, Minn.: World Resource.

Zabin, L.S., and K. Kiragu. 1998. "The Health Consequences of Adolescent Sexual and Fertility Behavior in Sub-Saharan Africa." *Studies in Family Planning* 2(June 29): 210–32.

Zhang, Junsen, and Roland Strum. 1994. "When Do Couples Sign the One-Child Certificate in Urban China?" *Population Research and Policy Review* 13: 69–81.

Zwingle, Erla. 1998. "Women and Population." *National Geographic*, October: 35–55.

Chapter 15

Amnesty International. 1995. *Human Rights Are Women's Right*. New York: Amnesty International USA.

Armitage, Richard L. 1989. "Red Army Retreat Doesn't Signal End of U.S. Obligation." *Wall Street Journal*, February 7: A20.

Barke, Richard P., Hank Jenkins-Smith, and Paul Slovic. 1997. "Risk Perceptions of Men and Women Scientists." *Social Science Quarterly* 78: 167–76.

BICC (Bonn International Center for Conversion). 1998. "Chapter Six." *Conversion Survey, 1998*. Bonn, Germany: BICC.

Bothwell, Robert. 1999. "Defence Research." In *The Canadian Encyclopedia: Year 2000 Edition*, edited by James H. Marsh, pp. 645. Toronto: McClelland and Stewart, Inc.

Brown, Seyom. 1994. *The Causes and Prevention of War*. New York: St. Martin's Press.

Burns, Mike. 1998. "The Irish Peacemaker: Prime Minister Bertie Ahern Negotiates Historic Agreement." *Europe* 379: 10–5.

Calhoun, Martin L. 1996. "Cleaning up the Military's Toxic Legacy." *USA Today Magazine* 124: 60–4.

Canadian Global Almanac. 2000. Edited by Susan Girvan. Toronto: Macmillan Canada.

Card, Claudia. 1997. "Addendum to 'Rape as a Weapon of War.'" Hypatia 12: 216–8.

Carneiro, Robert L. 1994. "War and Peace: Alternating Realities in Human History." In Studying War: Anthropological Perspectives, edited by S.P. Reyna, and R.E. Downs, pp. 3–27. Langhorne, Penn.: Gordon and Breach Science Publishers.

Cauffman, Elizabeth, Shirley Feldman, Jaime Waterman, and Hans Steiner. 1998. "Posttraumatic Stress Disorder among Female Juvenile Offenders." Journal of the American Academy of Child and Adolescent Psychiatry 37: 1209–17.

Cobb, Terry, and Bill McAndrew. 1990. Battle Exhaustion: Soldiers and Psychiatrists in the Canadian Army, 1939–1945. Montreal: McGill-Queens University Press.

Cohen, Ronald. 1986. "War and Peace Proness in Pre- and Postindustrial States." In Peace and War: Cross-Cultural Perspectives, edited by M.L. Foster, and R.A. Rubinstein, pp. 253–67. New Brunswick, N.J.: Transaction Books.

Cohen, William. 1998. "We Are Ready to Act Again." Washington Post, August 23: C1.

Collins, Anne. 1988. In the Sleeps Room: The Story of the CIA Brainwashing Experiments in Canada. Toronto: Lester and Orpen Dennys.

Cooney, Mark. 1997. "From War to Tyranny: Lethal Conflict and the State." American Sociological Review 62: 316–38.

Corrado, Raymond R. 1992. "Political Crime in Canada." In Criminology: A Canadian Perspective, 2nd ed., edited by Rick Linden, pp. 419–50 in Toronto: Harcourt Brace and Company.

Curtis, James E., and Ronald D. Lambert. 1994. "Ideology, Elites and Social Change." In Sociology, edited by Lorne Tepperman, James E. Curtis, and James Richardson, pp. 710–755. Toronto: McGraw-Hill Primis.

Department of National Defence. 1999. "The Legacy." November 20 <www.dnd.ca>.

———. 2000. January 2 <www.dnd.ca>.

Dixon, William J. 1994. "Democracy and the Peaceful Settlement of International Conflict." American Political Science Review 88(1): 14–32.

Doyle, Michael. 1986. "Liberalism and World Politics." American Political Science Review 80(December): 1151–69.

Eddy, Melisa. 1999. "Violence Explodes in Kosovo." Daily Reflector, January 18: A1, A9.

Enders, Walter, and Todd Sandler. 1993. "The Effectiveness of Anti-Terrorism Policies: A Vector-Autoregression-Intervention Analysis." American Political Science Review 87(4): 829–44.

"Fast New Gizmos Can Unearth Them Safely: How to Reduce Land Mine Causalities." 1998. U.S. News and World Report, December 27: 60.

Forrow, Lachlan, Bruce Blair, Ira Hefland, George Lewis, Theodore Postol, Victor Sidel, Barry Levy, Herbert Abrams, and Christine Cassel. 1998. "Accidental Nuclear War—A Post–Cold War Assessment." New England Journal of Medicine 338: 1326–31.

Funke, Odelia. 1994. "National Security and the Environment." In Environmental Policy in the 1990s: Toward a New Agenda, 2nd ed., edited by Norman J. Vig, and Michael E. Kraft, pp. 323–45. Washington, D.C.: Congressional Quarterly, Inc.

Gardner-Outlaw, Tom, and Robert Engelman, 1997. "Sustaining Water, Easing Scarcity: A Second Update." Population Action International Report. <www.populationaction.org/why_pop/water/water.html>.

Gentry, John. 1998. "Military Force in an Age of National Cowardice." Washington Quarterly 21: 179–92.

Gibbs, Nancy. 1994. "Cry the Forsaken Country." Time, August 1: 27–37.

Gioseffi, Daniela. 1993. Introduction to On Prejudice: A Global Perspective, edited by Daniela Gioseffi, pp. xi–1. New York: Anchor Books, Doubleday.

Harris, Paul. 1996. "Military Advising is Growing Industry." Insight on the News 12: 12–4.

Hayman, Peter, and Douglas Scaturo. 1993. "Psychological Debriefing of Returning Military Personnel: A Protocol for Post-Combat Intervention." Journal of Social Behavior and Personality 8(5): 117–30.

Hooks, Gregory, and Leonard E. Bloomquist. 1992. "The Legacy of World War II for Regional Growth and Decline: The Effects of Wartime Investments on U.S. Manufacturing, 1947–72." Social Forces 71(2): 303–37.

INTERPOL. 1998. "Frequently Asked Questions about Terrorism." <www.kenpubs.co.uk/INTERPOL.COM/English/faq>.

Klingman, Avigdor, and Zehava Goldstein. 1994. "Adolescents' Response to Unconventional War Threat Prior to the Gulf War." Death Studies 18: 75–82.

Koerner, Brendan. 1998. "Creepy Crawly Spies: Tiny Robot Insects May Soon Serve as Military Scouts." U.S. News and World Report, September 14: 48–50.

Kyl, Jon, and Morton Halperin. 1997. "Q: Is the White House's Nuclear-Arms Policy on the Wrong Track?" Insight on the News 42: 24–8.

Laqueur, Walter. 1998. "The New Face of Terrorism." Washington Quarterly 21: 169–79.

Lewis, Bernard. 1990. "The Roots of Islamic Rage." Atlantic, September: 47–60.

"Light of Day in Bloody Eire." 1998. U.S. News and World Report, December 28: 78–9.

Lloyd, John. 1998. "The Dream of Global Justice." New Statesman 127: 28–30.

Maclean's. 2000a. "On Canadian Soil." January 24: 24–5.

———. 2000b. "The Mysterious Gulf War Illness." February 21: 52–4.

McGeary, Johanna. 1998. "Nukes...They're Back." Time, May 25: 34–9.

Miller, Susan. 1993. "A Human Horror Story." Newsweek, December 27: 17.

Moaddel, Mansoor. 1994. "Political Conflict in the World Economy: A Cross-National Analysis of Modernization and World-System Theories." American Sociological Review 59 (April): 276–303.

Mylvaganam, Senthil. 1998. "The LTTE: A Regional Problem or a Global Threat?" Crime and Justice International 14: 1–2.

National Gulf War Resource Center. 1997. "Who Has Gulf War Syndrome?" Fall: 7–8. <www.gulfwar.self2/page7.html>.

Nelson, Murry R. 1999. "An Alternative Medium of Social Education—the 'Horrors of War' Picture Cards." Social Studies 88: 100–8.

Novac, Andrei. 1998. "Traumatic Disorders—Contemporary Directions." Western Journal of Medicine 169: 40–2.

Olick, Jeffery, and Daniel Levy. 1997. "Collective Memory and Cultural Constraints: Holocaust Myth and Rationality in German Politics." American Sociological Review 62: 921–36.

Paul, Annie Murphy. 1998. "Psychology's Own Peace Corps." Psychology Today 31: 56–60.

Perdue, William Dan. 1993. Systemic Crisis: Problems in Society, Politics and World Order. Fort Worth, Tex.: Harcourt Brace Jovanovich.

Pfefferbaum, Betty. 1997. "Posttraumatic Stress Disorder in Children: A Review of the Past 10 Years." Journal of the American Academy of Child and Adolescent Psychiatry 36: 1503–12.

Picard, Andre. 1995. "After Johnny Comes Marching Home." The Globe and Mail, April 8 <news.chaptersglobe.com/search97cgi/s97_cgi?action=viewandVdKVgwKey=%2Fjule>.

Porter, Bruce D. 1994. War and the Rise of the State: The Military Foundations of Modern Politics. New York: Free Press.

Renner, Michael. 1993a. "Environmental Dimensions of Disarmament and Conversion." In Real Security: Converting the Defense Economy and Building Peace, edited by Kevin J. Cassidy, and Gregory A. Bischak, pp. 88–132. Albany: State University of New York Press.

———. 1993b. "National Insecurity." In Systematic Crisis: Problems in Society, Politics and World Order, edited by William D. Perdue, pp. 136–41. Fort Worth, Tex.: Harcourt Brace Jovanovich.

Sagan, Carl. 1990. "Nuclear War and Climatic Catastrophe: Some Policy Implications." In Readings on Social Problems, edited by William Feigelman, pp. 374–88. Fort Worth, Tex.: Holt, Rinehart and Winston.

Scheff, Thomas. 1994. Bloody Revenge. Boulder, Colo.: Westview Press.

Shanahan, John J. 1995. "Director's Letter." Defense Monitor 24(6): 8. Washington, D.C.: Center for Defense Information.

SIPRI (Stockholm International Peace Research Institute). 1998. SIPRI Yearbook 1998: Armaments, Disarmament and International Security. Oxford: Oxford University Press.

Starr, J.R., and D.C. Stoll. 1989. "U.S. Foreign Policy on Water Resources in the Middle East." Washington, D.C.: The Center for Strategic and International Studies.

Statistical Abstract of the United States: 1998, 118th ed. U.S. Bureau of the Census. Washington, D.C.: U.S. Government Printing Office.

Statistics Canada. 1998. Canada Yearbook 1999. Ottawa: Minister of Industry.

Sutker, Patricia B., Madeline Uddo, Kevin Brailey, and Albert N. Allain, Jr. 1993. "War-Zone Trauma and Stress-Related Symptoms in Operation Desert Shield/Storm (ODS) Returnees." Journal of Social Issues 49(4): 33–50.

Sweet, Alec Stone, and Thomas L. Brunell. 1998. "Constructing a Supranational Constitution: Dispute Resolution and Governance in the European Community." American Political Science Review 92: 63–82.

Thompson, Allan. 1999. "Spend More or Do Less." National Post, December 11: K1.

Thompson, Mark. 1999. "Star Wars: The Sequel." Time Daily, 153(7): 1–3. February 22 <www.time.com>.

UCS (Union of Concerned Scientists). 1998. "Comprehensive Test Ban Treaty." <www.ucsusa.org/arms/ctbt.top.html>.

United Nations. 1998. "UN Peacekeeping Operations: 50 Years, 1948–1998." <www.uno.org/Depts/dpko/mail.html>.

USIS (United States Information Source). 1998. "Patterns of Global Terrorism: 1997." <www.usis.usemb.se/terror/rpt1997/review.html>.

World Commission on Environment and Development (Brundtland Commission). 1990. Our Common Future. New York: Oxford University Press.

Zimmerman, Tim. 1997. "Just When You Thought You Were Safe…Could a False Alarm Still Start a Nuclear War?" U.S. News and World Report, February 10: 38–40.

Bogardus, Emory, 257
Bohlen, Jim, 26
Boland, Reed, 467
Boles, Margaret, 445
Bond, David, 229
Bond, James T., 369–370, 381
Bongaarts, John, 462
Boroditsky, R., 40
Botkin, Jeffery R., 443
Bouchard, Lucien, 248–249
Boudreau, Francois A., 195
Bouton, Richard A., 283
Bowd, A., 256
Boyd, Monica, 252
Boyd, Neil, 230
Boyle, Thomas, 87
Bracey, Gerald W., 358
Bradley, Aaron, 491
Bradshaw, York, 180
Brady, P., 256
Braithwaite, John, 151
Brannock, J.C., 279
Brantingham, Paul, 102
Brazzini, D.G., 174
Brecher, Jeremy, 375
Breidenbach, Susan, 217
Breton, Raymond, 240, 247
Brienza, Julie, 159
Briere, J., 147
Briggs, Vernon M. Jr., 325
Brin, David, 442
Brinkerhoff, M.B., 141
Britt, Benjamin, 42
Broder, John, 494
Brookbank, Candace, 121, 134
Brooks-Gunn, Jeanne, 181, 326
Brown, Lester R., 455, 458–459, 463–464,
    468, 471–472, 475, 479, 482, 484
Brown, Louise, 436
Brown, Phil, 18
Brown, Rosemary, 213
Brown, Roy J., 396–398, 418
Brown, Seyom, 498, 500, 515
Browning, Christopher R., 147
Brunell, Thomas L., 514
Brydon-Miller, M., 18
Buchanan, J.D., 194–195
Buckhard, Paul, 476
Buckler, Grant, 427
Buffet, Warren, 317
Bulkeley, William M., 415–416
Bullard, Robert D., 477
Burger, Jerry M., 223
Burke, R.J., 211
Burnet, Jean, 271
Burns, Mike, 514
Burrows, Darryl, 18
Busby, Dean M., 146
Bush, Corlann G., 430
Bush, George, 511
Bushweller, Kevin, 402
Button, James W., 280, 285, 288, 2 96,
    300–301
Byck, R., 79

Cahill, Spenser, 170
Calasanti, Toni, 216
Caldas, Stephen, 398

Calhoun, Martin L., 507
Call, Kathleen, 396
Calment, Jeanne, 33
Came, Barry, 436
Cameron, Ewan, 503
Campaign for Nuclear Phase-Out, 480
Campbell, Bruce, 312–313, 317–320
Campbell, Kim, 212
Canada Mortgage and Housing Corpora-
    tion, 329
Canadian Acid Rain Program, 482
Canadian Association for Community
    Living, 397
Canadian Association for Independent
    Living Centres, 60
Canadian Association of Retired Persons,
    197
Canadian Cancer Society, 61, 89
Canadian Centre for Policy Alternatives,
    313
Canadian Centre on Disability Studies, 60
Canadian Centre on Substance Abuse, 49,
    65, 68, 71, 75, 77–78, 80, 83–84,
    86–88, 94
Canadian Child Care Association, 197
Canadian Coalition for the Rights of the
    Child, 39
Canadian Council on Rehabilitation and
    Work, 60
Canadian Council on Social Develop-
    ment, 56, 322–324, 386, 388–389, 391,
    396, 399, 402, 411, 414
Canadian Environmental Defence Fund,
    480
Canadian Environmental Network, 480
Canadian Federation of University
    Women, 56
Canadian Labour Congress, 55
Canadian Medical Association (CMA),
    52–53, 326
Canadian Nuclear Safety Commission,
    474
Canadian Nurses Association, 326
Canadian Paediatric Society, 326
Canadian Senior Citizens' Information
    and Services Centre, 197
Canadian Tobacco Manufacturer's
    Council, 68
Canale, M.C., 83
Caplan, Arthur, 439
Card, Claudia, 504
Card, David, 347
Carey, Gregory, 432, 436
Carney, James, 173–174
Carney, Larry S., 201
Carniero, Robert L., 495
Carroll, William K., 26
Carter, Jimmy, 500
Carvin, Andy, 415
Cassel, C., 195
Cassidy, B., 225
Caston, Richard J., 357, 375
Castro, Fidel, 508
Catania, Joseph A., 21
Catley-Carlson, Margaret, 463
Cauffman, Elizabeth, 504
CELA (Canadian Environmental Law
    Association), 474–476, 480

Centre for Addiction and Mental Health,
    65
Ceruzzi, Paul, 433
Chao, Ruth, 176
Chapman, B.E., 279
Charlton, Eda, 502
Chatters, Dave, 298
Chernos, Saul, 414, 416
Chesley, L., 144
Chesney-Lind, Meda, 121
Child and Family Canada, 197
Child Labour Coalition, 376
Children's Defense Fund, 197
Childwatch, 197
Chirot, Daniel, 499
Chisholm, Patricia, 381, 436
Chiu, Charlotte, 373
Chong, John, 263
Chossudovsky, Michel, 314, 374
Chow, Henry, 260
Chretien, Jean, 248
Chua-Eoan, Howard, 99
Cianni, Mary, 211
Cipriaso, Jon Cristian, 297
Clark, Campbell, 88
Clark, Charles, 159
Clark, Joe, 68
Clark, Lorraine, 144
Clark, Warren, 76, 327, 341, 345, 410
Clark, Wayne, 144, 159
Clarke, Adele E., 436
Clayton, Gary, 450
Claxton-Oldfield, Stephen, 259
Clements, Mark, 170
Cleveland, Gordon, 343
Cleveland, Rose, 281
Clinton, William, 93, 515–516
Coalition of Provincial Organizations of
    the Handicapped, 60
Cobb, Terry, 505
Cockerham, William C., 46, 48, 50
Cohen, Joel, 455
Cohen, Mark Nathan, 236
Cohen, Ronald, 492
Cohen, Warren, 418
Colasanto, Diane, 202
Coleman, James, 368
Coleman, John R., 22
College of Family Physicians, 326
Collins, Anne, 503
Collins, Chiquita, 46
Columbo, John Robert, 237–238
Comas-Diaz, Lillian, 223
Common Frontiers, 480
Company of Young Canadians, 332
Comstock, George, 130
Confucius, 466
Conklin, John E., 119, 126
Conlon, R.T., 60
Conrad, Peter, 380, 430
Consumers Association of Canada, 55
Conte, Jon R., 146, 149
Conway, John F., 148, 161
Cook, Kaye V., 216
Cook, Nick, 494
Cooley, Charles, 15
Coombs, Robert H., 88
Cooney, Mark, 492

Cooper, Kathleen, 476
Cooper, M., 89
Cooper, Mary H., 459, 465
Cooper, M., 49
Corak, Miles, 19, 329–331
Corrado, Raymond, 509
Cote, Paul, 26
Council of Canadians with Disabilities, 60
Council of Ontario Universities, 394
Council on Aging of Ottawa-Carleton, 197
Cowan, Mary Rose, 264
Cowgill, Donald, 170
Coyne, Andrew, 310
Cranston, Kevin, 276, 296, 299
Crauford-Lewis, M., 243
Crawford, Maria, 144
Creese, Gillian, 33
Culbert, Lori, 278
Cummings, Elaine, 172
Currid, Cheryl, 217
Curtis, James E., 23, 391, 510

Dahrendorf, Ralf, 14
Dai, S.Y., 184
Daisley, B., 397
Dalecki, Michael G., 282, 295
Daly, M., 144
Danaher, Kevin, 361–362
Da Pont, M., 380
Das Gupta, T., 201
Daub, Shannon, 318
Davin, N.F., 393
Davies, Robertson William, 385
Davis, Kingsley, 311
Deal, Angela G., 143
DeAngelis, Tori, 190
DeBare, Ilana, 217
De Cecco, John P., 277
Decima Research, 84
Defence for Children International, 197
DeGrandpre, R., 277
DeGuia, T. 70
DeJong, William, 134–135
Dembo, Richard, 96
D'Emilio, John, 281, 300
Demo, David H., 160, 293, 295
Demont, John, 253
Deng, Francis M., 316
Dennis, Richard J., 94
Denton, Margaret, 213
Department of National Defence, 497, 501, 514
Desjardins, Andrea, 470
Desrochers, Daniel, 65
DeStefano, Linda, 202
Dickens, Charles, 3
DiIulio, John, 102, 132
Dionis, Joanna, 489
Disabled Actions Women's Network, 60
Dixon, William J., 499
Dobash, R.E., 141
Dobash, R.P., 141
Doell, R.G., 278
Doerr, A., 243–244
Doherty, Gillian, 342
Donakowski, D.W., 256
Donnelly, Liam, 229–230
Dordick, Gwendolyn A., 22

Dosanjh, Ujjal, 292
Douglas, Tommy, 50, 51
Dovidio, John F., 257
Downs, Donald, 379
Doyle, Michael, 499
Drakes, Shellene, 319–320
Drentea, Patricia, 224
Dreidger, Leo, 238
D'Souza, Dinesh, 400
Dubowitz, Howard, 150
Duchesne, Doreen, 114
Duke, Steven, 93
Duke Engineering and Services Canada, 473–474
Dumas, J., 251
Duncan, Greg, 326
Dunst, Carl J., 143
Durkheim, Emile, 11, 12, 106, 279, 361, 422, 428
Duster, Troy, 93
Dwyer, Victor, 230, 397

Earth Council, 482
Easley, Margaret, 85
Eddy, Melissa, 509
Edison, Marcia, 268
Edwards, Bob, 477
EGALE (Equality for Gays and Lesbians Everywhere), 290–292, 294, 296–297, 300
Ehrenfeld, David, 436
Eibert, Mark D., 448, 450
Eichler, Margrit, 221
Eisenhower, Dwight D., 496
Eitzen, Stanley, 383
Ekos Research Associates, 387
Eliany, Marc, 78
Elder Adult Resource Services, 197
Elliot, D., 147
Elliott, Jean Leonard, 160
Elmer-Dewitt, Philip, 436
Emery, B.C., 146
Emmons, C.A., 195
Enders, Walter, 508
Engelman, Robert, 499
Environics Research Group, 383, 481–482
Environmental Action, 480
Environmental Defense Fund, 480
Epstein, Gerald, 357
Epstein, Norman, 85
Erikson, Kai T., 106
Errington, J., 224
Esses, V.M., 256
Esterberg, K., 281
Etzioni, Amitai, 236
Evans, John, 102
Everett, Sherry A., 39
Eyerman, R., 26

Facal, Joseph, 249
Faison, Seth, 126
Families Against Deadbeats, 344
Fan, Pi-Ling, 207
Fang, Bay, 432
Farhi, Paul, 130
Fast., J., 380
Fattah, Ezzat A., 103
Faulkner, Anne H., 276, 296, 299

Favazzo, Armando R., 42
Fawcett, D., 322–323
Feagin, Clairece B., 76
Feagin, Joe R., 76
Feather, Norman T., 375
Fedorowycz, Orest, 99, 111, 132, 145, 149
Fee, Elizabeth, 39
Fekete, John, 400
Felderhoof, John, 315
Felson, Marcus, 104, 123, 133
Fenna, Donald, 434
Fennell, Tom, 76, 314
Fichten, Catherine S., 411
Fiebert, Martin S., 220
Fields, Jason, 181
Fife, R., 94
Figert, Anne, 18
Fine, Sean, 176, 179–180
Finkelstein, Ken, 315
Finkle, Jason L., 476
Fisher, Brandy E., 470, 478
Fisher, John, 296–299
Fitzgerald, Louise F., 231
Fitzhugh, T.V., 244
Fix, Janet L., 443
Flavin, Christopher, 464
Fleras, Augie, 160, 361
Flexnor, Joe, 377
Foote, David, 198
Forrow, Lachlan, 506
Foster, Burk, 85
Foundation for Equal Families (FFEF), 297
Fowler, T., 79
Fox, Maggie, 425
Frank, Barney, 298
Frank, James G., 7
Franklin, Benjamin, 171
Franklin, Sarah, 285
Frechette, M., 106
Frederick, Judith A., 157–158
Freedman, Estelle B., 281
Free the Children, 182–183
Freitas, Frances Anne, 415
French, Hilary, 464
Frideres, James S., 243
Friedan, Betty, 186, 199
Friedman, Dorian, 129
Friends of the Earth, 480
Funke, Odelia, 506, 511, 517

Gaertner, Samuel L., 257
Gagan, David, 229
Gairdner, William, 161
Galbraith, John Kenneth, 318
Galinsky, Ellen, 381
Gallagher, P.E., 283
Gans, Herbert J., 312
Gardner, Gary, 458–460, 464, 479
Gardner-Outlaw, Tom, 499
Garey, M., 131
Garfinkel, Paul, 65
Garlinghouse, P.A., 283
Garnets, L., 284
Gaskell, Jane, 219, 500
Gates, Bill, 317
Gay and Lesbian Association of Retiring Persons, 197
Geddes, John, 450, 436, 438

Stones, Michael J., 196
Stout, James W., 164
Stover, Dawn, 472
Stowe, Emily Howard, 224
Straus, Murray A., 141, 143, 375
Streeten, Paul, 326
Strong, Marilee, 42
Stuckless, Janice, 116–117
Strum, Roland, 467
Stubbs, John, 229–230
Such, P., 237
Sullivan, A., 293
Sullivan, Theresa A., 375
Sullivan, Thomas, 85
Sunoo, Brenda, 445
Sunter, S., 407
Sutherland, Edwin, 110
Sutker, Patricia B., 505
Suzuki, David, 235
Swartz, Joel, 119
Sweet, Alec Stone, 514
Switzer, Jacqueline Vaughn, 462–463, 481
Swol, Karen, 133–134
Sylvan Learning Systems, 418
Szasz, Thomas, 39

Tait, Heather, 220, 391
Tam, Tony, 207
Tannen, Deborah, 221
Tasker, Fiona L., 295
Tator, Carol, 238
Tauber, C.M., 193
Taylor, Paul, 431
Terenzini, Patrick T., 268
Thirunarayanapuram, Desikan, 47
Thomas, Jennifer, 128
Thomas, W.I., 15
Thompson, Cooper, 285
Thompson, Dick, 449
Thompson, Kendrick S., 85
Thompson, Mark, 492–493, 515
Thompson, Myron, 298
Thomson, Kenneth R., 317
Thurow, Lester C., 198
Tibbets, Janice, 108
Tilly, Chris, 341, 344, 346
Toffler, Alvin, 445
Tomaskovic-Devey, Donald, 207
Toronto Board of Education, 399
Townson, Monica, 185, 188, 318
Tremblay, Pierre, 299
Trevethan, S., 141, 144
Trivette, Carol M., 143
Troper, Harold, 249–250, 252
Troyer, Ronald J., 5
Trudeau, Pierre, 239
Tserkonivnitska, Marina, 211, 216
Tubman, J., 85
Tuxill, John, 478

Ukers, William H., 5
Underwood, Anne, 126
UNICEF, 36, 197, 326, 376
Union of Concerned Scientists, 480

United Council on Welfare Fraud, 314
United Nations, 100–101, 201–202, 205, 209, 212–213, 215, 218, 224, 263, 308, 311, 326, 349–351, 355, 376, 400, 426, 459, 461, 466–467, 486, 509, 511–512, 514, 516
Urquhart, Terry, 59, 60

Vajpeyi, Dhirendra K., 479
Vanderlinden, Loren, 476
Van Dyck, C., 79
Vanier, Georges, 491
Vanier Institute of the Family, 193
Vanin, S., 220
Van Kammen, Welmoet B., 96
Van Kempen, Eva T., 317
Van Willigen, Marieke, 224
Verbrugge, Lois M., 47
Viano, C. Emilio, 147
Victoria Youth Pride Society, 297
Visschedijk, Jan, 38, 46
Vobejda, Barbara, 216
Vonnegut, Kurt, 304

Wagner, Betsy, 281
Waite, L.J., 158
Waldie, Paul, 419
Waldorf, D., 85
Wallace, Bruce, 445, 447
Wallen, W.K., 83
Wallenstein, S., 195
Waller, Douglas, 494
Walsh, Barent W., 44
Walsh, G.W., 83
Walshok, Mary Lindenstein, 430
Wappel, Tom, 298
Warner, Barbara, 108
Waterman, C., 144
Watkins, Susan Cotts, 462
Watson, Catherine, 407–408
Webb, Julie, 418
Weber, Max, 15
Webster, I., 73, 79
Wechsler, Henry, 74
Weil, Michelle, 445
Weinberg, Alvin, 11, 427
Weinberg, Martin S., 435
Weinfeld, Morton, 58, 502
Weir, L., 295–296
Weisbrot, Mark, 311
Weissberg, Roger P., 175
Weitz, Rose, 47, 48
Weitzman, Murray S., 348
Welter, Cole H., 443–444
West, Cornell, 139, 159, 380
Weston, Kath, 294
Wheeler, Michael L., 269–270
Whipple, Evangeline, 281
White, I.L., 118, 219
White, Helene Raskin, 89
Whitla, W., 212
Whitley, B.E. Jr., 282, 285
Wilde, Candee, 217
Wildman-Hanlon, D., 195

Wigton, R.S., 195
Wilkins, K., 47, 223
Williams, Christine L., 113, 212
Williams, David R., 46
Williams, Eddie N., 254
Williams, John E., 201, 211–212, 223
Williams, Karen, 294–295
Williams, Linda, 113
Willinsky, J., 219
Willis, Diane J., 146–147
Willms, Douglas, 176
Wilmut, Ian, 438
Wilson, Doug, 25
Wilson, John, 16
Wilson, John K., 400
Wilson, Susanah, 144
Wilson, William Julius, 269, 331
Wine, J.D., 225
Winks, Robin W., 238
Winner, Langdon, 441, 450–451
Winnipeg Police Service, 87
Winzer, Margaret, 398
Witters, Weldon, 66
Wolf, E.M., 164
Wootton, Barbara, 207
World Bank, 308
World Commission on Environment and Development, 517
World Health Organization, 33, 34, 35, 36, 63, 308, 326, 468, 475
World Resources Institute, 475, 480–481
World Watch Institute, 480
World Wildlife Fund, 480
Wright, David, 33
Wright, Erik Olin, 209
Wright, Marylyn P., 372
Wysong, Earl, 70

Yalnizyan, A., 319
Yanz, Linda, 365–366, 375
Yee, M., 385
Yeh, T.S., 195
Yogis, J.A., 295
Young, Margaret, 318

Zabin, L.S., 463
Zack, Naomi, 236, 239
Zagaroli, Lisa, 117
Zalcberg, J.R., 194–195
Zdanowicz, Y.M., 83
Zhang, Junsen, 467
Ziedonis, Douglas, 88
Zigler, Edward, 150
Zimmerman, Marc A., 219
Zimmerman, Tim, 515
Zimring, F.E., 100
Zinn, Howard, 266
Zinn, Maxine Baca, 383
Zollo, B., 195
Zuckerman, H., 215
Zundel, Ernst, 264
Zwerling, Craig, 489
Zwingle, Erla, 464
Zylicz, Z., 195

organization child, 390
poverty and, 46–47, 176, 178, 180–181, 317, 319–321, 324, 344–347, 351
sexual exploitation, 112, 114–115, 119, 171, 181, 183, 286, 327, 330–331, 363, 376, 460
special needs, 149, 163, 178–179, 342, 396–398
Chiefdoms, 492
Chronic conditions, 33, 47
Circumcision, female, 202
Citizenship, 254–255
gay activism, 24–25, 277, 279–280, 282, 297–301
gender inequities, 212–215, 378
legislation, 254–255
Clarity Act, 248–249
Class, social. See Socioeconomic class
Classic rape, 113
Climate change, 423, 461–462, 471–472, 475, 486
Cloning, 325, 438–439, 448–449
Cocaine, 65–66, 79–80
crime–drug use relationship, 85–87
criminalization of, 66, 68–69
juvenile crime, 80–83
Cohabitation, 138. See Families
Cold War, 493, 498, 507, 515
Collaborative research, 18
Colonialism, 236, 238
Communication, male-female differences, 221
Community policing, 133
Comprehensive Test Ban Treaty (CTBT), 515–516
Compressed workweek, 381
Computer-aided manufacturing (CAM), 432
Computer crime, 18, 119, 126, 431–432
Computer hacking, 431
Computers
in education, 407, 411–414, 433–434
gender differences, 217, 430–431
in health care, 60–62
research methods, 21
security, 442–443
telecommuting, 381, 432
warfare and, 493–494
Conduct problems. See Behaviour problems
Conflict. See Domestic violence; War and conflict
Conflict perspective, 13–14
age inequality, 172, 198
crime and violence, 23, 108–109
education, 390–392
employment issues, 361–362, 382
environmental problems, 460–462, 479
family problems, 80–83, 139–140
gender inequality, 203–204
health care, 38–39
poverty, 312–314
race and ethnic relations, 255–256
sexual orientation, 280
substance abuse, 68–69
technology, 429–430, 450

war and conflict, 496, 516
Consumer culture, 461, 468–469, 480–481, 483–486
affluenza, 485–486
planned obsolescence, 461
Consumer products
safety issues, 13–14, 117–119, 429, 470–471, 476
technology, 481
Contingent workers, 375
Contraception, 8, 38–39, 161, 164, 424, 426–427, 430, 436, 444, 464–466
maternal and infant health, 35–38, 444, 464
population control, 461–462
Control theory, 107–108
Convergence hypothesis, 356
Controlled Drugs and Substances Act, 78–79, 92–93
Conventional crime, defined, 110
Corporal punishment, 66, 147–148, 327, 365
Corporate crime, 115, 117–119
Corporate multinationalism, 357–358
Corporate murder, 119
Corporate violence, 13–14, 115, 117–118
Corporate welfare, 312–313, 351
Corporations, 312–314, 354
attitudes toward, 359–360
charitable contributions, 349
downsizing and relocation, 314, 357, 361, 375
and employees, 361–362
environmental injustice, 361, 477
family-based empires, 320
global financial control, 357
government policy influence, 313–314, 318, 357, 361–362
job elimination, 314, 357, 361, 375
medical and health issues, 357, 367–371, 378–380
military-industrial complex, 496
product safety issues, 13–14, 117–119, 429, 470–471, 476
technological innovations, 448–449
Covenant marriage, 160
Crime
action strategies, 128–133
community programs, 129–130
criminal justice policy, 130–133, 151
children and, 112, 114–115, 119, 147, 163, 171, 183
costs, 65, 94, 126–128, 131
computer, 18, 119, 126, 431, 442
criminal activities survey, 105–106
criminal harassment, 144
definition, 102
demographic patterns, 111–112, 120–126
domestic. See Domestic violence; Familicide; Homicide; Stalking
drunk driving, 9, 15, 24
gender and, 93, 111–112, 120–121
global perspective, 65–66, 100–101
hate crimes, 235, 260, 264–266, 296–297
juvenile delinquency, 85–87, 120, 150

legislation, 78–79, 92–93, 120, 175, 177, 260
media violence, 130, 147, 150
methadone treatment programs and, 94–95
perceptions of, 99–100, 259
schools and, 296–297
statistics, sources of, 98, 101–104
substance abuse and, 65, 85–87, 90–93, 96
theories, 104–110
types of crime, 110–120, 235, 260, 264–266
street crime, property, 113–114
street crime, violent, 110–113, 122
terrorism, 508–509, 512, 516
vice, 113–115
white-collar, 115, 117–119, 127–128, 135
young offenders, 107, 111–112, 120, 123–124, 175, 177
youth programs, 129
Crime rates, 99–101
Crime Stoppers, 129
Criminal harassment, 144
Criminal justice system
costs of crime, 94, 126–128, 131
drug-related offenses, 85–87, 90–94, 96
effectiveness of, 134–135
therapeutic communities in, 90
rehabilitation versus incapacitation, 93, 96, 132, 269, 408
Crude divorce rate, 154
Cultural assimilation, 236, 239
Cultural genocide, 391, 393–394
Cultural imperialism, 390–391
Cultural lag, 429
Cultural origins of homophobia, 284–286, 296
Cultural sexism, 216, 218–221
Cultural transmission of prejudice, 166, 235, 257–259, 281–282, 298
Culture
consumer. See Consumer culture
definitions of wealth and poverty, 308–310, 314, 316
elements of, 6–9
environmental problems, causes of, 461–462, 480–481
and family, 137, 163
divorce, 154–158
domestic violence, 147–149, 150
socialization function of school, 155
technology and, 445
Culture of poverty, 176, 316–317
Cumulative trauma disorders, 367, 379
Custody, child, 154, 159, 160–161, 165, 214–215, 225, 293–296
Culture wars, 400
Cybernation, defined, 425

Data smog removal, 446–447
Date rape, 112–113
Debt relief, 350
Decriminalization of drug use, 65
Deemed suspect, 237
De facto segregation, 238
Deforestation, 422, 471, 475, 478

homophobia, 285
men's movement, 225
self-concept, income and, 223
sexual abuse, 147
sexual harassment of, 229–231, 228
socialization of and domestic violence, 224
Malnutrition, 308, 325, 350, 463–464. *See also* Nutrition
Malthusian theory, 460
Manifest functions, 12
Manners, elements of culture, 8
Marijuana, 8, 65–66, 69–70, 77–78, 89
legal issues, 69, 78–79, 86, 94
juvenile crime, 80–83
use of in Canada, 77–78
Marital rape, 4, 136, 144, 149
Market basket measure, 309
Marriage. *See also* Families
covenant, 160
interracial, 236, 237, 242
marital status and poverty, 158
same-sex, 137–139, 291–293, 296
Marxist theories. *See* Conflict perspective
Master status, 6, 110, 362
defined, 6
homosexuality label, 281
work role and, 6
Mater familias, 138
Materialism, 480. *See also* Consumer culture
Maternal and child health, 163–164. *See also* Children; Childcare; Environment; Feminization of Poverty; Health; Infant Mortality; Poverty; Pregnancy; Work/Employment
Maternal mortality rates, 36–37, 341, 380. *See also* Families; Work/Employment
Maternity leave, 214
Math and science, 219, 401. *See also* Technological Revolution; Technology
MDMA, 80
Mechanical solidarity, 422
Mechanization, defined, 425
Media
crime reporting, 130, 259
domestic violence prevention, 4, 150
elderly, portrayals of, 174
greenwashing, 462
and prejudice, 4, 130, 259, 359
and sexism, 130, 216, 220
and social beliefs, 430
societal legitimation, 130
substance abuse, 39, 49, 57, 59, 68, 76, 430
worker safety, 378
Mediation, 512–514
Media violence, 130, 147, 150
Medical care. *See* Health and health care
Medicalization, 39
Medical model of drug use, 66
Medical use of marijuana, 78, 94
Medicare, 50–52, 335
Melting pot, 239
Men. *See* Gender differences; Males
Men's movement, 225
Mental disorders, 19, 34, 37, 39, 58, 280
Mental health, 34

children, 140, 146, 163, 408
child labourers, 365
divorce, negative consequences, 158–159
domestic violence and, 146–147, 151–153
elderly, 34, 173, 190, 192, 381
gender and, 48, 146–147, 223, 233
posttraumatic stress disorder and, 504–505
poverty and, 46, 163, 326
stigma, 280
substance abuse and, 151
technology and, 444–445
unemployment and, 375–376
Mental status
elderly, 34, 173, 190, 192
labelling and, 39, 280, 285
measurement of, 34
Methadone, 94–95
Microsociety schools, 412
Micro sociology, 14–15
Military, 492–494
Military-industrial complex, 496
Military spending, 225, 350, 457, 492–494
Militias, 497
Minimum wage, 321, 347, 349, 362–363, 365, 376–377
Minority (age group), 198
Minority (social groups), defined, 166–167
Mitigated accountability, 175
MK-Ultra, 503
Modernization, defined, 422
Modernization theory, 170
Modern racism, defined, 258
Mommy tracks, 211–212
Montreal Massacre, 25
Morbidity, 34–35
Mores, elements of culture, 9
Mortality rates, 35–37, 46, 58, 76, 173, 185, 223
infants, children, and youth, 35, 49, 365
maternal and infant health, 35–38, 47, 161, 364
workplace, 367–368
Mothers Against Drunk Driving (MADD), 9, 15, 95
Multiculturalism, 239–240, 260, 271
Multiculturalism Act, 240, 269
Multicultural education, 266–267, 388–389, 399–400
Multilateral Agreement on Investments (MAI), 362
Multinationalism, corporate. *See* Corporations
Multiple chemical sensitivity, 471
Mutually assured destruction, 515

Narcotics Anonymous, 89–90
Narcotics Control Act, 93
National Child Benefit (NCB), 357–358
National Child Benefit Supplement (NCBS), 337–338
Nationalism, 500
National organizations. *See* Activism
Needle torture, 391
Negative sanctions, 9, 221

Neglect, 141, 146–147
Neighbourhood watch programs, 129
New ageism, 189
No-fault divorce, 156
Non-Smoker's Health Act, 74, 76–77
Normalization, 397–398
Norms and sanctions, 7, 9
North American Free Trade Agreement, 356–357, 361
Nuclear Nonproliferation Treaty, 515–516
Nuclear power, 481
Nuclear waste, 433, 472, 507
Nuclear terrorism, 516
Nuclear weapons, 506, 514–516
Nuclear winter, 423, 490, 506, 515
Nunavut Act, 243
Nutrition
child labourers, 179–183, 354, 363–367, 376–379
environmental problems, 463–464
investment in human capital, 207, 349–351
organic food, 481
poverty and, 461–462, 308, 325–326, 338

Occupational health and safety. *See* Health and health care
Occupational roles, 362
Occupational sex segregation, 210–212
October Crisis, 509
Official Languages Act, 247
Oklahoma City bombing, 265
Old age. *See* Elderly
Old-young minorities, 169–170
One drop of blood rule, 244
Open skies agreement, 367
Operation Identification, 129
Operational definition of variable, 19
Opium, 66, 69
Opium and Drug Act, 79
Organ replacement, 56–57, 59–60
Organic solidarity, 422
Organization child, 390
Organized crime, 101, 115
Organized labour, 354–355, 366, 376–378
Overt discrimination, defined, 260
Ozone layer destruction, 470–471

Paradox of productivity, 451
Parenting. *See also* Divorce; Family; Single-parent families
changing attitudes toward, 163, 212
childcare assistance, 341–343
child support enforcement, 343–344
educational assistance, 340–341
employment insurance, 338–340
family allowance and child benefits, 336–338
fatherlessness, 163
gender inequality, 228
minimum wage, 347–344
moral and interpersonal education, 411–412
poverty and, 150, 163, 316, 320–321, 326–327, 342, 344
public assistance and welfare programs, 334–349

Student activism, 24–26, 300–301
Student loan programs, 340–341
Students Against Drunk Driving (SADD), 95
Subcultural theories, 107
Subculture, 170, 431
Subjective elements of social problems, 4
Subsidized housing, 328–329
Substance abuse, 3, 19, 40, 58, 64, 97
 Aboriginal peoples, 49, 58, 80, 84
 action strategies, 90–95
 alcohol, 4, 16, 49, 64, 66, 68, 72, 73
 among homeless, 80–83
 cocaine, 65–66, 79–80
 collective action, 92–95
 crime, 65, 85–87, 111, 126, 132, 134, 150
 deregulation, 68–69
 deviant label and, 69–70
 domestic violence and, 81, 85, 149–150
 drugs used, 57, 71–83
 during pregnancy, 48
 economic costs of, 87
 education and, 48–49, 74
 family, 65, 84–85, 137, 146, 151, 154–158
 gender differences, 84
 global context, 65–66
 government regulation, 69, 78–79, 90–94, 165
 health costs of, 65, 87, 89
 inhalants, 84
 juvenile crime, 81–83
 legalization, 94
 marijuana, 8, 65–66, 69–70, 77–78
 poverty and, 49, 327
 prescription drugs, 84
 societal costs and consequences, 65, 68, 126
 sociological perspectives, 67–70
 street youth and, 80–83
 theories, 70–71
 tobacco, 37, 39, 46, 66, 74–77, 93, 95, 165, 180
 treatment alternatives, 89–90, 92, 94–95
 unemployment and, 375
Sudden infant death syndrome, 36, 89, 326
Suicide, 3, 44–45, 100, 243
 divorce and, 158
 domestic violence and, 146, 153
 gay and lesbian youth, 297, 299
 gender differences, 44, 223
 physician-assisted, 194–195
 posttraumatic stress disorder and, 504–505
 substance abuse and, 65, 89
 youth, 32, 44–45, 89, 158, 178, 385
Survey research, 20–21
Sustainable development, 487
Sweatshops, 363
Symbolic interactionism, 14–16
 age inequality, 172–174, 198
 ageism, 198
 crime and violence, 109–110
 defined, 14–16

education, 392
 employment/unemployment, 362
 environmental problems, 462–463
 family problems, 140
 gender inequality, 204
 health care, 39
 poverty, 314–317
 race and ethnic relations, 256–257
 sexual orientation, 281
 substance abuse, 69–70, 89–90, 95
 technology, 430–432
 war and conflict, 496–497
Symbols
 elements of culture, 6, 9
 symbolic interaction perspective, 14–16

Taxation/tax policy
 and corporate welfare, 312–313
 and polluting practices, 482, 486
Tax evasion, 314–316
Tax fraud, 314
Tax havens, 313, 315–316
Teachers
 male, 206, 231–232, 401–402
 minority, 399
 self-fulfilling prophecy, 392
Teacher-student interactions, 218–219, 392
Technological fix, 416, 427, 488
Technological revolution, 217, 425
 action strategies, 448–450
 computers, 217, 431, 433–434
 global context, 425–427, 432
 information highway, 434–444
 science and biotechnology, 435–439
 science, ethics, and law, 448
 societal consequences, 170, 422–423, 425, 427–429, 439–448
 theory, 428–432
 war and, 491, 493–494, 501
 workplace, 430, 432–433, 443
Technology
 defined, 425
 gender inequities, 217, 427, 430, 432
 health care, 61–62
Technology-induced diseases, 444–445
Technology Partnerships Canada, 313
Technophobia, 445
TeleCampus, 415
Telecommuting, 381, 432
Telemedicine, telepathology, teleradiology, 61–62
Terrorism, 508–509, 512, 516
Tertiary prevention strategies, domestic violence, 153–154
Tertiary work sector, 358
Theory, 11–17
 conflict, 13–15. See also Conflict theory
 structural-functionalist, 11–13, 17. See also Structural-functionalism
 symbolic interactionist, 14–16. See also Symbolic Interactionism
Tobacco Act, 76
Tobacco industry, 68, 76, 93, 95
Tobacco use, 46, 74–77, 93, 180
 health costs, 37, 76–77, 89, 165

health issues, 37, 39, 66, 76, 87–88
 during pregnancy and after delivery, 76, 165
Toxic waste, 471–474
Training. See Work/employment; Education
Triad dispute resolution, 514

Underclass, defined, 331
Underemployment, 375
Under-5 mortality rates, 35–36
Unemployment, 3, 65, 344, 362, 374–376, 407, 409. See also Work/employment
 corporate downsizing and relocation, 314
 poverty, 318
 school dropouts, 407
 technology and, 374, 443
 youth, 180–181, 338
Uniform Crime Reports, 102–103
Unions, 354–355, 362, 377–378, 432
United Nations, 3, 355, 376, 509, 511–514

Vaccinations, 32, 42, 258, 273
Vagrancy laws, 109
Values, 8, 19, 498–499. See also Culture
Variables, defining, 19
Verstehen, 13
Viagra, 38–39
Vice crimes, 113–115
Victimization surveys, 99, 103, 127–128, 131, 141
Victimless crimes, 113–115
Violence. See Corporate Violence; Crime; Domestic Violence; Familicide; Gay Bashing; Hate Crimes; Homicide; Violent Crime
Violent crime, 21, 49, 94, 139–141, 143–154, 156, 165, 178, 195–197
Virtual elite, 443
Virtual reality, 425, 441
Visible minorities, defined, 204–242, 261, 323–324
Volunteer work, activism, 26–27, 349, 373, 411, 486

Wages. See Income, wages, salaries
War, defined, 491
War and conflict
 action strategies, prevention, 509–516
 arms control, 514–516
 causes of, 423, 497–500
 death and disability, 499, 501–504, 512
 defense against aggression, 499–500
 development of civilization, 492
 environmental impact of, 506–507
 global context, 491
 global security scenarios, 509
 industrialization, 492–493
 information warfare, 442, 494
 mediation and arbitration, 512, 514
 military spending, 225, 350, 457, 492–495, 505
 nationalism, 500
 post-Cold War era, 507–509
 poverty, 325, 349–350
 problems caused by, 442, 550

To the owner of this book

We hope that you have enjoyed Mooney et al.'s *Understanding Social Problems,*
First Canadian Edition (0-17-616839-7), and we would like to know as much
about your experiences with this text as you would care to offer. Only through
your comments and those of others can we learn how to make this a better text
for future readers.

School _____ Your instructor's name _____

Course _____ Was the text required? _____ Recommended? _____

1. What did you like the most about *Understanding Social Problems?*

   _____
   _____
   _____

2. How useful was this text for your course?

   _____
   _____
   _____

3. Do you have any recommendations for ways to improve the next edition of
   this text?

   _____
   _____
   _____

4. In the space below or in a separate letter, please write any other comments
   you have about the book. (For example, please feel free to comment on
   reading level, writing style, terminology, design features, and learning aids.)

   _____
   _____
   _____
   _____

Optional

Your name _____ Date _____

May Nelson Thomson Learning quote you, either in promotion for
Understanding Social Problems or in future publishing ventures?

Yes _____ No _____
Thanks!

You can also send your comments to us via e-mail at
college@nelson.com

PLEASE TAPE SHUT. DO NOT STAPLE.

TAPE SHUT

TAPE SHUT

- - - FOLD HERE - - -

NELSON

THOMSON LEARNING ™

MAIL ▷POSTE
Canada Post Corporation
Société canadienne des postes
Postage paid   Port payé
if mailed in Canada si posté au Canada
Business Reply   Réponse d'affaires
0066102399   01

TAPE SHUT

TAPE SHUT

0066102399-M1K5G4-BR01

NELSON THOMSON LEARNING
HIGHER EDUCATION
PO BOX 60225 STN BRM B
TORONTO ON M7Y 2H1